Here are your

1999 Year Book
Cross-Reference Tabs

For insertion in your WORLD BOOK set

Put these Tabs in the appropriate volumes of your **World Book Encyclopedia** now. Then, when you later look up some topic in **World Book** and find a Tab near the article, you will know that one of your **Year Books** has newer or more detailed information about that topic.

How to use these Tabs

First, remove this page from **THE YEAR BOOK**.

Begin with the first Tab, **ARMED FORCES**. Take the A volume of your **World Book** set and find the **Armed Forces** article in it. Moisten the **ARMED FORCES** Tab and affix it to that page.

Glue all the other Tabs in the appropriate **World Book** volume.

The 1999 World Book

YEAR BOOK

The Annual Supplement to The World Book Encyclopedia

■■■ A REVIEW OF THE EVENTS OF 1998 ■■■

World Book, Inc.

a Scott Fetzer company

Chicago

www.worldbook.com

World Book, Inc.
525 W. Monroe
Chicago, IL 60661

ISBN: 0-7166-0499-X
ISSN 0084-1439
Library of Congress Catalog Card Number: 62-4818

Printed in the United States of America.

Staff

EDITORIAL

Executive Editor
Darlene R. Stille

Managing Editor
Scott Thomas

Senior Editors
Jay Lenn
Kristina Vaicikonis

Staff Editors
Tim Frystak
Al Smuskiewicz
Peter Uremovic

Contributing Editors
David Dreier
Mark Dunbar
Jennifer Parello

Editorial Assistant
Ethel Matthews

Cartographic Services
H. George Stoll, Head
Wayne K. Pichler,
Manager,
Cartographic Database
Susan E. Ryan,
Staff Cartographer

Index Services
David Pofelski, Head
Pam Hori

Statistical Services
Jay Powers, Head

Permissions Editor
Janet Peterson

ART

Executive Director
Roberta Dimmer

Design
Brenda B. Tropinski,
Senior Designer,
Year Book

Cari L. Biamonte
Senior Designer

Don Di Sante,
Designer

Photography
Sandra M. Dyrlund
Senior Photographs
Editor

Sylvia Ohlrich
Photographs Editor

Marc Sirinsky
Photographs Editor

Art Production Assistant
Jon Whitney

RESEARCH SERVICES

**Director of Research Services
and Product Development**
Paul Kobasa

Researchers
Karen A. McCormick
Mitchell C. Bassler
Cheryl J. Graham

Library Services
Jon Fjortoft, Head

PRODUCTION

Manufacturing/Pre-Press
Sandra Van den Broucke,
Director
Barbara Podczerwinski,
Manufacturing Manager
Randi Park
Senior Production
Manager

Proofreaders
Anne Dillon
Roxanne Rakoczy

Text Processing
Curley Hunter
Gwendolyn Johnson

EXECUTIVE VICE PRESIDENT AND PUBLISHER
Michael Ross

Contributors

Contributors not listed on these pages are members of the editorial staff.

- **ADDY, PREMEN,** M.A., Ph.D.; Editor, *India Weekly.* **[Hinduism]**

- **ALEXIOU, ARTHUR G.,** B.S.E.E., M.S.E.E.; Senior assistant secretary, UNESCO/IOC. **[Ocean]**

- **ALI, JAVED,** M.A., J.D.; Management analyst, Research Planning Incorporated. **[Armed forces** Special Report: **Chemical and Biological Weapons]**

- **ANDREWS, PETER J.,** B.A., M.S.; Free-lance writer. **[Chemistry]**

- **APSELOFF, MARILYN FAIN,** B.A., M.A.; Professor of English, Kent State University, Ohio. **[Literature for children]**

- **ASKER, JAMES R.,** B.A.; Washington Bureau Chief, *Aviation Week & Space Technology* magazine. **[Space exploration]**

- **BARBER, PEGGY,** B.A., M.L.S.; Associate executive director for communications, American Library Association. **[Library]**

- **BARNHART, BILL,** B.A., M.S.T., M.B.A.; Financial markets columnist, *Chicago Tribune.* **[Stocks and bonds]**

- **BARRETT, NORMAN.,** M.A.; Free-lance writer. **[Soccer** Special Report: **The 1998 World Cup; Soccer]**

- **BAYNHAM, SIMON,** B.A., M.A., Ph.D.; Consultant, Research Institute for the Study of Conflict and Terrorism, London. **[Africa and African country articles]**

- **BOULDREY, BRIAN,** B.A., M.F.A.; Free-lance editor and instructor. **[Disabled; Nobel prizes; People in the news; Pulitzer prizes; San Francisco]**

- **BOYD, JOHN D.,** B.S.; Economics reporter, *Bridge News.* **[Economics** Special Report: **Asian Economic Crisis— Global Contagion; Economics; International trade; Manufacturing]**

- **BRADSHER, HENRY S.,** A.B., B.J.; Foreign affairs analyst. **[Asia and Asian country articles]**

- **BRETT, CARLTON E.,** B.A., M.S., Ph.D.; Professor of geology and biology, University of Rochester. **[Paleontology]**

- **BRODY, HERB,** B.S.; Senior editor, *Technology Review* magazine. **[Internet]**

- **BUERKLE, TOM,** B.A.; Correspondent, *International Herald Tribune.* **[Europe** Special Report: **European Union; Europe and Western European nation articles]**

- **CAMPBELL, GEOFFREY A.,** B.J.; Free-lance writer. **[Courts; Human rights; Supreme Court of the United States]**

- **CAMPBELL, LINDA P.,** B.A., M.S.L.; Senior reporter, legal affairs, *Fort Worth Star-Telegram.* **[Courts; Human rights; Supreme Court of the United States]**

- **CARDINALE, DIANE P.,** B.A.; Assistant communications director, Toy Manufacturers of America. **[Toys and games]**

- **CASEY, MIKE,** B.S., M.A.; Assistant editor, *Kansas City Star.* **[Automobile]**

- **CORNELL, VINCENT J.,** B.A., M.A., Ph.D.; Associate professor of religion, Duke University. **[Islam]**

- **DeFRANK, THOMAS M.,** B.A., M.A.; Washington bureau chief, *New York Daily News.* **[Armed forces]**

- **DILLON, DAVID,** B.A., M.A., Ph.D.; Architecture critic, *The Dallas Morning News.* **[Architecture]**

- **DIRDA, MICHAEL,** B.A., M.A., Ph.D.; Writer and editor, *The Washington Post Book World.* **[Literature, World; Poetry]**

- **DUCKHAM, DAVID,** Former British Lion and England Rugby Union International player; marketing consultant. **[Rugby]**

- **EATON, WILLIAM J.,** B.S., M.S.; Curator, Hubert H. Humphrey Fellowship Program, University of Maryland. **[U.S. government articles]**

- **ELLIS, GAVIN,** Editor, *The New Zealand Herald.* **[New Zealand]**

- **FARR, DAVID M. L.,** D.Phil.; Professor emeritus of history, Carleton University. **[Canada; Canadian provinces; Canadian territories; Canada, Prime Minister of]**

- **FISHER, ROBERT W.,** B.A., M.A.; Free-lance writer. **[Labor and employment]**

- **FITZGERALD, MARK,** B.A.; Midwest editor, *Editor & Publisher* magazine. **[Newspaper]**

- **FOX, THOMAS C.,** B.A., M.A.; Publisher, *National Catholic Reporter.* **[Roman Catholic Church]**

- **FRICKER, KAREN,** B.A., M.A.; Free-lance theater writer. **[Theater** Special Report: **A New Broadway Takes Center Stage; Theater]**

- **FRIEDMAN, EMILY,** B.A.; Health-policy and ethics analyst, *Journal of the American Medical Association.* **[Health-care issues]**

- **GADOMSKI, FRED,** B.S., M.S.; Meteorologist, Pennsylvania State University. **[Weather]**

- **GATTY, BOB,** Vice President of Communications and Marketing, Food Distributors International. **[Food]**

- **GIBSON, ERIC,** B.A.; Assistant editor Leisure & Arts page, *The Wall Street Journal.* **[Art]**

- **GOLDEN, JONATHAN J.,** B.A., M.J.; Ph.D. student, Brandeis University. **[Judaism]**

- **GOLDNER, NANCY,** B.A.; Free-lance dance critic. **[Dance]**

- **GRIFFITHS, PAUL J.,** B.A., M.Phil., Ph.D.; Professor of the philosophy of religions, University of Chicago. **[Buddhism]**

- **HARAKAS, STANLEY SAMUEL,** B.A., M.Div., Th.D.; Professor emeritus, Holy Cross Greek Orthodox School of Theology. **[Eastern Orthodox Churches]**

- **HAVERSTOCK, NATHAN A.,** A.B.; Affiliate scholar, Oberlin College. **[Latin America and Latin American country articles]**

- **HELMS, CHRISTINE,** B.A., Ph.D.; Writer and Middle East analyst. **[Middle East and Middle Eastern country articles; North African country articles]**

- **HENDERSON, HAROLD,** B.A.; Staff writer, Chicago *Reader.* **[Chicago]**

- **HOFFMAN, ANDREW J.,** B.S., M.S., Ph.D.; Assistant professor of organizational behavior, Boston University. **[Environmental pollution]**

- **JOHANSON, DONALD C.,** B.S., M.A., Ph.D.; Director and professor, Institute of Human Origins. **[Anthropology]**

- **JONES, TIM,** B.S.; Media writer, *Chicago Tribune.* **[Telecommunications]**

- **KENNEDY, BRIAN,** M.A.; Free-lance journalist. **[Australia, Australia, Prime Minister of, Australian rules football]**

- **KHNG, PAULINE,** B.A., M.A.; Honorary fellow, Centre for Southeast Asian Studies, University of Hull. **[Singapore]**

- **KILGORE, MARGARET,** B.A., M.B.A.; Editor, Phillips-Van Buren, Incorporated. **[Los Angeles]**

- **KING, MIKE,** Reporter, *The Montreal Gazette.* **[Montreal]**

- **KLINTBERG, PATRICIA PEAK.,** B.A.; Washington editor, *Farm Journal.* **[Agriculture]**

- **KRONHOLZ, JUNE,** B.S.J.; Staff reporter, *The Wall Street Journal.* **[Education]**

- **LAWRENCE, ALBERT,** B.A., M.A., M.Ed.; President, OutExcel! **[Chess]**

- **LEWIS, DAVID C.,** M.D.; Professor of medicine and community health, Brown University. **[Drug abuse]**

- **LITTLE EAGLE, AVIS A.,** A.A.S.; Editor, *Indian Country Today.* **[Indian, American]**

- **LYE, KEITH,** B.A., F.R.G.S.; Free-lance author and editor **[Cricket]**

- **MARCH, ROBERT H.,** A.B., M.S., Ph.D.; Professor of physics and liberal studies, University of Wisconsin at Madison. **[Physics]**

- **MARSCHALL, LAURENCE A.,** B.S., Ph.D.; Professor of physics, Gettysburg College. **[Astronomy]**

- **MARTY, MARTIN E.,** Ph.D.; Director, Public Religion Project, University of Chicago. **[Protestantism]**

- **MATHER, IAN J.,** B.A., M.A.; Diplomatic editor, *The European,* London. **[Ireland; Northern Ireland; United Kingdom; United Kingdom, Prime Minister of]**

- **MAUGH, THOMAS H., II,** Ph.D.; Science writer, *Los Angeles Times.* **[Biology]**

- **McLEESE, DON,** B.A., M.A.; Columnist/critic-at-large, *Austin American-Statesman.* **[Popular music]**

- **MESSENGER, ROBERT,** B.A.; Editor, *New Criterion.* **[City; Crime; Literature, American; Washington, D.C.]**

- **MINER, TODD J.,** B.S., M.S.; Meteorologist, Pennsylvania State University. **[Weather]**

- **MORITZ, OWEN,** B.A.; Urban-affairs editor, *New York Daily News.* **[New York City]**

- **MORRIS, BERNADINE,** B.A., M.A.; Free-lance fashion writer. **[Fashion]**

- **MULLINS, HENRY T.,** B.S., M.S., Ph.D.; Professor of Earth science, Syracuse University. **[Geology]**

- **MUTUA, MAKAU WA,** LL.B. LL.M. S.J.D.; Director of the Human Rights Center, State University of New York, Buffalo. **[Human rights** Special Report: **A Common Standard— 50 Years of Defending Human Rights for All]**

- **NESBITT, ELEANOR M.,** M.A., M.Phil., Ph.D.; Lecturer in religious education, University of Warwick. **[Sikhism]**

- **NGUYEN, J. TUYET,** M.A.; United Nations correspondent, Deutsche Presse-Agentur. **[Population; United Nations]**

- **OGAN, EUGENE,** B.A., M.A., Ph.D.; Professor emeritus of anthropology, University of Minnesota. **[Pacific Islands]**

- **PAETH, GREGORY,** B.A.; Television and radio writer, *The Cincinnati Post.* **[Radio]**

- **REID, RON,** B.A.; Sportswriter, *The Philadelphia Inquirer.* **[Sports articles]**

- **ROSE, MARK J.,** B.A., M.A., Ph.D.; Managing editor, *Archaeology* magazine. **[Archaeology]**

- **ROSENSTIEL, TOM,** A.B., M.S.; Director, Project for Excellence in Journalism. **[Newspaper** Special Report: **Tabloid Journalism—Yesterday and Today]**

- **RUBENSTEIN, RICHARD E.,** B.A., M.A., J.D.; Professor of conflict resolution and public affairs, George Mason University. **[Terrorism]**

- **SARNA, JONATHAN D.,** Ph.D.; Joseph H. & Belle R. Braun Professor of American Jewish History, Brandeis University. **[Judaism]**

- **SAVAGE, IAN,** B.A., M.A., Ph.D.; Assistant professor of economics and transportation, Northwestern University. **[Aviation; Transportation]**

- **SEGAL, TROY,** B.A.; Free-lance writer. **[Television]**

- **SHAPIRO, HOWARD,** B.S.; Travel editor, *The Philadelphia Inquirer.* **[Philadelphia]**

- **SOLNICK, STEVEN L.,** B.A., M.A., Ph.D.; Assistant professor of political science, Columbia University. **[Baltic states and other former Soviet republic articles]**

- **STEIN, DAVID LEWIS,** B.A., M.S.; Urban affairs columnist, *The Toronto Star.* **[Toronto]**

- **STOCKER, CAROL M.,** B.A.; Reporter, *The Boston Globe.* **[Gardening]**

- **STUART, ELAINE,** B.A.; Managing editor, Council of State Governments. **[State government]**

- **TANNER, JAMES C.,** B.S.J.; Former news editor—energy, *The Wall Street Journal.* **[Energy supply]**

- **TATUM, HENRY K.,** B.A.; Associate editor, editorial page, *The Dallas Morning News.* **[Dallas]**

- **THOMAS, PAULETTE,** B.A.; Staff writer, *The Wall Street Journal.* **[Bank]**

- **TONRY, MICHAEL,** A.B., LL.B.; Professor of law and public policy, University of Minnesota Law School. **[Prison]**

- **von RHEIN, JOHN,** B.A., B.A.; Classical- music critic, *Chicago Tribune.* **[Classical music]**

- **WALTER, EUGENE J., Jr.,** B.A.; Free-lance writer. **[Conservation; Zoos]**

- **WATSON, BURKE,** B.A.; Assistant suburban editor, *Houston Chronicle.* **[Houston]**

- **WOLCHIK, SHARON L.,** B.A., M.A., Ph.D.; Professor of political science and international relations, George Washington University. **[Eastern European country articles]**

- **WOODS, MICHAEL,** B.S.; Science editor, *The Toledo* (Ohio) *Blade* and *Pittsburgh Post-Gazette.* **[AIDS; Computer; Drugs; Electronics; Magazine; Medicine; Mental health; Public health and safety]**

- **WRIGHT, ANDREW G.,** B.A., Senior editor, *Engineering News-Record.* **[Building and construction]**

- **WUNTCH, PHILIP,** B.A.; Film critic, *The Dallas Morning News.* **[Motion pictures]**

- **ZIMRING, FRANKLIN E.,** B.A., J.D.; Director, Earl Warren Legal Institute and law professor, University of California at Berkeley. **[Courts** Special Report: **Marking Time on Death Row]**

Contents

▲ Page 281

◀ Page 342

◀ Page 151

▼ Page 323

The Year's **Major News Stories**

From economic crises in Asia and Russia to a sex scandal in the White House that resulted in impeachment proceedings against President Bill Clinton, 1998 was a year of memorable news events. On these three pages are stories that the editors picked as some of the most important of the year, along with details on where to find information about them in this volume.

The Editors

U.S. and British forces attack Iraq

In December, United States and British forces launch air and missile strikes against Iraq, claiming that Iraqi President Saddam Hussein continued to block United Nations investigations of Iraq's programs to build weapons of mass destruction. See **Iraq,** page 239; **Middle East,** page 280; **Armed Forces** Special Report: **Chemical and Biological Weapons,** page 56.

Glenn back in orbit

Former astronaut and U.S. Senator John H. Glenn, Jr. (D., Ohio), who in 1962 was the first American to orbit the Earth, returns to space in October aboard the space shuttle Discovery at the age of 77. See **Space Exploration,** page 379.

Impeaching the president

The House of Representatives in September receives a report and 36 boxes of documents from Independent Counsel Kenneth Starr, who had investigated President Bill Clinton for four years. The House on December 19 voted to impeach President Clinton on one charge of perjury and one charge of obstruction of justice. See **Congress of the United States,** page 128; **United States, President of the,** page 434.

Terrorist bombs rip American embassies

August 7 terrorist bombings of U.S. embassies in Nairobi, Kenya, *left,* and Dar es Salaam, Tanzania, kill at least 224 people, including 12 Americans. See **Africa,** page 39; **Kenya,** page 253; **Terrorism,** page 402; **United States, Government of the,** page 429.

Economic woes in Asia and Russia

An economic crisis that swept much of Asia in 1997 deepens in 1998, raising worries that the entire global economy could be dragged into recession. Meanwhile, Russia teeters on the brink of economic collapse. See **Asia,** page 66; **Economics** Special Report: **Asian Economic Crisis—Global Contagion,** page 170; **International trade,** page 235; **Russia,** page 358.

Newt Gingrich steps down

In response to the poor showing of Republican congressional candidates in November's midterm elections, Newt Gingrich (R., Ga.), the controversial speaker of the House of Representatives, gives up his post and announces his resignation from Congress. See **Congress of the United States,** page 128.

There is rejoicing in Belfast in May after voters in Ireland and Northern Ireland overwhelmingly approve a peace agreement between Northern Ireland, Ireland, and Great Britain. The pact was aimed at bringing decades of conflict and violence to an end. See **Ireland,** page 239; **Northern Ireland,** page 308.

A peace accord for Northern Ireland

The ravages of Hurricane Mitch

The Choluteca River in Honduras swells with rainwater in October in the aftermath of Hurricane Mitch, the worst storm—and the worst natural disaster—ever to hit Latin America. Mitch killed an estimated 10,000 to 20,000 people in Honduras, Nicaragua, El Salvador, and Guatemala. See **Latin America,** page 258; **Weather,** page 438.

Mideast peace pact

In October, Israel's Prime Minister Benjamin Netanyahu and Palestinian leader Yasir Arafat sign a U.S.-brokered peace agreement. Israel agrees to withdraw from 13 percent of the West Bank and release hundreds of jailed Palestinians in return for a crackdown on terrorism and an end to calls for Israel's destruction. See **Israel,** page 240; **Middle East,** page 280.

Maris's home-run record falls

In an exciting home-run derby, Mark McGwire of the St. Louis Cardinals and Sammy Sosa of the Chicago Cubs go head to head in a race to topple Roger Maris's 1961 seasonal record of 61 homers. McGwire takes the prize with 70 home runs. Sosa hits 66. See **Baseball,** page 86.

1998 YEAR IN BRIEF

A month-by-month listing of the most significant world events that occurred during 1998.

1 **Mohammed Rafiq Tarar** is sworn in as president of Pakistan. A former senator and Supreme Court judge, Tarar was overwhelmingly elected president on December 31, 1997, by members of the National Assembly.

A law banning smoking in all California bars, nightclubs, and gambling casinos goes into effect at midnight. The legislature in California banned smoking in all other indoor public places in 1995.

4 **Israeli Foreign Minister David Levy** resigns from Prime Minister Benjamin Netanyahu's coalition government, leaving Netanyahu with only a 61 to 59 majority in the Knesset, the Israeli parliament. On January 1, Levy publicly protested the Netanyahu government's disinterest in social welfare programs and its performance in negotiating peace with the Palestinians.

Daniel arap Moi wins a fifth, five-year term as president of Kenya in an election that domestic and international observers describe as "flawed and chaotic" but essentially honest.

6 **Algeria rejects** a United Nations offer to conduct an international inquiry into the on-going massacre of civilians by Islamic militant groups. Observers estimate that between 60,000 and 80,000 people have been murdered in Algeria since 1992.

7 **A federal jury deadlocks,** after deliberating for 13 hours, over how active a role Terry L. Nichols played in the planning of the April 19, 1995, bombing of the Oklahoma City Federal Building, which resulted in the death of 168 people. The deadlock allows Nichols, who was convicted on Dec. 23, 1997, of conspiring to bomb the building and of involuntary manslaughter, to escape the death penalty.

8 **The Indonesian stock market** drops 19 percent, the largest one-day loss yet in the current Southeast Asian economic crisis, which began in July 1997.

Ramzi Ahmed Yousef, convicted of planning the Feb. 26, 1993, World Trade Center bombing that resulted in the death of six people and the injury of hundreds, is sentenced to life in prison plus 240 years.

9 **Chancellor of Germany** Helmut Kohl concedes that the unemployment rate cannot be halved as Kohl had promised in January 1996. Unemployment reached 11.8 percent in December 1997, its highest level since Adolf Hitler took power in Germany in 1933.

11 **Sonia Gandhi,** widow of an assassinated prime minister of India and daughter-in-law of another, announces that she will enter politics to campaign for Congress Party candidates in India's upcoming parliamentary election. Since the deaths of Indira Gandhi in 1984 and Rajiv Gandhi in 1991, the power of the Congress Party has declined, and politics in India, which has had three coalition governments since 1996, has splintered among small parties based largely on religion and caste.

12 **More than 3 million people** in the eastern third of Canada and hundreds of thousands in upstate New York and northern New England remain without electricity following days of freezing rain that has left the landscape coated in ice.

17 **Iraqi President Saddam Hussein,** on the seventh anniversary of the beginning of the Persian Gulf War, threatens to evict all United Nations weapon inspectors from Iraq.

20 **Two University of Massachusetts** scientists, James Robl and Steven Stice, announce the birth of twin Holstein calves, Charlie and George, that were cloned from the cells of cow fetuses.

21 **President Bill Clinton denies** sexual involvement with 24-year-old Monica Lewinsky, a former White House intern, after the *Washington Post* reported that independent counsel Kenneth Starr is investigating allegations concerning a relationship.

22 **Pope John Paul II** meets with Cuban President Fidel Castro after opening his mission to Communist Cuba with a mass attended by between 60,000 and 80,000 people.

A car swerves around downed tree limbs and power lines in Watertown, New York, on Jan. 10, 1998, after an ice storm crippled upstate New York, northern New England, and the eastern third of Canada.

Theodore J. Kaczynski acknowledges that he is the Unabomber and pleads guilty to all charges made against him by the federal government. He will be sentenced to life in prison with no hope of parole for mailing bombs that killed 3 people and maimed 28 others.

24 Hundreds of German demonstrators brawl in the streets of Dresden over an exhibit—"War of Extermination: Crimes of the Wehrmacht from 1941 to 1944"—showing German soldiers during World War II (1939–1945) killing Jews and other civilians.

25 The Denver Broncos win the National Football League championship by beating the Green Bay Packers 31 to 24 in Super Bowl XXXII in San Diego.

27 U.S. President Bill Clinton, addressing Congress, declares the state of the union sound and proposes increased spending on social programs and a plan to rescue Social Security.

28 Twenty-six people accused of conspiring to assassinate Prime Minister of India Rajiv Gandhi in 1991 are found guilty and sentenced to be hanged. Nearly 300 witnesses testified in the trial, which lasted six years.

31 Petr Korda of the Czech Republic beats Chile's Marcelo Rios in straight sets to win the Australian Open tennis championship. Martina Hingis of Switzerland wins the women's title by beating Spain's Conchita Martinez, also in straight sets.

2 **President Bill Clinton** sends the first balanced U.S. federal budget in nearly 30 years—earmarked at $1.73 trillion—to Congress.

The Centers for Disease Control announce that death from AIDS fell by 44 percent in the first half of 1997.

3 **Karla Faye Tucker** is executed by lethal injection after being on death row in Texas for 15 years. She is the second woman to be executed in the United States since the resumption of capital punishment in 1977.

A U.S. Marine jet on a training flight in northern Italy slices through the cable of a ski lift in the Dolomite Mountains, causing a suspended cable car to plunge 370 feet (111 meters) down a mountain, killing all 20 passengers.

4 **An earthquake** registering 6.1 strikes a hilly, agricultural region in northwest Iraq, 200 miles (322 kilometers) north of Kabul, the capital, leaving as many as 4,500 people dead and 30,000 people homeless.

6 **President Bill Clinton** and British Prime Minister Tony Blair warn the president of Iraq, Saddam Hussein, that if he continues to bar United Nations inspection teams from looking for chemical and biological weapons, Iraq faces the prospect of a substantial military response.

7 **The 1998 Winter Olympics** in Nagano, Japan, open in a public celebration, attended by the emperor and empress of Japan, that reflects traditional Japanese culture as well as cutting-edge technological innovation.

United Nations Secretary General Kofi Annan, *left*, brokers a deal with Saddam Hussein, president of Iraq, *right*, on Feb. 22, 1998, to allow UN teams to resume weapon inspections in Iraq.

9 **Eduard Shevardnadze,** president of Georgia, survives an attempt on his life when his motorcade is attacked in Tbilisi, the capital, with antitank grenades and heavy machine-gun fire.

12 **A federal district judge** declares unconstitutional the line item veto, which allows the president of the United States to individually veto tax and spending items in a bill without rejecting an entire piece of legislation.

15 **Some 100 leaders of Sierra Leone's** ousted military junta are imprisoned in Freetown, the capital, after surrendering to West African peacekeeping troops. Peacekeeping troops, led by Nigerian officers, on February 13, took control of Freetown, which is reported to be calm and little damaged by the fighting.

16 **A China Air jet crashes** into a row of houses just short of the runway at Chiang Kai Shek Airport outside Taipei, Taiwan, killing 9 people on the ground and all 197 people aboard the plane.

17 **The U.S. women's hockey team** wins the gold medal in the first women's ice hockey competition in Olympic history, finishing the games 6–0.

18 **Secretary of State** Madeleine Albright, Secretary of Defense William Cohen, and National Security Adviser Samuel Berger, speaking before an audience at Ohio State University in Columbus, face protests as they attempt to sell the Clinton Administration's stance toward possible military intervention in Iraq.

19 **The National Research Council** announces that nearly 22,000 people die annually of lung cancer caused by inhalation of radon.

20 **Eight hours after Great Britain** and Ireland suspend Sinn Fein, the political wing of the Irish Republican Army (IRA), from Northern Ireland peace talks, a bomb explodes outside a police station in the village of Moira, southwest of Belfast. Sinn Fein, as a condition for admittance to the peace talks, had pledged that the IRA would suspend use of terrorist tactics.

22 **President Saddam Hussein** of Iraq agrees, after a three-hour meeting with United Nations Secretary General Kofi Annan, to lift the Iraqi ban on UN arms inspections at all presidential properties.

23 **Tornadoes** with winds as high as 260 miles (418 kilometers) per hour hit central Florida in a path running from Daytona Beach on the Atlantic Ocean to Tampa Bay on the Gulf of Mexico. Forty-two people are killed and more than 200 are injured.

President Bill Clinton tentatively accepts a deal brokered by United Nations Secretary General Kofi Annan and agreed to by Iraqi President Saddam Hussein that allows UN weapons inspectors immediate and unconditional access to whatever Iraqi sites they chose to examine for weapons of mass destruction.

24 **Kim Dae-Jung** is inaugurated president of South Korea and begins his term by calling for cooperation and reconciliation with North Korea. The 73-year-old Kim, who is assuming control of a country in economic crisis, announces a series of economic reforms.

Another round of torrential rains hits the California coast, triggering more flash floods and mud slides, which wash away or bury houses, highways, and cars. Tornadoes, rare in southern California, touch down in Long Beach and Huntington Beach. Between the central coast and the Mexican border, at least seven people are killed in storm-related accidents. In Los Angeles, a record 13.68 inches (34.75 centimeters) of rain has fallen since February 1.

26 **The U.S. Senate** votes 51 to 48 to continue to debate election finance reform. The vote to not vote blocks the legislation until at least 1999.

27 **A British Home Office** minister announces to the House of Lords that Queen Elizabeth II does not object to changing the law of succession to allow the British throne to pass to the monarch's oldest child, whether male or female.

1 **An estimated 250,000 citizens** of rural Great Britain, including farmers and landowners as well as fox hunting enthusiasts and other hunters, flood central London to demonstrate against a Labour Party bill that would outlaw hunting with hounds.

3 **Microsoft Corporation Chairman** Bill Gates admits in testimony before a Senate committee that Microsoft does restrict its Internet partners from dealing with Microsoft's competitors. The United States Justice Department is considering a suit against Microsoft for forcing personal computer manufacturers to load only Microsoft's World Wide Web browsing program.

5 **Scientists with the Lunar Research** Institute, in Gilroy, California, announce that an unmanned American spacecraft has detected evidence of water on the moon. The water, in the form of ice crystals mixed in dirt, may exist in sufficient quantities to sustain lunar colonies.

6 **The three surviving Dionne** quintuplets, Cecile, Annette, and Yvonne, accept a $2.8-million settlement from the Canadian province of Ontario, which in the 1930's had removed the first surviving quintuplets from their parents and placed them on public display.

8 **A storm system** over the United States produces blizzard conditions from Wisconsin through Kansas in the Midwest and thunderstorms and torrential rain in the South. Nebraska is blanketed under a foot (31 centimeters) of snow, and Iowa receives as much as 18 inches (45 centimeters), stranding motorists on interstate highways behind drifts 12 feet (3.6 meters) high.

10 **General Augusto Pinochet** steps down as commander of the Chilean army after 25 years of wielding power. During the years of his military junta, more than 3,000 of Pinochet's political opponents either died under mysterious circumstances or disappeared.

11 **The Red Cross withdraws** from Kosovo after receiving repeated anonymous death threats against the only outside aid workers in Yugoslavia's highly troubled southernmost province. Red Cross workers were also the only outside observers in an area where approximately 75 ethnic Albanians were killed in the recent government sweep against separatist rebels.

12 **A group of astronomers** from Johns Hopkins University in Baltimore, the University of California at Berkeley, and the Keck Observatory in Hawaii announce the discovery of a galaxy that is the most distant object yet observed from Earth. It is approximately 12.2 billion light-years from Earth.

14 **The attorneys general** of more than 30 U.S. states reach an agreement with the American Family Publishers specifying that the sweepstakes company pay participating states $50,000 each to settle charges of deceptive advertising.

15 **President K. R. Narayanan of India** invites Atal Bihari Vajpayee, leader of the Hindu nationalist party, to form a coalition government after two weeks of backroom politicking, following an inconclusive parliamentary election.

17 **Zhu Rongji,** who has guided economic policy in China for five years, is named prime minister of China by the National People's Congress meeting in Beijing.

19 **Senior U.S. State Department** officials reveal that President Bill Clinton, at the urging of Pope John Paul II, will ease certain restrictions on humanitarian aid and travel to Cuba, including those regulations imposed after Cuban aircraft shot down two private planes in 1996.

20 **A tornado,** striking just before dawn, cuts a swath through five counties in northeastern Georgia, killing 11 people as it rampages through more than 400 houses and mobile homes, 11 poultry farms, and 2 schools.

23 **Russian President Boris Yeltsin**, returning to the political stage after another bout of ill health, announces on television that he has fired his entire cabinet, including Prime Minister Viktor Chernomyrdin, long considered the president's political heir apparent.

President Bill Clinton and Hillary Rodham Clinton appear with Ghanaian President Jerry Rawlings (right) before a massive crowd on March 23, 1998, in Accra, Ghana. The Clintons wear kente cloths, the traditional fabric of Ghana.

President Bill Clinton, in Ghana on the first leg of a six-nation tour of Africa, momentarily steps down from the podium above Independence Square in Accra, the capital, to shake hands in the crowd. In response, the throng, estimated at more than 1 million people, surges forward, trampling through steel barriers and over people in the front. Secret Service agents extricate the shaken president and whisk him from the scene.

24 **Two boys**, 11 and 13 years old, empty a Jonesboro, Arkansas, school by pulling a fire alarm and shoot into the crowd exiting the building. Four students and one teacher die.

25 **Italian paleontologists** reveal the existence of a baby dinosaur fossil in which details of the animal's soft anatomy are preserved. Previously, only fragments of fossilized dinosaur tissue have been available for study.

The European Commission declares that 11 European countries—Austria, Belgium, Finland, France, Ireland, Germany, Italy, Luxembourg, the Netherlands, Portugal, and Spain—have qualified economically to join the European Union's single currency, which is scheduled to go into effect in January 1999.

27 **Russian President Boris Yeltsin** announces that he has appointed a 35-year-old technocrat and reformer, Sergei Kiriyenko, prime minister. The Russian president publicly threatens to dissolve parliament if Kiriyenko is not quickly granted parliamentary approval.

29 **Archaeologists in Israel** announce that they have discovered the ruins of a structure dating from 50 to 70 B.C., which they believe to be the earliest known synagogue.

17

1 A judge of the U.S. District Court in Little Rock, Arkansas, dismisses Paula Corbin Jones's civil suit against President Bill Clinton. The suit alleged that Jones was sexually harassed and suffered emotional distress as a result of an alleged 1991 encounter in a Little Rock hotel room between Jones, then a state of Arkansas employee, and Clinton, then governor of Arkansas.

2 The *tankan* quarterly, a business survey conducted by the Bank of Japan, reports that the Japanese economy is either on the brink of recession or already in recession. The report sends the Japanese stock market into its biggest drop yet in 1998. Norio Ohga, chairman of the Sony Corporation, responds to the market drop by announcing that "the Japanese economy is on the verge of collapse."

5 President Kim Dae-Jung of South Korea agrees to send delegates to Beijing for an April 11 meeting with North Korea to discuss food and agricultural problems, including the current severe food shortage in North Korea. The meeting will be the first time in four years that the two countries have communicated officially.

6 Citicorp, a bank, and Travelers Group, an insurance company, announce their intention to merge, despite federal laws prohibiting such combinations. The merger will involve a $70-billion stock swap, the largest such transaction in history.

The Dow Jones Industrial Average of selected stocks listed on the New York Stock Exchange closes above 9,000 for the first time in history.

A mother and her daughters walk through a Roman Catholic neighborhood in Belfast, Northern Ireland, on April 11, 1998, the day after peace talks produced an accord to settle years of conflict between Catholics and Protestants.

8 **A worldwide survey,** conducted by an international team of botanists and conservationists over a 20-year period, reveals that at least 1 in every 8 known plant species on Earth is threatened with extinction.

9 **Tens of thousands of Islamic** pilgrims—in Mecca for the *hajj,* the annual pilgrimage that is one of Islam's holiest rituals—stampede in 100 °F (38 °C) heat during the traditional "stoning of the devil" ceremony, which involves hurling pebbles at pillars that symbolize the temptations of Satan. At least 118 people fall to their death from a bridge or are trampled to death.

10 **Twenty-two months of peace talks** produce an accord, called the Belfast or Good Friday Agreement, designed to end the deadly conflict in Northern Ireland between Roman Catholics and Protestants. The agreement provides for a 108-seat National Assembly in which Protestants and Catholics are to govern jointly.

12 **Mark O'Meara birdies three** of the final four holes of the Masters, in Augusta, Georgia, to win his first major Professional Golf Association (PGA) tournament.

15 **The legendary head** of Cambodia's Khmer Rouge, Pol Pot, dies in his bed in a thatched hut in the mountains of northern Cambodia. He was being held under house arrest by his former followers, Khmer Rouge guerrillas, who had convicted him of crimes against humanity in 1997.

17 **Islamic factions waging civil war** in Afghanistan agree to a cease-fire. The agreement calls for an exchange of prisoners and face-to-face talks between the factions, including the Taliban, an ultraconservative, militant group that currently holds two-thirds of Afghanistan.

20 **Israeli Prime Minister** Benjamin Netanyahu and Palestinian leader Yasir Arafat agree to travel to London and meet with U.S. Secretary of State Madeleine Albright in an effort to revive the stalled peace process.

21 **An astronomer** at the Jet Propulsion Laboratory in Pasadena, California, reports that astronomers have observed planets being formed from a swirling disk of gas and dust around a young star. These observations suggest that planetary systems may be common in the universe, increasing the possibility of life existing beyond Earth.

22 **The Irish Parliament in Dublin** votes overwhelmingly to approve the Northern Ireland peace accord, which was agreed to in Belfast on April 10. Among its other provisions, the agreement calls on Great Britain to formally renounce claims over that part of the island that is now the Irish Republic. It calls on the Irish Republic to amend its constitution to renounce claims of sovereignty over Northern Ireland.

24 **The Communist-dominated Duma**, the lower house of the Russian parliament, caves in to President Boris Yeltsin and approves his candidate for prime minister, Sergei Kiriyenko.

26 **The Roman Catholic** auxiliary bishop of Guatemala City, Juan Gerardi Conedera, is murdered in his residence two days after issuing a scathing report on human rights violations during Guatemala's civil war, which ended in December 1996.

The German People's Union (DVU) takes 12.9 percent of the vote in state elections in Saxony-Anhalt, qualifying DVU, which has links to Germany's neo-Nazi movement, for seats in the state assembly. The DVU vote is the highest tallied by an extreme-right party in Germany's post-World War II history. Chancellor Helmut Kohl's governing Christian Democrats receive 22 percent of the vote, down more than 12 percent from the last state elections in 1994.

27 **The Security Council** of the United Nations (UN) votes to extend sanctions against Iraq because of its failure to fully comply with UN demands for evidence of disarmament. Before the vote, Iraq threatened to disrupt future arms inspections if the sanctions were not lifted.

1 **Former Rwandan prime minister** Jean Kambanda confesses before a United Nations war crimes tribunal, meeting in Tanzania, that he is guilty of committing genocide against members of the Tutsi tribe in Rwanda as well as against moderate members of his own Hutu clan. Kambanda, who faces a maximum sentence of life in prison, promises to testify against former colleagues in the Rwandan government in connection with the 1994 mass killings of at least 500,000 people.

2 **Wim F. Duisenberg** of the Netherlands is appointed first head of the European Union's (EU) new central bank. The central bank was created to oversee the EU single currency, which is to go into effect in January 1999.

6 **The chairmen of Daimler-Benz AG** and the Chrysler Corporation announce that the Stuttgart, Germany-based maker of Mercedes-Benz automobiles will acquire Chrysler in a $36-billion merger. The purchase is the largest acquisition of an American company by a foreign buyer in history.

8 **The U.S. Department of Labor** announces that unemployment in the United States in April 1998 dropped to 4.3 percent, the nation's lowest unemployment level since 1970.

11 **Indian Prime Minister** Atal Bihari Vajpayee announces that India had detonated three nuclear devices in underground tests in India's Thar Desert, in the northwest part of the country. The largest of the three was a hydrogen bomb, a weapon of enormous power. The announcement, which also confirms that India conducted its first nuclear tests in 1974, generates immediate international condemnation.

12 **Indonesian soldiers kill 12 students** during what had been a peaceful demonstration that had spilled onto the streets of Jakarta, the capital, from a college campus. When the approximately 10,000 student demonstrators, demanding the resignation of President Suharto, refused to clear public thoroughfares, they were attacked with clubs and shot at by troops.

13 **India detonates two nuclear** devices at the underground testing site in the country's northwestern Thar Desert where three similar tests were conducted on May 11. President Bill Clinton announces that the United States is imposing wide-ranging economic sanctions on India, including the suspension of nearly all American aid.

14 **Riots erupt throughout Jakarta,** throwing the Indonesian capital into chaos. At least 1,000 people, civilian and military personnel, die as a result of the rioting.

Frank Sinatra, who was widely hailed as the greatest popular singer of his generation, dies in Los Angeles at the age of 82.

15 **Brush and forest fires,** driven by a combination of drought, heat wave, and high winds, burn out of control in El Salvador, Honduras, Nicaragua, Guatemala, and in every Mexican state except Baja California. The smoke and clouds of cinders mixed with urban pollution trigger environmental alerts from Mexico City northeast into Texas, where officials of 50 counties issue health warnings.

17 **New York Yankees pitcher** David Wells strikes out 27 batters in a row to pitch a perfect game against the Minnesota Twins. The feat marks the 15th perfect game in major league history.

18 **The U.S. Justice Department** and the attorneys general of 20 states launch antitrust suits in United States District Court against the Microsoft Corporation of Redmond, Washington, for attempting to control access to the Internet and World Wide Web through Microsoft's near monopoly in personal computer operating systems.

21 **President Suharto of Indonesia** resigns his office after 32 years in power. Vice President B. J. Habibie immediately takes the presidential oath. The Suharto resignation comes in the wake of the grave Asian economic crisis, which has brought the Indonesian economy to the edge of collapse, triggering weeks of daily public protests.

22 **The citizens of Northern Ireland** and the Irish Republic vote overwhelmingly for a referendum approving the Belfast Agreement, a peace accord designed to end hundreds of years of conflict between Roman Catholics and Protestants in Northern Ireland.

24 **Eddie Cheever** wins the Indianapolis 500 by overtaking Buddy Lazier, who finishes second, in the final laps of the event.

Hong Kong voters turn out in record numbers for the first election in the city since China regained control of the former British colony at midnight on June 30, 1997. Many prodemocracy politicians, who were ousted from office by the Chinese government in Beijing, the capital, only hours after the handover at midnight on June 30, 1997, are reelected to Hong Kong's Legislative Council.

25 **Russia's prime minister,** Sergei Kiriyenko, publicly reassures foreign investors that Russia will meet financial obligations and is working to promote tax reform and reduce borrowing.

27 **Russia's Central Bank**, attempting to head off economic crisis, raises interest on treasury bills to 90 percent and the interest on loans to other banks from 50 to 150 percent.

29 **The Congress of the Philippines** declares Joseph Estrada president, 18 days after the disputed May 11 election. Estrada succeeds President Fidel Ramos.

30 **Pakistan, ignoring worldwide** condemnation, detonates a nuclear device in an underground test in the same mountainous desert region where it detonated five similar nuclear devices on May 28.

Demonstrators in Jakarta carry a man shot by police on May 14, 1998, the third straight day of riots against President Suharto's government. Suharto topples from power on May 21 after 32 years in office.

1 **Hundreds of ethnic Albanians** living in Yugoslavia's Kosovo Province flee across the border to Albania in the wake of the latest Serbian attack on members of the Kosovo Liberation Army, which seeks independence for the province. Using both police and army forces, the Belgrade government of Slobodan Milosevic is attempting to retain control of the province by crushing the militants.

3 **More than 100 people are killed** when passenger cars from a German Railways express train, traveling at 125 miles (200 kilometers) per hour, derail near Eschede in northern Germany. The cars crash into a concrete column supporting a highway overpass, causing it to collapse.

5 **Japanese and U.S. physicists** announce that they have discovered the existence of mass in the neutrino, a subatomic particle that is so light that scientists had assumed it was without mass. The discovery suggests that neutrinos may make up much of the mass of the universe.

Attorney General Janet Reno announces that the Justice Department will not prosecute physicians who prescribe lethal drugs to the terminally ill.

6 **Serbian forces shell the villages** of Babaloc, Gramocel, and Shaptej in Yugoslavia's Kosovo Province and torch hundreds of houses in the region. Additional attacks on ethnic Albanians by government forces and police are reported near the Macedonian border.

7 **The Press Trust of India** reports that more than 2,500 Indians have died as a result of the current, record-breaking heat wave, which began on May 12. In New Delhi, the capital, temperatures climbed as high as 124 °F (51 °C).

8 **U.S. Vice President Al Gore** announces that global temperature records have been broken in each of the first five months of 1998. The 1998 record high temperatures follow 1997 temperatures that were the highest recorded since people began measuring temperature with thermometers in the mid-1800's.

9 **President Boris Yeltsin** of Russia promises Chancellor Helmut Kohl of Germany that Yeltsin will intercede with Slobodan Milosevic, the Serbian leader of Yugoslavia, to end Serbian attacks on ethnic Albanians living in Yugoslavia's Kosovo Province.

12 **A Japanese government official** announces that the Japanese economy, which is the world's second largest, is officially in recession.

14 **Michael Jordan** of the Chicago Bulls steals the ball with only 5.2 seconds remaining in Game 6 of the National Basketball Association (NBA) championship and sinks an 18-foot (5.5-meter) pull-up jump shot, defeating the Utah Jazz by 87 to 86. The win provides the Bulls with their third NBA championship in a row and sixth championship during the 1990's.

15 **Stock markets around the world** shudder in response to Japan's June 12 announcement that its economy is officially·in a recession. In New York City, the Dow Jones Industrial average closes down 207 points. The Japanese currency, the yen, falls to another record low against the dollar, sparking new fears that the current economic crisis in Asia is spreading to the West.

President Bill Clinton debates with Jiang Zemin, president of China, on human rights issues during a news conference on June 27, 1998, in Beijing. Clinton began a five-day state visit to China on June 25.

22 **A team of U.S. astronomers** announce the discovery of a planet about the size of Jupiter, but twice its mass, orbiting Gliese 876, a sun only 15 lights-years from our sun. It is the first discovery of a planet orbiting a low-mass star, the most common star type in the Milky Way. The discovery has led to speculation that planetary systems similar to our own may be a common feature of the galaxy.

25 **The U.S. Supreme Court,** nearing the end of its current term, rules six to three that attorney-client privilege does not end with death. In another ruling, the court declares the line-item veto unconstitutional. The court also decides that the government may deny grants to artists whose work is by "general standards" deemed indecent.

27 **President Bill Clinton,** in China on a state visit, and Chinese President Jiang Zemin engage in a debate over human rights, including China's crackdown on dissidents during the 1989 Tiananmen Square demonstrations, during a news conference that is broadcast nationally on Chinese television.

16 **Yugoslav President** Slobodan Milosevic meets with Russian President Boris Yeltsin in Moscow and agrees to concessions that will ease his government's current military campaign against ethnic Albanians in the Serbian province of Kosovo.

17 **The Federal Reserve Bank** of New York sells dollars to buy approximately $2 billion worth of Japanese yen on international currency markets. The rare U.S. move from dollars to yen is an attempt to boost the sliding value of the yen, which declined to another record low on June 15. Japan also buys at least $2 billion in yen on international markets. which analysts claim has spread to Russia and Eastern Europe.

18 **President Bill Clinton appoints** Richard C. Holbrooke, who was the chief American negotiator in the 1995 Bosnia peace agreement, to the post of U.S. Ambassador to the United Nations.

20 **EuroLee Janzen wins** the U.S. Open for a second time, with a score of 68, one stroke over Payne Stewart.

Andres Pastrana defeats Horacio Seerpa to be elected president of Colombia.

29 **Serbian troops** launch a series of attacks on separatist rebels in the Serbian province of Kosovo, where as much as 90 percent of the population is of ethnic Albanian ancestry. Diplomats view the new offensive as putting an end to their latest efforts to negotiate a cease-fire between the Serbs and the Kosovo Liberation Army guerrillas, who currently control approximately 40 percent of the state. NATO officials have threatened to carry out air strikes against the Belgrade government of Slobodan Milosevic if Serbian forces do not withdraw from Kosovo, where the fighting has left hundreds dead.

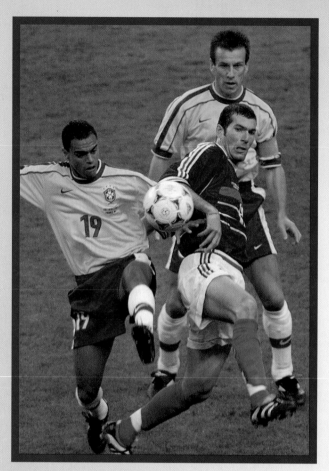

Zinedine Zidane of France (right) battles Brazil's Denilson for control of the ball on July 12, 1998, in the final game of the soccer World Cup 98. France, which hosted the games, scored a major upset by winning the event.

2 **Residents of Volusia and Brevard** counties in northeast Florida continue to flee their houses as whole towns are threatened by wildfires, which burn through the countryside despite the efforts of hundreds of firefighters. More than 30,000 people have been evacuated since July 1.

4 **Jana Novotna** of the Czech Republic wins her first Wimbledon championship by beating Nathalie Tauziat of France, 6-4, 7-6.

5 **Pete Sampras** defeats Goran Ivanisevic of Croatia—6-7 (2-7), 7-6 (11-9), 6-4, 3-6, 6-2—to take his fifth Wimbledon title and his eleventh Grand Slam championship.

8 **At least 19 people are killed** in riots between ethnic groups in Lagos, Nigeria's commercial capital, in the wake of the sudden death on July 7 of Moshood Abiola, imprisoned leader of the opposition to the West African country's current military regime.

12 **France beats Brazil** to capture the World Cup in the soccer championship's biggest upset in half a century.

Three brothers, ages 10, 9, and 7, are burned to death in Ballymoney, Northern Ireland, the result of a firebomb thrown into their house. Police suggest the attack was made by Protestants, upset by bans on marching through Catholic neighborhoods.

13 **Prime Minister Ryutaro Hashimoto** of Japan resigns in response to the severe losses the Liberal Democratic Party suffered in parliamentary elections on July 12. Political observers interpret the vote as a blunt demand for greater leadership to revive Japan's ailing economy.

The International Monetary Fund and World Bank conclude agreements with Russian officials that provide Russia with nearly $17 billion in additional loans in 1998 and 1999. In total, the Russian economy is now backed with $22.6 billion in loans intended to stave off further economic crises, prop up the ruble, and steady shaky international markets.

15 **Dallas [Texas] County Health** and Human Services officials declare a state of emergency due to a heat wave that pushed temperatures to above 100 °F (38 °C) for 10 straight days.

16 **A federal appeals court** in Washington, D.C., rejects an attempt by the Clinton Administration to block the grand jury testimony of Secret Service officials on their knowledge of the nature of President Bill Clinton's relationship with Monica Lewinsky, a former intern at the White House.

17 **The remains of the last czar** of Russia, Nicholas II, his wife, Alexandra, and 3 of their 5 children are buried beside those of his ancestors in Saints Peter and Paul Cathedral in St. Petersburg. The remains were authenticated by DNA testing, conducted by British and American scientists.

Three *tsunamis* (enormous waves caused by an earthquake) crash into Papua New Guinea's northern coast, killing an estimated 3,000 people in an area with between 8,000 and 10,000 residents. The last and largest of the three waves was estimated to be 33 feet (10 meters) high.

18 **President Bill Clinton** announces that the U.S. government will spend $250 million to buy 80 million bushels of wheat, in an attempt to push up prices to aid American farmers, who the president describes as being "in crisis."

20 **General Abdulsalam Abubakar**, president of Algeria since the death of General Sani Abacha in June 1998, declares that presidential elections will be held in the next three months and power will be handed to a civilian government on May 29, 1999.

21 **A 700-foot (213-meter) construction** elevator tower collapses at approximately the level of the 22nd floor of the Conde Nast Headquarters under construction on New York City's Times Square. Hundreds of residents and workers are evacuated, and the Times Square area is closed to traffic leaving what is normally the busiest section of New York City eerily quiet.

24 **A gun battle** takes place inside the U.S. Capitol, in Washington, D.C., when a 41-year-old man opens fire when asked to walk through a metal detector. Exchanging shots with the gunman, two Capitol police officers are killed and a tourist is wounded before the gunman is subdued.

The foreign minister of Japan, Keizo Obuchi, is named president of the ruling Liberal Democratic Party (LDP), ensuring that he will be Japan's next prime minister.

26 **More than 50 crosses appear** outside the walls of Auschwitz, the World War II (1939–1945) Nazi German concentration camp and extermination center near what is now Oswiecim, Poland. The crosses are believed to be part of a campaign by a group of Polish Roman Catholics, who claim the right to maintain Christian symbols at a place where Christians as well as Jews were murdered. Jewish groups claim that Auschwitz is the world's largest Jewish cemetery and should not reflect non-Jewish faiths.

29 **Massive flooding of China's** Yangtze River has resulted in the widespread contamination of drinking water, exposing millions of Chinese to a variety of diseases. Weeks of rain have resulted in the flooding of millions of acres, driving millions of people from their houses and leaving at least 3,000 dead.

2 **Indian and Pakistani forces** exchange intense artillery fire in the disputed border area of the Indian state of Kashmir. At least 80 people, mostly civilians, die in the barrage.

3 **Thirty-two people die** in Bombay, India, when a seven-story, concrete apartment building collapses, leaving a pile of rubble 20 to 30 feet (6 to 9 meters) high. In the last three years, eight major structures have collapsed in Bombay.

4 **Canadian officials sign a treaty** with West Coast Canadian Indians that guarantees the Nisga people control over specified lands in British Columbia, as well as the right to establish and govern a nation on those lands.

6 **Monica Lewinsky,** a 25-year-old, former White House intern, answers questions before a grand jury in Washington, D.C., about the nature of her relationship with President Bill Clinton. On July 28, independent council Kenneth Starr announced that he had granted Lewinsky immunity from federal prosecution in exchange for her promise to testify.

7 **Powerful car bombs,** set by unknown terrorists, explode outside the American embassy in Nairobi, Kenya. The explosions kill at least 213 people, including 12 Americans, and wound more than 5,000. Minutes before the blast, a similar bomb exploded outside the American embassy in Dar es Salaam, the capital of Tanzania, killing 11 and injuring 72.

12 **A Titan 4A rocket**, carrying a spy satellite for the U.S. National Reconnaissance Office, blows up 40 seconds after being launched, creating a spectacular fireball 20,000 feet (6,096 meters) over the Atlantic Ocean near Cape Canaveral, Florida.

13 **Rebels, believed to be backed by** the government of neighboring Rwanda, reach the outskirts of Kinshasa, capital of the Congo, after only 10 days of insurrection. Inga Dam, the largest generator of hydroelectricity in Africa, is seized, and electrical power in Kinshasa is cut off.

15 **A car bomb explodes** in the Northern Ireland town of Omagh, killing 29 people and shattering a cease-fire in effect for over a year.

16 **King Hussein issues a decree** from a hospital bed in Rochester, Minnesota, that gives his brother and heir, Crown Prince Hassan, the constitutional power to reorganize the government of Jordan. Hussein was undergoing treatment for cancer.

17 **President Bill Clinton admits** in a television address that he misled grand jury prosecutors and the public about his relationship with Monica Lewinsky, a former White House intern. The president characterizes the relationship as "wrong" and "not appropriate." Earlier in the day, the president testified for more than four hours before prosecutors under the direction of independent counsel Kenneth Starr, who had spent four years investigating the personal and professional lives of the president and Mrs. Clinton.

The government of Russia attempts to stave off economic collapse by permitting banks to postpone for 90 days the repayment of $43 billion in short-term foreign debts and by allowing the value of the ruble to float on international monetary markets.

18 **A mountain, turned to mud** by heavy rains, collapses and slides over two Himalayan villages in India's northern Uttar Pradesh state. More than 200 people are buried alive.

Russia's Bank of Moscow and Bank Imperial suspend the sale of American dollars in an attempt to stop the downward slide of the ruble.

20 **U.S. cruise missiles are launched** from ships in the Arabian and Red seas at targets in Afghanistan and Sudan. U.S. government officials describe the target in Afghanistan as a terrorist training camp and the target in the Sudan as a factory where chemical weapons are fabricated. President Bill Clinton characterizes the operation as an "act of self-defense" and "retribution" for the August 7 bombings of American embassies.

The U.S. Embassy in Nairobi, Kenya (left) and an office building and a bank, are destroyed on August 7 by powerful car bombs set by terrorists. Minutes before the blast, a similar bomb exploded outside the American embassy in Dar es Salaam, Tanzania.

22 **The president of Uganda**, Yoweri K. Museveni, issues a warning that he will invade the Democratic Republic of the Congo if troops from Angola and Zimbabwe are not immediately withdrawn from Congo.

23 **Russian President Boris Yeltsin** replaces Sergei Kiriyenko, who has held office as prime minister for only five months, with Viktor Chernomyrdin, who was himself dismissed as prime minister on March 23.

25 **The ruble goes into free fall** on Moscow currency exchanges, tumbling 9 percent against the dollar before the Russian Central Bank intervenes by suspending trading.

26 **Hurricane Bonnie hits land** at the mouth of North Carolina's Cape Fear River with winds of 100 miles (161 kilometers) per hour and very heavy rains.

27 **Government officials** in Kuala Lumpur release statistics confirming that the Malaysian economy shrank in the second quarter of 1998 by 6.8 percent and is in severe recession. In Seoul, the Bank of Korea issues a statement that the South Korean economy, which contracted by 6.6 percent in the second quarter, is also officially in recession.

28 **The Tokyo Stock Exchange** drops 3.5 percent, ending the week at its lowest level since 1986. During the week of August 23, the value of all stocks on the Tokyo exchange fell by a total of $241 billion.

29 **More than 6,000** Northwest Airlines pilots go out on strike, grounding the airline's fleet of 400 planes.

A Cuban Tupolev-143 jet catches fire and explodes on a third take-off attempt from the Quito, Ecuador, airport, killing 79 of 90 people aboard.

2 All 229 passengers and crew aboard Swissair Flight 111, bound for Geneva from New York City, die when the plane crashes into the Atlantic Ocean off the southeast shore of Nova Scotia.

5 North Korea, the first Communist country in history in which power is transferred from one generation of a family to another, officially declares Kim Jong Il "Great Leader." Kim Jong Il is the eldest son of Kim Il Sung, Great Leader of North Korea from 1948 until his death in 1994.

7 Russian central bank chairman Sergei Dubinin resigns in the wake of the current financial crisis in which the value of the ruble has fallen from 6 to the dollar to 20 to the dollar in less than one month.

9 Independent counsel Kenneth W. Starr sends to the U.S. Congress 36 cartons of grand-jury testimony, videotapes, and a report that summarizes his four-year, $40-million investigation into the lives of President Bill Clinton and First Lady Hillary Rodham Clinton.

10 Russian President Boris Yeltsin withdraws Viktor S. Chernomyrdin from parliamentary consideration for prime minister and nominates Foreign Minister Yevgeny Primakov.

Iran announces that it holds the militant Taliban movement, currently in control of much of Afghanistan, responsible for the deaths of nine Iranian diplomats killed on August 8 in a consulate in Mazar-i-Sharif, a city in northern Afghanistan.

On Sept. 9, 1998, police officers deliver to the House of Representatives 36 cartons of grand-jury testimony and documents related to Independent Counsel Kenneth Starr's 4-year, $40-million investigation of President Bill Clinton.

11 **The lower house of the Russian** parliament, the Duma, confirms Yevgeny Primakov as prime minister.

12 **Floodwaters in Bangladesh,** which have covered much of the country for more than two months, begin to recede. The massive flooding of the Brahmaputra, Ganges, and Jamuna rivers has left 900 people dead and displaced one-quarter of the country's 124 million people since July 10.

16 **The Basque separatist group ETA** announces an "indefinite" cease-fire in its 30-year battle for independence from Spain. More than 800 deaths have been attributed to terrorist attacks by ETA and other militant Basque nationalist parties.

18 **Prime Minister Keizo Obuchi** announces that leaders of Japan's two largest political parties have agreed on a series of radical economic reforms. The reforms, which include the nationalization of insolvent banks, are part of an effort to prop up Japan's economy, which is undergoing its worst recession since World War II (1939–1945).

20 **Malaysian police,** wearing black ski masks and brandishing machine guns, arrest former Deputy Prime Minister Anwar Ibrahim hours after Anwar led a demonstration that was characterized as the largest in the city's history. Demanding reform of the government of Prime Minister Mahathir bin Mohamad, Anwar has attracted increasingly bigger crowds in the weeks since Mahathir fired his former protege on charges of corruption, treason, sedition, and sexual indecency.

Cal Ripken, Jr., third baseman for the Baltimore Orioles, voluntarily sits out his first Orioles' game since 1982, establishing an endurance record of starting in 2,632 consecutive games.

21 **President Bill Clinton's** August 17 grand jury testimony regarding the nature of his relationship with a former White House intern, Monica Lewinsky, is broadcast in its entirety on national television.

24 **Saudi Arabia expels Afghanistan's** chief ambassador to Riyadh, the capital, and recalls its own envoy from the Afghan capital, Kabul. Afghanistan is charged with providing a haven to a known terrorist, Osama bin Laden, who Saudi Arabia banished for attempting to overthrow the monarchy. The United States has accused bin Laden of organizing the August bombings of American embassies in Kenya and Tanzania, which resulted in the deaths of more than 220 people.

The foreign minister of Iran announces that his government has disassociated itself from the death threat imposed on the Indian-born, British novelist Salman Rushdie. In 1989, the Ayatollah Khomeini, who headed the revolutionary government of Iran, branded Rushdie's novel *The Satanic Verses* blasphemous to Islam and issued a fatwa, or religious edict, that offered a reward to anyone who assassinated the author.

25 **Hurricane Georges crashes** across the Florida Keys with winds over 100 miles (161 kilometers) per hour, causing widespread flooding, but no reported deaths. In its rampage across the Caribbean before hitting the Keys, Georges left more than 500 people dead and billions of dollars in damage in its wake.

27 **German voters elect** liberal Social Democrat Gerhard Schroeder chancellor, turning out Helmut Kohl. Kohl, a conservative, supervised the unification of East and West Germany and held power for 16 years.

St. Louis Cardinals' first baseman Mark McGwire hits two home runs in the final game of the Cardinals' 1998 season, bringing his 1998 home run total to 70. McGwire broke the previous single-season home-run record of 61, held by Roger Maris since 1961, on Sept. 8, 1998.

30 **United States President Bill Clinton** announces that the U.S. government ends fiscal year 1998 with a budget surplus of approximately $70 billion. The surplus is the first since 1969 and the largest in U.S. history.

3 **Australia's conservative** government, led by Prime Minister John Howard, wins reelection, but with a diminished majority in Parliament.

4 **Brazil reelects President Fernando** Henrique Cardoso, who is credited with ending Brazil's crippling inflation.

7 **The United States Department** of Health and Human Services announces that the number of U.S. citizens who died from AIDS in 1997 was down 47 percent from 1996 and was at its lowest level since 1987.

8 **The U.S. House of Representatives** votes 258 to 176 to launch a full-scale inquiry into whether President Bill Clinton should be impeached.

9 **The Italian government**, under the leadership of Prime Minister Romano Prodi, collapses in a parliamentary confidence vote of 313 to 312. Prodi held office for 2½ years, Italy's second-longest lived government since World War II (1939-1945).

12 **Japan's parliament passes** legislation designed to save the Japanese banking industry, which may hold as much as $1 trillion in bad debt.

13 **Special envoy** Richard C. Holbrooke of the United States discloses that he and Yugoslav President Slobodan Milosevic have come to terms over a cease-fire in Kosovo Province. The agreement averts the immediate threat of a North American Treaty Organization (NATO) air strike against Milosevic's forces.

14 **U.S. Attorney General Janet Reno** and FBI Director Louis Freeh announce that they have charged Eric Robert Rudolph with three 1996 bombings in Atlanta, Georgia, including the bombing at the 1996 Summer Olympics. Rudolph was previously charged with the Jan. 29, 1998, bombing of an abortion clinic in Birmingham, Alabama.

16 **The Nobel Committee** announces that John Hume and David Trimble, Roman Catholic and Protestant leaders in Northern Ireland, are to be awarded the Nobel Peace Prize for their efforts on behalf of the Belfast Accord.

17 **More than 15 inches** (38 centimeters) of rain falls over central Texas in six hours, sending creeks and rivers over their banks in 60 Texas counties and closing dozens of highways and expressways. Twenty-two people die in the floods statewide.

19 **A Palestinian hurls two grenades** at a crowd of Israeli soldiers in a crowded bus station in Beersheba, wounding more than 60 people, some seriously. The attack is believed to be an attempt to disrupt Israeli-Palestinian peace talks currently underway in the United States.

The government of Russia releases figures confirming that the number of Russians living in poverty has risen to 44.3 million people—30 percent of the population—from 31 million one year before. Russian government economists define the poverty line as a monthly income of $31 or less.

20 **The president of BankAmerica** Corporation, David Coulter, announces his resignation in light of a $372-million loss to the bank under his direction. The loss resulted from an unsecured loan that Coulter made in 1997 to a hedge fund, D. E. Shaw & Company. Hedge funds put investors' money into highly risky ventures in the hopes of spectacular returns.

The New York Yankees complete their 1998 season of 125 victories by winning the World Series with a four-game sweep over the San Diego Padres.

23 **Palestinian leader Yasir Arafat** and Israeli Prime Minister Benjamin Netanyahu sign an agreement that breathes life back into the 1993 Oslo Accords, reopening the possibility an independent Palestinian state. The agreement commits Israel to withdraw from 13 percent of the West Bank over the next 12 weeks. In return, the Palestinians pledged to take steps to curb terrorism and to amend their charter, which currently calls for the destruction of the Israeli state.

25 **Typhoon Babs hits Taiwan** and Hong Kong with more than 20 inches (50 centimeters) of rain and 80-mile- (128-kilometer-) per-hour winds. Babs smashed

Senator John Glenn prepares to board the space shuttle Discovery at Kennedy Space Center in Florida on Oct. 29, 1998, for his first return to space since orbiting the Earth in 1962.

into the Philippines on October 22, leaving 400,000 people homeless and more than 190 people dead.

26 **President Jamil Mahaud of Ecuador** and Alberto Fujimori of Peru sign a peace treaty ending a boundary dispute that had triggered three wars in 50 years.

27 **The United Nations** world population report reveals that 21 million of the 30 million people worldwide infected with HIV reside in Africa.

29 **The space shuttle Discovery lifts** off from Cape Canaveral, Florida, with an international crew of seven astronauts, including space pioneer John Glenn.

The flight is the 121st U.S. space mission since John Glenn first orbited Earth in February 1962.

30 **Gale force winds** and torrential rains from Hurricane Mitch sweep across Honduras, Guatemala, El Salvador, and Belize, forcing the evacuation of thousands of people in Central America. Floods and mud slides triggered by the deluge trapped thousands more without power, food, or drinkable water. In Nicaragua, the pounding rain fills the crater of Casita Volcano, forming a lake that triggers the collapse of the crater walls. A river of water and mud flows down the sides of the volcano and buries entire villages, killing as many as 2,000 people.

Speaker of the House of Representatives Newt Gingrich, a Republican from Georgia, waves to a crowd in Washington, D.C. on November 6 after announcing that he will resign as speaker of the House and will leave Congress in January 1999

2 The death toll from Hurricane Mitch exceeds 10,000 people. Another 10,000 people remain missing. The storm, which stalled over Honduras, Nicaragua, Guatemala, El Salvador, and Belize for nearly a week in late October, dumped as much as 24 inches (61 centimeters) of rain every 24 hours, triggering massive flooding and mudslides.

3 Democrats show strength in midterm elections, picking up five seats in the House of Representatives and holding their ground in the Senate. The election marks the first time since 1934 that the party of a sitting U.S. president gained seats in Congress in a midterm election. Republicans maintain their control of governorships but lose major posts in California, Iowa, and Minnesota.

4 A United States federal grand jury returns a 238-count indictment charging Saudi exile Osama bin Laden with conspiring to bomb two U.S. embassies in Africa in August and with a series of acts of terrorism against Americans abroad. The U.S. government offers a $5-million reward for information leading to the arrest of bin Laden.

5 Scientists for the first time cultivate human cells—called human embryonic stem cells—that are capable of developing into many of the body's 210 different types of cells, researchers announce in the journal *Science*. The cells, derived from fertilized human eggs, can divide indefinitely when grown outside the body without the signs of age that afflict other cells. Researchers hope to use the cells to grow tissue for human transplants.

6 **Speaker of the U.S. House** Newt Gingrich (R., Georgia) announces that he will not seek reelection as speaker of the House and will leave Congress when his term expires in January 1999. Gingrich orchestrated the Republican takeover of Congress in 1994, but his Republican colleagues blamed him for the party's unexpected losses in the November 3 mid-term elections.

7 **United States Senator John Glenn** returns to Earth after a nine-day mission on the space shuttle Discovery. Glenn, the world's oldest astronaut at age 77, served as a subject of geriatric research on the mission. In 1962, Glenn became a national hero for being the first American to circle the planet.

9 **Representative** Robert L. Livingston of Louisiana locks up the votes to become the next speaker of the House of Representatives.

11 **The Israeli Cabinet approves** a new Israeli-Palestinian peace accord, which calls for an Israeli troop withdrawal from 13 percent of the West Bank in exchange for a Palestinian crackdown on violent militants.

13 **President Bill Clinton** agrees to pay Paula Corbin Jones $850,000 to drop her lawsuit claiming that he had sexually harassed her in 1991 when he was still governor of Arkansas.

14 **President Bill Clinton** cancels a planned military strike on Iraq just hours before it was set to begin. The cancellation is in response to President Saddam Hussein's vague promise, made in a letter to the United Nations, that Iraq will allow inspections of weapon sites.

19 **The Judiciary Committee** of the U.S. House of Representatives opens impeachment hearings against President Bill Clinton with testimony by independent counsel Kenneth Starr on the nature of the president's relationship with Monica Lewinsky, a former White House intern. Starr defended his four-year, $40-million investigation into the political, financial, and private lives of President Clinton and Hillary Rodham Clinton.

20 **The attorneys general** of 46 states agree to settle their lawsuits against U.S. tobacco companies for $206 billion, which the states will share over a period of years. The states had sued cigarette manufacturers to recover Medicaid money spent treating diseases related to smoking.

22 **Foreign Minister Mohammed Saeed** al-Sahhaf announces that Iraq does not intend to honor its November 14 promise to cooperate with international arms inspectors and will not allow inspectors to see documents related to its weapons program.

23 **The European Union votes to lift** its 32-month ban on beef from Great Britain. The EU had placed British beef exports under a worldwide ban in 1996 when some British cows were found to carry a disease linked to Creutzfeldt-Jakob disease, a fatal, degenerative, brain disorder in human beings.

24 **A spokesperson for the U.S.** Department of Justice announces that Attorney General Janet Reno has concluded that there is insufficient evidence to appoint an independent counsel to investigate Vice President Al Gore's role in fund raising during the 1996 presidential election.

25 **Great Britain's highest court** rules that General Augusto Pinochet's status as the former ruler of Chile does not make him immune from arrest. Pinochet had been held in Britain at the request of a Spanish court, which sought his extradition on grounds of genocide and terrorism committed against Spanish citizens during Pinochet's rule from 1973 to 1990.

The government of Prime Minister Mesut Yilmaz of Turkey falls in a parliamentary confidence vote taken after the prime minister was accused of helping gangsters buy a state-owned bank.

28 **President Jacques Chirac of France** announces that United Nations Secretary General Kofi Annan has secured promises from eight African leaders to sign a cease-fire in Congo's civil war.

4 **The space shuttle Endeavour carries** into orbit the first U.S.-built section of a planned international space station, which is expected to cost more than $100 billion. During the 12-day mission, astronauts onboard Endeavour attach the U.S. module to a Russian-built section of the station already in orbit.

7 **Attorney General Janet Reno** announces that she will not seek the appointment of an independent counsel to investigate President Bill Clinton's role in a Democratic advertising campaign for the 1996 election.

8 **Scientists in Japan report** that they cloned eight calves from cells gathered from a single cow. Only four of the calves survived.

9 **Scientists in South Africa announce** the discovery of what they describe as the best preserved skeleton yet found of an early member of the human family. The scientists estimated the age of the skeleton at between 3.2 million and 3.6 million years old.

11 **The Judiciary Committee** of the U.S. House of Representatives votes along party lines to send to the House three articles recommending impeachment against President Bill Clinton. The Republican-controlled committee charges Clinton of committing *perjury* (lying under oath) during testimony on August 17, 1998, before a grand jury investigating his relationship with Monica Lewinsky, a former White House intern. In a second article of impeachment, the committee charges Clinton with committing perjury in his deposition in the Paula Jones sexual harassment case in 1997. A third article accuses Clinton of trying to influence witnesses in the Lewinsky matter. The next day, the committee votes a fourth article of impeachment accusing President Clinton of abuse of power.

Biologists announce that they have deciphered the full genetic programming of a multicelled animal. Scientists hope the discovery will pave the way for mapping the entire human genetic code. The genetic code of the animal—a microscopic roundworm—gives scientists their first glimpse of the information needed to develop, operate, and maintain a multicellular animal.

12 **President Bill Clinton flies to Israel** to revive a peace accord signed in October by Israeli Prime Minister Benjamin Netanyahu and Palestinian leader Yasir Arafat. Netanyahu, who lost much of his political support by agreeing to cede more land to the Palestinians, threatens to break the accord.

16 **President Bill Clinton orders** a series of air and missile strikes against Iraq. Iraq refused to live up to its promise of allowing the United Nations to conduct on-site inspections to ensure the dismantling of weapons of mass destruction. The attack begins at about 11 p.m. Baghdad time with a wave of more than 200 Tomahawk missiles, most launched against centers believed to be used for manufacturing or storing weapons of mass destruction.

19 **The U.S. House of Representatives** votes to impeach President Bill Clinton, marking the second time in U.S. history that a president has faced a Senate trial to remove him from office. House members pass two articles of impeachment with a vote of 228 to 206 on a charge of lying under oath and 221 to 212 on a charge of obstructing justice during the investigation of his relationship with Monica Lewinsky. House Democrats failed in their efforts to win House approval of a move to censure the president as an alternative to impeachment.

Congressman Robert Livingston of Louisiana, whom the Republican majority had nominated for speaker of the U.S. House of Representatives, admits to having extramarital affairs and announces that he will not run for speaker. He also intends to resign from the House in mid-1999.

The United States ends its campaign of air and missile strikes on Iraq. President Clinton and Prime Minister Tony Blair of Great Britain proclaim they have achieved their goal of degrading Iraq's military machine. Iraqi officials pledge to never allow the return of United Nations arms inspectors.

Republican Henry J. Hyde (right) of Illinois, chairman of the House Judiciary Committee, hands articles of impeachment to Gary Sisco (left), secretary of the Senate, on December 19 after the House of Representatives voted to impeach President Bill Clinton.

20 **A 27-year-old woman** in Houston gives birth to the last of eight infants, the first known surviving set of octuplets. The first child, a girl, was born on December 8. The smallest of the infants died on December 27, and the others remained in critical condition.

21 **An overwhelming majority** of the Israeli parliament votes to dissolve the government of Prime Minister Benjamin Netanyahu. Earlier in the day, members of parliament agreed to withdraw a scheduled vote of no-confidence in Netanyahu's government, which by law would have forced parliament to hold elections within 60 days.

23 **More than a third** of California's annual citrus crop is destroyed by a freeze, and growers say that orange prices in supermarkets will triple by the end of the year. The cold spell, which began on December 21, is the worst since 1990.

24 **Serbian forces break** a two-month cease-fire as they launch an assault on separatist guerrillas in Podujevo, Serbia, in northern Kosovo Province. International monitors, who are in Kosovo to encourage talks between the government and the rebels, state that it may be pointless to continue their peace efforts.

Ocean

Space

People in the News

Geology

Astronomy

Architecture

Biology

South Africa

Transportation

Nobel Prizes

Economics

Canada

New York City

Chemistry

Disasters

Popular Music

Archaeolo

1998 UPDATE

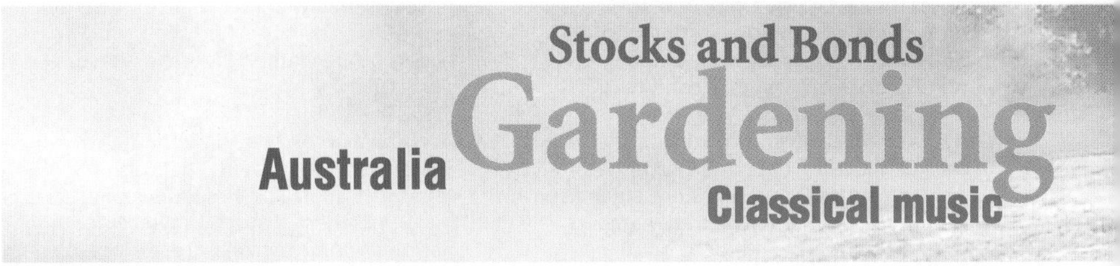

Stocks and Bonds

Gardening

Australia

Classical music

The major events of 1998 are summarized in more than 250 alphabetically arranged articles, from "Afghanistan" to "Zoos." Included are Special Reports that offer in-depth looks at subjects ranging from the Asian economic crisis to the life and career of Frank Sinatra. The Special Reports can be found on the following pages under their respective Update article titles.

Afghanistan. The Taliban, a fundamentalist Muslim militia group composed primarily of Pashtuns, Afghanistan's largest ethnic group, captured the city of Mazar-i-Sharif in August 1998, a major victory in its war against an alliance of several small ethnic groups. The capture of Mazar-i-Sharif gave the Taliban control of nearly the entire country.

In 1996, the Taliban captured Afghanistan's capital, Kabul, and formed a new national government. By late 1998, the Taliban held all of Afghanistan except for a northeastern area, which remained under Tajik control. In 1998, the United Nations (UN) intensified efforts to negotiate peace between the warring factions. The Taliban withdrew from the talks in May.

In August, two days after they took control of Mazar-i-Sharif, the Taliban captured Taloqan, the capital of Takhar province and a stronghold of the Tajik ethnic minority, but Tajiks led by Ahmed Shah Massoud recaptured the province in October.

The Taliban also captured Pul-i-Khumri, the base for the Ismaili Muslim religious sect's armed forces. In September, the Taliban captured Bamiyan, the center of the Hazara ethnic group. Reports by United Nations observers and human rights groups said the Taliban slaughtered thousands of Hazaras in Mazar-i-Sharif and Bamiyan.

Dozens of U.S. missiles struck targets in Afghanistan and Sudan on August 20 in what U.S. President Bill Clinton described as an act of self-defense against terrorist plots and retribution for the August 7 bombings of U.S. embassies in East Africa. The missiles destroyed what U.S. officials described as a terrorist training complex southeast of Kabul. United States security officials said the site was run by Osama bin Laden, an exiled Saudi millionaire linked to a host of terrorist activities. The leader of the Taliban, Mullah Mohammad Omar, condemned the bombings and promised to shelter bin Laden.

Tension with relief groups. The Taliban damaged its relations with international aid agencies in 1998 by refusing to relax restrictions on women and refusing to cooperate with aid organizations in Afghanistan. The strict Islamic rule imposed by the Taliban made it difficult for foreign aid workers to supply Afghanistan with food and medicine. UN aid workers left Afghanistan in March, and most aid workers in Kabul left the country in July. Some workers later returned.

An earthquake shook Takhar province on February 4, killing an estimated 4,500 people. An earthquake on May 30 in Badakshan province killed nearly 4,000 people. □ Henry S. Bradsher

See also **Asia** (Facts in brief table); **Iran;
Disasters.**

Taliban gunners fire at opposition forces on Aug. 2, 1998, near Shibarghan in a campaign to capture Mazar-i-Sharif, the last major city outside Taliban control. The Taliban took Mazar-i-Sharif on August 8.

Although several African leaders spoke of an African *renaissance* (revival) in 1998, the year was overshadowed by an escalation of political and military conflict in many parts of the continent. In 1998, at least one in four African countries was involved in either civil war or regional conflict, according to a United Nations (UN) report. The report also noted that half of all deaths from conflicts worldwide occurred in Africa. The fighting posed serious challenges for the Organization of African Unity (OAU), an association of more than 50 African nations, which celebrated its 35th anniversary in 1998. In 1992, the OAU had made the prevention of conflict a central plank in its strategy for regional development in preparation for the arrival of the 2000's.

In 1998, various African governments continued to intervene in the domestic affairs of their neighbors, including Sierra Leone, Guinea-Bissau, and Lesotho. In the Democratic Republic of the Congo (formerly Zaire), ethnic animosities drew in nearly all surrounding countries. Equally worrisome was the eruption of hostilities between neighboring states—most notably Ethiopia and Eritrea.

More positive events in Africa in 1998 included a trip to the continent by United States President Bill Clinton and First Lady Hillary Rodham Clinton and the restoration of a democratically elected government in Sierra Leone. Nigeria seized an opportunity to return to civilian rule with the June death of military dictator Sani Abacha. Abacha had seized power in November 1993 after a former military leader annulled the results of democratic elections held earlier that year.

President Clinton's visit to six African states —Ghana, Uganda, Rwanda, South Africa, Botswana, and Senegal—between March 23 and April 2, 1998, was the most comprehensive tour of the continent ever undertaken by a U.S. president. The countries were chosen for their commitment to democratic government and economic reform, with the exception of Rwanda, which was included to highlight U.S. concern for the 1994 *genocide* (mass murder) of 500,000 Tutsi. Kenya, Zimbabwe, and Nigeria were conspicuous by their absence from Clinton's itinerary. The governments of Kenya and Zimbabwe were under pressure to institute democratic reforms and Nigeria continued to be ruled by a military dictatorship.

During Clinton's three-hour stopover in Rwanda, he admitted that the international community must bear some of the blame for the 1994 slaughter of some 500,000 people. He said that

the outside world "did not act quickly enough after the killing began." In Uganda, Clinton apologized for U.S. participation in the slave trade and for the American treatment of Africa during the *Cold War* (the intense rivalry between the United States and the former Soviet Union from 1945 to 1991). He added that the United States and Russia had a special responsibility to Africa because they had previously sacrificed the needs of Africans to U.S. and Soviet strategic interests.

The highlight of Clinton's tour was his stay in South Africa from March 26 to March 28, 1998, the first state visit to that country by a U.S. president. Clinton's visit underlined America's support for South Africa's remarkable transformation from *apartheid* (racial separation) to democracy and black-majority rule.

Bomb blasts. On August 7, two car bombs exploded within minutes of each other outside the U.S. embassies in Nairobi, Kenya, and Dar es Salaam, Tanzania. The blasts killed at least 224 people—12 of them Americans. Thousands more were injured.

United States investigators accused Islamic extremist Osama bin Laden, a Saudi Arabian living in exile in Afghanistan, of masterminding the attack. The United States retaliated on August 20 by launching missile strikes on what were described as a terrorist base camp in Afghanistan and a factory for making components of chemical weapons in Sudan.

On October 7, a federal grand jury in New York City indicted four men in connection with the bombings. Two of the suspects had been charged on September 28 with conspiring to bomb and murder U.S. citizens and with carrying out the bombing in Nairobi. The three suspects in custody pleaded not guilty. The fourth suspect remained at large.

Turmoil in central Africa. The second civil war in the Democratic Republic of the Congo in three years erupted in August, renewing the regional conflict that had engulfed Africa's Great Lakes region in 1996 and 1997. Rwanda and Uganda, which had helped Congo's President Laurent Kabila seize power in 1997, threw their support to anti-Kabila forces in 1998. Both countries accused Kabila of harboring insurgents who, they said, were trying to overthrow their governments. As the crisis worsened, troops from Angola, Zimbabwe, and Namibia arrived to support Kabila.

Other civil conflicts. Conditions in Angola worsened in 1998 as rebel forces led by Jonas

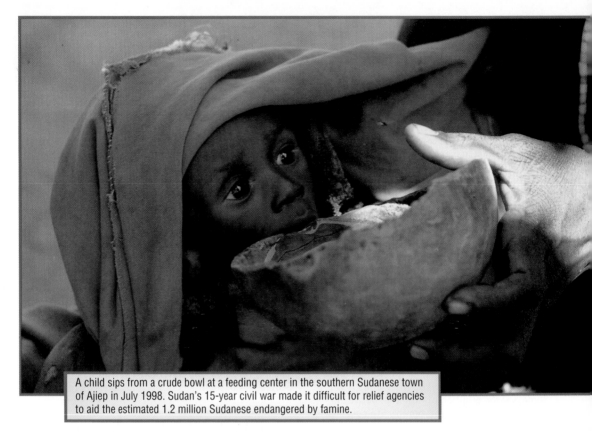

A child sips from a crude bowl at a feeding center in the southern Sudanese town of Ajiep in July 1998. Sudan's 15-year civil war made it difficult for relief agencies to aid the estimated 1.2 million Sudanese endangered by famine.

Savimbi attempted to recover territory controlled by the national army. Combat was concentrated in the diamond-rich northeast, resulting in an exodus of at least 30,000 refugees into neighboring countries.

In Sierra Leone, democratically elected President Ahmed Tejan Kabbah, who was toppled by an army *coup* (overthrow) in 1997, was restored to power on March 10, 1998, by a Nigerian-led military force. However, guerrillas loyal to the former military regime continued to wage a war of opposition in the countryside.

The Guinea-Bissau army mutinied against the elected government of President Joao Bernardo Vieira on June 7. Troops from neighboring Guinea and Senegal intervened in support of Vieira. The conflict resulted in the deaths of hundreds of soldiers and civilians and sent at least one-third of the country's population fleeing their homes, many to Senegal. On November 2, the two sides signed a cease-fire agreement, which called for the immediate deployment of peacekeeping troops from the Economic Community of West African States, a multinational coalition, and the formation of a government of national unity. In addition, presidential elections were scheduled for March 1999.

Border disputes soured political relations between a number of African states during 1998.

In southern Africa, Botswana and Namibia argued over the ownership of two small islands in the Linyanti River on Botswana's northern border with Namibia.

Following clashes between armed troops along the Linyanti and Chobe rivers, the two countries agreed in May to submit the disagreement to the International Court of Justice (ICJ), the UN's highest judicial body, in the Netherlands. A hearing was set for early 1999.

In June 1998, the ICJ also agreed, at the request of Cameroon, to rule on a long-standing boundary dispute between Cameroon and Nigeria over the oil-rich Bakassi Peninsula. The ICJ's decision to intervene followed clashes earlier in the year between the two countries' security forces. Nigeria's opposition to the court's involvement raised doubts about whether the ICJ's ruling would resolve the conflict.

War in the Horn of Africa. A boundary disagreement between Ethiopia and Eritrea, two of Africa's poorest countries, led to renewed fighting on May 6. At issue was 150 square miles (390 square kilometers) in the barren and remote Yirga Triangle, which Eritrea claimed Ethiopia had annexed. The boundary there had never been formally settled between the two countries.

By June, the two states were locked in a full-scale air war. The brunt of the fighting was concentrated along a wide front of the border region. As the crisis grew, the OAU attempted to persuade Ethiopia's prime minister, Meles Zenawi, and Eritrea's president Isaias Afworki, to accept a U.S.-Rwandan peace plan calling for the withdrawal of troops and arbitration.

Meanwhile, embassy officials representing a number of Western nations asked that their citizens leave the region, especially Eritrea's capital, Asmara, which had been the target of several bombing raids by Ethiopian fighter planes. By late June, when major attacks ended, the war had claimed hundreds of lives and led to the displacement of thousands of people. In November, the United States initiated another round of negotiations, as troops and weapons remained massed along each side of the border.

South Africa intervenes in Lesotho. On September 22, about 600 South African soldiers, led by paratroop units in armored vehicles, entered the tiny mountainous kingdom of Lesotho after repeated appeals for foreign intervention from Lesotho's Prime Minister Pakalitha Mosisili. Lesotho, an independent nation, is entirely surrounded by South Africa. Also on September 22, about 200 troops from Botswana entered Lesotho under the umbrella of the 14-nation Southern African Development Community (SADC).

The military operation followed weeks of unrest in Lesotho triggered by parliamentary elections held on May 23. Mosisili had been accused of rigging the elections, in which his ruling Lesotho Congress for Democracy party won an overwhelming victory. On September 11, a pro-opposition army faction had staged a mutiny that had forced the army's top commanders into exile.

South Africa justified its intervention on the basis of SADC's declared policy against army mutinies and coups. Many of Lesotho's citizens, however, viewed the action as an unwarranted invasion. The South African army encountered considerable opposition from both civilian looters and Lesotho army rebels. At least 100 people died before order was restored.

On October 2, Mosisili and the rebels agreed that Mosisili's government would remain in power until new elections were held within 18 months. Under South African mediation, the parties also agreed that the foreign troops, by then numbering 3,200, would remain in Lesotho until the country's own security forces were able to maintain order.

Economic developments. In its annual report released in May, the African Development Bank (AfDB), an international lending organization, estimated that Africa's economic growth in 1998 would average 5 percent, compared with 3.7 percent in 1997. The bank reported that during the previous three years, four-fifths of African countries had achieved positive economic growth. At the beginning of the 1990's, one-third of African nations were in economic decline.

However, the AfDB added that the financial crisis in Asia could depress the prices of certain African commodities, such as copper, cobalt, and other minerals. Falling commodity prices would reduce growth rates in countries such as South Africa and Zambia that depended heavily on their exports. Observers also noted that the resumption of civil conflict in Central Africa would undermine the continent's economic prospects.

Africa's foreign debt, which stood at about $315 billion in 1997, continued to sap the continent's capacity to import and invest. Africa spent more on debt repayments than on health care in 1998. Although Africa accounted for only 10 percent of the world's people in 1998, its population growth rate—2.8 percent per year—remained the highest among the world's continents, with each woman having an average of six children.

Health issues. Although tuberculosis remained the leading single infectious killer of Africans during 1998, the human immunodeficiency virus (HIV), which causes AIDS, continued to plague the continent. In 1998, about two-thirds of all HIV-infected people worldwide—about 21 million people—lived in Sub-Saharan Africa, according to a joint report by the United Nations Program on AIDS and the World Health Organization.

The report estimated that 87 percent of the world's HIV-infected children lived in Africa. Zimbabwe emerged as the African country most devastated by AIDS, with 25 percent of adults between the ages of 15 and 49 infected with HIV. Life expectancy in Zimbabwe fell from 61 to 39 years since 1993, according to a November 1998 report by the U.S. Bureau of the Census.

Conservation. Rapid population growth and the resulting overcultivation of land continued to exert enormous pressures on Africa's natural environment. Increased demands for firewood contributed to further deforestation, soil erosion, and *desertification* (spread of desert).

In August, the World Wildlife Fund (WWF), a conservation organization based in Geneva, Switzerland, announced that the rhinoceros, which had been in danger of being hunted to extinction, was making a comeback. According to WWF estimates, Africa's rhinoceros population rose to more than 11,000 in 1997 from less than 10,000 in 1995. The WWF credited effective antipoaching and conservation programs in such countries as South Africa, Zimbabwe, Namibia, and Kenya for reversing the trend.

☐ Simon Baynham
See also the various African country articles.

Country	Population	Government	Monetary unit*	Foreign trade (million U.S.$) Exports[†]	Imports[†]
Algeria	29,806,000	President Liamine Zeroual; Prime Minister Ahmed Ouyahia**	dinar (58.12 = $1)	12,621	8,690
Angola	12,212,000	President Jose Eduardo dos Santos	readj. kwanza (257,128.00 = $1)	2,989	1,140
Benin	5,900,000	President Mathieu Kerekou	CFA franc (556.61 = $1)	424	635
Botswana	1,620,000	President Festus Mogae	pula (4.32 = $1)	2,100	1,500
Burkina Faso	11,119,000	Popular Front Chairman, Head of State, & Head of Government Blaise Compaore	CFA franc (556.61 = $1)	306	700
Burundi	6,937,000	President Pierre Buyoya	franc (485.00 = $1)	84	121
Cameroon	14,389,000	President Paul Biya	CFA franc (556.61 = $1)	2,047	1,245
Cape Verde	424,000	President Antonio Mascarenhas Monteiro; Prime Minister Carlos Wahnon Veiga	escudo (99.69 = $1)	9	252
Central African Republic	3,555,000	President Ange Patasse	CFA franc (556.61 = $1)	171	175
Chad	6,904,000	President Idriss Deby	CFA franc (556.61 = $1)	251	220
Comoros	724,000	President Mohamed Taki Abdoulkarim	franc (417.46 = $1)	22	69
Congo (Brazzaville)	2,809,000	President Denis Sassou-Nguesso	CFA franc (556.61 = $1)	1,176	671
Congo (Kinshasa)	48,042,000	President Laurent Kabila	new zaire (217,500.00 = $1)	592	424
Djibouti	616,000	President Hassan Gouled Aptidon; Prime Minister Barkat Gourad Hamadou	franc (177.72 = $1)	16	219
Egypt	66,547,000	President Hosni Mubarak; Prime Minister Kamal Ahmed al-Ganzouri	pound (3.40 = $1)	3,921	13,210
Equatorial Guinea	430,000	President Teodoro Obiang Nguema Mbasogo; Prime Minister Serafin Seriche Dougan	CFA franc (556.61 = $1)	175	292
Eritrea	3,816,000	President Isaias Afworki	Ethiopian birr	81	404
Ethiopia	60,053,000	President Negasso Gidada	birr (6.99 = $1)	422	1,142
Gabon	1,161,000	President El Hadj Omar Bongo; Prime Minister Paulin Obame	CFA franc (556.61 = $1)	2,712	881
Gambia	1,217,000	Head of State Yahya Jammeh	dalasi (10.87 = $1)	14	278
Ghana	19,016,000	President Jerry John Rawlings	cedi (2,345.00 = $1)	1,252	2,175
Guinea	7,308,000	President Lansana Conte	franc (1,243.00 = $1)	725	775
Guinea-Bissau	1,142,000	President Joao Bernardo Vieira	CFA franc (556.61 = $1)	21	63
Ivory Coast (Cote d'Ivoire)	15,684,000	President Henri Konan Bedie	CFA franc (556.61 = $1)	4,071	2,918
Kenya	30,738,000	President Daniel T. arap Moi	shilling (59.60 = $1)	2,054	3,273
Lesotho	2,216,000	King Letsie III; Prime Minister Pakalitha Mosisili	maloti (5.56 = $1)	218	1,100
Liberia	3,339,000	President Charles Taylor	dollar (1 = $1)	667	5,800

Country	Population	Government	Monetary unit*	Foreign trade (million U.S.$)	
				Exports[†]	Imports[†]
Libya	5,965,000	Leader of the Revolution Muammar Muhammad al-Qadhafi; General People's Committee Secretary (Prime Minister) Muhammad Ahmad al-Manqush	dinar (0.39 = $1)	11,213	5,356
Madagascar	14,125,000	President Didier Ratsiraka	franc (5,115.00 = $1)	223	478
Malawi	11,724,000	President Bakili Muluzi	kwacha (44.98 = $1)	481	623
Mali	11,806,000	President Alpha Oumar Konare; Prime Minister Ibrahim Boubacar Keita	CFA franc (556.61 = $1)	542	684
Mauritania	2,450,000	President Maaouya Ould Sid Ahmed Taya	ouguiya (203.10 = $1)	437	222
Mauritius	1,154,000	President Sir Cassam Uteem; Prime Minister Navinchandra Ramgoolam	rupee (24.81 = $1)	1,751	2,278
Morocco	28,548,000	King Hassan II; Prime Minister Abderrahmane Youssoufi	dirham (9.24 = $1)	6,987	9,511
Mozambique	17,703,000	President Joaquim Alberto Chissano; Prime Minister Pascoal Manuel Mocumbi	metical (11,495.00 = $1)	168	784
Namibia	1,663,000	President Sam Nujoma; Prime Minister Hage Geingob	rand (5.56 = $1)	1,450	1,550
Niger	10,093,000	President, Niger National Council, Ibrahim Bare Mainassara; Prime Minister Ibrahim Assane Mayaki	CFA franc (556.61 = $1)	268	377
Nigeria	121,513,000	Head of State, Chairman, Federal Executive Council Abdulsalam Abubakar	naira (21.89 = $1)	18,614	7,997
Rwanda	7,261,000	President Pasteur Bizimungu	franc (317.98 = $1)	87	297
São Tomé and Príncipe	141,000	President Miguel Trovoada	dobra (2,390.00 = $1)	8	26
Senegal	8,993,000	President Abdou Diouf; Prime Minister Mamadou Lamine Loum	CFA franc (556.61 = $1)	925	1,190
Seychelles	75,000	President France Albert Rene	rupee (5.43 = $1)	53	233
Sierra Leone	4,833,000	President Ahmad Tejan Kabbah	leone (1,850.00 = $1)	47	212
Somalia	11,811,000	No functioning government	shilling (2,620.00 = $1)	81	81
South Africa	44,223,000	State President Nelson Mandela	rand (5.56 = $1)	29,964	31,939
Sudan	30,392,000	President Umar Hasan Ahmad al-Bashir	pound (1,826.00 = $1)	556	1,185
Swaziland	928,000	King Mswati III; Prime Minister Barnabas Sibusiso Dlamini	lilangeni (5.56 = $1)	700	831
Tanzania	32,211,000	President Benjamin William Mkapa; Prime Minister Frederick Sumaye	shilling (670.72 = $1)	718	1,336
Togo	4,527,000	President Gnassingbe Eyadema	CFA franc (556.61 = $1)	346	501
Tunisia	9,363,000	President Zine El Abidine Ben Ali; Prime Minister Hamed Karoui	dinar (1.08 = $1)	5,559	7,914
Uganda	23,204,000	President Yoweri Kaguta Museveni; Prime Minister Kintu Musoke	shilling (1,233.50 = $1)	555	1,317
Zambia	10,204,000	President Frederick Chiluba	kwacha (2,145.00 = $1)	1,403	1,523
Zimbabwe	11,989,000	President Robert Mugabe	dollar (37.50 = $1)	2,397	2,817

*Exchange rates as of Nov. 6, 1998, or latest available data.   †Latest available data.
**Resigned on December 14; replaced by Smail Hamdani.

Agriculture.

Farmers in the United States in 1998 experienced the downside of the Federal Agricultural Improvement and Reform (FAIR) Act. The act, passed by Congress in 1996, ended government restrictions on planting corn, cotton, rice, and wheat and reduced federal income subsidies to farmers. The act gave farmers the freedom to plant crops to meet market demands. However, instead of earning high prices for grain, U.S. farmers in 1998 watched grain prices hit a 10-year low. Instead of continued growth in export markets, they saw international markets contract. Drought, record heat, and floods also contributed to farmers' troubles.

A Marietta, South Carolina, farmer inspects his strawberry crop during an unseasonable cold snap in March 1998. Sprinklers coat the plants with water, which turns to ice and protects them from the cold air.

The U.S. Congress passed a $5.9-billion emergency farm aid package in 1998 and provided additional tax cuts for farmers. The government also gave away record amounts of grain—about 4 million metric tons of wheat alone—and provided $4.8 billion in export credits to ensure that buyers abroad would keep exports flowing.

World farm production. World grain production declined in every commodity except oilseeds, but diminished demand flattened prices. According to a U.S. Department of Agriculture report in December, world wheat production in 1998 totaled 586 million metric tons, down 4 percent from 1997. Higher wheat production in Canada and the European Union, an organization of 15 European countries, failed to offset weather-related losses in Australia, India, and Russia.

Production of small grains, including corn, rye, grain sorghum, barley, oats, millet, and mixed grains, fell 1 percent from 1997 levels to 882 million metric tons. The drop was the result of production shortfalls in the former Soviet Union and Eastern Europe. Global rice production in 1998 declined by 2 percent to 377 million metric tons due to flooding in China and Texas.

Global oilseed production rose by 1 percent to 288 million metric tons due to record planted acreage in the United States and a record crop. Smaller cotton crops in China, Egypt, and the United States cut global cotton production by 8 percent to 84 million bales.

U.S. farm production continued to shift as a result of the FAIR Act. U.S. farmers in 1998 harvested the largest soybean crop ever, at 2.76 billion bushels; the second-largest corn crop, at 9.84 billion bushels; and the third-largest rice crop, at 180 million metric tons. The 1998 wheat harvest totaled 2.5 billion bushels, the same as in 1997.

Exports. Reduced international demand, stemming primarily from economic turmoil in Asia—the fastest growing U.S. export market—cut U.S. exports and farm prices in nearly every category. In the first eight months of 1998, exports to Asia fell by 29 percent. In total, U.S. farmers saw exports decline by $3.1 billion to $54.4 billion. Exports of red meat and poultry, however, increased by 2 percent.

Reduced feed use in financially strapped Russia and South Korea resulted in smaller purchases of U.S. grain. Improved harvests in Pakistan and the countries of North Africa, former U.S. customers, also cut demand for U.S. crops.

The ensuing crash of commodity prices hit nearly every sector. In 1998, average U.S. farm prices fell by 25 percent for corn and soybeans and by 33 percent for wheat. These were the lowest prices in 10 years for corn, the lowest in 4 years for soybeans, and the lowest in 7 years for wheat. Hog prices, adjusted for inflation, fell to their lowest level in U.S. history, due to a record-setting supply and a significant reduction in packing plant capacity. Only rice prices held firm, the result of record domestic use and strong exports. Despite a weather-damaged cotton crop of 13.5 million bales, 28 percent less than in 1997, the decline in supply failed to trigger a price increase.

Russian woes. The devaluation of the Russian ruble in August 1998 seriously reduced the purchasing power of Russian consumers. Until then, Russian purchases of U.S. poultry had been running 122 percent above 1997 levels. The financial crisis came as Russia harvested a drought-reduced wheat crop of 28.5 million metric tons, 35 percent below 1997 levels. In addition, barley production, at 10 million metric tons, was off by 50 percent.

Russia's total grain production of 49 million metric tons, the lowest in 50 years, resulted in higher prices and a further reduction in livestock inventories. On Nov. 4, 1998, the U.S. government announced a 3.1-million-metric-ton food aid package for Russia, consisting of wheat, corn, soybeans, rice, pork, beef, and nonfat dry milk.

Farm aid. Beginning in August, Congress began pumping additional subsidies into U.S. farms to help stem the effects of low commodity prices. On August 12, President Clinton signed a law that allowed farmers to receive 1999 crop direct payments provided by the FAIR Act as early as Oct. 1, 1998. This money was in addition to $5.7 billion in federal subsidies for 1998 already distributed under the FAIR Act. On October 21, the president signed emergency legislation that provided $2.85 billion in direct payments because of low prices. Another $2.4 billion for weather-related 1998 crop losses was to be distributed in early 1999.

The need for emergency aid highlighted the weaknesses in the U.S. crop insurance program, which offered protection against bad harvests but was no help when prices fell. Although price protection insurance called Crop Revenue Coverage was available in 1998, it was costly and not well understood. Just 65 percent of U.S. cropland was protected by crop insurance in 1998. The federal government earmarked $400 million of the $2.4 billion in disaster loss funds to help farmers pay for insurance for 1999 crops.

Protectionism. The export slump fed a growing protectionist sentiment that led the House of Representatives on Sept. 25, 1998, to reject legislation that would have renewed Clinton's "fast-track" authority to negotiate trade agreements, including those involving agricultural products. The authority, which had expired in 1994, allowed the Administration to negotiate trade pacts without consulting Congress. After negotiations were completed, Congress had the right to approve or reject, but not alter, the agreement.

In another display of protectionist sentiment, five states along the U.S. border with Canada in September 1998 began interfering with shipments of Canadian agricultural products to the United States. A record drop in the value of the Canadian dollar relative to the U.S. dollar and low U.S. cattle and grain prices fueled a percep-

tion that Canadian farmers were shipping excessive amounts of their products to the United States, driving prices down even further.

On September 15, South Dakota became the first state to order state police to conduct thorough inspections of trucks from Canada. Trucks that violated highway safety or food safety laws were not permitted to enter. Within one week, Idaho, Minnesota, Montana, and North Dakota had instituted similar policies. In addition, groups of farmers in several states blocked highways and rail lines to prevent the entry of Canadian farm products. The action stopped only when the U.S. government initiated new talks with Canada over many long-simmering border issues.

Clean-water battles. The stand-off between the Clinton Administration and the Republican-controlled Congress on environmental issues led to President Clinton's announcement on February 19 of a "clean-water action plan." One of its components was a requirement that all livestock operations be regulated to prevent water pollution by 2005. Congress appropriated $200 million to help states enact the plan. However, Congress also reduced funding for the Environmental Quality Incentives Program, which helps U.S. farmers pay the cost of water quality improvements, from $200 million to $174 million.

☐ Patricia Peak Klintberg

AIDS. Officials from the United States Centers for Disease Control and Prevention (CDC) in Atlanta, Georgia, reported in October 1998 that the number of deaths from acquired immune deficiency syndrome (AIDS) in the United States during 1997 dropped by a record 47 percent. According to the CDC, 16,685 people died of AIDS-related causes in 1997, compared with 31,130 in 1996. Officials attributed the reduction to an extremely effective combination drug treatment called Highly Active Antiretroviral Therapy (HAART). HAART interferes with the reproduction of the human immunodeficiency virus (HIV), which causes AIDS, and allows people infected with HIV to live longer and healthier lives.

HIV infections. No such decline occurred in the number of new HIV infections in the United States, the CDC cautioned in April 1998. The infection rate remained at about 40,000 new cases annually. In addition, a higher proportion of new infections were occurring in minority groups and women, the CDC said in June. From June 1994 to June 1997, African Americans, who made up 12 percent of the U.S. population in 1998, accounted for 57 percent of new HIV infections. Women of all races between ages 13 and 24 accounted for 44 percent of new HIV infections.

Global AIDS. The United Nations AIDS Program (UNAIDS) reported in June 1998 that the

AIDS epidemic continued to expand in developing countries. According to UNAIDS, about 90 percent of new cases and deaths from AIDS in 1997 occurred in developing countries. By early 1998, the number of HIV-infected people worldwide reached 30 million. About 2.3 million deaths from AIDS occurred worldwide in 1997.

Vaccine. The first full-scale clinical trials of an AIDS vaccine called AIDSvax began in the United States, Canada, and Thailand in June 1998. VaxGen Inc., a pharmaceutical company in South San Francisco, California, said the four-year trials would test the vaccine on 7,500 uninfected volunteers at high risk of exposure to HIV because of intravenous drug use or sexual relations with HIV-infected people.

HIV in infants. The CDC reported in February that a shorter version of a complex drug treatment can reduce by half the transmission of HIV from mothers to infants during childbirth. The $50-per-patient treatment was expected to help about 500,000 HIV-infected infants per year born in developing countries, where people cannot afford the longer therapy, costing about $800 per patient per year. In June, UNAIDS announced it planned to treat 30,000 pregnant, HIV-infected women in 11 developing countries.   □ Michael Woods

Air pollution. See **Environmental pollution.**
Alabama. See **State government.**
Alaska. See **State government.**

Albania continued to experience political and civil turmoil in 1998. The opposition Democratic Party boycotted parliament for much of the year. In January, Prime Minister Fatos Nano and other leaders of Albania's ruling Socialist Party charged the opposition with inciting civil unrest.

In August, former president and Democratic Party leader Sali Berisha urged his supporters to "fight dictatorship with all means" and to overthrow Nano's government. On September 12, Azem Hajdari, a prominent Democratic Party member, was assassinated by unidentified gunmen. The next day, Nano and his cabinet fled their offices after some 2,000 protesters attacked the main government building in Tirana, the capital. One protester was killed and four guards were wounded in gun battles in the premier's offices.

Nano, facing rioting and discord in his own coalition, resigned on Sept. 28, 1998. He was replaced by Pandeli Majko, the Socialist Party leader. Majko a 30-year-old reformer, was a respected figure who had worked to bridge the gap between the government and the opposition after the financial crisis that struck Albania in 1997.

Albania's economy began to recover in the first half of 1998. In September, the International Monetary Fund (a United Nations-affiliated organization that provides short-term credit to member nations) estimated that Albania's *gross domes-*

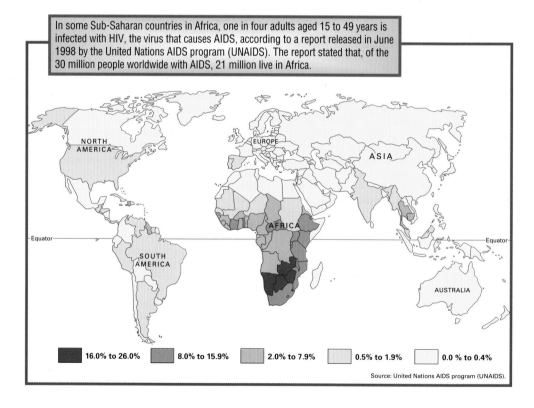

In some Sub-Saharan countries in Africa, one in four adults aged 15 to 49 years is infected with HIV, the virus that causes AIDS, according to a report released in June 1998 by the United Nations AIDS program (UNAIDS). The report stated that, of the 30 million people worldwide with AIDS, 21 million live in Africa.

16.0% to 26.0%   8.0% to 15.9%   2.0% to 7.9%   0.5% to 1.9%   0.0 % to 0.4%

Source: United Nations AIDS program (UNAIDS).

Armed citizens patrol the streets of Daira de Ramika, a town west of the Algerian capital, Algiers, in January 1998, after the massacre of local citizens. More than 1,000 people were murdered by Islamic extremists in Algeria in a two-week period in January during the holy month of Ramadan.

tic product (the value of all goods and services produced in a country in a year) would grow by 10 percent for 1998, the highest growth rate in Eastern Europe.

Kosovo crisis. Albanian leaders condemned the government of Yugoslavia for using military force to suppress an armed separatist movement among ethnic Albanians in Kosovo, a region in the Yugoslav republic of Serbia. Kosovo's population is 90 percent ethnic Albanian. Albanian leaders urged the Kosovo Liberation Army to use restraint in its demands for independence. As the violence escalated, however, Albania urged the United States and the Euopean Union, an organization of 15 Western European nations, to resolve the conflict militarily. In March, the North Atlantic Treaty Organization (NATO) refused Albania's request to deploy NATO troops along its border with Yugoslavia but pledged aid for refugees from Kosovo. By October 1998, some 20,000 refugees from Kosovo had crossed into Albania.

On December 14, Serbian border guards and separatist rebels engaged in a five-hour firefight along the Albanian-Yugoslav border. At least 30 ethnic Albanian guerrillas were killed. Yugoslavia accused Albania of aiding the Kosovo separatists in terrorist operations. □ Sharon L. Wolchik

See also **Europe** (Facts in brief table); **Yugoslavia.**

Algeria. In September 1998, Algerian President Liamine Zeroual unexpectedly announced that he would hold presidential elections before February 1999. Many observers were stunned by the announcement and speculated that Zeroual's early departure was due to a power struggle with hard-line elements in the military. The hard-liners were in favor of a more aggressive approach in dealing with Islamic militants in Algeria. The militants began waging war against the government in 1992, when the military canceled parliamentary elections that the Islamic Salvation Front (known as the FIS), an Islamic extremist group, was expected to win. By 1998, violence against civilians and clashes between Islamic militants and government forces had claimed as many as 80,000 lives.

In December 1998, Algerian Prime Minister Ahmed Ouyahia resigned under criticism from hard-liners. Zeroual named Smail Hamdani, a senator and former ambassador, to replace Ouyahia. Hamdani was to lead a caretaker government whose primary task was to prepare for the 1999 presidential elections.

Violence. In a two-week period in January 1998, during the Muslim holy month of Ramadan, more than 1,000 people were killed by Islamic extremists in Algeria. Violence continued throughout 1998 despite the government's announcement that security forces had killed Khalifi Athmane, the leader of the radical Armed Islamic Group (known as the GIA), on July 8. The GIA was suspected of having been responsible for some of the deadliest attacks in the Algerian conflict.

In September, a United Nations (UN) fact-finding mission that visited Algeria in July and August condemned the terrorist activities of Islamic militants. It also noted that the Algerian government could improve its own human-rights record.

Singer killed. In June, Algerians were outraged when Matoub Lounes, a popular singer and member of Algeria's Berbers, an ethnic minority, was ambushed and killed in Tizi Ouzou, the center of Berber culture, east of Algiers. The GIA claimed responsibility for the murder. Lounes, an advocate of secular democracy, had condemned both the Islamic radicals and the government. He also condemned legislation recognizing Arabic as the primary language in Algeria, a law that went into effect days after his death.

Women. In April, the Islamic Supreme Council, Algeria's highest religious authority, decreed that women who became pregnant after being abducted and raped by Islamic extremists could not obtain abortions. The decree overturned an earlier council ruling that would have permitted such abortions. At least 1,600 Algerian women have been raped by extremists since 1994.

In August 1998, approximately 100 women who were attempting to find missing sons demonstrated at a human-rights office in Algiers. Nearly 1,800 young men, many of them Muslim extremists or sympathizers, have disappeared since June 1991. The Algerian Human Rights League accused the army of "forced disappearances, extrajudicial killings, [and] torture."

Oil and gas. Algerian officials predicted in August 1998 that oil and gas revenues would drop to $12 billion in 1998 from $13.6 billion in 1997. The drop was attributed to the severe decline in 1998 of world oil prices, which were the lowest in more than 10 years. Algeria's oil and gas sector provides more than 90 percent of the country's foreign trade and some 50 percent of the government's revenues. A series of bombings that damaged Algeria's gas pipelines in 1998 triggered government concern about the security of oil and gas facilities.

Europe. A French court in February 1998 convicted 36 Islamic extremists for a 1995 bombing campaign in France that killed 9 people and injured more than 200. The extremists, GIA supporters, hoped the bombs would drive France into ending its support of the Algerian government.   □ Christine Helms

See also **Africa** (Facts in brief table).

Angola. See Africa.

Animal. See Biology; Conservation; Zoos.

Anthropology. In May 1998, a research team led by zoologist Meave Leakey of the National Museums of Kenya announced the oldest fossil evidence for *bipedalism* (walking on two feet). The researchers dated a *tibia* (shinbone) of *Australopithecus anamensis,* a hominid whose remains were discovered by Leakey in 1995 in Kenya, to between 4.07 million and 4.17 million years ago. (Hominids are species in the human family.) Anatomical details indicate that *A. anamensis* was capable of bipedal walking.

Although Leakey originally had dated the fossils to approximately 4 million years ago, some scientists believed them to be younger. The discovery of additional Kenyan fossils between 1995 and 1997 enabled her team to confirm the primitive status of *A. anamensis,* and more accurate geological dating techniques allowed the researchers to determine a reliable age for the fossils. Previously, the oldest evidence for hominid bipedalism came from 3.6-million-year-old fossil footprints in Laetoli, Tanzania. The prints were left by *Australopithecus afarensis,* a species best known from a skeleton, nicknamed "Lucy," discovered in Ethiopia in 1974.

Talking Neanderthals? Research announced in April 1998 by scientists at Duke University in Durham, North Carolina, provided evidence that Neanderthals, prehistoric humans that became extinct 30,000 years ago, may have been capable of speech. Scientists had previously thought that Neanderthals were unable to speak.

Duke researchers Richard Kay, Matthew Cartmill, and Michelle Balow measured the *hypoglossal canal* (a canal at the base of the skull through which nerve fibers pass to the tongue) in the skulls of apes, prehistoric humans, and modern humans. Their measurements showed that Neanderthals and certain earlier types of humans had hypoglossal canals much larger than those in apes and within the range of sizes seen in modern humans. This finding indicated that human speech may have originated as early as 300,000 years ago.

Evolution side branch. In July, paleoanthropologists Lee Berger of the University of Witwatersrand in South Africa and Henry McHenry of the University of California at Davis reported their discovery that *Australopithecus africanus* was more apelike than previously thought. *A. africanus* was a hominid that lived between 2.5 million and 3 million years ago. The research was based on analyses of both newly found and previously known specimens recovered from Sterkfontein Cave in South Africa.

The researchers found that the arms of *A. africanus* were longer in proportion to its body than the arms of *A. afarensis,* the presumed ancestor of *A. africanus.* Some scientists said this indicated that *A. africanus* was adapted to a tree-dwelling lifestyle and belonged to a side branch of human evolution not ancestral to modern humans. Berger and McHenry, however, speculated that *A. africanus* was a human ancestor, and *A. afarensis* may have belonged to a side branch.

Cranium clues. In June, paleontologists led by Ernesto Abbate of the University of Florence in Italy reported finding a *cranium* (upper part of the skull) that indicated some features of modern skulls appeared as long ago as 1 million years. The cranium, found in the African state of Eritrea, has large brow ridges and other characteristics of *Homo erectus*, a human species that became extinct about 400,000 years ago. However, the upper rear portion of the cranium is shaped somewhat like the skulls of modern humans. Other fossil and geological evidence at the site of the find indicated that the cranium may be 1 million years old.

Best-preserved skeleton? Paleontologist Ronald Clarke of the University of Witwatersrand announced in December that he had discovered what may be one of the most complete skeletons ever found of an early hominid. The specimen, embedded in stone in Sterkfontein Cave in South Africa, is an australopithecine at least 2.6 million years old.   ☐ Donald C. Johanson

See also **Archaeology.**

Archaeology. In April 1998, a team of scientists reported evidence suggesting that *Neolithic* (late Stone Age) *nomads* (members of tribes who move from place to place) in northern Africa made astronomical observations between 5,000 and 7,000 years ago. The team, which included anthropologist Fred Wendorf of Southern Methodist University in Dallas, Texas, and astrophysicist J. McKim Malville of the University of Colorado in Boulder, excavated a complex arrangement of stones spread over an area measuring 1.8 by 0.75 miles (2.9 by 1.2 kilometers) in the Sahara, some 500 miles (804 kilometers) south of Cairo, Egypt. The complex included a circle of small stones 12 feet (3.7 meters) wide. The circle contained two pairs of larger stones that marked two lines of sight—a north-south line and a line pointing in the direction of the sunrise on the *summer solstice* (longest day of the year) 6,000 years ago. (The position of the solstice sunrise changes over time.) The site also included 10 slabs of stone, each 9 feet (2.7 meters) tall, arranged in lines oriented perfectly in north-south and east-west directions.

The researchers believed the Neolithic nomads had abandoned the site by 2800 B.C. By this time, the wet climate that created the temporary lakes used by the herders had become dry, changing the area into a desert.

A team led by French historian Francoise Dunand (left) retrieves mummies from 2,000-year-old tombs built for the working-class near Luxor, Egypt. Studies made on the mummies in 1998 revealed arthritis of the spinal column and stunted growth, conditions suggesting lives of hard labor and poor nutrition.

Burial in Pyramid of the Moon. In October 1998, archaeologists reported finding a skeleton, possibly of an ancient ruler, within the Pyramid of the Moon at Teotihuacan, north of Mexico City. Teotihuacan dominated the Central Valley of Mexico from the end of the first century B.C. to approximately A.D. 750.

The burial chamber, which dates to about A.D. 100, is within an early temple that was later covered by three other structures. The final structure was the Pyramid of the Moon, built in approximately A.D. 250. The archaeologists, from the University of Tokyo in Japan, the National Autonomous University of Mexico, the University of the Americas in Mexico, and other institutions, found more than 150 objects believed to be offerings buried with the body. These included jadeite figurines, flaked obsidian pieces, pyrite mirrors, and the remains of two jaguars. The tomb was the only undisturbed major burial site yet found at Teotihuacan.

Settlement not dependent on farming. Archaeologists Robert J. Hard of the University of Texas at San Antonio and John R. Roney of the Bureau of Land Management in Albuquerque, New Mexico, reported in March 1998 that their excavations revealed that the rise of settled village life in the southwestern United States and northwestern Mexico was not necessarily dependent on agriculture. Archaeologists have traditionally believed that early settlements were dependent on farming.

Hard and Roney were studying Cerro Juanaquena, site of a prehistoric terraced village south of the U.S.-Mexican border. Their excavations at the site uncovered grinding stones, animal bones, ash, and other domestic refuse that suggested settled habitation. Food remains found at the site included corn, wild squash, wild plant seeds, and the bones of pronghorn antelope. The size of the grinding stones indicated that wild plant seeds were more important than corn.

The archaeologists dated the site to approximately 1000 B.C., more than 1,000 years before scientists believed hunter-gatherers in the area became farmers and village dwellers. The researchers said that hunting and gathering apparently made sedentary life possible at Cerro Juanaquena without dependence on agriculture.

Monks Mound surprise. Archaeologist William Woods of Southern Illinois University in Edwardsville reported in March 1998 that drilling in Monks Mound at Cahokia, Illinois, had revealed a layer of limestone or sandstone cobbles deep within the terraced earthen pyramid. The discovery of the stone layer surprised archaeologists, because stone does not occur naturally at Cahokia. The stones had been transported to the area from several miles away.

Monks Mound, which was built sometime between A.D. 950 and 1150, is 100 feet (30.5 meters) tall—the largest prehistoric earthen construction in the Americas. The stone layer, which is at least 32 feet (9.8 meters) in length, lies 40 feet (12.2 meters) beneath the surface of the mound's second terrace. Archaeologists speculated that the stone layer was a platform used for ritual activities.

Lewis and Clark campsite. In September 1998, archaeologist Ken Karsmizki of the Museum of the Rockies in Bozeman, Montana, announced that he had discovered the location of a campsite used by the Meriwether Lewis and William Clark party during its exploration from 1804 to 1806 of what is now the Northwestern United States. The campsite, dating from 1805 and located on the Missouri River near Great Falls, Montana, was the first expedition campsite to be verified.

Karsmizki found a tent stake, an iron push pin, and a gun flint that he dated from the time of Lewis and Clark. He also found three stone fire pits, which were arranged in a line and spaced 50 feet (15.2 meters) apart—indicating a large, regimented camp. No other large expedition using military-style camps went this far up the Missouri River until 1832.   □ Mark Rose

See also **Anthropology; Geology.**

Architecture. The most spectacular architectural event of 1998 in the United States was the October reopening of New York City's Grand Central Terminal. Constructed in 1913 as the gateway to New York City, the terminal quickly became an American landmark as well as an essential transit station. However, as long-distance train travel declined, the station deteriorated, becoming a dreary place for the hundreds of thousands of commuters who passed through it daily.

In 1968, Penn Central Transportation Company, the terminal's owner, announced plans to build a multistory office tower above it. Spurred by a coalition of preservationists, New York City designated the station as an official landmark and banned the construction of the tower.

The $197-million restoration project, by the New York City architectural firm of Beyer Blinder Belle, included the terminal's dramatic Great Hall with its star-spangled zodiac ceiling and adjacent waiting room. The architects also lined the concourses with more than 100 shops and restaurants in order to reconnect Grand Central to the city and to make it a destination for tourists as well as commuters.

In the works. In July 1998, a design for a World War II Memorial in Washington, D.C., won approval from the National Capital Planning Commission, the agency that oversees federal de-

Visitors admire New York City's newly restored Grand Central Terminal after a rededication ceremony on Oct. 1, 1998. The renovation of the train terminal—a national landmark built in 1913—cost nearly $200 million.

velopment in Washington. The commission had rejected the memorial's original design, by architect Friedrich St. Florian, in 1997. The first version would have stretched 300 feet (90 meters) across the National Mall, interrupting the view between the Lincoln Memorial and the Washington Monument. The latest version of the memorial was designed with a sunken plaza surrounded on three sides by a circular retaining wall punctured by two ceremonial arches.

New Reagan Building. The $818-million Ronald Reagan Building and International Trade Center opened in Washington, D.C., in May 1998. Among federal buildings, the 3.1-million-square-foot (288,000-square-meter) Reagan Building is second in size only to the Pentagon, headquarters of the Department of Defense, in Arlington, Virginia. Architect James Freed, of Pei Cobb Freed & Partners of New York City, covered the Reagan Building in the same creamy limestone used in neighboring neoclassical buildings but detailed it in a crisp, modern way. At the center of the structure, Freed created a dramatic steel-and-glass atrium, surrounded by showrooms, shops, and restaurants. Critics praised the atrium's transparency and sociability, rare among federal buildings. The building houses three federal agencies as part of a strategy to concentrate far-flung federal agencies in downtown Washington.

Boston's new federal courthouse, by Henry N. Cobb of Pei Cobb Freed & Partners, represents a return to the early-American tradition of locating the most important civic buildings on the most important sites. The $163-million courthouse, which opened in September, is constructed of solid red brick, like neighboring warehouses along Boston Harbor. The side facing the waterfront, however, is a seven-story, 33,000-square-foot (3,100-square-meter) concave glass wall, which was intended, according to Cobb, to convey the idea that justice is open and accessible. Within the building, glass-walled corridors form an interior street. At the center of the courthouse is a nine-story rotunda featuring bold, monochromatic paintings by American artist Ellsworth Kelly. A public entrance from a waterfront park leads to a cafeteria, exhibition spaces, and a public day-care center.

Concert halls. Two major concert halls opened in the United States in 1998. The $67-million Nancy Lee and Perry R. Bass Performance Hall in Fort Worth, Texas, designed by architect David M. Schwarz of Washington, D.C., was more reminiscent of opera houses of the late 1800's than the late 1900's. With 50-foot (15-meter) limestone angels holding 16-foot (5-meter) gold-leafed trumpets hovering over the front entrance and an 80-foot (24-meter) dome with hand painted murals, Bass Hall resides firmly in the Euro-

pean classical tradition. Its 2,056 seats are arranged in five tiers, with an abundance of wood, white plaster, and brass trim. The hall, which opened in May, became the home of the Fort Worth Symphony Orchestra, the Fort Worth Dallas Ballet, the Fort Worth Opera, and the Van Cliburn International Piano Competition.

Seattle's Benaroya Hall, which opened in September, was designed exclusively for concert music. Mark Reddington of the Seattle firm LMN Architects created a 2,500-seat main hall and a 540-seat recital hall, plus an interior concourse lined with shops, restaurants, and coffee bars. The hall's most dramatic feature is a cylindrical glass lobby that offers dramatic views of Puget Sound and the downtown-Seattle skyline.

The 1998 Pritzker Prize was awarded to 60-year-old Italian architect Renzo Piano, whom the jury praised for his rare melding of art, architecture, and engineering into a truly remarkable synthesis. Piano gained international recognition in 1978 when he and British architect Richard Rogers completed the Georges Pompidou Center in Paris. His first U.S. building was the Menil Collection in Houston. Other notable projects include the Cy Twombly Gallery in Houston and the Kansai International Airport in Osaka, Japan. □ David Dillon

See also **Art.**

Argentina.
Economic analysts credited the policies of President Carlos Saul Menem's administration for easing the impact of the 1998 global economic crisis on Argentina. The decision in 1991 to fix the value of the peso to the United States dollar was credited for forcing the Argentine government to live within its means and control inflation throughout 1998.

Nonetheless, economic turmoil in other countries threatened Argentina. Worried about a drop in trade with Brazil, which buys approximately 30 percent of Argentine exports, Menem negotiated more than $8 billion in loans from international lenders in September to ensure that the government could survive a severe economic slowdown. This credit was expected to complement a $2.8-billion line of credit from the International Monetary Fund, a United Nations agency that grants loans to member nations.

1999 elections. Seeking to capitalize on high approval ratings at home and abroad, Menem sought support for a constitutional amendment that would have enabled him to run for a third term as president in October 1999. His maneuvering to accomplish this goal, however, triggered a split within his own Justicialist (Peronist) Party. Menem resolved the conflict in July 1998 by withdrawing his bid for reelection.

Eduardo Duhalde, the governor of Buenos

Aires province, was the frontrunner for the Peronist Party, which scheduled primary elections for 1999. Fernando de la Rua, the mayor of the capital, Buenos Aires, became the main opposition candidate by winning the primary election for the center-left Alliance Coalition on Nov. 29, 1998.

Crimes of the past. On January 15, Alfredo Astiz, a retired navy captain, was arrested after boasting to a reporter about participating in a death squad that tortured and killed political dissidents, including two French Roman Catholic nuns and a Swedish teen-age girl in 1977. Astiz avoided prosecution because of a 1987 law that provided immunity for lower-ranking officers accused of human-rights violations committed during Argentina's military rule from 1976 to 1983. Astiz's comments in 1998, however, led President Menem to strip the officer of his rank and military pension.

The government announced in January that it would demolish the Navy Mechanics School in Buenos Aires, the scene of tortures and executions during the military regime's so-called "dirty war" against political opponents. Human-rights groups protested the plans and demanded that the government convert it into a museum to commemorate the people who died there. A federal judge blocked the demolition, and the matter remained unresolved through 1998.

In February, government investigators discovered Swiss bank accounts, allegedly containing millions of dollars pillaged from political prisoners during the dirty war. One account belonged to Antonio Domingo Bussi, governor of the northern province of Tucuman. Bussi, a former general, was reprimanded by an Argentine court for failing to report his assets on income tax records, but the governor was spared impeachment because of his popularity with the provincial legislature.

Extraditions. On June 17, Argentina extradited Dinko Sakic to face charges of crimes against humanity in his native Croatia. Sakic commanded the largest Nazi concentration camp in Croatia during World War II (1939–1945). Sakic's wife, Nada, who served as a camp guard, was extradited in November 1998.

Iran implicated in bombings. On May 15, Argentine Foreign Minister Guido Di Tella announced the expulsion of seven employees of the Iranian embassy in Buenos Aires on grounds that embassy officials had been involved in the 1992 bombing of the Israeli embassy and the 1994 bombing of a Jewish community center in Buenos Aires. At least 115 people were killed in the attacks.   ☐ Nathan A. Haverstock

See also **Economics** Special Report: **Asian Economic Crisis—Global Contagion; Latin America** (Facts in brief table).

Arizona. See State government.

Arkansas. See State government.

Armed forces. The United States and Great Britain launched a series of air and missile strikes against military and security targets in Iraq beginning on Dec. 16, 1998, after United Nations (UN) inspectors reported that they had been denied full access to suspected chemical and biological weapons sites. The U.S. cruise missile and bomber attacks were aimed at halting Iraq's capacity for building weapons of mass destruction.

Relations between the United States and Iraq had been tense throughout 1998, following continued Iraqi reluctance to allow UN inspectors full access to suspected weapons sites. In February, President Bill Clinton ordered a build-up of U.S. military forces in the Persian Gulf and threatened to launch an air strike against Iraq. On February 22, UN Secretary General Kofi Annan and Iraq Deputy Premier Tariq Aziz signed an agreement permitting UN inspectors access to suspected Iraqi weapons sites. The United States was prepared to launch an air strike against Iraq in mid-November when the government in Baghdad again barred UN inspections. The strike was called off following a last-minute agreement. The air strikes launched in December were triggered by a report from UN Special Commission head Richard Butler. The report accused Iraq of continuing to block access to weapons sites and information.

Terrorist targets. President Clinton ordered missile attacks against suspected terrorist targets in Afghanistan and Sudan on Aug. 20, 1998. The attacks were in retaliation for the August 7 terrorist bombings of American embassies in Kenya and Tanzania. The bombings killed 224 people, including 12 Americans.

U.S. naval vessels in the Red Sea and Arabian Sea launched approximately 75 cruise missiles during the attack. The missiles struck an alleged terrorist training complex near Khost, Afghanistan, and a factory in Khartoum, Sudan. U.S. officials claimed that the factory manufactured chemical weapon components, including nerve gas, and that both targets were funded by Osama bin Laden, an exiled Saudi Arabian.

Courts-martial proceedings against two U.S. Marine Corps officers were postponed in October until 1999. Captain Richard Ashby, a pilot, and Captain Joseph Schweitzer, a navigator, were charged with killing 20 people when their EA-6B Prowler surveillance aircraft cut the cable of a ski gondola near Cavalese, Italy, on Feb. 3, 1998. Prosecutors said that the plane was flying too low for conditions. The plane was on a low-level training mission when the accident occurred. It hit the gondola cable at a height of 370 feet (110 meters) in an area where military aircraft were prohibited from flying below 1,000 feet (300 meters). Defense attorneys said that maps and flight instructions did not warn of the cable.

Ashby and Schweitzer were both charged with 20 counts of involuntary manslaughter and negligent homicide, in addition to damage to military and private property and dereliction of duty. The military dismissed charges against two other crew members who were in the plane at the time of the accident but had no control over the aircraft.

McKinney demoted. Former Sergeant Major of the Army Gene C. McKinney, the Army's highest-ranking enlisted soldier, was convicted in a military court on one count of obstruction of justice in March 1998. He was acquitted on 18 other counts of obstructing justice and sexual misconduct with five female soldiers and a Navy enlisted woman. McKinney had been reduced in rank in 1997 to command sergeant major after he was first charged. The court reduced his rank an additional grade, to master sergeant, and allowed him to retire with full retirement pay.

In February 1997, retired Sergeant Major Brenda Hoster, McKinney's former public relations assistant, alleged that McKinney had made unwanted sexual advances to her in 1996. Five other enlisted women later accused McKinney of the same conduct. The alleged victims claimed that the verdict reflected sexual bias in the military. McKinney, the first African American to hold the rank of sergeant major of the Army, argued that the charges were racially motivated.

Ralston reappointed. In January 1998, Secretary of Defense William S. Cohen reappointed Air Force General Joseph W. Ralston to a second two-year term as vice chairman of the Joint Chiefs of Staff. Ralston had withdrawn as a candidate for chairman in 1997 because of an extramarital relationship he had in the 1980's.

New sexual misconduct guidelines were announced on July 29, 1998, by Defense Secretary Cohen. Under the new rules, adultery remained unacceptable conduct, but commanding officers were given discretion to decide if a particular case of adultery undermined military discipline and order. The policy also created tougher guidelines for fraternization, prohibiting such activities as dating or business enterprises between officers and enlisted personnel.

Training exercises. Defense Secretary Cohen announced in June 1998 that male and female recruits would continue to train together throughout most of the military. However, drill instructors would be subject to greater scrutiny in an effort to avoid a repeat of sexual misconduct charges involving Army recruits and drill sergeants in 1996 and 1997. Under the decision, the Marine Corps was allowed to continue its practice of training men and women separately.

Cohen directed recruits' superiors to ensure the safety and privacy of men and women by placing them on separate floors or in separate areas of barracks. Cohen's plan ignored the recommendations of an advisory commission that urged the armed forces to return to same-sex basic training exercises. The commission had concluded that training men and women together resulted in less effective work relations.

Base closings. The Senate Armed Services Committee in May 1998 rejected Defense Secretary Cohen's request to create an independent commission to identify military bases that could be closed. The Clinton Administration supported holding two rounds of base closings, chosen by a commission, in the years 2001 and 2005. Cohen estimated that the cuts could save $21 billion by 2015. Cohen told lawmakers that unless additional base closures were approved, the Defense Department would have to cut billions of dollars in spending for new weapons in order to remain within budget.

Declining troop levels, shrinking military budgets, and increased peacekeeping duties stretched the U.S. military to its limit in 1998. As overseas deployments expanded and field training operations decreased, some military officials expressed concern that the overall readiness of the armed forces was suffering. In February, General Henry H. Shelton, chairman of the Joint Chiefs of Staff, assured the U.S. Congress that the military was at an acceptable level of preparedness in the event of a crisis.

In September, however, Defense Secretary Cohen and the Joint Chiefs of Staff announced that an increase in the defense budget was necessary unless major weapons programs or overseas deployments were eliminated. Some members of Congress accused Shelton and the chiefs of the Air Force, Army, Marine Corps, and Navy of being untruthful during the February defense budget hearings. The chiefs countered that the readiness of the U.S. armed forces had steadily declined throughout 1998 as military personnel—especially military pilots—left the service for more lucrative civilian jobs.

Defense budget. The Department of Defense submitted its $257.3-billion budget for fiscal year 1999 to Congress on Feb. 2, 1998. The largest single weapons request was approximately $4 billion for the continued development of a ballistic missile defense system. Money was also allocated to support peacekeeping operations, particularly in the Balkans and the Persian Gulf.

On October 17, President Clinton signed a $250-billion defense spending bill. The legislation provided funds for a variety of new weapons programs. A $520-billion spending bill signed by the president on October 22 included an additional $9 billion for peacekeeping operations and the ballistic missile defense system.

An honor guard passes before the draped and fenced-off Tomb of the Unknowns at Arlington National Cemetery in Virginia during the exhumation of an unknown Vietnam War veteran. The remains were identified in June 1998 as those of First Lieutenant Michael Blassie.

Naval vessels. President Clinton on July 25, 1998, commissioned the U.S.S. *Harry S Truman,* in Norfolk, Virginia. The $4.5-billion Nimitz-class nuclear-powered aircraft carrier was 1 of 13 U.S. aircraft carriers on active duty in 1998.

The Navy announced in April that the third and final Seawolf-class nuclear submarine would be named the U.S.S. *Jimmy Carter.* The submarine was scheduled to join the fleet in 2001. Carter, the 39th president of the United States, was a Naval Academy graduate and the only president to serve as a submarine officer.

"Mighty Mo" retired. The U.S.S. *Missouri,* the battleship on which Japanese officials formally surrendered, ending World War II (1939–1945), arrived in Hawaii on June 22, 1998. The Honolulu-based Missouri Memorial Association planned to refurbish the *Missouri* and open it as a museum in 1999. The *Missouri* was anchored 1,000 feet (300 meters) away from the memorial erected above the U.S.S. *Arizona,* which was sunk during the Japanese attack on Pearl Harbor on Dec. 7, 1941.

Command changes. Louis Caldera was sworn in on July 2, 1998, as secretary of the Army. Caldera, a 1978 graduate of the United States Military Academy, replaced Togo West, Jr., who was appointed President Clinton's secretary of veterans affairs.

In November 1998, Richard Danzig was sworn in as secretary of the Navy. Danzig replaced John Dalton, who announced his retirement in June.

The Senate Armed Services Committee in July rejected Florida State Senator Daryl Jones as President Clinton's nominee as secretary of the Air Force. Former U.S. Air Force reserve colleagues accused Jones, a graduate of the Air Force Academy near Colorado Springs, Colorado, of falsifying his resume.

"Unknown Soldier" identified. The remains of a serviceman from the Vietnam War (1957–1975), buried in 1984 at the Tomb of the Unknowns at Arlington National Cemetery in Virginia, were identified in June 1998 as those of First Lieutenant Michael Blassie. Blassie was an Air Force pilot whose attack jet was shot down in South Vietnam in 1972.

The remains were removed from the Tomb of the Unknowns in May 1998 after a lengthy investigation concluded that they probably belonged to one of two Americans who had been shot down near An Loc in South Vietnam. DNA testing confirmed Blassie's identity. Blassie's remains were reinterred with full military honors in a St. Louis, Missouri, cemetery in July 1998.

☐ Thomas M. DeFrank

See also **Armed forces** Special Report: **Chemical and Biological Weapons; Terrorism.**

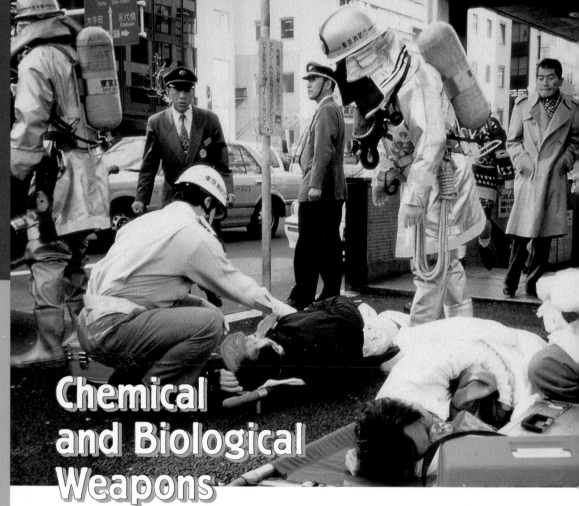

Chemical and Biological Weapons

The spread of chemical and biological weapons caused grave concern to the world on the verge of the new century.

By Javed Ali

In February 1998, the United States and Great Britain appeared to be on the threshold of initiating military action against Iraq. International tensions had been building since October 1997, when United Nations (UN) inspections of Iraqi weapons facilities came to a halt after Iraqi President Saddam Hussein ordered American inspectors to leave the country. Inspectors affiliated with the world body were attempting to verify if Iraq had complied with UN demands that it destroy all chemical, biological, and nuclear weapons and all facilities for making such weapons. These demands had resulted from Iraq's 1990 invasion of Kuwait and subsequent defeat in the 1991 Persian Gulf War. Although the UN managed in early 1998 to craft a deal with Iraq to resume inspections and avoid a military showdown, international concerns over Iraqi weapons programs did not go away. In April 1998, UN inspectors said they discovered a mustard chemical agent, capable of destroying lung tissue, in Iraqi artillery shells. In June, U.S. tests found evidence that Iraq had placed the deadly nerve agent VX inside ballistic missiles during the Persian Gulf War. In August 1998, President Hussein again stopped cooperating with UN inspectors.

The crisis over the inspection of Iraqi weapons facilities drew attention to what intelligence and defense experts have labeled a major threat to international security—the proliferation of chemical and biological weapons. According to unclassified U.S. intelligence and military documents, 22 to 24 nations had offensive chemical weapons programs at various stages of development in 1998, and 10 to 12 nations had offensive biological weapons programs. Although not all of the nations suspected by the government of having these weapons programs were known to private arms experts, many were. Among the nations with possible chemical and biological programs listed by the Henry L. Stimson Center, a research institution concentrating on international security issues, were Egypt, Iran, Iraq, Libya, and North Korea. For less developed countries, these weapons are attractive because they are inexpensive to produce and seemingly increase a nation's international clout. The United States and other more developed countries, on the other hand, considered stopping the proliferation of these weapons an urgent priority.

Arms control experts have also expressed concern about the use of chemical and biological weapons by terrorist groups and individuals with political or religious motivations. The justification for such concerns was demonstrated in March 1995 when Aum Shinrikyo, a Japanese doomsday cult, released chemical agents in a Tokyo subway, killing 12 people and injuring 5,000. In August 1998, U.S. President Bill Clinton ordered the destruction of a factory in Sudan that allegedly produced substances that could be used to make chemical weapons for terrorists.

Rescue workers wearing breathing equipment tend to victims of a 1995 nerve-gas attack in a Tokyo subway, *left*. The attack, carried out by a Japanese terrorist group, killed 12 people and injured 5,000.

Historical perspective

While all of these issues and concerns brought chemical and biological agents to the public's attention, their use in warfare is not new. Historians note that during the Middle Ages, armies hurled disease-infested corpses over city walls to start epidemics. During the French and Indian war (1754-1763), British soldiers distributed smallpox-infested blankets to North American Indians sympathetic to the French.

The emergence of sophisticated chemical industries in the early 1900's prompted nations to develop chemicals as agents of warfare. The most extensive use of chemical agents in history occurred during World War I (1914-1918), when both Axis and Allied powers employed such weapons. The result was more than 100,000 fatalities and 1 million casualties.

In the mid-1930's, Italian forces used chemical weapons against local troops in Abyssinia (now Ethiopia), and Japanese forces began using chemical and biological weapons against the Chinese in Manchuria. During World War II (1939-1945), all the major powers—the United States, Great Britain, the Soviet

Countries with chemical and biological weapons

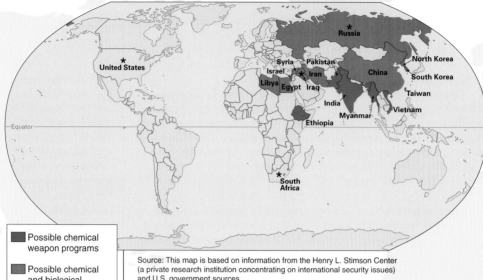

Possible chemical
weapon programs

Possible chemical
and biological
weapon programs

★ Countries that have
acknowledged hav-
ing had chemical
and biological pro-
grams in the past

Source: This map is based on information from the Henry L. Stimson Center
(a private research institution concentrating on international security issues)
and U.S. government sources.

The author:
Javed Ali is a manage-
ment analyst at Re-
search Planning, In-
corporated, in Falls
Church, Virginia, and
the principal author of
*Jane's U.S. Chemical-
Biological Defense
Guidebook.*

Union, Germany, and Japan—possessed chemical and biological
arsenals. But aside from Japan's activities in China, which continued into the 1940's, there is no recorded use of chemical or biological agents during the war.

The most shocking use of chemical weapons in the modern
era took place during the Iran-Iraq War (1980-1988), when
thousands of people, including civilians as well as combatants,
died through exposure to various agents. Both Iran and Iraq employed these weapons during the conflict.

Chemical weapons

Chemical weapons contain toxic chemical compounds manufactured through various processes. There are four major categories
of chemical weapons, each of which triggers a unique set of responses in humans. Blister agents, such as the mustard gas used
during World War I, blister skin and destroy mucous mem-
branes, including the lining of the lungs. Blood agents, such as
cyanide, deprive human tissues of oxygen, leading to respiratory
failure and paralysis. Choking agents, including phosgene and
diphosgene, cause fluid to accumulate in the lungs. Nerve agents,
such as sarin and VX, disrupt nerve transmission, leading to
heart and lung failure.

Chemical weapons go into effect within minutes or hours,
depending on the type and purity of the agent used and the route
by which the agent enters the body. Nerve agents are the fastest
acting and most deadly chemical agents. Just 3/10,000 of an
ounce (10 milligrams) of VX absorbed through the skin will kill
a 170-pound (77-kilogram) man within 5 to 15 minutes.

There are many ways in which chemical weapons can be delivered—some of them technologically challenging, others quite
simple. Technologically advanced delivery systems include ballis-

Chemical weapons and their effects

The active agents used in chemical weapons are toxic chemical compounds manufactured through various production methods.

AGENT	EFFECT
Blister agents lewisite mustard nitrogen mustard	Blistering of skin, destruction of mucous membranes (such as in lungs)
Blood agents cyanide hydrogen cyanide	Deprives body cells of oxygen, leading to respiratory failure and paralysis
Choking agents diphosgene phosgene	Triggers accumulation of fluid in the lungs
Nerve agents sarin soman tabun VX	Disrupts nerve transmission, leading to heart and lung failure

Biological weapons and their effects

The active agents used in biological weapons are living microorganisms or toxins produced by microorganisms.

AGENT	EFFECT
Bacteria anthrax	Respiratory distress, shock, death
brucellosis	Fever, joint and muscle pain, fatigue
cholera	Gastrointestinal distress, loss of fluids, collapse
plague	Pneumonia, bleeding of skin and mucous membranes, lymph node pain
Q fever	Fever, respiratory distress, joint and muscle pain
Viruses ebola	Vomiting, massive internal bleeding
smallpox	Blisters, bleeding of skin and mucous membranes
Toxins aflatoxin	Liver failure
botulinum	Respiratory paralysis
ricin	Convulsions, circulatory failure

tic and cruise missiles, bombs, and mortars and artillery. However, chemical agents can also be delivered by aircraft-mounted agricultural spray tanks and hand-held and portable spraying devices.

Each chemical agent reacts differently when released into the environment. Chemical weapons such as sarin and hydrogen cyanide are very *volatile* (degrade rapidly after exposure to the environment) and quickly lose their effectiveness after release. VX and mustard are less volatile and remain effective long after being released. Such agents can continue to contaminate the environment for weeks, posing a hazard for anyone who enters the area. Even volatile chemicals can be made to last longer in the environment by adding substances called stabilizers.

Nations interested in developing chemical weapons in the 1990's had more than 80 years accumulation of relevant scientific research at their disposal. The production of blister, blood, and choking agents involves methods of chemical synthesis that have existed since World War I. The production of nerve agents is based on chemical technologies developed by German and British researchers during World War II.

Biological weapons

While chemical weapons consist of *inanimate* (nonliving) chemical compounds, biological weapons are made of living organisms, such as viruses and bacteria, or of toxic substances, such as botulinum, derived from living organisms. Different types of biological agents have different effects on people. Certain agents can kill up to 90 percent of an exposed population. This group includes the much-feared anthrax bacterium, which causes a fatal lung inflammation when inhaled. Other agents, while less lethal than anthrax, are still deadly. The toxin ricin, derived from castor bean seeds, causes death through circulatory failure.

A crop duster releases chemical pesticides over a farm field, *above.* The same types of aircraft-mounted spray tanks used to release agricultural pesticides can be used to release harmful chemical and biological agents over human populations.

The fungus-derived toxin aflatoxin kills by triggering liver failure. Certain biological agents, including the brucellosis and Q fever bacteria, cause debilitating symptoms, such as fever, pain, and fatigue, but do not kill.

Although chemical weapons produce their effects within minutes or hours, the symptoms caused by biological weapons are usually delayed. Depending on the biological agent, the amount used, and the method of delivery, symptoms may not appear for days, weeks, or even months. This delay is the main reason why biological weapons have been long considered ideal for covert warfare, terrorist attacks, and sabotage.

Delivery methods for biological weapons are similar to the methods available for chemical weapons, including bombs, missiles, artillery and mortar rounds, and aircraft-mounted spray tanks. However, the successful delivery of biological weapons is much more complicated than the release of chemical agents. Because biological agents, other than toxins, are living organisms, a range of environmental factors—including humidity, sunlight, and wind direction and speed—are critical in determining whether the organisms will survive their release.

Biological weapons in relatively small quantities have the potential to infect vast numbers of people. Just 110 pounds (50 kilograms) of anthrax bacteria released from an aircraft over a city of 500,000 people could kill as many as 95,000 individuals and sicken 120,000 others, according to the World Health Organization, an agency of the United Nations based in Geneva, Switzerland.

The procedures for producing biological weapons have been long known to scientists. Most bacteria can be grown with fermentation techniques, in which sugar compounds or other *organic* (carbon-based) substances are broken down through bacterial action. Viruses can be cultivated in eggs, mouse brains, or tissue cultures. Some microorganisms used in weapons can be obtained from biological-supply companies or even from nature. And the most rudimentary lab equipment—culture medium, petri dishes, and a small incubator—is all that is needed to grow them.

Proliferation among nations and terrorists

The ease and affordability of producing chemical and biological weapons are only two of the reasons for their proliferation among nations. Possession of such weapons, which can be as potentially destructive as medium-sized nuclear devices, provides a strategic lever that developing countries can use against more technologically sophisticated nations. Besides using chemical and biological weapons to threaten or intimidate neighboring countries, weaker nations may use such weapons to make more powerful aggressors think twice before initiating military action. These weapons may also be used as bargaining chips to be negotiated away in return for favorable economic, diplomatic, or political concessions from more powerful states.

Chemical and biological weapon production facilities and storage sites are easy and inexpensive to build and difficult to detect and destroy. Biological weapons can be produced in college laboratories, hospitals, or even breweries. The ability to blend such production facilities into the background gives biological weapons an advantage over more conspicuous technologies, such as those needed to make nuclear weapons.

Although U.S. intelligence officials estimate that as many as 24 nations have chemical weapons programs and as many as 12 nations have biological weapons programs, few details have been made public about which countries have what weapons. Nevertheless, proliferation experts believe that most of these countries are concentrated in a region ranging from the Middle East to China—a part of the world where there have been intense, long-lasting political disputes among numerous nations. Iraq alone has acknowledged producing hundreds of tons of mustard and nerve agents, 5,020 gallons (19,000 liters) of the toxin that causes botulism, 2,110 gallons (8,000 liters) of anthrax, 630 gallons (2,400 liters) of aflaxtoxin, and smaller quantities of other biological agents. (While Iraq claims to have de-

U.S. soldiers in France practice using gas masks during World War I (1914-1918). Chemical weapons caused 1 million casualties in the war.

stroyed all of these weapons, this claim was not verified by UN inspectors in 1998.)

U.S. intelligence officials have indicated that the proliferation of chemical and biological weapons among terrorists is at least as worrisome as proliferation among nations. The activities of the Japanese cult Aum Shinrikyo demonstrated that any group with enough funds, organizational skill, and technological sophistication is capable of initiating chemical or biological attacks on civilians or government institutions.

Controlling proliferation and managing danger

Despite the proliferation of chemical and biological arsenals in the 1990's, experts have long maintained that international agreements have been important in helping thwart the use and spread of these weapons. The first international arms control agreement to address chemical and biological weapons was the 1925 Geneva Protocol, signed by more than 100 nations. Under terms of the protocol, countries agreed never to use such weapons. However, the protocol had a number a weaknesses, including the absence of penalties for violating the treaty and mechanisms for enforcing it.

In 1969, U.S. President Richard Nixon announced that the United States would unilaterally destroy all of its biological weapons, which was accomplished by 1975. Other nations then began considering a new international treaty dealing with biological agents. In 1972, the United States, the Soviet Union, and Great Britain negotiated the Biological and Toxin Weapons Convention, the first agreement banning the use, production, acquisition, and transfer of biological weapons, as well as research on such weapons. By late 1998, the treaty had been signed by more than 150 countries and ratified by more than 140. However, this treaty, too, lacked a mechanism for enforcement or verification. Negotiations to strengthen the treaty were carried out in Geneva in 1998.

In 1993, the Chemical Weapons Convention, prompted by the use of chemical agents during the Iran-Iraq War, was signed by 137 countries in Paris. The treaty, which by late 1998 had been signed by more than 160 countries and ratified by more than 120, bans research on chemical weapons and the production, acquisition, use, stockpiling, and transfer of chemical weapons. Moreover, the treaty has an enforcement mechanism, known as the Organization for the Prohibition of Chemical Weapons (OPCW), which carries out inspections on both military and civilian chemical facilities in participating countries.

However, OPCW inspections are imperfect because possession of a weapons-type chemical agent does not necessarily imply it is being used in weapons. The same chemical agents are also used in such legitimate civilian products as insecticides, gasoline additives, and dyes.

To help ensure compliance, the Chemical Weapons Convention requires participating countries to implement legislation criminalizing prohibited activities. Although the United States

had not yet implemented such legislation in 1998, the U.S. military had begun destroying its large chemical arsenal under a directive issued by the U.S. Congress in the late 1980's.

Russia, like the United States, has ratified both the Chemical and Biological Weapons Conventions. However, unlike the United States, Russia had made little disarmament progress as of 1998. United States arms experts have suggested that internal political and financial difficulties have prevented Russia from destroying any of the more than 40,000 tons (36 million kilograms) of chemical weapons the Soviet Union produced during the Cold War (mid-1940's to early 1990's). Arms experts are also concerned that less-than-stringent security at Russian storage sites might enable terrorists to acquire material for weapons. Arms authorities harbor similar concerns about Russian stockpiles of biological weapons, which were produced in enormous quantities by the Soviet Union.

Federal officials in the United States are training local police, fire, emergency response, and health care personnel on how to respond to chemical and biological attacks. In May 1998, President Clinton ordered the strengthening of American defenses against both terrorist attacks and germ warfare. Among the steps he announced was the development and stockpiling of antibiotics and vaccines to protect U.S. civilians from biological agents.

Arms control authorities believe that the steps taken to combat the proliferation of chemical and biological weapons, while imperfect, have laid a valuable foundation on which to build more effective defense and control strategies. However, they also warn that because chemical and biological weapons provide an easy, inexpensive way for developing countries, such as Iraq, to strengthen their international clout, these lethal instruments will remain a focus of the world's concern in years to come.

Prompted by fears of an Iraqi chemical weapons attack, an Israeli family, *top,* protects itself with gas masks during the 1991 Persian Gulf War. U.S. marines leaving for the Gulf conflict, *top right,* are vaccinated against a number of microbial diseases, including anthrax. Anthrax is a severe respiratory illness caused by a bacterium believed to be in Iraq's arsenal in 1991.

Armenia. President Levon Ter-Petrosyan resigned on Feb. 3, 1998, amid fierce opposition to his plan for ending the war with neighboring Azerbaijan. As a cease-fire between the two nations began its fifth year in May 1998, Armenian troops continued to occupy the Armenian enclave of Nagorno-Karabakh and surrounding territory in Azerbaijan. Ter-Petrosyan had endorsed a European plan to withdraw Armenian troops first and resolve the region's political status later, but Armenian nationalists and hard-liners objected to any compromise that did not guarantee autonomy for Nagorno-Karabakh.

On March 30, Prime Minster Robert Kocharyan was elected president. Kocharyan was forced into a runoff against Karen Demirchyan, the former head of Armenia's Communist Party. Demirchyan had won a surprising 31 percent of the vote on the first ballot, signaling growing nostalgia among voters for the economic and political stability of the Soviet era. After his election, Kocharyan named Finance and Economy Minister Armen Darbinyan as the new prime minister.

Kocharyan's election was a blow to negotiations with Azerbaijan, however. Kocharyan, who led the breakaway government of Nagorno-Karabakh in 1997, resisted compromise over the status of the territory. ☐ Steven L. Solnick

See also **Asia** (Facts in brief table); **Azerbaijan.**

Art. In 1998, the art world was dominated by the issue of art plundered from public and private collections throughout Europe by the Nazi government of Germany before and during World War II (1939-1945). Much of the art was confiscated from Jews who were later killed by the Nazis. Since the mid-1990's, a growing number of heirs of Jewish vicitims have taken steps to reclaim lost possessions.

Efforts to restore the looted art to its original owners or their heirs or to provide restitution proved difficult. In nearly all cases, the current owners of the art purchased the objects in good faith, without knowing that the objects were looted. In addition, the original owners or their heirs often lacked proof of ownership because the records were destroyed in the war. Other complications included the huge expense of pressing legal claims and the lack of established guidelines for resolving ownership issues.

Schiele case. On Jan. 7, 1998, Manhattan District Attorney Robert M. Morgenthau issued a grand jury subpoena that prevented the Museum of Modern Art (MOMA) in New York City from returning to Austria two paintings by Austrian artist Egon Schiele. The paintings had been part of an exhibition of Schiele's work at MOMA. Morgenthau acted on behalf of two families who claimed that the paintings had been stolen from

their families by the Nazis. The paintings had been loaned to MOMA by the Leopold Museum in Vienna, Austria.

The Leopold Museum offered to abide by the findings of an international tribunal to be convened to examine the case. The families, however, insisted that the paintings remain in the United States in order to ensure a fair ruling. MOMA immediately went to court to win the paintings' release. On May 13, a judge in New York City ruled that MOMA could return the paintings to Austria. In December 1998, Morgenthau's office continued to appeal the decision, and an investigation of the case continued.

Museum sued. On July 31, the heirs of Paul Rosenberg, a well-known Jewish art dealer in Paris in the 1930's, sued the Seattle Art Museum for the return of "Odalisque" (1925) by the French artist Henri Matisse. The suit was the first filed against an American museum by those seeking the recovery of Nazi-looted art. The Rosenberg family contended that in 1941 the Nazis had confiscated the painting from Rosenberg, who fled to the United States during World War II. The Seattle Art Museum, in turn, sued Knoedler & Company, the prestigious New York City art gallery that in 1954 had bought the painting in Paris and then sold it to private collectors. The collectors had donated the painting to the Seattle Museum in 1996. The daughter of the collectors contacted the Rosenberg family in 1997 after finding the painting in a book on Nazi-looted art.

Degas settlement. In August 1998, the Art Institute of Chicago, the heirs of the original owners of a landscape by French impressionist Edgar Degas, and the painting's most recent owner reached the first settlement involving Nazi-confiscated art in the United States. In 1995, relatives of the original owners, Dutch collectors Friedrich and Louise Gutmann, discovered that the Degas landscape was owned by Chicago business executive Daniel C. Searle, a member of the board of directors of the Art Institute of Chicago. Searle had purchased the painting in 1987 for $850,000. The Gutmanns died in Nazi concentration camps in the 1940's.

In 1996, the Gutmann heirs sued Searle. Under an agreement announced in August 1998, however, Searle donated the painting to the Art Institute. In return, the Art Institute agreed to pay the Gutmann heirs a total of approximately $550,000—half the 1998 value of the painting.

Museum guidelines. In June, the Association of Art Museum Directors, a professional body that represents the 170 largest art museums in North America, issued guidelines to help museums resolve claims involving art looted during World War II. The guidelines called for the creation of databases to help identify stolen works

Classic motorcycles, *left,* line the galleries of the Solomon R. Guggenheim Museum in New York City for the motorcycle art show that ran from June through September 1998. The interior spiral of the Frank Lloyd Wright-designed museum, *below,* is wrapped in chrome for the exhibit, which celebrated the motorcycle as a cultural icon of the 1900's.

of art; a review of the ownership of objects in their collections and of objects about to be bought, donated, or borrowed; and the timely resolution of any claims on objects in their collection. The Art Dealers Association of America issued similar guidelines later in 1998.

International agreement. In December, delegates from 44 countries met in Washington, D.C., and approved the first international agreement on the restoration of Nazi-looted art. The guidelines, which were not legally binding, called for governments to reveal all official records on stolen art, to make efforts to identify stolen art, and to negotiate "a just and fair solution" to valid claims.

NEA reprieve. Congressional opponents of the National Endowment for the Arts (NEA), a federal arts-funding agency, failed in 1998 to eliminate the agency. Instead, the United States Congress approved an agency budget of $98 million for fiscal year 1998-1999.

In the late 1980's and early 1990's, many conservative members of Congress were outraged by the NEA's decision to provide financial support for art that some people considered obscene or sacrilegious. In May 1998, Congress confirmed William J. Ivey, executive director of the Country Music Foundation of Nashville, as the new chairman of the NEA.

Supreme Court ruling. In June 1998, the U.S. Supreme Court upheld a 1990 law requiring the NEA to take "general standards of decency" into account when awarding grants. However, the court also ruled that the law contained only "advisory language" and so did not actually prohibit the NEA from funding art that some might consider obscene or otherwise objectionable.

Important exhibitions of 1998 included retrospectives devoted to Finnish modernist architect Alvar Aalto, French painter Pierre Bonnard, and American painter Jackson Pollock by MOMA; British painter Edward Burne-Jones by the Metropolitan Museum of Art in New York City; and American sculptor Alexander Calder at the San Francisco Museum of Modern Art. American pop artist Chuck Close was the subject of an exhibition at the Museum of Contemporary Art in Chicago, while the Whitney Museum of American Art in New York City mounted a retrospective of the works of abstract expressionist Mark Rothko. Other important exhibitions included "Monet in the 20th Century," organized by the Museum of Fine Arts in Boston; "Edo: Art in Japan, 1615–1868" at the National Gallery of Art in Washington, D.C.; "China: 5,000 Years" at the Solomon R. Guggenheim Museum in New York City; and "Delacroix: The Late Work" at the Philadelphia Museum of Art.   □ Eric Gibson

See also **Architecture.**

Asia

The economies of several Asian countries went into recession in 1998 as an economic crisis, which began in 1997, intensified and shook financial markets around the world. The crisis contributed to political upheaval, social unrest, widespread hunger, and armed conflicts.

Economic crisis. In the 1970's and 1980's many Asian countries led the world in economic growth. In 1997, however, Thailand's economy crashed, abruptly halting a decade of rapid growth and triggering a financial crisis throughout Asia.

Across East Asia in 1998, economic output fell, unemployment rose, and the values of stock and currencies plunged. Banks, unable to collect debts, cut back on new loans, forcing many businesses into bankruptcy. Some banks closed. Other faltering banks—in Japan, South Korea, and Thailand, for example—remained open but only with the help of government subsidies.

Economies in South Asia were weakened by a decline in trade with the once booming economies of East Asia. Falling currency values reduced the cost of products made in East Asia, lessening the demand for South Asian exports.

By early 1998, the economic contagion spread beyond the Pacific Rim to markets around the world. The growing crisis caused foreign investors to pull out of Asia, resulting in a dramatic drop in stock prices. Some stock markets tumbled to less than half their 1997 values.

Economists hoped that Japan, the world's second-largest economy, would bail out the troubled region by pumping money into Asian countries. Japan, however, was crippled by a banking crisis. Japan had entered an economic slowdown in the early 1990's that had left many banks with unpaid loans on undervalued property. The government's efforts to overhaul problem banks and institute economic reforms failed, and in 1998, Japan experienced its most serious financial crisis since the end of World War II (1939–1945). Most Asian countries were greatly affected by Japan's downturn because of their extensive trade, foreign investment, and credit links with Japan.

Malaysia and Hong Kong sought refuge from the economic crisis by abandoning parts of the capitalist system that had made their economies rich. On Sept. 2, 1998, Malaysia attempted to shield its economy from the effects of an unpredictable international financial market by imposing strict controls on its currency and stock markets.

Hong Kong, which maintained a separate

A child in Jakarta, Indonesia, scavenges through one of the city's garbage dumps in August 1998, looking for food. Hunger was widespread in Indonesia in 1998, the result of the economic crisis that devastated Asian stock and currency markets.

Country	Population	Government	Monetary unit*	Foreign trade (million U.S.$)	
				Exports[†]	Imports[†]
Afghanistan	23,731,000	No functioning government	afghani (4,750.00 = $1)	188	616
Armenia	3,726,000	President Robert Kocharian	dram (503.05 = $1)	248	661
Australia	18,758,000	Governor General William Deane; Prime Minister John Howard	dollar (1.59 = $1)	62,901	65,910
Azerbaijan	7,801,000	President Heydar A. Aliyev	manat (3,950.00 = $1)	781	794
Bangladesh	128,558,000	President Mustafizur Rahman; Prime Minister Sheikh Hasina Wajed	taka (48.50 = $1)	3,297	6,621
Bhutan	1,756,000	King Jigme Singye Wangchuck	ngultrum (42.30 = $1)	71	114
Brunei	300,000	Sultan Sir Hassanal Bolkiah	dollar (1.63 = $1)	2,273	1,915
Cambodia (Kampuchea)	11,052,000	King Norodom Sihanouk; Prime Minister Ung Huot; Prime Minister Hun Sen	riel (3,730.00 = $1)	464	1,400
China	1,265,413,000	Communist Party General Secretary and President Jiang Zemin; Premier Zhu Rongji	renminbi (8.28 = $1)	182,690	142,377
Georgia	5,500,000	President Eduard Shevardnadze	lari (not available)	140	250
India	986,026,000	President Kircheril Raman Narayanan; Prime Minister Atal Behari Vajpayee	rupee (42.30 = $1)	33,900	40,358
Indonesia	206,491,000	President Bacharuddin Jusuf Habibie	rupiah (8,300.00 = $1)	53,444	41,693
Iran	71,569,000	Leader of the Islamic Revolution Ali Hoseini-Khamenei; President Mohammad Khatami-Ardakani	rial (3,000.00 = $1)	21,300	13,300
Japan	125,922,000	Emperor Akihito; Prime Minister Keizo Obuchi	yen (118.18 = $1)	421,053	338,840
Kazakhstan	17,457,000	President Nursultan Nazarbayev	tenge (76.60 = $1)	6,366	4,275
Korea, North	25,121,000	Korean Workers' Party General Secretary Kim Chong-il	won (2.20 = $1)	805	1,240
Korea, South	46,262,000	President Kim Tae-chung; Prime Minister Kim Chong-pil	won (1,311.50 = $1)	136,741	144,615
Kyrgyzstan	4,960,000	President Askar Akayev	som (18.60 = $1)	380	439
Laos	5,296,000	President Khamtai Siphandon; Prime Minister Sisavat Keobounphan	kip (3,682.00 = $1)	323	690
Malaysia	21,398,000	Paramount Ruler Tuanku Ja'afar ibni Al-Marhum Tuanku Abdul Rahman; Prime Minister Mahathir bin Mohamad	ringgit (3.80= $1)	78,253	78,418

economy from China, had grown rich from wide-open trade without governmental intervention. As its stock market plummeted in 1998, the local government in Hong Kong abandoned its free-market principles. In August, the Hong Kong government purchased $15 billion worth of stock in an effort to keep the market from diving. The move, however, failed to keep Hong Kong's economy from sinking into recession. Property values fell sharply, and unemployment reached a 15-year high of 5 percent.

Hunger. The economic crisis, combined with drought and massive flooding, cut agricultural production in 1998, leaving many people hungry and unable to pay for food. International aid workers reported acute hunger in parts of Indonesia.

Nuclear tests. India and Pakistan, which had fought three wars since the two nations were created by partition in 1947, conducted a series of nuclear tests in May 1998. India had exploded its first nuclear device in 1974, but had halted testing after the United States threatened to impose harsh economic sanctions.

India's announcement on May 11, 1998, that it had conducted underground nuclear tests star-

Country	Population	Government	Monetary unit*	Foreign trade (million U.S.$)	
				Exports[†]	Imports[†]
Maldives	269,000	President Maumoon Abdul Gayoom	rufiyaa (11.77 = $1)	73	349
Mongolia	2,556,000	President Natsagiy Bagabandi; Prime Minister Janlaviin Narantsatsralt	tugrik (817.61 = $1)	423	439
Myanmar (Burma)	49,447,000	Prime Minister, State Peace and Development Council Chairman Than Shwe	kyat (6.15= $1)	866	2,261
Nepal	23,603,000	King Birendra Bir Bikram Shah Dev; Prime Minister Girija Prasad Koirala	rupee (68.33 = $1)	385	1,442
New Zealand	3,683,000	Governor General Sir Michael Hardie-Boys; Prime Minister Jennifer Shipley	dollar (1.86 = $1)	14,052	14,520
Pakistan	152,766,000	President Rafia Tara Prime Minister Nawaz Sharif	rupee (57.10 = $1)	8,717	11,595
Papua New Guinea	4,596,000	Governor General Sir Silas Atopare; Prime Minister William Skate	kina (2.14 = $1)	2,137	1,696
Philippines	71,654,000	President Joseph Estrada	peso (40.00 = $1)	20,417	34,122
Russia	146,120,000	President Boris Yeltsin; Prime Minister Yevgeny Primakov	ruble (15.80 = $1)	87,368	67,619
Singapore	2,919,000	President Ong Teng Cheong; Prime Minister Goh Chok Tong	dollar (1.63 = $1)	125,023	132,445
Sri Lanka	19,034,000	President Chandrika Kumaratunga; Prime Minister Sirimavo Bandaranaike	rupee (67.27 = $1)	4,666	5,839
Taiwan	22,106,000	President Lee Teng-hui; Vice President Lien Chan	dollar (32.55 = $1)	116,000	102,400
Tajikistan	6,603,000	President Emomali Rahmonov; National Assembly Chairman Safarali Rajabov	ruble (750.00 = $1)	785	797
Thailand	60,626,000	King Phumiphon Adunyadet; Prime Minister Chuan Likphai	baht (36.67= $1)	55,526	72,168
Turkmenistan	4,361,000	President Saparmurat Niyazov	manat (not available)	1,939	777
Uzbekistan	24,320,000	President Islam Karimov	som (85.85 = $1)	4,388	4,523
Vietnam	79,247,000	Communist Party General Secretary Le Kha Phieu; President Tran Duc Luong; Prime Minister Phan Van Khai	dong (13,899.00 = $1)	7,256	11,144

*Exchange rates as of Nov. 6, 1998, or latest available data.
†Latest available data.

tled the world, even though India's new Hindu nationalist government had vowed during the 1998 election campaign to resume developing nuclear weapons. Pakistan retaliated on May 28 by detonating its own series of nuclear devices.

Both countries developed missiles capable of delivering nuclear warheads. However, observers noted that it would take both countries years to build nuclear weapons small enough to fit on the missiles.

North Korea tried to launch what it claimed to be a satellite in August 1998, an act that ignited international concern about the country's mis-sile program. The satellite was attached to a medium-range missile that broke up over Japan. The missile firing angered Japanese officials, who initially suspected that the rocket launch was a hostile act. According to intelligence agencies, the launch suggested that North Korea had developed the technology for rockets that could reach any part of Japan.

Political turmoil. Many people in Asia blamed the economic crisis on government officials, which resulted in the ouster of several governments. In May, riots sparked by Indonesia's faltering economy forced Asia's longest-serving ruler, President Suharto, to resign. Vice President Bacharuddin Jusuf Habibie succeeded Suharto, who had ruled Indonesia for 32 years. Elections brought new political leaders to India, the Philippines, and South Korea. Parliaments confirmed prime ministers in China, Japan, Mongolia, and Nepal.

Smoke from forest fires caused health problems in Asia in 1998 and contributed to severe smog over metropolitan areas. Corporations had deliberately set fires in jungles in 1997 to clear land for growing trees for palm oil, rubber, or pulp wood. The fires in Indonesia and Malaysia had burned out of control, blanketing much of Southeast Asia in smoke. Government officials ordered the corporations to stop setting fires, but the fires continued to rage in 1998, aided by drought conditions. By March, smoky haze once again spread over parts of Indonesia, Malaysia, and Singapore.

Floods killed thousands of people in Asia in 1998, devastated crops, and swallowed entire villages in China, India, Bangladesh, and North Korea. Flooding and landslides in northern and eastern India killed nearly 1,000 people and affected the lives of millions of others. In Bangladesh, which experienced its worst floods in 10 years, more than 900 people were killed. China experienced its worst flooding in 40 years when the Yangtze River and two other rivers overflowed, resulting in the death of approximately 3,000 people.

Environmentalists blamed the massive flooding on environmental damage, in particular the excessive cutting of forestland. Logging caused erosion and an increased runoff of rain. The mud carried by the runoff filled riverbeds, causing water levels to rise.

Brunei. Sultan Hassanal Bolkiah of Brunei, an oil-rich Islamic monarchy on Borneo, engaged in a bitter family feud in 1998 and struggled to keep his country's once booming economy from being devastated by falling oil prices. Oil and natural gas sales generated 90 percent of the government's income. In 1997, oil pumped nearly $2 billion into Brunei's economy. In 1998, oil revenue fell at least 20 percent.

Hassanal, who had ruled the country since Brunei gained independence from Great Britain in 1984, blamed many of the economic problems on his brother, Prince Jefri. The sultan accused Jefri, a former finance minister, of mishandling the family's $60 billion in investments.

On July 29, 1998, the sultan dismissed Jefri as head of Brunei's state investment agency and its largest conglomerate, the Amedeo Development Corporation. The company had lost $16 billion under Jefri's stewardship, according to a 1998 audit.

Jefri, who went into self-imposed exile in the United States, blamed his rift with the royal family on Islamic fundamentalists who, he claimed, played an influential role in Brunei's government. In ceremonies on August 10, the sultan proclaimed his 24-year-old son, Prince al-Muhtadee Billah, as Brunei's heir apparent.

Bhutan, a small Buddhist monarchy in the eastern Himalaya, took a major step toward constitutional government in 1998. The king, Jigme Singye Wangchuck, who had been an absolute ruler, voluntarily issued an edict stating that the National Assembly could force the king's abdication by a two-thirds vote of no-confidence. The Assembly ratified the edict on July 7.

Laos. The National Assembly named Khamtai Siphandon as president of Laos on February 24. He succeeded Nouhak Phoumsavan as head of the Communist state. Khamtai was replaced as prime minister by Sisavat Keobounphan.

The 210-megawatt Nam Theun-Hinboun Dam began generating electricity in Laos on April 4, an act that international aid groups considered to be a major step toward economic development of the small, impoverished nation. However, Laos remained dependent on foreign aid in 1998, and its currency, the kip, fell sharply in value.

Mongolia. A seven-month stalemate ended in December when the Mongolian parliament elected the mayor of Ulan Bator, Janlaviin Narantsatsralt, as prime minister. Narantsatsralt took office on December 9, succeeding Tsakhiagiin Elbegdorj, who had continued in office in a caretaker capacity since his resignation in July. Elbegdorj had succeeded Mendsaikhan Enkhsaikhan, who resigned in April.

The parliament fought bitterly over the selection of a new prime minister. One candidate, Sanjaasuregiin Zorig, was murdered on October 2. Police suspected Zorig's murder was politically motivated.

Nepal. King Birendra Bir Bikram Shah Dev appointed Girija Prasad Koirala prime minister of the Himalayan kingdom of Nepal in April 1998, after Surya Bahadur Thapa resigned from office on April 10. Koirala, leader of the Congress Party, was supported by one faction of Communists. Another Communist faction conducted rural guerrilla warfare and demanded that Nepal oust King Birendra and become a republic.

An American company abandoned a $9-billion plan to generate electricity in Nepal, citing political instability and government delays. King Birendra Bir Bikram Shah Dev said Nepal would seek other foreign investment to harness Himalayan rivers with hydroelectric-power dams.

☐ Henry S. Bradsher

See also the various Asian country articles; **Economics** Special Report: **Asian Economic Crisis.**

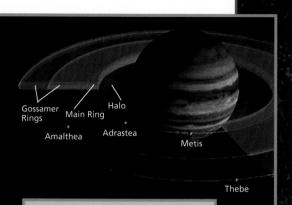

Gossamer Rings · Main Ring · Halo · Amalthea · Adrastea · Metis · Thebe

The rings of Jupiter are revealed and their formation explained in an illustration released in September 1998 by the National Aeronautics and Space Administration (NASA). With data provided by Galileo, a spacecraft circling Jupiter since 1995, astronomers concluded that the rings are formed from dust kicked up by meteoroids that collide with Jupiter's moons. The astronomers reported that Jupiter has four rings, not three as they had previously believed.

A Hubble Space Telescope image captures an object (circled) that some astronomers believe is the first planet outside the solar system to be observed from Earth. Astronomer Susan Terebey and her colleagues at the Extrasolar Research Corporation in Pasadena, California, released the image in May 1998. They believe it is a large planet near a double-star system of the Milky Way Galaxy.

Astronomy. In 1998, astronomers reported the probability of ice on the moon and discovered how the rings of Jupiter were formed. They observed new planets, recorded powerful gamma rays from a magnetic star, and found evidence that the universe is likely to expand forever.

Ice on the moon. In March, scientists with the U.S. National Aeronautics and Space Administration's (NASA's) Lunar Prospector mission announced that the moon-orbiting satellite had detected large amounts of frozen water at both lunar poles. According to the scientists, as much as 10 billion tons (9 billion metric tons) of water could be present on the moon in the form of ice crystals mixed with dirt. Lunar Prospector, orbiting the moon at a height of about 62 miles (100 kilometers), carried instruments that analyzed the chemical composition of the lunar surface. The instruments showed what some scientists believed was evidence of ice in deep polar craters shielded from the sun. Differing scientists noted that other elements on the moon could have produced such readings. The finding fueled speculation that lunar colonies might be able to satisfy their water needs from the lunar soil.

Jupiter's rings. In September, scientists at Cornell University in Ithaca, New York, and the National Optical Astronomy Observatories in Tucson, Arizona, announced that they had determined the origin of Jupiter's rings by analyzing data from NASA's Galileo spacecraft, orbiting the

planet since 1995. The rings, discovered in 1979 when the Voyager spacecraft passed by the planet, circle Jupiter like the rings of Saturn. Unlike Saturn's rings, which are wide and bright, Jupiter's rings are narrow and faint. While Saturn's rings are composed of chunks of rock and ice, Jupiter's are made of dust particles.

Voyager images showed only three rings around Jupiter—a thin main ring, a broader inner ring called the halo, and a transparent outer ring called the gossamer ring. The new images from Galileo revealed that Jupiter's gossamer ring is actually two rings, one embedded in the other. The pictures also revealed that dust from two of Jupiter's smaller moons, Amalthea and Thebe, which orbit near the gossamer ring, is the same kind of dust that is found in the rings. Scientists decided that the dust is pulverized material from the two moons, kicked off the surface by the impact of meteoroids. The larger main ring of Jupiter is probably formed by dust produced by meteoroid collisions with other Jovian moons.

New planets. Astronomers Geoffrey Marcy at San Francisco State University and Paul Butler at the Anglo-Australian Observatory near Sydney, announced in September 1998 the discovery of two planets orbiting nearby stars—HD210277 in the constellation Aquarius and HD187123 in the constellation Cygnus. The astronomers did not see the new planets directly but detected them by observing their stars, which wobbled slightly as the planets orbited them. Twelve new planets orbiting stars similar to the sun have been discovered using this method since 1995.

Astronomers noted that the new planets are not likely to harbor life. Most are similar in size to Jupiter—several hundred times more massive than Earth—and either so close to or far from their stars that planetary surface temperatures would be too hot or too cold for life. However, the planet around HD210277 has an orbit only a little farther from its star than Earth has from the sun—the first planet found at such a distance. Its discovery led scientists to speculate that Earth-like planets may be common in the Milky Way.

Magnetar. On Aug. 27, 1998, Earth was bombarded by a burst of *gamma rays,* electromagnetic radiation more intense than visible or ultraviolet light or X rays. The powerful radiation drove detectors on several orbiting spacecraft off scale and disrupted some radio transmissions on Earth. The rays never reached the ground because they were absorbed by the atmosphere. Astronomers traced the radiation to a star named SGR1900+14, located about 20,000 light-years from Earth in the Milky Way. A light-year is the distance light travels in a year, about 5.9 trillion miles (9.5 trillion kilometers). SGR1900+14 is a rare type of neutron star called a *magnetar* (a star that has collapsed under its own weight to only a few miles in diameter, intensifying its magnetic field to a level billions of times greater than Earth's).

Ever-expanding universe. In January, two teams of researchers, one at the Lawrence Berkeley National Laboratory in California and the other at the Harvard-Smithsonian Center for Astrophysics in Cambridge, Massachusetts, independently announced the conclusion that the universe may expand forever. Both teams had observed exploding stars called supernovae, which are among the brightest objects in the universe, in very distant galaxies and measured the speeds at which they moved away from the Milky Way. Combining the known distance of a supernova with its speed allowed the scientists to measure the expansion rate of the universe. By comparing the universe's rate of expansion in the past with its current expansion rate, they noted that, while the universe is currently expanding more slowly than in the past, it has not slowed sufficiently to ever collapse in on itself. From this information, they theorized that the universe is likely to expand forever.   □ Laurence A. Marschall

See also **Space exploration.**

Australia

Australia continued to enjoy relative prosperity in 1998, despite an economic crisis among its Asian trading partners. Although the ruling Liberal-National party coalition government held a majority of 23 seats in the House of Representatives, it did not have a majority in the Senate, the house of review for all legislation. Prime Minister John Howard's government was forced to depend on the support of independent senators to pass key legislation. In the October federal election, the coalition government was reelected, but with a reduced majority.

The main issue of the 1998 federal election campaign was the Liberal-National coalition's policy of reforming Australia's indirect taxation system. The coalition proposed abolishing a variety of wholesale taxes and replacing them with a 10-percent tax on all goods and services. Most analysts, recalling that a proposal to introduce such a tax had cost the coalition control of Parliament in 1993, believed that the policy was risky. Public opinion polls forecast a swing to Labor.

The Labor Party did enjoy a number of victories in the 1998 election, held on October 3. However, Prime Minister Howard's coalition held onto enough seats to be reelected, but with a much reduced majority. The coalition won 80 seats. Australian Labor Party (ALP) won 67 seats, and an independent won 1 seat.

The recently formed One Nation Party was the big loser in the election. The party had a platform of restricted immigration, reduced assistance for *Aborigines* (native Australians), and a 2-percent flat "easy tax." The founder of the party, Pauline Hanson, failed to be reelected to Parliament. Hanson first gained national attention when the Liberal Party withdrew its endorsement of her in 1996 because of her outspoken views on race. Nevertheless, in 1996 she had won the seat as an independent and went on to found her own political party.

In 1998, both Hanson and her party suffered from Australia's preferential system of voting, which required voters to rank all candidates in order of preference on their ballots. The main parties refused to give One Nation any of their second preferences. Although Hanson won the largest primary vote in the newly created Blair seat, she failed in the election because the Labor and Liberal parties both directed their preferences against her. While several other One Nation Party candidates received a healthy proportion of the primary vote in various electorates, the party managed to win only one seat, a place in the Senate for one of its Queensland candidates. Sydney resident David Oldfield, a high-profile party leader, failed in his attempt to win a Senate seat.

State elections. When Queenslanders went to the polls in state elections on June 13, they gave 23 percent of the vote to the One Nation Party. The party gathered much of its support from electors in rural seats, where voters were disillusioned with the National Party's stand on such issues as restrictive gun laws. Queensland voters elected 11 members of the One Nation Party, unseating National Party premier Rob Borbidge. The ALP won 44 seats in the 149-seat

Parliament, and its leader, Peter Beattie, was named premier.

On August 29, Tasmanian voters gave the Labor Party control of their state government, and Jim Bacon became the new state premier. In a referendum held in conjunction with the federal election in October, voters in the Northern Territory rejected a proposal to become Australia's seventh state.

To become a republic? A constitutional convention called to discuss the merits of changing Australia from a constitutional monarchy to a republic opened in Canberra, the capital, on February 2. Under the existing constitution, the head

On Australia's first Sorry Day, May 26, 1998, Lyall Dennison, the son of an Aborigine taken from his family under the country's former assimilation policy, reads from a book of apologies made to Aborigines by Australians who chose to renounce such policies.

Members of the Australian House of Representatives

The House of Representatives of the 39th Parliament convened on Nov. 10, 1998. When it convened, the House of Representatives consisted of the following members: 67 Australian Labor Party, 64 Liberal Party of Australia, 16 National Party of Australia, and 1 independent. This table shows each legislator and party affiliation. An asterisk (*) denotes those who served in the 38th Parliament.

Australian Capital Territory
Annette Ellis, A.L.P.*
Bob McMullan, A.L.P.*

New South Wales
Tony Abbott, L.P.*
Anthony Albanese, A.L.P.*
John Anderson, N.P.*
Peter Andren, Ind.*
Larry Anthony, N.P.*
Bruce Baird, L.P.
Kerry Bartlett, L.P.*
Bronwyn Bishop, L.P.*
Laurence Brereton, A.L.P.*
Alan Cadman, L.P.*
Ross Cameron, L.P.*
Ian Causley, N.P.*
Janice Crosio, A.L.P.*
John Fahey, L.P.*
Laurie Ferguson, A.L.P.*
Timothy Fischer, N.P.*
Joel Fitzgibbon, A.L.P.*
Joanna Gash, L.P.*
Jill Hall, A.L.P.
Michael Hatton, A.L.P.*
Kelly Hoare, A.L.P.
Joe Hockey, L.P.*
Colin Hollis, A.L.P.*
Bob Horne, A.L.P.
John Howard, L.P.*
Kay Hull, N.P.
Julia Irwin, A.L.P.
Jackie Kelly, L.P.*
Mark Latham, A.L.P.*
Tony Lawler, N.P.
Michael Lee, A.L.P.*
Jim Lloyd, L.P.*
Stephen Martin, A.L.P.*
Robert McClelland, A.L.P.*
Leo McLeay, A.L.P.*
Daryl Melham, A.L.P.*
Allan Morris, A.L.P.*
Frank Mossfield, A.L.P.*
John Murphy, A.L.P.
Gary Nairn, L.P.*
Garry Nehl, N.P.*
Brendan Nelson, L.P.*
Tanya Plibersek, A.L.P.
Roger Price, A.L.P.*
Philip Ruddock, L.P.*
Stuart St. Clair, N.P.
Alby Schultz, L.P.
Andrew Thomson, L.P.*
Mark Vaile, N.P.*
Danna Vale, L.P.*

Northern Territory
Warren Snowdon, A.L.P.

Queensland
Arch Bevis, A.L.P.*
Mal Brough, L.P.*
Kay Elson, L.P.*
Craig Emerson, A.L.P.
Warren Entsch, L.P.*
Teresa Gambaro, L.P.*
Gary Hardgrave, L.P.*
David Jull, L.P.*
Robert Katter, N.P.*
De-Anne Kelly, N.P.*
Cheryl Kernot, A.L.P.
Peter Lindsay, L.P.*
Kirsten Livermore, A.L.P.
Ian Macfarlane, L.P.
Margaret May, L.P.
John Moore, L.P.*
Paul Neville, N.P.*
Bernie Ripoll, A.L.P.
Kevin Rudd, A.L.P.
Con Sciacca, A.L.P.
Bruce Scott, N.P.*
Peter Slipper, L.P.*
Alexander Somlyay, L.P.*
Kathy Sullivan, L.P.*
Wayne Swan, A.L.P.
Cameron Thompson, L.P.
Warren Truss, N.P.*

South Australia
Neil Andrew, L.P.*
David Cox, A.L.P.
Alexander Downer, L.P.*
Trish Draper, L.P.*
Martyn Evans, A.L.P.*
Christine Gallus, L.P.*
Christopher Pyne, L.P.*
Rodney Sawford, A.L.P.*
Patrick Secker, L.P.
Andrew Southcott, L.P.*
Barry Wakelin, L.P.*
Trish Worth, L.P.*

Tasmania
Dick Adams, A.L.P.*
Duncan Kerr, A.L.P.*
Michelle O'Byrne, A.L.P.
Harry Quick, A.L.P.*
Sid Sidebottom, A.L.P.

Victoria
Kevin Andrews, L.P.*
Fran Bailey, L.P.*
Phillip Barresi, L.P.*
Bruce Billson, L.P.*
Anna Burke, A.L.P.
Bob Charles, L.P.*
Peter Costello, L.P.*
Simon Crean, A.L.P.*
Michael Danby, A.L.P.
Gareth Evans, A.L.P.*
Martin Ferguson, A.L.P.*
John Forrest, N.P.*
Petro Georgiou, L.P.*
Steve Gibbons, A.L.P.
Julia Gillard, A.L.P.
Alan Griffin, A.L.P.*
David Hawker, L.P.*
Harry Jenkins, A.L.P.*
David Kemp, L.P.*
Louis Lieberman, L.P.*
Jenny Macklin, A.L.P.*
Stewart McArthur, L.P.*
Peter McGauran, N.P.*
Peter Nugent, L.P.*
Gavan O'Connor, A.L.P.*
Neil O'Keefe, A.L.P.*
Peter Reith, L.P.*
Michael Ronaldson, L.P.*
Nicola Roxon, A.L.P.
Bob Sercombe, A.L.P.*
Sharman Stone, L.P.*
Lindsay Tanner, A.L.P.*
Andrew Theophanous, A.L.P.*
Kelvin Thomson, A.L.P.*
Gregory Wilton, A.L.P.*
Michael Wooldridge, L.P.*
Christian Zahra, A.L.P.

Western Australia
Kim Beazley, A.L.P.*
Julie Bishop, L.P.
Graham Edwards, A.L.P.
Jane Gerick, A.L.P.
Barry Haase, L.P.
Carmen Lawrence, A.L.P.*
Jann McFarlane, A.L.P.
Judi Moylan, L.P.*
Geoffrey Prosser, L.P.*
Stephen Smith, A.L.P.*
Wilson Tuckey, L.P.*
Mal Washer, L.P.
Kim Wilkie, A.L.P.
Daryl Williams, L.P.*

Members of Australia's 4x200-meter men's freestyle relay swim team celebrate their gold-medal victory and new world record at the 8th World Championships in Perth on Jan. 13, 1998.

of state is Queen Elizabeth II of the United Kingdom, who, in theory, appoints a governor general as her representative in Australia. While the queen is formally consulted about the appointment, the governor general is usually chosen by the prime minister. The prime minister is responsible for running the country on a day-to-day basis. The governor general signs bills into law and has reserve powers over the armed forces but is usually a figurehead.

Half of the 152 delegates attending the two-week convention were elected by Australian voters, who chose 46 republicans and 27 monarchists. The 76 nonelected delegates were chosen by federal and state parliaments and community groups.

Some prorepublican delegates at the convention advocated that Australia should have a president elected by popular vote. This model was favored in public-opinion polls. The dominant Australian Republican Movement (ARM), led by lawyer and merchant banker Malcolm Turnbull, favored a minimalist approach to constitutional revision on the grounds that the fewer changes made in the present system, the more likely a revised constitution would be to succeed with voters. The ARM advocated a simple change from an appointed governor general to an appointed president. The group proposed that the presiden-

tial candidate be chosen by the prime minister from a list submitted by the public and community organizations. The candidate would then be appointed after approval by a two-thirds majority of Parliament members.

Convention delegates agreed that, in the proposed republic, the president would have powers similar to those of the present governor general. He or she would be an Australian citizen who was qualified to become a member of the House of Representatives. The term of office would be five years. Other resolutions of the convention included a new preamble to the constitution that would mention Australia's original inhabitants and an affirmation of equality before the law of all people, regardless of gender. It would also recognize Australia's cultural diversity.

Convention delegates also agreed that Australia would retain the name *Commonwealth of Australia* and would remain a member of the Commonwealth of Nations, an association of countries that were once part of the British Empire. Many delegates who favored the country's becoming a republic said they would like to see the British Union Jack, the national flag of the United Kingdom, dropped from the corner of the Australian flag and a new design chosen for the new republic. However, the convention determined that there would be no attempt to alter

The Ministry of Australia*

John Howard—prime minister

Tim Fischer—minister for trade; deputy prime minister

Alexander Downer—minister for foreign affairs

Peter Costello—treasurer

John Anderson—minister for transport and regional services

Robert Hill—minister for the environment and heritage; leader of the government in the Senate

Richard Alston—minister for communications, information technology and the arts; deputy leader of the government in the Senate

Peter Reith—minister for employment, workplace relations and small business; leader of the House

Jocelyn Newman—minister for family and community services

John Moore—minister for defence

Michael Wooldridge—minister for health and aged care

John Fahey—minister for finance and administration

David Kemp—minister for education, training and youth affairs; vice president of the Executive Council

Nick Minchin—minister for industry, science and resources

Daryl Williams—attorney general

Mark Vaile—minister for agriculture, fisheries and forestry

Philip Ruddock—minister for immigration and multicultural affairs

*As of Nov. 1, 1998.

Premiers of Australian states

State	Premier
New South Wales	John Carr
Queensland	Peter Beattie
South Australia	John Olsen
Tasmania	Jim Bacon
Victoria	Jeff Kennett
Western Australia	Richard Court

Government leaders of Australian mainland territories

Australian Capital Territory	Kate Carnell
Northern Territory	Neil Conn

the Australian flag without a general vote by the electorate.

The delegates voted, 75-71, to adopt the model proposed by the ARM, though not all delegates participated in the voting. Prime Minister Howard promised that the issue would go before the Australian people in a referendum to be held late in 1999. Queen Elizabeth indicated that she would accede to the people's wishes.

The economy. The budget presented by Treasurer Peter Costello on May 12 sought to achieve a budget surplus, despite concerns about the impact of the economic crisis affecting Australia's Asian trading partners. Growth in 1998 was forecast to continue at 3 percent, and inflation was expected to remain below 3 percent. While the government hoped that unemployment would fall, it remained above 8 percent.

Costello noted that Australia's most pressing economic problem remained its trade deficit, which in 1998 was more than 5 percent of *gross domestic product* (the value of all goods and services produced in a country in a given year). A trade deficit occurs when a country imports more goods than it exports to other countries. Figures released in May showed that sales to Australia's Asian trading partners, except for Singapore, had taken a sharp downturn in the first three months of the year. The value of the Australian dollar fell below U.S. $.60 in June and remained unsteady throughout 1998.

Investments. On June 16, Australia's leading insurance organization, AMP, became Australia's fourth-largest public company and was listed on the Australian Stock Exchange. The company's more than 2 million policyholders shared the company's assets in the form of shares.

The sale in 1997 of part of Telstra, Australia's government-owned telecommunications company, had proved popular with shareholders. However, in 1998, the opposition Labor Party blocked legislation that would have enabled the government to sell off the rest of the company. The legislation failed to pass the Senate by one vote on July 11.

Aborigines. The government of Australia set aside May 26 as Sorry Day, in which books signed by more than 1 million Australians were presented to Aboriginal representatives at ceremonies in various parts of the country. The people who signed the books apologized for past government policies that had removed hundreds of thousands of Aboriginal children from their parents. An Aboriginal flag flew over the national Parliament building for the day. Not everyone joined in the ceremonies. Prime Minister John Howard expressed his personal sympathy for past wrongs but refused to apologize on behalf of all Australians.

On July 8, the government passed its "Wik" legislation in the upper house with the help of independent Tasmanian Senator Brian Harradine, after 18 months of stalemate. The 10-point legislation was the result of a native title land claim made by the Wik people to the High Court of Australia in December 1996. The court had ruled that Aboriginal groups still held ownership rights over land that the government had leased to individual farmers and large agricultural companies. The Wik legislation was introduced in Parliament after farming groups demanded that the government protect their leases from land-rights claims by Aborigines.

The Labor Party opposed the Wik legislation. Aboriginal groups also opposed it, despite claims by Prime Minister Howard that the plan was a fair compromise for both Aborigines and farmers.

Essential services. On July 28, 1998, the New South Wales Health Department announced that it had found evidence of two parasitic microbes, *giardia* and *cryptosporidium,* in Sydney's water supply. Most of the 3.7 million residents of Australia's largest city spent the next month and a half boiling water before using it. Despite the discovery of the potentially harmful parasites, no outbreak of illness was recorded. However, Sydney Water, the company that operates the city's water supply system, did not lift its water-boil warning until September 19. An embarrassed state government ordered an independent inquiry into how the water supply came to be contaminated.

On September 25, an explosion at Victoria's main gas plant killed two workers and injured eight others. The state's 1.5 million customers were without gas for more than a week. The ban on the use of gas affected both households and industries. The state government called for an inquiry into the causes of the accident.

Industrial dispute. On April 17, 1998, Patrick Stevedores, one of Australia's two main cargo-handling companies, set off a prolonged industrial dispute when it fired its entire work force of 1,400 employees. All workers who were laid off were members of the Maritime Union of Australia. The company claimed that the union's restrictive work practices had cost the company millions of dollars in lost revenue.

To replace the union workers, Patrick hired workers employed by a company backed by the National Farmers' Federation. The Maritime Union claimed that many of these workers had been secretly trained with the knowledge of the Minister for Workplace Relations, Peter Reith. The minister denied knowledge of the scheme.

The union took the company to court, alleging that Patrick had acted illegally. Work on the waterfront returned to normal on May 8, after the company reinstated union workers. In return, the union accepted that half its members would be laid off. A formal agreement was signed in June.

Weather. Drought conditions, which had affected many parts of eastern Australia in early 1998, gave way to floods in many areas in August. New South Wales was particularly hard hit. Wollongong suffered millions of dollars worth of damage when a storm struck the coastal city in August.

Yachting disaster. The Sydney-to-Hobart (Tasmania) yacht race ended in tragedy on December 28 when winds of 90 miles (145 kilometers) per hour and 33-foot (10-meter) swells struck the racing fleet. Australian authorities confirmed that four sailors died and two others were presumed drowned. While more than 50 people had to be rescued, 39 yachts managed to finish the race.

Commonwealth Games held in Kuala Lumpur, the capital of Malaysia, attracted national attention in Australia. At the close of the games on September 20, Australia had captured 198 medals, including 80 gold medals. Great Britain took 136 medals, including 36 golds. Australian swimmer Susan O'Neill won 6 gold medals and boosted her medal tally to a record 10 golds during the games. Heather Turland, a 38-year-old mother of four from Bowral, New South Wales, won the women's marathon.   □ Brian Kennedy

See also **Asia** (Facts in brief table).

Australia, Prime Minister of. In

1998, John Howard, leader of the Liberal-National party coalition, was reelected to a second term as prime minister of Australia. Howard, leader of the Liberal Party, had became prime minister in 1996, when the coalition first defeated the Australian Labor Party.

In the Oct. 3, 1998, election, the coalition defeated the Labor Party again, but by a narrower margin. The Labor Party won a greater overall percentage of the vote in the election, but failed to win sufficient seats in the House of Representatives to form a government.

Prime Minister Howard's tax reform plan, which he had proposed in August 1998, stirred controversy. The plan, which was to simplify Australia's tax system and make the country's economy more competitive, centered on a 10-percent goods-and-services tax—the first consumption tax in Australia's history. The plan also called for cuts in personal income taxes.

According to political analysts, the plan lost the coalition a significant number of votes in the October elections. After the election, Prime Minister Howard announced that passing the 10-percent goods-and-services tax would become a primary goal of his second term.   □ Brian Kennedy

See also **Australia.**

Australian rules football. A crowd of more than 94,000 people watched the 1998 Australian Football League (AFL) grand final between the North Melbourne Kangaroos and the Adelaide Crows at the Melbourne Cricket Ground on September 26. The Kangaroos, who were the firm favorites after compiling 11 straight wins during the regular season, led in the first half only to be beaten in the end by 35 points. The Crows scored 15 goals and 15 behinds for a total of 105 points. The Kangaroos scored 8 goals and 22 behinds for 70 points. Andrew McLeod, a Darwin-born Aboriginal player for the Crows, repeated his 1997 grand final effort by collecting the Norm Smith medal as the match's best and fairest player. Robert Harvey of the St. Kilda Saints won his second successive Brownlow Medal as the best and fairest player for the 1998 AFL season.

Local premierships. In South Australia, the premiership was won by Port Adelaide 11.9 (75) over Sturt 9.12 (66). In Western Australia, East Fremantle 20.10 (130) defeated West Perth 13.9 (87). The Tasmanian Football League grand final was won by Launceston 14.16 (100) over Clarence 6.15 (51). In the Northern Tasmanian Football League, South Launceston 9.11 (65) defeated East Devonport 9.4 (58). In Queensland, Southport 12.15 (87) won the premiership over Morningside 11.10 (76).   □ Brian Kennedy

Austria assumed a greater role in European affairs in 1998. The country held the rotating presidency of the European Union (EU) in the second half of the year, the first time it had done so since joining the 15-nation bloc in 1995.

Austria's EU presidency sought to strengthen the EU's ability to act decisively in foreign affairs. At a summit meeting in Vienna in December 1998, EU leaders discussed plans for a new foreign-policy department based in Brussels. Leaders hoped the department would enable the EU to adopt common foreign-policy positions.

Austria also initiated a debate about the possible creation of a common EU defense policy, convening the first meeting of EU defense ministers in Vienna in November. Chancellor Viktor Klima deferred reviewing Austria's own neutrality until after parliamentary elections in 1999. The People's Party, the junior partner in Austria's coalition government, urged in 1998 that Austria join the North Atlantic Treaty Organization, saying neutrality did not make sense in light of Austria's EU membership. Klima responded that Austria contributed to European security by staying neutral and maintaining relations with Russia.

EU economic policy also underwent a significant change during Austria's presidency. At a summit meeting in Portschach, Austria, in October, EU leaders agreed that the bloc should shift its emphasis to economic growth and employment. The shift was a response to Europe-wide discontent after years of policies focused on cutting budget deficits and inflation in order to prepare for a single currency, the euro. Many EU governments felt the policies were no longer desirable after 11 EU countries qualified in May to launch the euro in 1999, and with unemployment in EU countries at about 10 percent.

Economy. Austria's economy strengthened during 1998, supported by low interest rates and an accelerating economic recovery among the country's European neighbors. Economic output was expected to grow by 3.2 percent, and the country's unemployment rate remained one of the lowest in Europe at around 4.4 percent.

Turmoil among Roman Catholics in Austria continued in 1998 despite a three-day visit by Pope John Paul II in June. Support for the church had waned in the mid-1990's after Cardinal Hans Hermann Groer was accused of sexually abusing a number of young clergymen. In addition, 500,000 Austrians signed a petition demanding church reforms, including the ordination of women and an end to celibacy for priests. The crowd of 50,000 at the pope's open-air mass in Vienna was smaller than expected.   □ Tom Buerkle

See also **Europe** (Facts in brief table); **Europe** Special Report: **European Union.**

Automobile. The United States auto industry experienced another strong year in 1998. Through September, sales of cars and light trucks ran 1.7 percent ahead of 1997's totals. Automotive industry analysts predicted in late 1998 that 15.3 million cars and trucks would be sold by the end of the year. The increased sales, however, came at a price for the automobile manufacturers. Car companies offered low-interest rates and generous cash-back incentives to lure customers into dealer showrooms.

Breaking a long trend in which sedans, hatchbacks, and coupes were the most popular sellers, consumers in 1998 opted for vans, pickup trucks, and sport-utility vehicles. Sales of light trucks totaled 5.5 million by Sept. 30, 1998, a 7.7-percent increase compared with the same period in 1997. Car sales for the first nine months of 1998 totaled 6.2 million, 3.2 percent less than a year earlier.

Top sellers. The Toyota Camry was the best-selling automobile in the United States in 1998 for the second consecutive year. By October, Camry sales had reached 340,434 units. The Honda Accord ranked second, with sales of 335,154 units. The Ford Taurus ranked third with sales of 317,011 units.

Foreign competitors. Foreign automakers gained U.S. market share at the expense of General Motors Corporation (GM) and Ford Motor

New car models in 1998 featured more powerful engines in both luxury automobiles and redesigned classics.

The redesigned 1999 Rolls Royce Silver Seraph, *above,* featured a new body powered by a 6.0-liter 12-cylinder engine. The 1999 New Volkswagen Beetle, *left,* featured a 4-cylinder, 115-horsepower engine. In 1998, Rolls-Royce Motor Cars was purchased for $572 million by BMW, edging out Volkswagen in a battle for owner-ship of the luxury car company.

Ford Motor Company continued to focus on sport-utility vehicles (SUV's) in 1998.The 1999 Lincoln Navigator, *right,* featured a powerful 8-cylinder, 260-horsepower engine and 4-wheel drive. Its design was meant to attract motorists wanting a vehicle that combined the dash of an SUV with the luxury of the 1999 Lincoln Town Car, *bottom.*

Company. The Big Three (GM, Ford, and Chrysler) took 70.5 percent of the U.S. market share during the first nine months of 1998, compared with 71.7 percent for the same period in 1997.

Honda did particularly well in the first nine months of 1998, with sales of 761,064 units, 7.5 percent ahead of the same period in 1997. The redesigned Accord was credited with much of the increase in sales volume. A new sport-utility vehicle from Mercedes-Benz helped boost the German automaker's sales to 125,273 units, 56.5 percent ahead of the same period in 1997.

Big Three. In 1998, GM officials watched profits drop and the company's market share fall, largely as a result of two United Automobile Workers (UAW) union strikes. Approximately 3,400 UAW workers at a metal-stamping plant in Flint, Michigan, went on strike on June 5. Another 5,800 UAW members at a Flint engine parts and dashboard components facility joined the strike on June 11. At the center of the dispute was the UAW's position of protecting workers' jobs and GM's stance of improving efficiency.

The walkouts cut off the flow of parts to GM's assembly operations. GM shut down 26 of their 29 North American assembly plants and conducted massive layoffs. The loss of production also left GM dealerships short of vehicles. On July 28, both sides reached a tentative agreement that workers ratified the following day. Analysts reported that the strike showed the UAW's resolve to protect jobs and GM's determination to withstand a long walkout. The strike cost GM more than $2 billion in the second and third quarters.

GM's profits through the first nine months of 1998 slipped to $1.18 billion from the $4.96 billion earned in the first three quarters of 1997. GM's market share through September 1998 fell to 29.3 percent, compared with 31.3 percent for the same period in 1997.

Ford car and truck sales reached 2.9 million units by September 1998, 1 percent ahead of the first nine months of 1997. Sales of the most popular vehicle in the United States, the F-series truck, rose to 588,799 units, or 9.8 percent above the same period in 1997. Sales of such other light trucks as the Expedition and Ranger also increased. The rising sales, coupled with Ford's aggressive cost-cutting measures, boosted the company's profits to $4.9 billion through the first nine months of 1998, compared with $4.5 billion during the same period in 1997.

On Sept. 11, 1998, Ford announced that Alex Trotman would retire as chairman, president, and chief executive officer on Jan. 1, 1999. He was replaced as chairman by William Clay Ford, Jr. Ford, the great-grandson of company founder Henry Ford, had held various positions at Ford since 1979. The company also announced that Jacques Nasser, who ran Ford's automotive operations, would be president and chief executive officer.

Chrysler entered 1998 as the nation's number three automaker, but ended the year as part of Daimler-Benz AG of Germany, another sign of the globalization of the industry. The two companies announced the merger, worth more than $32 billion, on May 7. Company officials claimed that the merger would benefit both companies. The new company, DaimlerChrysler AG, expected to save $1.4 billion in 1999 by sharing distribution, research, and purchasing. Analysts suggested that Daimler would acquire Chrysler's quick design and production techniques, while Daimler's financial assets would cushion Chrysler during economic downturns. Stock from the new company was trading on international stock exchanges on November 17.

Chrysler reported a strong first nine months of 1998, with profits of $2.7 billion, compared with $1.9 billion for the same period in 1997. The company's market share grew with the sales of its new Dodge Durango, the Ram pickup, and Dodge Dakota.

New vehicles. Manufacturers in 1998 raced to meet consumers' appetites for new trucks. GM introduced its new full-size pickup trucks, the Chevrolet Silverado and GMC Sierra. Chrysler's Jeep Division redesigned the Grand Cherokee. Toyota introduced its largest truck, the Tundra.

Return of the Beetle. A new version of a classic automobile was introduced in March 1998. Volkswagen's 1998 New Beetle, also commonly known as a "bug" because of its appearance, featured a 4-cylinder, 115-horsepower engine with a top speed of 120 miles (195 kilometers) per hour. The new Beetle received rave reviews from automotive experts and consumers. Many praised the smooth ride of the new vehicle. Others cited the nostalgia brought on by the Beetle, which first experienced popularity in the 1960's.

On May 15, 1998, however, Volkswagen voluntarily recalled all new Beetles that had been sold in 1998 to correct electrical wiring in the engine compartment that posed a potential fire hazard. The recall affected approximately 8,500 new Beetles in the United States and 1,600 in Canada.

Union issues. UAW members in June reelected Stephen Yokich as president of the union. Yokich was scheduled to face a challenge in 1999 when the union negotiates with the Big Three to replace a contract that was due to expire in September 1999. Analysts predicted that the union and GM would have significant problems reaching an agreement in light of the strikes in Flint in 1998 and walkouts at GM plants since 1997.

☐ Mike Casey

See also **Transportation.**

Eddie Cheever celebrates his first Indianapolis 500 win, on May 24, 1998, with the traditional drink of milk. It was Cheever's first victory in a 19-year racing career.

Automobile racing.

Discord between the Indy Racing League (IRL) and Championship Auto Racing Teams (CART) continued in 1998. The IRL and CART remained separated by their choice of chassis design and engine formula. The IRL required all teams to use chassis and engines built by league suppliers and banned use of turbocharged engines.

In November, the IRL announced engine specifications for the 2000 season, which some fans thought might unite the leagues. The IRL reduced engine size from 4 liters to 3.5 liters, bringing them closer to the 2.65-liter engines used by CART teams. The IRL, however, would not allow drivers to lease engines from a manufacturer, a program continued by CART.

The 82nd Indianapolis 500, held at the Indianapolis Motor Speedway in Indiana on May 24, 1998, was won by Eddie Cheever. It was Cheever's first victory in his 19-year career. Many fans noted that the veteran Cheever took the checkered flag against a field heavily staffed with rookies and second-year drivers. Only 18 of the 33 cars that had started the race finished. With 58 laps run under 12 different caution flags, more than 25 percent of the distance was run at the sluggish speed of 80 miles (130 kilometers) per hour. The average overall speed was 145 miles (232 kilometers) per hour.

CART. An expanded, 19-event CART season ran from March through November and included races in Australia, Brazil, and Canada. Alex Zanardi of Italy was the most successful driver on the circuit, winning six times in his first 12 starts. On September 6, Zanardi went on to win his second consecutive series title.

NASCAR fans saw more competitive races in the popular 33-race Winston Cup stock-car series. The season's most poignant victory on the National Association for Stock Car Auto Racing (NASCAR) circuit occurred on February 15, when veteran driver Dale Earnhardt ended 20 years of frustration by winning the Daytona 500, arguably the premier NASCAR event, for the first time. His average speed of 172 miles (275 kilometers) per hour was the third fastest in NASCAR history.

Jeff Gordon captured his third Winston Cup title on November 1 after winning the AC Delco 400 at North Carolina Speedway in Rockingham. Gordon was the youngest three-time champion and the first racer since 1994 to clinch the championship before the end of the season.

Formula One. The Grand Prix season consisted of 16 races—12 in Europe and one each in Argentina, Brazil, Canada, and Japan. The final race of the season, the Japanese Grand Prix, was held on Nov. 1, 1998, in Suzuka, Japan. Mika Hakkinen of Finland battled Michael Schumacher of Germany for the Formula One championship during the season. Hakkinen claimed the title during the Japanese Grand Prix after a tire on Schumacher's car exploded, forcing him from the race.

Endurance. A team that included two-time Indy 500 champion Arie Luyendyk of the United States, Didier Theys of Belgium, and Mauro Baldi of Monaco gave Ferrari the victory in the 24 Hours of Daytona on February 1. It was Ferrari's first victory in the race since 1972. The team covered 711 laps and 2,531 miles (4,072 kilometers). Second place went to the GT-1 division Porsche 911 team of Danny Sullivan, a former Indy and Daytona champion, Allan McNish of Scotland, Jorg Mueller of Monaco, and Dirk Mueller and Uwe Alzen, both of Germany.

On June 7, 1998, in France, a Porsche factory-model team finished in first place for the third straight victory in the LeMans 24 Hours. The winning car, driven by Allan McNish, Stephane Ortelli, and Laurent Aiello, covered 2,972 miles (4,782 kilometers) with an average lap speed, including pit stops, of 124 miles (200 kilometers) per hour.

Dragsters. The National Hot Rod Association (NHRA) sponsored a 23-race series in 1998. Season champions were Gary Scelzi in the top fuel division, John Force in funny cars, and Warren Johnson in the pro stock division.   □ Ron Reid

Aviation. The severe economic crisis in Asia in 1998 had a chilling effect on the region's airline industry. The economic recession resulted in a decrease in the demand for business travel and tourism. The devaluation of Asian currencies also cut into profits. While most revenues were collected in local currencies, the airlines paid most bills in United States dollars. The financial crisis led companies to lay off employees, cancel many international flights, return leased aircraft, and delay orders for new aircraft.

Major carriers—such as Cathay Pacific Airlines of Hong Kong, Japan Air Lines, and All Nippon Airlines, also of Japan—announced substantial financial losses. In Indonesia, at least three airlines declared bankruptcy in 1998. Philippine Airlines (PAL), Asia's oldest commercial airline, ceased operation in September after a brief pilots' strike hurt the company's already strained finances. Although PAL resumed limited service, the future of the company remained uncertain.

In response to declining demands for service, many European and Australian airlines reduced flights to Asia. The decline in the airline industry ironically coincided with the opening of new airports in the region that had been under construction during Asia's economic boom earlier in the 1990's. Malaysia opened its Kuala Lumpur International Airport in June 1998. Hong Kong opened the Chek Lap Kok International Airport in July, replacing a downtown airport that was famous for its risky approach between highrises.

Industry partnerships. In November 1998, Northwest Airlines Corporation of Minneapolis, Minnesota, purchased 46 percent of the voting shares in Continental Airlines, Inc., of Houston. The new partnership would allow passengers to book some connecting flights between the two airlines and to accumulate frequent-flier points that could be redeemed with either company. The U.S. Department of Justice challenged the acquisition, claiming it was anticompetitive.

When the new deal was first announced in January, other airlines sought ways to offer similar services to customers. American Airlines of Dallas-Fort Worth and US Airways of Arlington, Virginia, announced a partnership that offered passengers a joint frequent-flier program and other shared services, even though the two companies remained separate entities.

Labor troubles. On August 29, pilots at Northwest Airlines launched a strike that lasted nearly two weeks. A disagreement over wage increases focused on the pilots' requests for a one-time payment to make up for a 15.5-percent pay cut that the pilots agreed to in 1993, when the airline was on the verge of bankruptcy. Pilots also demanded assurances that they would not lose their jobs because of Northwest's commitments

to its regional commuter airline affiliates and the company's foreign affiliate, KLM Royal Dutch Airlines of the Netherlands.

In Canada, the federal government's mediation failed to prevent a strike by pilots at Air Canada on September 2. The dispute over pay and working conditions was settled 12 days later, when the airline's 2,100 pilots accepted a package that included improvements in pay, pensions, and scheduling, as well as a bonus and clothing allowance.

Low-cost airlines. Two low-cost airlines, the resuscitated Pan American World Airways of Miami and Western Pacific Airlines of Colorado Springs, Colorado, ceased operations in February 1998 after announcing bankruptcy. Pan American later emerged from bankruptcy as a charter service under new ownership. In June, US Airways responded to strong competition from low-cost airlines on the East Coast by introducing its own low-cost, no-frills MetroJet service.

Aircraft manufacturing. The European consortium Airbus Industrie in 1998 captured half of the world market for new jet orders, primarily because of the success of its midsized Airbus A-320 series of twin-engine jets. Airbus also scored a big success in August, when British Airways announced that it would forsake its long-time supplier, the Boeing Company of Seattle, Washington, for the Airbus short-range jets. Boeing in 1998 remained the industry's primary supplier of long-range jets with its 747, 767, and 777 models. Late in the year, however, canceled orders by Asian customers led Boeing to announce layoffs and a reduced production schedule.

Aircraft safety. In October 1998, the U.S. Federal Aviation Administration ordered airlines to replace the electrical wiring that passes through fuel tanks of Boeing 747's after investigators determined that the July 1996 explosion of Trans World Airlines flight 800 may have been caused by the ignition of fuel vapors in the nearly empty center fuel tank. The accident killed 230 people on a Paris-bound Boeing 747 off Long Island, New York.

Swissair Flight 111, bound for Geneva from New York City on Sept. 2, 1998, crashed into the Atlantic Ocean near Halifax, Nova Scotia, after the pilot reported smoke in the cockpit. All 229 passengers and crew members died in the accident.

New airport name. On February 6, President Bill Clinton signed into law a bill renaming the recently renovated National Airport in Arlington, Virginia, the Ronald Reagan Washington National Airport after the former U.S. president. The event caused a stir among many airline employees, because President Reagan had fired some 11,000 striking air traffic controllers in 1981.

☐ Ian Savage

See also **Building and construction; Labor and employment; Transportation.**

Azerbaijan. Voters in Azerbaijan elected Heydar Aliyev to a second term as president on Oct. 11, 1998. Aliyev, 75, who headed Azerbaijan's Communist Party during the Soviet era, won 76 percent of the vote. Five top opposition candidates boycotted the balloting, calling the election laws unfair. International observers reported "serious irregularities" during the election.

The accession of a more hard-line government in neighboring Armenia frustrated efforts to settle the long-standing conflict over the Armenian enclave of Nagorno-Karabakh. Armenian troops continued to occupy Azerbaijani territory in the fifth year of the cease-fire between the two countries. A near agreement on a phased withdrawal of Armenian troops collapsed in February 1998 when Armenia's president resigned under intense pressure by political opponents who objected to the withdrawal.

Azerbaijani officials in November 1998 put off a decision to construct a major oil pipeline from Baku, the capital, to the Georgian Black Sea port of Supsa. The United States advocated a longer route ending in Turkey, which is a member of the North Atlantic Treaty Organization, the military alliance of Western nations. □ Steven L. Solnick

See also **Armenia; Asia** (Facts in brief table).

Bahamas. See **West Indies.**

Ballet. See **Dance.**

Bangladesh. Mounting crime in 1998 caused concern among Bangladesh's business community as well as among human-rights groups. The six chambers of commerce in Bangladesh released a joint statement in May acknowledging that "trade and industry is deeply worried over the breakdown of law and order and increasing criminalization of the society."

Human-rights groups reported increased incidences of politically motivated violence and crime in Bangladesh in 1998, and the U.S. Department of State accused the country of rampant human-rights violations. Human-rights officials charged that opponents of the government were often detained and abused without being charged with a crime.

Demonstrations. A demonstration against a government agreement to settle a lengthy separatist movement in southeastern Bangladesh turned violent on June 9 when government supporters attempted to block demonstrators near the capital, Dhaka. In late June, government opponents organized a general labor strike against the agreement, which led to clashes that left more than 200 people injured.

The June 9 demonstration was the largest of its kind since the 1996 government protests led by Hasina Wajed, head of the Awami League. Hasina had organized strikes that forced the res-

Children carry precious fresh water through floodwaters in Dhaka, Bangladesh, in September 1998. More than two months of monsoon, the longest rainy season in memory, left two-thirds of the country under water.

ignation of then-Prime Minister Khaleda Ziaur Rahman.

The Awami League, in coalition with the Jatiya Party, formed a new government in June 1996, headed by Hasina. On August 10, 1998, the Jatiya Party left the coalition and launched demonstrations against the government, charging it with law violations, including using police to repress government opponents.

BNP ends boycott. In February 1998, the Bangladesh National Party (BNP) ended its boycott of parliament and resumed its participation in the government. The BNP began the boycott in protest of Hasina's policies in August 1997.

Verdict. A judge sentenced 15 former military commanders to death on Nov. 8, 1998, for the 1975 assassination of Bangladesh's independence leader, Mujibur Rahman. Rahman, Hasina's father, was prime minister when he was killed.

Bangladesh's monsoon floods in mid-1998 lasted more than two months and were the worst in memory. Massive floods left more than 900 people dead and inundated two-thirds of the country. The monsoon waters wiped out thousands of rice crops waiting to be harvested, damaged more than 1 million houses, and left more than 22 million people homeless.

☐ Henry S. Bradsher
See also **Asia** (Facts in brief table).

Bank. The United States banking industry began 1998 with strong profits. The Federal Deposit Insurance Corporation (FDIC), a government agency that insures deposits at U.S. banks and savings and loans, reported that in the first six months of the year, the nation's 10,779 banks and savings associations posted profits of $32 billion. The FDIC said that the second quarter of 1998—April through June—was the sixth straight quarter of record earnings. Favorable interest rates and a strong economy boosted earnings.

Bank mergers. In April, the banking industry witnessed a wave of the biggest mergers ever announced. The merging banks believed that combining would enable them to reduce costs by cutting administrative expenses and cushion their operations against sour regional trends by making loans across the United States. The mergers also continued a trend of banks and other financial services companies crossing industry borders.

On April 6, Citicorp of New York City, the second-largest U.S. bank, and Travelers Insurance Group Inc. of Hartford, Connecticut, a leading insurance and brokerage firm, announced a deal to become Citigroup, Inc. If approved by government regulators, the new Citigroup, with combined assets of almost $700 billion, would be the world's largest financial services company. On April 13, NationsBank Corp. of Charlotte, North

Carolina, and BankAmerica Corp. of San Francisco reported the formation of a $570-billion bank to be called BankAmerica. It ranked first among U.S. banks in terms of deposits. On April 13, Banc One Corp. of Columbus, Ohio, and First Chicago NBD Corp. of Chicago announced the creation of a company with $30 billion in assets. The new Banc One ranked second only to the new Citigroup in the number of credit card accounts.

Heavy losses in overseas lending, especially in Asia and Russia—whose economies were reeling—reduced bank profits in the second half of 1998. BankAmerica forecast trading losses of $330 million, while Bankers Trust New York Corp. of New York City projected a $350-million loss. Republic New York Corp. of New York City said Russia's financial problems cost the bank $155 million. Credit Suisse First Boston, Inc., of Boston reported losing $400 million in Russian lending. Worst hit was Citigroup, which reported $1 billion in losses from investments in Russia and the bond market. Citigroup projected its third-quarter net income at about $700 million, significantly less than the combined $1.5-billion net income for Citicorp and Travelers for the third quarter of 1997.

Hedge bailout. Banks also recorded mounting losses in hedge-fund investments—largely unregulated investments that are highly sensitive to currency and interest-rate fluctuations. On Sept. 23, 1998, the Federal Reserve System (the Fed), the nation's central bank and top banking regulator, stepped in to stem losses in a high-risk hedge fund, Long-Term Capital Management LP of Greenwich, Connecticut. On behalf of large, wealthy clients, the fund had invested in risky overseas markets and currencies, primarily in Russia and Asia. As these economies stumbled, Capital Management piled up losses and seemed headed for insolvency.

In response, the Fed persuaded several banks and investment houses to raise $3.5 billion to bolster the fund. Some members of the U.S. Congress criticized the Fed's intervention, arguing that the bailout was unfairly protecting wealthy investors. Alan Greenspan, chairman of the Fed, argued that the collapse of the fund could have damaged national economies, including that of the United States. Greenspan also pointed out that the bailout involved no public money.

Rate cut. With global economic concerns mounting, the Fed on September 29 cut the Federal Funds rate for the first time since January 1996, to 5.25 percent from 5.5 percent. A key short-term interest rate, the Federal Funds rate is the rate that banks charge each other for overnight lending. The Federal Funds rate affects the prime rate, the rate banks charge their best customers, as well as the interest rates on most con-

Officials of the Bank of Japan, the country's central bank bow in greeting to prosecutors in March 1998. The prosecutors were conducting a probe of the bank as part of an investigation of bribery allegations at a number of Japanese banks.

sumer loans. The cut was a signal that the Fed was more worried about a global recession than about inflation.

Glass-Steagall survives. In 1998, Congress came close to overturning the Glass-Steagall Banking Act of 1933, the primary law governing the businesses in which U.S. banks may engage. On May 13, 1998, the House of Representatives by a vote of 214 to 213 passed legislation that would have made it easier for banks, securities firms, and insurance companies to enter one another's businesses. The bill died in the Senate in October, however, partly because of disagreements over provisions to protect low-income banking customers. Consumer groups opposed the legislation, arguing it would have rolled back rules that ban banks from charging high fees for checking accounts with less than $1,000.

Banking industry officials argued that changes in U.S. banking laws were needed to reflect recent changes in how Americans save, invest, and borrow. For example, an increasing number of U.S. households keep their savings in mutual funds—funds composed of groups of stocks, which typically pay higher interest rates than banks do but also carry a greater risk of losses. The Fed reported that from 1980 to 1997, banks' share of U.S. household financial assets fell from 90 percent to 55 percent. During the same peri-

od, mutual funds' share of household money rose from 10 percent to 44 percent.

Bank competition. On Aug. 7, 1998, President Bill Clinton signed a new law allowing federally chartered credit unions to provide services to members from outside their group. Credit unions are nonprofit banking associations that offer low-cost financial services only to members. About half of the 11,500 credit unions in the United States operate under federal charters. Under the new Credit Union Membership Access Act, a credit union for teachers could accept members from unrelated companies that had no more than 3,000 employees.

The legislation overrode a February ruling by the U.S. Supreme Court striking down a 1982 policy change by the National Credit Union Administration (NCUA), which supervises federally chartered credit unions. In a reinterpretation of the 1934 law establishing credit unions, the NCUA had allowed credit unions to accept members from unrelated companies. The 1934 law had limited credit union membership to those sharing a common occupational bond or residing within a specific community. As a result of the policy change, credit unions had significantly boosted their membership. □ Paulette Thomas

See also **Economics; Economics** Special Report: **Asian Economic Crisis—Global Contagion.**

Baseball. A spellbinding quest for the home- run record and the highest victory total by any team in 92 years made 1998 one of the greatest seasons in the history of major league baseball. Attendance for the regular season totaled 70,589,505—the highest in history. In July, team owners elected Bud Selig as commissioner of major league baseball. Selig had been the acting commissioner since 1992. Fans of the Florida Marlins, the 1997 World Series champions, found the 1998 season a big disappointment after H. Wayne Huizenga, the team's owner, gutted his roster of star players to diminish his payroll. The result was a team that finished with a 54-108 win-loss record, the worst in baseball history for a defending champion.

Home-run derby. First-baseman Mark McGwire of the St. Louis Cardinals and right-fielder Sammy Sosa of the Chicago Cubs thrilled both passionate and casual baseball fans with their race to break Roger Maris's single-season record of 61 home runs, set in 1961. McGwire tied the 60 home runs Babe Ruth hit in 1927 on Sept. 5, 1998, against the Cincinnati Reds. McGwire tied Maris on September 7, hitting number 61 off Cubs' pitcher Mike Morgan.

McGwire broke Maris's record the following night with a 341-foot (104-meter) line drive off Chicago's Steve Trachsel. The record-breaking ball barely cleared the left-field fence and was McGwire's shortest homer since 1993. After rounding the bases to a standing ovation, the slugger scooped up his 10-year-old son, Matthew, the Cardinals' batboy, in a joyous bear hug. He then jumped into the stands to hug the sons and daughters of Roger Maris. McGwire also embraced his rival, Sosa.

McGwire and Sosa were tied with 66 home runs each on Sept. 25, 1998, before McGwire belted two home runs in each of his last two games. McGwire hit his final home run off the first pitch thrown to him by Carl Pavano of the Montreal Expos. That shot left him with a season total of 70 home runs.

Sosa ended the season with 66 home runs and 158 runs batted in (RBI's)—the most RBI's since Ted Williams and Vern Stephens each batted in 159 runs in 1949.

Regular season. The New York Yankees compiled a win-loss record of 114-48 during the 1998 season—the best record since the Cubs won 116 games in 1906. New York finished 22 games ahead of the runner-up Boston Red Sox in the American League (AL) Eastern Division—the largest winning margin ever for the storied team.

The Cleveland Indians (89-73) took the AL Central Division title by nine games, and the Texas Rangers (88-74) won the AL Western Division crown by three games. Boston (92-70) won a spot in the division play-offs as the AL "wild-card" entry because their record was the best among AL teams that did not win a division title. In the National League (NL), the Atlanta Braves (106-56), Houston Astros (102-60), and San Diego Padres (98-64) won the Eastern, Central, and Western divisions, respectively, by 18, 12½, and 9½ games. The Cubs qualified for post-season play for the first time since 1989 by beating the San Francisco Giants, 5-3, in a special wild-card tie-breaker. The game was necessary because both the Cubs and Giants finished the regular season with identical records (89-73). The victory boosted the Cubs' win total to 90 games.

Play-offs. In the AL division play-offs, the Yankees ousted Texas in a three-game sweep, and Cleveland beat Boston, 3 games to 1. In the NL division series, Atlanta swept Chicago in three games and San Diego defeated Houston, 3 games to 1. The Yankees advanced to the World Series for the second time in three seasons by beating Cleveland, 4 games to 2, in the AL championship series. San Diego was a surprise winner in the NL championship series, beating Atlanta, 4 games to 2.

World Series. The World Series opened on Oct. 17, 1998, in New York City's Yankee Stadium. The home team won a 9-6 victory over San Diego after Yankees first-baseman Tino Martinez's grand-slam home run led to seven runs in the seventh inning. The Yankees were even more powerful the following night, pounding out 16 hits in a 9-3 victory. Yankees' starting pitcher Orlando "El Duque" Hernandez allowed only one run in seven innings of work in the game. On October 20 in San Diego, Yankees third baseman Scott Brosius, who was later named Most Valuable Player of the World Series, homered twice to carry his team to a 5-4 victory. New York finished the Padres off on October 21 with a 3-0 victory behind pitcher Andy Pettitte.

The four-game sweep gave the Yankees their 24th World Series championship—the most ever won by a professional sports team in the United States or Canada. The sweep, however, was bad news for the Fox Network, which televised the series. The four-game series had an average rating of 14.1, the smallest television audience ever for a World Series. One rating point represents 1 percent of U.S. households with a TV. As a result, the Fox network was forced to offer millions of dollars in free airtime to advertisers.

Stars. On May 6, Kerry Wood, a 20-year-old rookie pitcher with the Cubs, struck out 20 batters in a 2-0 victory over Houston. The strikeouts, coming in Wood's fifth major league start, were an NL record for a single game. On May 17, David Wells of the Yankees pitched a *perfect game* (a game in which the pitcher retires all opposing

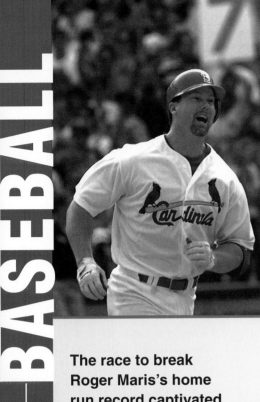

The St. Louis Cardinals' Mark McGwire, *left*, rounds the bases after hitting his 70th home run of the season and 457th of his career on Sept. 27, 1998.

The race to break Roger Maris's home run record captivated fans in 1998.

On Sept. 8, 1998, St. Louis Cardinals' first-baseman Mark McGwire slammed his 62nd home run of the season, breaking Roger Maris's record of 61 home runs, set in 1961. The muscular, 34-year-old slugger went on to hit 70 home runs in 1998. "Big Mac" was the first major league player to hit at least 50 homers in three consecutive seasons.

Baseball fans spent much of the 1998 season captivated by the race between McGwire, the Seattle Mariners' Ken Griffey, Jr., and the Chicago Cubs' Sammy Sosa to break Maris's record. While McGwire hit home runs in the first four games of April, Sosa did not become a contender in the race until he hit 20 home runs in June. This established a new major league record for home runs in a single month. Griffey fell behind in July. By the end of August, Sosa had 54 home runs to McGwire's 55. Sosa hit his 62nd homer just five days after McGwire broke Maris's record.

After the record was broken, fan interest shifted to see which slugger would finish the season with the most homers. McGwire and Sosa each had 66 with just two games to go in the regular season. McGwire ended the suspense by knocking out two home runs in each of his last two games, hitting his 70th on September 27.

Sosa ended the season with 66 home runs and was named the National League's Most Valuable Player. Griffey hit 56 homers in 1998.

The Chicago Cubs' Sammy Sosa, *above,* watches his 62nd home run of the season fly over the wall at Chicago's Wrigley Field on September 13. Sosa ended the season with 66 home runs.

Final standings in major league baseball

American League

American League champions—
New York Yankees (defeated Cleveland, 4 games to 2)
World Series champions—
New York Yankees (defeated San Diego, 4 games to 0)

Eastern Division	W.	L.	Pct.	G.B.
New York Yankees	114	48	.704	—
Boston Red Sox*	92	70	.568	22
Toronto Blue Jays	88	74	.543	26
Baltimore Orioles	79	83	.488	35
Tampa Bay Devil Rays	63	99	.389	51

Central Division				
Cleveland Indians	89	73	.549	—
Chicago White Sox	80	82	.494	9
Kansas City Royals	72	89	.447	16½
Minnesota Twins	70	92	.432	19
Detroit Tigers	65	97	.401	24

Western Division				
Texas Rangers	88	74	.543	—
Anaheim Angels	85	77	.525	3
Seattle Mariners	76	85	.472	11½
Oakland Athletics	74	88	.457	14

Offensive leaders

Batting average	Bernie Williams, New York	.339
Runs scored	Derek Jeter, New York	127
Home runs	Ken Griffey, Jr., Seattle	56
Runs batted in	Juan Gonzalez, Texas	157
Hits	Alex Rodriguez, Seattle	213
Stolen bases	Rickey Henderson, Oakland	66
Slugging percentage	Albert Belle, Chicago	.655

Leading pitchers

Games won	Roger Clemens, Toronto; David Cone, New York; Rick Helling, Texas (tie)	20
Earned run average (162 or more innings)—	Roger Clemens, Toronto	2.65
Strikeouts	Roger Clemens, Toronto	271
Saves	Tom Gordon, Boston	46
Shut-outs	David Wells, New York	5
Complete games	Scott Erickson, Baltimore	11

Awards†

Most Valuable Player	Juan Gonzalez, Texas
Cy Young	Roger Clemens, Toronto
Rookie of the Year	Ben Grieve, Oakland
Manager of the Year	Joe Torre, New York

National League

National League champions—
San Diego Padres (defeated Atlanta, 4 games to 2)

Eastern Division	W.	L.	Pct.	G.B.
Atlanta Braves	106	56	.654	—
New York Mets	88	74	.543	18
Philadelphia Phillies	75	87	.463	31
Montreal Expos	65	97	.401	41
Florida Marlins	54	108	.333	52

Central Division				
Houston Astros	102	60	.630	—
Chicago Cubs*	90	73	.552	12½
St. Louis Cardinals	83	79	.512	19
Cincinnati Reds	77	85	.475	25
Milwaukee Brewers	74	88	.457	28
Pittsburgh Pirates	69	93	.426	33

Western Division				
San Diego Padres	98	64	.605	—
San Francisco Giants	89	74	.546	9½
Los Angeles Dodgers	83	79	.512	15
Colorado Rockies	77	85	.475	21
Arizona Diamondbacks	65	97	.401	33

Offensive leaders

Batting average	Larry Walker, Colorado	.363
Runs scored	Sammy Sosa, Chicago	134
Home runs	Mark McGwire, St. Louis	70
Runs batted in	Sammy Sosa, Chicago	158
Hits	Dante Bichette, Colorado	219
Stolen bases	Tony Womack, Pittsburgh	58
Slugging percentage	Mark McGwire, St. Louis	.752

Leading pitchers

Games won	Tom Glavine, Atlanta	20
Earned run average (162 or more innings)—	Greg Maddux, Atlanta	2.22
Strikeouts	Curt Schilling, Philadelphia	300
Saves	Trevor Hoffman, San Diego	53
Shut-outs	Greg Maddux, Atlanta	5
Complete games	Curt Schilling, Philadelphia	15

Awards†

Most Valuable Player	Sammy Sosa, Chicago
Cy Young	Tom Glavine, Atlanta
Rookie of the Year	Kerry Wood, Chicago
Manager of the Year	Larry Dierker, Houston

*Qualified for wild-card play-off spot.
†Selected by the Baseball Writers Association of America.

batters in succession) to beat the Minnesota Twins, 4-0. Only 14 other pitchers had managed that feat since 1880. Philadelphia Phillies pitcher Curt Schilling struck out seven Florida Marlins on Sept. 26, 1998, to become the fifth pitcher in major league history to record back-to-back 300-strikeout seasons.

On September 20, Baltimore Orioles third-baseman Cal Ripken, Jr., sat out his team's final home game of the season to end his record playing streak at 2,632 consecutive games. Ripken, 38, began his streak on May 30, 1982. On Aug. 24, 1998, Barry Bonds of the Giants hit his 400th career home run, making him the first major league player to hit 400 home runs and steal 400 bases. By the end of the season, Bonds had 411 homers and 445 stolen bases.

Hall of Fame. Don Sutton, who compiled a record of 324-256 during 23 seasons as a pitcher with the Los Angeles Dodgers and other teams, was elected to the Baseball Hall of Fame in January. Sutton ranked fifth on the career strikeout list, with 3,574. Also elected to the Hall of Fame in 1998 were Larry Doby, first African American player in the American League; "Bullet" Joe Rogan, a former Negro League pitcher; George Davis, a shortstop in the late 1800's and early 1900's; and Lee MacPhail, Jr., the former president of the American League.   □ Ron Reid

See also **People in the news** (McGwire, Mark).

Basketball. Professional basketball during the 1997-1998 season took on a familiar look, when the Chicago Bulls won the National Basketball Association (NBA) title for the sixth time in eight seasons under coach Phil Jackson. The Bulls tied the Utah Jazz for best record during the NBA's 82-game regular season, each with 62 wins and 20 losses. The Bulls topped the Central Division as the Jazz topped the Midwest Division.

The Los Angeles Lakers led the league as highest-scoring team, averaging 105.5 points per game. The Lakers shared their Pacific Division title with the Seattle SuperSonics after both teams finished the season with a 61-21 record. The Miami Heat took the Atlantic Division championship.

The Bulls moved through the first two rounds of the Eastern Conference play-offs with little trouble, beating the New Jersey Nets (3 games to 0) and the Charlotte Hornets (4 to 1). The Indiana Pacers, however, challenged the Bulls and took the series to a seventh and final game before Chicago prevailed (4 to 3). The Jazz won the Western Conference for the second straight season by defeating the Houston Rockets (3 games to 2), the San Antonio Spurs (4 to 1), and the Lakers (4 to 0).

The Bulls were vulnerable going into the best-of-seven finals after almost losing to the Pacers. Many fans and sports writers believed that the Bulls' dynasty of the 1990's was over when the Jazz won the first game in Salt Lake City, 88-85 in overtime. Chicago rebounded with a 93-88 victory in Game 2 when Karl Malone, the veteran Utah forward, missed 11 of 16 attempted shots.

Utah lost Game 3 in Chicago, 96-54. The Jazz scored the fewest points ever in an NBA finals game. The Bulls took a 3-1 series lead with an 86-82 victory in Game 4, but Malone brought the Jazz back with 39 points in an 83-81, Game 5 victory.

The series returned to Salt Lake City for Game 6 on June 14. Jordan scored 45 points to spark an 87-86 victory. With 5.2 seconds left in the game, he stripped the ball from Malone, raced to the other end of the court, and hit the jump shot that gave Chicago a one-point lead and their sixth NBA championship.

People. Michael Jordan won the league's most valuable player (MVP) award for the fifth time. He was named MVP in both the regular season and in the playoffs. Larry Bird, in his first year as coach, was named the NBA's coach of the year.

Tim Duncan, the 7-foot (210-centimeter) San Antonio Spurs forward who was the No. 1 choice of the NBA draft, was named NBA's rookie of the year. Duncan averaged 21.1 points and 11.9 rebounds per game during the regular season. The Atlanta Hawks' 7-foot-2 (218-centimeter) Dikembe Mutombo was the NBA's top defensive player

The 1997-1998 college basketball season

College tournament champions

NCAA	(Men)	Division I: Kentucky
		Division II: UC Davis
		Division III: Wisconsin-Platteville
	(Women)	Division I: Tennessee
		Division II: North Dakota
		Division III: Washington (Missouri)
NAIA	(Men)	Division I: Georgetown (Ky.)
		Division II: Bethel College (Ind.)
	(Women)	Division I: Union (Tenn.)
		Division II: Walsh (Ohio)
NIT	(Men)	Minnesota

Men's college champions

Conference	School
America East	Delaware*
Atlantic Coast	Duke (reg. season)
	North Carolina (tournament)
Atlantic Ten	
Eastern Division	Temple
Western Division	Xavier (Ohio)*
Big East	
Big East 7	Syracuse
Big East 6	Connecticut*
Big Sky	Northern Arizona*
Big South	N.C.-Asheville (reg. season)
	Radford (tournament)
Big Ten	Michigan State (reg. season)
	Michigan (tournament)
Big Twelve	Kansas*
Big West	
Eastern Division	Utah State*
Western Division	Pacific (Calif.)
Colonial	William & Mary (reg. season)
	Richmond (tournament)
Conference USA	
American Division	Cincinnati*
National Division	Memphis
Ivy League	Princeton†
Metro Atlantic	Iona*
Mid-American	Eastern Michigan (tournament)
East Division	Akron
West Division	Ball State—Western Michigan (tie)
Mid-Continent	Valparaiso*
Mid-Eastern	Coppin State (reg. season)
	S. Carolina State (tournament)
Midwestern	Detroit (reg. season)
	Butler (tournament)
Missouri Valley	Illinois State*
Northeast	LIU-Brooklyn (reg. season)
	Fairleigh Dickinson (tournament)
Ohio Valley	Murray State*
Pacific Ten	Arizona†
Patriot League	Lafayette (reg. season)
	Navy (tournament)
Southeastern	
Eastern Division	Kentucky*
Western Division	Mississippi
Southern	Davidson (tournament)
North Division	Appalachian State
South Division	Tenn.-Chattanooga
Southland	Nicholls State*
Southwestern	Texas Southern (reg. season)
	Prairie View (tournament)
Sun Belt	South Alabama*
Trans America	
East Division	Charleston (S.C)*
West Division	Georgia State
West Coast	Gonzaga (reg. season)
	San Francisco (tournament)
Western	Las Vegas (tournament)
Mountain Division	Utah
Pacific Division	Texas Christian

*Regular season and conference tournament champion.
†No tournament played.

National Basketball Association standings

Eastern Conference

Atlantic Division

	W.	L.	Pct.	G.B.
Miami Heat*	55	27	.671	—
New York Knicks*	43	39	.524	12
New Jersey Nets*	43	39	.524	12
Washington Wizards	42	40	.512	13
Orlando Magic	41	41	.500	14
Boston Celtics	36	46	.439	19
Philadelphia 76ers	31	51	.378	24

Central Division

	W.	L.	Pct.	G.B.
Chicago Bulls*	62	20	.756	—
Indiana Pacers*	58	24	.707	4
Charlotte Hornets*	51	31	.622	11
Atlanta Hawks*	50	32	.610	12
Cleveland Cavaliers*	47	35	.573	15
Detroit Pistons	37	45	.451	25
Milwaukee Bucks	36	46	.439	26
Toronto Raptors	16	66	.195	46

Western Conference

Midwest Division

	W.	L.	Pct.	G.B.
Utah Jazz*	62	20	.756	—
San Antonio Spurs*	56	26	.683	6
Minnesota Timberwolves*	45	37	.549	17
Houston Rockets*	41	41	.500	21
Dallas Mavericks	20	62	.244	42
Vancouver Grizzlies	19	63	.232	43
Denver Nuggets	11	71	.134	51

Pacific Division

	W.	L.	Pct.	G.B.
Seattle SuperSonics*	61	21	.744	—
Los Angeles Lakers*	61	21	.744	—
Phoenix Suns*	56	26	.683	5
Portland Trail Blazers*	46	36	.561	15
Sacramento Kings	27	55	.329	34
Golden State Warriors	19	63	.232	42
Los Angeles Clippers	17	65	.207	44

Individual leaders

Scoring

	G.	F.G.	F.T.	Pts.	Avg.
Michael Jordan, Chicago	82	881	565	2,357	28.7
Shaquille O'Neal, Los Angeles	60	670	359	1,699	28.3
Karl Malone, Utah	81	780	628	2,190	27.0
Mitch Richmond, Washington	70	543	407	1,623	23.2
Antoine Walker, Boston	82	722	305	1,840	22.4
Shareef Abdur-Rahim, Vancouver	82	653	502	1,829	22.3
Glen Rice, Charlotte	82	634	428	1,826	22.3
Allen Iverson, Philadelphia	80	649	390	1,758	22.0
Chris Webber, Sacramento	71	647	196	1,555	21.9
David Robinson, San Antonio,	73	544	485	1,574	21.6

Rebounding

	G.	Off.	Def.	Tot.	Avg.
Dennis Rodman, Chicago	80	421	780	1,201	15.0
Jayson Williams, New Jersey	65	443	440	883	13.6
Tim Duncan, San Antonio	82	274	703	977	11.9
Dikembe Mutombo, Atlanta	82	276	656	932	11.4
D. Robinson, San Antonio	73	239	536	775	10.6
Karl Malone, Utah	81	189	645	834	10.3
Anthony Mason, Charlotte	81	177	649	826	10.2
Antoine Walker, Boston	82	270	566	836	10.2
Arvydas Sabonis, Portland	73	149	580	729	10.0

*Made play-offs
NBA champions—Chicago Bulls
(defeated Utah Jazz, 4 games to 2)

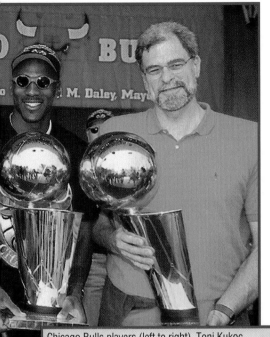

Chicago Bulls players (left to right), Toni Kukoc, Ron Harper, Dennis Rodman, Scottie Pippen, and Michael Jordan, and coach, Phil Jackson (right), pose with Chicago's six NBA championship trophies during a celebration in Chicago on June 16, 1998.

for the third time in four seasons. Chicago's Dennis Rodman led the league in rebounds for the seventh straight year. Rodman averaged 15 rebounds per game.

Bulls coach Phil Jackson announced on June 21 that, after nine seasons, he would not return as coach. In July, Jackson refused an offer from team management to return to the team, paving the way for Tim Floyd, Iowa State's former basketball coach, to take over as Bulls head coach.

Labor strife. NBA team owners began a lockout of players on July 1 that lasted through the rest of 1998. The lockout evolved from a disagreement between players and owners over money and forced the cancellation of more than 300 games in 1998. Issues included the players' share of league revenues and a clause that allowed a team to resign one of its own players for any amount of money, regardless of salary caps.

The owners claimed that the NBA would no longer prosper if salaries continued to exceed the $100-million level paid to some players. The players' union claimed that NBA revenues were still growing. During the lockout, teams and players were prohibited from making any sort of trade, signing any contracts, or practicing. By the end of December, neither side had agreed to a compromise, threatening the cancellation of the entire season in 1999.

Professional women. In its second year, the Women's National Basketball Association (WNBA), which expanded to 10 teams in 1998, continued to fight for significant attendance and television ratings through a 30-game regular season. The Houston Comets won their second straight WNBA title on September 1, defeating the Phoenix Mercury, 80-71, to take the championship series, 2 games to 1.

The American Basketball League (ABL) expanded to nine teams in 1998 and held a 44-game second season. On March 15, the Columbus Quest took the ABL championship for a second year by defeating the Long Beach Stingrays, 86-81, in a 3 games to 2 series.

Midway through its third season, the ABL announced on December 22 that it had canceled the remainder of the season and filed for bankruptcy. The ABL was unable to get the necessary television exposure and sponsorship support to compete with the rival WNBA.

College men. North Carolina (30-3) was the lone number-1 seed to reach the NCAA Final Four in San Antonio in March. North Carolina joined Kentucky (29-4), Utah (25-3), and Stanford (26-4). Utah advanced to the NCAA championship game with a 65-59 victory over North Carolina. Kentucky also qualified for the third time in four seasons, barely getting by Stanford in overtime, 86-85. Utah led the final game by 10 points at halftime before Kentucky launched a comeback, winning 78-69.

Voters named Antawn Jamison of North Carolina player of the year and Michigan State's Tom Izzo coach of the year. The consensus All-America team included Jamison, Mike Bibby and Miles Simon of Arizona, and Raef LaFrentz and Paul Pierce of Kansas.

College women. The University of Tennessee (33-0) dominated women's college basketball in 1998 to win the NCAA championship for the third straight year. North Carolina State (21-6), Louisiana Tech (26-3), and Arkansas (21-10) also made it to the Final Four. In the championship game held on March 29 in Kansas City, Missouri, Tennessee defeated Louisiana Tech 93-75.

Chamique Holdsclaw of Tennessee was named women's player of the year while Tennessee Coach Pat Summit was named coach of the year for the sixth consecutive year. Most selectors named Holdsclaw, Nykesha Sales of the University of Connecticut, Ticha Penicheiro of Old Dominion, Alicia Thompson of Texas Tech, and Tracy Reid of North Carolina to the All-America team.

International. The United States won the 13th women's world basketball championship by beating Russia, 71-65, on June 7. Yugoslavia won the men's world championship with a 64-62 victory over Russia. □ Ron Reid

Belarus. The isolation of Belarus from the international community deepened during 1998, owing largely to the rule of President Aleksandr Lukashenko. In April, Lukashenko's government ordered ambassadors from 22 countries to vacate their residences in the diplomatic compound on the outskirts of the capital, Minsk. Government officials called the evictions temporary and tied them to municipal repairs scheduled for the area. However, diplomats suspected that Lukashenko, who lived nearby, intended to claim the entire wooded compound for his own use.

Diplomatic battle. Western diplomats refused to leave their embassies, calling the eviction order a violation of the 1961 Vienna Convention on diplomatic relations, which said that diplomatic missions are immune from search or requisition. The diplomats' fears were confirmed in June 1998 when Lukashenko declared the compound a "presidential residence" and said that utilities would be cut off to force the diplomats to leave. In protest, eight countries permanently recalled their diplomats. After Lukashenko reaffirmed his position, the European Union (EU), an organization of 15 Western European nations, and the United States banned all travel visas for Belarusian officials in July. The government of Belarus rescinded the eviction order in October.

Further isolation. International financial institutions registered their disapproval of the Belarusian government by ending direct relations. In April, the International Monetary Fund (IMF), a United Nations-affiliated organization that provides short-term credit to member nations, recalled its representative to Belarus after releasing just $70 million in credits out of $300 million originally pledged. The World Bank, a United Nations agency that provides long-term loans to countries for development, recalled its representative in August. Both agencies said that Belarus had taken too few steps toward reforming its economy.

Economy. Despite the skepticism of international experts, Belarusian economic officials claimed that the economy grew by 11 percent in 1998. Because Belarus maintained one of the most closed economies of all the former Soviet republics, the international financial crisis of 1998 had a milder effect on it than on neighboring Russia. However, the ongoing economic troubles in Russia, Belarus's major trading partner, posed a grave threat to Belarus.

Reunification pledge. On Dec. 25, 1998, Lukashenko and Russian President Boris Yeltsin signed a declaration pledging to unify Belarus and Russia as a single country. The declaration offered few details about the merger, however, and politicians in both former Soviet republics expressed opposition. ☐ Steven L. Solnick

See also **Russia.**

Belgium. A brief escape by Belgium's most notorious criminal suspect destabilized the government in 1998. Marc Dutroux, the alleged leader of a criminal ring uncovered in 1996, escaped in April 1998 while awaiting trial on charges of abducting and sexually abusing six girls and killing four of them. Police recaptured Dutroux within four hours. However, the incident magnified public concern about police incompetence and government corruption. A parliamentary committee had criticized the police after the initial crimes for failing to prevent the deaths of the girls despite numerous leads to Dutroux.

Immediately after the escape attempt, Interior Minister Johan Vande Lanotte and Justice Minister Stefaan De Clerck took responsibility for the incident by resigning. In May, the government and opposition parties agreed to create a unified federal police force and to establish an independent council to supervise the judicial system.

Bribery trial. Several former government ministers, including Willy Claes, who was also secretary-general of the North Atlantic Treaty Organization, were convicted on corruption charges in December in Belgium's biggest political scandal. The men, members of the country's two socialist parties, were found guilty of accepting more than $3 million in political party contributions in 1988 and 1989 from French and Italian

Belgium's most notorious criminal suspect, Marc Dutroux, returns to jail after his escape in April 1998.The escape of Dutroux, who is accused of sexually abusing and killing girls, ignited public concern about police corruption and government incompetence.

defense companies in return for contracts. Claes received a three-year suspended sentence.

Bank takeovers. ING Groep N.V., the largest bank and insurer in the Netherlands, acquired Banque Bruxelles Lambert S.A., Belgium's second-largest bank, for $4.4 billion in January 1998. In June, Fortis AG, a Belgian-Dutch insurance and banking company, bought Generale de Banque S.A., Belgium's largest bank, for $14.2 billion. Both ING and Fortis claimed the takeovers would help them compete across Europe after the introduction of the single currency, the euro, in 1999.

Economy. Belgium benefited from an upturn in the European economy in 1998. Output was expected to grow by 2.8 percent, while unemployment dropped to less than 9 percent. Belgium also was approved, in May 1998, to join 10 other European Union countries in launching the euro, despite the fact that its national debt stood at 120 percent of gross domestic product, twice the debt ceiling specified in the Maastricht Treaty on European Union. The government promised to continue to restrain public spending to cut the debt in half in about 15 years.   □ Tom Buerkle

See also **Europe** (Facts in brief table); **Europe** Special Report: **European Union.**

Belize. See Latin America.

Benin. See Africa.

Bhutan. See Asia.

Biology. In July 1998, biologists at the University of Hawaii in Honolulu led by Ryuzo Yanagimachi reported that they had created more than 50 mice that were *clones* (genetic duplicates) of adult mice. The report was the first published study to confirm the results of the 1996 Scottish experiment that produced the lamb Dolly, the first clone of an adult mammal.

Yanagimachi's group extracted the *nuclei* (the part of cells that contain genetic material) from body cells taken from the ovaries of a group of adult mice. They also removed the nuclei from egg cells taken from another group of mice. The scientists then injected the nuclei from the ovary cells into the egg cells. The resulting cells were placed into the wombs of yet another group of mice, where they developed into animals genetically identical to the mice from which the nuclei were obtained.

In December 1998, scientists led by animal-reproduction researcher Yukio Tsunoda of Kinki University in Japan announced that they had produced eight calves through cloning. The calves were among 19 that five groups of Japanese researchers had reportedly produced since July. Many of these animals died soon after birth. Japanese researchers were interested in cloning as a way to produce large numbers of cattle with high-quality beef or larger milk production.

Mouse *clones* (genetically identical mice) surround the donor of genetic material used to create them. In July 1998, scientists at the University of Hawaii in Honolulu announced that they had produced more than 50 such mouse clones.

Amphibian deaths. An international team of biologists announced in June 1998 that it had identified a species of fungus that the team believed was responsible for the deaths of large numbers of frogs and toads in Panama and Australia. The discovery of this fungus provided scientists with supporting evidence to help explain the worldwide decline, first reported in the 1980's, of many amphibian populations, including frogs, toads, and salamanders. Most scientists attribute amphibian declines to a combination of factors, including natural population fluctuations, disease, destruction of wetlands, pollution from agricultural pesticides, and increased levels of ultraviolet radiation from the sun.

The fungus, a member of the chytrid class, was discovered on the skin of dead frogs and toads by a group of biologists led by Lee Berger of the Australian Animal Health Laboratory near Melbourne, Australia. When the researchers scraped the fungus off the animals and placed it in a tank with healthy frogs, the frogs died within two weeks. The researchers theorized that the fungus prevents frogs from absorbing oxygen through the skin, causing suffocation.

How the fungus could appear in such widely separated locations as Panama and Australia remained a mystery. Some experts speculated that scientific researchers who traveled around the world conducting studies may have inadvertently carried the fungus, spreading it from one amphibian group to another. In 1998, a task force began developing a code of practice for field workers to minimize further transmission.

Eggshell thinning. In the 1970's, the pesticide dichloro-diphenyl-trichloroethane (DDT) was banned in many countries because it was linked to the thinning and breaking of egg shells of *birds of prey* (birds, such as eagles, that hunt and eat other animals). A study published in April 1998 indicated that the shells of some birds had begun thinning long before DDT was introduced in the late 1940's.

Ornithologist (bird biologist) Rhys E. Green of the Royal Society for the Protection of Birds in Edinburgh, Scotland, examined thousands of museum specimens of eggs dating back to 1850 from four species of British thrushes. He reported that shell thickness had declined by 2 to 11 percent, depending upon the species, between 1850 and 1998. For three of the species, the decline occurred at a steady rate over the entire period. For one of the species—the thrush known in Great Britain as the blackbird—egg shells started to get thicker again around 1960.

Green argued that the thinning may have been caused by acid rain resulting from industrialization. Acid rain is produced when sulfur-dioxide or nitrogen-oxide emissions from the combustion of fossil fuels react with water vapor in the atmosphere. Such rain reduces the calcium content of leaf litter consumed by worms. When eaten by thrushes, such worms would provide the birds with reduced levels of calcium, leading to egg shells that are thin and fragile. Green speculated that blackbird egg shells may have begun to thicken in the 1960's because of clean-air legislation passed in the 1950's.

Carbon dioxide and trees. Trees may grow as much as 12 percent faster when exposed to the levels of carbon dioxide that environmentalists predict will be in the atmosphere in the mid-2000's, researchers at Duke University in Durham, North Carolina, reported in August 1998. The researchers, conducting the first open-air test of the higher carbon dioxide levels thought to be likely from continued burning of fossil fuels, encircled three patches of North Carolina pine forest with rings of pipes 60 feet (18 meters) tall that injected the surrounding air with extra carbon dioxide. Computers controlled the emissions to maintain a carbon-dioxide level approximately 1.5 times greater than normal. Three similar patches of forest with normal carbon dioxide levels were monitored as controls.

The scientists found that the trees receiving the extra levels of carbon dioxide grew 12 percent faster than the trees in the control patches.

Increased levels of carbon dioxide spur plant growth by increasing the rate of *photosynthesis* (the process by which plants create food using carbon dioxide and sunlight). According to the researchers, if the world's forests were to grow at the accelerated rate found in this study, trees might absorb 20 percent of the 16.5 billion tons (15 billion metric tons) of carbon dioxide projected to be released to the atmosphere in 2050.

Rafting iguanas. In October 1998, biologists reported that a group of at least 15 iguanas had apparently traveled 200 miles (322 kilometers) from the island of Guadeloupe to the island of Anguilla in the Caribbean Sea on trees uprooted by a hurricane. The accidental trip of these large lizards confirmed one suspected mechanism by which isolated islands are populated by new species of animals.

After interviewing witnesses who saw the reptiles coming ashore in October 1995, biologist Ellen J. Censky of the Connecticut State Museum of Natural History in Storrs, Connecticut, tracked down 15 green iguanas, though she said she suspected there were more. This species, which is common on Guadeloupe, had not been observed on Anguilla before. Censky concluded that the animals and the trees they lived in were probably blown into the sea in September 1995 and carried to Anguilla by prevailing currents. Censky found at least one pregnant female iguana, suggesting that the animals would establish a self-sustaining population in their new home.

Killer dolphins. Bottlenosed dolphins, the sweet-tempered stars of marine shows, apparently practice a form of *infanticide* (infant killing) on the young of their own species, researchers from the United States and Scotland reported independently in July 1998. While studying the nature of injuries to dead baby dolphins washed onto shore, scientists from the Armed Forces Institute of Pathology in Washington, D.C., and the University of Aberdeen and Inverness Veterinary Centre in Scotland found a pattern of injuries consistent with dolphin attacks. The dolphin calves had broken bones, ripped tissues, and bruised organs similar to those previously observed in harbor porpoises killed by dolphins.

Although the researchers were not sure why the young dolphins were killed, they speculated that the killers were adult males looking for mates. A female dolphin is generally not sexually responsive while she is still tending a young calf. Previous studies, however, have shown that females can become fertile again within one to two weeks after losing an infant. Biologists speculated that adult males would improve their own chances of producing offspring by killing the offspring of other males.   □ Thomas H. Maugh II

Competitors set off on the ninth and final leg of the 7th Whitbread Round the World yacht race on May 22, 1998. The Swedish yacht *EF Language* (foreground), skippered by Paul Cayard of San Francisco, won three of the first six legs to clinch the overall victory.

Boating. On July 3, 1998, the 115-foot (35-meter) powerboat *Cable & Wireless Adventurer* cut almost eight days off the round-the-world boating record set by the United States submarine U.S.S. *Triton* in 1960. The 26,000-mile (41,800-kilometer) journey, which included stops in 11 countries, took 74 days, 20 hours, and 58 minutes. Anticipation for the upcoming America's Cup race built throughout 1998, with a record 16 international yacht clubs registering for the 1999 race.

The 7th Whitbread Round the World yacht race, which began and ended in Southampton, England, covered 31,600 nautical miles (58,500 kilometers) and took more than eight months to complete. Ten 64-foot (19.5-meter) yachts of similar construction left Southampton on Sept. 21, 1997, on a 7,350-nautical mile (13,600-kilometer) leg to Capetown, South Africa, the longest of the nine-leg race. Almost a month later, *EF Language*, a Swedish yacht named for a multinational educational products firm, won the first leg. The victory proved an omen, as *EF Language* went on to win three of the first six legs, securing the overall lead. *EF Language* had a leg to spare when it finished sixth in the eighth leg in May 1998.

EF Education, with an all-female crew, and *Silk Cut,* a prerace favorite, lost their masts on the fifth leg from New Zealand to Brazil in February. Both were forced to retire from leg five. The race ended on May 24, 1998, with *EF Language* 138 points ahead of second-place finisher *Merit Cup* from Monaco. *Swedish Match* placed third.

Other sailboat races. In May 1998, Randy Smyth and Jason Sneed teamed up to win the 13-leg Worrell 1000 catamaran race from Florida to Virginia for the second straight year. On June 23, the 79-foot (24-meter) maxi-yacht *Alexia* beat 161 other boats to win the 41st Newport-Bermuda sailboat race, covering 635 miles (1,022 kilometers) in 90 hours, 56 minutes, and 16 seconds.

Stormy seas claimed the lives of four crew members in Australia's Sydney-to-Hobart yacht race on December 28. Two more were presumed drowned. While more than 50 people had to be rescued, 39 boats managed to finish the race.

Powerboats. On July 12, 1998, in Detroit, Dave Villwock again piloted *Miss Budweiser* to victory in the Gold Cup race, the premier event on the American Power Boat Association circuit. Villwock averaged 140.3 miles (225.8 kilometers) per hour to beat the runner-up, *Miss Chrysler Jeep*, by a wide margin. It was *Miss Budweiser's* 12th Gold Cup victory and her third in four years. Villwock became the sixth driver to win three straight Gold Cups. ☐ Ron Reid

Bolivia. See Latin America.

Books. See Literature for children; Literature, American; Literature, World.

Bosnia-Herzegovina. Citizens of Bosnia-Herzegovina voted in September 1998 elections for members of Bosnia's parliament and the three-person federal presidency. Zivko Radisic, a moderate, defeated hard-liner Momcilo Krajisnik in the race for the Serbian seat of the presidency, while nationalist Ante Jelavic replaced moderate Kresimir Zubak in the Croatian seat. Alija Izetbegovic easily won reelection to the Muslim seat.

The Organization for Security and Cooperation in Europe, the body overseeing the national election, disqualified approximately 200 candidates in the weeks before the election. Four candidates from the nationalist Croatian Democratic Union of Bosnia-Herzegovina were disqualified because they had received biased support from Croatian television broadcasts. Two Serbian candidates were disqualified for their role in preventing the burial of a Muslim cleric in August.

Bosnian Serbs also voted in September in presidential elections for the Bosnian Serb republic. (Under the 1996 Dayton Agreement that ended the Bosnian War [1992-1995], Bosnia was divided into a Bosnian Serb republic and a Muslim-Croat federation.) Despite the support of Western governments, moderate President Biljana Plavsic lost to Nikola Poplasen, leader of the ultranationalist Serbian Radical Party.

Postwar recovery. In February 1998, officials of the North Atlantic Treaty Organization (NATO) extended the mandate of its 31,000 peace-keeping troops in Bosnia through the end of 1998. Clashes between ethnic groups erupted throughout the year, as refugees returning to their towns or villages were attacked. The United Nations High Commissioner for Refugees reported in August that some 500,000 refugees from the Bosnian War had returned to the country in 1998, but most had not returned to their prewar homes. An estimated 1.3 million refugees have yet to return.

In December, NATO troops arrested Radislav Krstic, a senior Bosnian Serb military commander under indictment by the International Criminal Tribunal for the Former Yugoslavia, based in The Hague, Netherlands. Krstic, the most prominent figure arrested for war crimes to date, was accused of genocide for directing the 1995 assault on the town of Srebrenica.

Economy. Bosnia's unemployment rate officially stood at 60 percent in 1998. However, experts estimated that unemployment was closer to 80 percent. In January, the European Union, an organization of 15 Western European nations, agreed to give the Serb Republic a $6.6-million loan. The World Bank, a United Nations agency that provides long-term loans to countries for development, approved a $17-million credit to improve infrastructrure.   □ Sharon L. Wolchik

See **Croatia; Europe** (Facts in brief table).

Botswana continued to uphold its reputation for good economic management and democratic political stability during 1998. In May, the African Development Bank, an international lending organization, estimated that the southern African country would experience an average annual economic growth rate of about 6.5 percent over the next five years, fueled chiefly by a continued increase in diamond production. Diamonds constituted 80 percent of Botswana's export earnings. However, key challenges include an estimated 21 percent unemployment rate and the AIDS epidemic. About 25 percent of all adults in Botswana were infected with the human immunodeficiency virus (HIV), which causes AIDS.

Peaceful transition. On March 31, Sir Ketumile Masire stepped down as president of Botswana after 18 years in power, one of only a few African leaders who have left office voluntarily. Vice President Festus Mogae succeeded him on April 1. Mogae had previously served as finance minister. Mogae's move into the presidency was designed to boost the chances of his ruling Botswana Democratic Party (BDP) in parliamentary elections scheduled for 1999.

New vice president. Ian Khama, former commander of the Botswana Defense Force, was formally elected as the country's new vice president by the National Assembly on July 13, 1998. Khama had been appointed vice president on April 1, one day after resigning from the military, but was unable to assume his new position officially until he had been elected to the National Assembly. In a by-election held on July 4, Khama won by a landslide. Khama, the oldest son of Botswana's first president, Seretse Khama, was also paramount chief of Botswana's largest clan, the Bamangwato. Most analysts agreed that the combination of Mogae and Khama, who represented major factions within the BDP, would help heal party rifts before the elections.

Clinton's visit. Botswana's position as Africa's oldest democracy earned the country a stop on United States President Bill Clinton's trip to Africa in March and April. Clinton praised Masire for helping to build one of Africa's strongest economies, and officials of the two countries discussed environmental and mineral issues.

Border tensions. On January 21, officials from Botswana and Namibia met to discuss a boundary dispute over two small, largely uninhabited islands in the Linyanti and Chobe rivers, which separate northern Botswana from northeastern Namibia. The dispute had led to several shooting incidents between troops from the two countries. On May 6, the two sides agreed to settle the matter through the International Court of Justice in the Netherlands.   □ Simon Baynham

See also **Africa** (Facts in brief table).

Bowling. Walter Ray Williams, Jr., of Stockton, California, took 1998 Player of the Year honors for the third straight season on the men's Professional Bowlers Association (PBA) tour. Aleta Sill of Dearborn, Michigan, ended the season with nearly $1 million in career earnings on the Professional Women's Bowlers Association (PWBA) tour.

Televised bowling moved away from its traditional presentation to a new one-hour format broadcast by CBS. In an attempt to attract a younger audience, spectators at these events sat in a horseshoe configuration, loudly cheering the competitors, who wore live microphones. The telecasts also featured tiny cameras set up behind the pins, to show each approaching ball.

The performances of Walter Ray Williams, Jr., and Parker Bohn III of Jackson, New Jersey, highlighted the 1998 PBA Tour. Williams won five titles and was the leading money winner on the tour, with $222,900. At the U.S. Open on April 11, 1998, in Fairfield, Connecticut, Williams led the field with a total of 14,294 pins—the highest ever for a single tournament. He beat Tim Criss, 221-189, in the title match.

Bohn, who finished second on the earnings list, completed only the second nationally televised perfect game during the American Bowling Congress (ABC) Masters tournament on May 9. However, he lost the title match to Mike Aulby, 224-192. On September 20, Bohn won the Japan Cup for the second time, in Tokyo. He defeated Steve Jaros in the title match, 238-226.

PWBA. Aleta Sill became the first woman to win the bowling triple crown twice, when she won the U.S. Open at Fairfield. Sill rolled eight straight strikes to beat Tammy Turner, 276-151. For the first time, four competitors in the 23-tournament PWBA Tour earned in excess of $100,000 for the season. The group included Carol Gianotti-Block of Perth, Australia, who led with $136,150; Aleta Sill with $120,005; Carolyn Dorin-Ballard with $115,978; and Dede Davidson with $113,400. In other major competitions, Lynda Norry won the Women's International Bowling Congress Queens tournament, Yvette Smith took the Hammer Players title, and Julie Gardner won the Sam's Town Invitational.

Seniors. Pete Couture of Titusville, Florida, won an unprecedented four tournaments and earned a record $117,300 for 1998. His victories included the ABC Senior Masters tournament and the Showboat Senior Open in Naples, Florida, which was the first PBA event ever to shorten its format. Couture was declared the winner of the tournament after 27 games, due to the approach of Hurricane Georges. Johnny Petraglia won the PBA Senior National Championship in Jackson, Michigan, in August. □ Ron Reid

Boxing. More boxing news occurred outside the ring during 1998 than from competition between fighters in major bouts. The ongoing suspension of Mike Tyson, the fight game's best-known heavyweight, and the legal troubles of Don King, the controversial promoter, largely overshadowed the few bouts that won public attention. Adding to the confusion, the year began with well over 100 "world champions" because boxing continued to be fragmented into at least nine different sanctioning organizations. The current state of the sport was perhaps best exemplified by the announcement in 1998 of plans to stage a so-called "Geezer Bout" in January 1999 between former heavyweight champions George Foreman, 50, and Larry Holmes, 49, who reigned in the 1970's and 1980's.

Tyson and King. Tyson's license to box in Nevada had been revoked in 1997, as a result of biting Evander Holyfield's ears during a match in Las Vegas. Tyson spent 1998 attending to several lawsuits and attempting to regain his license. On March 5, he filed a $100-million suit against King, alleging that the promoter had robbed him of millions of dollars over a 10-year period.

King underwent a 10-week trial on insurance fraud charges in New York City before being acquitted on July 10. It was the second time King

World champion boxers

World Boxing Association Division	Champion	Country	Date won
Heavyweight	Evander Holyfield	U.S.A.	11/96
Light heavyweight	Roy Jones	U.S.A.	7/98
	Lou Del Valle	U.S.A.	9/97
Middleweight	William Joppy	U.S.A.	1/98
	Julio Cesar Green	U.S.A.	8/97
Welterweight	James Page	U.S.A.	10/98
	Vacant	—	—
Lightweight	Jean-Baptiste Mendy	France	5/98
	Orzubek Nazarov	Russia	10/93
Featherweight	Antonio Cermeno	Venezuela	10/98
	Vacant	—	—
	Freddie Norwood	U.S.A.	4/98
Bantamweight	Johnny Tapia	U.S.A.	12/98
	Nana Konadu	Ghana	6/97
Flyweight	Mauricio Pastrana*	Venezuela	10/98
	Hugh Soto	Argentina	5/98
	Jose Bonilla	Venezuela	11/96
World Boxing Council Division	Champion	Country	Date won
Heavyweight	Lennox Lewis	United Kingdom	2/97
Light heavyweight	Roy Jones	U.S.A.	8/97
Middleweight	Hassine Cherifi	U.S.A.	5/98
	Keith Holmes	U.S.A.	3/96
Welterweight	Oscar de la Hoya	U.S.A.	4/97
Lightweight	Cezar Bazan	Mexico	6/98
	Steve Johnston	U.S.A.	3/97
Featherweight	Luisito Espinosa	Philippines	12/95
Bantamweight	Joichiro Tatsuyoshi	Japan	12/98
	S. Singmanassak	Thailand	8/96
Flyweight	Manny Pacquiao	Philippines	12/98
	Chatchai Sasakul	Thailand	11/97

*Interim champion

was tried on charges of attempting to defraud the insurance company Lloyd's of London out of $350,000 following the cancellation of a fight involving Julio Cesar Chavez. The first case against King had ended in a mistrial in 1995.

Tyson applied for a boxing license in New Jersey on July 17, 1998. At a July 23 appearance before the New Jersey State Athletic Control Board, Tyson became enraged by repeated questions about why he had bitten Holyfield. Tyson withdrew his application in August. He then asked the Nevada State Athletic Commission to restore the boxing license it had revoked in July 1997. On October 13, a 122-page psychiatric report, ordered by the Nevada commission, concluded that Tyson was depressed and lacked self-esteem but was mentally fit to return to boxing. On October 19, the commission voted to restore Tyson's license.

Other divisions. On June 13, Oscar De La Hoya beat Patrick Charpentier of France on a third-round technical knockout (TKO) to retain his World Boxing Council (WBC) welterweight title. De La Hoya defended his title again on September 18, beating Chavez on an eighth-round TKO in Las Vegas. Roy Jones defeated Lou Del Valle to unify the WBC and World Boxing Association (WBA) light heavyweight titles July 18 in New York City. He defended them both on November 14 against Canada's Otis Grant.   □ Ron Reid

Brazil. On Oct. 4, 1998, President Fernando Henrique Cardoso, 67, of the Social Democratic Party won election to a second, four-year term. Political experts believed that Brazilian voters granted Cardoso a second term with the hope that the man who had led them out of rampant inflation in 1994 could perform another economic miracle—stabilize a badly troubled economy.

On the eve of the 1998 elections, national unemployment stood at a 15-year high of more than 8 percent—and as high as 19 percent in the industrial state of Sao Paulo. Cardoso, nevertheless, assured investors at home and abroad that he would carry out long-delayed fiscal reforms in his second term. The reforms included overhauling Brazil's nearly bankrupt social security system and overstaffed civil service. Such promises were essential for Brazil to reach an agreement on November 13 on a $41.5-billion bailout package with the International Monetary Fund, a United Nations agency located in Washington, D.C., that provides short-term credit to member nations.

Developing crisis. Against the backdrop of a global economic crisis, Cardoso walked a tight wire during 1998, playing to two distinct audiences. One group, foreign investors, had an enormous stake in Brazil's economy. U.S. banks, for example, had invested a record $27.2 billion in Brazil as of March 1998. These banks watched the Brazilian economic crisis closely since they had already written off enormous losses on loans to other countries, including as much as $6.8 billion to Russia alone.

Cardoso backtracked on promises of fiscal reform to appeal to the electorate. The president spent money where he had promised to trim it, including $400 million to boost the wages of civil servants, $5 billion to build low-cost housing, and $4 billion to assist farmers in drought-stricken northeast Brazil.

Cardoso's administration further heightened fears abroad by dipping into its foreign reserves in order, as some economists noted, to prop up a grossly overvalued currency, the real. By September, the government was depleting foreign reserves by about 1 billion dollars a day. The government also increased interest rates to more than 40 percent. The crisis triggered a flight of foreign capital from Brazil, dried up business investment, and threw even more Brazilians out of work.

Deaths of presidential aides. Cardoso lost two of his closest advisers in April. Communications Minister Sergio Roberto Viera da Motta, 57, died on April 19 of complications from a long-term illness. A founder of the president's party, da Motta was the chief architect of a plan to privatize Brazil's state-owned telecommunication system. Luis Eduardo Magalhaes, 43, the leader of the president's party in the lower house of Congress, died of a heart attack on April 21. He had been a key player in garnering congressional support for economic reform, including the streamlining of the civil service and the updating of the country's labor and social security laws.

Telephone industry privatized. In spite of da Motta's death, plans proceeded for the sale of the government's controlling shares in Telecomunicacoes Brasileiras S.A., also known as Telebras. The government divided Telebras into 12 separate companies and auctioned them off on July 29 for more than $19 billion. Telefonica of Spain, Portugal Telecom, and the MCI Communications Corporation of the United States formed a loose business alliance that provided $11.6 billion of the total sale price.

Unknown tribe. In April, officials of Brazil's Federal Indian Bureau discovered a previously unknown Indian tribe living in a remote area of the Amazon rain forest. Spotting the tribe's village from the air, the officials estimated that the group consisted of about 200 people who lived by fishing and hunting.

□ Nathan A. Haverstock

See also **Economy** Special Report: **Asian Economic Crisis—Global Contagion; Latin America** (Facts in brief table); **Russia.**

British Columbia. See Canadian provinces.
Brunei. See Africa.

Buddhism. In 1998, troubles escalated between the governing Sinhalese Buddhists in Sri Lanka and the country's ethnic minority Tamils. On January 25, three Tamil suicide bombers attacked the Temple of the Tooth, a holy site in Kandy, Sri Lanka, that houses a tooth that the devout believe belonged to the Buddha. The bombers killed 13 people and injured at least 20 others. The relic was not damaged in the attack.

Taiwan. On April 9, Buddhist monks in India presented Taiwan with another tooth believed to be from the remains of the Buddha. The tooth, a gift intended to bring blessings to Taiwan, had reportedly been taken from a temple in Tibet during China's Cultural Revolution in the 1960's. Taiwan's Buddhists received the tooth with public prayer and celebration. China, which claims sovereignty over Taiwan, questioned the authenticity of the tooth, claiming that only two authentic relics exist—the one in Sri Lanka and another in Beijing.

Protests. On March 10, 1998, six Tibetans began a hunger strike in New Delhi, India, in an attempt to persuade the United Nations (UN) General Assembly to discuss Chinese rule in Tibet. They also argued that the UN should act upon its own 1961 resolution that demanded an end to human rights violations in Tibet. The Dalai Lama, the exiled leader of Tibetan Buddhists, visited the strikers in April. He expressed admiration for their goals but disapproved of their methods. On April 27, Indian police took the six individuals to the hospital. In protest to the police intervention, Thupten Ngodup, a former Buddhist monk, publicly set fire to himself. He died two days later.

In May, the Dalai Lama's government-in-exile, located in Dharmsala, India, reported that Chinese guards had fired upon prisoners at Drapchi prison in Lhasa, Tibet. A Buddhist monk, four nuns, and another inmate died in attacks on prisoners that were allegedly intended to squelch demonstrations for Tibetan independence.

Western leaders called on China in 1998 to begin talks with Tibetans on human rights issues. In October, Chinese leaders signed the UN International Covenant on Civil and Political Rights, a treaty that binds participating nations to an agreement to honor human rights. By the end of 1998, the Chinese government had yet to ratify the treaty.

Fund-raising scandal. In February, Maria L. Hsia was indicted in the United States on federal charges of illegal fund-raising for the U.S. Democratic Party at a Buddhist temple in California. The indictment focused on an event that Vice President Al Gore attended in 1996. Allegedly, Hsia solicited $55,000 from guests for the Democratic National Committee and then reimbursed individuals from temple funds.   □ Paul J. Griffiths

See also **China; Democratic Party; Sri Lanka.**

Building and construction. Hong Kong opened its Chek Lap Kok International Airport on July 6, 1998. The airport rests on a 3,084-acre (1,248-hectare) man-made island that was constructed from two smaller, natural islands. The airport's passenger terminal, designed by British architect Sir Norman Foster, is the largest enclosed space ever built, capable of holding five Boeing 747's tip to tip. Despite well-publicized problems with the baggage handling system, the airport easily accommodated one of the world's heaviest transit rates, estimated at 35 million passengers annually. The airport was designed to handle up to 87 million people annually.

Construction on the $21-billion transportation hub also included rail lines and roads. In May, the airport authority opened one of the approaches to the airport, the 1.5-mile (2.4-kilometer) Ting Kau Bridge. The suspension bridge features twin steel decks hanging from three towers.

Japan's Akashi Kaikyo Bridge, the world's longest suspension bridge, opened to automobile traffic on April 4. Spanning 12,831 feet (3,911 meters), the bridge connects Kobe on the main island of Honshu to Awaji Island. The bridge is suspended from two towers that stand 6,532 feet (1,991 meters) apart, a span that marked another engineering record. Engineers designed the bridge to withstand earthquakes that measure as much as 8.5 on the Richter scale.

The European Union (EU), a group of 15 Western European nations, opened a new $500-million parliament building in Strasbourg, France, in May. Designed by Paris-based Architecture Studio Europe, the complex sits atop a concrete mat measuring 1.6 million cubic feet (45,500 cubic meters). Supporting piles were extended 46 feet (14 meters) into the ground. The complex includes a 17-story cylindrical office building connected by walkways to the 138-foot (42-meter) tall egg-shaped debating chamber, made of steel and concrete and covered on the outside with cedar and oak planks. The new facility serves as the permanent headquarters for the EU's 626 parliamentary delegates.

Los Angeles railway. In October 1998, the first of 25 phases of the $1.9-billion Alameda Corridor was completed in the Los Angeles metropolitan area. When completed, the 20-mile (32-kilometer) rail line will consolidate three separate rail lines from the ports of Los Angeles and Long Beach to downtown Los Angeles. It is expected to unclog freight congestion at one of North America's busiest Pacific coast ports. Transportation officials predicted that trade activity would increase from $157 billion to $253 billion annually by 2001, the scheduled completion date for the project.

Plans for the Alameda Corridor include nearly 50 new bridges, 200 automobile overpasses, and

Japan's Akashi Kaikyo Bridge, the longest suspension bridge in the world, opens to automobile traffic on April 4, 1998. The bridge connects the city of Kobe on the main Japanese island of Honshu to the much smaller Awaji Island.

a trench for rail lines below street level. Engineers estimated that trains will move at about 40 miles (64 kilometers) per hour through the corridor and that the new rail system would save motorists 15,000 hours a day that is currently spent waiting at railroad crossings.

The Arizona Diamondbacks, Phoenix's professional baseball team, opened the $354-million, 49,500-seat Bank One Ballpark in March. It was the first U.S. stadium with natural grass under a retractable roof. To open the six-panel stadium roof, three panels are pulled by cables and stacked at either end of the opening. Cables also pull the panels shut. When the roof is in place, the stadium's air conditioning system can cool the seating area from 110 °F to 80 °F (43 °C to 27 °C) in less than four hours.

The roof was intended to open or close in five minutes, but problems caused primarily by the stretching of the cables did not allow the process to work as smoothly as expected. Contractors tightened the cables several times and made other improvements on the roof throughout 1998.

Highway projects. On July 1, two segments of E-470, a privately financed toll road, opened in the Denver, Colorado, metropolitan area. The project, scheduled for completion in 2001, was designed to wrap around the eastern suburbs, linking the Denver International Airport with the north and south ends of Interstate 25, which runs directly through Denver. The highway was also planned to provide rapid access between the airport and interstates 70 and 76.

The 1998 openings added a total of 17.2 miles (27.7 kilometers) to the 46.7-mile (75.2-kilometer) project. A 5.3-mile (8.5-kilometer) segment was completed in 1991. The new roads opened with state-of-the-art electronic technology for collecting tolls, automatically billing regular tollway users and ticketing speeding drivers.

Boston's $10.8-billion Central Artery/Tunnel Project, designed to relieve the city's chronic downtown traffic congestion, began above-ground construction in the spring of 1998. The project, also known as the Big Dig, has two major components. One part, an 8-to-10 lane underground expressway, was designed to replace a six-lane, 40-year-old elevated highway. The other portion is a tunnel system—including the Ted Williams Tunnels, which opened in 1995—that was designed to link Interstate 90 south of downtown Boston with Logan Airport in East Boston.

In 1998, builders concentrated on the interchanges linking new and existing highways and two bridges over the Charles River. Officials expected to have nearly 50 percent of the project finished by the end of 1998 and all of the work completed by 2004. ☐ Andrew G. Wright

See also **Architecture; Transportation.**

Bulgaria. Prime Minister Ivan Kostov identified administrative reform and privatization as his government's priority projects for 1998. However, tensions between the ruling coalition and the opposition Bulgarian Socialist Party, which was ousted as the ruling party in 1997 after mass protests, prevented the legislature from passing many important pieces of legislation.

Despite Kostov's promises to accelerate economic restructuring, privatization continued to lag. However, several banks were privatized in 1998, and the government announced its intention in July to privatize 51 percent of the national telecommunications company. Officials also projected that 85 percent of state-owned businesses would be privatized by the end of the year.

Economy. The stabilization program enacted in 1997 began to produce positive results in Bulgaria in 1998. Analysts expected the *gross domestic product* (the total value of goods and services produced by a country in a given year) to grow by 3.5 to 4 percent in 1998. After sharp declines in 1997, foreign investment in Bulgaria rebounded in 1998 and was expected to exceed $1 billion by year's end. In January, the World Bank agreed to loan Bulgaria $400 to $600 million over the next three years, and, in September, the International Monetary Fund (IMF) approved $864 million in credit to help Bulgaria meet its medium-range economic goals. The World Bank and IMF are institutions affiliated with the United Nations that offer loans and credit to member nations.

Foreign affairs. Bulgaria's leaders continued to campaign for membership in the European Union (EU), a political and economic alliance of 15 Western European countries, and in the North Atlantic Treaty Organization (NATO). In September, at the request of the EU, Bulgaria agreed to shut down its only nuclear power plant in 2004. The Bulgarian military began creating new standards in 1998 in cooperation with NATO. On October 11, Bulgaria granted permission for NATO warplanes to use the country's airspace in case air strikes against Yugoslavia became necessary.

Bulgaria resolved an ongoing dispute with Gazprom, the state-owned Russian gas company, in April, signing a new agreement regarding the natural gas pipeline that supplies Bulgaria and several neighboring countries. Bulgarian leaders also signed an agreement with the Royal Dutch-Shell Group in April to build a new natural gas pipeline across Bulgaria that would connect Turkmenistan and Germany. ☐ Sharon L. Wolchik

See also **Europe** (Facts in brief table); **Yugoslavia.**

Burkina Faso. See Africa.

Burma. See Myanmar.

Bus. See Transportation.

Business. See Bank; Economics; Labor; Manufacturing.

Secretary of Health and Human Services Donna Shalala throws out the first baseball of the 1998 professional baseball season at the Baltimore Orioles opening game on March 31, 1998.

Cabinet, U.S. Secretary of Energy Federico F. Pena resigned his Cabinet position in June 1998, citing personal and family reasons for leaving. Pena had served as secretary of transportation during President Bill Clinton's first term (1993–1997). President Clinton selected Bill Richardson, U.S. ambassador to the United Nations, to replace Pena.

The Senate confirmed Richardson, a Democrat and former U.S. representative from New Mexico, for the energy post in July 1998. Richardson said that he would "bring a sense of activism" to the department. His agenda included focusing on international energy issues and encouraging less-developed countries to act on global warming.

Babbitt probe. On February 11, Attorney General Janet Reno asked a three-judge federal panel to name a special prosecutor to investigate whether Interior Secretary Bruce Babbitt lied to Congress about his department's 1995 rejection of a casino gambling project involving three Chippewa Indian tribes in Wisconsin. In 1998, Republicans alleged that the Department of the Interior had turned down the request under pressure from President Clinton's White House staff because Indian tribes opposed to the plan had allegedly contributed to Clinton's 1996 reelection campaign. Wisconsin tribes that had opposed the casino application also donated $286,000 to the

Democratic Party after the project was rejected.

Babbitt testified on Jan. 29, 1998, before the House Committee on Oversight and Reform, that the application rejection was based on department policy and not because of political intervention by presidential aides. Carol Elder Bruce, a Washington, D.C., trial lawyer, was named independent counsel in the case on March 19.

Kickback charges. Attorney General Reno asked a three-member panel of federal judges on May 11 to appoint an independent counsel to investigate charges made in 1997 by Laurent Yene, an African-born businessman, that Labor Secretary Alexis M. Herman had accepted money in 1996 while she was director of the White House Office of Public Liaison.

Yene alleged that Herman accepted the money in exchange for lining up clients for a company that he owned. On Jan. 15, 1998, Herman denied the allegations. On May 26, a federal judicial panel appointed Ralph I. Lancaster, Jr., a trial attorney from Portland, Maine, as independent counsel to investigate the allegations.

☐ William J. Eaton

See also **People in the news** (Richardson, Bill); **United States, Government of the; United States, President of the.**

California. See Los Angeles; San Francisco; State government.

Cambodia.

The Cambodian People's Party (CPP), headed by Prime Minister Hun Sen, won 41 percent of the vote in the July 1998 elections. The CPP captured 64 of 122 seats in the parliament, falling short of the two-thirds needed to form a new government. The two main opposition candidates, Prince Norodom Ranariddh and Sam Rainsy, charged the CPP with using fraud, violence, and intimidation to win the election.

The National United Front for an Independent, Neutral, Peaceful, and Cooperative Cambodia (FUNCINPEC) Party, headed by Ranariddh, won 43 seats in the parliament with 32 percent of the vote. A party headed by Rainsy won 15 seats with 14 percent of the vote in Cambodia's first parliamentary election in five years.

FUNCINPEC had won control of the National Assembly in 1993, but it was forced to form a coalition government with the CPP when Hun Sen refused to give up his party's control over the government. Ranariddh became the first prime minister of the coalition government, and Hun Sen was named second prime minister.

In July 1997, Hun Sen staged a *coup* (military overthrow), ousting Ranariddh and stripping FUNCINPEC of its power in parliament. According to a team of observers from the United Nations, Hun Sen's forces murdered at least 40 FUNCINPEC leaders during the coup.

Election protests. A handful of international monitors hastily declared the July 1998 elections fair. However, Ranariddh and Rainsy claimed that the CPP used violence and intimidation against its opposition. Ranariddh and Rainsy charged that Cambodian television and radio, which were controlled by Hun Sen, publicized only CPP candidates, and the CPP appointed village chiefs to limit protests from opposition parties. The National Election Committee, which was dominated by Communist supporters of Hun Sen, rejected charges of voter fraud.

After demonstrations in the capital, Phnom Penh, demanding the ouster of Hun Sen, the highest appeals body, the Constitutional Council, which Hun Sen also controlled, dismissed the appeals of opposition parties. In November, Ranariddh agreed to a coalition government headed by Hun Sen, with Ranariddh as leader of the National Assembly.

Pol Pot, the former leader of the Khmer Rouge, died at age 73 on April 15, apparently of a heart attack. In 1997, the Khmer Rouge had convicted him of ordering the murder of government officials. As leader of the Khmer Rouge, Pol Pot oversaw the deaths of more than 1.5 million people when the Communist group ruled Cambodia in the 1970's. □ Henry S. Bradsher

See also **Asia** (Facts in brief table).

The body of Pol Pot, the Khmer Rouge leader who oversaw the deaths of more than 1.5 million Cambodians in the 1970's, is displayed after his death on April 15. Pol Pot had been held under house arrest by the Khmer Rouge since 1997.

Quebec's uncertain future in the federation dominated the Canadian political scene in 1998.

New Quebec leader. In early 1998, Daniel Johnson led the Liberal Party in Quebec. Poll after poll had shown that he and his party were unlikely to win the next provincial election. On March 2, Johnson stunned the province by resigning his post. Many political experts believed that Johnson had never held the confidence of Prime Minister Jean Chretien, the national leader of the Liberal Party, who blamed Johnson for the near-defeat of the federalist option in a 1995 referendum on Quebec's independence.

The vacancy in the province's Liberal leadership put pressure on Quebecer Jean Charest, then national leader of the Progressive Conservative Party, to assume Johnson's position. Many in Quebec believed that the popular Charest was the only political figure in the province who could defeat Quebec's charismatic Premier Lucien Bouchard and his separatist Parti Quebecois (PQ). Charest hesitated for several weeks before announcing on March 26, 1998, his intention to seek the post. Declaring that he had never seen a contradiction between being a proud Canadian and a proud Quebecer, Charest was enthusiastically accepted by Quebec's Liberals on April 30.

The campaign. Public opinion polls of Quebec voters conducted in mid-1998 showed that support for separation was at its weakest level in several years. Nevertheless, on October 13, Bouchard placed the issue squarely before voters by announcing he would hold provincial elections in November, about a year before he was legally obliged to do so. Bouchard, who had succeeded Jacques Parizeau as head of the PQ government in 1996, said he did not want to anger voters by "living on borrowed time."

In the campaign, Charest stressed his belief that Quebecers were tired of constitutional wrangling and that another referendum was not needed. Charest and the Liberals also tried to exploit public unhappiness with the PQ's deep budget cuts that had reduced provincial spending on health care, education, and other social services.

Bouchard, realizing that another referendum was unpopular with Quebec voters, announced that he would hold another vote on independence only if "winning conditions" existed. He asserted that Quebecers wanted a premier who would stand up for Quebec in dealings with the federal government and promised to press for restrictions on the federal government's social policy initiatives under provincial jurisdiction.

Polls showed Charest and the Liberals trailing in the campaign, but the results of the voting on Nov. 30, 1998, imitated those of the 1994 election. The PQ took 76 seats in Quebec's 125-member legislature. The Liberals won 48 seats, and the Action Democratique, a small third party, won 1 seat. While the Liberals won slightly more of the popular vote than the PQ, their strength was concentrated in areas such as Montreal, with a greater number of English-speaking and ethnic voters. The PQ gained its solid majority in the legislature because French-speaking Quebecers constitute a majority in more than 70 of the province's 125 electoral districts.

As a result of the election, the separatist PQ government continued in office, but without the landslide victory Bouchard wanted as the first of his "winning conditions" for a future referendum. Charest became opposition leader. The question of whether Quebec would remain in the federation remained unresolved.

Secession ruling. In an Aug. 20, 1998, ruling on the legality of *secession* (the act of formally withdrawing from a nation), the nine justices of the Supreme Court of Canada—four of them French-speaking and three from Quebec—delivered unanimous decisions on three questions that the federal government had asked the court to

consider in 1996. First, as Canada's constitution has no provision for secession, did Quebec have the authority to leave the federation? Second, did international law give Quebec the right to secede? Third, in a conflict between domestic and international law, which law took precedence?

On the first question, the court stated that any action on the part of Quebec to move toward secession must be in accordance with the constitution. Because the constitution contains no provision covering secession, such a step would "violate the Canadian legal order." The court noted, however, that Canadians outside Quebec could not ignore the fact that a majority

A pedestrian in Ottawa makes his way through branches downed by a January 1998 ice storm that was called Canada's worst disaster of modern times. The storm toppled hundreds of thousands of trees and power lines from Ontario to New Brunswick, cutting off power to 3 million people and causing billions of dollars worth of damage.

of Quebecers might express their desire through a legal referendum to secede from the Canadian federation. In such a situation, the federal government and the provincial governments would be obliged to negotiate the terms of Quebec's independence. In these negotiations, the judges wrote, all parties would have to safeguard principles that underlay the political and social order of Canada, including federalism, democracy, the rule of law, and individual and minority rights.

On the second question, the court dismissed the argument that international law gave Quebec the right of secession. International law, the court wrote, recognizes secession only when a people are prevented from exercising their political rights because of their colonial status or because of severe oppression. Quebec did not fall into either of these categories. The province was a founding and equal member of the Canadian federation. Its people had rights similar to those enjoyed by other Canadians. On the third question, the court stated that because Quebec had no right of secession under either domestic or international law, there was no conflict between the two. The court refrained from discussing how the difficult aspects of the secession process could be settled. The justices wrote that these matters would have to be decided by the "political actors" in the process.

Reaction. Both federalists and separatists were encouraged by certain aspects of the decision. Many analysts praised the Supreme Court ruling as a sensible compromise in a difficult situation. By ruling that Quebec's claim to self-determination could be realized legally, the court had avoided humiliating Quebec nationalists and giving the separatists ammunition for the forthcoming election. However, legal experts believed that the decision reaffirmed the federalist position that Quebec could not simply leave Canada by voting to do so in a popular referendum. Secession could be achieved only through complex negotiations whose process and outcome satisfied all parties in the federation.

Bouchard and the PQ accepted the court's ruling even though the Quebec government had refused to participate in hearings on the issue. The PQ argued that the Supreme Court's decision had validated the referendum process that Quebec had followed in 1995. The federal government responded to the decision by dropping its hardline tactic of stressing the risks and costs of separation and returning to emphasizing the need for a new balance of powers in the federation.

Party standings. The Liberals maintained a comfortable majority in the House of Commons in 1998. In a by-election held on March 30, they took a seat from the right-wing Reform Party in British Columbia to bring their total seats in the House of Commons to 156. (The death of Liberal Shaughnessy Cohen in December reduced the number to 155 again.) The Reform Party (official opposition) held 59 seats. Bloc Quebecois held 45. The New Democratic Party held 21. The Progressive Conservative Party held 19. There was one independent in the House.

Jean Charest's move to the Quebec Liberal Party meant that a new head was needed for the federal Progressive Conservative Party. On November 14, the party chose Joe Clark, who had served as prime minister in 1979 and 1980.

The Canadian economy, strong at the beginning of 1998, was damaged by shocks result-

1998 Canadian population estimates

Province and territory populations

Alberta	2,760,847
British Columbia	3,928,338
Manitoba	1,122,827
New Brunswick	744,050
Newfoundland	545,410
Northwest Territories	67,451
Nova Scotia	912,923
Ontario	11,039,341
Prince Edward Island	136,556
Quebec	7,239,088
Saskatchewan	990,633
Yukon Territory	32,097
Canada	29,508,216

City and metropolitan area populations

	Metropolitan area	City
Toronto, Ont.	4,425,581	2,475,956
Montreal, Que.	3,375,925	1,031,474
Vancouver, B.C.	1,937,934	543,830
Ottawa-Hull	1,040,220	
Ottawa, Ont.		332,850
Hull, Que.		64,173
Edmonton, Alta.	871,591	622,732
Calgary, Alta.	851,473	795,982
Quebec, Que.	682,953	170,018
Winnipeg, Man.	669,881	620,953
Hamilton, Ont.	634,641	327,660
London, Ont.	405,823	331,534
Kitchener, Ont.	394,359	183,740
St. Catharines-Niagara	375,690	
St. Catharines, Ont.		132,081
Niagara Falls, Ont.		77,595
Halifax, N.S.	337,457	115,602
Victoria, B.C.	311,264	75,189
Windsor, Ont.	285,752	202,707
Oshawa, Ont.	281,719	140,836
Saskatoon, Sask.	222,398	196,602
Regina, Sask.	194,427	181,122
St. John's, Nfld.	174,957	102,467
Sudbury, Ont.	161,646	92,723
Chicoutimi-Jonquière	160,262	
Chicoutimi, Que.		62,985
Jonquière, Que.		56,435
Sherbrooke, Que.	150,168	78,236
Trois-Rivières, Que.	141,472	48,943
Thunder Bay, Ont.	125,813	113,889
Saint John, N.B.	125,655	72,465

Source: World Book estimates based on data from Statistics Canada.

ing from the economic turmoil in Asia, a lengthy strike by General Motors workers, and a steady loss of consumer confidence as economic uncertainty grew. The economy grew by only 1.8 percent for the first two quarters, with an estimated growth rate of 3.2 percent for the year.

The economy in 1998 also was troubled by a decline in the value of the Canadian dollar. On January 3, the dollar fell to a record low of 68.19 cents U.S. On the same day, the Bank of Canada, the country's central bank, raised its benchmark interest rate—the rate charged to commercial banks—to 5 percent to halt sales of the dollar, despite worries that the increase would dampen economic growth. The bank also began buying large amounts of Canadian currency in order to stabilize the Canadian dollar. However, investors looking for a safer haven moved steadily out of Canadian and into U.S. investments. On August 26, the Canadian dollar fell to a new low of 63.88 cents U.S. The next day, the bank raised its benchmark interest rate by a full percentage point, to 6 percent, and bought more currency.

Many analysts linked the fall in the Canadian dollar to declining world commodity prices that lowered earnings for Canadian oil, metals, forest products, and wheat. Despite Canada's efforts to diversify its economy, world financial markets still viewed the value of the Canadian dollar as closely tied to commodity prices.

Although the Canadian dollar's decline meant higher prices for consumers, inflation was not a problem in 1998. It hovered around 1 percent. Unemployment reached 8.3 percent in autumn.

Budget. Finance Minister Paul Martin on February 24 introduced Canada's first balanced budget since 1970. In announcing the $151-billion budget for fiscal year 1998-1999 (April 1, 1998, to March 31, 1999), Martin proudly reminded Canadians that the federal deficit had stood at a record $45 billion only four years before. Higher tax revenues and a lower interest rate on the national debt—benefits of Canada's healthy economy—had helped the Liberal government fulfill its 1993 election promise to eliminate the country's annual operating deficit.

One highlight of what Martin called an "education budget" was the establishment of a $2.5-billion, 10-year college scholarship fund. Beginning in 2000, the fund was slated to provide an estimated 100,000 needy college students with up to $15,000 apiece. Martin also offered $7.2 billion in tax cuts to those Canadians whose real after-tax income had fallen by 7 percent since 1989. The cuts, to be phased in over four years, were targeted mostly at lower- and middle-income Canadians. The budget also included funds for gradually reducing the country's massive $583-billion national debt.

Provincial pressures. On Oct. 14, 1998, Martin reported a $3.5-billion surplus for fiscal year 1997-1998. Provincial finance ministers immediately demanded a share of the surplus. The ministers asked the federal government to restore $6 billion in payments for social programs cut since 1994. They also demanded that the federal government pay a greater share of employment insurance premiums and increase funding for more economically troubled provinces.

Martin, however, used the surplus to lower the national debt, the first such reduction since 1970. He also insisted that uncertainties about corporate tax revenues—vulnerable because of Canada's economic slowdown—warranted fiscal caution. Martin did agree, however, to consider modest increases in funding for health care.

Foreign affairs. In a vote on Oct. 5, 1998, Canada was chosen to fill one of the ten elected seats on the United Nations Security Council. Foreign minister Lloyd Axworthy stated that Canada intended to support reforms that would make the Security Council more accountable to the General Assembly.

During 1998, Canadian officials continued to press for wider acceptance of the convention banning antipersonnel land mines, signed in Canada in December 1997. By November 1998, 52 countries had ratified the treaty, more than the number needed for its implementation in March 1999. Nations that did not sign the treaty included Russia, Israel, the United States, and China.

Canadian officials also took a leading role in drafting a treaty creating the world's first permanent war-crimes tribunal. The new court was to be based in The Hague, Netherlands, and was to have the authority to prosecute genocide, crimes against humanity, and war crimes. On July 17, 1998, at a meeting in Rome, 120 countries voted in favor of establishing the court. The treaty must be ratified by 60 countries to take effect.

Trouble in the salmon fisheries. The salmon-fishing season in the Northwest Pacific Ocean in 1998 triggered renewed conflict between Canada and the United States. A Canadian ban on fishing for endangered coho salmon in British Columbia and the negotiation of two short-term agreements between Canada and Washington state raised hope that the region's governments would agree on a plan to protect seriously depleted salmon stocks. British Columbia, however, bitterly attacked the ban and agreements as disastrous for its fishing industry.

Representatives from Canada and the United States attempted throughout 1998 to renew the 1985 Pacific Salmon Treaty, which had laid down guidelines to ensure the conservation and equitable division of stocks of five types of salmon. Disputes over dwindling salmon stocks had led

Members of the Canadian House of Commons

The House of Commons of the first session of the 36th Parliament convened on Sept. 22, 1997. As of Dec. 15, 1998, the House of Commons consisted of the following members: 155 Liberal Party, 59 Reform Party, 45 Bloc Québécois, 21 New Democratic Party, 19 Progressive Conservative Party, and 1 Independent. This table shows each legislator and party affiliation. An asterisk (*) denotes those who served in the 35th Parliament.

Alberta
Diane Ablonczy, Ref.*
Rob Anders, Ref.*
Leon E. Benoit, Ref.*
Cliff Breitkreuz, Ref.*
Rick Casson, Ref.
David Chatters, Ref.*
Ken Epp, Ref.*
Peter Goldring, Ref.
Deborah Grey, Ref.*
Art Hanger, Ref.*
Grant Hill, Ref.*
Rahim Jaffer, Ref.
Dale Johnston, Ref.*
Jason Kenney, Ref.
David Kilgour, Lib.*
Eric Lowther, Ref.
Preston Manning, Ref.*
Ian McClelland, Ref.*
Anne McLellan, Lib.*
Bob Mills, Ref.*
Deepak Obhrai, Ref.
Charlie Penson, Ref.*
Jack Ramsay, Ref.*
Monte Solberg, Ref.*
Myron Thompson, Ref.*
John Williams, Ref.*

British Columbia
Jim Abbott, Ref.*
David Anderson, Lib.*
Chuck Cadman, Ref.
Raymond Chan, Lib.*
John Cummins, Ref.*
Elizabeth Davies, N.D.P.
Harbance Singh Dhaliwal, Lib.*
John Duncan, Ref.*
Reed Elley, Ref.
Paul Forseth, Ref.*
Hedy Fry, Lib.*
Bill Gilmour, Ref.*
Jim Gouk, Ref.*
Gurmant Grewal, Ref.
Richard M. Harris, Ref.*
Jim Hart, Ref.*
Jay Hill, Ref.*
M. Sophia Leung, Lib.
Gary Lunn, Ref.
Keith Martin, Ref.*
Philip Mayfield, Ref.*
Grant McNally, Ref.
Ted McWhinney, Lib.*
Val Meredith, Ref.*
John Reynolds, Ref.
Nelson Riis, N.D.P.*
Svend J. Robinson, N.D.P.*
Werner Schmidt, Ref.*
Mike Scott, Ref.*
Lou Sekora, Lib.
Darrel Stinson, Ref.*
Chuck Strahl, Ref.*
Randy White, Ref.*
Ted White, Ref.*

Manitoba
Reg Alcock, Lib.*
Lloyd Axworthy, Lib.*
Bill Blaikie, N.D.P.*
Rick Borotsik, P.C.
Bev Desjarlais, N.D.P.
Ronald J. Duhamel, Lib.*
John Harvard, Lib.*
Howard Hilstrom, Ref.
Jake E. Hoeppner, Ref.*
David Iftody, Lib.*
Inky Mark, Ref.
Pat Martin, N.D.P.
Rey D. Pagtakhan, Lib.*
Judy Wasylycia-Leis, N.D.P.

New Brunswick
Gilles Bernier, P.C.
Claudette Bradshaw, Lib.
Jean Dubé, P.C.
Yvon Godin, N.D.P.
John Herron, P.C.
Charles Hubbard, Lib.*
Andy Scott, Lib.*
Greg Thompson, P.C.
Angela Vautour, N.D.P.
Elsie Wayne, P.C.*

Newfoundland
George S. Baker, Lib.*
Gerry Byrne, Lib.*
Norman Doyle, P.C.
Bill Matthews, P.C.
Fred J. Mifflin, Lib.*
Lawrence D. O'Brien, Lib.*
Charlie Power, P.C.

Northwest Territories
Ethel Blondin-Andrew, Lib.*
Nancy Karetak-Lindell, Lib.

Nova Scotia
Scott Brison, P.C.
Bill Casey, P.C.
Michelle Dockrill, N.D.P.
Gordon Earle, N.D.P.
Gerald Keddy, P.C.
Wendy Lill, N.D.P.
Peter Mackay, P.C.
Peter Mancini, N.D.P.
Alexa McDonough, N.D.P.
Mark Muise, P.C.
Peter Stoffer, N.D.P.

Ontario
Peter Adams, Lib.*
Sarkis Assadourian, Lib.*
Jean Augustine, Lib.*
Sue Barnes, Lib.*
Colleen Beaumier, Lib.*
Réginald Bélair, Lib.*
Mauril Bélanger, Lib.*
Eugène Bellemare, Lib.*
Carolyn Bennett, Lib.
Maurizio Bevilacqua, Lib.*
Raymond Bonin, Lib.*
Paul Bonwick, Lib.
Don Boudria, Lib.*
Bonnie Brown, Lib.*
John Bryden, Lib.*
Sarmite Bulte, Lib.
Charles Caccia, Lib.*
Murray Calder, Lib.*
John Cannis, Lib.*
Elinor Caplan, Lib.
M. Aileen Carroll, Lib.
Marlene Catterall, Lib.*
Brenda Chamberlain, Lib.*
Hec Clouthier, Lib.
David M. Collenette, Lib.*
Joe Comuzzi, Lib.*
Sheila Copps, Lib.*
Roy Cullen, Lib.*
Paul DeVillers, Lib.*
Stan Dromisky, Lib.*
Arthur C. Eggleton, Lib.*
John Finlay, Lib.*
Joe Fontana, Lib.*
Roger Gallaway, Lib.*
John Godfrey, Lib.*
Bill Graham, Lib.*
Herb Gray, Lib.*
Ivan Grose, Lib.*
Albina Guarnieri, Lib.*
Mac Harb, Lib.*
Tony Ianno, Lib.*
Ovid L. Jackson, Lib.*
Jim Jones, P.C.
Joe Jordan, Lib.
Jim Karygiannis, Lib.*
Stan Keyes, Lib.*
Bob Kilger, Lib.*
Gar Knutson, Lib.*
Karen Kraft Sloan, Lib.*
Walt Lastewka, Lib.*
Derek Lee, Lib.*
Judi Longfield, Lib.
Steve Mahoney, Lib.
Gurbax Singh Malhi, Lib.*
John Maloney, Lib.*
John Manley, Lib.*
Sergio Marchi, Lib.*
Diane Marleau, Lib.*
Larry McCormick, Lib.*
John McKay, Lib.
Dan McTeague, Lib.*
Peter Milliken, Lib.*
Dennis J. Mills, Lib.*
Maria Minna, Lib.*
Andy Mitchell, Lib.*
Ian Murray, Lib.*
Lynn Myers, Lib.
Robert D. Nault, Lib.*
John Nunziata, Ind.*
Pat O'Brien, Lib.*
John O'Reilly, Lib.*
Gilbert Parent, Lib.*
Carolyn Parrish, Lib.*
Janko Peric, Lib.*
Jim Peterson, Lib.*
Beth Phinney, Lib.*
Jerry Pickard, Lib.*
Gary Pillitteri, Lib.*
David Pratt, Lib.
Carmen Provenzano, Lib.
Karen Redman, Lib.
Julian Reed, Lib.*
John Richardson, Lib.*
Allan Rock, Lib.*
Brent St. Denis, Lib.*
Benoît Serré, Lib.*
Alex Shepherd, Lib.*
Bob Speller, Lib.*
Paul Steckle, Lib.*
Christine Stewart, Lib.*
Jane Stewart, Lib.*
Paul Szabo, Lib.*
Andrew Telegdi, Lib.*
Paddy Torsney, Lib.*
Rose-Marie Ur, Lib.*
Tony Valeri, Lib.*
Lyle Vanclief, Lib.*
Joseph Volpe, Lib.
Tom Wappel, Lib.*
Susan Whelan, Lib.*
Bryon Wilfert, Lib.
Bob Wood, Lib.*

Prince Edward Island
Wayne Easter, Lib.*
Lawrence MacAulay, Lib.*
Joe McGuire, Lib.*
George Proud, Lib.*

Quebec
Hélène Alarie, B.Q.
Mark Assad, Lib.*
Gérard Asselin, B.Q.*
André Bachand, P.C.
Claude Bachand, B.Q.*
Eleni Bakopanos, Lib.*
Michel Bellehumeur, B.Q.*
Stéphane Bergeron, B.Q.*
Yvan Bernier, B.Q.*
Robert Bertrand, Lib.*
Bernard Bigras, B.Q.
Pierre Brien, B.Q.*
René Canuel, B.Q.*
Serge Cardin, B.Q.
Martin Cauchon, Lib.*
Yvon Charbonneau, Lib.
Jean Chrétien, Lib.*
Jean-Guy Chrétien, B.Q.*
Denis Coderre, Lib.
Paul Crête, B.Q.*
Madeleine Dalphond-Guiral, B.Q.*
Pierre de Savoye, B.Q.*
Maud Debien, B.Q.*
Odina Desrochers, B.Q.
Stéphane Dion, Lib.*
Nunzio Discepola, Lib.*
Claude Drouin, Lib.
Antoine Dubé, B.Q.*
Gilles Duceppe, B.Q.*
Maurice Dumas, B.Q.*
Sheila Finestone, Lib.*

Raymonde Folco, Lib.
Ghislain Fournier, B.Q.
Alfonso Gagliano, Lib.*
Christiane Gagnon, B.Q.*
Michel Gauthier, B.Q.*
Jocelyne Girard-Bujold, B.Q.
Maurice Godin, B.Q.*
Monique Guay, B.Q.*
Michel Guimond, B.Q.*
André Harvey, P.C.
Marlene Jennings, Lib.
Francine Lalonde, B.Q.*
René Laurin, B.Q.*
Raymond Lavigne, Lib.*
Ghislain Lebel, B.Q.*
Réjean Lefebvre, B.Q.*
Clifford Lincoln, Lib.*
Yvan Loubier, B.Q.*
Richard Marceau, B.Q.
Jean-Paul Marchand, B.Q.*
Paul Martin, Lib.*
Marcel Massé, Lib.*
Réal Ménard, B.Q.*
Paul Mercier, B.Q.*
Gilbert Normand, Lib.
Denis Paradis, Lib.*
Bernard Patry, Lib.*
Gilles-A. Perron, B.Q.
Pierre S. Pettigrew, Lib.*
Pauline Picard, B.Q.*
Louis Plamondon, B.Q.*
David Price, P.C.
Lucienne Robillard, Lib.*
Yves Rocheleau, B.Q.*
Jacques Saada, Lib.
Benoît Sauvageau, B.Q.*
Caroline St-Hilaire, B.Q.
Diane St-Jacques, P.C.
Guy St-Julien, Lib.
Yolande Thibeault, Lib.
Stéphan Tremblay, B.Q.*
Suzanne Tremblay, B.Q.*
Daniel Turp, B.Q.
Pierrette Venne, B.Q.*

Saskatchewan
Chris Axworthy, N.D.P.*
Roy Bailey, Ref.
Garry Breitkreuz, Ref.*
Ralph E. Goodale, Lib.*
Allan Kerpan, Ref.*
Derrek Konrad, Ref.
Rick Laliberte, N.D.P.
Lee Morrison, Ref.*
Lorne Nystrom, N.D.P.
Jim Pankiw, Ref.
Dick Proctor, N.D.P.
Gerry Ritz, Ref.
John Solomon, N.D.P.*
Maurice Vellacott, Ref.

Yukon Territory
Louise Hardy, N.D.P.

The Ministry of Canada*

Jean Chrétien—prime minister
Lawrence MacAulay—solicitor general of Canada
Don Boudria—leader of the government in the House of Commons
Lloyd Axworthy—minister of foreign affairs
Pierre Pettigrew—minister of human resources development
Arthur Eggleton—minister of national defence
Herb Dhaliwal—minister of national revenue
Lyle Vanclief—minister of agriculture and Agri-Food Canada
Alfonso Gagliano—minister of public works and government services;
    deputy leader of the government in the House of Commons
Jane Stewart—minister of Indian affairs and Northern development
David Anderson—minister of fisheries and oceans
Alasdair Graham—leader of the government in the Senate
Herb Gray—deputy prime minister
Sheila Copps—minister of Canadian heritage
Lucienne Robillard—minister of citizenship and immigration
John Manley—minister of industry
Allan Rock—minister of health
Paul Martin—minister of finance
David Michael Collenette—minister of transport
Marcel Massé—president of the Treasury Board;
    minister responsible for infrastructure
Stéphane Dion—president of the Queen's Privy Council for Canada;
    minister of intergovernmental affairs
Ralph Goodale—minister of natural resources and minister
    responsible for the Canadian Wheat Board
Anne McLellan—minister of justice; attorney general of Canada
Hedy Fry—secretary of state (multiculturalism/ status of women)
Gilbert Normand—secretary of state (agriculture and agri-food,
    fisheries and oceans)
Ethel Blondin-Andrew—secretary of state (children and youth)
Fred Mifflin—minister of veterans affairs; secretary of state
    (Atlantic Canada Opportunities Agency)
Christine Stewart—minister of the environment
David Kilgour—secretary of state (Latin America and Africa)
Raymond Chan—secretary of state (Asia-Pacific)
Ronald Duhamel—secretary of state (science, research, and
    development; Western economic diversification)
Jim Peterson—secretary of state (international financial institutions)
Claudette Bradshaw—minister of labour
Martin Cauchon—secretary of state (Economic Development
    Agency of Canada for the Regions of Quebec)
Andrew Mitchell—secretary of state (parks)
Sergio Marchi—minister for international trade
Diane Marleau—minister for international cooperation;
    minister responsible for la Francophonie

*As of Dec. 31, 1998.

Premiers of Canadian provinces

Province	Premier
Alberta	Ralph Klein
British Columbia	Glen Clark
Manitoba	Gary Filmon
New Brunswick	Camille Thériault
Newfoundland	Brian Vincent Tobin
Nova Scotia	Russell MacLellan
Ontario	Mike Harris
Prince Edward Island	Patrick George Binns
Quebec	Lucien Bouchard
Saskatchewan	Roy Romanow

Government leaders of territories

Northwest Territories	Jim Antoine
Yukon Territory	Piers MacDonald

Federal spending in Canada
Estimated budget for fiscal 1998-1999*

Department or agency	Millions of dollars†
Agriculture and agri-food	1,691
Canadian heritage	2,427
Citizenship and immigration	723
Environment	502
Finance	62,854
Fisheries and oceans	1,052
Foreign affairs and international trade	3,131
Governor general	12
Health	1,877
Human resources development	25,360
Indian affairs and northern development	4,426
Industry	3,582
Justice	818
National defence	9,383
National revenue	2,377
Natural resources	658
Parliament	299
Privy Council	165
Public works and government services	3,743
Solicitor general	2,588
Transport	1,130
Treasury board	1,554
Veterans affairs	1,964
Total	**132,316**

* April 1, 1998, to March 31, 1999.
† Canadian dollars; $1 = U.S. $0.65 as of Oct. 23, 1998.

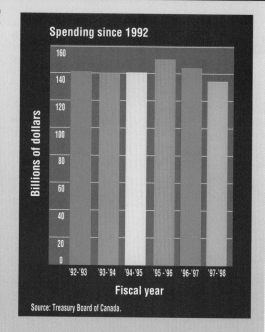

Spending since 1992

Source: Treasury Board of Canada.

both countries to disregard the treaty since 1993. Conservationists predicted a drastic decline in the 1998 salmon harvest, due in large part to warmer ocean temperatures caused by the El Nino current. The British Columbia catch was expected to decline from 20 million salmon in 1997 to 10 million in 1998.

On June 26, Canada and Washington state announced a one-year agreement to restrict the catch of chinook salmon bound for Washington's rivers to 50 percent of 1997 levels and the catch of coho salmon migrating to spawning grounds in British Columbia's Upper Thompson River to 22 percent of 1997 levels. On July 3, 1998, Canada and Washington agreed to limit their catch of sockeye salmon for one year. British Columbia criticized the agreements, calling them too restrictive and an unfair burden on provincial fishers. Disagreement over the extent to which coho salmon were endangered led to a breakdown in talks between Canada and Alaska on July 9.

As talks to renew the Pacific Salmon Treaty dragged on, Canada took action on its own. On June 19, Fisheries Minister David Anderson essentially banned all fishing for coho salmon in British Columbia and ordered fishermen of other types of salmon to release any coho they caught. Under the plan, the entire Pacific coast of British Columbia was divided into zones, with boundaries that

changed during the salmon-fishing season according to the movement of the fish. In some zones, commercial fishing was prohibited. In others, it was permitted during certain hours using certain types of nets and hooks. British Columbia angrily insisted that the federal government should not have imposed the ban until bargaining with the United States was completed.

Anderson also offered $400 million in grants to British Columbia fishermen to abandon fishing for the 1998 season. Over the summer, about 1,100 vessel owners, representing 37 percent of the fleet, tied up their boats in return for a lump-sum payment of $6,500. Later in the year, Anderson offered larger grants to try to persuade one-third of British Columbia's 3,000 fishing-boat owners to give up their licenses permanently.

There was little doubt that British Columbia's small, independent fishers would be more severely affected by the cutbacks than would larger, corporate-owned vessels. It was also clear, however, that the Canadian government was prepared to take steps to prevent the West Coast fishery from collapsing the way that the cod fishery of Newfoundland had in the late 1980's.

☐ David M. L. Farr

See also **Canada, Prime Minister of; Canadian provinces; Canadian territories; Montreal; Toronto.**

Canada, Prime Minister of. Jean

Chretien, leader of the governing Liberal Party, reached the midpoint of his second term as Canada's prime minister in 1998. Beyond striving to maintain Canadian unity throughout the year, Chretien's ruling Liberal Party government offered a thin legislative program and avoided a number of controversial issues, such as physician-assisted suicide. Yet the prime minister's approval rating remained high, at about 65 percent.

Chretien was criticized on several issues in 1998, including being out of touch with the concerns of the Canadian people. As the Canadian dollar tumbled in value during the summer, Chretien dismissed worries about Canadians' standard of living. Instead, the prime minister emphasized the increases in tourism and exports resulting from a cheaper dollar.

During 1998, Chretien strongly defended the responsibility of the federal government to lay down national standards for and retain management of public health care. Chretien resisted the demands of the provincial premiers for a share in the administration of medicare as well as a mechanism for resolving policy disputes. He stated he would never surrender the national government's authority to make social policy affecting all Canadians. □ David M. L. Farr

See also **Canada.**

Canadian provinces. Canada's 10 prov-

inces exercised tight controls over their budgets in 1998. A number of provincial governments, however, managed to allocate more funds for health care and education, areas that had been neglected during previous years of austerity.

Alberta. Although declining oil prices reduced government revenues, the Progressive Conservative Party (PCP) government of Premier Ralph Klein forecast a surplus of $165 million for fiscal year 1998-1999 (April 1, 1998, to March 31, 1999). (All amounts are in Canadian dollars.) The 1997-1998 surplus had been $2.6 billion. Surpluses in two consecutive years allowed Treasurer Stockwell Day to reduce personal income tax rates in the budget, which was presented in February. The cut, retroactive to January 1, reduced the income tax payable by Albertans by 1.5 percent, to 44 percent of the federal tax. Day also announced increased spending on education, social services, job training, and road construction. The grants represented a reversal of the government's previous insistence on paying off the provincial debt—one of the lowest in Canada—before boosting spending levels.

The Supreme Court of Canada ruled in April that Alberta's Individual Rights Protection Act of 1973 violated the Canadian Charter of Rights and Freedoms, Canada's bill of rights, by not protect-

ing people against discrimination because of sexual orientation. The rights act covers such factors as race, age, religion, physical and mental disability, and family status. The court's ruling overturned an Alberta Court of Appeal's decision in favor of a college in Edmonton, the capital, that in 1991 had fired an employee after learning he was gay. Despite some party opposition, Premier Klein accepted the ruling and did not invoke the so-called "notwithstanding clause" of the Canadian constitution that allows provincial governments to suspend certain rights.

In March 1998, widespread public protests forced Klein's government to abandon an attempt to use the notwithstanding clause to limit compensation for victims of a provincial sterilization program. Between 1928 and 1972, about 2,800 Albertans were sterilized without their permission under provincial legislation targeting people with severe mental handicaps. In June 1998, Alberta agreed, in an out-of-court settlement, to pay $48 million to 504 of the victims. Victims who believed the settlement was inadequate were permitted to take their case to court.

British Columbia. The Nisga'a people of British Columbia, after a struggle of more than 100 years, moved closer in 1998 to winning title to a small section of their ancestral lands in northwestern British Columbia. In a vote held in November, the Nisga'a overwhelmingly approved a treaty signed in July by representatives of the band and federal and provincial officials. The treaty, which also required approval by Canada's Parliament, was the first native land claim settled in British Columbia in the 1900's.

Under the terms of the treaty, the Nisga'a were to receive about 750 square miles (2,000 square kilometers) in the remote Nass River Valley, control of the area's forest and fishery resources, and $490 million in compensation. They were to gain the right to elect officials to regulate land use, public works, and public safety. In return, the Nisga'a were to give up their exemption from income and sales taxes. The treaty followed a unanimous decision by the Supreme Court of Canada in December 1997 recognizing the validity of oral histories and traditions in establishing native land claims.

The British Columbia economy, which enjoyed the strongest growth in Canada in the early and mid-1990's, stumbled in 1998. Resource industries such as lumber, which accounted for one-third of the province's exports, were hard hit by economic turmoil in Asia. Critics of the New Democratic Party (NDP) government of Premier Glen Clark also blamed high taxes and strict environmental regulations for the province's stagnant economy.

The provincial budget of $20.5 billion for fiscal year 1998-1999, introduced in March 1998, included a $95-million deficit. To stimulate economic growth, the budget included tax cuts for businesses and for wage earners at the top and bottom of the income scale, though the cuts were spread over three years.

Manitoba. Two of the oldest grain cooperatives on the Canadian prairies merged in July, in an effort to meet increasingly stiff competition in the grain-handling business. Manitoba Pool Elevators and the Alberta Wheat Pool, which had combined sales of $3.4 billion in 1997, formed Agricore. The new company became the second-largest of Canada's five grain-handlers, after the Saskatchewan Wheat Pool. The wheat pools were formed by farmers in the 1920's to obtain better prices for members.

A 1998 government report confirmed charges that efforts to protect Winnipeg, Manitoba's capital, during the disastrous Red River flood in the spring of 1997 worsened flooding in some communities south of the city. To safeguard the southwestern side of Winnipeg, workers had constructed a 25-mile- (40-kilometer-) long dike. The barrier created a lake that stretched 55 miles (90 kilometers) south to the U.S. border.

The province's fourth consecutive balanced budget, announced in March 1998 by Finance Minister Eric Stefanson, included increased funding for health, education, and programs to reduce child poverty. The budget included an income tax cut that brought the provincial income tax rate down 2 percent, to 50 percent of the federal tax.

New Brunswick, Canada's only legally bilingual province, gained a new premier in May when Camille Theriault was selected as the leader of the ruling Liberal Party. Theriault, New Brunswick's first Acadian (French-speaking) premier since 1970, was sworn into office on May 14, 1998. He succeeded Ray Frenette, who had served as interim premier since the retirement of Premier Frank McKenna in 1997.

The new premier inherited a potentially explosive dispute with New Brunswick's Indians over logging rights. In April 1998, the New Brunswick Court of Appeal overturned a lower court ruling that had upheld a 1726 treaty giving the Indians unlimited rights to harvest trees on the province's public lands. Responding to the new court ruling, the government ordered Indians who were logging on public lands without a permit to cease operations. When the Indians refused, the government seized trucks loaded with Indian-cut logs.

In June 1998, the Theriault government gave the Tobique First Nation, New Brunswick's second-largest native band, 5 percent of the total 1998 harvest from the province's public lands, worth about $14 million. Other native groups reached similar agreements with the government, averting a confrontation that would have imperiled the province's forestry industry, which produced about $2.8 billion in revenues in 1998.

Newfoundland, which had the highest unemployment rate in Canada, suffered new setbacks in 1998 when funds for the $1.9-billion Atlantic Groundfish Strategy (TAGS) program ran out. The TAGS program provided income supports for about 40,000 fishers and fishery plant workers who became unemployed after a 1992 federal ban on cod, haddock, and flatfish fishing. The ban, originally intended to last two years, had been imposed to allow regeneration of seriously depleted fishing stocks in the North Atlantic Ocean.

In June 1998, the Canadian government announced a $730-million aid package for the fishing industry in the Atlantic provinces (New Brunswick, Newfoundland, Nova Scotia, and Prince Edward Island) and Quebec. Newfoundland, the hardest hit by the collapse of cod fishing, was to receive about two-thirds of the money. The funds were to be used to support voluntary retirement plans for cod fishers, provide job training for out-of-work fishing crews, and assist fishing communities with high unemployment rates. The aid package also included lump-sum payments for people dependent on the TAGS program. Many fishers angrily denounced the new package as inadequate.

Although fishing crews were permitted to catch a limited amount of cod off the southern coast of Newfoundland during the summer of 1998, fishery experts found no evidence that cod stocks were reviving. In April, the federal Committee on the Status of Endangered Wildlife in Canada placed cod on Canada's endangered species list.

Nova Scotia's governing Liberal Party and the opposition New Democratic Party (NDP) each won 19 seats in legislative elections in March 1998. The election results were a stunning setback for the Liberals, who had taken 40 seats in the 1993 election. In that contest, the NDP had won only 3 seats. In the 1998 election, the Progressive Conservative Party (PCP) picked up the remaining 14 seats. Observers attributed the Liberals' losses to the austerity policies instituted to improve Nova Scotia's weak financial position. The NDP had capitalized on public discontent with spending cuts that resulted in hospital closings, increased taxes, and salary rollbacks for hundreds of public servants.

Vowing not to enter into a coalition with one of the other parties, Russell MacLellan, leader of the Liberal Party, continued as premier, though his government remained vulnerable to confidence votes. In June 1998, all but one PCP mem-

Families of the victims of Swissair Flight 111 visit Peggys Cove, Nova Scotia, near the site of the crash that claimed 229 lives. The Sept. 2, 1998, crash was the worst air disaster ever to take place in Canadian territory.

ber voted with the Liberals in approving a new provincial budget.

Ontario. Major changes to Ontario's $14-billion educational system went forward in 1998. Premier Mike Harris's PCP government took over educational financing from local school boards, introduced a new curriculum, and revised working conditions for teachers, increasing class time and capping class size. Nearly 8,000 teachers, many of them unhappy at the changes, took early retirement. Strikes delayed the opening of some schools in September as teachers' unions and school boards struggled to settle new contracts for the 1998-1999 school year.

In July 1998, a provincial court handed the Harris government a setback when it struck down a section of the 1997 education restructuring act that deprived Roman Catholic school boards of the right to collect taxes. Canada's 1867 constitution gave religious groups the right to raise public taxes for their schools. The court ruled in 1998 that taking away the self-financing of separate school boards would destroy their independence and change the character of the education they provided. The government announced it would appeal.

The Harris government continued to implement the personal income tax cuts that were the centerpiece of its policies when it won office in 1995. A final tax cut went into effect in July 1998, six months ahead of schedule. The change made the provincial tax rate 40.5 percent of the federal rate, compared with 58 percent in 1995.

The provincial budget, introduced in May 1998, projected a $4.2-billion deficit in fiscal year 1998-1999 and forecast the elimination of the deficit by 2000-2001. Opposition parties claimed the deficit would have been eliminated earlier if the government had not pressed forward with tax cuts. The budget included modest spending increases for health, in recognition of public dissatisfaction with the government's perceived haste to restructure the health-care system.

Public outcry over the poor living conditions of the three surviving Dionne quintuplets led the Harris government to award the sisters $4 million in 1998. The five sisters, born in 1934 to a poor farmer and his wife in northern Ontario, had been under the care of the provincial government from 1934 to 1943. Although a trust fund was established for them, the sisters never received any benefits from it. In March 1998, Harris presented the three sisters with the money and agreed to an investigation of possible misappropriations from the fund.

Prince Edward Island. The PCP government of Premier Pat Binns continued to move slowly toward balancing the provincial budget. The budget, presented in March, contained a deficit of $3.4 million on a spending plan of $782.2 million. The PCP's victory in legislative elections in 1996 had resulted in large part from public anger with austerity measures imposed by the previous NDP government. Health care was the largest single item in the budget, which contained no tax changes and few new spending proposals.

Quebec. A deadly ice storm—the worst natural disaster in modern Canadian history—struck southern Quebec, eastern Ontario, and parts of New Brunswick from Jan. 5 to Jan. 9, 1998. The storm, which left at least 25 people dead, dumped almost 4 inches (10 centimeters) of freezing rain on the region, depositing a thick layer of ice on electric transmission towers and lines. Some 3 million people lost power and heat when the weight of the ice snapped towers and power lines. The strong winds and subzero temperatures that followed the storm complicated efforts to restore power. As many as 75,000 people were still without electricity four weeks after the storm. Property owners in Quebec and Ontario filed approximately 700,000 claims, the largest number of claims for any Canadian natural disaster. The insurance payout exceeded $1.14 billion. Hydro-Quebec's costs for repairing its power transmission network were expected to reach $815 million.

An improving economy reduced Quebec's operating deficit for the second consecutive year, down to $1.1 billion for fiscal year 1998-1999 from $5.8 billion when the Parti Quebecois (PQ) took office in 1994. The budget contained no major tax or spending changes. The government promised large tax cuts when the deficit was eliminated, which the PQ forecast would occur in fiscal year 1999-2000.

Saskatchewan. The provincial government released its fifth consecutive balanced budget in March 1998. Finance Minister Eric Cline announced that Saskatchewan's income taxes would be reduced by 2 percent to 48 percent of the federal rate, effective July 1. The budget provided increases for child welfare, education, and highways as well as $500 million to reduce the $12.1-billion provincial debt. Revenues for the year were forecast at $5.15 billion, with a small surplus of $21 million.

The Saskatchewan Party, formed in August 1997 by eight disaffected Liberal and PCP members of the provincial legislature, elected Elwin Hermanson, a former Reform Party member, as its first leader in April 1998. In 1997, the right wing Saskatchewan Party had displaced the Liberals in the legislature to become the official opposition to the ruling NDP government.

□ David M. L. Farr

See also **Canada; Montreal; Toronto.**

Canadian territories. The Northwest Territories in 1998 prepared for the creation of the territory of Nunavut on April 1, 1999. Nunavut was to be formed from the eastern part of the Northwest Territories, an area largely populated by Inuit, a people native to the region. Nunavut was to cover an area twice the size of Ontario, Canada's second-largest province, and to have a population of about 25,000. During 1998, the Nunavut Implementation Committee and the Territories' government oversaw preparations for the election of a new legislature and the hiring and training of managers for Nunavut's administration.

The premier of the Northwest Territories, Don Morin, resigned on November 26, after an investigation disclosed he had failed to remove himself from government discussions about property he owned. A new premier, Jim Antoine, was chosen by consensus from the members of the legislature, which does not have political parties.

Canada's first diamond mine opened in October 1998 near Lac de Gras, northeast of Yellowknife, capital of the Northwest Territories. When fully operational in 2002, the Etaki mine was expected to account for about 6 percent of annual world diamond production, worth about $500 million (Canadian dollars). Because secondary processing accounts for 80 percent of revenues in the diamond industry, the territorial government insisted that the Etaki complex also include a sorting and valuation facility.

Yukon. The Yukon's largest employer, the Anvil Range mine at Faro, closed on Jan. 16, 1998, because of falling world prices for its zinc and lead output. Shut down in 1996 for more than one year, the mine had struggled after reopening in November 1997. Tourism emerged as a major element in the Yukon's economy in 1998, with a growing number of visitors coming to see the territory's spectacular landscape.

Resources transfer. In November, the Yukon took control of its gas and oil rights from the federal government, the first step in the transfer of responsibility for all land and resource management to the territory by 1999. Many Yukoners had believed that the fact that they were not allowed to manage their own resources relegated them to second-class status within Canada.

The Yukon's budget for fiscal year 1997-1998 was presented on February 23 by the government leader, Piers McDonald. With declining revenue caused by reduced transfer payments from the federal government, the budget planners forecast a deficit of $8.7 million. Total revenues for fiscal year 1997-1998 were estimated at $437 million, of which 65 percent came from the federal government.   □ David M.L. Farr

Cape Verde. See Africa.

Chemistry. The discovery of a new chemical compound that fights fever, pain, and inflammation like aspirin, but does not irritate the stomach or kidneys like aspirin, was announced by researchers at Vanderbilt University School of Medicine in Nashville, Tennessee, in May 1998. The compound, acetoxyphenyl alkylsulfide (APHS), was the latest and most powerful of a new class of experimental aspirin substitutes that are called COX-2 inhibitors.

Aspirin works by inactivating an enzyme called cyclooxygenase-2 (COX-2)—a protein substance that promotes inflammation, pain, and fever. Aspirin also inactivates a second enzyme, called cyclooxygenase-1 (COX-1), which is needed for normal tissue function. The blocking of this enzyme can lead to stomach ulcers and kidney problems.

The researchers found that APHS was 60 times more effective than aspirin at knocking out COX-2 in tests on laboratory animals. In the same tests, APHS was approximately six times less likely to inactivate COX-1.

Animal tests of APHS continued in 1998 at G. D. Searle & Company, a St. Louis, Missouri, drug firm. These tests were expected to eventually provide a clearer indication of how effective APHS would be in humans. Although researchers did not anticipate APHS becoming available to the public any time soon, they hoped that other COX-2 inhibitors—some of which were undergoing human tests in 1998—would begin entering the market in 1999. The beneficial effects of the other COX-2 inhibitors, however, did not seem to be as long-lasting as those of APHS.

Synthetic sea shells. A new chemical technique to imitate the intricate, curved shapes found in nature was announced in April 1998, when chemist Geoffrey A. Ozin displayed tiny spheres, knots, spirals, tops, and doughnuts that he and his co-workers at the University of Toronto had created. The objects, made from silicon dioxide, or silica (the compound that makes up quartz), resembled diatoms, microscopic aquatic organisms with exquisite, symmetrical patterns on their surfaces.

Most materials that are chemically fabricated have flat surfaces with regular, crystalline shapes, such as cubes or hexagons. Curved materials are extremely difficult to create through chemical reactions and usually have to be shaped by mechanical or physical methods. Ozin's team replicated nature's curved shapes by using chemical processes similar to those used to produce the liquid crystals found in digital watch displays.

The researchers first prepared a foamlike solution of various chemical compounds and silica. By altering the solution's salt concentration and acidity, the chemists caused the molecules in the foam's bubbles to arrange themselves into different shapes. These molecules acted as a type of scaffolding to which the silica molecules in the solution attached, forming the tiny, curved diatomlike objects.

Although these tiny "sea shells" may not be as impressive as larger ones found at the beach, they have more practical applications. Curved objects of the right shapes might be used to separate biological compounds in the preparation of medicines. These materials might also be used as the basis for chemical sensors, to clean up toxic wastes, and even to help make better batteries.

Beetle-baby chemists. Immature squash beetles defend themselves with a chemical-production method similar to one used by human researchers. This finding was reported by chemist Jerrold Meinwald and his colleagues at Cornell University in Ithaca, New York, in July 1998. The squash beetle (*Epilachna borealis*) pupa (the stage in the life of an insect between the larval and winged adult stage) produces hundreds of different chemical toxins based on three simple compounds.

Although the immobile, uncamouflaged beetle pupa appears to be defenseless against attack, hungry ants or wasps that approach it may be treated to a soup of noxious molecules. When predators come into contact with the chemicals that sit in drops on tiny hairs on the pupa, they frantically run away, trying to clean off the toxins as they flee.

Meinwald, using chemical analytical techniques, discovered that the compounds on the pupal hairs consist of an ever-changing mixture of several hundred—possibly even several thousand—discrete chemicals. He speculated that the chemical variety made it more difficult for predators to adapt to the toxic defense. Meinwald also found that some of the compounds contained unusually large chemical ring structures. While most other natural compounds, such as hormones and flavorings, have rings made of five or six atoms each, rings in some of the beetle compounds have more than 200 atoms each.

The squash beetle strategy resembles a method of research, called combinatorial chemistry, that was developed in the mid-1990's. Chemists employing this method use a small set of basic chemicals to randomly create a large number of variations of compounds known to be active. Each of the variations is then tested for a potential use as a drug, pesticide, or other practical application.

Chemists suggested that squash beetle chemical production could provide a new approach to the manufacture of insect repellents to which pests would have difficulty adapting themselves.

☐ Peter J. Andrews

Chess champion Garry Kasparov of Russia, whom most experts considered the best player in the world, formed a new world chess organization in April 1998. The World Chess Council (WCC) was expected to bring an end to the Professional Chess Association (PCA), which Kasparov founded in 1993. The PCA had not conducted a tournament since 1996. Kasparov, who had not defended his PCA title since 1995, was defeated in a nontitle match in 1997 by Deep Blue, a supercomputer developed by International Business Machines Corporation of Armonk, New York.

Alexei Shirov of Spain was scheduled to play Kasparov in a title match in October 1998, but the match was postponed after the WCC failed to secure sponsors for the event.

FIDE champion. Anatoly Karpov of Russia defeated Viswanathan Anand of India in January to retain the title of the other official world chess organization—World Chess Federation (FIDE). Karpov won $1.37 million in the match, which was held in Lausanne, Switzerland. FIDE cancelled plans to host a second world championship in late 1998, which would have forced Karpov to defend his title twice in the same year.

The 33rd Chess Olympiad, a biennial competition involving teams from more than 100 nations, was held from September 26 to October 13 in the Russian city of Elista. Russia won the gold medal; the United States took the silver; and Ukraine captured the bronze.

Tournaments. On August 9 in Kailua-Kona, Hawaii, Judit Polgar of Hungary became the first woman to win the U.S. Open Championship. Boris Gulko of Fairlawn, New Jersey, who had been tied with Polgar in the U.S. Open but lost on tie-break points, won the U.S. Masters Tournament in Honolulu, Hawaii, on July 29. On March 29 in Las Vegas, Nevada, Julian Hodgson of England won the National Open Chess Tournament. At a combined event held in Denver, Colorado, Nick de Firmian of Denmark won the U.S. Chess Championship on November 18. Irina Krush, 14, of New York City won the U.S. Chess Women's Championship on November 15.

Young champions. Ten-year-old Hikaru Nakamura, of White Plains, New York, became the youngest U.S. chess master in history in April 1998, according to a ranking from the U.S. Chess Federation. Igor Shliperman, 18, of Rego Park, New York, won the U.S. Junior Championship on July 20. Shelby School of Payson, Arizona, was named best team at both the U.S. Elementary School Championship in Peoria, Illinois, on April 26 and at the U.S. National Junior High Championship held in Phoenix on May 3. Masterman School of Philadelphia won the team championship at the 1998 National High School Championship in Los Angeles on May 10.   □ Al Lawrence

Chicago. Students in Chicago's public elementary schools made gains on standardized reading and mathematics tests in 1998—progress that Mayor Richard M. Daley called "wonderful, exciting news." School superintendent Paul Vallas expressed hope for more progress. He predicted that half of the school's students would perform at their appropriate grade level within a few years.

Not everyone interpreted the improved scores as a success. Critics claimed that the scores might have been higher because Chicago schools no longer allowed "social promotion"—advancing failing students to higher grades to keep them with their classmates. Consequently, grade-level appropriate scores on standardized tests may not reflect the expected age-level appropriate skills.

The Museum Campus—a new 57-acre (23-hectare) park linking the Adler Planetarium, the Field Museum of Natural History, and the John G. Shedd Aquarium—opened in May southeast of downtown Chicago. The project, which took 11 years to complete and rerouted sections of Lake Shore Drive away from Lake Michigan, allows people to walk between the three museums and between the campus and the city's downtown.

Development projects. In April, the city's Department of Planning and Development unveiled a plan for a 17-mile (27-kilometer) trail along the once heavily polluted Chicago River. The proposed trail was planned to connect the city's southwest side, downtown, and far northwest side.

In June, the Chicago Plan Commission approved a $600-million development project—including a 60-story apartment complex, movie theaters, and retail stores—planned for a downtown neighborhood between Michigan Avenue and the lakefront. Developers scaled back their original plans after area residents complained to city officials about the existing congestion in the area.

Beetle infestation. In July, city officials discovered that Asian longhorn beetles were infesting trees in the city's north side Ravenswood and Lincoln Park neighborhoods and nearby suburbs. The beetles lay eggs under bark, and their larvae tunnel into trees, eventually killing them. Hundreds of trees were scheduled to be cut and burned in an effort to keep the beetles from spreading into more of the metropolitan area.

Commonwealth Edison Company, which supplies Chicago's electricity, began shutting down its 25-year-old twin nuclear reactors at suburban Zion, Illinois, in January. Under pressure from lower-cost electricity producers and federal safety regulators, the company closed the plant 15 years ahead of schedule.

Archbishop Francis George of the Archdiocese of Chicago was made a cardinal of the Roman Catholic Church on February 21. His appointment by Pope John Paul II capped the archbishop's swift rise through the church's hierarchy. George was the sixth consecutive Chicago archbishop to be named to the 123-member College of Cardinals, the group of leaders responsible for selecting the next pope.

Sports. The Chicago Bulls won their sixth National Basketball Association championship in eight years by defeating the Utah Jazz on June 14. During the baseball season, Chicago Cubs right-fielder Sammy Sosa hit 66 home runs, surpassing the record of 61 home runs set by Roger Maris in 1961 and leading his team into the division play-offs for the first time in nine years. Sosa's achievement was surpassed by the St. Louis Cardinal's Mark McGwire, who hit 70 home runs during the 1998 season.

Deaths. Margaret Hillis, former director of the Chicago Symphony Chorus and one of the nation's foremost chorus masters, died on Feb. 4, 1998, at age 76. She founded the chorus in 1957 and served as director until 1994. During her tenure, Hillis won nine Grammy awards.

Beloved sports broadcaster Harry Caray died on Feb. 18, 1998, at age 83. During a career that spanned more than 50 years, he called games for the St. Louis Cardinals, Oakland Athletics, Chicago White Sox, and Chicago Cubs. "He was the voice of summer," wrote *Chicago Tribune* columnist Bob Verdi. Jack Brickhouse, another admired figure in sports broadcasting, died on Aug. 6, 1998, at age 82. From the 1940's to the 1980's, Brickhouse announced games for the Chicago Cubs and White Sox baseball teams and the Chicago Bears football team.

☐ Harold Henderson

See also **Baseball; Basketball; City; Deaths.**

Children's books. See **Literature for children.**

Chicago's Museum Campus—a new park linking the city's lakefront museums—opens in May 1998. The park, created by rerouting a section of Lake Shore Drive away from the lake, provides convenient access to the museums and lakefront from the city's downtown.

Chile. General Augusto Pinochet Ugarte, military dictator of Chile from 1973 to 1990, was arrested in London on Oct. 16, 1998. Pinochet's arrest and extradition had been sought by Spanish authorities, who charged him with human rights abuses. More than 3,000 dissidents were killed or "disappeared" in Chile during Pinochet's rule.

On November 25, the Law Lords, the highest British appeals court, determined that Pinochet was not immune from prosecution as a former head of state. On December 17, the Law Lords dismissed the ruling and scheduled a new hearing for January 1999, because one of the justices had not declared his affiliation with Amnesty International, a London-based human rights group.

On September 11, the 25th anniversary of Pinochet's military *coup* (takeover), Chilean filmmaker Patricio Guzman rereleased his 1978 documentary *The Battle of Chile,* which had exposed the Pinochet regime to international criticism. He also released *Chile: Obstinate Memory,* which is based on interviews of Chileans conducted in 1995.

In mid-1998, Chile cut $685 million from its national budget after being hit by a 35-percent drop in the price of copper and an estimated $500-million loss in copper sales to trading partners in Asia. Copper accounts for 42 percent of Chile's export earnings. ☐ Nathan A. Haverstock

See also **Latin America** (Facts in brief table).

China experienced severe flooding in the summer of 1998, when the Yangtze River and two other rivers swelled to record levels. The flooding resulted in the deaths of more than 3,000 people and destroyed 6 million houses. It forced the evacuation of 14 million people and affected the lives of 240 million people—nearly one-fifth of China's population. Chinese officials estimated that flood damage exceeded $20 billion.

Floodwaters wrecked crops and caused landslides that swallowed whole villages. To fight the floods, the army deployed more troops than on any occasion since 1949, when the Communist-led army won a civil war that resulted in the founding of the People's Republic of China.

According to officials, the Yangtze River, long known as China's "river of sorrow" for its devastating floods, had not flooded so severely since 1954, when 30,000 people died. In the summer of 1998, eight rain-fueled flood crests swept down the 3,900-mile (6,276-kilometer) long river, overwhelming large cities and villages in the central part of the country.

Flooding in the Songhau and Nen rivers was the worst on record in northeast China. Sandbags protected the Daqing area, which produced more than one-third of China's oil, but neighboring towns were devastated by flood water.

Environmental deterioration contributed to the unusually fierce flooding conditions in 1998, according to officials. Logging on upper reaches of the Yangtze caused erosion and an increased run-off of rain. The mud carried by the run-off filled the river's bed and reduced its capacity to hold water. Land once used as reservoirs for river overflow had been turned into crop land by farmers, and poorly maintained dikes and dams were unable to restrain racing waters, creating a situation ripe for disaster.

New prime minister. China's parliament, the National People's Congress (NPC), elected Zhu Rongji as prime minister on March 17. Zhu, who had guided China's economic policy through the 1990's, succeeded Li Peng, who had served out the maximum two five-year terms as prime minister allowed by the Chinese constitution. The NPC named Li as its new chairman.

Zhu, a 69-year-old electrical engineer and industrial planner, joined the Communist Party in 1949. In the 1950's, he was condemned by the Communists after he criticized party policy. The party banished Zhu to a work farm during the Cultural Revolution (1966–1976).

Zhu began his climb to power under Deng Xiaoping, China's paramount leader from 1980 until his death in 1997. Zhu's background in economics proved useful to Deng, who was determined to restructure China's economy. In 1988, Zhu became mayor of Shanghai, China's largest city.

In 1991, Deng selected Zhu as a deputy prime minister, a position in which he was given broad authority to rein in China's economy. Zhu enforced strict austerity measures and embarked on an unpopular policy of tightly limiting loans and curbing government spending. Economists lauded Zhu's efforts, which reduced inflation while maintaining a high and steady growth rate.

Leadership selected. In March 1998, the NPC formally reelected Jiang Zemin to a second five-year term as president of China and chairman of the Central Military Commission—the top ranking leadership position in China. The NPC confirmed 55-year-old Hu Jintao as vice president, the youngest person ever to hold the office. Political observers considered Hu, a hydroelectrical engineer who had been the head of the Communist Party in Tibet since 1989, a rising star in Chinese politics.

Economic reforms. In March 1998, Zhu called for sweeping economic reforms, vowing to make ailing state-owned industries solvent, overhaul the country's banking system, and cut government staff in half. He pledged to make these changes within three years.

Zhu announced a plan to reshape state-owned industries, most of which were grossly overstaffed and in debt. He proposed using

A man floats past a school after flood waters from the swollen Yangtze River inundated the central Hunan province in August. Flooding in 1998 resulted in the deaths of more than 3,000 people and caused an estimated $20 billion in damage.

mergers, staff cuts, bankruptcies, and improved management to transform the 79,000 state companies into globally competitive conglomerates.

In the banking plan, Zhu proposed creating a system modeled on the American federal reserve system, giving the central bank control over commercial banks. The new system would free banks from the political pressure that had forced them in the past to make bad loans to state companies.

Zhu vowed to cut 4 million government jobs, explaining that public money had been consumed by excess salaries and wasteful spending projects. He also promised to eliminate subsidized housing, a benefit popular with Chinese workers, many of whom earned less than $100 a month in 1998.

With China's economy weakened by the Asian economic crisis, the government indicated in July that it would delay reforms to state industries and housing subsidies. An official newspaper reported that rents would not increase in 1998. The government had expected the economy to grow by 8 percent, but a drop in consumer spending, billions of dollars in flood costs, and the widening financial crisis in Asia threatened this growth.

Crime and corruption. In March, 45 percent of the delegates at the NPC refused to support the report of the nation's chief prosecutor describing his achievements in combating crime and corruption. Delegates said the vote, which was the largest protest ever recorded in China's parliament, reflected a general attitude that the government had not been effective in fighting crime.

On July 31, Chen Xitong, a former mayor and Communist Party head of Beijing, the capital, was sentenced to 16 years in prison for embezzling state funds, taking bribes, and abusing power.

Chen was the most senior Chinese leader to be jailed since the Gang of Four, a radical group of Communists who were ousted from power in 1976.

War on smuggling. Jiang announced in July 1998 that his government would form a new anti-smuggling police force. According to Zhu, some $12 billion in foreign goods were smuggled into China annually, leading to massive losses of tax revenue and hindering the growth of industries. Zhu said the worst offenders were companies operated by the Communist Party, the police, and the People's Liberation Army (PLA).

On July 22, Jiang ordered the PLA, which includes the army, navy, and air force, to relinquish its sprawling multibillion-dollar commercial empire, claiming it was the only way to combat the epidemic of smuggling. He hoped that this transformation would make the army more professional, by turning its focus from money making back to military preparedness.

In 1998, the PLA ran an empire of more than 15,000 companies, ranging from farms and textile factories to hotels and international corporations, with an annual turnover of $15 billion. Without this income, the PLA would be forced to rely on its official budget, which was $11 billion in 1998. Jiang proposed other military reforms, including reducing the size of the army from 3 million to 2.5 million soldiers. On November 29, the Communist Party ordered its various units and government ministries to forfeit their business enterprises.

Clinton visit. United States President Bill Clinton visited China in June. The Chinese government, departing from its usual censorship, televised a debate between Jiang and Clinton and broadcast Clinton criticizing China's human rights record on two occasions. In a news conference at the end of his trip, Clinton called Jiang a visionary leader who could be the figure who leads China to democracy.

Human rights. The number of criminals executed in China dropped significantly in 1998 after the passage of the Criminal Procedure Code in 1997, according to a 1998 report by Amnesty International, a London-based human rights group. The report emphasized, however, that China continued to execute far more people than any other nation. The report estimated that there were 3,000 executions in 1997, down from 4,367 in 1996.

In October 1998, China signed an international covenant calling for freedom of speech and assembly. The government subsequently arrested people who forged a China Democratic Party out of a nationwide network of political activists.

Hong Kong. Voters turned out in record numbers in May 1998 to return to office pro-

democracy candidates ousted by China after Great Britain turned over its former colony in June 1997. More than 50 percent of registered voters in Hong Kong voted for the Legislative Council in 1998, shattering the previous voter turnout record of 39 percent in 1991.

Martin Lee, a prominent prodemocracy politician, and his Democratic Party candidates, won 13 of the 20 elective seats and received about half of the popular vote. The pro-Beijing Liberal Party won only 3 percent of the vote.

China disbanded Hong Kong's last freely elected Legislative Council on July 1, 1997, because the government in Beijing objected to changes made in the electoral laws by the former British governor. China substituted a Provisional Legislature composed of pro-Beijing politicians.

The British government said in 1998 that it was "broadly satisfied" with the way that China was governing Hong Kong. However, some observers questioned China's promise to adhere to Hong Kong's British system of law when local officials decided in March not to prosecute a politically well-connected newspaper publisher on corruption charges. Many residents feared that the use of Communist Party influence would erode their legal protections.   □ Henry S. Bradsher

See also **Asia** (Facts in brief table); **Economics** Special Report: **Asian Economic Crisis; Taiwan.**

City. The financial crises that afflicted Japan and Southeast Asia in 1998 triggered economic problems in many cities in Asia. The economic trouble resulted in a sharp cut in the cost of living in several of these cities. Rankings by the Corporate Resources Group (CRG), a business consultancy based in Geneva, Switzerland, revealed that Hong Kong replaced Tokyo as the most expensive city in which to live in 1998. Tokyo had been ranked as the most expensive city for several consecutive years. CRG found that 5 of the 10 most costly cities in 1998 were in China. In contrast, Seoul, South Korea, fell from the 7th to the 46th spot, and Singapore fell from the 8th to the 13th position. These cities were characteristic of many in Southeast Asia that experienced steep drops in their cost of living due to economic recession.

CRG annually ranks 150 cities throughout the world by comparing the city-by-city rents and costs of 145 types of goods and services. CRG gives each city a numerical rating compared with New York City, which is assigned a base-line rating of 100. Hong Kong's rating in 1998 was 157.4, meaning that its cost of living was approximately 57 percent higher than that of New York City. The nine most expensive cities after Hong Kong included Tokyo (154.3), Beijing (153.1), Moscow (151.3), Shanghai (144.9), Osaka, Japan (140.9), Guangzhou, China (122.8), St. Petersburg, Russia

50 largest cities in the United States

Rank	City	Population*
1.	New York, N.Y.	7,380,906
2.	Los Angeles, Calif.	3,553,638
3.	Chicago, Ill.	2,721,547
4.	Houston, Tex.	1,744,058
5.	Philadelphia, Pa.	1,478,002
6.	San Diego, Calif.	1,171,121
7.	Phoenix, Ariz.	1,159,014
8.	San Antonio, Tex.	1,067,816
9.	Dallas, Tex.	1,053,292
10.	Detroit, Mich.	1,000,272
11.	San Jose, Calif.	838,744
12.	Indianapolis, Ind.	746,737
13.	San Francisco, Calif.	735,315
14.	Jacksonville, Fla.	679,792
15.	Baltimore, Md.	675,401
16.	Columbus, Ohio	657,053
17.	El Paso, Tex.	599,865
18.	Memphis, Tenn.	596,725
19.	Milwaukee, Wis.	590,503
20.	Boston, Mass.	558,394
21.	Washington, D.C.	543,213
22.	Austin, Tex.	541,278
23.	Seattle, Wash.	524,704
24.	Nashville, Tenn.	511,263
25.	Cleveland, Ohio	498,246
26.	Denver, Colo.	497,840
27.	Portland, Ore.	480,824
28.	Fort Worth, Tex.	479,716
29.	New Orleans, La.	476,625
30.	Oklahoma City, Okla.	469,852
31.	Tucson, Ariz.	449,002
32.	Charlotte, N.C.	441,297
33.	Kansas City, Mo.	441,259
34.	Virginia Beach, Va.	430,385
35.	Honolulu, Hawaii	423,475
36.	Long Beach, Calif.	421,904
37.	Albuquerque, N. Mex.	419,681
38.	Atlanta, Ga.	401,907
39.	Fresno, Calif.	396,011
40.	Tulsa, Okla.	378,491
41.	Las Vegas, Nev.	376,906
42.	Sacramento, Calif.	376,243
43.	Oakland, Calif.	367,230
44.	Miami, Fla.	365,127
45.	Omaha, Nebr.	364,253
46.	Minneapolis, Minn.	358,785
47.	St. Louis, Mo.	351,565
48.	Pittsburgh, Pa.	350,363
49.	Cincinnati, Ohio	345,818
50.	Colorado Springs, Colo.	345,127

*1996 estimates (latest available).
Source: U.S. Bureau of the Census.

50 largest metropolitan areas in the United States

Rank	Metropolitan area	Population*
1.	Los Angeles-Long Beach, Calif.	9,127,751
2.	New York, N.Y.	8,643,437
3.	Chicago, Ill.	7,733,876
4.	Philadelphia, Pa.-N.J.	4,952,929
5.	Washington, D.C.-Md.-Va.-W.Va.	4,563,123
6.	Detroit, Mich.	4,318,145
7.	Houston, Tex.	3,791,921
8.	Atlanta, Ga.	3,541,230
9.	Boston-Worcester-Lawrence-Lowell-Brockton, Mass.	3,263,060
10.	Dallas, Tex.	3,047,983
11.	Riverside-San Bernadino, Calif.	3,015,783
12.	Minneapolis-St. Paul, Minn.-Wis.	2,765,116
13.	Phoenix-Mesa, Ariz.	2,746,703
14.	Nassau-Suffolk, N.Y.	2,660,285
15.	San Diego, Calif.	2,655,463
16.	Orange County, Calif.	2,636,888
17.	St. Louis, Mo.-Ill.	2,548,238
18.	Baltimore, Md.	2,474,118
19.	Pittsburgh, Pa.	2,379,411
20.	Seattle-Bellevue-Everett, Wash.	2,234,707
21.	Cleveland-Lorain-Elyria, Ohio	2,233,288
22.	Oakland, Calif.	2,209,629
23.	Tampa-St. Petersburg-Clearwater, Fla.	2,199,231
24.	Miami, Fla.	2,076,175
25.	Newark, N.J.	1,940,470
26.	Denver, Colo.	1,866,978
27.	Portland, Ore.-Vancouver, Wash.	1,758,937
28.	Kansas City, Mo.-Kan.	1,690,343
29.	San Francisco, Calif.	1,655,454
30.	San Jose, Calif.	1,599,604
31.	Cincinnati, Ohio-Ky.-Ind.	1,597,352
32.	Norfolk-Virginia Beach-Newport News, Va.	1,540,252
33.	Fort Worth-Arlington, Tex.	1,526,578
34.	Indianapolis, Ind.	1,492,297
35.	San Antonio, Tex.	1,490,111
36.	Sacramento, Calif.	1,482,208
37.	Milwaukee-Waukesha, Wis.	1,457,655
38.	Columbus, Ohio	1,447,646
39.	Fort Lauderdale, Fla.	1,438,228
40.	Orlando, Fla.	1,417,291
41.	Charlotte-Gastonia, N.C.-Rock Hill, S.C.	1,321,068
42.	New Orleans, La.	1,312,890
43.	Bergen-Passaic, N.J.	1,311,331
44.	Salt Lake City-Ogden, Ut.	1,217,842
45.	Las Vegas, Nev.-Ariz.	1,201,073
46.	Buffalo-Niagara Falls, N.Y.	1,175,240
47.	Hartford, Conn.	1,144,574
48.	Greensboro-Winston-Salem-High Point, N.C.	1,141,238
49.	Providence-Fall River-Warwick, R. I.	1,124,044
50.	Nashville, Tenn.	1,117,178

*1996 estimates (latest available).
Source: U.S. Bureau of the Census.

(115.1), Dalian, China (112.9), and London (111.6). The least expensive city surveyed by CRG was Harare, Zimbabwe (43.0), where the cost of living was only 43 percent that of the cost in New York City.

New York City remained the most expensive city in the United States in 1998 and ranked 21st in the world, up from 31st in 1997. Rounding out the list of the five most expensive U.S. cities were Miami, Florida (87.0), Los Angeles (86.1), Chicago (85.8), and Honolulu, Hawaii (85.7). San Francisco (85.1) ranked sixth. The most expensive Canadian city to live in was Toronto (74.3). In the rankings of European cities, Moscow, St. Petersburg, and London topped the list, followed by Geneva and Zurich , in Switzerland. Sydney (78.9) was the most expensive city in Australia.

In South America, cost of living was highest in Sao Paulo, Brazil (102.9), Buenos Aires, Argentina (100.1), and Rio de Janeiro, Brazil (95.6). Luanda, Angola (105.5), led Africa in expense, followed by Dar es Salaam, Tanzania (103.1), and Cairo, Egypt (98.1). The most expensive city in the Middle East was Tel Aviv, Israel (100.5). Amman, Jordan, and Abu Dhabi, United Arab Emirates (both at 96.0), ranked second and third in the region.

Urban sprawl and automobiles. A number of cities around the world in 1998 experimented with new ways to reduce traffic congestion, which was becoming more of a problem as urban sprawl increased. Urban sprawl is the development of a city over an increasingly large region. As residential properties spread into surrounding areas, people relied more on automobiles for transportation between home and places of employment, education, recreation, and other activities. Car ownership in 1998 continued to increase in developed countries—particularly in the United States, where there were almost 750 cars for every 1,000 people.

As traffic jams piled up in 1998, officials in many cities studied Singapore's innovative approaches to the problem. Since 1975, Singapore has adopted various measures to control traffic. In 1998, the Singapore government began requiring cars to be equipped with *transponders* (devices that can transmit or receive radar or other signals), into which a driver inserted a prepaid cash card. Electronic sensors on the highway detected the transponder and charged the driver a fee, which was greater during times of traffic congestion than at other times of the day. San Diego, California, in 1998 tackled traffic congestion on Interstate Highway 15, on which a driver had the choice of using free, congested lanes or entering toll lanes, whose costs varied depending on the volume of traffic.

In July, John Prescott, deputy prime minister of Great Britain, proposed a plan to let local gov-

50 largest urban centers in the world

Rank	Urban center*	Population
1.	Tokyo-Yokohama, Japan	29,344,000
2.	Mexico City, Mexico	26,176,000
3.	Sao Paulo, Brazil	23,715,000
4.	Seoul, South Korea	20,736,000
5.	New York City, U.S.	14,642,000
6.	Bombay, India	14,585,000
7.	Osaka-Kobe-Kyoto, Japan	14,195,000
8.	Calcutta, India	13,589,000
	Rio de Janeiro, Brazil	13,589,000
10.	Teheran, Iran	13,132,000
11.	Buenos Aires, Argentina	12,633,000
12.	Manila, Philippines	12,211,000
13.	Jakarta, Indonesia	12,100,000
14.	Cairo, Egypt	11,943,000
15.	Lagos, Nigeria	11,314,000
16.	Delhi, India	11,100,000
17.	Moscow, Russia	10,977,000
18.	Los Angeles, U.S.	10,593,000
19.	Karachi, Pakistan	10,454,000
20.	Paris, France	8,788,000
21.	London, U.K.	8,701,000
22.	Lima, Peru	8,646,000
23.	Istanbul, Turkey	8,341,000
24.	Taipei, Taiwan	8,076,000
25.	Bogota, Colombia	7,449,000
26.	Shanghai, China	7,399,000
27.	Essen, Germany	7,289,000
28.	Bangkok, Thailand	7,194,000
29.	Madras, India	7,033,000
30.	Chicago, U.S.	6,557,000
31.	Pusan, South Korea	6,294,000
32.	Bangalore, India	6,279,000
33.	Santiago, Chile	6,094,000
34.	Dhaka, Bangladesh	5,969,000
35.	Beijing, China	5,941,000
36.	Hong Kong, China	5,910,000
37.	Lahore, Pakistan	5,487,000
38.	Tianjin, China	5,192,000
39.	Nagoya, Japan	5,186,000
40.	Kinshasa, Congo	5,151,000
41.	Madrid, Spain	4,968,000
42.	Baghdad, Iraq	4,953,000
43.	Milan, Italy	4,821,000
44.	Belo Horizonte, Brazil	4,802,000
45.	St. Petersburg, Russia	4,721,000
46.	Barcelona, Spain	4,693,000
47.	Shenyang, China	4,591,000
48.	Ahmadabad, India	4,565,000
49.	Hyderabad, India	4,503,000
50.	Ho Chi Minh City, Vietnam	4,306,000

*An urban center is a continuous built-up area, similar to a metropolitan area, having a population density of at least 5,000 persons per square mile (1,900 per square kilometer).

Source: 1998 estimates based on data from the U.S. Bureau of the Census.

ernments charge fees for using roads and spend the revenue on improving public transportation. In October, officials in Paris sponsored a "leave your car at home" day to raise awareness of increasing traffic problems. Public transportation was free during the day, and cars were banned from the city's downtown area.

Other urban sprawl problems. Traffic congestion was one of several consequences of urban sprawl examined in a September report by the Sierra Club, an environmental group based in San Francisco. The report analyzed data from a number of institutions, including the U.S. Census Bureau, U.S. Department of Transportation, and American Farmland Trust, a conservation group based in Washington, D.C. The negative consequences of urban sprawl cited by the report included long commutes to work due to traffic congestion; loss of farms, forests, and other green spaces because of urban development; increased flooding from loss of water-absorbing wetlands; and higher taxes to support schools, roads, and water and sewer services. The report also noted that sprawl intensifies the flight of the middle class to the suburbs, which concentrates poverty in dense urban areas.

According to the report, the 10 large U.S. cities (populations of more than 1 million) in which the threats of urban sprawl were greatest in 1998 were—in consecutive order—Atlanta, Georgia; St. Louis, Missouri; Washington, D.C.; Cinncinnati, Ohio; Kansas City, Missouri; Denver, Colorado; Seattle; Minneapolis-St. Paul, Minnesota; Ft. Lauderdale, Florida; and Chicago. The five most threatened medium-sized U.S. cities (populations between 500,000 and 1 million) were Orlando, Florida; Austin, Texas; Las Vegas, Nevada; West Palm Beach, Florida; and Akron, Ohio. Small cities in which urban sprawl was a growing problem included McAllen, Texas; Raleigh, North Carolina; Pensacola, Florida; Daytona Beach, Florida; and Little Rock, Arkansas.

United States city economies. The National League of Cities, a Washington, D.C.-based organization that seeks to improve the quality of life in U.S. cities, reported that 1998 was the fifth consecutive year in which most U.S. cities showed signs of improving fiscal health. Seventy percent of the 314 city governments surveyed reported they were better able to meet their financial needs in 1998 than in 1997. In addition, 62 percent of the municipalities responded that they expected to be even better off in 1999.

Despite the generally bright outlook, many city officials were concerned that the rate of increase in city revenues was well below that of state and federal revenues. Between 1988 and 1997, state revenues grew by 67 percent and federal revenues were up by 80 percent. During the same period, municipal revenue growth increased by only 46 percent. Many officials blamed the disparity on stagnant property taxes.

Berlin. New office towers, government buildings, and hotels continued to spring up in Berlin, Germany, in 1998 in preparation for the transfer of the seat of the national government from Bonn in 1999. Despite the construction, however, Berlin's economy shrank by 0.6 percent in the first half of 1998, and city officials expected the economic slowdown to continue through 1999. Officials were also disappointed that few businesses had relocated to Berlin as of 1998.

What makes greatness? *Cities in Civilization,* a 1,000-page study of the history of cities by Sir Peter Hall, a professor of urban planning at University College in London, was published in 1998. The study, the result of 15 years of research by Hall, sought to answer the question, "What makes a particular city, at a particular time, suddenly become immensely creative, exceptionally innovative?" Hall examined 21 cities—from ancient Athens and Rome to modern London and Los Angeles—in search of an answer. Hall concluded there was no simple formula for urban greatness. He suggested instead that culture, economics, and technology create a complex mixture that makes cities thrive.   □ Robert Messenger

Civil rights. See **Human rights.**

Classical music. In June 1998, delegates meeting in St. Paul, Minnesota, at the annual conference of the American Symphony Orchestra League, an association of 350 amateur and professional orchestral groups, challenged the popular notion that classical music is dying. They argued that although classical music faces a number of challenges, including smaller audiences and declining financial support, these challenges can be overcome. Polly Kahn, education director for the New York Philharmonic, said that the Philharmonic was expanding its efforts to reach young inner city audiences to compensate for the fact that most music programs in New York City's public schools have been pared down or eliminated. She noted that over the past four years, the orchestra's outreach activities had tripled, and more than one-third of its players now participate regularly in community outreach programs.

Reaching out to kids. The American Symphony Orchestra League launched an Internet site in 1998 to invite children into the world of serious music. The Web site (www.playmusic.org) includes interactive games in which children can learn about orchestras and musical instruments. The league also began to air a series of public service announcements on television in 1998. The first announcement, airing in September, intercut scenes of children playing sports with scenes of

Conductor Zubin Mehta and the cast of Puccini's opera *Turandot* acknowledge the audience's applause at the opera's first performance in China in September 1998. Puccini's opera about a Chinese princess was staged in Beijing's Forbidden City, once the palace compound of Chinese emperors.

young orchestra musicians to show that both sports and music are fun and rewarding pastimes involving teamwork and practice.

Turandot plays in China. *Turandot,* the final opera written by the Italian composer Giacomo Puccini (1858-1924), was performed in September 1998 in Beijing, China, in an elaborate new production staged by Chinese film director Zhang Yimou. The production cost $15 million and involved more than 350 singers, musicians, and support staff from Italy's Maggio Musicale Fiorentino, in addition to hundreds of Chinese extras. Zubin Mehta conducted the work. The opera was performed in the courtyard of a 500-year-old temple in the Forbidden City, an area of Beijing where China's emperors formerly lived.

Although *Turandot,* about a Chinese princess and the man who wins her love, is set in a fairy-tale China, Communist officials had long forbidden it to be performed. They considered the opera to be an example of decadent Western art. On opening night, some 4,000 spectators paid as much as $1,500 each for seats to the performance, which was recorded for worldwide television, radio, and videotape release.

New operas and vocal music. The most heavily promoted operatic premiere in 1998 was *A Streetcar Named Desire,* presented by the San Francisco Opera in September. This opera, the first by the American composer and conductor Andre Previn, has a libretto by Philip Littell that is based on the classic drama by the American playwright Tennessee Williams. In April, the Minnesota Opera presented the first fully orchestrated staging in North America of *Transatlantic,* a satire written in 1930 by American composer George Antheil about the buying and selling of the United States presidency. *Monsters of Grace,* a "multimedia" opera composed by Philip Glass in collaboration with director Robert Wilson, premiered in April in Los Angeles. The opera includes a 3-D (three-dimensional) video that requires the audience to wear special glasses to see the special effects. *Chaos,* Michael Gordon's "science-fiction opera," which includes rock, jazz, and classical elements, had its first performance in October 1998 at the Kitchen Center in New York City.

An unprecedented number of new operas by American women composers appeared in 1998. *Patience and Sarah,* by composer Paula M. Kimper and librettist Wende Persons, premiered in July at New York City's Lincoln Center Festival. The opera, based on a 1972 cult novel by Isabel Miller, depicts a romance between two Puritan women in the early 1800's. In August 1998, Deborah Drattell attended the premiere of her music drama, *Lilith,* presented by the Glimmerglass Opera in Cooperstown, New York. The drama is about a spiritual battle between Eve and Lilith, Adam's first wife according to Jewish mystical literature. Libby Larsen's *Eric Hermannson's Soul,* with a libretto by Chas Rader-Shieber based on a short story by the American author Willa Cather, was produced by Opera Omaha in November.

In January, *Evidence of Things Not Seen,* a cycle of 36 songs featuring singers accompanied by piano, was heard for the first time at the New York Festival of Song. The 95-minute song cycle, by Ned Rorem, widely considered to be America's greatest living composer of art songs, includes text by 24 different authors.

New orchestral and instrumental music. In October, the Cleveland Orchestra under Christoph von Dohnanyi presented the world premiere of the *Emerson Concerto for Piano and Orchestra,* a "reconstruction" of works by the American composer Charles Ives (1874–1954). Ives scholar David G. Porter compiled the concerto using material taken from various Ives keyboard pieces. Alan Feinberg was the piano soloist. The British composer Sir Harrison Birtwistle's latest symphonic creation, *Exody (23:59:59),* was premiered in February 1998 by the Chicago Symphony Orchestra under conductor Daniel Barenboim. The subtitle of the work, which is concerned with time, refers to the final second before midnight.

The Nixon Tapes, John Adams's 51-minute concert suite drawn from his 1987 opera *Nixon in China,* had its first performance in July at the Aspen (Colorado) Music Festival. The performance featured baritone James Maddalena as President Richard Nixon and tenor John Duykers as Communist Party chairman Mao Zedong. In January 1998, Hugh Wolff conducted the St. Paul (Minnesota) Chamber Orchestra in the premiere of the Chinese-born composer Bright Sheng's *Postcards.* The work is based on Chinese folk music. In May, Kurt Masur led the New York Philharmonic in the world premiere of the American composer David Del Tredici's *The Spider and the Fly,* a cantata for soprano, baritone, and orchestra.

Masur takes London position. Kurt Masur announced in November that he had accepted a five-year appointment as principal conductor of the London Philharmonic Orchestra. Masur was scheduled to begin the assignment in 2000. He also planned to continue his conducting duties with the New York Philharmonic until 2002.

Notable deaths. Alfred Schnittke, one of the former Soviet Union's most prolific composers, died in August at age 63. Composer Sir Michael Tippett, a leading figure in British music, died in January at age 93. Renowned German-born conductor Klaus Tennstedt died in January at age 71.

☐ John von Rhein

See also **Popular music.**

Clinton, Bill. See United States, President of the.

Clothing. See Fashion.

Coal. See Energy supply.

Grammy Award winners in 1998

Classical Album, Premieres—*Cello Concertos (Works of Danielpour, Kirchner, Rouse);* Yo-Yo Ma, cello; Philadelphia Orchestra, David Zinman, conductor.

Orchestral Performance, *Berlioz: Symphonie Fantastique;* Cleveland Orchestra and Chorus, Pierre Boulez, conductor.

Opera Recording, *Wagner: Die Meistersinger von Nurnberg;* Chicago Symphony Orchestra and Chorus, Sir Georg Solti, conductor.

Choral Performance, *Adams: Harmonium/Rachmaninoff: The Bells;* Atlanta Symphony Orchestra, Robert Shaw, conductor.

Classical Performance, Instrumental Solo with Orchestra, *Premieres—Cello Concertos (Works of Danielpour, Kirchner, Rouse);* Yo-Yo Ma, cello; Philadelphia Orchestra, David Zinman, conductor.

Classical Performance, Instrumental Solo without Orchestra, *Bach: Suites for Solo Cello, Nos. 1-6;* Janos Starker, cello.

Chamber Music Performance, *Beethoven: The String Quartets;* Emerson String Quartet.

Small Ensemble Performance, *Hindemith: Kammermusik No. 1;* Berlin Philharmonic members, Claudio Abbado, conductor.

Classical Vocal Performance, *An Italian Songbook;* Cecilia Bartoli, mezzo-soprano; James Levine, piano.

Classical Contemporary Composition, *Adams: El Dorado;* John Adams.

Colombia. On Aug. 7, 1998, Andres Pastrana Arango, of the Conservative Party, was sworn in as president of Colombia for a four-year term. In the week leading up to Pastrana's heavily guarded inauguration, about 200,000 leftist rebels carried out daring and often well-coordinated attacks in 17 of Colombia's 32 provinces.

The wave of violence claimed the lives of 143 Colombian soldiers and police officers and an unknown number of rebels and civilians. One attack by the Revolutionary Armed Forces of Colombia (FARC) destroyed a United States-supported counternarcotics base in the southern city of Miraflores.

Peace initiatives. The administration of outgoing President Ernesto Samper failed to make progress in reaching peace with rebel forces before Samper left office. The crisis was dramatically demonstrated on March 2, when the Colombian Army suffered one of its worst defeats since civil strife began in the mid-1960's. FARC rebels ambushed an elite 150-member army battalion in the jungles of southern Caqueta, killing 70 men and taking 27 prisoners.

Amid continued bloodshed, most Colombians welcomed the idea of peace talks between the government and rebel leaders. During the presidential campaign, citizens took to the streets by the hundreds of thousands—waving white handkerchiefs, napkins, even sheets—demanding an end to civil strife.

Pastrana immersed himself in peace efforts even before taking office. On July 9, 1998, he met with FARC leaders and promised to demilitarize five municipalities in south-central Colombia as a condition for launching peace talks. On November 1, shortly before Colombian troops were to withdraw, 800 FARC rebels seized the southern city of Mitu near the Brazilian border. An estimated 150 soldiers and policemen and an unknown number of rebels were killed in the battle.

In August, the National Council on Peace, a nongovernment organization of civilian leaders in Colombia, met in Mainz, Germany, with representatives of another rebel force, the National Liberation Army (ELN). In return for unspecified concessions, the ELN agreed to future talks on suspending its campaign against the Cano Limon-Covenas pipeline. The ELN had reportedly bombed this economically vital pipeline 532 times since it opened in 1986.   □ Nathan A. Haverstock

See also **Latin America** (Facts in brief table); **People in the news** (Pastrana, Andres).

Colorado. See State government.

Common Market. See Europe.

Commonwealth of Independent States. See Armenia; Azerbaijan; Belarus; Georgia; Kazakhstan; Russia; Tajikistan; Ukraine; Uzbekistan.

Comoros. See Africa.

In August 1998, Apple Computer, Inc., debuted the iMac, an easy-to-use personal computer that incorporated the central processing unit, monitor, and modem in a single, futuristically designed unit. The iMac was intended mainly for Internet use and did not come equipped with a floppy-disk drive.

Computers. On May 18, 1998, the U.S. Department of Justice and 20 individual states filed suit in federal court against Microsoft Corporation of Redmond, Washington. The suit charged Microsoft, developer of the immensely popular Windows *operating system* (the master control program that coordinates the operations of a computer), with engaging in competitive practices that violated federal antitrust laws. Justice Department attorneys accused Microsoft of forcing computer makers who wished to install Windows on their computers to also install Microsoft's Internet Explorer *Web browser* (a program that enables computers to access the World Wide Web). The Justice Department argued that such tactics helped Internet Explorer take a large share of the Web browser market away from Netscape Communications Corporation of Mountain View, California. Netscape's Navigator browser had dominated the market until 1996. Microsoft denied the charges and contested them in a series of legal actions.

Windows 98, a new version of the Windows operating system for personal computers, went on sale in June 1998. An estimated 1 million units were sold during its first month on the market. In 1998, various versions of Windows were in use on approximately 90 percent of all personal computers worldwide. Windows 98 featured an interface that closely integrated a Web browser with the operating system. However, some industry experts regarded Windows 98 as merely a thinly disguised update of its predecessor, Windows 95.

A new breed of Apple. In 1998, Apple Computer, Inc., of Cupertino, California, continued to regain the momentum it had lost in recent years. In August, Apple introduced the iMac, a new personal computer aimed at the emerging market for powerful but inexpensive machines. Apple built state-of-the-art technology into the iMac, yet sold it for under $1,300. Like the original Macintosh computer, the product that revolutionized personal computing in 1984, the iMac was an all-in-one computer, with the monitor and other components built into one case.

Y2K problem. In June 1998, a report by a U.S. House of Representatives subcommittee gave the 24 largest federal agencies a failing grade in their efforts to solve the computer glitch known as the Year 2000 (Y2K) problem. Many older computers used in government were originally programmed to read only the last two digits of a year. As a result, these computers might misread the year 2000 as 1900 and not function properly. The report said that the agencies must speed up their efforts to make critical computer systems Y2K compliant by Jan. 1, 2000. ☐ Michael Woods

See also **Internet**.

Congo (Kinshasa) in 1998 suffered through a second civil war in less than three years. The fighting dashed the promises of peace and eventual prosperity in the former Zaire raised by the overthrow in May 1997 of long-time dictator Mobutu Sese Seko. The new conflict again drew in a number of Congo's neighbors, some of whom found themselves fighting against former allies.

Rebel attacks. The uprisings began in early August 1998 in the Kivu provinces of eastern Congo. As in 1996, the rebellion was launched by members of the Congolese Tutsi community in response to persecution from government-controlled Hutu forces. Within weeks, the Tutsi-dominated governments of Rwanda and Uganda, which had helped Congo's current president, Laurent Kabila, seize power from Mobutu, sent troops to support the rebels. The two countries turned against Kabila in 1998 because Kabila had purged Tutsis from his government and had failed to stop attacks on Rwanda by Congo-based Hutu militants. The governments of Angola, Zimbabwe, and Namibia supported Kabila in the conflict.

In southwest Congo, the embattled Kabila faced another revolt led by Bizima Karaha, his former foreign minister. By late August, rebel groups had thrown a military *cordon* (circle of

Tutsi rebels in eastern Congo launch an uprising in August 1998 against Congo President Laurent Kabila. The Tutsi-dominated Rwandan government backed the rebellion after Kabila failed to end attacks on Rwanda by Congo-based Hutu militants.

soldiers) around Kinshasa, the capital, causing more than 1,000 foreign nationals to flee the country. The forces of Angola, Namibia, and Zimbabwe kept Kinshasa from falling into rebel hands.

Karaha and other opposition forces claimed that Kabila was corrupt, had fostered ethnic hatred, failed to revive the economy, and shut them out of the political process by banning political parties. On March 19, United States Secretary of State Madeleine K. Albright delivered a strongly worded warning to Kabila, urging him to democratize his country or risk losing U.S. support.

Diplomatic initiatives. As the civil war gathered momentum, President Nelson R. Mandela of South Africa convened a meeting on August 23 to negotiate a cease fire. It was the first of many failed attempts. The first peace talks to include a rebel delegation, held in early November in Zimbabwe, collapsed when Kabila refused to attend.

On November 6, Mandela persuaded Rwanda, which had publicly denied involvement in the Congolese conflict, to admit its support of the rebels. However, a diplomatic solution appeared increasingly remote, and rebel leaders vowed to fight on unless an overall political settlement was reached with Kabila directly.

☐ Simon Baynham
See also **Africa** (Facts in brief table); **Rwanda.**

Congress of the United States.

On Dec. 19, 1998, the U.S. House of Representatives voted 228 to 206 to impeach President Bill Clinton on one charge of perjury before a federal grand jury. The House also voted 221 to 212 to impeach the president on one charge of obstruction of justice. At issue in the impeachment proceedings against President Clinton was whether he lied under oath or obstructed justice in trying to conceal his relationship with Monica Lewinsky, a former White House intern.

It was only the second time the House of Representatives conducted a presidential impeachment vote in its 209-year history. (In 1868, the House impeached President Andrew Johnson, who was eventually acquitted in a trial conducted by the U.S. Senate.)

Proceedings leading to impeachment. The president admitted on August 17 that he had misled his family and the nation about the nature of his relationship with Lewinsky. The president's admission on live television drew widespread condemnation from many politicians, mainly Republicans, who demanded his resignation.

The charges of perjury, obstruction of justice, and abuse of power were made against the president by Independent Counsel Kenneth Starr in a 445-page report that was delivered to the House of Representatives in September. The report was the product of Starr's four-year, $40-million investigation into the political, business, and personal lives of President Clinton and First Lady Hillary Rodham Clinton. Starr's report charged the president with 11 impeachable offenses, all involving either perjury or obstruction of justice. The report contained explicit details of alleged encounters between Clinton and Lewinsky. Both Starr's report and a four-hour videotape of Clinton's unprecedented grand jury testimony were made available to the public.

Several leading Democrats in Congress denounced the president's conduct, but only a few members of the Democratic Party supported calls for removing President Clinton from office. Many congressional Republicans insisted that lying under oath to a grand jury, as Starr had alleged in his report, was enough to justify impeachment.

On October 8, the House voted 258 to 176 to authorize the House Judiciary Committee to launch an impeachment inquiry into charges that President Clinton lied under oath and tampered with witnesses to conceal the inappropriate relationship. Thirty-one Democrats joined 227 House Republicans in the vote.

The Judiciary Committee opened hearings on November 19. Among those who testified was Kenneth Starr, who was applauded by Republican members of the committee and criticized by Democratic members.

On December 11 and 12, all 16 Democrats on the Judiciary Committee voted against sending articles of impeachment to the House of Representatives. All 23 Republicans (with the exception of one member on one ballot) voted to recommend impeachment.

Elections. Democrats gained five seats in the House and avoided major losses in the Senate in the November 3 election. With the economy in good shape, most incumbents from both political parties in House and Senate races were returned to office. However, the Democratic victories in the House represented the first time since 1934 that the party of a sitting president had gained seats in a midterm election. Political experts suggested that the unusual election outcome may have been due to the public's dissatisfaction with the impeachment proceedings against the president. According to opinion polls, the majority of the public approved of Clinton's performance as president and opposed the impeachment, which was generally regarded as highly partisan.

Republicans retained control of the House and Senate in the 106th Congress, which convened in January 1999. Democratic gains, however, cut the Republican majority in the House to 223 seats against the Democrats' 211 seats, with one independent who usually voted with the Democrats.

Members of the United States Senate

The Senate of the first session of the 106th Congress consisted of 45 Democrats and 55 Republicans when it convened on Jan. 6, 1999. The first date in each listing shows when the senator's term began. The second date in each listing shows when the senator's term expires.

State	Term	State	Term	State	Term
Alabama		**Louisiana**		**Ohio**	
Richard C. Shelby, R.	1987-2005	John B. Breaux, D.	1987-2005	Mike DeWine, R.	1995-2001
Jeff Sessions, R.	1997-2003	Mary L. Landrieu, D.	1997-2003	George V. Voinovich, R.	1999-2005
Alaska		**Maine**		**Oklahoma**	
Theodore F. Stevens, R.	1968-2003	Olympia Snowe, R.	1995-2001	Don Nickles, R.	1981-2005
Frank H. Murkowski, R.	1981-2005	Susan M. Collins, R.	1997-2003	James M. Inhofe, R.	1994-2003
Arizona		**Maryland**		**Oregon**	
John McCain III, R.	1987-2005	Paul S. Sarbanes, D.	1977-2001	Ron Wyden, D.	1996-2005
Jon Kyl, R.	1995-2001	Barbara A. Mikulski, D.	1987-2005	Gordon Smith, R.	1997-2003
Arkansas		**Massachusetts**		**Pennsylvania**	
Tim Hutchinson, R.	1997-2003	Edward M. Kennedy, D.	1962-2001	Arlen Specter, R.	1981-2005
Blanche Lambert Lincoln, D.	1999-2005	John F. Kerry, D.	1985-2003	Rick Santorum, R.	1995-2001
California		**Michigan**		**Rhode Island**	
Dianne Feinstein, D.	1992-2001	Carl Levin, D.	1979-2003	John H. Chafee, R.	1976-2001
Barbara Boxer, D.	1993-2005	Spencer Abraham, R.	1995-2001	Jack Reed, D.	1997-2003
Colorado		**Minnesota**		**South Carolina**	
Ben N. Campbell, R.	1993-2005	Paul D. Wellstone, D.	1991-2003	Strom Thurmond, R.	1955-2003
Wayne Allard, R.	1997-2003	Rod Grams, R.	1995-2001	Ernest F. Hollings, D.	1966-2005
Connecticut		**Mississippi**		**South Dakota**	
Christopher J. Dodd, D.	1981-2005	Thad Cochran, R.	1978-2003	Thomas A. Daschle, D.	1987-2005
Joseph I. Lieberman, D.	1989-2001	Trent Lott, R.	1989-2001	Tim Johnson, D.	1997-2003
Delaware		**Missouri**		**Tennessee**	
William V. Roth, Jr., R.	1971-2001	Christopher S. (Kit) Bond, R.	1987-2005	Fred Thompson, R.	1994-2003
Joseph R. Biden, Jr., D.	1973-2003	John Ashcroft, R.	1995-2001	Bill Frist, R.	1995-2001
Florida		**Montana**		**Texas**	
Bob Graham, D.	1987-2005	Max Baucus, D.	1978-2003	Phil Gramm, R.	1985-2003
Connie Mack III, R.	1989-2001	Conrad Burns, R.	1989-2001	Kay Bailey Hutchison, R.	1993-2001
Georgia		**Nebraska**		**Utah**	
Paul Coverdell, R.	1993-2005	J. Robert Kerrey, D.	1989-2001	Orrin G. Hatch, R.	1977-2001
Max Cleland, D.	1997-2003	Chuck Hagel, R.	1997-2003	Robert F. Bennett, R.	1993-2005
Hawaii		**Nevada**		**Vermont**	
Daniel K. Inouye, D.	1963-2005	Harry M. Reid, D.	1987-2005	Patrick J. Leahy, D.	1975-2005
Daniel K. Akaka, D.	1990-2001	Richard H. Bryan, D.	1989-2001	James M. Jeffords, R.	1989-2001
Idaho		**New Hampshire**		**Virginia**	
Larry E. Craig, R.	1991-2003	Robert C. Smith, R.	1990-2003	John W. Warner, R.	1979-2003
Mike Crapo, R.	1999-2005	Judd Gregg, R.	1993-2005	Charles S. Robb, D.	1989-2001
Illinois		**New Jersey**		**Washington**	
Richard J. Durbin, D.	1997-2003	Frank R. Lautenberg, D.	1982-2001	Slade Gorton, R.	1989-2001
Peter Fitzgerald, R.	1999-2005	Robert G. Torricelli, D.	1997-2003	Patty Murray, D.	1993-2005
Indiana		**New Mexico**		**West Virginia**	
Richard G. Lugar, R.	1977-2001	Pete V. Domenici, R.	1973-2003	Robert C. Byrd, D.	1959-2001
Evan Bayh, D.	1999-2005	Jeff Bingaman, D.	1983-2001	John D. Rockefeller IV, D.	1985-2003
Iowa		**New York**		**Wisconsin**	
Charles E. Grassley, R.	1981-2005	Daniel P. Moynihan, D.	1977-2001	Herbert Kohl, D.	1989-2001
Tom Harkin, D.	1985-2003	Charles E. Schumer, D.	1999-2005	Russell D. Feingold, D.	1993-2005
Kansas		**North Carolina**		**Wyoming**	
Sam Brownback, R.	1996-2005	Jesse A. Helms, R.	1973-2003	Craig Thomas, R.	1995-2001
Pat Roberts, R.	1997-2003	John Edwards, D.	1999-2005	Mike Enzi, R.	1997-2003
Kentucky		**North Dakota**			
Mitch McConnell, R.	1985-2003	Kent Conrad, D.	1987-2001		
Jim Bunning, R.	1999-2005	Byron L. Dorgan, D.	1992-2005		

Members of the United States House of Representatives

The House of Representatives of the first session of the 106th Congress consisted of 211 Democrats, 223 Republicans, and 1 independent (not including representatives from American Samoa, the District of Columbia, Guam, Puerto Rico, and the Virgin Islands), when it convened on Jan. 6, 1999. There were 203 Democrats, 227 Republicans, 1 independent, and 4 vacancies when the second session of the 105th Congress convened. This table shows congressional district, legislator, and party affiliation. Asterisk (*) denotes those who served in the 105th Congress; dagger (†) denotes "at large."

Alabama
1. Sonny Callahan, R.*
2. Terry Everett, R.*
3. Bob Riley, R.*
4. Robert Aderholt, R.*
5. Bud Cramer, D.*
6. Spencer Bachus, R.*
7. Earl Hilliard, D.*

Alaska
†Donald E. Young, R.*

Arizona
1. Matt Salmon, R.*
2. Ed Pastor, D.*
3. Bob Stump, R.*
4. John Shadegg, R.*
5. Jim Kolbe, R.*
6. J. D. Hayworth, R.*

Arkansas
1. Marion Berry, D.*
2. Vic Snyder, D.*
3. Asa Hutchinson, R.*
4. Jay Dickey, R.*

California
1. Mike Thompson, D.
2. Wally Herger, R.*
3. Douglas Ose, R.
4. John Doolittle, R.*
5. Robert T. Matsui, D.*
6. Lynn Woolsey, D.*
7. George E. Miller, D.*
8. Nancy Pelosi, D.*
9. Barbara Lee, D.*
10. Ellen Tauscher, D.*
11. Richard Pombo, R.*
12. Tom Lantos, D.*
13. Fortney H. (Peter) Stark, D.*
14. Anna Eshoo, D.*
15. Tom Campbell, R.*
16. Zoe Lofgren, D.*
17. Sam Farr, D.*
18. Gary Condit, D.*
19. George Radanovich, R.*
20. Calvin Dooley, D.*
21. William M. Thomas, R.*
22. Lois Capps, D.*
23. Elton Gallegly, R.*
24. Brad Sherman, D.*
25. Howard McKeon, R.*
26. Howard L. Berman, D.*
27. James E. Rogan, R.*
28. David Dreier, R.*
29. Henry A. Waxman, D.*
30. Xavier Becerra, D.*
31. Matthew Martinez, D.*
32. Julian C. Dixon, D.*
33. Lucille Roybal-Allard, D.*
34. Grace Napolitano, D.
35. Maxine Waters, D.*
36. Steven Kuykendall, R.
37. Juanita Millender-McDonald, D.*
38. Steve Horn, R.*
39. Edward Royce, R.*
40. Jerry Lewis, R.*
41. Gary Miller, R.
42. George E. Brown, Jr., D.*
43. Kenneth Calvert, R.*
44. Mary Bono, R.*
45. Dana Rohrabacher, R.*
46. Loretta Sanchez, D.*
47. C. Christopher Cox, R.*
48. Ronald C. Packard, R.*
49. Brian Bilbray, R.*
50. Bob Filner, D.*
51. Randy (Duke) Cunningham, R.*
52. Duncan L. Hunter, R.*

Colorado
1. Diana DeGette, D.*
2. Mark Udall, D.
3. Scott McInnis, R.*
4. Bob Schaffer, R.*
5. Joel Hefley, R.*
6. Tom Tancredo, R.

Connecticut
1. John Larson, D.
2. Sam Gejdenson, D.*
3. Rosa DeLauro, D.*
4. Christopher Shays, R.*
5. James H. Maloney, D.*
6. Nancy L. Johnson, R.*

Delaware
†Michael Castle, R.*

Florida
1. Joe Scarborough, R.*
2. Allen Boyd, D.*
3. Corrine Brown, D.*
4. Tillie Fowler, R.*
5. Karen Thurman, D.*
6. Clifford B. Stearns, R.*
7. John Mica, R.*
8. Bill McCollum, R.*
9. Michael Bilirakis, R.*
10. C. W. Bill Young, R.*
11. Jim Davis, D.*
12. Charles Canady, R.*
13. Dan Miller, R.*
14. Porter J. Goss, R.*
15. Dave Weldon, R.*
16. Mark Foley, R.*
17. Carrie Meek, D.*
18. Ileana Ros-Lehtinen, R.*
19. Robert Wexler, D.*
20. Peter Deutsch, D.*
21. Lincoln Diaz-Balart, R.*
22. E. Clay Shaw, Jr., R.*
23. Alcee Hastings, D.*

Georgia
1. Jack Kingston, R.*
2. Sanford Bishop, D.*
3. Mac Collins, R.*
4. Cynthia A. McKinney, D.*
5. John Lewis, D.*
6. Newt Gingrich, R.**
7. Bob Barr, R.*
8. Saxby Chambliss, R.*
9. Nathan Deal, R.*
10. Charlie Norwood, R.*
11. John Linder, R.*

Hawaii
1. Neil Abercrombie, D.*
2. Patsy T. Mink, D.*

Idaho
1. Helen Chenoweth, R.*
2. Mike Simpson, R.

Illinois
1. Bobby Rush, D.*
2. Jesse L. Jackson, Jr., D.*
3. William O. Lipinski, D.*
4. Luis Gutierrez, D.*
5. Rod R. Blagojevich, D.*
6. Henry J. Hyde, R.*
7. Danny Davis, D.*
8. Philip M. Crane, R.*
9. Janice Schakowsky, D.
10. John Edward Porter, R.*
11. Gerald Weller, R.*
12. Jerry F. Costello, D.*
13. Judy Biggert, R.
14. J. Dennis Hastert, R.*
15. Thomas W. Ewing, R.*
16. Donald Manzullo, R.*
17. Lane A. Evans, D.*
18. Ray LaHood, R.*
19. David Phelps, D.
20. John Shimkus, R.*

Indiana
1. Peter J. Visclosky, D.*
2. David McIntosh, R.*
3. Tim Roemer, D.*
4. Mark Souder, R.*
5. Steve Buyer, R.*
6. Danny L. Burton, R.*
7. Edward A. Pease, R.*
8. John Hostettler, R.*
9. Baron Hill, D.
10. Julia M. Carson, D.*

Iowa
1. Jim Leach, R.*
2. Jim Nussle, R.*
3. Leonard Boswell, D.*
4. Greg Ganske, R.*
5. Tom Latham, R.*

Kansas
1. Jerry Moran, R.*
2. Jim Ryun, R.*
3. Dennis Moore, D.
4. Todd Tiahrt, R.*

Kentucky
1. Edward Whitfield, R.*
2. Ron Lewis, R.*
3. Anne Northup, R.*
4. Kenneth Lucas, D.
5. Harold (Hal) Rogers, R.*
6. Ernie Fletcher, R.

Louisiana
1. Robert L. Livingston, R.††
2. William J. Jefferson, D.*
3. W. J. (Billy) Tauzin, R.*
4. Jim McCrery, R.*
5. John Cooksey, R.*
6. Richard Hugh Baker, R.*
7. Chris John, D.*

Maine
1. Thomas Allen, D.*
2. John Baldacci, D.*

Maryland
1. Wayne T. Gilchrest, R.*
2. Robert Ehrlich, Jr., R.*
3. Benjamin L. Cardin, D.*
4. Albert Wynn, D.*
5. Steny H. Hoyer, D.*
6. Roscoe Bartlett, R.*
7. Elijah Cummings. D.*
8. Constance A. Morella, R.*

Massachusetts
1. John W. Olver, D.*
2. Richard E. Neal, D.*
3. James McGovern, D.*
4. Barney Frank, D.*
5. Martin Meehan, D.*
6. John Tierney, D.*
7. Edward J. Markey, D.*
8. Michael Capuano, D.
9. John Joseph Moakley, D.*
10. William Delahunt, D.*

Michigan
1. Bart Stupak, D.*
2. Peter Hoekstra, R.*
3. Vernon Ehlers, R.*
4. Dave Camp, R.*
5. James Barcia, D.*
6. Frederick S. Upton, R.*
7. Nick Smith, R.*
8. Debbie Stabenow, D.*
9. Dale E. Kildee, D.*
10. David E. Bonior, D.*
11. Joseph Knollenberg, R.*
12. Sander M. Levin, D.*
13. Lynn Rivers, D.*
14. John Conyers, Jr., D.*
15. Carolyn Kilpatrick, D.*
16. John D. Dingell, D.*

Minnesota
1. Gil Gutknecht, R.*
2. David Minge, D.*
3. Jim Ramstad, R.*
4. Bruce F. Vento, D.*

*Announced resignation Nov. 6, 1998.   ††Announced resignation Dec. 19, 1998

5. Martin O. Sabo, D.*
6. William P. Luther, D.*
7. Collin C. Peterson, D.*
8. James L. Oberstar, D.*

Mississippi
1. Roger Wicker, R.*
2. Bennie Thompson, D.*
3. Charles Pickering, R.*
4. Ronnie Shows, D.
5. Gene Taylor, D.*

Missouri
1. William L. (Bill) Clay, D.*
2. James Talent, R.*
3. Richard A. Gephardt, D.*
4. Ike Skelton, D.*
5. Karen McCarthy, D.*
6. Pat Danner, D.*
7. Roy Blunt, R.*
8. Jo Ann Emerson, R.*
9. Kenny Hulshof, R.*

Montana
†Rick Hill, R.*

Nebraska
1. Doug Bereuter, R.*
2. Lee Terry, R.
3. Bill Barrett, R.*

Nevada
1. Shelley Berkley, D.
2. Jim Gibbons, R.*

New Hampshire
1. John E. Sununu, R.*
2. Charles Bass, R.*

New Jersey
1. Robert E. Andrews, D.*
2. Frank LoBiondo, R.*
3. H. James Saxton, R.*
4. Christopher H. Smith, R.*
5. Marge Roukema, R.*
6. Frank Pallone, Jr., D.*
7. Bob Franks, R.*
8. William Pascrell, D.*
9. Steven Rothman, D.*
10. Donald M. Payne, D.*
11. Rodney Frelinghuysen, R.*
12. Rush Holt, D.
13. Robert Menendez, D.*

New Mexico
1. Heather Wilson, R.*
2. Joe Skeen, R.*
3. Thomas Udall, D.

New York
1. Michael Forbes, R.*
2. Rick Lazio, R.*
3. Peter King, R.*
4. Carolyn McCarthy, D.*
5. Gary L. Ackerman, D.*
6. Gregory Meeks, D.
7. Joseph Crowley, D.
8. Jerrold Nadler, D.*
9. Anthony Weiner, D.
10. Edolphus Towns, D.*
11. Major R. Owens, D.*
12. Nydia Velázquez, D.*
13. Vito J. Fossella, R.*

14. Carolyn Maloney, D.*
15. Charles B. Rangel, D.*
16. José E. Serrano, D.*
17. Eliot L. Engel, D.*
18. Nita M. Lowey, D.*
19. Sue Kelly, R.*
20. Benjamin A. Gilman, R.*
21. Michael R. McNulty, D.*
22. John Sweeney, R.
23. Sherwood L. Boehlert, R.*
24. John McHugh, R.*
25. James Walsh, R.*
26. Maurice Hinchey, D.*
27. Thomas Reynolds, R.
28. Louise M. Slaughter, D.*
29. John J. LaFalce, D.*
30. Jack Quinn, R.*
31. Amo Houghton, R.*

North Carolina
1. Eva Clayton, D.*
2. Bob Etheridge, D.*
3. Walter Jones, Jr., R.*
4. David Price, D.*
5. Richard Burr, R.*
6. Howard Coble, R.*
7. Mike McIntyre, D.*
8. Robert Hayes, R.
9. Sue Myrick, R.*
10. Cass Ballenger, R.*
11. Charles H. Taylor, R.*
12. Melvin Watt, D.*

North Dakota
†Earl Pomeroy, D.*

Ohio
1. Steve Chabot, R.*
2. Rob Portman, R.*
3. Tony P. Hall, D.*
4. Michael G. Oxley, R.*
5. Paul E. Gillmor, R.*
6. Ted Strickland, D.*
7. David L. Hobson, R.*
8. John A. Boehner, R.*
9. Marcy Kaptur, D.*
10. Dennis Kucinich, D.*
11. Stephanie Jones, D.
12. John R. Kasich, R.*
13. Sherrod Brown, D.*
14. Thomas C. Sawyer, D.*
15. Deborah Pryce, R.*
16. Ralph Regula, R.*
17. James A. Traficant, Jr., D.*
18. Bob Ney, R.*
19. Steven LaTourette, R.*

Oklahoma
1. Steve Largent, R.*
2. Tom Coburn, R.*
3. Wes Watkins, R.*
4. J. C. Watts, R.*
5. Ernest Jim Istook, R.*
6. Frank Lucas, R.*

Oregon
1. David Wu, D.
2. Greg Walden, R.
3. Earl Blumenauer, D.*
4. Peter A. DeFazio, D.*
5. Darlene Hooley, D.*

Pennsylvania
1. Robert Brady, D.*
2. Chaka Fattah, D.*
3. Robert A. Borski, Jr., D.*
4. Ron Klink, D.*
5. John Peterson, R.*
6. Tim Holden, D.*
7. W. Curtis Weldon, R.*
8. Jim Greenwood, R.*
9. E. G. (Bud) Shuster, R.*
10. Donald Sherwood, R.
11. Paul E. Kanjorski, D.*
12. John P. Murtha, D.*
13. Joseph Hoeffel, D.
14. William J. Coyne, D.*
15. Patrick Toomey, R.
16. Joseph Pitts, R.*
17. George W. Gekas, R.*
18. Michael Doyle, D.*
19. William F. Goodling, R.*
20. Frank Mascara, D.*
21. Philip English, R.*

Rhode Island
1. Patrick Kennedy, D.*
2. Robert Weygand, D.*

South Carolina
1. Mark Sanford, R.*
2. Floyd Spence, R.*
3. Lindsey Graham, R.*
4. James DeMint, R.
5. John M. Spratt, Jr., D.*
6. James Clyburn, D.*

South Dakota
†John Thune, R.*

Tennessee
1. William Jenkins, R.*
2. John J. Duncan, Jr., R.*
3. Zach Wamp, R.*
4. Van Hilleary, R.*
5. Bob Clement, D.*
6. Bart Gordon, D.*
7. Ed Bryant, R.*
8. John S. Tanner, D.*
9. Harold E. Ford, Jr., D.*

Texas
1. Max Sandlin, D.*
2. Jim Turner, D.*
3. Sam Johnson, R.*
4. Ralph M. Hall, D.*
5. Pete Sessions, R.*
6. Joe Barton, R.*
7. Bill Archer, R.*
8. Kevin Brady, R.*
9. Nick Lampson, D.*
10. Lloyd Doggett, D.*
11. Chet Edwards, D.*
12. Kay Granger, R.*
13. William Thornberry, R.*
14. Ron Paul, R.*
15. Rubén Hinojosa, D.*
16. Silvestre Reyes, D.*
17. Charles W. Stenholm, D.*
18. Sheila Jackson Lee, D.*
19. Larry Combest, R.*
20. Charlie Gonzalez, D.
21. Lamar S. Smith, R.*

22. Tom DeLay, R.*
23. Henry Bonilla, R.*
24. Martin Frost, D.*
25. Ken Bentsen, D.*
26. Richard K. Armey, R.*
27. Solomon P. Ortiz, D.*
28. Ciro Rodriguez, D.*
29. Gene Green, D.*
30. Eddie Bernice Johnson, D.*

Utah
1. James V. Hansen, R.*
2. Merrill Cook, R.*
3. Christopher Cannon, R.*

Vermont
†Bernard Sanders, Ind.*

Virginia
1. Herbert H. Bateman, R.*
2. Owen B. Pickett, D.*
3. Robert Scott, D.*
4. Norman Sisisky, D.*
5. Virgil Goode, D.*
6. Robert Goodlatte, R.*
7. Thomas J. (Tom) Bliley, Jr., R.*
8. James P. Moran, Jr., D.*
9. Rick C. Boucher, D.*
10. Frank R. Wolf, R.*
11. Thomas Davis III, R.*

Washington
1. Jay Inslee, D.
2. Jack Metcalf, R.*
3. Brian Baird, D.
4. Doc Hastings, R.*
5. George Nethercutt, R.*
6. Norman D. Dicks, D.*
7. Jim McDermott, D.*
8. Jennifer Dunn, R.*
9. Adam Smith, D.*

West Virginia
1. Alan B. Mollohan, D.*
2. Robert E. Wise, Jr., D.*
3. Nick J. Rahall II, D.*

Wisconsin
1. Paul Ryan, R.
2. Tammy Baldwin, D.
3. Ron Kind, D.*
4. Gerald D. Kleczka, D.*
5. Thomas Barrett, D.*
6. Thomas E. Petri, R.*
7. David R. Obey, D.*
8. Mark Green, R.
9. F. James Sensenbrenner, Jr., R.*

Wyoming
†Barbara Cubin, R.*

Nonvoting representatives
American Samoa
Eni F. H. Faleomavaega, D.*

District of Columbia
Eleanor Holmes Norton, D.*

Guam
Robert Underwood, D.*

Puerto Rico
Carlos Romero-Barceló, D.*

Virgin Islands
Donna Christian-Green, D.

Democratic candidates did better than expected in open congressional seats, with only one incumbent Democrat losing reelection. Among Republicans, Bill Redmond of New Mexico, Vince Snowbarger of Kansas, and Jon Fox of Pennsylvania lost their seats in the House.

In the Senate, the Republicans' 55 to 45 majority remained unchanged, which dashed GOP (for Grand Old Party) hopes of achieving a filibuster-proof 60-seat majority. The GOP suffered two major losses in Senate races and won an important victory. In New York, Congressman Charles E. Schumer, a Democrat, defeated Republican Senator Alfonse M. D'Amato. In North Carolina, Democrat John Edwards captured Lauch Faircloth's Senate seat. In a bid for a second term, Carol Moseley-Braun (D., Illinois) lost to Republican Illinois state Senator Peter Fitzgerald.

Gingrich leaves Congress. On November 6, Speaker of the House Newt Gingrich (R., Georgia) announced that he would resign both as speaker of the House and as a U.S. representative. Many House Republicans had blamed Gingrich for allowing Democratic gains in the House in the November elections. Other Republicans claimed that the speaker made too many concessions to Democratic leaders in the fiscal 1998-1999 spending bill. Gingrich had been elected to the House in 1979. During the 1994 congressional election campaigns, he led a Republican movement that included a call for cuts in government spending to achieve a balanced federal budget. The strategy gave Republicans control of the House for the first time in 40 years.

Gingrich's abrupt departure from the speaker's chair and from Congress came after many House Republicans revealed that he would face strong opposition if he tried to retain his position. The speaker announced that he had based his decision on the hope of unifying what had become a divided Republican Party.

Livingston announcement. Republican representatives in November 1998 unanimously selected Robert L. Livingston (R., Louisiana), a 21-year House veteran and chairman of the House Appropriations Committee, to succeed Gingrich as speaker. On December 19, Livingston stunned the House by announcing that he would not run for speaker and would resign from Congress in six months. His decision followed an admission that he had been involved in extramarital relationships.

New leadership. The GOP retained Richard K. Armey (R., Texas) as House majority leader. Armey fought off challenges by representatives Jennifer Dunn of Washington, Steve Largent of Oklahoma, and J. Dennis Hastert of Illinois. Tom DeLay of Texas held his position as majority whip without a challenge. Republicans in the House se-

lected J. C. Watts of Oklahoma as chairman of the Republican Conference and Thomas Davis III of Virginia as chairman of the national Republican Congressional Committee. The GOP leadership had announced that the party's priorities in the 106th Congress would be focused on tax cuts and social security funding.

Following the November elections, Democrats reelected Representative Richard A. Gephardt of Missouri as House minority leader and Representative David E. Bonior of Michigan as minority whip. Democrats selected Representative Martin Frost of Texas as Democratic Caucus chairman and Representative Robert Menendez of New Jersey as caucus vice chairman. The Democratic leadership announced that the party would attempt to build on its November victories to retake control of the House in 2000.

The leadership in the Senate remained unchanged in the wake of the November 1998 elections. Senator Mitch McConnell of Kentucky, chairman of the National Republican Senatorial Committee, easily withstood a challenge from Senator Chuck Hagel of Nebraska. Majority Leader Trent Lott of Mississippi, Assistant Majority Leader Don Nickles of Oklahoma, Republican Conference chairman Connie Mack III of Florida, and Republican policy chairman Larry E. Craig of Idaho were reelected without opposition.

Senate Democrats reelected Thomas A. Daschle of South Dakota as their minority leader, Harry M. Reid of Nevada as minority whip, and Robert G. Torricelli of New Jersey as head of the party campaign committee.

IRS reform. Congress joined President Clinton in 1998 to reform the Internal Revenue Service (IRS) in an effort to make the IRS more taxpayer friendly. The legislation created 74 new rights for taxpayers, including restricting some IRS collection methods, shifting the burden of proof from the taxpayer to the IRS on disputes that go to court, and creating a nine-member board to supervise the IRS. The changes were expected to reduce federal revenues by approximately $12.9 billion by 2008.

Transportation plan. In May 1998, Congress approved a massive six-year, $217-billion bill to construct highways and mass transit facilities. The president signed the legislation, known as the Transportation Equity Act for the 21st Century (TEA-21) in June 1998. TEA-21 earmarked approximately $173 billion for highway construction, $41 billion for mass transit service, and $2 billion for highway safety. TEA-21 provided a 40-percent increase in spending over its successor, the Intermodal Surface Transportation Efficiency Act of 1991, which expired in 1997.

Tobacco legislation. The Senate failed to pass a $516-billion antitobacco bill in 1998 that

A Capitol Hill police officer places a card on the Capitol steps in memory of Officer Jacob Chestnut and Special Agent John Gibson, who were killed on July 24, 1998, during a shooting spree in the Capitol. The gunman was charged with two counts of murder.

was designed to carry out a highly-publicized 1997 agreement to settle smoking-related lawsuits against the tobacco industry. Lawmakers could not agree on what provisions to include in the bill. The bill would have raised the federal tax on cigarettes by $1.10 a pack over a five-year period. It also would have given the U.S. Food and Drug Administration broad powers to regulate tobacco products and place new restrictions on tobacco advertising. Tobacco companies attacked the bill as a costly tax increase.

Welfare benefits. The Senate voted 92 to 8 in May 1998 and the House voted 364 to 50 in June to restore food stamps benefits to about 250,000 of the 935,000 legal immigrants who had lost eligibility when the welfare system in the United States was revised in 1996. The 1996 legislation made all legal immigrants ineligible for food stamps. The 1998 legislation provided $818 million through 2003 to restore food stamps for immigrants who were in the United States prior to 1996. President Clinton signed the new legislation in June 1998.

Reagan airport. Congress passed a bill in January, which President Clinton signed into law on February 6, renaming Washington National Airport the Ronald Reagan Washington National Airport in honor of former President Ronald Reagan. The airport is located in Virginia, across the Potomac River from Washington, D.C.

Officers killed. Two Capitol Police officers were killed on July 24, 1998, in a shoot-out with a lone gunman at the U.S. Capitol Building. Officer Jacob Chestnut, 58, and Special Agent John Gibson, 42, a plain-clothes officer assigned to protect House Majority Whip DeLay, were killed by the gunman, Russell E. Weston Jr., 41, of Rimini, Montana. Weston was injured in the shootout. A Virginia woman visiting the Capitol was also injured by stray gunfire. It was the deadliest attack since Congress first began meeting in the Capitol in 1800 and the first shooting within the building since 1954.

Federal prosecutors charged Weston with two counts of murdering a law enforcement officer. A federal judge will determine in 1999 whether Weston is mentally competent to stand trial.

Chestnut and Gibson were the first Capitol Police officers to be killed while on duty at the Capitol. In a rare honor, both their coffins lay in state in the Rotunda prior to funeral services, and both men were buried in Arlington National Cemetery in Virginia.   □ William J. Eaton

See also **Democratic Party; Elections; People in the news** (Starr, Kenneth); **Republican Party; Taxation; United States, Government of the; United States, President of the.**

Connecticut. See **State government.**

Conservation. In April 1998, the World Trade Organization (WTO), a Geneva, Switzerland-based organization that resolves international trade disputes, ruled that the United States violated international trade laws by using trade sanctions to enforce turtle conservation. The WTO noted that it was illegal for one country to force another country to protect endangered wildlife. The U.S. law in question prohibited the importation of shrimp from countries whose shrimping boats did not use special devices to protect endangered sea turtles from being trapped in trawling nets. Approximately 150,000 sea turtles drown each year after becoming entangled in nets not equipped with turtle excluder devices (TED's). In October, the WTO upheld its April ruling, turning down an appeal by the United States.

The WTO ruling came in response to a challenge to the U.S. law filed by India, Pakistan, Malaysia, and Thailand, which all claimed that the law discriminated unfairly against their shrimp exports. In August, the Clinton Administration revised U.S. import guidelines to require individual boats bringing shrimp into the United States to have TED's, rather than demanding that each country require the devices on their shrimping boats. Conservationists complained that this policy shift was more difficult to enforce and would result in less effective protection for sea turtles than the old policy.

Spare the trees. The South American nation of Suriname announced in June that it was classifying 4 million acres (1,620,000 hectares) of virgin tropical forest—more than 10 percent of the country's total area—as permanently protected. Suriname hoped the preserve would attract needed funds from travelers eager to enjoy its spectacular wildlife and botanical treasures. Suriname also said it would invite *bioprospecting* (searching for plants from which medically useful substances could be extracted) by major pharmaceutical firms.

Conservationists consider tropical forests among the world's most threatened ecosystems. Agriculture, mining, and logging have stripped vast areas of tropical forests, leaving the regions dry, barren, and vulnerable to fires. In the first six months of 1998, nearly 40 million acres (16.2 million hectares) of tropical forest were consumed by fires in Brazil, Mexico, Central America, Africa, and Indonesia, causing major air pollution. Unlike many other nations, Suriname resisted the enormous profits offered by foreign timber concerns interested in its rain forest resources. Environmentalists hoped that Suriname's example would be followed by larger countries, such as Brazil and Indonesia, where rain forests are rapidly disappearing.

Wildlife smugglers. In May, a three-year undercover operation initiated by the U.S. Customs Service resulted in the arrest or indictment of more than 40 members of a wildlife smuggling ring in Colorado, Missouri, Tennessee, and Texas. Agents in the operation rescued hundreds of rare parrots and monkeys, a mountain lion, and a Mexican lynx. It was the largest exotic animal case ever conducted by the Customs Service. Agents from the U.S. Fish and Wildlife Service (USFWS) and law enforcement authorities from Canada, Australia, New Zealand, and Panama participated in the operation.

The smugglers captured the animals in various countries and planned to sell them illegally to exotic pet fanciers in at least 9 states and 10 other countries. Officials calculated the value of the animals at hundreds of thousands of dollars.

Wolf release. The USFWS in March released 11 Mexican gray wolves into the Blue Range Wolf Recovery Area, a 7,000-square-mile (18,000-square-kilometer) region within the Apache National Forest in Arizona and Gila National Forest in New Mexico. The Mexican gray wolf was eradicated from its Southwest range during the 1970's, primarily because ranchers regarded it as a threat to domestic livestock. The released wolves belonged to three family groups that were raised in captivity.

By November 1998, five of the released animals had been found dead, one was missing and presumed dead, and five had been returned to captivity. One male wolf was shot and killed by a camper in April, and his mate was recaptured and brought back into the captive population. Authorities said the other dead wolves had also apparently been shot, though officials did not know who killed the animals. The penalty for killing a Mexican gray wolf, which is classified as endangered by the USFWS, is a $100,000 fine and up to six months in prison. Some of the wolves were returned to captivity after they strayed too close to ranches and other human settlements.

In May, one adult pair produced the first recorded birth of a Mexican gray wolf in the wild in the United States in more than 50 years. Unfortunately, the pup's mother was killed in August. Biologists said the pup apparently later died.

Despite the setback, biologists released two more pairs of wolves in December and planned to release several more wolves in 1999. Biologists hoped to eventually establish a self-sustaining wild population of approximately 100 wolves.

Everglades restoration. The U.S. Army Corps of Engineers announced a plan in October 1998 to rescue the endangered Everglades ecosystem in south Florida by restoring the natural flow of water that is the foundation for the system. This biologically diverse ecosystem was threatened by a combination of water diversion projects, agricultural pollution, and land development. The restoration plan, which required the approval of Congress before it could begin, was to be paid for by both the federal government and the State of Florida. Proponents hoped the work would begin by 2002.

In May 1998, Florida Governor Lawton Chiles vetoed two bills that would have stalled the Everglades restoration efforts. One measure required state legislators to approve every detail of the scheme. The second bill required the Army Corps and the South Florida Water Management District to apply state rather than federal law when condemning and purchasing private land to be used for water storage and purification in the restoration. Florida law, unlike federal law, pays landowners, such as industries that own sugar cane operations, higher-than-market prices for their land.

Conservationists scored another victory in September, when a federal judge in Miami ruled that state and federal agencies should speed up their antipollution work in the Everglades. The ruling also compelled the Environmental Protection Agency to review the legality of a law that allowed farmers to discharge harmful levels of agricultural fertilizer into the Everglades.

Breathing room. The densely populated New York metropolitan area received a breath of fresh air in February when a coalition of state and federal agencies and private foundations completed the purchase of Sterling Forest, 15,800 acres (6,400 hectares) of rugged woodlands 40 miles (64 kilometers) northwest of New York City. Zurich Insurance of Switzerland, the owner from whom the property was purchased, had planned to build a development for 35,000 residents on the land. The deal required more than five years of negotiations and cost the federal government, the states of New York and New Jersey, and several private donors $55 million.

Sterling Forest, with small mountains, lakes, and dense stands of trees, is the largest remaining piece of open land in the New York metropolitan area and home to thousands of migratory birds as well as black bears, white-tailed deer, and bobcats. The forest will become a park. The purchase also protected a major watershed supplying more than 2 million residents in northern New Jersey.

Zurich Insurance retained ownership of 2,250 acres (911 hectares) of the forest, on which it planned to build hundreds of houses as well as commercial buildings. Conservationists hoped to eventually obtain this land as well, keeping the entire forest intact. They began a fund-raising campaign in 1998 to acquire the remaining land.

□ Eugene J. Walter, Jr.

Costa Rica. On May 8, 1998, Miguel Angel Rodriguez of the Social Christian Unity Party was sworn in for a four-year term as president of Costa Rica. In July, Rodriguez launched a series of forums intended to allow Costa Rican labor organizations, businesses, political parties, and independent social agencies to help set priorities for his administration. Although the public generally approved of the program, some critics said the attempt to reach consensus about certain issues hampered Costa Rica's legislature.

The consensus forums revealed that most Costa Ricans favored a mixed public and private economy and the gradual privatization of large state-owned companies. Other priorities that emerged from the forums included providing grade school children access to computers and developing ecotourism, a tourist industry aimed at not overburdening the environment.

On October 4, the World Bank, a United Nations agency that provides loans to developing countries, praised Costa Rica for achieving life expectancy and infant mortality rates that are comparable to those of countries with much higher per-capita incomes. In its annual report, the World Bank attributed this success to a decades-long government effort to provide information about sanitation and health.   □ Nathan A. Haverstock

See also **Latin America** (Facts in brief table).

Courts. On June 4, 1998, United States District Court Judge Richard Matsch sentenced Terry L. Nichols to life in prison for his role in the 1995 bombing of the Alfred P. Murrah Federal Building in Oklahoma City, Oklahoma. A federal jury in Denver, Colorado, had convicted Nichols in December 1997 of conspiring with Timothy J. McVeigh to bomb the Oklahoma City federal building. A jury in 1997 sentenced McVeigh to death for his role in the attack.

Matsch also sentenced Nichols to six years in prison for each of eight involuntary manslaughter convictions in connection with the deaths of eight federal law enforcement officers killed in the bombing. Jurors in 1997 had acquitted Nichols of charges that he helped carry out the attack, which killed 168 people and injured more than 500 others.

Unabomber. A federal judge on May 4, 1998, sentenced Theodore J. Kaczynski to four life terms in prison plus 30 years for a series of mail-bombings that killed three people and injured more than 20 others during a 17-year bombing campaign. The bombing spree ended in 1996 with Kaczynski's arrest at the Montana cabin where he lived. Kaczynski, an antitechnology fanatic who had been dubbed the "Unabomber," pleaded guilty on Jan. 22, 1998, to 13 federal charges stemming from the attacks.

Microsoft lawsuit. A federal trial began on October 19 to determine whether Microsoft Corporation of Redmond, Washington, violated federal antitrust laws. On May 18, the U.S. Justice Department and attorneys general from 20 states filed a federal lawsuit against Microsoft, the world's largest creator of computer software, alleging that it had violated antitrust laws that were designed to prevent any one business from developing too much power over competitors.

Justice Department attorneys argued that Microsoft should be prohibited from requiring computer makers who use Microsoft's popular Windows *operating system* (the master control program that coordinates the operations of a computer) to install Microsoft's Internet Explorer *Web browser* (a program that enables computers to access the World Wide Web). Microsoft attorneys denied the allegations. Officials argued that Microsoft could not separate the company's Web browser from the operating system.

Tobacco litigation. The U.S. Congress in 1998 failed to pass legislation that would have ended dozens of state lawsuits against cigarette makers because lawmakers could not agree on what provisions to include in the bill. The failure meant that a $368.5-billion national settlement reached in 1997 between the federal government and tobacco manufacturers did not go into effect.

However, some states independently reached agreements with tobacco companies. Texas officials in July 1998 finalized a $17.6-billion settlement, which was to be paid over 26 years. In May, tobacco companies agreed to pay $6.1 billion to Minnesota over 25 years. The companies also agreed to pay $469 million to health insurer Blue Cross-Blue Shield of Minnesota over a five-year period. On November 20, cigarette makers and the attorneys general of 46 states agreed to a $206-billion settlement of state lawsuits. Under the agreement, tobacco company payments would be distributed to the states over a 25-year period beginning in 2000.

Tobacco regulations. The 4th U.S. Circuit Court of Appeals in Richmond, Virginia, ruled in August 1998 that the U.S. Food and Drug Administration (FDA) did not have the authority to regulate cigarettes and smokeless tobacco as a dangerous substance. The court ruled that it was up to Congress to impose restrictions. In 1996, the FDA had ruled that nicotine was a drug and fell under the agency's jurisdiction. The agency had planned a series of restrictions on the advertising and marketing of tobacco.

World Trade Center. U.S. District Court Judge Kevin Duffy on Jan. 8, 1998, sentenced Ramzi Ahmed Yousef to life imprisonment plus 240 years in prison for masterminding the 1993

Susan McDougal is escorted to federal court in June 1998, where a judge released her from prison. McDougal was originally jailed for refusing to cooperate in Kenneth Starr's investigation of President Bill Clinton and Hillary Clinton.

bombing of the World Trade Center in New York City and for a 1994 airplane bombing. The Trade Center bombing killed six people and injured more than 1,000 others. The bombing of a Philippines airliner killed a Japanese passenger. During a 1995 airplane bombing trial, prosecutors had claimed that Yousef was plotting to bomb American passenger airplanes traveling in the Far East. In addition to imposing the life sentence, the judge fined Yousef $4.5 million and ordered him to pay $250 million to the bombing victims.

Implants. Attorneys for Dow Corning Corporation of Midland, Michigan, agreed on July 8, 1998, to a tentative agreement to settle legal claims against the company made by about 170,000 women. Under the tentative agreement, which was filed in bankruptcy court in November, Dow Corning would pay $3.2 billion to those women who claimed that they had suffered various health problems caused by silicone breast implants.

Dow Corning, which was once the nation's largest implant producer, declared bankruptcy in 1995. If approved, the settlement would enable Dow Corning to restructure and end its bankruptcy.

Defamation. A jury in a Poughkeepsie, New York, court on July 13, 1998, found three men liable for defaming Steven Pagones, a former county prosecutor. The men had claimed that Pagones helped abduct and rape a teenaged girl in 1987. On July 29, 1998, the jury ordered civil rights activists Reverend Al Sharpton, Alton Maddox, and C. Vernon Mason—who served as advisers to the alleged victim—to pay Pagones $345,000 in damages. A state grand jury in 1988 determined that the teenager's story was a hoax and that Pagones did not assault her.

☐ Geoffrey A. Campbell
and Linda P. Campbell

See also **Computers; Courts Special Report: Marking Time on Death Row; Crime; State government; Supreme Court of the United States.**

Marking Time on Death Row

The United States faces difficult questions as the number of executions continues to increase.

By Franklin E. Zimring

In February 1998, the state of Texas executed Karla Fay Tucker, a 38-year-old convicted murderer. In April, the state of Virginia put Angel Breard, a citizen of Paraguay, to death. These two executions triggered international responses that reflected the continuing tensions surrounding *capital punishment* (the death penalty for a crime) both in the United States and around the world.

Tucker was the first woman executed in the state of Texas since the Civil War (1861–1865). Worldwide pleas for clemency preceded the execution. Breard had been convicted on charges of murder and attempted rape. The execution, which many people claimed violated an international treaty, triggered mass protests in Central and South America.

Many legal experts agreed that the controversies surrounding these executions grew out of conflicting trends in the United States and the rest of the Western industrialized world. Most Western, industrialized nations have abandoned the use of the death penalty, but the number of people executed in the United States has continued to increase—from 25 executions in 1987 to 74 in 1997.

As recently as 1947, the majority of all nations used the death

penalty to punish and deter violent crime. By 1997, however, the number of nations that continued to execute criminals had dipped below 100. Of the 193 countries reporting in 1997 to Amnesty International, a London-based human rights group, 79 had abolished capital punishment completely. Of the remaining 114 countries that retained the death penalty, 23 had not actually carried out an execution in at least 10 years.

Most Western nations abandoned the use of the death penalty in the years following World War II (1939–1945). Many Europeans came to believe that the Holocaust—the systematic extermination of some 6 million European Jews, Gypsies, and homosexuals by Nazi Germany during World War II—demonstrated that it was wrong for a state to hold the power to kill its own citizens.

In the early 1970's, the United States was among those Western, industrialized nations that prohibited capital punishment. The Supreme Court had voted in 1972 to ban the death penalty, as it was then imposed, as a form of cruel and unusual punishment in violation of the 8th and 14th amendments to the U.S. Constitution. In 1976, the Supreme Court approved new state laws designed to meet the earlier objections, and the death penalty was reinstated.

Crime and punishment

In the years since 1976, the U.S. Congress passed laws specifying a number of capital offenses. In 1988, for example, Congress passed a law imposing the death penalty on persons who committed murder during a drug-related felony. In 1994, it passed a bill that added nearly 60 offenses to the list of crimes punishable by death. These included murders committed by an escaped federal prisoner and murders that resulted from the smuggling of illegal immigrants.

While federal law mandates the death penalty for a number of offenses, less than 1 percent of those persons sentenced to death in the United States since 1988 were tried in federal courts. In 1997, only 16 people were sentenced to death under federal law. One of those was Timothy McVeigh, who was convicted in 1997 of the 1995 bombing of the Alfred P. Murrah Federal Building in Oklahoma City, Oklahoma. No person convicted of a capital offense in a federal court has been actually put to death since 1964.

In the American federal system, the U.S. Constitution assigns most of the responsibility for defining crime and enforcing the law to the states. The federal government provides basic rules, including constitutionally guaranteed rights, but states determine criminal penalties. And criminal penalties, including capital punishment, vary widely among the 50 states.

In 1998, 12 U.S. states had no death penalty on their books. The 38 states with death penalty laws provided that only certain forms of aggravated murder were punishable by death. Of the 38 states with death penalty statutes, 29 actually carried out executions in the years since 1976. Of those 29 states, 6 conducted 70 percent of all executions. In 1997, one state—Texas—put 37 prisoners to death, a number equal to all other states combined.

The arguments put forth by human rights advocates and by capital punishment proponents were rooted, for the most part, in personally held beliefs that cannot be verified with statistical evidence. Both sides of the issue have jumped, therefore, on various circumstances surrounding the use of capital punishment in the United States in the late 1990's to bolster their arguments. These circumstances included the inconsistency with which executions have been carried out; the unequal application of the death penalty among racial minorities; the ever-growing number of prisoners waiting on death row; the long delays between when people are sentenced and actually put to death; and the financial costs involved.

The author:

Franklin E. Zimring is director of the Earl Warren Legal Institute, and a law professor at the University of California, Berkeley.

Human rights issues

Most capital punishment opponents viewed the death penalty as a human rights issue and saw execution as an example of the destructive power of government. They argued that a modern democratic state did not have the right to execute its citizens, regardless of cause. When proponents of the death penalty pointed to the heinous nature of certain crimes, the human rights advocates responded that they were missing the fundamental issue. The advocates claimed that a state that renounces its power to kill citizens was a better place to live than a state where the government claimed the right to execute in the interest of punishing criminals.

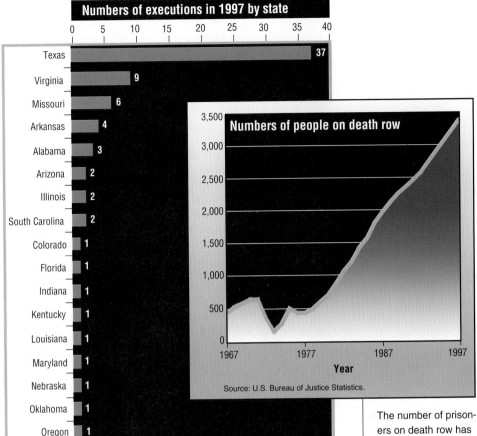

Numbers of executions in 1997 by state

State	Executions
Texas	37
Virginia	9
Missouri	6
Arkansas	4
Alabama	3
Arizona	2
Illinois	2
South Carolina	2
Colorado	1
Florida	1
Indiana	1
Kentucky	1
Louisiana	1
Maryland	1
Nebraska	1
Oklahoma	1
Oregon	1

Numbers of people on death row

Source: U.S. Bureau of Justice Statistics.

Source: Death Penalty Information Center, Washington, D.C.

Death penalty proponents responded to the human rights advocates with the argument that capital punishment was justifiable in the same way that killing in self-defense or killing in war was justifiable. According to this argument, all human beings have a right to defend themselves. Societies of human beings have the right of self-defense as well, through the use of capital punishment.

Proponents maintained that execution was an appropriate, even a logical, response by society toward the individual who kills. They argued that taking the life of a killer satisfies both the victims' survivors and the general public's need for closure. This argument was rooted in the traditions of Western Civilization, growing from the Old Testament, biblical concept of "an eye for an eye."

Deterring crime

Some proponents also argued that the death penalty deters crime, pointing out that the murder rate in the United States in the 1990's decreased as the number of people executed for capital crimes increased. Opponents of capital punishment responded—and many proponents agreed—that statistical conclusions about how capital

The number of prisoners on death row has continued to increase since 1976, when the U.S. Supreme Court declared capital punishment constitutional. The increase in executions has been accompanied by an increase in the number of persons sentenced to death.

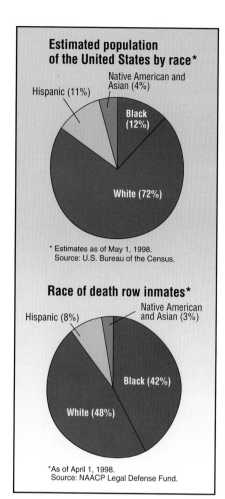

Estimated population of the United States by race*

Native American and Asian (4%)

Hispanic (11%)

Black (12%)

White (72%)

* Estimates as of May 1, 1998.
Source: U.S. Bureau of the Census.

Race of death row inmates*

Hispanic (8%)

Native American and Asian (3%)

Black (42%)

White (48%)

*As of April 1, 1998.
Source: NAACP Legal Defense Fund.

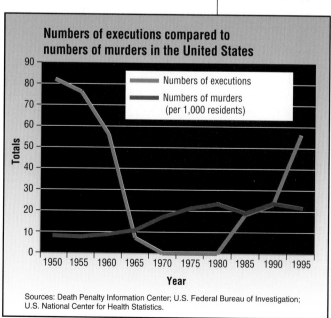

Numbers of executions compared to numbers of murders in the United States

Numbers of executions

Numbers of murders (per 1,000 residents)

Totals

Year

Sources: Death Penalty Information Center; U.S. Federal Bureau of Investigation; U.S. National Center for Health Statistics.

punishment affects the crime rates were inconclusive. Many criminologists, including those who favored capital punishment, have admitted that they have been unable to produce "convincing studies" that track the relationship between the death penalty and the crime rate.

Dwayne Smith, a criminologist at the University of North Carolina at Charlotte and editor of the journal *Homicide Studies*, has suggested that such factors as poverty, gun availability, alcohol use, and policing techniques have greater influence in reducing the crime rate than does the death penalty. Smith has also written that the decline in murder and violent crime rates in the mid- to late-1990's may be attributed in part to the number of people put in prison in the early to mid-1990's. Because there were fewer potential murderers on the streets, there were fewer murders committed. According to the U.S. Bureau of Justice Statistics, a division of the U.S. Department of Justice, the nation's adult prison population grew from 773,919 state and federal inmates in 1990 to 1,244,554 inmates in 1997. Smith also noted that because criminals on the street are more likely to be murdered than noncriminals, prison keeps them from being killed themselves.

Inconsistencies in executions

The inconsistency with which the death penalty has been applied from state to state has frustrated many death penalty opponents. Opponents point out the inequity in a system in which a person convicted of murder in one state is more likely to be put to death than a person convicted of the same type of murder in another state. Proponents responded that all of the states should carry out executions as allowed by the 1976 U.S. Supreme Court decision. Such inconsistencies in the application of the death penalty from state to state were based in the provisions of the U.S. Constitution as well as peculiarities of the American justice system.

Methods of execution also varied from state to state. Some people believed that certain methods of execution were physically painful and considered them to be cruel and unusual punishment. For example, in 1998 Florida and Georgia legislators authorized electrocution as the only method of execution. Maryland and Mississippi law specified lethal injection or the gas chamber. Delaware and New Hampshire authorized lethal injection or hanging. In Utah, either lethal injection or a firing squad were authorized methods of execution. The majority of states used lethal injection as the primary method of execution.

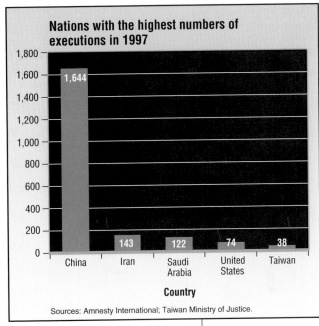

Nations with the highest numbers of executions in 1997

Country

Sources: Amnesty International; Taiwan Ministry of Justice.

Capital punishment opponents have long asserted that the death penalty should be abolished in the United States because it is not only applied inconsistently from state to state, but from person to person. They argued that in the United States, race is too often a motivating factor in whether a person is convicted of murder and sentenced to death. They back their argument on the following U.S. Bureau of Justice statistics: In 1997, 42 percent—1,400 people—of the total number of inmates—3,400 people—on death row in the United States were black Americans. In the same year, black Americans made up 12 percent of the total U.S. population, according to the U.S. Census Bureau. According to capital punishment opponents, the discrepancy between the percentage of black Americans on death row and blacks in the general population was a strong indication that justice in the United States is not color blind. Proponents of capital punishment countered that race was not a factor because the U.S. justice system prosecuted cases without regard for the race of the defendant or the victim, and that an equally large number of homicide arrests were blacks.

According to Amnesty International, a London-based human rights organization, the United States conducted the fourth-highest number of executions in 1997. China, Iran, Saudi Arabia, and the United States accounted for 84 percent of all reported executions worldwide in 1997.

A growing problem

The ever-growing number of inmates on death row provided one of the worst problems associated with the death penalty in the 1990's and was the unavoidable result of some basic patterns. During the 1990's, approximately 20,000 murders were committed annually. Approximately 1 percent of the people committing those murders—some 200 people—were sentenced annually to death. Although the number of people sentenced to death was a small fraction of the total number convicted of murder in the Unit-

COURTS

SPECIAL REPORT

States with the death penalty in 1997

States with Death Penalty

States without Death Penalty

Methods of execution by state

State	Method
Alabama	Electrocution
Arizona	Lethal injection or gas chamber
Arkansas	Lethal injection or electrocution
California	Lethal injection or gas chamber
Colorado	Lethal injection
Connecticut	Lethal injection
Delaware	Lethal injection or hanging
Florida	Electrocution
Georgia	Electrocution
Idaho	Lethal injection or firing squad
Illinois	Lethal injection
Indiana	Lethal injection
Kansas	Lethal injection
Kentucky	Lethal injection or electrocution
Louisiana	Lethal injection
Maryland	Lethal injection or gas chamber
Mississippi	Lethal injection or gas chamber
Missouri	Lethal injection or gas chamber
Montana	Lethal injection
Nebraska	Electrocution
Nevada	Lethal injection
New Hampshire	Lethal injection or hanging
New Jersey	Lethal injection
New Mexico	Lethal injection
New York	Lethal injection
North Carolina	Lethal injection or gas chamber
Ohio	Lethal injection or electrocution
Oklahoma	Lethal injection
Oregon	Lethal injection
Pennsylvania	Lethal injection
South Carolina	Lethal injection or electrocution
South Dakota	Lethal injection
Tennessee	Lethal injection or electrocution*
Texas	Lethal injection
Utah	Lethal injection or firing squad
Virginia	Lethal injection or electrocution
Washington	Lethal injection or hanging
Wyoming	Lethal injection

* Tennessee authorizes lethal injection for those sentenced after January 1, 1999. Convicts on death row prior to that date choose between the electric chair and lethal injection.

Sources: U.S. Bureau of Justice Statistics; Death Penalty Information Center; state departments of corrections.

ed States, the total was still greater than the number of executions carried out in any one year since the 1930's. Between 1993 and 1997, the number of annual executions averaged 50 persons.

The result of this steady increase in condemned prisoners was a steady growth in the death row population in the United States, a population that reached approximately 3,400 persons in 1998. If the states were to carry out a total of 50 executions per year, it would take 68 years to execute the 1998 death row population, even if no new death sentences were imposed. The largest number of executions in the United States in the 1900's occurred in 1933, when 199 persons were executed. Some experts maintained that if 199 inmates on death row were executed each year, the annual addition of an almost equal number of prisoners to death row would do little to reduce the existing population.

When executions do occur in the United States, they are often conducted a decade or more after the condemned prisoners have been convicted of a capital crime. Such delays, mostly due to the appeals process available in the American court system, have been a continuing source of controversy in the capital punishment debate.

Due process of law

Underlying the appeals process is the concept of *due process of law* (the legal steps and measures to which a person is entitled to protect himself or herself). Due process exists to make certain that the innocent are not wrongly punished. The innocent are occasionally found guilty by the U.S. justice system. According to statistics published in November 1998 as part of a national conference on wrongful convictions and the death penalty, 75 people condemned to death had been found innocent and released from death rows since 1972.

Due process also gives guilty persons every chance to demonstrate legal errors. A death sentence cannot be carried out unless a convicted person has been accorded due process and has exhausted all available appeals at both the state and federal levels. However, the process is usually long and expensive. So long as the appeals process can be extended, a defendant may postpone an execution.

Federal laws passed by Congress in 1994 and 1996 reduced some delays. The laws limited appeals by death row inmates and reduced some federal court powers to hear death penalty cases. However, some legal experts argued in the 1990's that keeping defendants out of federal court after they have had a limited opportunity to raise issues may speed the process, but at a price. Although reducing access to court hearings saves time and money, it also increased the chance of an innocent person being executed if a judge cannot hear all claims of legal error. To give the American public a truly swift and efficient system of capital punishment, significant effort to keep the process error free would, by necessity, have to be abandoned. To give the public the absolute guarantee of due process and error-free administration of justice would, in effect, rule out use of capital punishment.

Expensive proposition

According to several studies reported during the 1990's, the cost of a death penalty case to a state averaged $2 million. Most of the total involved trial and prison costs, rather than the act of actually putting a person to death. A 1993 study by researchers at Duke University in Durham, North Carolina, for example, found that each death penalty conviction and execution costs the state of North Carolina $2.16 million more than the average cost of life imprisonment. A separate study reported that a death penalty sentence averaged $2.3 million in Texas—approximately three times the cost of imprisoning someone in a single cell at the highest security level for 40 years. Several legal experts have suggested that capital punishment combined with due process of the law is not cost effective.

As long as the death penalty exists as a method of punishing murderers in the United States—where concern that an innocent person might be executed is interwoven into the legal system—the lengthy appeals process will continue, causing long delays. In turn, those delays will result in an ever increasing backlog of prisoners on death row, a situation that will continue to frustrate supporters and opponents of capital punishment alike.

Cricket. Australia solidified its reputation as the world's top test match-playing nation during the 1997-1998 cricketing year. The Australians began by winning home test series against New Zealand in November-December 1997 and South Africa in December 1997-February 1998. In January 1998, they also took the one-day Carlton and United series, beating South Africa in two of the three matches. However, the Australians lost twice in a three-match series in India. The key to India's success was the brilliant batting of India's Sachin Tendulkar, who scored two centuries and finished the series with 416 runs at an average of 111.50. Tendulkar's performance supported the view of many observers that he was cricket's best batsman since the legendary Sir Donald Bradman, who captained Australia in the 1930's and 1940's.

West Indies, on a tour of Pakistan in November 1997, suffered a crushing defeat, losing two tests by an inning and a third by 10 wickets. Wasim Akram and Mushtaq Ahmed turned in fine bowling performances for Pakistan, while Aamer Sohail, Inzamam-al-Haq, and Ijaz Ahmad scored heavily. Courtney Walsh bowled well for West Indies, but apart from Carl Hooper, who scored the only century for the visitors, the West Indian batting was disappointing.

West Indies faced England from January-April 1998. In an exciting six-test series, fast bowlers Curtley Ambrose and Courtney Walsh devastated English batting, helping West Indies to triumph by 3 tests to 1. After 52 tests as England's captain, Michael Atherton resigned his post following the final match in Antigua. England's one-day captain, Adam Hollioake, fresh from leading his side to victory in the Champions Trophy in Sharjah, United Arab Emirates, fared no better in the one-day series, as West Indies defeated England, 4-1.

The English season was dominated by a five-test series against South Africa from May through August. South Africa's punishing schedule between October 1997 and March 1998 had included 11 test matches in four series—three of which were played away from home—and three major one-day competitions. England, led by Alec Stewart, triumphed in a closely contested series with South Africa by 2 tests to 1. Allan Donald had an outstanding series for South Africa, taking 33 wickets, while Jonty Rhodes delighted spectators with his spectacular fielding. South Africa took some consolation in winning a three-match, one-day series.

Adam Hollioake was replaced as captain by Alec Stewart for the Emirates Triangular series in August 1998, where one-day world champion Sri Lanka met England and South Africa. Sri Lanka defeated England in the final. The enthusiasm of English fans was muted when Sri Lanka won a single test by 10 wickets in the last international match of the English summer. But cricket lovers enjoyed the magnificent stroke play of Sanath Jayasuriya and the astonishing spin bowling of Muttiah Muralitharan, who had 16 wickets for 220 runs, the fifth best test figures of all time. The attractive style of cricket played by Sri Lanka won them many English fans.

In December 1998, Australia defeated England, 2-0, after only the third test in the Ashes series. This was Australia's sixth consecutive Ashes win and the earliest victory ever in the series.

High-tech umpiring. A major issue in international cricket in 1998 was highlighted during the England-South Africa series, when several umpiring decisions were shown to be incorrect by television replays. Cricket authorities already accept a third umpire in televised matches, who views a television replay to rule on close calls concerning run-outs. Some authorities wish to go further and give these umpires the right to rule on such matters as bat-pad catches, catches by the wicket-keeper, and some leg-before-wicket decisions. Others argue that the use of television replay weakens the authority of the umpires, whose decisions have traditionally been regarded as final. They also argue that replays slow the pace of the game.

One-day cricket. The view that one-day cricket is becoming a very different game from test matches and other longer forms of the sport was underlined by Steve Waugh's appointment to captain Australia in one-day internationals ahead of test-captain Mark Taylor, together with Adam Hollioake's captaincy of England both in the one-day internationals in the West Indies and in the Champions Trophy held in the United Arab Emirates. This view has been reinforced by the fact that established test players are being replaced in one-day matches by one-day specialists. However, some countries, notably Sri Lanka, still play much the same side in both forms of cricket.

Women's cricket. Australia's defeat of New Zealand in the final of the Women's World Cup, held at Eden Gardens, Calcutta, in December 1997, was Australia's fourth victory in five World Cup attempts. Australia's prowess was also demonstrated during a tour of England in 1998, when the team won all five one-day internationals, even though the three tests were high-scoring draws.

A landmark event for women's cricket took place in September 1998, when the Marylebone Cricket Club, traditionally the guardian of the *laws* (rules) of cricket, voted to end 211 years of men-only membership. Although 10 women were to be annually elected honorary members, most women will have to join the waiting list, which currently means that they will have to wait about 18 years for admission.

☐ Keith Lye

Crime statistics released in November 1998 by the Federal Bureau of Investigation (FBI) revealed that serious crime in the United States declined 4 percent in 1997, compared with 1996 statistics. According to the FBI Uniform Crime Reporting Program, which collects crime statistics from law enforcement agencies nationwide, violent crime —murder, robbery, aggravated assault, and rape—decreased by a total of 3 percent. Property crime—motor vehicle theft, larceny, and burglary—fell by 2 percent.

The FBI reported that both murders and robberies fell by 7 percent in 1997 compared with 1996 statistics. Aggravated assault fell by 1 percent. Rape decreased less than 1 percent. Motor vehicle theft fell by 3 percent. Larceny dropped 2 percent. And burglary dropped by 2 percent. The FBI report revealed that crime fell by 5 percent in Northeastern states, by 2 percent in Southern and Western states, and by 1 percent in Midwestern states, compared with crime in 1996.

Criminologists in 1998 continued to study reasons for the decrease, including improved police tactics, a strong economy, a decreased interest in gangs, and a growing prison population that resulted in the removal of criminals from society.

Questionable data. Some experts suggested the possibility that falling crime rates were the result of falsely reported statistics. They cited Philadelphia, where police authorities had withdrawn crime statistics from the national system maintained by the FBI for 1996, 1997, and the first half of 1998. The Philadelphia police department had discovered that some officers had downgraded serious crimes into less serious incidents. Similar allegations were raised in 1998 in Atlanta, New York City, and Boca Raton, Florida.

Some police officials in the United States argued that decreasing crime statistics put pressure on departments to show continuing lower crime rates. Other police officials, including the FBI, countered that the nationwide statistics reflected a true decrease in crime.

Young criminals. On March 24 in Jonesboro, Arkansas, two boys, aged 11 and 13, went on a shooting spree outside their school. Law enforcement officials reported that the boys set off a fire alarm to lure students out of Westside Middle School and onto the playground before firing into the crowd from nearby woods. Four girls and a teacher were killed, and 10 people were wounded in the attack. A judge convicted the boys of juvenile delinquency in August and ordered that they remain in juvenile detention until age 21.

On April 24, a 14-year-old boy killed a teacher and wounded three other people after the boy opened fire at an eighth-grade graduation dance

Law-enforcement officers remove the body of one of five victims after two boys opened fire on students and teachers outside a school in Jonesboro, Arkansas, on March 24, 1998.

in Edinboro, Pennsylvania. On May 19, 1998, an 18-year-old high school student fatally shot another student in a school parking lot in Fayetteville, Tennessee.

On May 21, a 15-year-old student in Springfield, Oregon, shot and killed two classmates and injured more than 20 other people in a high school cafeteria. Authorities said that the student also murdered his parents. Authorities charged the boy with 4 counts of aggravated murder, 26 counts of attempted aggravated murder, 6 counts of first-degree assault, 18 counts of second-degree assault, unlawful possession of a firearm, unlawful manufacture of a destructive device, possession of a destructive device, and first-degree theft. A trial was scheduled for 1999. If convicted, the boy faced life in prison.

Criminologists in 1998 debated possible explanations for the increase in juvenile violence. Some experts suggested the availability of guns in the United States. Some suggested a declining family structure, while still others blamed an American culture focused on glorifying violence in movies, on television, and in music.

Hate crimes made headlines in 1998 following two murders that received national attention. Although laws differ from state to state, a hate crime is generally viewed as one committed because of the victim's race, ethnic background, religion, or sexual orientation.

Three white men were arrested and charged with murder in June following the death of an African American man in Jasper, Texas. Authorities said that the victim, James Byrd, Jr., 49, had been beaten, chained to the back of a pickup truck, and dragged for 2 miles (3.2 kilometers). Authorities alleged that the three suspects had ties to a white-supremacist movement. The incident sparked concern about racial violence.

In October, Matthew Shepard, a 21-year-old college student who was openly gay, was beaten to death by two men in Laramie, Wyoming. Authorities said that Shepard was tied to a fence and severely beaten because of his sexual orientation. He later died from his injuries. Two suspects in the case were charged with first-degree murder, kidnapping, and robbery.

Following the incident, U.S. Attorney General Janet Reno called on the U.S. Congress to pass a federal hate crimes statute that covered sexual orientation. Federal law in 1998 allowed for the prosecution of hate crimes in cases where victims were attacked because of their race, religion, or ethnicity. Reno supported extending prosecution to crimes where victims were targeted because of gender, disability, or sexual orientation.

□ Robert Messenger

See also **Courts; Courts** Special Report: **Marking Time on Death Row; Prison.**

Croatia. United Nations (UN) peacekeeping forces returned eastern Slavonia to Croatian control on Jan. 15, 1998. An estimated 80,000 refugees—mostly Croats and some ethnic Serbs who had fled from their homes when Serbian rebels seized the region in 1991—began to return. By late March 1998, some 60,000 Serbs who had been living in eastern Slavonia since the hostilities, including refugees from other parts of Croatia and Bosnia-Herzegovina, had fled the region. International officials criticized the government of President Franjo Tudjman for failing to allow Serb refugees to freely reenter Slavonia and protect them from Croats. A senior German official in April called for sanctions against Croatia after reports that border guards were refusing to grant passage to Serb refugees. In June, Croatia's parliament approved a new program to facilitate the return of refugees. However, Western officials continued to watch Croatia's policies toward refugees closely throughout the year.

Domestic affairs. A controversial 22-percent value-added tax (VAT) went into effect in Croatia on Jan. 1, 1998. In contast to value-added taxes in other European countries, Croatia's VAT had no exemptions or lower rates. Union workers in January threatened to strike to protest the tax. In August, farmers in eastern Croatia blocked a local main road to protest the VAT's impact on their profits. The farmers demanded that the government renegotiate a 1997 deal on federal wheat purchases, taking the new tax into consideration.

In response to the Tudjman government's repudiation of Western criticism of its leadership, opposition leaders in March called for early elections. The government survived a no-confidence motion introduced by opposition parties in June.

Foreign affairs. Officials of the European Union (EU), an alliance of 15 European nations, said in March that in order for Croatia to improve relations with Europe, it would have to comply with the peace agreements regarding eastern Slavonia and Bosnia-Herzegovina, expedite the return of refugees, and improve internal democracy and ethnic reconciliation. United States Secretary of State Madeleine Albright made similar remarks during a visit to Croatia in August.

In May, Foreign Minister Mate Granic, while on an official visit to Israel, apologized for Croatia's persecution of Jews in the Holocaust. In September, Croatia and Bosnia-Herzegovina reached an agreement regarding Bosnia's use of the port of Ploce. In November, Croatia and Slovenia resolved their ongoing dispute over the Krsko nuclear power plant in Slovenia. Croatia had helped Slovenia build the facility when both countries were part of Yugoslavia.   □ Sharon L. Wolchik

See also **Bosnia-Herzegovina; Europe** (Facts in brief table).

Cuba. Pope John Paul II, head of the Roman Catholic Church, began a five-day visit to Cuba on Jan. 21, 1998. During his tour, the pope called on the government to end the suppression of religious and personal liberties in Cuba. He also criticized the 36-year United States embargo against Cuba, which he claimed created hardships, especially for the poor.

Many world leaders credited the pope's visit for easing tensions between Cuba and its neighbors. Responding to a request by the pope, Cuba released some 300 prisoners, including political dissidents and elderly or ill criminal offenders. About 70 prisoners on the pope's list remained in jail for "reasons of national security."

Foreign relations. Guatemala, which had severed ties with Cuba in 1959 after Cuba's Communist revolution, reestablished diplomatic relations in January 1998. In April, the Dominican Republic also restored diplomatic relations, which had ended in 1961. Haiti, which had reestablished diplomatic ties in 1996, reopened its embassy in Havana, the Cuban capital, on Feb. 7, 1998.

On March 19, U.S. President Bill Clinton announced the resumption of U.S. flights to Cuba for humanitarian aid and family emergencies. The United States had halted such flights after Cuban jet fighters shot down two unarmed civilian planes in February 1996. Clinton also adopted a policy allowing Cuban Americans to send $300 every three months to family members living in Cuba.

Prime Minister Jean Chretien of Canada began a three-day visit to Cuba on April 26, 1998. Cuba promised Chretien that it would pay a Canadian insurance company $10 million for assets seized following the 1959 revolution. Political analysts believed that similar moves for U.S. companies could help lead to the lifting of the U.S. embargo.

President Fidel Castro of Cuba made a six-day tour of English-speaking nations in the Caribbean in August 1998. In Grenada, he was enthusiastically welcomed at the airport. During the 1983 U.S. invasion of Grenada intended to oust Communist influences, the airport had been the scene of fighting between U.S. forces and a Cuban military brigade that was helping to build the facility.

Conflicts. On Aug. 25, 1998, seven Cuban exiles in the United States were indicted in San Juan, Puerto Rico, on charges of conspiring to assassinate Castro in 1997. On Sept. 14, 1998, the U.S. Federal Bureau of Investigation arrested eight men and two women in Miami, Florida, on charges of spying for Cuba. Their primary target was allegedly the U.S. Southern Command in Miami, which oversees U.S. military operations in Latin America. ☐ Nathan A. Haverstock

See also **Latin America** (Facts in brief table); **Roman Catholic Church.**

Cuban President Fidel Castro welcomes Pope John Paul II to Cuba at the beginning of the pope's five-day visit in January 1998.

Cyprus. A breakdown in talks to reunite the Greek and Turkish sections of Cyprus as well as the planned delivery of Russian antiaircraft missiles to the Greek Cypriot government threatened to ignite a wider conflict between Greece and Turkey in 1998. Cyprus was divided in 1974 after Turkey invaded the Mediterranean island in response to the overthrow of the Cypriot president by Greek military officers. In 1983, the Turkish minority of Cyprus declared the northern one-third of the island to be the Turkish Republic of Northern Cyprus. With the exception of Turkey, this entity has never been recognized by the international community. The southern, Greek-dominated Republic of Cyprus has widespread international recognition.

Reunification talks. Talks sponsored by the United States to reunify Cyprus broke down in May 1998, when Rauf Denktash, the Turkish Cypriot leader, demanded that the north be recognized as a state. He also demanded that southern Cyprus withdraw its application for membership in the European Union (EU), an organization of 15 Western European countries. Denktash had previously refused an offer by Greek Cypriot leader Glafcos Clerides to include Turkish representatives in EU talks considering the Cypriot bid for membership in 1998.

Supporters of reunification feared that Turkish Cypriots preferred stronger ties to Turkey rather than federation with the south. They noted that in July, Turkish President Suleyman Demirel inaugurated a project in which ships would regularly tow huge water-filled balloon-like bags to northern Cyprus from Turkey. The project was designed to provide northern Cyprus with 245 million cubic feet (7 million cubic meters) of fresh water. In 1998, Cyprus, which is heavily dependent on the water-intensive industries of tourism and agriculture, was hit by its worst drought of the century. Despite the drought, southern Cyprus rejected Turkey's offer to supply water.

Russian missiles. On December 29, President Clerides announced the cancellation of plans to deploy Russian S-300 surface-to-air missiles in southern Cyprus. Earlier in the year, Turkish officials threatened to destroy the missiles if they were deployed. The Turks viewed the missiles as a threat to Turkey's air superiority over Cyprus.

Tensions regarding Cypriot airspace escalated in June after Greece and Turkey each sent warplanes over the airspace of its rival. In December, the United Nations Security Council called for a reduction in weapons and troops in Cyprus and for a resumption of reunification talks.

◻ Christine Helms

See also **Middle East** (Facts in brief table); **Turkey.**

Czech Republic. President Vaclav Havel, elected to another five-year term in January 1998, underwent emergency surgery in April. After having additional surgery in July, Havel collapsed in August and nearly died of blood poisoning brought on by pneumonia. After his recovery, he resumed an active role in the political affairs of the Czech Republic.

The center-left Czech Social Democratic Party (CSSD) won the largest share of the vote—32.3 percent—in elections to the lower chamber of parliament in June 1998. The Civic Democratic Party (ODS) of Vaclav Klaus, who resigned as prime minister in 1997, took 27.7 percent of the vote, despite the fact that Klaus's government had collapsed in November 1997. The Communist Party ran third, with 11 percent, followed by the Christian Democratic Union, with 9 percent of the vote. The Freedom Union party, formed in January 1998 by former leaders of the Civic Democratic Party, received 8.6 percent of the vote.

New government. In July, President Havel named Milos Zeman, who was speaker of the lower chamber of parliament and leader of the CSSD, prime minister, after the CSSD struck a deal with the ODS to form a minority government. The two parties agreed that they would consult on important issues, and the ODS agreed not to support no-confidence votes against the new government. Zeman's government supported many of the political and economic reforms that had occurred in the Czech Republic since the collapse of Communism in Czechoslovakia in 1989. (The Czech Republic and Slovakia became separate nations in 1993.) However, Zeman's government pledged to slow the privatization of banks and other state-owned enterprises and to increase welfare spending in order to ease the financial hardships brought on by the shift to a market economy.

In Senate elections held in November 1998, the CSSD won only 3 of 27 open seats in the 81-seat body. Overall, the party lost 3 of the 26 Senate seats it held before the election.

Economy. Analysts predicted in October that inflation would reach 8 percent by the end of 1998 and that the nation's *gross domestic product* (the total value of goods and services produced in a given year) would drop 2 percent by year end. Unemployment stood at 6.8 percent in October.

Foreign affairs. The new government supported the country's move toward closer political and economic ties with the West. However, relations with Germany were strained in August, after Zeman made remarks criticizing Germany's inclusion of *Sudeten Germans* (ethnic Germans who were expelled from their homes in Czech territory after World War II [1939–1945]) on a new ethnic reconciliation panel. ◻ Sharon L. Wolchik

See also **Europe** (Facts in brief table).

Jubilant fans climb Prague's landmark St. Wenceslas statue in February 1998 to celebrate the Czech Republic hockey team winning its first Olympic gold medal in a 1-0 upset over Russia on Feb. 23.

Dallas.

Dallas. Dallas voters narrowly approved a referendum on Jan. 17, 1998, for a $230-million professional sports and entertainment arena northwest of the city's downtown. The arena was planned to accommodate the Dallas Stars hockey team and the Dallas Mavericks basketball team. The referendum designated the city's share of the expenses at $125 million, which the city planned to raise with an increased hotel room tax and a new fee on vehicle rentals. In October, Mavericks majority owner Ross Perot, Jr., announced plans for a $500-million real estate project next to the planned arena that included office towers, retail stores, hotels, and apartments.

Cowboys coach quits. Barry Switzer resigned on January 9 as coach of the Dallas Cowboys professional football team. He had been under fire from fans and some team players, including quarterback Troy Aikman and fullback Daryl Johnston, for allegedly being too lax about discipline. The Cowboys won the Super Bowl in 1996 and three division titles since Switzer's tenure began in 1994. In the 1997 season, however, the team had 6 wins and 10 losses. In February 1998, the Cowboys announced that former Pittsburgh Steelers offensive coordinator Chan Gailey would coach the Dallas team.

Trinity River project. On May 2, Dallas voters approved a $543.5-million bond issue, the largest in the city's history, which included $246 million for improvements to the flood-prone area along the Trinity River, on the south side of the city. Plans included construction of new toll roads along both sides of the river to ease traffic congestion, a lake in the flood plain, and an expansion of flood-control systems. The bond issue also included funds for a new police headquarters building and other public projects.

Southern Dallas. Nine banks announced on April 24 that they would lend $1.5 billion to private investors over the next five years for development projects in southern Dallas. Although nearly half the city's population resided south of downtown in 1998, the area represented only 16 percent of the city's tax base. Mayor Ron Kirk, who had made balanced economic growth a top priority in recent years, praised the banks' commitment.

African American judge. Former Dallas City Attorney Sam Lindsay was sworn in as a federal judge for the Northern District of Texas on September 11. His appointment marked the first time an African American had held such a position in the 119-year history of the district.

School scandal. On February 4, Yvonne Gonzalez, former superintendent of the Dallas Independent School District, was sentenced to 15 months in federal prison after she pleaded guilty to misapplying school funds to pay for furniture in her office and apartment. Federal investigators discovered the diversion of funds in 1997 while conducting a wider probe, which Gonzalez had requested, of criminal wrongdoing in the public schools. She had resigned in September 1997.

The Roman Catholic Diocese of Dallas agreed in July 1998 to pay $23.4 million of a $119.6-million judgment in a 1997 sexual abuse lawsuit. The diocese had been found guilty of gross negligence, fraud, and reckless disregard for the safety of others in its handling of sexual abuse accusations against parish priest Rudy Kos. The settlement brought the total amount the Diocese of Dallas and its insurers agreed to pay to the 12 victims in the Kos controversy to more than $30 million. In March 1998, Kos was sentenced to life in prison for sexually molesting minors.

Considering the Olympics. In October, a 50-member delegation from Dallas, which included Mayor Kirk, attended the United States Olympic Congress in Phoenix, Arizona, to promote the city's first bid for the Summer Olympic Games. Dallas had the largest delegation of the nine cities at the conference concerning the 2012 games. With a deadline for final bids not due until March 2000, Dallas did not make an official bid. The winning U.S. city will be presented to the International Olympic Committee in the fall of 2000. □ Henry Tatum

See also **City; Houston.**

Dance. Mark Morris's staging of the opera *Platee,* performed only three times in June at the Zellerbach Hall in Berkeley, California, was the most critically acclaimed dance performance of 1998. It made a great impression not only for its choreographic invention and the sensitive way that Morris directed the singers, but also for Morris's ability to make a cruel story charming.

Platee, composed by Jean-Philippe Rameau in 1745, tells the tale of an ugly amphibian creature, Platee, who fancies herself to be attractive to all men, including the god Jupiter. Jupiter pretends to be in love with the monstrous-looking frog in order to teach his wife, Juno, a lesson.

As usual, Morris updated the opera, setting some of the scenes in a tavern filled with bawdy sailors and prostitutes and placing others in a swamp teeming with creepy-crawly animals. Elaborate costumes by fashion designer Isaac Mizrahi enhanced Morris's conception.

Morris's unhappy experience with his first Broadway show, *Capeman*—the story of a gang murder—which opened in January 1998 and closed about eight weeks later, did not deter Morris or his Mark Morris Dance Group from having an otherwise fruitful year. The company premiered *Medium* on February 13 at the Byham Theater in Pittsburgh, Pennsylvania. Set to a score by American composer John Harbison in tribute

The Royal Swedish Ballet of Stockholm performs *Skating Rink*, a classic dance from 1922, as part of the company's 225th anniversary celebration in June 1998. The company reconstructed the piece, which was once part of the repertoire of the *avant-garde* (ahead of its time) Les Ballets Suedois.

to Austrian composer Franz Peter Schubert, this unusually lyric dance was well received as it toured the United States with other Morris dances. Morris himself danced one of his signature roles, Dido, in the opera *Dido and Aeneas* by English composer Henry Purcell.

American Ballet Theater. Jointly financed productions once again helped the American Ballet Theater (ABT) mount the full-length extravaganzas that were the centerpieces of its major season of 1998, at the Metropolitan Opera House in New York City. The first of its new ballets during the eight-week run, which began May 11, was *The Snow Maiden*. It was choreographed by Ben Stevenson, director of the Houston Ballet, and had its premiere in Houston on March 12.

The Snow Maiden, based on a Russian fairy tale about the ill-fated love between a fantasy creature and a mortal, is set to various works by Russian composer Peter Ilich Tchaikovsky. It starred the Bolshoi Ballet's Nina Ananiashvili at its premiere in Houston and again in New York City. Apart from Ananiashvili's dancing, critics found the production bland.

A far more rousing work was *Le Corsaire*. This reconstruction of an 1837 work by Marius Petipa was adapted from a 1997 production by the Boston Ballet. With further streamlining of its complicated plot about treacherous pirates,

Le Corsaire premiered on June 19, 1998, and was a smash hit. The ballet offers several roles for virtuoso male performers and entered ABT's repertory just at the moment when the company has a wealth of such dancers, including Angel Corella, Ethan Stiefel, Vladimir Malakhov, Jose Manuel Carreno, Julio Bocca, and Parrish Maynard.

While ABT concentrated on lavish, full-length productions at the Met, it was more artistically adventurous during its season from October 27 to November 8 at New York City's City Center Theater. Twyla Tharp's *Known by Heart* was the most illustrious of the new works.

The New York City Ballet celebrated its 50th anniversary in 1998. The year began on a sour note, however, when the troupe, which rarely tours, canceled plans to tour all 50 states beginning on July 4. The company was unable to raise the $4 million needed to finance the tour. In September and October, however, the City Ballet salvaged some of its grand plan by performing in Berkeley and Orange County, California; in Houston; and on four campuses in upstate New York.

The City Ballet presented a revival of Jerome Robbins's *Les Noces* on May 20 at its home theater, the New York State Theater. This production sparked controversy because Robbins used a taped recording of the score by Russian composer Igor Stravinsky instead of a live orchestra.

The City Ballet's winter season began on November 24 with the same program that the troupe danced at its first performance in 1948. Afterward, all of the group's former dancers were invited onto the stage to take a bow.

The Martha Graham Dance Company, which had fallen on hard times since Graham's death in 1991, took steps to preserve Graham's now rarely performed and endangered repertory. In May 1998, artistic director Ron Protas established the Martha Graham Trust to license the choreographer's works to other companies and provide dancers expert in Graham's techniques to supervise those productions. The Colorado Ballet, which danced *Appalachian Spring* from October 17 to 24 in Denver, was the first American troupe to benefit from the arrangement.

European visitors. Boris Eifman's Ballet of St. Petersburg, which performed at New York's City Center Theater for a week in April, offered a rare look at contemporary Russian ballet. Eifman focused on protagonists with tumultuous inner lives, mixed acrobatics with traditional ballet, and used cinematic techniques in his ballets. For his first American visit, Eifman presented *Tchaikovsky: The Mystery of Life and Death*, which explores the tragic themes in that composer's music and life, and *Red Giselle*, which is based on the life of a famous Russian ballerina, Olga Spessivtseva, who went mad.

William Forsythe's Frankfurt Ballet presented *Eidos: Telos* on December 2 through December 6 during the Brooklyn Academy of Music's Next Wave Festival. It was the German company's first U.S. engagement in 10 years. Based on the mythological character Arachne, the work is the kind of complex multimedia affair favored by the experimental choreographer.

The Ballet Nacional de Cuba paid its first visit to the United States in 19 years in January 1998, when it performed at New York City's City Center and at the Orange County Performing Arts Center in Costa Mesa, California. The troupe danced a version of *Cinderella* by Cuban choreographer Pedro Consuegra with music by Austrian composer Johann Strauss, Jr.

Jerome Robbins, one of the greatest choreographers of the 1900's as well as an enduring bright light on Broadway, died on July 29, 1998, at age 79. Beginning with *On the Town* in 1944, Robbins produced a steady and stunning array of smash musicals. But it was his association with the New York City Ballet, from 1948 until his death, that gave Robbins the most challenging outlet for his creativity. Working with choreographer George Balanchine, Robbins added an American vernacular touch to the classical profile of the company. He was also ballet's great humorist.

□ Nancy Goldner

■ Deaths

in 1998 included those listed below, who were Americans unless otherwise indicated.

Abacha, Sani (1943–June 8), Nigerian dictator who was notorious for the corruption and harshness of his five-year regime and the irony of his role as a peacekeeper in West Africa.

Abzug, Bella (1920–March 31), labor and civil rights lawyer, politician, and feminist icon who represented New York City's West Side in Congress for three terms in the 1970's.

Ambler, Eric (1909–October 22), English author of suspense and spy novels who is credited with raising the thriller to the level of serious literature.

Amory, Cleveland (1917–October 14), social historian and animal rights activist who wrote several best-selling books, including *The Cat and the Curmudgeon.*

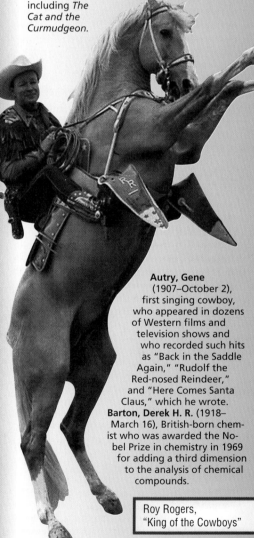

Autry, Gene (1907–October 2), first singing cowboy, who appeared in dozens of Western films and television shows and who recorded such hits as "Back in the Saddle Again," "Rudolf the Red-nosed Reindeer," and "Here Comes Santa Claus," which he wrote.

Barton, Derek H. R. (1918–March 16), British-born chemist who was awarded the Nobel Prize in chemistry in 1969 for adding a third dimension to the analysis of chemical compounds.

Roy Rogers, "King of the Cowboys"

Bettmann, Otto (1903– May 1), curator of rare books who fled Germany in 1935 with more than 25,000 photographs and prints with which he formed the Bettmann Archive.

Bono, Sonny (1935– January 5), song-writer and singer who with former wife Cher recorded a number of hits, including "I Got You, Babe." In 1988, Bono was elected mayor of Palm Springs, California, and in 1994 and 1996 to the U.S. Congress.

Alice Faye, actress

Buffalo Bob Smith, "Howdy-Doody host

Brickhouse, Jack (1916–August 6), amiable sports announcer whose career from the 1940's to 1981 included broadcasts of more than 5,000 Chicago Cubs and White Sox baseball games.

Bridges, Lloyd (1913–March 10), actor who appeared in a variety of films, including *High Noon,* but was best known for the underwater adventure television series "Sea Hunt" and for being the father of actors Beau and Jeff Bridges.

Brimsek, Frankie (1915–November 11), hockey goalie who was inducted into both the Canadian and American hockey halls of fame.

Buffalo Bob Smith (Robert Schmidt) (1917–July 30), creator and sidekick of Howdy Doody—as well as Clarabell the Clown, Phineas T. Bluster, and Flub-a-Dub—with whom Buffalo Bob appeared from 1947 to 1960 on one of television's most enduring children's programs.

Buscaglia, Leo (1925–June 12), author of 15 self-help books and lecturer who became famous preaching the power of love on public television.

Caray, Harry (1919–February 18), sports announcer with the St. Louis Cardinals, Oakland A's, Chicago White Sox, and Chicago Cubs. Caray was as well known for his renditions of "Take Me Out to the Ball Game" as he was for his rousing play-by-play.

Carmichael, Stokely (Kwame Ture) (1941–November 15), black activist who helped redirect the civil rights movement from nonviolent civil disobedience into a more confrontational mode with his call in 1966 for "black power."

Carret, Philip (1896–May 26), legendary Wall Street investor who is credited with shaping the investment pool that became known as the mutual fund. Carret worked at his Wall Street office until one month before his death at age 101.

Carter, Betty (1930–September 26), vocalist and composer whose unusual style set the standard for jazz singing. Her 1961 rendition of "Baby, It's Cold Outside" with Ray Charles became a classic of jazz music.

Castaneda, Carlos (1925?–April 27), leader of the New Age movement of the 1960's whose writings were praised by some as serious anthropology and dismissed by others as products of an overwrought imagination.

Chiles, Lawton (1930–December 12), governor of Florida whose political career as a moderate Democrat was marked by a concern for environmental issues and fiscal responsibility.

Helen Wills Moody, tennis player

Sony Bono,
congressman and singer

Stokely Carmichael,
civil-rights activist

Clark, Dane (1913–September 11), actor best known for his roles as tough, but likable sailors and pilots in World War II movies. Clark aspired to play the "Joe Average" of film characters.

Cleaver, Eldridge (1935–May 1), writer whose influential prison memoir *Soul on Ice* was seen in the late 1960's as giving voice to the collective rage of African Americans.

Clifford, Clark (1906–October 10), political adviser to four presidents and secretary of defense in the Johnson Administration. Clifford helped organize the North Atlantic Treaty Organization and the Marshall Plan.

Commager, Henry Steele (1902–March 2), influential historian and teacher whose scholarly writing reflected his belief in the U.S. Constitution and humanity's ability to reason and learn.

Cookson, Dame Catherine (1906–June 11), British writer of popular fiction who drew on her own impoverished childhood for the inspiration to write more than 90 novels.

Costa, Lucio (1902–June 13), Brazilian architect who in the 1950's planned Brazil's capital, Brasilia.

Diemer, Walter E. (1905–January 8), gum company employee who in 1928 accidentally invented bubble gum.

Douglas, Marjory Stoneman (1890–May 14), environmentalist who was known for her 1946 bestseller *The Everglades: River of Grass.*

Duncan, Todd (1903–February 28), African American baritone who created the role of Porgy in George Gershwin's *Porgy and Bess.*

Ewbank, Weeb (1907–November 17), only football coach in history who led teams—the Baltimore Colts in 1958 and the New York Jets in 1968—to championships in both the National and American football leagues.

Faye, Alice (1915–May 9), actress who starred in more than 30 films, most of them 20th Century Fox musicals, in the late 1930's and early 1940's.

Fell, Norman (1924–December 14), film and television actor best known for his role as the landlord on the sitcom "Three's Company."

Flock, Tim (1924–March 31), stock-car racer who won the 1952 and 1955 Nascar Winston Cup series and took 40 of the 190 Winston Cup races he entered, a career record that remains unbroken.

Friendly, Fred (1915–March 3), producer and former president of CBS news who with Edward R. Murrow was credited with inventing the television documentary with such landmark programs as "See It Now" and "Harvest of Shame."

Fujita, Tetsuya (1920–Nov. 19), meteorologist who devised the scale by which tornado severity is rated and discovered how violent down-bursts of air can trigger airplane crashes

Gellhorn, Martha (1908–February 15), journalist and novelist who covered the Blitz in London and landed on the beach in Normandy on D-Day during World War II. Gellhorn was the only one of Ernest Hemingway's four wives to leave him.

Roddy McDowall, actor

Alan B. Shepard, Jr., astronaut

Goldhaber, Gertrude Scharff (1911–February 2), physicist whose discoveries laid much of the groundwork for the understanding of nuclear fission and the structure of atomic nuclei.

Goldman, James (1927–October 28), novelist, screenwriter, and playwright who wrote *The Lion in Winter* and the book for Stephen Sondheim's *Follies.*

Goldwater, Barry M. (1909–May 29), politician who served 30 years in the U.S. Senate and ran for president against Lyndon Johnson in 1964. Goldwater's philosophy of less government at home and anti-Communism abroad laid the foundation for modern U.S. conservatism.

Gore, Albert, Sr. (1907–December 5), liberal Democrat who represented Tennessee in the House and Senate and was the father of Vice President Al Gore.

Gorman, Carl (1908?–February 5), artist who with other Navajo Indians transformed their native language during World War II into a code that the Japanese were never able to break.

Griffith Joyner, Florence (1959–September 21), track-and-field athlete who won three gold medals at the 1988 Summer Olympics.

Hartman, Phil (1948–May 28), Canadian-born comedian known for his impersonations of Bill Clinton on television's "Saturday Night Live" and his role on "Newsradio."

Hickson, Joan (1906–October 17), English actress whose greatest fame came as Miss Marple in the BBC television series based on the Agatha Christie character.

Holzman, William "Red" (1920–November 13), Hall-of-Fame basketball coach who led the New York Knicks to two NBA championships.

Howell, Mary (1932–February 5), physician and Harvard Medical School's first woman associate dean. Howell championed medical careers for women, particularly in *Why Would a Girl Go into Medicine?*

Hughes, Ted (1930–October 28), poet laureate of Great Britain who was as well-known as the husband of American poet Sylvia Plath as he was for his own work.

Kane, Bob (1915–November 3), cartoonist who in 1939 created the comic-book character Batman.

Kazan, Alfred (1915–June 5), literary critic and writer best known for his 1942 review of American literature, *On Native Grounds.*

Kukui, Kenichi (1918–January 9), Japanese theoretical and physical chemist who received the Nobel Prize in chemistry in 1981 for explaining how certain properties of the orbit of electrons affect the chemical reactivity of a molecule.

Kurosawa, Akira (1910–September 6), internationally acclaimed Japanese film director whose movies, such as *Rashomon, Seven Samurai,* and *Ran,* were known for integrating Japanese folklore and Western styles of acting and storytelling.

Lewis, Shari (1934–August 2), ventriloquist and puppeteer who with Lamb Chop, Charlie Horse, and Hush Puppy captured the hearts of children with a combination of humor and teaching.

Lord, Jack (1920–January 21), actor who played Steve McGarrett on the television series "Hawaii Five-O."

Luckman, Sid (1916–July 5), football star at Columbia University and Chicago Bears quarterback who, in the 1940's, introduced the T-formation offense under the tutelage of George Halas.

Marshall, E. G. (1910–August 24), actor whose 50-year career included roles in the original 1942 Broadway production of *The Skin of Our Teeth,* the film *12 Angry Men,* and the television series, "The Defenders" and "The New Doctors."

McCartney, Linda (1941–April 17), photographer, singer, and animal rights activist who was married to Beatle Paul McCartney.

McDonald, Dick (1909–July 14), restaurateur who with brother Maurice invented the fast-food

Florence Griffith Joyner, Olympic runner

restaurant in 1948 with the first McDonald's in San Bernardino, California.

McDowall, Roddy (1928–October 3), actor whose career spanned more than 60 years. McDowall made more than 130 films, including boyhood roles in *How Green Was My Valley* and *Lassie Come Home* and adult roles *Cleopatra* and *Planet of the Apes.*

Merrill, Bob (1921–February 16), tunesmith who wrote "How Much Is That Doggie in the Window?" and lyrics for *Funny Girl.*

Merritt, Theresa (1923?–June 12), actress and singer whose career stretched from Billy Rose's 1943 production of *Carmen Jones* to a role in television's "That's My Mama" and August Wilson's 1984 Broadway musical *Ma Rainey's Black Bottom.*

Mitchell, William Ormond (1914–February 25), writer who became a symbol of Canada's West for his short stories, radio scripts, and such novels as *Who Has Seen the Wind.*

Moody, Helen Wills (1905–January 1), tennis player who was ranked No. 1 in the world for eight straight years, won 31 Grand Slam titles between 1923 and 1938, and enjoyed a 180-match winning streak between 1927 and 1933.

Moore, Archie (1913–December 9), professional boxer who held the world light-heavyweight title nine years, longer than any fighter in history.

Moss, Jeffrey (1942–Sept. 24), cocreator of "Sesame Street" and creator of Cookie Monster and Oscar the Grouch.

Murray, Jerome (1912–January 7), inventor whose creations included everything from the

Barry Goldwater, senator

George Wallace, politician

electric carving knife to the peristaltic pump that made open-heart surgery and kidney dialysis possible.

Murray, Jim (1919–August 16), Pulitzer Prize-winning sports writer and cofounder of *Sports Illustrated.*

Newhouser, Hal (1921–November 10), Hall of Fame pitcher for the Detroit Tigers and the only major league pitcher to win two consecutive Most Valuable Player awards.

Nitschke, Ray (1936–March 8), Green Bay Packer middle linebacker in the team's glory days in the 1960's who was elected to the Pro Football Hall of Fame in 1978.

Nolan, Jeanette (1911–June 15), actress whose career stretched from her 1948 film debut playing Lady Macbeth to her role as Robert Redford's mother in *The Horse Whisperer* in 1998.

O'Sullivan, Maureen (1911–June 23), film actress best known for playing Jane to Johnny Weissmuller's Tarzan and as mother to real-life daughter Mia Farrow in *Hannah and Her Sisters.*

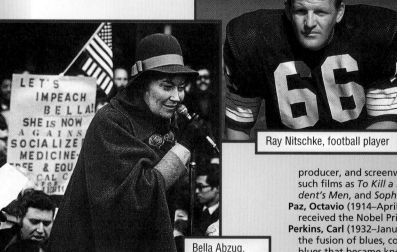

Ray Nitschke, football player

Bella Abzug, congresswoman and women's rights activist

Pakula, Alan J. (1928–November 19), film director, producer, and screenwriter who was known for such films as *To Kill a Mockingbird, All the President's Men,* and *Sophie's Choice.*

Paz, Octavio (1914–April 19), Mexican writer who received the Nobel Prize in literature in 1990.

Perkins, Carl (1932–January 19), musician involved in the fusion of blues, country, and rhythm-and-blues that became known as "rockabilly" and who wrote "Blue Suede Shoes."

Porsche, Ferdinand (1909–March 27), German industrialist and Porsche A.G. chairman who designed the sports car he named for his family.

Powell, Lewis (1907–August 25), U.S. Supreme Court justice whose moderate stance made him a pivotal figure on the court from 1972 until 1987.

Rabbitt, Eddie (1941–May 7), singer and songwriter who between 1976 and 1990 had 34 Top-10 singles and 17 No. 1 hits on the Billboard country chart, including "I Love a Rainy Night."

Ray, James Earl (1928–April 23), man who was convicted of assassinating Martin Luther King, Jr.

Rebozo, Bebe (1912–May 8), Florida millionaire, whose friendship and business dealings with Richard Nixon came under intense scrutiny during the Watergate scandal of 1972 to 1974.

Reines, Frederick (1918–August 26), physicist who with a colleague in 1951 was the first to detect neutrinos, a kind of subatomic particle.

Robbins, Jerome (1918–July 29), celebrated choreographer known for such ballets as "The Cage" and "Afternoon of a Faun," and for the staging and choreography of such Broadway musicals as *The King and I* and *West Side Story.*

Rogers, Roy (1911–July 6), actor and singer whose easy-going "King of the Cowboys" persona tamed the West, with the help of his wife Dale Evans, in more than 90 movies and 100 television shows of the 1940's and 1950's.

Rolle, Esther (1920?–November 17), actress who was best known for Florida, the strong-willed character she portrayed on television's "Maude" and "Good Times" in the 1970's,

Shepard, Alan B., Jr. (1923–July 21), astronaut who, on May 5, 1961, was the first American in space, served on the crew of Apollo 14, and became one of the 12 men to have walked on the Moon.

Sinatra, Frank (1915–May 14), singer hailed for transforming popular music into an art form while transforming himself from 1940's pop superstar into an icon of swinging sophistication.

Smythe, Reg (1917–June 13), British cartoonist who in 1957 created the "Andy Capp" comic strip, which was reputed to be based on Smythe's parents.

Lloyd Bridges, actor

Tammy Wynette, country-western singer

Sobek, Joseph (1918–March 27), tennis and squash professional who invented racquetball.

Spilhaus, Athelstan (1911–March 30), South African-born geophysicist who invented a device to measure ocean temperatures, balloons to measure atmospheric waves, and more than 3,000 toys.

Spock, Benjamin (1903–March 15), physician whose handbook, *Dr. Spock's Baby and Child Care,* recommended common sense over rules and a rigid schedule and sold millions of copies in the post-World War II (1939–1945) baby-boom years.

Stickney, Dorothy (1896?–June 2), stage actress who played Vinnie Day opposite her husband, Howard Lindsay, in *Life with Father* for 3,224 performances, the longest run of a nonmusical in Broadway history.

Suzuki, Shinichi (1898–January 27), musician and teacher who created the "Suzuki Method"—a system in which music, like language, is learned by imitating sounds, rather than studying notes.

Tippett, Sir Michael (1905–January 8), British composer of complex, highly inventive music, including operas, oratorios, and symphonies.

Thompson, Kay (1902–July 2), musician and writer who created "Eloise," a stage and storybook character whose adventures terrorize her fellow residents in New York City's Plaza Hotel.

Udall, Morris (1922–December 12), liberal Democrat from Arizona who served in Congress for 30 years. Udall was known for his support of environmental issues and government reform.

Ulanova, Galina (1910–March 22), celebrated Russian ballerina for whom Prokofiev wrote *Romeo and Juliet* and two other ballets.

Von Ohain, Hans (1911–March 13), German engineer who independently coinvented (with Frank Whittle working simultaneously in Great Britain) the aviation gas turbine, or jet engine.

Wallace, George C. (1919–September 13), four-term Alabama governor well-known for his original stance against racial segregation and three bids for the U.S. presidency.

Shari Lewis, puppeteer

Ward, Helen (1916–April 21), singer with the Benny Goodman band in the 1930's who made hits of "Goody Goody," and "These Foolish Things."

Wells, Junior (Amos Blackmore) (1934–January 15), harmonica player and singer who played a major role in developing the Chicago blues style of the late 1950's and 1960's.

West, Dorothy (1907–August 16), novelist who played an integral part in the Harlem Renaissance of the 1920's and worked late in her career with editor Jacqueline Kennedy Onassis.

Wilson, Carl (1946–February 7), singer and musician who played lead guitar with the Beach Boys and was the lead vocalist for such hits as "God Only Knows" and "Good Vibrations."

Wilson, Flip (1933–November 25), comedian and 1970's variety show host who created the flamboyant characters Geraldine and the Reverend Leroy of the Church of What's Happening Now.

Wood, Beatrice (1895–March 12), ceramic artist whose relationships with Man Ray, Francis Picabia, and Marcel Duchamp earned her the title "Mama of Dada." She provided the inspiration for Francois Truffaut's film *Jules et Jim* and the character Rose in James Cameron's *Titanic*.

Wynette, Tammy (1942–April 6), singer whose hits, including "Stand By Your Man," and "D-I-V-O-R-C-E," established her as one of the queens of country western music.

Yankovic, Frank (1915–October 14), accordionist and bandleader who was crowned Polka King in 1948 and maintained the title for 50 years.

Young, Robert (1907–July 21), film and television actor who appeared in dozens of movies but was best known for his television roles as the ideal father in "Father Knows Best" and ideal physician in "Marcus Welby, M.D."

Youngman, Henny (1906–February 24), stand-up comedian who became famous for his rapid fire delivery of jokes and one-liners, including his signature "Take my wife—please."

Democratic Party. Many members of the Democratic Party, particularly Democrats running for the U.S. Congress in the November election, spent much of the 1998 campaign attempting to distance themselves from President Bill Clinton. On August 17, Clinton, speaking live on television, admitted that he had been involved in a relationship with Monica Lewinsky, a former White House intern. The scandal was expected to cost the Democrats seats in both the Senate and House of Representatives.

The Democratic Party, however, did considerably better in the elections than most political experts had predicted. Party leaders, no longer afraid of a backlash in the wake of the presidential scandal, softened their stance toward the president and sided with him during the impeachment hearings conducted in November and December by the House of Representatives Judiciary Committee.

On December 11 and 12, all 16 Democrats on the Judiciary Committee voted against sending articles of impeachment to the House of Representatives. All 23 Republicans (with the exception of one member on one ballot) voted to recommend impeachment. On December 19, the full House approved two articles of impeachment. All but five Democrats in the House voted against impeaching President Clinton.

Congressional elections. In the November elections, Democrats gained five seats in the U.S. House of Representatives and held off anticipated Republican gains in the Senate. The election reduced the majority in the House to 223 Republicans versus 211 Democrats, with one independent who usually voted with Democrats. In the Senate, Republicans retained a 55-to-45 majority.

Democrats won two major Senate victories on November 3. In New York, Congressman Charles E. Schumer, a Democrat, defeated Republican Senator Alfonse M. D'Amato. In North Carolina, Democrat John Edwards captured Lauch Faircloth's Senate seat in an upset that left North Carolina's senior senator, Jesse A. Helms, the only Republican holding a statewide office.

The Democrats suffered a major Senate loss in Illinois, where Carol Moseley-Braun, who had been the first African American woman elected to the Senate, was defeated by Peter Fitzgerald, a conservative Republican state senator.

State elections. In California, Lieutenant Governor Gray Davis became the first Democrat to be elected governor since Jerry Brown in 1978. In Alabama, Democrat Don Siegelman took the governor's mansion from Republican Fob James, Jr. In South Carolina, Democrat Jim Hodges beat Republican Governor David Beasley.

Fund-raising. Inquiries into President Clinton's 1996 reelection campaign continued to haunt the Democratic Party in 1998. The Democratic Party announced in 1997 that it had returned more than $3 million in contributions that it had deemed illegal or inappropriate. About three-quarters of the contributions had been raised by Asian American businessmen John Huang, Johnny Chung, and Charles Yah Lin Trie. Many of the contributions that were returned to donors came from individuals or businesses located in Asia.

A grand jury on Jan. 28, 1998, indicted Trie on charges of soliciting campaign contributions to the Democratic Party from individuals or companies in Asia, which were barred from making contributions to political campaigns in the United States. On February 5, Trie pleaded not guilty in federal court. Chung pleaded guilty on March 16 to federal charges of using false donors to conceal $20,000 in illegal contributions to the 1996 Clinton-Gore reelection campaign. On Dec. 14, 1998, a federal judge sentenced Chung to five years' probation.

Ban lifted. The Democratic National Committee (DNC) in January 1998 lifted a year-long, self-imposed ban on accepting contributions from noncitizens who were legal residents of the United States. The DNC had restricted itself after returning contributions.

Debt reduction. In January, DNC Finance Chairman Alan Solomont announced that the Democratic Party had reduced its debt from $13.4 million to $9.4 million at the end of 1997. The DNC reported that most of the debt was related to its defense during the fund-raising scandal. The DNC credited an intensive fund-raising campaign led by President Clinton for reducing the debt. In March 1998, the DNC reported that it would give 7.5 percent of the money raised at Democratic fund-raisers to state parties in states in which DNC benefits had been conducted.

Clinton, Gore cleared. Attorney General Janet Reno announced on Nov. 24, 1998, that she would not appoint an independent counsel to investigate whether Vice President Al Gore lied to Justice Department officials during a 1997 investigation of fund-raising phone calls for the DNC made from the vice president's government office. Reno reported that she found no reasonable grounds that Vice President Gore misled investigators examining alleged fund-raising abuses.

On Dec. 7, 1998, Reno said that she would not appoint a special prosecutor to investigate President Clinton's role in an advertising campaign during the 1996 election.   □ William J. Eaton

See also **Congress of the United States; Elections; Republican Party; State government; United States, President of the.**

California Governor-elect Gray Davis greets supporters in Los Angeles following his victory in the Nov. 3, 1998, election. Davis, who had been California's lieutenant governor, became the first Democrat to win a gubernatorial election in that state since 1978.

Denmark. Danes opted for stability in domestic and foreign policy in voting held during 1998. In March, the center-left government of Prime Minister Poul Nyrup Rasmussen was reelected over the center-right opposition, led by the Liberal Party. Rasmussen's coalition of Social Democrats, Radical Liberals, and several allied left-wing parties won 90 seats in the 179-seat parliament. Rasmussen had vowed to maintain the welfare system and to continue the economic policies that gave Denmark one of the strongest economies of the 15-nation European Union (EU). The Liberal Party campaigned for cuts in income taxes, which in 1998 were among the highest in Europe, and for reduced welfare spending. The extreme right-wing, anti-immigrant Danish People's Party, which argued that non-European immigrants were becoming too great a burden on the welfare system, won 13 seats.

European Union. In a referendum held in May, Danes endorsed the EU's Treaty of Amsterdam. The vote was considered a major test for the treaty, which EU members had agreed to in June 1997. The treaty was designed to prepare the EU for new members from Eastern and Southern Europe. Danes had rejected the Maastricht Treaty on European Union in 1992, a move that resulted in financial instability across Europe and forced the Danish government to renegotiate the treaty to allow Denmark to stay out of the single currency, opposed by many Danes.

The economy continued to boom in 1998. Growth was forecast to be about 2.4 percent, and unemployment was projected to be about 4.2 percent. The strong economy brought on the country's first general strike in 13 years, however. In April and May, some 500,000 workers in the construction, transportation, and manufacturing industries demanded more vacation time and a bigger pay increase. The government agreed to some of the demands to end the strike.

In June and September, the government announced tax increases and spending cuts to the 1999 budget. The moves were aimed at maintaining the strength of the Danish currency, the krone, an important consideration in light of the country's decision not to join 11 other EU nations in launching a single currency. The government left open the possibility of joining the currency in the future.

The first road and rail link from the Danish mainland to the island of Sjaelland, where Copenhagen, the capital is located, was opened in June 1998. Named the Fixed Link across the Great Belt, the project included a tunnel and two bridges, including the 4-mile (6.5-kilometer) East Bridge, the longest suspension bridge in Europe and the second-longest in the world.   □ Tom Buerkle

See also **Europe** (Facts in brief table); **Europe** Special Report: **European Union.**

A diver searches Copenhagen harbor in January 1998 for the head of the vandalized statue of the Little Mermaid, which commemorates the character from a Hans-Christian Andersen story. The head was eventually recovered and the statue restored.

Disabled. The United States Supreme Court ruled in June 1998 that state prison inmates were protected by the 1990 Americans with Disabilities Act (ADA). The case was filed by Ronald Yeskey. Yeskey was unable to participate in a Pennsylvania prison boot camp program, which would have qualified him for an early parole, because he had *hypertension* (high blood pressure). The court agreed with Yeskey's claim that his exclusion from the program violated the ADA.

The ruling allowed Yeskey to sue the prison over his prolonged confinement. Experts said the court's decision had implications for inmates with many kinds of disabilities, including those with HIV, the virus that causes AIDS.

Diseases. The Supreme Court ruled in June that people who carry HIV or have other health conditions—but show no symptoms—were protected against discrimination by the ADA. The decision was made in the case of Sidney Abbott, a woman whose dentist refused to fill a cavity outside a hospital setting because she had HIV. The court agreed with Abbott's argument that it would be unethical for her to reproduce, therefore, she was disabled and covered by the ADA. Analysts claimed that, by making reproduction grounds for discrimination, the court's decision could help women win insurance coverage for birth control.   □ Brian Bouldrey

Disasters. A study issued on November 27 by the Worldwatch Institute, an environmental research group, and Munich Re, a company that insures insurance companies, reported that disasters resulting from violent weather in the first 11 months of 1998 caused a record $89 billion in damages worldwide. The total exceeded the cost of weather-related disasters worldwide in all of the 1980's.

Disasters that resulted in 25 or more deaths in 1998 included the following:

Aircraft crashes
February 2—Mindanao Island, Philippines. A Philippine DC-9 crashes into a mountain 8,200 feet (2,500 meters) high on a flight from Manila to Cagayan de Oro, killing all 99 passengers and 5 crew members aboard.
May 5—Northern Peru. Seventy-five of 87 passengers and crew members aboard a Peruvian Air Force jet chartered by Occidental Petroleum Corporation die when the Boeing 737, flying in heavy rain, crashes into the Amazon jungle.
September 2—Nova Scotia. All 229 passengers and crew aboard Swissair Flight 111, bound for Geneva from New York City, die when the plane crashes into the Atlantic Ocean off the southeast shore of Nova Scotia. The wide-bodied MD-11 jet, which broke up on impact with the ocean, was minutes away from completing an emergency landing.

December 11—Southern Thailand. A Thai Airways jetliner crashes in a swamp during a rainstorm as it attempts to land, killing 101 of the 146 passengers and crew members aboard.

Earthquakes
January 10—Hebei Province, China. An earthquake of 6.2 intensity rocks dozens of villages near the Great Wall, 150 miles (240 kilometers) north of Beijing. The quake kills 50 people, injures nearly 12,000, and leaves 44,000 homeless.
February 4—Takhar and Badakhshan provinces, Afghanistan. An earthquake registering 6.1 strikes a hilly, agricultural region 200 miles (320 kilometers) northeast of Kabul, the capital, leaving about 4,500 dead and 30,000 homeless.
May 22—Central Bolivia. Two earthquakes, with respective magnitudes of 5.9 and 6.8, level hundreds of structures in Aiquile and Totora, towns approximately 250 miles (400 kilometers) east of La Paz, leaving at least 80 people dead. More than 150 aftershocks continue to shake the colonial-era towns, listed as national historical monuments for their adobe architecture, for 12 hours after the initial quakes.
May 30—Takhar and Badakhshan provinces, Afghanistan. An earthquake registering 6.9 hits northeastern Afghanistan, destroying as many as 100 villages and leaving some 4,000 people dead. The same area was hit by a quake on February 4.
June 28—Adana, Turkey. More than 100 people die when flimsily constructed apartment buildings in Adana, Ceyhan, and other towns in southern Turkey collapse during an earthquake with a magnitude of 6.3.

Explosions and fires
February 14—Cameroon. More than 100 people are killed when railroad tank cars explode after two trains collide on the outskirts of Yaounde, the capital of Cameroon, on the west coast of Africa. Before the explosion, the victims, many of them cabdrivers, had rushed into the wreckage to collect fuel gushing from the tankers ruptured by the collision.
April 4—Donetsk, Ukraine. A methane gas explosion in the deep Skachinskoho coal mine, located 390 miles (630 kilometers) southeast of Kiev, kills 63 of the 264 miners working at approximately 3,600 feet (1,100 meters) underground. Seventeen people died in a methane gas explosion in the same mine in August 1992.
October 17, Nigeria. An explosion at an oil pipeline 180 miles (290 kilometers) southeast of Lagos, Nigeria, kills more than 700 people, destroys several villages, and scorches crops in surrounding fields. The explosion is blamed on thieves attempting to siphon oil from the line by punching holes in it.

Shipwrecks
March 31—Yemen. At least 180 Somali refugees drown when their boat, carrying 182 passengers and 6 crew members, sinks in the Gulf of Aden off the coast of Yemen.
April 1—Nigeria. A boat en route from Nigeria to Gabon overturns in rough waters off Africa's

Children make their way through the ruins of buildings destroyed by an earthquake and its aftershocks in northeastern Afghanistan in February 1998. The earthquake, which registered a magnitude of 6.1, caused the deaths of approximately 4,500 people and left 30,000 homeless.

west coast. Only 20 of the 300 passengers aboard survive.

April 1—Sudan. At least 55 Sudanese military recruits drown when a boat, overloaded with passengers, tips over in the Blue Nile. Recruits, numbering in the hundreds, overran the ship in an attempt to escape military training, which is mandatory in the long-running civil war between northern and southern Sudan.

June 12—Guinea-Bissau. More than 200 people fleeing fighting between government troops and renegade forces in the West African country of Guinea-Bissau drown when they attempt to escape by boat to the coastal Bijagos Islands.

September 18—Manila, the Philippines. At least 60 people drown in heavy seas swept by tropical storm Vicki when a ferry with 430 people aboard sinks in Manila Bay, 40 miles (64 kilometers) south of Manila, the capital.

Storms and floods

February 23—Central Florida. Tornadoes with winds as high as 260 miles (420 kilometers) per hour hit central Florida in a path running from Daytona Beach on the Atlantic Ocean to Tampa Bay on the Gulf of Mexico. As many as 10 funnels cut swaths 50 miles (80 kilometers) wide through Seminole, Osceola, Orange, Brevard, and Volusia counties, shredding mobile homes and destroying hundreds of houses. At least 38 people are killed and more than 250 injured.

March 3—Pakistan. Torrential rains, which began on March 1, trigger flash floods across southwestern Pakistan, sweeping thousands of houses into riverbeds, which are typically dry, and drowning more than 300 people. An additional 1,500 are missing and feared dead.

March 24—West Bengal, India. A tornado with winds of 115 miles (185 kilometers) per hour accompanied by torrential rains drives through several villages in eastern India, killing at least 106 people, including 16 children who die when a school collapses. More than 500 people are missing and 1,100 are injured.

March 25—Ecuador. More than 175 people in the area of Calceta, a town 124 miles (200 kilometers) southwest of Quito, drown in flash floods resulting from extremely heavy rainfall.

April 8—Southeastern United States. Tornadoes, roaring through Mississippi, Alabama, and Georgia, kill 43 people. The most severe damage and 32 of the fatalities are concentrated in Jefferson County, Alabama, west of Birmingham, where tornadoes with winds estimated to top 250 miles (400 kilometers) per hour cut a 1-mile- (1.6 kilometer-) wide swath 15 miles (24 kilometers) long.

May 6—Salerno and Avellino provinces, Italy. Days of heavy rain trigger massive rock and mud slides in Campania region villages south of Naples, killing at least 142 people and leaving more than 1,500 homeless.

June 9—Western India. A cyclone moves into the Gulf of Kutch from the Arabian Sea and tears into western India, killing more than 700 people and leaving many hundreds homeless. The death toll is highest around the port of Kandla, which is hit by a 12-foot (3.7-meter) tidal wave.

July 17—Papua New Guinea. Three *tsunamis* (huge waves often caused by underwater earthquakes), the last and largest estimated to be 33 feet (10 meters) high, crash into Papua New Guinea's northern coast, killing an estimated 3,000 people in an area of between 8,000 and 10,000 residents. The vast majority of the victims are children. The walls of water may have been triggered by two earthquakes, 20 minutes apart, centered approximately 12 miles (19 kilometers) offshore.

July 27—China. The Yangtze River crests for the third time in July, reaching its highest level in 44 years. Weeks of rain result in the flooding of millions of acres in Hunan, Hubei, and Jiangxi provinces, where millions of people have been driven from their houses and at least 3,000 people have died.

September 8—Chiapas, Mexico. Governor Roberto Albores Guillen declares the State of Chiapas a disaster zone after six days of heavy rain caused 15 rivers to overflow their banks, producing massive flooding that left at least 120 people dead and 25,000 homeless.

September 12—Bangladesh. Floodwaters, which have covered much of the country for more than two months, begin to recede, according to the Flood Forecast and Warning Center. The massive flooding of the Brahmaputra, Ganges, and Jamuna rivers has left 900 people dead and displaced one quarter of the country's 124 million people since July 10.

September 24—The Caribbean. Hurricane Georges drives toward Cuba and the Florida Keys after tearing across the island of Hispaniola, leaving at least 200 people dead and 100,000 homeless in the Dominican Republic. Sugar, banana, rice, and coffee crops are severely damaged in both the Dominican Republic and Haiti. In its rampage across the Caribbean, the hurricane has killed more than 500 people and caused billions of dollars in damage.

October 31—Central America. A tropical storm that has been stalled over Honduras, Nicaragua, Guatemala, El Salvador, and Belize for nearly a week continues to dump as much as 24 inches (61 centimeters) of rain every 24 hours, triggering mud slides and massive flooding. In Honduras and Nicaragua, entire villages are wiped out. Central American officials estimate that more than 10,000 people have been killed in the storm, which began as Hurricane Mitch with winds 180 miles (290 kilometers) per hour.

November 22–December 7—Eastern and Central Europe. At least 180 people die—most of them in Poland and Romania—from sub-zero temperatures and blizzard conditions.

Other disasters

April 9—Mecca, Saudi Arabia. More than 2 million Islamic pilgrims, in Mecca for the *hajj*, the annual pilgrimage that is one of Islam's holiest rituals, stampede in 100 °F (38 °C) heat during the traditional "stoning of the devil" ceremony, which involves hurling pebbles at pillars that symbolize the temptations of Satan. More than 100 people fall to their deaths from a bridge or are trampled to death.

June 3—Eschede, Germany. More than 100 people are killed when a German Railways express train, traveling at 125 miles (200 kilometers) per hour, derails in northern Germany and crashes into a concrete column supporting a highway overpass, causing it to collapse. Two of the train's cars are crushed under tons of concrete.

June 6—Taipei, Taiwan. A team from the U.S. Centers for Disease Control and Prevention aids in the investigation of an intestinal virus that has killed 30 babies. Scientists believe as many as 200,000 infants on the island were infected with the virus during the week of May 31.

June 7—New Delhi, India. More than 2,500 people die in India in a record-breaking heat wave that began on May 12. In New Delhi, the capital, temperatures climbed as high as 124 °F (51 °C).

August 3—Bombay, India. Thirty-two people die when a seven-story, concrete apartment building collapses, leaving a pile of rubble 20 to 30 feet (6 to 9 meters) high. Since 1995, eight major structures have collapsed in Bombay, where officials estimate 18,000 structurally unsafe buildings house as many as 1.2 million people.

October 18—Egypt. A commuter train running between Alexandria, Egypt, and Kafr el-Sheik jumps its tracks at a station southeast of Alexandria, plows through a crowded platform and kills 30 people.

November 26—Punjab, India. More than 200 people die and 260 are injured when an express passenger train en route to Calcutta collides with cars that had uncoupled accidentally from a mail train on its way to New Delhi.

Drug abuse. A public-health study reported in September 1998 that the number of college students in the United States who engaged in binge drinking remained constant at about 40 percent from 1993 to 1997. Binge drinking is defined, for men, as consuming at least five drinks within a few hours and, for women, as consuming four drinks. The 1997 College Alcohol Study by the Harvard University School of Public Health in Boston noted that educational and disciplinary programs aimed at reducing binge drinking as well as the well-publicized deaths of a number of college students from alcohol abuse had failed to discourage the practice. According to the study, 42.7 percent of the 14,521 students interviewed were identified as binge drinkers, compared with 44.1 percent in 1993.

The study also found increases in both the number of students who drank to get drunk and the number who abstained from alcohol. According to the study, 53.2 percent of students surveyed reported drinking to get drunk in 1997, compared with 39.4 percent in 1993. The number of students who said they avoided alcohol altogether rose to 19 percent from 15.6 percent between 1993 and 1997.

Drug use. Although the overall number of Americans using illegal drugs did not change in 1997, drug use among people ages 12 to 17 rose slightly, according to the 1997 National Household Survey on Drug Abuse. The study, published in August 1998 by the U.S. Department of Health and Human Services, was based on a survey of 24,500 Americans age 12 and over. The researchers found that 6.4 percent of those questioned—about 14 million people—reported using illegal drugs at least once in the 30 days prior to the interview, compared with 6.1 percent in 1996. The number using illicit drugs increased to 11.4 percent from 9 percent in 1996 among people ages 12 to 17. The increase was particularly noticeable among 12- and 13-year-olds, 3.8 percent of whom admitted using illegal drugs, compared with 2.2 percent in 1996.

Marijuana ranked as the most commonly used drug, both overall and among teen-agers. In 1997, 9.4 percent of youth ages 12 to 17 used marijuana. The 1997 figure was up from 7.1 percent over 1996 and nearly double the 1992 figure.

The number of people in the United States using cocaine remained fairly constant from 1996 to 1997 at 1.5 million. Heroin use increased between 1992 and 1997. Officials estimated that 325,000 people in the United States used heroin in 1997. Approximately 74 percent of illicit drug users in 1997 were white, and 22 percent were black or Hispanic. Male drug users outnumbered females by about two to one.   □ David Lewis

Drugs. In March 1998, the United States Food and Drug Administration (FDA) approved the sale of Viagra, or sildenafil citrate, the first pill to treat *impotence* (the inability to maintain an erection). Impotence affected as many as 30 million men in the United States in 1998.

Physicians wrote more than 3.6 million prescriptions for Viagra, sold by Pfizer, Incorporated, of New York City, in the first four months it was available. Clinical trials in more than 4,000 men had shown that Viagra was effective in approximately 70 percent of patients. Viagra works by increasing blood flow to the penis.

The popularity of the drug led to controversies over whether health insurance companies should reimburse patients for the medicine, which cost between $7 and $10 per tablet. Many health insurers either limited reimbursement for Viagra or refused to pay for it. Concerns also arose about the drug's safety. By late November, the FDA confirmed that approximately 130 American men taking Viagra had died. The agency said that most of the men had risk factors for cardiovascular disease, and some had taken nitrate medications, which the FDA and Pfizer had previously warned should not be taken while using Viagra. In November, the FDA warned physicians to be cautious about prescribing Viagra to patients with heart disease or high blood pressure, and

Pfizer added similar warnings to the drug's label. The FDA maintained that Viagra was safe when used properly.

Thalidomide returns. In July, the FDA approved thalidomide, a drug banned worldwide since the 1960's, for the treatment of *leprosy,* or *Hansen's disease* (an infectious disease that may cause blindness and crippling deformities). However, the approval of the drug meant that U.S. physicians could also prescribe thalidomide for other diseases, including cancer and AIDS, for which it showed some promise. The drug was to be sold by Celgene Corporation, of Warren, New Jersey, under the name of Thalomid.

In the 1960's, physicians in Europe and certain other parts of the world prescribed thalidomide as a sedative for pregnant women. Many of these women bore children with severe birth defects. In 1998, the FDA required that men and women taking Thalomid be instructed on the use of effective methods of birth control. In addition, women taking the drug were required by the FDA to undergo regular pregnancy tests.

Super aspirin. The FDA gave Merck and Company, Incorporated, of Whitehouse Station, New Jersey, permission in May 1998 to sell Aggrastat, or tirofiban, a medication that prevents the blood clots that cause most heart attacks. Aggrastat was the first in a new family of medicines, termed "super aspirins," approved to treat people with *unstable angina pectoris* (a severe form of chest pain that occurs in people with advanced coronary artery disease). A heart attack results when a blood clot blocks an artery in the heart.

Unstable angina had previously been treated with aspirin and the blood thinner heparin. Despite this treatment, many patients still had heart attacks. Aggrastat works by interfering with a protein that holds blood clots together.

New TB drug. In June, the FDA approved the first new drug for pulmonary tuberculosis since 1973. Pulmonary tuberculosis is a highly contagious lung infection that is the most common form of tuberculosis (TB) in the United States.

The drug, rifapentine, sold as Priftin by Hoechst Marion Roussell, Incorporated, of Kansas City, Missouri, is used with other TB drugs to fight drug-resistant strains of TB, which caused growing concern among physicians worldwide in the 1990's. The World Health Organization, a United Nations agency, forecast that 30 million people would die from TB worldwide in the 1990's. According to the Centers for Disease Control and Prevention in Atlanta, Georgia, approximately 19,000 cases of TB occurred in the United States in 1997, many involving TB strains resistant to traditional drugs.

Hepatitis C. The FDA approved new drug therapy in June 1998 for hepatitis C patients who have relapses following other treatments. Hepatitis C is a viral disease of the liver that affects approximately 4 million Americans. The new therapy, known as Rebetron, is a combination of two antiviral medications made by Schering-Plough Corp. of Kenilworth, New Jersey. The FDA said that Rebetron was not a cure for hepatitis C, but suppressed the virus better than existing treatments. The agency cautioned, however, that Rebetron could have serious side effects, including *anemia* (blood thinning) and depression.

Cancer drug hope. In May, news reports about cancer research at Boston Children's Hospital raised hopes that a group of drugs called angiogenesis inhibitors might become an important treatment for cancer. The Boston researchers said that the drugs caused tumors to shrink in mice by halting the growth of new blood vessels that the tumors needed in order to grow and spread. However, researchers at the National Cancer Institute in Bethesda, Maryland, said in November that they had been unable to obtain such results in similar experiments with the drugs. Scientists hoped additional research would clarify the effects that angiogenesis inhibitors may have on tumors. ☐ Michael Woods

See also **AIDS; Drug abuse; Medicine.**

Eastern Orthodox Churches.

On Jan. 13, 1998, St. Therapon Chapel, a sacred Eastern Orthodox shrine in Istanbul, Turkey, was looted and burned, and the chapel's caretaker was killed. The crime followed a December 1997 bombing at the Patriarchal Center, the headquarters of the Ecumenical Patriarchate of the Orthodox Church in Constantinople (Istanbul). The attacks led Orthodox leaders to question the Turkish government's commitment to protecting the Orthodox church in Turkey, where a majority of the people are Muslims. Turkish authorities made no arrests but maintained that the crimes had been thoroughly investigated.

Reconciliations. The Bulgarian Orthodox Church, which had split in 1996, was reunited on Oct. 5, 1998. A dissident group of bishops led by Metropolitan Pimen declared their repentance to the Holy Synod of the Bulgarian Church and acknowledged the authority of Patriarch Maxim. The conflict had begun in 1992, when the Bulgarian government invalidated the former Communist government's approval of Maxim's 1971 election and chose Pimen to head a new synod.

A 30,000-member Greek Orthodox group based in Astoria, New York, was united with the Greek Orthodox Archdiocese of America on April 7, 1998. The conflict between the two groups was based on the use of different calendars and, consequently, different days of religious observances. The Greek Orthodox Church adopted the Gregorian calendar, the one used throughout most of the world, in 1924. The splinter group follows the Julian calendar, the one used by all Christians until 1582. The unification pact allowed the "Old Calendarists" to continue using the Julian calendar.

Book burning. Bishop Nikon of Yekaterinburg, Russia, allegedly ordered the burning of "heretical" books on May 5, 1998, at a local seminary. The event caused alarm among many Orthodox Christians because the books were written by three respected Orthodox theologians.

The remains of Czar Nicholas II, four of his six family members, and four servants were buried on July 17, 1998, in Saints Peter and Paul Cathedral in St. Petersburg, Russia. Exactly 80 years before, Communist revolutionaries had executed the last Russian monarch and his household at Yekaterinburg. Russian Orthodox officials voiced doubts about the authenticity of the remains, even though they had been identified through genetic tests.

Archbishop Basil, head of the Polish Orthodox Church, died Feb. 11, 1998, at age 84. Archbishop Seraphim of Athens, Greece, died May 8, after 24 years in office, longer than any Church of Greece leader.   □ Stanley Samuel Harakas
    See also **Russia.**

Economics.
The world economy slowed in 1998 as a contagious financial crisis and recession spread across much of Asia, devastated Russia, leaped to Brazil, and threatened the economies of most major industrial nations by autumn 1998. Eventually, many countries, led by the United States, cut interest rates to fuel economic growth and avert downturns. By the end of 1998, the worldwide economic outlook had improved, but economists predicted a broader global slowdown in 1999.

Economists debated whether the world's leading central banks—government agencies that control each nation's money supply and influence how fast an economy can grow—had restricted money growth too much in 1998. Other economists maintained that the central banks had followed a prudent course of action until financial market distress during the summer foreshadowed a more ominous phase of the world crisis.

In summer 1998, Great Britain's Bank of England raised interest rates to ward off potential inflation, but by autumn the bank cut rates sharply as the risk of recession increased. The U.S. Federal Reserve System (the Fed), the central bank of the United States, considered raising rates in the spring as U.S. economic growth hit a rapid 5.5 percent annual pace in the first three months of 1998. On September 29, the Fed made the first of

three cuts in short-term interest rates, reducing a key rate by one-quarter of a percentage point. The cut was the first made by the Fed since 1996.

Central bankers in nations not hurt by the economic crisis were concerned in 1998 that strong consumer demand in their own economies might trigger a pickup in overall *inflation rate* (the pace of price increases). However, the crisis brought a sharp price decline worldwide to basic commodities and many intermediate and finished goods. The result lowered consumer price inflation in nations that were growing but weakened industries that depended on such income.

Farming, mining, energy, and forestry industry profits plunged in such developed nations as Australia, Canada, and the United States, as once-thriving Asian markets suffered and global demand shrank. Factory output weakened as the prices of such products as steel, chemicals, and computer memory chips dropped due to competition from less-expensive imports made in developing countries. In such hard-hit nations as Russia, where people desired imports of food and manufactured goods, deflation fueled a downward financial spiral that overwhelmed the economies. China also experienced a slowdown in growth, though the nation remained the primary Asian country to dodge recession in 1998.

Worldwide economic growth. The International Monetary Fund (IMF), a United Nations affiliate that provides economic guidance and loans to member nations, repeatedly scaled back estimates of economic growth in 1998. In October, the IMF projected the average 1998 growth in major industrial countries at 2.1 percent compared with a 2.9-percent gain in 1997.

The IMF calculations were worse for most European industrial nations, where a 1.4 percent growth pace was expected for 1998 following 4.2 percent growth in 1997. Growth in developing nations worldwide, the IMF projected, would weaken to 2.3 percent in 1998 from 5.8 percent in 1997. The projections, however, obscured economic downturns in Hong Kong, Indonesia, Japan, Malaysia, Russia, and South Korea. The economies of several Caribbean and Central American countries also suffered following a hurricane in October 1998. In late 1998, Brazil, Latin America's largest economy, began moving toward recession.

Many economists blamed the IMF for making financial matters worse through the year. IMF conditions for loans were blamed for ruining local currencies and forcing nations to enforce harsh measures that hit people at the worst possible time. An IMF-required end to food and energy subsidies for millions of impoverished Indonesians led to riots that forced President Suharto of Indonesia to resign from office in May after 32 years in power. Critics claimed that the IMF help did not prevent Russia from defaulting on debt in August, which ignited a global market panic. Malaysia also rebelled against IMF policies by curbing the free movement of money in and out of the country.

The IMF's critics argued that the agency's vision was too narrow. They said that growth-oriented policies were needed to get the world past the crisis point, rather than initiating hard reforms that undercut growth in the short run.

Stock market turmoil. The U.S. stock market peaked on July 17 when the Dow Jones Industrial Average—a composite of the stock prices of 30 major companies traded on the New York Stock Exchange—closed at a record high of 9337.97. Instability in foreign economies, however, led many investors in late July and August to sell stocks. In August, Russia froze payments on several billion dollars worth of debts after its unit of currency, the ruble, plunged to approximately half its value. Investors worried that more countries might also freeze payments on their debts, forcing the stock market into a tailspin. In the United States, the Dow Industrials plunged 512 points on August 31—a 19-percent drop from the record set on July 17.

The United States economy had already slowed to a 1.8-percent growth pace for the April to June quarter, in part due to the impact of the foreign economic crisis. Many economists feared that the United States could enter a recession or a period of very weak growth. President Bill Clinton labeled the turmoil the worst financial threat the world had faced since the end of World War II (1939-1945). The Fed cut interest rates three times beginning in September 1998, spurring rate cuts from many other nations. As the U.S. economy improved to a 3.9-percent pace from July through September, recession fears decreased. The Dow rebounded and climbed on November 23 to a new record high of 9374.27.

Foreign economies. Germany, a key European economy, was among those nations that initially resisted cutting rates in autumn 1998. Voters in September elected a more liberal administration to replace conservative leaders. The new leaders pushed for interest-rate stimulus to curb a high unemployment rate.

The 11 countries deemed economically qualified to join the EU's single currency—Austria, Belgium, Finland, France, Ireland, Germany, Italy, Luxembourg, the Netherlands, Portugal, and Spain—announced on Dec. 3, 1998, that they would cut interest rates.   ☐ John D. Boyd

See also **Economics** Special Report: **Asian Economic Crisis; Europe** Special Report: **European Union; International Trade; Manufacturing.**

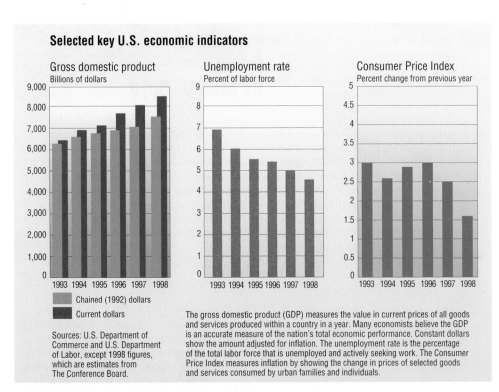

Selected key U.S. economic indicators

Gross domestic product — Billions of dollars
Unemployment rate — Percent of labor force
Consumer Price Index — Percent change from previous year

Chained (1992) dollars
Current dollars

Sources: U.S. Department of Commerce and U.S. Department of Labor, except 1998 figures, which are estimates from The Conference Board.

The gross domestic product (GDP) measures the value in current prices of all goods and services produced within a country in a year. Many economists believe the GDP is an accurate measure of the nation's total economic performance. Constant dollars show the amount adjusted for inflation. The unemployment rate is the percentage of the total labor force that is unemployed and actively seeking work. The Consumer Price Index measures inflation by showing the change in prices of selected goods and services consumed by urban families and individuals.

Many investors expected a quick resolution to the economic crisis in Southeast Asia in 1997. By mid-1998, economists realized that the health of the global economy was at stake.

Asian Economic Crisis— Global Contagion

By John D. Boyd

In the early weeks of June 1998, observers of the world's financial markets watched in disbelief as the value of the Japanese currency, the yen, fell to a record eight-year low against the United States dollar. For days, advisers to President Bill Clinton debated the wisdom of helping Japan through its dangerous financial crisis. Finally, on June 17, the president, on the advice of U.S. Treasury Secretary Robert E. Rubin, authorized the conversion of about $2 billion into yen, to help calm the global market and prevent the yen from falling even further in value.

How did Japan—the largest economy in Asia and the second-largest in the world—fall to such a disastrous low? And what compelled the United States to come to the aid of its most powerful economic rival? The answers lie in a crisis that began in 1997 in the economies of several small southeastern Asian nations that, through most of the 1990's, had been models of fast-paced growth. The turmoil then spread and deepened, triggering Japan's worst recession since World War II (1939-1945), the decline of Russia from market boom to financial collapse, a sharp downturn for the once-thriving

Hong Kong economy, and a substantial slowdown for the economy of China. The crisis drove political leaders from power in Thailand, South Korea, Indonesia, Japan, and Russia. Although the crisis periodically cooled, it would then strike another country or return to one it had ravaged earlier. It leaped from Indonesia to Russia and from Russia to Brazil. By the autumn of 1998, the decline was slowing the economies of the United States, Europe, and Canada as well.

How the crisis began

Most accounts of the Asian economic crisis, as it came to be called, charted its beginning to the sudden collapse of Thailand's currency, the baht, on July 2, 1997. Although the baht crisis was a crucial milestone, economists pointed out that the stage had been set earlier. Throughout the early 1990's, Thailand had been one of a group of countries called "Asian tigers" for their fiercely charging economic growth. Businesses in these countries expanded so rapidly in the boom years that they overbuilt their manufacturing capacity, borrowing heavily in the process. However, the value of the Thai baht in global currency markets—and that of many other Southeast Asian currencies—still reflected the strength they had built up in the boom years. Meanwhile, the Japanese yen had weakened as Japan compiled a muddled economic record at best. So the overbuilt tigers saw prices for their products erode from excess capacity and competition from a weak yen. That curbed income from exports, made it harder to keep up payments on the heavy borrowing that had fueled their capital spending surge, and undercut the value of financial assets from stocks to office property to government bonds.

By mid-1997, Thai leaders faced their first budget deficit in many years, and Thailand was short on financial reserves to back up the baht's value to foreign investors and currency speculators. Its leaders admitted the country would need a bailout from the International Monetary Fund (IMF), a United Nations-affiliated organization located in Washington, D.C., that provides short-term credit to member nations. The Thai government decided to allow the market to freely set the baht's value instead of continuing to spend government funds to prop it up, but hiked interest rates to try to entice foreign capital to remain in baht holdings.

That decision, which went into effect on July 2, 1997, was disastrous. Speculators in droves sold off their Thai holdings, causing the baht's value to collapse by more than 30 percent against the U.S. dollar. Many Thai businesses found that their debts had become too expensive to repay. Many debtors defaulted, causing banks to fail. Government revenues dropped because of the loss of corporate taxes.

As the Thai economy crumbled, financial analysts saw clearly that other Asian tigers were also overextended and vulnerable to sharp devaluations. Even though the fast-growth years had spread prosperity to millions, many Southeast Asian countries were riddled with interlocking economic relationships that favored a few insiders or big businesses. These favored few borrowed and bought

A street vendor in Bangkok, Thailand, *preceding page*, in January 1998 pauses to rest beside her wares. The shop window behind her reflects the attempts of merchants to sell their goods despite the record low level to which the Thai currency, the baht, had fallen.

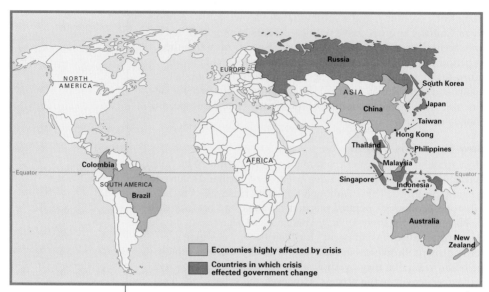

Economies highly affected by crisis

Countries in which crisis effected government change

Areas affected by the crisis

The crisis that began in Southeast Asia affected the economies of many nations throughout the world in 1997 and 1998. In some countries, such as Indonesia, Japan, Thailand, South Korea, and Russia, the faltering economy also resulted in changes in— or in some cases, the fall of—governments.

The author:

John D. Boyd is an economics reporter for *Bridge News* and the author of many articles on international trade, economics, and manufacturing.

from each other, resisting attempts by outsider companies from the United States and elsewhere to enter their markets. This system included large business conglomerates that dominated South Korea and what critics called the "crony capitalism" that bestowed wealth on a minority in Indonesia.

Such practices, abetted at times by corrupt government officials, were so widespread across Asia that governments and financial systems there rarely let weak companies fail so healthier ones could emerge through market competition. In boom years, these countries resisted dismantling systems that appeared to work so well. When hard times hit, the same relationships made their economies more vulnerable and in greater need of basic retooling to get back on a growth track.

The crisis deepens

During the summer of 1997 and into autumn, deep currency declines spread quickly to the Philippines, Malaysia, Singapore, Indonesia, Hong Kong, and South Korea, slashing the value of investments in company stocks, government and private debt securities, and real estate. Governments raised interest rates in a desperate attempt to keep foreign investors from withdrawing their funds. However, high rates also priced loans out of reach for businesses to borrow money to keep operating. Factories closed and workers were laid off.

The disaster might have been contained at that point, if not for the fact that the region's preeminent economy—Japan's—was itself already in trouble. Japan's government, in a move that was widely criticized as a fundamental economic-policy blunder, had significantly raised sales taxes on April 1, 1997. The country's economy had just emerged from years of stagnation. However, after the tax hike, consumers immediately cut their spending, and the economy sank into a severe contraction from which it could not recover. By early 1998, Japan was clearly in a deep recession. Since Japan bought goods from the rest of the region, and its banks funded business throughout Pacific Rim nations, a painful Japanese downturn starting in spring 1997 was ominous for the growth prospects in the rest of Asia by the time the baht's devaluation ignited the contagion crises.

With no hope of containing the disaster themselves, Southeast Asia's cash-strapped governments scrambled for loans to tide them over. Many requested money from the IMF, even though the IMF forced borrowers to adopt tough austerity programs that usually included hikes in interest rates and taxes to shore up national budgets—steps that would deepen economic downturns at first. Thailand quickly signed an IMF plan, as did several other nations whose currencies collapsed soon after the baht. But the world financial community treated each currency collapse as a problem limited to individual nations—much like the Mexican peso collapse of December 1994—while actually the Asian crisis had become an unpredictable contagion. The world was awakened on Oct. 27, 1997, by a steep sell-off in Hong Kong's Hang Seng stock index—long considered a bulwark against the tide. World markets shook in response.

Within days, markets stabilized and were recovering in most major industrial nations outside Asia. However, among Asian tigers, the turmoil continued. In November 1997, Thailand's prime minister, Chavalit Yongchaiyudh, resigned under fire for his handling of the economic crisis. The new prime minister, Chuan Leekpai, said his country would not recover from its financial shocks until 2000.

Also in November 1997, the currency fever ravaged South Korea, the world's 11th-largest economy. As the country

Some key events in the crisis

- Early 1990's—The "Asian tiger" nations borrow heavily to finance a period of rapid growth, eventually overbuilding their manufacturing capacity.
- Mid-1990's—The value of the Japanese yen falls against both the U.S. dollar and the currencies of Asian neighbors, måking Japanese goods less expensive on world markets compared with goods from other Asian nations.
- April 1, 1997—Japan raises the sales tax, throwing its economy into an immediate downturn and putting more pressure on Asian neighbors.
- July 2, 1997—Thailand's government devalues its currency, the baht, setting off a negative chain reaction as global investors start to flee Southeast Asian holdings.
- Week of July 11, 1997—The Philippine currency, the peso; Malaysia's currency, the ringgit; and Singapore's dollar plunge in value.
- August 14, 1997—Indonesia's currency, the rupiah, falls sharply.
- Oct. 27, 1997—Hong Kong stock market falls by 13.7 percent, bringing its total losses for the month to 40 percent.
- November 20, 1997—South Korea's currency, the won, drops sharply.
- June 17, 1998—The United States intervenes to support the Japanese yen, but its value continues to fall. Japan has admitted its economy is in recession.
- Mid-1998—The economies of the United States, Canada, and European Union nations slow as commodity prices fall and markets are flooded with cheap Asian goods.
- August 17, 1998—Russia defaults on $40 billion in loans. Its currency, the ruble, collapses.
- August 28, 1998—The Hong Kong government announces that its economy is in recession.
- September 1998—Brazil's economy reels when investors once again flee emerging markets, draining billions in foreign reserve funds.
- September 1998—Japan, the United States, and Canada cut key interest rates to boost their economies by increasing the money supply.
- Oct. 7, 1998—Japan's parliament begins passing bank-debt reforms, sending the value of the yen up against the dollar. The dollar falls 8 percent, the largest drop in 25 years.
- Oct. 15, 1998—The U.S. Federal Reserve cuts interest rates for the second time in just over two weeks. Stock markets worldwide turn markedly higher as fragile investor confidence begins to rebuild.

Officials of Sanyo Securities Co. Ltd., a Japanese brokerage firm, bow in apology in November 1997 as they announce that their company has begun bankruptcy proceedings. The recession in Japan—the world's second-largest economy—prolonged and increased the crisis in Southeast Asia.

rapidly lost reserves defending its currency, the won, and the economy plunged into recession, its leaders at first resisted the need for help. But they were soon forced to request the largest IMF-led bailout in history—$57 billion. In December, angry South Korean voters went to the polls to replace President Kim Yong Sam, whose term had ended. For the first time, they ousted the ruling party and elected a once-imprisoned dissident, Kim Dae Jung.

In early 1998, Indonesia—the world's fourth-most-populous country with more than 200 million people—was in high-stakes talks with the IMF to renegotiate the tough conditions the IMF had attached to loans approved in October 1997. Much of the country's wealth was concentrated in the hands of friends and relatives of long-time strongman President Suharto, but now millions of suddenly impoverished Indonesians saw their food and fuel prices surge under the IMF program. As Indonesia lurched toward revolution that spring, business activity ground to a halt. For weeks the crisis worsened, and more than 1,200 people died in rioting before Suharto resigned on May 21, 1998. He was replaced by Vice President B. J. Habibie. While the political crisis ebbed, the economic crisis deepened.

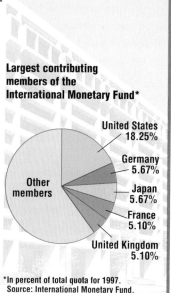

The International Monetary Fund

During the Asian economic crisis, many countries turned for help to the International Monetary Fund (IMF), an international organization headquartered in Washington, D.C. The IMF was formed in 1944 to help stabilize the world financial system and foster trade after World War II (1939-1945). The IMF helped its more than 180 member nations by providing short- and medium-term loans as they restructured their debts. Its sister organization, the World Bank, issued long-term loans to fund infrastructure development.

Largest contributing members of the International Monetary Fund*

United States 18.25%
Germany 5.67%
Japan 5.67%
France 5.10%
United Kingdom 5.10%
Other members

*In percent of total quota for 1997.
Source: International Monetary Fund.

In late spring 1998, some observers thought that the worst may have passed and that the major economic fires in Asia were being put out. Although the Asian crisis would certainly continue and the countries hardest hit would take years to return to prosperity, many economists thought the crisis could be managed without much further deterioration. That view soon changed, as it became clear that such nations as Japan, China, and Russia faced increasing economic pressure. Despite robust overall growth of the U.S. economy, the effects of the Asian crisis were undercutting some key U.S. industries and beginning to cloud Europe's solid growth outlook as well.

By mid-1998, severe recessions were underway in economies that had been fairly strong just 18 months earlier—those of Japan, South Korea, Indonesia, and Hong Kong. China had reclaimed Hong Kong, a city on its southern Pacific coastline, after more than 150 years of British rule in July 1997. Although investors feared that China's mainland Communist government would interfere with the city's legendary commercial prowess, China assured traders it would protect its new financial jewel by maintaining Hong Kong's independent economy. China itself was still closed in many ways. The government controlled the value of its currency, the yuan, and limited the ability of global money managers to move in and out of yuan holdings. Hong Kong's dollar, on the other hand, traded somewhat freely, but its managers kept the currency fairly stable by pegging it to the U.S. dollar and using a "currency board" system—a mechanism that automatically boosts domestic interest rates when speculators try to bid the local currency down.

So it was a cruel irony that in mid-1998 Hong Kong officials conceded that their economy was in recession. Mainland China's economy had suffered setbacks from the Southeast Asian damage and had slowed, but its official annual growth rate was still over 5 percent. Thus, mainland China was helping Hong Kong, rather than the other way around.

The role of "hot money" in the crisis

The reason for the ironic role reversal is a key one in understanding the overall Asian crisis and why the crisis posed an ever-greater threat to the rest of the world as 1998 progressed. At its core was a factor known as "hot money." Many Asian tigers had made it easy for investors around the world to pour money freely into Asian investments to help fuel their fast-growth economies when times were prosperous. However, those same fluid capital rules permitted such funds—known as hot money—to flow out with little hindrance to seek better returns elsewhere once the economies began teetering. Hot money fled the Thai baht and its related stocks and bonds, the Malaysian ringgit, Indonesian rupiah, South Korean won, and Philippine peso. It bailed out of Singapore and Hong Kong. It later weakened New Zealand and Australia, which were geographically near the trouble zone and sold goods to Asia.

But hot money did not burn China, because China did not allow the free flow of capital. The country's government could choose whether to devalue its currency or not. Thus, mainland China's insulation, often criticized in capitalist markets, kept the fever at bay. With the world's largest population and fast-growth policies tied to the rapid expansion of exports, China became a key player in the efforts of major world powers to halt the damage. World leaders urged China not to devalue the yuan, since that would set off a new round of currency crises and further destabilize Asia. China complied and served as a bulwark until mid-1998, when it began warning it would not tolerate unending declines in the Japanese yen.

Japan had experienced its most rapid growth during the 1980's, when Japanese banks lent huge sums of money to businesses at home and abroad. The funds fueled what became known as a "bubble economy" in Japan. Japanese households and companies alike piled up huge amounts of debt that later became a major drag on the economy. The bubble burst in the 1990's, plunging the country into a recession, which was eventually followed by sputtering growth. Fearful Japanese consumers, who had tucked any extra

Factors that contributed to the crisis

- Heavy debt in the private sector in many Southeast Asian countries.
- Increasing foreign debt among borrowing countries
- Close alignment of local Southeast Asian currencies to the U.S. dollar.
- Weakening economic performance of Southeast Asian nations.
- Currency speculation by foreign investors.
- Changing technologies in financial markets.
- Loss of confidence by people in many Southeast Asian nations in their leaders' ability to resolve the crisis.

Source: Library of Congress, Congressional Research Service report *The 1997-98 Asian Financial Crisis.*

The crisis spreads

By mid-1998, investors and economists realized that the economic downturn in Southeast Asia had grown into a global crisis, affecting nearly all the nations of the world.

Change in gross domestic product in selected world economies

U.S.
European Union
South Korea
Japan
Russia
Indonesia

Year

*Estimated.
Source: International Monetary Fund.

Russian soldiers in mismatched uniforms, *above,* harvest carrots beside collective farm workers near Ilyin-skoe, Russia, in September 1998. Members of the armed forces, as well as workers in many industries, went unpaid for months in 1998 because of the economic slowdown.

money into savings instead of spending it in ways that might spur economic growth, were starting to regain confidence when sales taxes were hiked in April 1997.

To stimulate the economy, Japan's central bank had cut interest rates to the lowest of any major country, but this failed to reignite consumer spending. Demand continued to weaken, more businesses failed, and more people lost jobs. Banks that were sitting on huge piles of bad loans kept extending repayment deadlines to keep their strapped borrowers afloat, but new lending shriveled. Such debt rollovers added to the financial burden so that by mid-1998, Japan's total bad debt was estimated at $1 trillion.

U.S. leaders urged Japan to dramatically attack its debt problem so that banks and government could pour healthy new loans into Japan's economy—as the United States had done on a smaller scale in the 1980's and early 1990's to deal with its own savings and loan crisis. They also strongly urged Japan to pass permanent tax cuts to give consumers and businesses the confidence to spend again and jump-start economic growth. Instead, Japan's ruling Liberal Democratic Party under Prime Minister Ryutaro Hashimoto offered a series of large economic stimulus packages

A South Korean, *left,* offers gold family heirlooms to the government in January 1998 as part of a national campaign in which private citizens helped the government repay foreign debt. More than 1.6 million Koreans contributed $1.1 billion worth of gold during the month.

People in Indonesia, *right,* strain to purchase subsidized goods at a Jakarta market in January 1998. When the government put an end to such subsidies and food and fuel prices soared, days of massive rioting pushed President Suharto into resigning in May.

that focused on boosting public works spending. The packages neither cleaned up the debt crisis nor offered permanent tax cuts.

The policy stalemate spurred a precipitous drop in the yen, making Japanese goods cheaper to buyers around the world. From China to the United States, it became harder for other nations to compete. Global trade of goods and prices of basic commodities had already been affected by the crisis among the Asian tigers. When much of Asia shifted from economic expansion to contraction in late 1997, prices fell further for petroleum, chemicals, minerals, metals, forest products, and farm goods as a global glut expanded sharply. Asian nations cut their purchases of raw materials and factory goods from the United States, Canada, and Europe, but flooded those markets with cheap Asian goods. The cycle fed on itself. As Asian imports flooded in, Western factories scaled back production because their customers were buying more from overseas. As factories slowed, they curbed purchases of domestic supplies and cut back on new hires or even laid off workers. Japan is one of the largest trading partners to the United States and a prime competitor to China, so as the yen kept falling, China warned it might have to devalue as well, and the United States felt compelled to act.

On June 17, 1998, the United States reversed a policy that had been in place during the Clinton administration. It intervened directly in global currency markets by joining Japan to buy yen and sell dollars, which spurred a brief rise in the yen. The world then waited for Japan to adopt dramatic new policies, but again

Japanese leaders deadlocked over tax cuts and took only initial steps to clean up bad debts. The yen began to sink again.

On July 12, Japanese voters dealt the ruling party an unexpected blow, slashing its number of seats in the upper house of parliament, and Hashimoto resigned. On July 24, the party elected Foreign Minister Keizo Obuchi as its leader and prime minister. Financial markets feared Obuchi would not sufficiently attack the problems, but he offered a platform of tax cuts and debt cleanup. Nevertheless, the yen kept dropping.

The role of the IMF

Throughout the Asian economic crisis, many nations turned to the International Monetary Fund for help with their problems. According to many critics, the IMF failed dismally. The IMF was formed, along with a sister organization called the World Bank, at a conference held in 1944 at Bretton Woods, New Hampshire. Officials from 44 countries created the agencies to help stabilize the world financial system and foster trade after World War II. The World Bank was to fund infrastructure development projects in needy countries by granting long-term loans. The IMF was to help countries with destabilized economies and currencies by giving them short- and medium-term financing as they restructured. These agencies had more than 180 member nations by the mid-1990's and operated out of Washington, D.C.

During the Asian crisis, the IMF provided loan packages to help borrower nations pay off foreign debts, but the attached conditions required borrowers to cut government subsidies; keep away from controls on free flow of capital; hike interest rates to defend the local currency; and open business ownership and trade to greater foreign investment. IMF critics pointed out, however, that the IMF's belt-tightening rules added to the economic pain of the Asian crisis. In Indonesia, for example, the rapid end to subsidies for consumer staples such as food and fuel destabilized the government. Critics began to call for major changes in the IMF's management and its economic policies. In the United States—the IMF's largest contributing member—Republican leaders in Congress refused to approve an IMF request for additional funds to bolster its drained reserves unless the IMF adopted reforms. Although the IMF continued to maintain that harsh conditions must be implemented to correct problems, the agency eventually loosened some of its program terms to borrowing nations. But at the annual fall meetings of the Bretton Woods agencies in Washington D.C. in October, many countries criticized IMF policies—which had been championed by the U.S. Treasury—and World Bank officials pointedly attacked the IMF's loan conditions as well.

A major bailout for Russia in July required the IMF to tap backup credit lines from the United States and other nations. When Russia rapidly went into a new round of crisis, the IMF lacked the funds to cover that nation's immediate needs. Russia devalued its ruble on August 17 and declared a 90-day suspension of payments on its foreign debt to commercial banks. On August 24, Russian President Boris Yeltsin dismissed his entire government and tried to reinstate Viktor Chernomyrdin as prime minister to attack the financial crisis. Chernomyrdin himself had been fired by Yeltsin from his position as prime minister just five months before. However, the Duma, the lower house of the Russian parliament, refused to accept Chernomyrdin and in September confirmed Yevgeny M. Primakov as prime minister instead. By the end of October, Yeltsin himself had withdrawn from the day-to-day duties of governing because of illness.

Late August was a critical turning point. Although Russia itself was a small part of the world economy, its effective default and ruble collapse triggered a new wave of pressure on Latin America— a much larger economic region with close trade ties to the United States and Europe. By August 28, global investors became so unnerved that many fled the U.S. stock market. The Dow Jones industrial average fell 512.61 points on September 1—the second-largest decline in the Dow's history—erasing all of the market's 1998 gains. The Japanese stock market dropped to a 12-year low in response. Malaysia suddenly adopted controls on capital flows and jailed its free-market finance minister. New currency worries emerged over the Venezuelan bolivar and Brazil's real. Meanwhile, the yen remained weak as Japan's parliament fought over bank reform plans.

The world reacts

Central banks around the world shifted within weeks from a lingering concern over long-term inflation risks to the rising risk that their economies might slow too much. The IMF slashed its growth estimates for the world economy both for 1998 and 1999, while private economists increasingly began to worry that the whole world could join Asia in recession. United States President Bill Clinton called the spreading crisis the biggest threat to the world financial system in 50 years and urged leading nations to agree on ways to fight it. Finally, Japan began new efforts to stimulate its economy with a September 1998 cut in its already low interest rates. That was soon followed by rate cuts in the United States, Canada, and Great Britain. Japan's parliament adopted a banking bailout plan, the U.S. Congress agreed to new IMF funding, and the U.S. Federal Reserve cut rates again in October and November. Germany's central bank—the most powerful in Europe—at first resisted rate cuts but came under heavy pressure for lower rates when a more liberal government came to power and wanted to curb high jobless levels, and as signs of a slowdown emerged. Germany was among 11 European nations that cut rates on December 3, coordinating their monetary policy ahead of launching a common currency—the euro—in January 1999.

Thus, as 1998 moved to a close, the major economic powers finally acted in ways that might eventually reverse the financial crisis. Yet a growing number of economists wondered if world leaders had waited too long and were throwing too few resources into the fight. Some urged widespread use of tax cuts and government guarantees of trade credit to boost purchasing power and confidence. With half the world already in recession, could the United States, Europe, and Latin America avoid the same fate in 1999?

Ecuador. On Aug. 10, 1998, Jamil Mahuad Witt, of the center-right Popular Democracy Party, was sworn in for a four-year term as president of Ecuador. Mahuad, who held a master's degree in public administration from Harvard University in Cambridge, Massachusetts, was a former mayor of Quito, Ecuador's capital. At his inauguration, he pledged to create 900,000 jobs, achieve an annual growth rate of 5 percent, and hold inflation to less than 10 percent during his term.

The new president's hopes were dashed, however, particulary by a severe drop in oil prices. Ecuador relied on oil exports for 44 percent of its national budget. In September, Mahuad devalued the national currency, the sucre, by 15 percent.

Heavy rains in 1998 left more than 285 people dead, most of them buried by landslides, according to government reports in June. The severe weather also destroyed bridges, roads, croplands, and some 5,000 houses. The government expected reconstruction costs to reach $3 billion. In February, a particularly heavy downpour caused a landslide that cracked Ecuador's most important oil pipeline. The subsequent explosion killed 11 people and severely burned at least 75 others. The accident also sent some 8,000 barrels worth of crude oil into a river near the northern port of Esmeraldas.   ☐ Nathan A. Haverstock

See also **Latin America** (Facts in brief table).

Education. The number of children in the United States attending public and private elementary and secondary schools reached a record 52.7 million in 1998. This number was a 500,000-student increase over the previous high of 52.2 million in 1997. The U.S. Department of Education (DOE) expected continued increases in enrollment, especially in grades 9 through 12. DOE predicted that 54.3 million children would attend public schools in 2008.

Local, state, and federal school spending increased 5 percent in 1998, according to the DOE. The DOE estimated that public schools would spend $347 billion in the 1998-1999 academic year.

Tuition voucher plans won a key victory in June 1998 when the Wisconsin Supreme Court ruled that Milwaukee children could use publicly funded vouchers to attend private schools. Milwaukee's voucher plan offered to pay tuition at private schools for up to 15,000 children from low-income families. Voucher proponents asserted that Milwaukee's plan would improve education by forcing public schools to compete with private schools for students. Opponents claimed that vouchers violated the separation of church and state guaranteed in the U.S. Constitution. They appealed the state court's decision to the U.S. Supreme Court.

In November, the Supreme Court declined to hear the Milwaukee case. Some legal authorities suggested that the court believed there should be more public debate on vouchers before it would hear such a case. The court's action disappointed both voucher opponents and supporters. Supporters had hoped a ruling in their favor would encourage state legislatures and the U.S. Congress to approve other programs. In May, Congress passed its first voucher legislation, which authorized a small scholarship program in Washington, D.C. President Bill Clinton vetoed the measure. Several state legislatures also introduced voucher legislation in 1998.

Privately funded vouchers. In July, a group of businessmen in San Antonio offered to send nearly every child in the 15,000-student Edgewood school district to a private school of their parents' choice. The offer angered the Edgewood school administration, because the schools had raised standardized test scores and graduation rates markedly in recent years. More than 700 children accepted the voucher offer. The Edgewood schools were expected to face an annual loss of up to $5 million in state funding.

Education savings accounts. President Clinton vetoed a bill in July that would have allowed parents to deposit up to $2,000 in a tax-free education savings account for each of their children. Because the accounts could be used for private-school tuition, supporters claimed the accounts gave parents greater educational choice. Opponents called them an assault on public schools.

Bilingual education was abolished for most California children after a voter initiative, called Proposition 227, passed with 61 percent of the vote in June. The vote ended a 30-year program of teaching children in their native language, which in most cases was Spanish, while gradually introducing them to English. Supporters of the measure claimed that bilingual education prevented children from becoming proficient in English.

The initiative required schools to substitute a year of English classes for bilingual programs and then place children in regular classes with their English-speaking peers. There were 1.4 million children with a limited ability to speak English in California in 1998.

Union merger rejected. In July, members of the National Education Association (NEA) voted not to merge with the American Federation of Teachers (AFT). The NEA, with 2.3 million members, and the AFT, with 900,000 members, were the two largest teachers' unions in the United States. Leaders of both unions said they wanted the merger so that the two groups could stop competing for members and turn their attention to fighting what they perceived as assaults on public education, including vouchers and education savings accounts. However, many NEA members said they were opposed to the merger because they feared losing representation in NEA's many committees and assemblies.

Remedial education. Trustees of the City University of New York City voted in May to end remedial classes at the university's 11 four-year campuses. In August, however, a state judge prevented the university from acting on the vote until the outcome of a lawsuit filed by opponents of the plan was decided. Opponents believed that ending remedial classes would hurt African Americans and new immigrants. People in favor of ending remedial classes argued that taxpayers should not have to pay again for instruction that should have occurred in high school. More than one-third of U.S. college freshmen needed remedial courses in reading, writing, or mathematics in 1998, according to DOE.

In 1998, Florida and Texas required applicants to state colleges who needed remedial education to take courses at community colleges before being considered for top-ranked universities. Oklahoma and Wisconsin authorized universities to charge students extra fees for remedial courses, and Massachusetts proposed that high schools pay for remedial classes that their graduates took in college.

Social promotion. In 1998, many school districts in the United States moved to toughen education requirements and end *social promotion* (passing a student on to the next grade even if he or she has failed the year's classwork). In Chicago, approximately 3,000 students were required to repeat the 8th grade in 1998.

Math and science rankings. Results released in 1998 revealed that 12th-graders in the United States ranked near the bottom among 21 industrialized countries in the Third International Math and Science Study. The study, consisting of tests administered in 1995 to students in the 4th, 8th, and 12th grades, was coordinated by the International Association for the Evaluation of Educational Achievement, a Netherlands-based organization of education ministries and research institutions. In the math exam, 12th-graders in the United States scored ahead of only Cyprus and South Africa. U.S. science scores trailed those of 15 other countries. Twelfth-graders in the Netherlands, Sweden, Denmark, and Switzerland scored the best in math. Sweden, the Netherlands, Iceland, Norway, and Canada ranked highest in science.

In contrast to the poor performance of American 12th-graders, U.S. 8th-graders in the study scored near average in relation to their international peers. U.S. 4th-graders did even better, ranking above average in math and near the top in science.

□ June Kronholz

Egypt. Egyptian Foreign Minister Amr Moussa criticized the United States in August 1998 for the American bombing of what U.S. officials claimed was a chemical-weapons factory in Sudan and a terrorist facility in Afghanistan. The U.S. officials said they had linked the two targets to Osama bin Laden, the alleged leader of an Islamic terrorist group that the U.S. government suspected was responsible for bombing two of its embassies in Africa earlier in August. Although Egypt had urged strong action against terrorism, Moussa asserted that the international community and "not just one country" should take such action. He also denied Sudanese reports that Egypt had aided the U.S. strike against Sudan.

Arab "mini-summit." In July, Egyptian President Hosni Mubarak hosted a summit in Cairo, the Egyptian capital, with Palestinian leader Yasir Arafat and Jordan's King Hussein. The summit demonstrated Arab anger with the United States for failing to pressure Israel into making concessions in the Arab-Israeli peace process, which had been stalemated since March 1997.

Anti-U.S. demonstrations. In December, anti-American demonstrations erupted at Cairo University when U.S. military forces launched air and missile strikes against Iraq. The United States claimed that Iraq had not cooperated with the United Nations Special Commission overseeing the dismantling and monitoring of Iraqi facilities for manufacturing chemical, biological, and nuclear weapons. Similar protests had erupted earlier in the year following U.S. threats to attack Iraq.

□ Christine Helms

See also **Israel; Middle East** (Facts in brief table); **Sudan; Terrorism.**

Egyptian workers, in 1998, complete a 10-year restoration of the Sphinx, the 4,500-year-old monument near the Pyramids of Giza. The project included replacing more than 12,000 limestone blocks along the torso and limbs of the sculpture.

El Salvador. In October 1998, the Farabundo Marti National Liberation Front (FMLN), a leftist party founded by former Salvadoran rebels, nominated former rebel leader Facundo Guardado as its presidential candidate for March 1999 elections. Hoping to attract the votes of women, the FMLN chose Maria Marta Valladares as his running mate. The incumbent National Republican Alliance nominated Francisco Flores.

Continued peace and the absence of political turmoil since the end of El Salvador's civil war in 1992 helped the country attract an estimated $1 billion in foreign investment in 1998. Salvadoran civil war refugees living in the United States, an estimated 25 to 30 percent of El Salvador's citizens, also made big contributions to the economy. In 1998, they sent home to families and friends an estimated $1.5 billion, much of it helping to feed and educate children.

On May 27, the U.S. State Department called on El Salvador to reopen its probe of the 1980 rape and murder of three U.S. Roman Catholic nuns and one Catholic layperson. Earlier in 1998, four of the five Salvadoran national guardsmen imprisoned for the crimes reported that they had acted on orders from high-ranking officers. In July, three of the guardsmen were released on parole. □ Nathan A. Haverstock

See also **Latin America** (Facts in brief table).

Elections. Democrats scored unexpected victories in off-year elections held in November 1998. Democrats won key gubernatorial races in Alabama, California, and South Carolina. The party also gained five seats in the United States House of Representatives and held the line in the U.S. Senate. The outcome of the election shattered Republican hopes of using a scandal involving President Bill Clinton and Monica Lewinsky, a former White House intern, to defeat Democratic candidates. The resulting furor among Republicans led Speaker of the House Newt Gingrich (R., Georgia), who had won reelection in the November race, to resign his post and leave the House to prevent a party-splitting battle over his leadership.

Congressional elections in the House reduced the Republican majority. In the new Congress, Republicans held 223 seats; Democrats, 211; with 1 independent who usually voted with the Democrats. In the Senate, Republicans retained their 55-seat majority. Two of President Clinton's sharpest Republican critics lost reelection bids. U.S. Representative Charles E. Schumer (D., New York) defeated Senator Alfonse M. D'Amato (R., New York), while Democrat John Edwards beat Senator Lauch Faircloth (R., North Carolina).

In Illinois, Senator Carol Moseley-Braun, a Democrat who was the first African American

woman elected to the Senate, lost to Republican State Senator Peter Fitzgerald. Ohio Governor George V. Voinovich, a Republican, captured the seat vacated by retiring Senator John H. Glenn, Jr., a Democrat. Other Republican winners included U.S. Representative Jim Bunning (R., Kentucky), who succeeded retiring Democratic Senator Wendell H. Ford, and U.S. Representative Michael Crapo (R., Idaho), who replaced retiring Republican Senator Dirk Kempthorne.

Democrats who won open Senate seats included former U.S. Representative Blanche Lambert Lincoln, who captured a seat in Arkansas vacated by retiring Democratic Senator Dale Bumpers. Former Democratic Governor Evan Bayh of Indiana, the son of former Senator Birch Bayh, replaced retiring Republican Senator Dan R. Coats.

Democrats predicted that the results of the November 1998 election put them in good shape to regain control of Congress in 2000.

Gubernatorial races. Republicans managed several gubernatorial victories in 1998. Of the 36 open governor's seats on the ballot, 23 were won by Republicans, 11 by Democrats, and 2 by independent candidates.

Two sons of former President George Bush were among those Republican candidates who captured governor's mansions. Texas Governor George W. Bush won reelection by a wide margin. Florida voters elected Jeb Bush as governor. Other Republicans winning first gubernatorial terms were Bill F. Owens of Colorado; Dirk Kempthorne of Idaho; George H. Ryan of Illinois; Mike Johanns of Nebraska; Kenny Guinn of Nevada; and Robert Taft of Ohio. Taft is the great-grandson of President William Howard Taft.

Republican governors reelected in 1998 included Jane Dee Hull of Arizona; Mike Huckabee of Arkansas; John G. Rowland of Connecticut; Bill Graves of Kansas; Paul Cellucci of Massachusetts; John Engler of Michigan; Gary E. Johnson of New Mexico; George E. Pataki of New York; Frank Keating of Oklahoma; Tom J. Ridge of Pennsylvania; Lincoln C. Almond of Rhode Island; William J. Janklow of South Dakota; Don Sundquist of Tennessee; Tommy G. Thompson of Wisconsin; and Jim Geringer of Wyoming.

Democrats won a major gubernatorial victory in California, where Lieutenant Governor Gray Davis defeated State Attorney General Dan Lungren. In Alabama, Lieutenant Governor Don Siegelman, a Democrat, ousted incumbent Governor Fob James, Jr. In South Carolina, Democrat Jim Hodges defeated Governor David Beasley. Voters elected Democrats Roy Barnes of Georgia and Tom Vilsack of Iowa to first terms as governor. Democratic governors winning reelection included Tony Knowles of Alaska; Benjamin J.

Jesse Ventura celebrates winning the Minnesota governor's race on Nov. 3, 1998. Ventura, a former professional wrestler who ran as a member of the Reform Party, defeated Democrat Hubert H. Humphrey III and Republican Norm Coleman.

Cayetano of Hawaii; Parris N. Glendening of Maryland; Jeanne Shaheen of New Hampshire; John Kitzhaber of Oregon; and Howard Dean of Vermont.

Voters in Minnesota elected Reform Party candidate Jesse Ventura, a former professional wrestler, to his first term as governor. Ventura defeated Democrat Hubert H. Humphrey III, son of the former Vice President Hubert H. Humphrey, Jr., and Republican Norm Coleman, mayor of St. Paul, Minnesota. Maine Governor Angus S. King, Jr., the nation's other independent governor, easily won reelection.

Ballot initiatives. Voters in Alaska and Hawaii approved measures in November 1998 banning same-sex marriages. Hawaii voters gave the legislature power to "reserve marriage to opposite-sex couples." Voters in Alaska approved a same-sex marriage initiative that amends the state constitution to limit marriage to "exist only between one man and one woman."

In Michigan, voters rejected an initiative to approve physician-assisted suicide. South Carolina voters abolished a 103-year-old constitutional ban on interracial marriages.   □ William J. Eaton

See also **Congress of the United States; Democratic Party; Republican Party; State government; United States, Government of the.**

Electric power. See Energy supply.

Electronics. Television stations in the United States began the transition to digital broadcasting in November 1998, when stations in most of the nation's 42 major TV markets began transmitting digital signals along with their traditional analog signal. All television stations in the United States were required to be broadcasting only digital signals by 2006.

Digital TV. Although digital TV signals require a smaller *bandwidth* (frequency range) than analog signals, the United States Federal Communications Commission (FCC) chose to retain the current bandwidth of U.S. TV channels. This led to disagreements among television networks about how the leftover space should be used. Some networks planned to present certain types of programming—movies or sports events, for example—in HDTV (high-definition television), a broadcasting format that uses the extra channel space to transmit more lifelike sound and pictures. Others announced plans to broadcast programs at a resolution comparable to today's analog TV but split up their channels to offer multiple programs. Certain digital broadcasters also planned to use the extra bandwidth to include such features as interactive capability with home computers, which also operate digitally.

Many television manufacturers introduced a digital model in 1998. These were primarily large-screen TV's, costing several thousand dollars. Manufacturers predicted that prices for digital sets would go down as demand increased.

V-Chip. The FCC announced in March 1998 the adoption of final technical standards for the V-chip, a feature that will be required in all TV sets sold in the United States with screens 13 inches (33 centimeters) and larger beginning in January 2000. The V-chip was designed to decode ratings for violence, sex, and profanity transmitted with TV signals and allow parents to program TV's to block channels broadcasting shows with content that they deemed undesirable. The adoption of V-chip standards allowed TV manufacturers to proceed with the production and sale of V-chip televisions and external V-chip boxes that can be connected to older TV sets.

New chips. In April 1998, National Semiconductor Corporation of Santa Clara, California, announced that it would begin manufacturing a new type of microprocessor by mid-1999 that puts most functions of a personal computer (PC) on a single chip. The chip was designed to handle a PC's graphics, audio, video, and other functions. Separate memory chips would still be needed, however. National Semiconductor predicted that this innovation would enable engineers to create a new generation of "smart" household appliances and consumer electronics products. The company also claimed that the "computer-on-a-chip" approach could one day reduce the retail price of a personal computer to less than $400.

In June 1998, International Business Machines Corporation (IBM) of Armonk, New York, began large-scale production of a new microprocessor chip that, according to company officials, could both cut prices and boost performance of cellular telephones and other portable electronic devices. The chip combined the conventional silicon material with germanium, a metallic element that conducts electricity so well that it could cut a chip's power needs by as much as 50 percent. In addition, IBM predicted that the new chip would permit engineers to consolidate many different components onto a single chip, reducing the size of electronic products.

MiniDisc. Sony Electronics Inc. reintroduced MiniDisc (MD) products in the United States in January 1998. MD's are a smaller, recordable version of the compact disc (CD). Like CD's, they record audio in a digital format, which results in better sound quality. MD's debuted in 1992 and were a hit with Japanese consumers but failed to catch on in the United States. Sony said it would market several home and portable MD player-recorders with new features aimed at greater consumer appeal.   □ Michael Woods

Employment. See Economics; Labor.
Endangered species. See Conservation.

Energy supply. World prices of crude oil fell to less than $10 a barrel in December 1998, down from more than $20 a barrel in early 1997. The low oil prices, caused by abundant supplies and a slackening in the growth of global energy demand, was matched by sharp reductions in the prices of many other fuels.

While major oil-consuming nations and fuel users reaped benefits from low energy prices, energy suppliers—particularly petroleum producers—suffered in 1998. The economies of the Organization of Petroleum Exporting Countries (OPEC), an association of 11 oil-exporting nations, were weak throughout the year. Some oil-exporting countries, including Venezuela and Russia, edged toward economic collapse in 1998. The business sectors of such United States oil-industry cities as Houston and Tulsa, Oklahoma, were hurt as profits of oil companies fell. Declining profits prompted many companies to plan mergers or find other ways to cut costs.

The bargain prices for fuel proved to be a boon for the U.S. economy. The United States, which consumes more petroleum than any other country, imported more than half the oil it used in 1998. The cheap crude helped to hold down the growing U.S. trade deficit and contributed to the nation's low inflation rate.

The inexpensive oil contributed to the lowest U.S. prices ever (adjusted for inflation and taxes) for gasoline, the chief petroleum product. Gasoline at pumps in the United States had averaged as much as $1.25 a gallon in 1997. The average price dropped to $1 a gallon by March 1998 and fell below $1 by December.

Prices of natural gas were also low for much of 1998. The Washington, D.C.-based Energy Information Administration (EIA), an agency of the U.S. Department of Energy, estimated that the wellhead price of gas averaged $1.80 per 1,000 cubic feet (28.6 cubic meters) through the first seven months of 1998, down from $2.13 in the first seven months of 1997.

Petroleum use. Global consumption of petroleum grew in 1998 but failed to make the 2-percent gains seen in previous years. Despite the slowdown in growth, consumers still burned gasoline, heating oil, and other petroleum-based products at a record average of 74.3 million barrels a day. A barrel of oil contains 42 gallons (159 liters).

The collapse of many Asian economies helped prevent oil use from reaching greater heights in 1998. China, Malaysia, Indonesia, South Korea, and other Asian nations in deep economic trouble during the year had formerly accounted for a significant part of the growth in oil demand. A relatively mild 1997-1998 winter in Europe and the United States helped curb petroleum con-

A fire rages at a blown-out oil well near Lovington, New Mexico, in March 1998. The fire, which began after well drillers accidentally struck a high-pressure pocket of natural gas, burned for eight days.

sumption in the industrial nations. Analysts said that world petroleum demand was likely to grow in 1999, though at a slower rate than previously projected.

Although the growth in oil demand slowed somewhat in 1998, supplies of oil increased. OPEC increased production by 10 percent at the beginning of 1998. The supply quickly overshot OPEC's market, causing OPEC to reverse course and voluntarily reduce output in an attempt to prop up sagging oil prices. Prices failed to recover, however, as new supplies poured in from outside OPEC. Production increased in the Caspian Sea region, the North Sea, and South America. Iraq began shipping more than 2 million barrels of oil a day in 1998 after the United Nations increased the

amount of oil the country was allowed to sell under UN sanctions imposed on Iraq after its 1990 invasion of Kuwait.

Coal consumption was up in the United States in 1998. The EIA said electric utility use of coal in the United States totaled 88 million tons (80 million metric tons) in July, 3 percent higher than the consumption level for July 1997. Coal production in the United States for all of 1998 rose for the second straight year. Through November, coal output reached more than 1 billion tons (907 million metric tons), 2.5 percent higher than a year earlier.

Natural gas was the only fossil fuel to show a decline in usage in 1998. The EIA reported that the United States burned slightly more than

17.44 trillion cubic feet (494 billion cubic meters) of natural gas during the first 10 months of the year, which was down from 17.76 trillion cubic feet (503 billion cubic meters) in the same period of 1997. However, a 1998 study by Hite, McNichol & Associates, a Houston-based oil and gas consulting firm, predicted that U.S. natural gas demand would expand 40 percent by 2020 due to increasing use of gas for industrial purposes and power generation.

Biggest merger. In December 1998, Exxon Corporation of Irving, Texas, announced that it planned to acquire Mobil Corporation of Fairfax, Virginia. The merger, if approved by the U.S. Federal Trade Commission, a government agency that works to maintain fair competition in the economy, would be the largest in U.S. history and create the largest oil company in the world. The new company, to be called the Exxon Mobil Corporation, would have more than 20 billion barrels in oil and gas reserves and a refining capacity of more than 5 million barrels a day. Lee Raymond, Exxon's chairman and chief executive, said the merger could cut $2.8 billion in company expenses, mostly through job eliminations and asset divestitures.   □ James Tanner

Engineering. See Building and construction.

England. See United Kingdom.

Environmental pollution. Representatives from more than 150 countries met in November 1998 in Buenos Aires, Argentina, and agreed to set rules for enforcing cuts in emissions of greenhouse gases by late 2000. Such gases, generated by the burning of fossil fuels, are blamed by many scientists for a gradual warming of the atmosphere. Scientists have warned that this warming might lead to the melting of glaciers and the flooding of coastal cities. Carbon dioxide, emitted from industrial sources and automobiles, is the primary greenhouse gas.

The emission cuts had been negotiated in December 1997 in Kyoto, Japan. The Kyoto Protocol, the treaty resulting from these negotiations, required industrialized nations to reduce emissions of carbon dioxide and five other greenhouse gases to an average of 5 percent below 1990 levels by 2012. The treaty required the United States, the world's leading emitter of greenhouse gases, to cut emissions by 7 percent below 1990 levels.

Although U.S. officials signed the Kyoto Protocol in November 1998, many members of the U.S. Senate, which must ratify the agreement, opposed the treaty. Treaty opponents feared that the implementation of the protocol's provisions would prove too costly for U.S. industry. They wanted certain market-based incentives added to the treaty to help reduce the costs of complying with the emission cutbacks. Opponents also objected to the fact that the protocol did not require China and other developing countries to reduce their greenhouse-gas emissions. Experts expected China to overtake the United States as the leading source of greenhouse gases in the early 2000's. During the Buenos Aires conference, Argentina and Kazakhstan became the first developing nations to accept binding targets and timetables for controlling emissions.

Low-emission vehicles. The race to mass-produce low-emission vehicles (LEV's) began in earnest in 1998. LEV's are automobiles that emit smaller amounts of carbon dioxide and *hydrocarbons* (substances that contribute to smog). Japan's Toyota Motor Corporation introduced the Prius, the world's first mass-produced "hybrid" vehicle, in Japanese markets in 1998. The car was powered by an electric motor at speeds up to 12 miles (19 kilometers) per hour—the period during which emissions from gas engines are highest in most cars. A 1.5-liter gasoline engine took over at higher speeds. In the Prius's first eight months on the market, more than 7,700 cars were sold. Toyota planned to introduce a similar hybrid vehicle in the United States by 2000.

Honda Motor Company of Japan responded to the Prius by introducing the LEV Accord. The car emits 70 percent less hydrocarbons than U.S. government regulations required in 1998.

In January, William C. Ford, chairman of the finance committee at Ford Motor Company in Dearborn, Michigan, said he believed that the first auto maker to reach the market with a reasonably priced alternative-fuel vehicle would gain a significant competitive advantage.

This shift in technology emphasis was driven by new pollution control standards. A number of states, including California, New York, Massachusetts, and Vermont, mandated that 10 percent of all new cars and light trucks sold after 2003 be zero-emission vehicles, which emit no hydrocarbons. The alternative-fuel market was also driven by such efforts as the Kyoto Protocol to reduce greenhouse gases. Automobiles contribute one-third of all carbon dioxide emissions in the United States.

Controlling smog. In September 1998, the U.S. Environmental Protection Agency (EPA) ordered 22 states to reduce emissions of nitrogen oxide gases by 28 percent by 2007. Nitrogen oxides are generated by the burning of fossil fuels. They mix with other chemicals to produce smog, the most pervasive air pollutant in the United States. Smog aggravates asthma and damages the lungs.

The move was the broadest regional effort to date to control smog. The EPA estimated that the program would cost industry approximately $1.7 billion annually. The costs were expected to be borne mainly by electric utility companies in the Midwest. However, downwind states in the Northeast were expected to benefit most from the smog cutbacks. Midwest governors called the new regulations unjustified and unaffordable, and they vowed to fight them.

Waterway pollution. In September 1998, the U.S. Department of Agriculture (USDA) and EPA proposed a draft plan to curb pollution of rivers, streams, and lakes by *nonpoint sources* (sources of pollution that cannot be pinpointed). The plan, which the agencies hoped to finalize and implement in 1999, following a period of public comment, imposed regulations on large-scale chicken, cattle, and hog farms to prevent waste from animal-feeding operations from entering waterways. The plan also called on small farms to voluntarily comply with the regulations.

The initiative was announced partly in response to the outbreak of disease in the Chesapeake Bay region in 1997. Environmentalists blamed a microbe in waste runoff from industrialized livestock operations for killing tens of thousands of fish and causing memory loss, skin abnormalities, and flulike symptoms in people who came in contact with the contaminated water. The new regulations were the first of many

planned by the Clinton Administration to restore and protect U.S. *watersheds* (areas draining into rivers, streams, or lakes).

Nuclear waste disposal. The U.S. Department of Energy received a federal license in May 1998 to bury plutonium and plutonium-contaminated clothing and equipment in the world's first deep, underground nuclear storage site. The radioactive materials were remnants of nuclear-weapons manufacturing. The site, called the Waste Isolation Pilot Plant, was excavated in salt beds 2,150 feet (655 meters) below the desert floor near Carlsbad, New Mexico. The agency planned to use the site to consolidate waste that had been stored for many years at temporary dumps in 16 states. Authorities expected the new repository to keep the plutonium safely sealed from the environment for 10,000 years.

The Energy Department also made progress on the development of a large nuclear waste disposal project at Yucca Mountain, near Las Vegas, Nevada. However, opponents of the project vowed to continue to wage a legal battle against it. Environmentalists warned that oil drilling in the Yucca Mountain area seriously compromised the safe storage of waste at the site. In 1998, there were 200 oil drilling wells in the vicinity.

Fish versus dams. A coalition of dam operators, a Maine shipbuilder, and environmental

Fish killed by a toxic mixture of lead, arsenic, and other metallic elements float on the surface of the Guadalquiver River outside Seville, Spain, in April 1998. Millions of cubic feet of toxic waste were released into the Guadiamar River after a nearby mine reservoir burst.

groups agreed in May to help pay the $8-million to $10-million cost of demolishing the Edwards Dam on the Kennebec River in Augusta, Maine. The agreement ended a dispute that began in November 1997, when the Federal Energy Regulatory Commission, the U.S. government agency that licenses hydroelectric power projects, ordered the dam's owner, Edwards Manufacturing Company, to tear down the 161-year-old dam. The ruling argued that the hindrance the dam posed to migratory salmon, sturgeon, striped bass, and other fish as they swam upstream to *spawn* (lay eggs) outweighed the benefit the dam provided in electricity generation. The 3.5-megawatt dam produced only one-tenth of 1 percent of Maine's electricity.

The demolition order marked the first time that the government refused to renew the license of a working hydroelectric dam whose owner wished to keep it in operation. The Federal Energy Regulatory Commission expected 550 dams to come up for relicensing by 2013. Many of these dams, particularly in Western states, hindered the spawning routes of migratory fish. Hydroelectric power provided 9 percent of U.S. energy needs in 1998.   □ Andrew Hoffman

See also **Conservation**.

Equatorial Guinea. See Africa.
Eritrea. See Africa.

Estonia. On Nov. 17, 1998, the Estonian parliament voted to ban so-called "electoral alliances" between political parties. The Estonian constitution specifies that a party must win at least 5 percent of the national vote to qualify for a seat in the legislature. To get around this law, parties had formed alliances, combining vote totals, to qualify for parliament without actually merging. Political analysts said that Prime Minister Mart Silmann's Coalition Party, facing national elections in March 1999, might not qualify for seats in parliament without the alliances.

Negotiations to resolve an international border dispute with Russia resumed in August 1998. Estonia wanted the new agreement to incorporate the borders set by the 1920 Treaty of Tartu, which would restore to Estonia lands in its northwestern Pskov region absorbed by Russia when the two countries were part of the Soviet Union.

Economic growth slowed from previous levels of 8 percent annually to a projected 4 to 5 percent in 1998. Economists had worried that such rapid growth, while attractive to foreign investors, could trigger inflation and trade deficits. Reduced demand from financially strapped Russian importers and the collapse of several Estonian banks contributed to the slowdown.   □ Steven L. Solnick

See also **Europe** (Facts in brief table); **Russia**.
Ethiopia. See Africa.

Europe

Eleven European nations embarked on an unprecedented economic initiative in 1998 by agreeing to launch a single currency, the euro. The project was designed to cement the economic and political integration of Western Europe, which began with the founding of the European Union (EU—an organization of 15 European nations) in 1957. The project also aimed at revitalizing Western Europe's competitiveness by promoting stability and trade across an economy that rivaled that of the United States in size. However, before the launch of the euro in January 1999, a new liberal government in Germany began advocating a shift in economic policy toward the fostering of jobs rather than the control of inflation.

Preparation for the launch of the euro
went smoothly, thanks to a strong economic recovery across most of Europe. Historically low interest rates and inflation helped boost consumer and business confidence, while the relative weakness of European currencies against the dollar stimulated exports by making Europe's goods cheaper on world markets. The European Commission, the executive agency of the 15-nation EU, forecast that economic growth in the bloc would accelerate to 2.9 percent in 1998 from 2.7 percent in 1997.

Growth fueled a continued improvement in government finances across Europe as tax revenues increased while welfare benefit payments eased. Government deficits were expected to average only 1.8 percent of *gross domestic product* (the value of all goods and services produced in a year) across the union, down from 2.3 percent in 1997.

When EU leaders met in Brussels in May 1998, they agreed that 11 countries—Austria, Belgium, Finland, France, Germany, Ireland, Italy, Luxembourg, the Netherlands, Portugal and Spain—fulfilled the economic requirements for monetary union and would participate in the launch of the euro in January 1999. Great Britain, Denmark, and Sweden declined to participate despite meeting the requirements. Greece was judged unqualified to participate.

Thousands of ethnic Albanian refugees from Kosovo, a province of Serbia, pour into Albania in June 1998, in the wake of fighting between Serb security forces and the Kosovo Liberation Army, a separatist guerrilla group.

Facts in Brief on European countries

Country	Population	Government	Monetary unit*	Foreign trade (million U.S.$) Exports†	Imports†
Albania	3,548,000	President Rexhep Mejdani; Prime Minister Pandeli Majko	lek (139.75= $1)	211	938
Andorra	75,000	Co-sovereigns bishop of Urgel, Spain, and the president of France; Prime Minister Marc Forne Molne	French franc & Spanish peseta	47	7,000
Austria	8,076,000	President Thomas Klestil; Chancellor Viktor Klima	schilling (11.68= $1)	57,824	67,324
Belarus	10,048,000	President Aleksandr Lukashenko	ruble (34,710.00= $1)	4,156	4,644
Belgium	10,273,000	King Albert II; Prime Minister Jean-Luc Dehaene	franc (34.25 = $1)	165,586	155,501
Bosnia-Herzegovina	3,947,000	Chairman of the collective presidency Zivko Radisic	dinar (not available)	152	1,100
Bulgaria	8,654,000	President Petar Stoyanov; Prime Minister Ivan Kostov	lev (1,653.00 = $1)	5,062	5,273
Croatia	4,457,000	President Franjo Tudjman	kuna (6.20 = $1)	4,341	9,123
Czech Republic	10,327,000	President Vaclav Havel; Prime Minister Milos Zeman	koruna (29.17 = $1)	22,503	26,987
Denmark	5,197,000	Queen Margrethe II; Prime Minister Poul Nyrup Rasmussen	krone (6.31 = $1)	48,042	44,208
Estonia	1,509,000	President Lennart Meri; Prime Minister Mart Silmann	kroon (13.28 = $1)	2,827	4,273
Finland	5,162,000	President Martti Ahtisaari; Prime Minister Paavo Lipponen	markka (5.05 = $1)	39,318	29,786
France	58,609,000	President Jacques Chirac; Prime Minister Lionel Jospin	franc (5.57 = $1)	288,867	267,698
Germany	81,664,000	President Roman Herzog; Chancellor Gerhard Schroeder	mark (1.66 = $1)	511,716	441,807
Greece	10,523,000	President Konstandinos Stephanopoulos; Prime Minister Konstandinos Simitis	drachma (279.47= $1)	10,970	25,509
Hungary	10,009,000	President Arpad Goncz; Prime Minister Viktor Orban	forint (214.35 = $1)	12,647	15,856
Iceland	277,000	President Olafur Grimsson; Prime Minister David Oddsson	krona (69.43 = $1)	1,852	1,992
Ireland	3,590,000	President Mary McAleese; Prime Minister Bertie Ahern	pound (punt) (0.67 = $1)	53,059	39,206
Italy	57,221,000	President Oscar Scalfaro; Prime Minister Massimo D'Alema	lira (1,642.25 = $1)	238,343	208,286
Latvia	2,504,000	President Guntis Ulmanis; Prime Minister Vilis Kristopans	lat (0.58 = $1)	1,672	2,720
Liechtenstein	31,000	Prince Hans Adam II; Prime Minister Mario Frick	Swiss franc	1,636	not available

Economic policy shift. The euro launch and Europe's economic health were the result of several years of politically controversial budget cutbacks and welfare reforms designed to enable EU countries to meet the single-currency requirements, which included low inflation and low budget deficits. With the launch of the euro secured, governments quickly turned their attention to Europe's continued high unemployment rate. Unemployment in EU countries in 1998 remained at approximately 10 percent, more than twice as high as the jobless rate in the United States, despite the creation of more than 1 mil-

lion new jobs. The shift in EU policy was forced by a new coalition government in Germany consisting of Social Democrats and Green party members elected in September. The new government, led by Chancellor Gerhard Schroeder, replaced the center-right government of Helmut Kohl.

Schroeder's finance minister, Oskar Lafontaine, urged the German central bank, the Bundesbank, to cut interest rates in order to promote growth and employment. Senior Bundesbank officials criticized Lafontaine, saying he was seeking to interfere with the independence of the bank and the European Central Bank, which opened in

Country	Population	Government	Monetary unit*	Foreign trade (million U.S.$) Exports[†]	Imports[†]
Lithuania	3,696,000	President Valdas Adamkus; Prime Minister Gediminas Vagnorius	litas (4.00 = $1)	3,860	5,644
Luxembourg	418,000	Grand Duke Jean; Prime Minister Jean-Claude Juncker	franc (34.25 = $1)	165,586	155,501
Macedonia	2,213,000	President Kiro Gligorov	denar (51.59 = $1)	1,147	1,627
Malta	373,000	President Ugo Mifsud Bonnici; Prime Minister Eddie Fenech Adami	lira (0.38 = $1)	1,640	2,556
Moldova	4,479,000	President Petru Lucinschi; Prime Minister Ion Ciubuc	leu (4.72 = $1)	843	1,148
Monaco	33,000	Prince Rainier III	French franc	no statistics available	
Netherlands	15,760,000	Queen Beatrix; Prime Minister Wim Kok	guilder (1.87 = $1)	194,011	177,376
Norway	4,391,000	King Harald V; Prime Minister Kjell Magne Bondevik	krone (7.36 = $1)	47,744	35,503
Poland	40,858,000	President Aleksander Kwasniewski; Prime Minister Jerzy Buzek	zloty (3.42 = $1)	25,751	42,308
Portugal	9,814,000	President Jorge Sampaio; Prime Minister Antonio Guterres	escudo (170.22 = $1)	22,783	32,822
Romania	22,698,000	President Emil Constantinescu; Prime Minister Radu Vasile	leu (9,862.00= $1)	8,428	11,275
Russia	146,120,000	President Boris Yeltsin; Prime Minister Yevgeny Primakov	ruble (15.80 = $1)	87,368	67,619
San Marino	26,000	2 captains regent appointed by Grand Council every 6 months	Italian lira	238,343	208,286
Slovakia	5,422,000	President (vacant); Prime Minister Mikulas Dzurinda	koruna (35.51 = $1)	8,791	10,271
Slovenia	1,945,000	President Milan Kucan; Prime Minister Janez Drnovsek	tolar (159.82= $1)	8,372	9,357
Spain	39,752,000	King Juan Carlos I; Prime Minister Jose Maria Aznar	peseta (141.20 = $1)	104,369	122,722
Sweden	8,894,000	King Carl XVI Gustaf; Prime Minister Goran Persson	krona (7.76 = $1)	82,737	65,491
Switzerland	7,374,000	President Ruth Dreifuss	franc (1.37 = $1)	72,506	71,075
Turkey	65,331,000	President Süleyman Demirel; Prime Minister Mesut Yilmaz	lira (290,771.50= $1)	23,075	42,931
Ukraine	51,134,000	President Leonid Kuchma	hryvna (3.75 = $1)	14,441	18,639
United Kingdom	59,056,000	Queen Elizabeth II; Prime Minister Tony Blair	pound (0.60 = $1)	281,079	306,564
Yugoslavia	10,755,000	President Slobodan Milosevic; Prime Minister Momir Bulatovic	new dinar (9.99 = $1)	1,842	4,102

*Exchange rates as of Nov. 6, 1998, or latest available data.   †Latest available data.

June to manage the euro. Lafontaine also proposed that EU countries relax their constraints on public spending in order to promote jobs. He called on the United States and Japan to join Europe to limit fluctuations between the euro, the dollar, and the yen. No formal decisions were made on those matters, but EU leaders agreed at a meeting in Austria in October that growth and employment should be the main goals of economic policy, not fighting inflation, which stood at less than 2 percent.

The Balkans. Conflict flared anew in the Balkans in 1998 as Serbia's armed forces sought to crush an independence movement in the province of Kosovo. About 90 percent of Kosovo's 2.2 million people are ethnic Albanians. Fighting erupted in March when Serbia sent police and military troops to Kosovo after several policemen were killed in attacks by the Kosovo Liberation Army, a guerrilla group seeking independence for the province. Observers believed hundreds of civilians were killed and an estimated 300,000 people fled to escape the attacks. The EU and the United Nations (UN) agreed to impose an arms embargo on Yugoslavia in March to try to force the country to negotiate a political settlement. In

A Ukrainian boy lays flowers at a World War II (1939-1945) monument at the War Museum in Kiev on May 9, 1998, the 53rd anniversary of the Allied Forces' defeat of Nazi Germany.

April, a "contact group" made up of the United States, Germany, France, Italy, Great Britain, and Russia froze Yugoslavia's overseas assets. As the crackdown continued, the North Atlantic Treaty Organization (NATO) threatened to carry out air strikes against Serbia unless the country consented to a cease-fire.

Yugoslav President Slobodan Milosevic and U.S. negotiator Richard Holbrooke finally reached an agreement to end the fighting . In an October accord, Serbia agreed to reduce its military and police presence in Kosovo to the levels that had prevailed before the fighting erupted, allow refugees to return home, admit international relief agencies to the province, and permit unarmed observers to monitor compliance.

EU enlargement. The European Union continued to explore expansion into the former Communist countries of Eastern Europe in 1998. In November, the EU began negotiating with Poland, the Czech Republic, Hungary, Estonia, Slovenia, and Cyprus. The EU did not promise an entry date, and several countries worried that their membership could be delayed for years by internal EU divisions over budget policy. Wealthier EU members, led by Germany and Great Britain, pushed for a reduction of the EU budget, while poorer countries, such as Spain, that benefit from EU farm and development subsidies, demanded

that payments be maintained. EU leaders hoped to agree to a budget in 1999 that would prepare the union for new members sometime after 2000.

Eastern Europe. In Hungary, candidates of the center-right Hungarian Civic Party defeated candidates of the Socialist Party, the successor to the Communist Party, in May 1998 elections. The Civic Party's leader, Viktor Orban, replaced Gyula Horn as the country's premier. Horn had promoted economic and political reform, including big cuts in welfare programs, that succeeded in making Hungary a candidate for membership in the EU and NATO. However, the election reflected discontent among people hurt by the reforms.

In the Czech Republic, similar discontent drove the conservative Civic Democratic Party from office in June when voters elected the country's first left-wing government since Communist rule ended in 1989. The Social Democrats won the largest bloc of seats in Parliament, and Milos Zeman, the party leader, was named prime minister. In January 1998, President Vaclav Havel was elected by Parliament to a new, five-year term.

In Slovakia, voters in September rejected the Socialist government of Vladimir Meciar, who had been criticized in the West for blocking democratic reforms. The former opposition leader, Mikulas Dzurinda, took over as prime minister at the head of a four-party coalition government and promised to revitalize democracy and improve ties with the West.

Merger boom. A record number of mergers and acquisitions took place in Europe in 1998 as companies prepared for intensified competition after the introduction of the euro. ING Barings, a Dutch bank, moved to become a continent-wide institution by buying Belgium's Banque Bruxelles Lambert S.A. and purchasing a controlling stake in Germany's BHF Bank. The London and Frankfurt stock exchanges agreed in July to an alliance that they hoped would lead to the formation of a single European stock market. In December, British drug maker Zeneca Group P.L.C. announced the purchase of Sweden's Astra A.B. to form a new pharmaceutical giant with a market value of $70 billion.

European companies also rushed to establish global presence by purchasing U.S. companies. Daimler-Benz AG of Germany, the maker of Mercedes-Benz automobiles, acquired U.S. automaker Chrysler Corp. to create DaimlerChrysler AG, the world's third-largest car manufacturer, with sales of $130 billion a year. Germany's Deutsche Bank AG offered $10 billion for Bankers Trust Corp., the eighth-largest U.S. bank. The new institution, if approved by government regulators, would result in the world's largest bank in terms of assets. British Petroleum Co. bought U.S.-based Amoco Corp. for $50 billion to strengthen its position as the world's third-largest oil company in terms of income.

Defense reorganization. Attempts to consolidate Europe's many national defense contractors around one or two European conglomerates were less successful in 1998. Defense ministers from Germany, France, Britain, Italy, and Spain told their contractors to prepare plans for consolidation, but work was stalled because Germany and Britain, whose main contractors were private companies, objected to the fact that the French government retained a controlling stake in its biggest contractor, Aerospatiale.

EU-U.S. trade. The European Union resolved one of its most serious policy disputes with the United States in 1998. Under an agreement reached in London in May between U.S. President Bill Clinton and British Prime Minister Tony Blair, who was acting as president of the EU, Clinton agreed to lift the U.S. threat of sanctions against European companies doing business in Iran and Libya. He also agreed to seek congressional approval to waive a separate set of U.S. sanctions on EU companies operating in Cuba. The deal, which built upon a temporary suspension of sanctions agreed to in 1997, committed European governments to step up cooperation in combating international terrorism and the proliferation of weapons of mass destruction. European na-

tions had regarded the sanctions as an illegal attempt by the U.S. government to impose U.S. laws on trading partners.

Trade relations worsened late in 1998 because of a dispute over bananas. The United States, with companies active in raising bananas in Central America, opposed EU trade rules that favored imports of bananas from former European colonies in Africa and the Caribbean. Ruling on the dispute in 1997, the World Trade Organization (WTO) had sided with the United States and demanded changes in the EU rules. In October 1998, the United States charged that Europe had failed to change its rules and threatened to impose 100 percent tariffs on a number of EU exports to the U.S. in 1999.

Human rights. In May 1998, European nations helped to forge an agreement by 120 countries at a United Nations conference in Rome to establish a permanent international court to prosecute cases of genocide, crimes against humanity, and war crimes.

Later in 1998, European nations set a more dramatic precedent that involved the former Chilean leader, Augusto Pinochet. While in Great Britain in October to discuss arms purchases and undergo back surgery, Pinochet was arrested in London following an extradition request from a Spanish judge. The judge wanted to try Pinochet in Spain for mass murder, hostage-taking, and torture following Pinochet's violent overthrow of the government of Salvador Allende in 1973. In November 1998, Britain's highest court, the Law Lords of the House of Lords, rejected Pinochet's claim of immunity as a former head of state. British Home Secretary (law enforcement minister) Jack Straw allowed the extradition proceedings to continue. Pinochet's lawyers successfully appealed the decision in December because one Law Lord had raised money for a human-rights organization that argued for extradition. A new panel of Law Lords was to give a final ruling in January 1999.

Beef ban. The European Union adopted a regulation on November 25 to end its ban on British beef exports, noting that Great Britain had taken adequate steps to protect consumers from the risks of "mad cow disease." The EU imposed the ban in 1996 after Britain acknowledged a possible link between the disease, formally known as bovine spongiform encephalopathy, and the fatal human brain condition, Creutzfeldt-Jakob disease. British beef exports were expected to resume in 1999.

◻ Tom Buerkle

See also **Europe** Special Report: **European Union** and the various European country articles.

Explosion. See **Disasters.**

Farm and farming. See **Agriculture.**

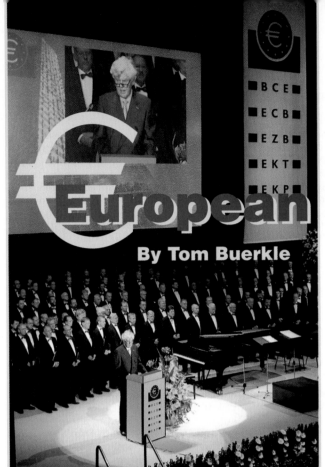

European Union

By Tom Buerkle

By 1998, the dream
of establishing a
single European
currency was ap-
proaching reality
as 11 nations pre-
pared to launch
the euro.

The author:
Tom Buerkle is a cor-
respondent for the
*International Herald
Tribune* and the author
of many articles on the
nations and econo-
mies of Europe.

E ven by the standards of European diplomacy, with its tradition of long, hard-fought negotiations on the brink of deadlines, the May 2, 1998, summit meeting in Brussels, Belgium,
was extraordinary. What had been scheduled as a lunchtime session
for the leaders of the 15 member nations of the European Union
(EU)—Austria, Belgium, Denmark, Finland, France, Germany,
Greece, Ireland, Italy, Luxembourg, the Netherlands, Portugal,
Spain, Sweden, and the United Kingdom—dragged on for nearly
12 hours. The mounting tension underscored the ambitious and
risky nature of the endeavor—the launch of Europe's first universal
currency in more than 1,500 years. Overcoming the skepticism of
many economists and frequent bouts of political turmoil, the leaders
of Europe ensured that the new currency, the euro, would be introduced by 11 EU countries on Jan. 1, 1999.

This economic and monetary union was the fulfillment of a cen-
turies-old dream and the crowning achievement of Europe's steady
move toward integration, which began shortly after World War II
(1939-1945). The EU was founded in 1957 on the principle that
close economic ties among the countries of Europe would foster
prosperity and prevent war. By mid-1998, the drive to launch the
euro had already produced tremendous economic change. It had
forced governments to reduce inflation, deficit spending, and interest rates and had triggered a boom in investment and takeovers by
corporations eager to win in the new, united European market.

Supporters believed the euro would continue to spur investment and competition across Europe, revitalizing the economy after years of lagging performance. But the single currency posed unprecedented challenges as well. In Europe, the task of managing a single monetary policy for countries with varying levels of wealth and growth and different histories of inflation and devaluation was daunting. The countries joining the euro would have to share sovereignty over some of the most important decisions a modern government can make, such as levels of public spending and tax rates. These countries would also give up their right to print paper money and mint coins, powerful symbols of nationhood.

In the wider world, the euro had the potential to rival the dollar as a global currency. The combined economy of the 11 countries adopting the euro would be the second largest in the world, after the United States. The management of the euro in relation to the dollar and the Japanese yen would greatly influence the flow of trade, investment, and jobs among the world's leading economies in the coming century.

How the idea of a single currency began

These were serious challenges, indeed. But the fact that the EU had succeeded in giving birth to the euro was already a major achievement. The seeds of the effort go back centuries. Charlemagne, who united most of Western Europe into the Holy Roman Empire, briefly unified Europe's primitive monies in 781, but the effort died with him. In 1865, France formed a currency union—called the Latin Monetary Union—with Italy, Belgium, and Switzerland. The countries minted gold and silver coins of the same size and weight. Greece joined a few years later, but the union collapsed in the early 1920's in the wake of financial pressures left by World War I (1914-1918).

Wim Duisenberg of the Netherlands, *preceding page,* president of the European Central Bank (ECB), addresses delegates attending the bank's opening ceremonies on June 30, 1998. The ECB was created to manage and maintain the price stability of the European Union's new single currency, the euro.

The real push for a single currency began in 1970, when Prime Minister Pierre Werner of Luxembourg drafted a plan for the European Economic Community (later renamed the European Union) to introduce a single currency. Werner believed that a single currency would make it easier for companies and consumers in a European common market to produce, sell, and buy goods by removing the cost and uncertainty of changing German marks, for example, to Italian lire or French francs. The plan was not implemented because of turmoil in the world economy and the oil crisis in 1973.

However, after the Berlin Wall—which symbolically divided Communist East Germany from non-Communist West Germany—collapsed in 1989, Chancellor Helmut Kohl of Germany and President Francois Mitterrand of France revived the idea of a single currency. They saw it as a means of keeping a newly unified Germany bound permanently inside the European Union and removing any temptation for Europe's largest economy to dominate its partners. Kohl's and Mitterrand's initiative led to the Treaty on European Union, which was signed by EU leaders in the Dutch city of Maastricht in March 1992. The treaty called for launching a single currency through a process known as economic convergence, whereby all EU

countries would strive to meet the same five requirements—low government deficits, low national debts, low inflation, low interest rates, and a stable exchange rate.

Challenges to a single currency

The treaty faced several challenges. Doubts about public support for the project coincided with a sharp rise in German interest rates. As a result, a wave of speculation spread through financial markets beginning in September 1992 that forced Britain, Italy, Spain, Portugal, Sweden, and Ireland to devalue their currencies. The financial turmoil also slowed many European economies to the verge of recession. It pushed unemployment to record highs of more than 12 percent in Germany, France, and Italy and to more than 20 percent in Spain. This turmoil made it more difficult for governments to fulfill the Maastricht economic requirements. But most European leaders remained committed to monetary union, believing it held the key to economic stability and prosperity.

The results of their determination were dramatic. Governments across Europe reduced their deficits by trimming welfare benefits and government subsidies, privatizing state-owned enterprises, and eliminating some of the burdensome regulations that slowed job creation and economic growth. Their efforts were reinforced by an economic recovery that strengthened in most EU countries through 1997 and 1998. As a result, governments succeeded in slashing their deficits from an average of 6.1 percent in 1993 to just 2.4 percent in 1997. By the time of the summit meeting in Brussels in May 1998, 11 countries—Austria, Belgium, Finland, France, Germany, Ireland, Italy, Luxembourg, the Netherlands, Portugal, and Spain—were judged to meet the five requirements for economic union. Those countries planned to launch the euro on Jan. 1, 1999, at the same value as the European currency unit, a weighted composite of EU currencies that was worth around $1.11 at the end of 1998.

Plans called for the euro to be made up of 100 cents. The Union agreed on the main design of notes and coins, leaving room for indi-

Birth of a currency

In the 1950's, the countries of Europe began preparing for a single currency, the euro, which was introduced in January 1999. Of the 15 countries that belonged to the European Union, 11 that were deemed to have met the requirements for joining the new currency chose to do so.

- **1957**—European Economic Community (EEC) is established by six nations to create a common market.

- **1979**—European Monetary System is organized to regulate the exchange rate of the currencies of the nine member countries of the European Community (EC), a successor to the EEC.

- **1986**—Single European Act, which requires EC countries to remove all barriers to the creation of a common market, goes into effect.

- **1992**—Maastricht Treaty transforms the EC into the European Union (EU), opens all internal borders, and commits the EC to Economic and Monetary Union by 1999.

vidual governments to print a national symbol or figure on one side. The notes and coins were not to go into circulation until 2002 because of the time needed for minting the new money and educating the public. Until then, the euro was to be mainly used for bookkeeping purposes among governments as people continued to use individual country currencies until July 2002. But the exchange rates between participating countries were to be fixed permanently from January 1999, making the single currency effective in practice.

The European Central Bank

The EU also created a European Central Bank to set interest rates for the 11-country euro zone and manage the new currency using gold and foreign currency reserves transferred from national central banks. This bank, based in Frankfurt, Germany, formally opened in June 1998.

Of the four EU countries that did not participate in the euro's launch, three—Britain, Sweden, and Denmark—did so voluntarily. Britain and Sweden were not yet prepared to commit themselves to the euro despite meeting most of the requirements, but Britain indicated it would strive to join the euro, most likely around the year 2002. Danish voters rejected the Maastricht treaty in a referendum in 1992. Still, Denmark pushed its government budget into surplus, surpassing the Maastricht requirements, to ensure that the Danish krone would remain stable against the euro. Greece, the Union's weakest economy and the only one to fail most of the Maastricht tests, made enough progress in economic reform that it could join the euro as early as 2001.

Despite all the progress, some uncertainty remained about how, or even whether, 11 or more countries could cooperate to manage a single currency. Germany, for instance, viewed the euro as a tool for

European Union members introducing new currency

Other European Union members

Eleven European Union nations launch the single currency in January 1999. Great Britain, Sweden, and Denmark chose not to participate in the initial launch. Greece did not meet the economic requirements for joining.

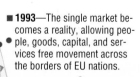

- **1993**—The single market becomes a reality, allowing people, goods, capital, and services free movement across the borders of EU nations.

- **1999**—The euro is launched. Although national currencies still circulate, the value of each is pegged to the euro.

- **1998**—The European Central Bank (ECB) is established, and 11 nations are selected to participate in the single currency.

- **2002**—Euro notes and coins are scheduled to replace national currencies over a six-month period.

spreading its low-inflation culture across all of Europe. France regarded the euro as a means of ending Germany's monetary domination of Europe and challenging the preeminence of the U.S. dollar in global markets. Those differences erupted at the May 2, 1998, Brussels meeting in a clash over the presidency of the European Central Bank. Chancellor Kohl supported the Dutch central banker Wim Duisenberg, while President Jacques Chirac argued in favor of Jean-Claude Trichet, the governor of the Bank of France. The result was a classic EU compromise. Duisenberg got the job, but with the understanding that he would step down halfway through his eight-year term to make way for Trichet.

Europe also lacked many of the features that enable the United States to live comfortably with the dollar. While Americans can move easily to different regions of their country in search of job opportunities, moving to a different region in the euro zone was more difficult for Europeans, because of cultural and linguistic differences. There also was no common budget in Europe to cushion the impact of regional slowdowns as there was in the United States. The federal budget helped Texans in the 1980's, for example, when the state fell into recession after oil prices collapsed.

European governments had the added complication of a so-called stability pact that set a permanent deficit ceiling of 3 percent of *gross domestic product* (GDP—the value of all goods and services produced in a country in a year). That ceiling could make recessions worse by forcing governments to cut spending or increase taxes just when the economy is slowing down.

Preparations for the euro increase

To overcome those built-in difficulties, European governments would have to cooperate on economic policy more closely than they had in the past. The finance ministers of the 11 euro countries began to do so in June 1998, holding monthly meetings to discuss the adoption of common tax rates, among other issues. Their task was made easier by a strong economic recovery, combined with low inflation and low interest rates, which postponed tough questions about how the euro countries would deal with economic difficulties. Growth in the 11 euro countries was expected to average 3.0 percent in 1998 and 2.6 percent in 1999, their best performance since the late 1980's and better than that of the United States.

Companies, meanwhile, wasted little time in preparing for the euro. In early 1998, ING Groep N.V., a Dutch bank and insurance company, acquired Banque Bruxelles Lambert S.A., the second-largest Belgian bank, as part of a growing wave of mergers by companies seeking to compete across the euro zone. Other European companies stepped up restructuring efforts modeled on those of U.S. corporations, consolidating production and distribution at fewer plants in Europe. They were driven by expectations of unprecedented competition across Europe when it became possible for consumers to directly compare the euro prices of such items as cars or dishwashers made in France and Germany, for example, rather than having them expressed in francs and marks.

Will monetary union succeed?

In the long run, the international test of monetary union can be expressed in simple terms. Can the euro challenge or even replace the dollar as the dominant international currency, just as the dollar replaced the British pound after World War I? It is far from an academic question. In the 1990's, the dollar was used in 80 percent of all foreign currency transactions around the globe. It accounted for almost 60 percent of foreign-currency reserves held by central banks. Global acceptance of the dollar allowed the United States to become the world's largest debtor, amassing a foreign debt of more than $1 trillion by 1997 at relatively low cost. If European exporters or oil-producing countries were to demand euros as payment, the cost of financing the U.S. trade deficit would rise and American living standards would decline.

With the euro countries accounting for just over 17 percent of global trade in mid-1998, which is slightly more than the United States, some erosion of the dollar's status seemed likely. Europeans will certainly benefit if they are able to conduct trade in their own currency, allowing the consortium Airbus Industrie, for example, to sell aircraft in euros rather than dollars.

The combined European stock markets were worth around $3.3 trillion, only one-third the size of the U.S. stock market. But they were still the world's second largest and they grew rapidly in the mid-1990's.

Economists have also raised serious questions about how the euro will affect international financial management. Many believed that a world with just three major currency zones—the dollar, the euro, and the yen—could be more volatile, with big swings in exchange rates that could affect the flow of investment and jobs around the globe. Closer coordination among governments might be able to moderate those pressures. Traditionally, however, European governments have found it difficult to speak with a single voice. Such economic powers as Germany, France, Italy, and Britain have not wanted to give up their seats in international forums. A potential warning for Europe came in June 1998, when the United States intervened in financial markets alongside Japan to support the value of the yen in an attempt to halt the Asian economic crisis. It was one of the most important international policy moves of the year, but European governments were not even consulted by officials in Washington or Tokyo.

With the successful launch of the euro behind it, the European Union still finds itself in uncharted territory full of economic and political challenges. To the Union's credit, it faces those challenges in the best economic shape it has been in for a decade. The euro stands as a proud symbol of what close cooperation among governments can achieve. That accomplishment, against steep economic odds and historical experience, may offer the best grounds for optimism about the future.

What changes will the euro bring?

- Competition was expected to revitalize the economy as businesses and consumers are able to buy and sell products and services much more easily across national borders.

- Borrowing and investing throughout Europe was expected to increase as a single capital market becomes possible for the first time.

- The euro may rival the U.S. dollar as a global currency, since the combined economy of the 11 euro nations becomes the second largest in the world.

- Managing a single monetary policy for countries of varying levels of wealth and different histories of inflation and devaluation is likely to provide a difficult challenge.

- Individual countries give up the right to print money and paper coins, important symbols of nationhood.

- The countries joining the euro have to share sovereignty over important decisions, such as levels of public spending and tax rates.

The trend toward casual business wear continued in 1998, with men favoring button-down shirts and khaki pants. For women, ankle-length skirts rivaled above-the-knee or thigh-high lengths in popularity. Men and women alike exchanged hand-held leather briefcases for casual shoulder models in nylon.

Fashion. In 1998, the fashion industry continued to long for the glory days of the 1980's, when elaborate clothes and such nuances as skirt lengths aroused women's passions. Sales in both the *haute couture* (made-to-order) and ready-to-wear markets remained flat as women's priorities shifted to comfort and practicality. When women sought designer merchandise, they often settled for a lipstick or handbag. Although fashion attracted more media attention than ever, the coverage failed to spur sales.

The industry, especially the haute couture branch in Paris, tried to fight back with extravagant presentations. John Galliano opened his fall 1998 show for Christian Dior with a chiffon-clad Pocahontas perched atop a full-scale antique steam train engine. At Givenchy, Alexander McQueen introduced his fall collection with a nearly nude Lady Godiva riding a horse through a simulated Amazonian rain forest. These shows and others made little impact beyond the press and produced little in the way of sales. The clothes simply did not seem relevant to most women.

American designers abroad. In contrast, American designer Oscar de la Renta achieved moderate success with his fall couture collection for Balmain. De la Renta focused on clothes that were wearable, not outrageous. Newly hired American designers also created a stir at French ready-to-wear firms, among them Michael Kors at Celine, Marc Jacobs at Louis Vuitton, and Narciso Rodriguez at Loewe. Alber Elbaz, who had worked for Geoffrey Beene before taking over at Guy Laroche in Paris, was tapped by Yves Saint Laurent in June to design his ready-to-wear collection.

Sportswear, or casual dressing, continued to be the biggest international theme in fashion among European and American designers alike. After decades of being dismissed as provincial by their European counterparts, American designers were praised for having a finger on the pulse of modern women.

Halston and Mizrahi stumble. The revival of Halston, a stellar name from the 1970's and early 1980's, fizzled in 1998, less than a year after the first styles from the newly resurrected Halston International began appearing in stores. After the death of the line's founder, Roy Halston Frowick, in 1990, Jack Setton and Marc Setton of Tropitex International in New York City acquired the rights to most of the Halston products and formed the new company. But first-year sales were disappointingly low. In April 1998, the Settons sold the company to the Catterton Group, an investment firm in Greenwich, Connecticut. In July, designer Randolph Duke was replaced by Kevan Hall, his assistant. At year-end, the company was operating on a much-reduced schedule.

Isaac Mizrahi, the American designer deemed most likely to embody the next generation of American fashion, announced in October that he was closing his design firm. Despite great popularity among retailers and the fashion press, Issac Mizrahi Company consistently lost money for its financier, Chanel Inc., the American arm of the French fashion house.

Trends in 1998. The popularity of jeans continued unabated, but teen-agers and young men and women supplemented their wardrobes with cargo pants. These pants, which are usually easy-fitting, come with deep pockets down each side.

After years of dominance by above-the-knee or thigh-high skirts, skirt-lengths shifted to the other extreme in 1998. During the summer, ankle-length skirts in thin chiffons rivaled miniskirts in popularity. For fall, stores were filled with longer skirts in heavier fabrics such as wool. The skirts were usually slim, though some were pleated for ease of movement. But no one expected the miniskirt to disappear.

Fur sales in the United States remained stagnant. Some observers blamed the relatively warm winter of 1997-1998, while others cited relatively high prices. Many designers, including some from the sportswear field, tried to boost fur sales by showing short jackets to complement long skirts, casual styles like pea coats and anoraks, and lots of offbeat colors like wine or blue. Still, the most successful use of fur was on collars, cuffs, and other trimmings. □ Bernadine Morris

Finland enjoyed a robust economy in 1998 as strong growth helped reduce unemployment and eliminate the government's budget deficit. The country qualified to join in the 1999 launch of a single currency, the euro, with 10 other member nations of the European Union (EU—an organization of 15 European nations). The Social Democratic government of Prime Minister Paavo Lipponen suffered through continued disclosures in 1998 about a long-running financial scandal.

The economy continued to benefit in 1998 from reforms adopted after the 1991 collapse of the Soviet Union virtually eliminated one of Finland's biggest export markets and sent the country into recession. Economists expected the economy to grow by 5 percent in 1998, one of the strongest growth rates in Europe.

Exports of electronic goods surged up nearly 50 percent in 1998, and Nokia Oy, the country's most successful high-tech company, overtook Motorola Inc. of the United States to become the world's leading maker of cellular telephones. Agreements between unions and industry to limit wage increases remained in place, ensuring that economic growth generated new jobs. The unemployment rate fell to about 11 percent in 1998, from 13.1 percent in 1997.

Budget. The strong economy transformed the government's finances, giving Finland a budget surplus for the first time since the late 1980's. The government reduced income taxes and cut spending on public works and other areas. The changes were part of a four-year plan designed to sustain growth, make Finland more competitive, and maintain a budget surplus of about 2 percent of *gross domestic product* (the value of all goods and services produced in a year).

Sundquist affair. Despite enjoying broad approval for its handling of the economy, the Lipponen government was shaken by new disclosures about Ulf Sundqvist, a former Social Democratic Party chairman who was fined for losses incurred by a bank he had managed during the 1980's. The affair had forced Budget Minister Arja Alho to resign in 1997 after she substantially reduced Sundquist's court-ordered fine. The Constitutional Committee of the Finnish Parliament—the nation's highest legal authority—investigated the affair and concluded in September 1998 that no laws had been broken. But Alho then revealed in an interview that Lipponen had played a major role in reducing the fine, a fact the prime minister had previously denied. The government defeated a measure of no confidence put forward by the opposition Center Party over the affair, but the Social Democrats' ratings slumped in the polls. □ Tom Buerkle

See also **Europe** (Facts in brief table); **Europe** Special Report: **European Union.**

Food. In August 1998, United States President Bill Clinton established the President's Council on Food Safety to develop a five-year plan to improve federal food safety activities. The move followed a report by the National Academy of Sciences in Washington, D.C., that recommended improved coordination of federal food safety programs. The council was composed of representatives from the Food and Drug Administration (FDA), the Department of Agriculture, and the Environmental Protection Agency. The council was also charged with overseeing the Joint Institute for Food Safety Research, which was established by Clinton in July to coordinate federal research into food safety.

New inspection system. The Clinton Administration announced in September that its new meat and poultry inspection system had cut the incidence of *Salmonella* contamination in chickens in half during the first six months of 1998. *Salmonella* is one of the most common illness-causing microbes in food. Before the Hazard Analysis and Critical Control Point (HACCP) program was implemented in January, testers in large poultry plants found *Salmonella* in 20 percent of broiler chickens. Tests performed six months after the program went into effect found the microbe in only 10.4 percent of broilers in plants using the HACCP system.

The HACCP system requires meat and poultry processors to identify points during the food production process where contamination might occur. The processors then must take action to head off contamination.

Unpasteurized juice warnings. In September, the FDA began requiring stores that sell unpasteurized apple juice and apple cider, which are not treated for disease-causing microorganisms, to post signs warning consumers of the potential health risks of these products. In November, the warning-sign requirement was extended to all unpasteurized fruit and vegetable juices. The warning reads "This product has not been pasteurized and, therefore, may contain harmful bacteria that can cause serious illness in children, the elderly, and persons with weakened immune systems." The FDA also required that every unpasteurized product carry a label with this warning by November 1999.

Irradiation concerns. The U.S. food industry wrestled in 1998 with the question of how to gain consumer acceptance for irradiation, a microbe-killing process approved for meat products in the United States in December 1997. Irradiation directs *gamma rays* (high-energy radiation waves) into food to kill bacteria. Although scientists assured the public that the procedure was safe and did not harm food, many consumers continued to express doubts about irradiation.

In July 1998, a report by the International Food Information Council, a multinational organization based in Washington, D.C., that conducts research on food safety and nutrition, concluded that additional consumer education was necessary to gain full acceptance. In September, the Grocery Manufacturers of America and the Food Marketing Institute, two Washington, D.C.-based food industry organizations, released a study indicating that consumers would accept irradiated food products if the products carried labels stating that irradiation kills harmful bacteria.

Fast food. A 1998 study by ACNielsen Corporation, a market research and analysis firm based in Stamford, Connecticut, revealed that annual spending on take-out meals in the United States had topped $100 billion. The study indicated that fewer than 4 out of 10 meals served in the United States included a home-cooked item. The researchers noted that adapting to this trend has required many supermarkets to devote more store space to precooked and partially cooked food products and less space to traditional items.

Food-firm mergers. Consolidations in the food industry intensified in 1998. The Food Institute, a research organization based in Fair Lawn, New Jersey, tracked a record 393 mergers and acquisitions of U.S. food firms during the first six months of 1998.　　　　☐ Bob Gatty

Football. Innovation and controversy characterized college football in 1998. Collegiate football officials came up with a new method—not quite a championship play-off series—to determine a national champion. Professional football was highlighted by John Elway's first Super Bowl victory in January and hurt by several high-profile officiating mistakes that altered the outcome of games.

College. The Bowl Championship Series (BCS) replaced the Bowl Alliance of the previous season in an attempt to answer the perennial question of "Who's No. 1?" The BCS system depended on a complex formula of points awarded on the basis of polls, computer rankings, strength of schedule factors, and win-loss records. The top eight teams under the BCS system qualified for the major bowl games, with No. 1 University of Tennessee (12-0) scheduled to meet No. 2 Florida State University (11-1) to decide the National Championship on Jan. 4, 1999, at the Fiesta Bowl in Tempe, Arizona.

The final matchup was hardly expected. Ohio State University (10-1) was ranked No. 1 in the preseason polls and remained atop the BCS standings for eight weeks. But the Buckeyes fell out of National Championship contention on Nov. 7, 1998, with a 28-24 home loss to Michigan State University, a 28-point underdog. Kansas State University (11-1) and the University of California at Los Ange-

University of Texas running back Ricky Williams poses with the 1998 Heisman Trophy, which he won as college football's best player. Williams compiled 6,279 rushing yards in his four-year collegiate career, a new record.

College conference champions

Division I-A

Conference	School
Atlantic Coast	Florida State—Georgia Tech (tie)
Big East	Syracuse
Big 10	Michigan—Ohio State—Wisconsin (tie)
Big 12	Texas A&M
Big West	Idaho
Conference USA	Tulane
Mid-American	Marshall
Pacific 10	UCLA
Southeastern	Tennessee
Western Athletic	Air Force

Division I-AA

Conference	School
Atlantic 10	Richmond
Big Sky	Montana
Gateway	Western Illinois
Ivy League	Pennsylvania
Metro Atlantic	Fairfield—Georgetown (tie)
Mid-Eastern	Florida A&M—Hampton (Va.) (tie)
Northeast	Monmouth (N.J.)
Ohio Valley	Tennessee State
Patriot	Lehigh
Pioneer	Drake
Southern	Georgia Southern
Southland	Northwestern State
Southwestern	Southern

Bowl games

Bowl	Winner	Loser
Alamo	Purdue 37	Kansas State 34
Aloha	Colorado 51	Oregon 43
Amos Alonzo Stagg (Div. III)	Mount Union (Ohio) 44	Rowan (N.J.) 24
Blue-Gray Classic	Gray 31	Blue 24
Citrus	Michigan 45	Arkansas 31
Cotton	Texas 38	Mississippi State 11
Fiesta	Tennessee 23	Florida State 16
Gator	Georgia Tech 35	Notre Dame 28
Heritage	Southern 28	Bethune-Cookman 2
Holiday	Arizona 23	Nebraska 20
Humanitarian	Idaho 42	Southern Mississippi 35
Independence	Mississippi 35	Texas Tech 18
Insight.com	Missouri 34	West Virginia 31
Las Vegas	North Carolina 20	San Diego State 13
Liberty	Tulane 41	Brigham Young 27
Micron PC	Miami 46	North Carolina State 23
Motor City	Marshall 48	Louisville 29
Music City	Virginia Tech 38	Alabama 7
Oahu	Air Force 45	Washington 25
Orange	Florida 31	Syracuse 10
Outback	Penn State 26	Kentucky 14
Peach	Georgia 35	Virginia 33
Rose	Wisconsin 38	UCLA 31
Sugar	Ohio State 24	Texas A&M 14
Sun	Texas Christian 28	USC 19
NCAA Div. I-AA	Massachusetts 55	Georgia Southern 43
NCAA Div. II	Northwest Missouri State 24	Carson-Newman (Tenn.) 6
NAIA	Azusa Pacific (Calif.) 17	Olivet Nazarene (Ill.) 14

All-America team (as picked by AP)

Offense
Quarterback—Cade McNown, UCLA
Running backs—Ricky Williams, Texas; Mike Cloud, Boston College
Wide receivers—Peter Warrick, Florida State;
    Torry Holt, North Carolina State
Tight end—Rufus French, Mississippi
Center—Craig Page, Georgia Tech
Other linemen—Kris Farris, UCLA; Aaron Gibson, Wisconsin;
    Rob Murphy, Ohio State; Matt Stinchcomb, Georgia.
All-purpose—David Allen, Kansas State
Place-kicker—Sebastian Janikowski, Florida State

Defense
Linemen—Corey Simon, Florida State; Tom Burke, Wisconsin;
    Anthony McFarland, Louisiana State; Montae Reagor, Texas Tech
Linebackers—Chris Claiborne, USC; Dat Nguyen, Texas A&M;
    Al Wilson, Tennessee; Jeff Kelly, Kansas State.
Backs—Champ Bailey, Georgia; Chris McAlister, Arizona;
    Antoine Winfield, Ohio State; Anthony Poindexter, Virginia
Punter—Joe Kristosik, Las Vegas

Player awards
Heisman Trophy (best player)—Ricky Williams, Texas
Lombardi Award (best lineman)—Dat Nguyen, Texas A&M
Outland Trophy (best interior lineman)—Kris Farris, UCLA

les (10-1) were also on pace to reach the championship game until December 5, when Kansas State suffered a 36-33 overtime loss to Texas A&M University (11-2) and UCLA fell, 49-45 to the University of Miami.

College football milestones. Joe Paterno, the head coach at Pennsylvania State University for 33 seasons, celebrated his 300th career victory on Sept. 12, 1998, when his Nittany Lions beat Bowling Green State University, 48-3. Paterno became the first coach to attain 300 wins at the same school. Prairie View A&M University ended the nation's longest losing streak—80 games—with a 14-12 victory over Langston University in Oklahoma City, Oklahoma, on September 26. The win was the Panthers's first since Oct. 28, 1989.

Ricky Williams, the University of Texas running back, won the 1998 Heisman Trophy by a landslide and became the first Texas player since Earl Campbell in 1977 to lead the nation in rushing. Williams broke Tony Dorsett's career rushing record, compiling a four-season total of 6,279 yards. Dorsett's 1973-1976 record of 6,082 yards, compiled at the University of Pittsburgh, stood for 22 years.

Before the season started, broadcaster Keith Jackson announced that he would retire after 32 years of announcing college football games for the ABC television network. Terry Bowden, for five years one of the most successful head coaches in Auburn University history, resigned on Oct. 23, 1998, during the team's worst season start in about 50 years. Former University of Notre Dame head football coach Lou Holtz accepted the head coaching job at the University of South Carolina in December.

Professional. The 1997-1998 National Football League (NFL) season ended in a moment of glory for John Elway, who wound up as the winning quarterback in the Super Bowl for the first time in his 15-year career with the Denver Broncos. Elway and the Broncos had lost in three earlier Super Bowls. Denver reached the play-offs as a wild-card entry and remained underdogs the rest of the way. On the first weekend of January, in the American Football Conference (AFC) play-offs, the Broncos beat the Kansas City Chiefs, 14-10, the day after the Pittsburgh Steelers eked out a 7-6 win over the New England Patriots.

In the National Football Conference (NFC) play-offs, the defending champion Green Bay Packers beat the Tampa Bay Buccaneers, 21-7, and the San Francisco 49ers ousted the Minnesota Vikings, 38-22. The Packers won the NFC title and a return trip to the Super Bowl with a 23-10 victory over the 49ers. The Broncos took the AFC championship for the first time in eight seasons by beating the Steelers, 24-21.

On January 25, in San Diego, California, Green Bay squared off against Denver in Super Bowl XXXII at Qualcomm Stadium. For the first time since 1984, the NFL title went to the AFC team. The Broncos powered their way to a 31-24 victory as the Packers tired in the late going. Denver's Terrell Davis rushed for 157 yards and three touchdowns to capture Most Valuable Player (MVP) honors.

The 1998-1999 season. In mid-January 1998, the league won a $17.6-billion, 8-year television contract from the CBS, Fox, ABC, and ESPN television networks. The deal increased the NFL's television rights fees by 100 percent, even though the participating networks acknowledged that they would lose money on the games. The owners also assured labor peace through 2003 by extending a collective bargaining deal with NFL players in March 1998.

As the season progressed, 21 teams lost their starting quarterback because of injury or poor performance. The temporary loss of Elway to injury hardly hurt the Broncos, however. They were unbeaten in their first 13 games and had hopes of becoming the first team since the 1972 Miami Dolphins to go undefeated and untied in the regular season. Denver's 20-16 loss to the New York Giants on Dec. 13, 1998, derailed this quest.

People. The season got underway with new head coaches at Buffalo (Wade Phillips), Indi-anapolis (Jim Mora), Oakland (Jon Gruden), and Dallas (Chan Gailey).

Kevin Gilbride became the season's first head coach to be fired when he was let go on October 13. On December 28, five more teams fired their head coach after disappointing seasons: Seattle (Dennis Erickson), Chicago (Dave Wannstedt); Carolina (Dom Capers), Baltimore (Ted Marchibroda), and Philadelphia (Ray Rhodes).

New NFL owners included Red McCombs at Minnesota and Al Lerner at Cleveland, where the reincarnated Browns will begin play in 1999. San Francisco's Eddie DeBartolo, Jr., put himself on suspension while under indictment in a federal gambling fraud case in Louisiana. DeBartolo later pleaded guilty to a felony charge and paid a $1-million penalty, which created a bitter, seven-month rift with Carmen Policy, the 49ers president who resigned and later signed on with Cleveland.

Many fans applauded the return to the NFL of Buffalo Bills quarterback Doug Flutie from eight seasons as a superstar in the Canadian Football League (CFL). Flutie earned the starting job after filling in for the injured Rob Johnson. Flutie's performance earned him a roster spot behind John Elway in the Pro Bowl, the NFL's annual contest between AFC and NFC all-stars.

Referees came under heavy criticism in 1998, after a number of calls drew outraged responses from fans. On Thanksgiving Day in Detroit, referee Phil Luckett tossed the coin before the overtime period of the Lions-Steelers game. As the coin was flipped, Pittsburgh's Jerome Bettis called "Tails," which came up. Luckett said he had heard Bettis say "Heads-tails." Detroit received the overtime kick-off, moved downfield, and won the game on a 42-yard field goal.

Luckett's crew drew criticism again on December 6, when they credited New York Jets quarterback Vinny Testaverde with the winning touchdown in a 32-31 victory over the Seattle Seahawks, even though TV replays conclusively showed that he had not crossed the goal line.

Other leagues. The Calgary Stampeders won the 86th Canadian Football League Grey Cup, edging the Hamilton Tiger-Cats, 26-24, on November 22 in Winnipeg, Manitoba. Calgary place-kicker Mark McLoughlin kicked a 35-yard field goal on the final play of the game to give Calgary its second Grey Cup title in four appearances since 1991. It was a sad finale for Hamilton, which had bounced back from a 2-16 record in 1997 to reach the CFL title game for the first time since 1989.

NFL Europe contested a 10-game season from April to June 1998 in five European cities. The Rhein Fire routed the Frankfurt Galaxy, 34-10, to win the World Bowl on June 14. Rhein quarterback Jim Arellanes, replacing the injured Mike Quinn, was the game's MVP. □ Ron Reid

National Football League final standings

American Conference

Eastern Division	W.	L.	T.	Pct.
New York Jets*	12	4	0	.750
Miami Dolphins*	10	6	0	.625
Buffalo Bills*	10	6	0	.625
New England Patriots*	9	7	0	.563
Indianapolis Colts	3	13	0	.188

Central Division	W.	L.	T.	Pct.
Jacksonville Jaguars*	11	5	0	.688
Tennessee Oilers	8	8	0	.500
Pittsburgh Steelers	7	9	0	.438
Baltimore Ravens	6	10	0	.375
Cincinnati Bengals	3	13	0	.188

Western Division	W.	L.	T.	Pct.
Denver Broncos*	14	2	0	.875
Oakland Raiders	8	8	0	.500
Seattle Seahawks	8	8	0	.500
Kansas City Chiefs	7	9	0	.438
San Diego Chargers	5	11	0	.313

*Made play-offs

National Conference

Eastern Division	W.	L.	T.	Pct.
Dallas Cowboys*	10	6	0	.625
Arizona Cardinals*	9	7	0	.563
New York Giants	8	8	0	.500
Washington Redskins	6	10	0	.375
Philadelphia Eagles	3	13	0	.188

Central Division	W.	L.	T.	Pct.
Minnesota Vikings*	15	1	0	.938
Green Bay Packers*	11	5	0	.688
Tampa Bay Buccaneers	8	8	0	.500
Detroit Lions	5	11	0	.313
Chicago Bears	4	12	0	.250

Western Division	W.	L.	T.	Pct.
Atlanta Falcons*	14	2	0	.875
San Francisco 49ers*	12	4	0	.750
New Orleans Saints	6	10	0	.375
Carolina Panthers	4	12	0	.250
St. Louis Rams	4	12	0	.250

*Made play-offs

Individual statistics

Leading scorers, touchdowns

	TD's	Rush	Rec.	Ret.	Pts.
Terrell Davis, Denver	23	21	2	0	138
Fred Taylor, Jacksonville	17	14	3	0	102
Robert Edwards, New England	12	9	3	0	72
Joey Galloway, Seattle	12	0	10	2	72
Keyshawn Johnson, N.Y. Jets	11	1	10	0	66

Leading scorers, kicking

	PAT att./made	FG att./made	Longest	Pts.
Steve Christie, Buffalo	41/41	33/41	52	140
Al Del Greco, Tennessee	28/28	36/39	48	136
Jason Elam, Denver	58/58	23/27	63	127
Adam Vinatieri, New England	32/32	31/39	55	127
John Hall, N.Y. Jets	45/46	25/35	54	120

Leading quarterbacks

	Att.	Comp.	Yds.	TD's	Int.
Vinny Testaverde, N.Y. Jets	421	259	3,256	29	7
John Elway, Denver	356	210	2,806	22	10
Neil O'Donnell, Cincinnati	343	212	2,216	15	4
Mark Brunell, Jacksonville	354	208	2,601	20	9
Doug Flutie, Buffalo	354	202	2,711	20	11
Drew Bledsoe, New England	481	263	3,633	20	14
Rich Gannon, Kansas City	354	206	2,305	10	6
Steve McNair, Tennessee	492	289	3,228	15	10
Dan Marino, Miami	537	310	3,497	23	15
Warren Moon, Seattle	258	145	1,632	11	8

Leading receivers

	Passes caught	Rec. yards	Avg. gain	TD's
O. J. McDuffie, Miami	90	1,050	11.7	7
Marshall Faulk, Indianapolis	86	908	10.6	4
Rod Smith, Denver	86	1,222	14.2	6
Keyshawn Johnson, N.Y. Jets	83	1,131	13.6	10
Carl Pickens, Cincinnati	82	1,023	12.5	5
Tim Brown, Oakland	81	1,012	12.5	9
Jimmy Smith, Jacksonville	78	1,182	15.2	8
Wayne Chrebet, N.Y. Jets	75	1,083	14.4	8
Frank Wycheck, Tennessee	70	768	11.0	2
Ben Coates, New England	67	668	10.0	6

Leading rushers

	Rushes	Yards	Avg.	TD's
Terrell Davis, Denver	392	2,008	5.1	21
Marshall Faulk, Indianapolis	324	1,319	4.1	6
Eddie George, Tennessee	348	1,294	3.7	5
Curtis Martin, N.Y. Jets	369	1,287	3.5	8
Ricky Watters, Seattle	319	1,239	3.9	9
Fred Taylor, Jacksonville	264	1,223	4.6	14
Jerome Bettis, Pittsburgh	316	1,185	3.8	3
Corey Dillon, Cincinnati	262	1,130	4.3	4
Antowain Smith, Buffalo	300	1,124	3.7	8
Robert Edwards, New England	291	1,115	3.8	9

Leading punters

	Punts	Yards	Avg.	Longest
Craig Hentrich, Tennessee	69	3,258	47.2	71
Tom Rouen, Denver	66	3,097	46.9	76
Chris Gardocki, Indianapolis	79	3,583	45.4	62
Bryan Barker, Jacksonville	85	3,824	45.0	65
Lee Johnson, Cincinnati	69	3,083	44.7	69

Individual statistics

Leading scorers, touchdowns

	TD's	Rush	Rec.	Ret.	Pts.
Randy Moss, Minnesota	17	0	17	0	106
Jamal Anderson, Atlanta	16	14	2	0	98
Terrell Owens, San Francisco	15	1	14	0	92
Emmitt Smith, Dallas	15	13	2	0	90
Antonio Freeman, Green Bay	14	0	14	0	86

Leading scorers, kicking

	PAT att./made	FG att./made	Longest	Pts.
Gary Anderson, Minnesota	59/59	35/35	53	164
Ryan Longwell, Green Bay	41/43	29/33	45	128
Richie Cunningham, Dallas	40/40	29/35	54	127
Morten Andersen, Atlanta	51/52	23/28	53	120
Jason Hanson, Detroit	27/29	29/33	51	114

Leading quarterbacks

	Att.	Comp.	Yds.	TD's	Int.
Randall Cunningham, Minnesota	425	259	3,704	34	10
Steve Young, San Francisco	517	322	4,170	36	12
Chris Chandler, Atlanta	327	190	3,154	25	12
Troy Aikman, Dallas	315	187	2,330	12	5
Steve Beuerlein, Carolina	343	216	2,613	17	12
Brett Favre, Green Bay	551	347	4,212	31	23
Charlie Batch, Detroit	303	173	2,178	11	6
Erik Kramer, Chicago	250	151	1,823	9	7
Trent Green, Washington	509	278	3,441	23	11
Jake Plummer, Arizona	547	324	3,737	17	20

Leading receivers

	Passes caught	Rec. yards	Avg. gain	TD's
Frank Sanders, Arizona	89	1,145	12.9	3
Antonio Freeman, Green Bay	84	1,424	17.0	14
Herman Moore, Detroit	82	983	12.0	5
Jerry Rice, San Francisco	82	1,157	14.1	9
Chris Carter, Minnesota	78	1,011	13.0	12
Michael Irvin, Dallas	74	1,057	14.3	1
Larry Centers, Arizona	69	559	8.1	2
Raghib Ismail, Carolina	69	1,024	14.8	8
Johnnie Morton, Detroit	69	1,028	14.9	2
Randy Moss, Minnesota	69	1,313	19.0	17

Leading rushers

	Rushes	Yards	Avg.	TD's
Jamal Anderson, Atlanta	410	1,846	4.5	14
Garrison Hearst, San Francisco	310	1,570	5.1	7
Barry Sanders, Detroit	343	1,491	4.3	4
Emmitt Smith, Dallas	319	1,332	4.2	13
Robert Smith, Minnesota	249	1,187	4.8	6
Duce Staley, Philadelphia	258	1,065	4.1	5
Gary Brown , N.Y. Giants	247	1,063	4.3	5
Adrian Murrell, Arizona	274	1,042	3.8	8
Warrick Dunn, Tampa Bay	245	1,026	4.2	2
Mike Alstott, Tampa Bay	215	846	3.9	8

Leading punters

	Punts	Yards	Avg.	Longest
Mark Royals, New Orleans	88	4,017	45.6	64
Brad Maynard, N.Y. Giants	101	4,566	45.2	63
Mitch Berger, Minnesota	55	2,458	44.7	67
Rick Tuten, St. Louis	95	4,202	44.2	64
Matt Turk, Washington	93	4,103	44.1	69

A giant figure representing one of the world's continents rolls down Paris's Champs Elysees during the opening celebration of the 16th World Cup soccer tournament. World Cup events were staged throughout France in June and July 1998.

France enjoyed a revival of confidence during 1998 after several years of pessimism and rising unemployment. Economic growth accelerated, creating new jobs, and France's victory in soccer's World Cup contributed to a sense of optimism.

The country in 1998 enjoyed its strongest economic growth since the late 1980's, with an expected increase of 3.1 percent. The economy benefited from a wider recovery among France's European neighbors, low interest rates, and stronger spending by French consumers. The solid growth helped bring the jobless rate down from 12.4 percent in 1997 to 11.7 percent in 1998.

Conservatives in disarray. The improved economy helped the governing Socialist Party of Prime Minister Lionel Jospin score gains in regional elections in March. The Socialists and their left-wing allies won 36.5 percent of the vote in the elections and emerged as the biggest party in most of the country's 22 electoral regions. The two center-right parties that supported President Jacques Chirac won 35.6 percent of the vote. The conservatives were split after the election when five senior members defied their party's orders and accepted support from the extreme right-wing National Front party to help them win the presidencies of five regional councils. The Front, which received 15.5 percent of the vote, ran a campaign that blamed France's 3.6 million immi-

grants for the country's crime and unemployment and opposed French involvement in the European Union, an organization of 15 European nations. Chirac condemned the five regional leaders and urged conservatives to renounce cooperation with the National Front.

Corruption scandals. The conservatives suffered another blow in August when a magistrate opened an investigation into allegations that the city of Paris gave bogus jobs to some 200 members of Chirac's Rally for the Republic party during the 1980's, when Chirac was the city's mayor. Alain Juppe, Chirac's deputy at the time and prime minister from 1995 to 1997, was placed under investigation. He denied any wrongdoing.

Scandal also affected the left when magistrates placed Roland Dumas, a leading Socialist and president of the country's Constitutional Council—France's highest legal body—under investigation in April 1998. Dumas's former mistress claimed she had been paid nearly $12 million by the French oil company Elf Aquitaine to persuade Dumas to approve a $2.7-billion sale of French frigates to Taiwan in 1991. Dumas, who was foreign minister at the time, denied the charges.

Business. The government agreed in May 1998 to what it hoped would be a final rescue plan for the troubled bank Credit Lyonnais. The plan—Europe's largest corporate bail-out in history—required the bank to reduce its operations by selling $104 billion in assets and to receive billions of dollars of government funds to guarantee its future. The government agreed to sell its 82-percent stake in the bank by the end of 1999. The government had already funded two previous rescue plans and spent more than $10 billion on the bank since 1995. The latest agreement raised the total cost of saving the bank to between $28 billion and $40 billion. The bank expanded rapidly in the late 1980's but nearly collapsed in the early 1990's because of bad loans. A Paris judge was investigating allegations of criminal activity by former bank executives.

The government moved to reorganize the French defense industry in July 1998 by arranging the merger of the state-owned aerospace company, Aerospatiale, with the Matra defense business subsidiary of the private group Lagardere. The merger created Europe's largest defense company, with sales of more than $13 billion in aircraft, missiles, and other equipment. The government also pledged to reduce its stake in the new company to less than 50 percent. Nevertheless, the government's retention of a sizable stake in the company impeded negotiations for a European defense merger involving Aerospatiale and two big private companies, British Aerospace PLC and Daimler-Chrysler Aerospace AG of Germany.

Christie's International PLC, the world's largest auction house, passed from British to French control in May when the retailer Francois Pinault agreed to buy the company for $1.2 billion. Pinault also owned France's largest department store chain, Pinault-Printemps-Redoute.

Cohabitation law. The National Assembly (lower house of Parliament) passed a bill in December giving unmarried couples the same tax status and right to social benefits as married couples. The bill, if passed by the Senate, would allow unmarried couples, including homosexuals, to register their union with the authorities. The government said the change would simply bring legislation into line with reality, since more than 2 million couples in France are unmarried and 39 percent of children are born out of wedlock. Conservatives and most churches opposed the bill, saying it undermined the institution of marriage. Many of the country's mayors said they would refuse to register homosexual unions.

Student protests. As many as 500,000 of the country's 2.6 million high-school students took to the streets during October and November to demand improvements in education, including more teachers to reduce overcrowding in classes and the repair of dilapidated buildings. The government responded by promising to spend an extra $750 million to fix buildings and hire 14,000 new supervisors and teachers' assistants.

Sports. France hosted one of the biggest international sporting events, soccer's World Cup, in 1998. The month-long competition attracted more than 3 million spectators and more than 1 billion television viewers worldwide during the final match. France upset the favored Brazilian team, which had won the cup in 1994 in the United States, winning 3-0 on July 12, 1998. For many French, the victory by a team that included several minority players was a boost for social unity. More than 1 million people celebrated the victory in the streets of Paris.

In contrast to the joy of the World Cup, the Tour de France bicycle race finished under a cloud of scandal over allegations of widespread drug abuse. Festina, the world's top-ranked cycling team, was expelled from the race after the team's massage therapist was arrested for possession of the artificial hormone EPO, a performance-enhancing drug. Police raided several other teams during the three-week race and arrested several riders, coaches, and team doctors on charges of illegal drug use. Five of the 20 remaining teams quit the race to protest the raids. On August 2, Marco Pantani won the race, the first Italian in 33 years to do so. ☐ Tom Buerkle

See also **Europe** (Facts in brief table); **Europe** Special Report: **European Union; Soccer** Special Report: **The 1998 World Cup; Sports.**

Gardening. Homeowners in the United States installed private pleasure gardens in 1998 on a scale not seen since the 1920's. Landscape design, which had long emphasized the natural look, suddenly veered toward formality as *espalier* (trellises or frameworks), vegetable *parterres* (ornamental arrangements), and *topiary* (shrubs or trees trimmed into ornamental shapes) made startling comebacks. *Pergolas* (shady places formed by plants on trellises), outdoor statuary, and stone terraces were also much in demand. The burble of artificial waterfalls and fountains became the wind chimes of the 1990's garden.

Many gardeners opened their grounds to the paying public for philanthropy. The Garden Conservancy, a national garden conservation organization, sold tickets to newer gardens in the United States to raise funds to preserve historic older private gardens.

Retail trends. Many large home-and-garden supply retailers added extensive greenhouses to their network of chain stores in 1998. In order to compete with the chains, the 12,000 independent retail nurseries in the United States focused on niche markets, such as new and unusual annuals and perennials. Tender exotics such as cannas, banana trees, and hibiscus were in demand as even northern gardeners experimented with tropical effects and bright colors.

Fighting infestations. Native American trees continued to suffer new ills in 1998. The pine pitch canker, a fungus first seen in 1986, rapidly spread through the Monterey pines planted along California's coast to hold the shoreline. Plant pathologist Tom Gordon of the University of California at Davis worked to identify the 15 percent of Monterey pines reportedly immune to the fungus so that they could be propagated.

Biological controls were used to combat a number of spreading alien pests. Scientists made plans to release parasitic wasps in Massachusetts in an attempt to reduce populations of European red lily beetles. The wasps were imported from France by researchers at the University of Rhode Island in Kingston to feed on the destructive beetles, which had spread throughout New England after appearing in a Boston garden in 1992. Researchers at the Connecticut Agricultural Experiment Station in Windsor ran trials in 1998 with Japanese ladybugs that feed on Asian woolly adelgids, insects that were wiping out native eastern hemlocks. Scientists at Cornell University in Ithaca, New York, released European beetles to try to combat the spread of purple loosestrife, a troublesome weed in the northeastern and north-central United States.

Flower shows and arboretums. The San Francisco Flower Show was staged at the cavernous Cow Palace for the second year in a row in 1998. The show, which came under new ownership in 1997, again won kudos for its captivating displays as well as ease of parking and access. In Memphis, the new Southern Family Flower Show was a great success at the Agricenter International complex.

Eighty acres (32 hectares) of the historic Elmwood Cemetery in Memphis were transformed in 1998 into the Carlisle S. Page Arboretum. A 60-acre (24-hectare) private garden on Martha's Vineyard, an island off the coast of Massachusetts, became the Polly Hill Arboretum, named after the amateur gardener who raised every plant on the property from seed. The arboretum has 73 hardy trees that are the largest of their species growing in New England.

Deaths. Plant geneticist David Goheen Leach, an internationally noted author, lecturer, and gardener, died on April 22. He introduced numerous varieties of rhododendrons, azaleas, and other woody ornamentals. Emily Whaley, who became a national gardening celebrity in 1997 with the publication of *Mrs. Whaley and her Charleston Garden,* died at her summer house in Flat Rock, North Carolina, in June at the age of 87.

☐ Carol Stocker

Gas and gasoline. See Energy supply.
Genetic engineering. See Biology; Medicine.

Geology. Geologists' current understanding of the West Antarctic Ice Sheet and how it may be affected by global warming was reviewed in May 1998 by Michael Oppenheimer, chief scientist at the Environmental Defense Fund in New York City. Many geologists and other scientists believe that the West Antarctic Ice Sheet is unstable and subject to *collapse* (rapid melting), which would cause the world's oceans to rise 13 to 20 feet (4 to 6 meters).

Oppenheimer concluded that the probability of major melting in the ice sheet during the 2000's was low but that the chances would increase dramatically in the 2100's and beyond. He contended, however, that complete disintegration of the West Antarctic Ice Sheet over the next 200 to 400 years was unlikely.

A more cautionary note was struck by geologist Reed P. Scherer and his colleagues at Uppsala University in Sweden, together with researchers at the California Institute of Technology in Pasadena. They reported in July 1998 that the ice sheet has collapsed at least once during the past 750,000 years, most likely during an *interglacial period* (a period between ice ages) slightly warmer than today.

The researchers reached their conclusion from a study of soil-core samples from the bottom of the ice sheet. The samples contained the remains of *diatoms* (one-celled marine algae) and significant quantities of a radioactive *isotope* (form) of the element beryllium. The isotope is created in the atmosphere and settles into the oceans, where it becomes incorporated into seabed deposits.

The samples revealed that the area now covered by the West Antarctic Ice Sheet was under water within the past 750,000 years. This finding suggested that the West Antarctic Ice Sheet could collapse if the global climate continues to grow warmer.

The causes of global warming. Geologists Michael E. Mann and Raymond S. Bradley of the University of Massachusetts in Amherst and Malcolm K. Hughes of the University of Arizona in Tucson reported in April 1998 the results of their research into the question of whether the warming of Earth during the 1900's has been due to human activities or is simply part of a long-term natural trend. The researchers determined global temperatures over the past 600 years by analyzing weather records, tree-ring data, and samples from ice cores and coral reefs. They found that 1990, 1995, and 1997 were the warmest years since at least 1400.

The scientists then evaluated the potential effects of *greenhouse gases* (gases that cause the atmosphere to retain solar heat that is reradiated by the Earth), solar energy, and gas and dust

Mount Etna in Sicily spews a fiery plume of lava into the air in July 1998, a display that experts feared could be a prelude to the volcano's first major eruption since 1992.

from exploding volcanoes on the atmosphere over a period of nearly 600 years. They determined that greenhouse gases, which are produced primarily as the result of such human activities as the burning of fossil fuels, did not exert a significant influence on atmospheric temperatures until the 1900's. By the late 1900's, the scientists found, those gases had apparently become the dominant mechanism of global climate change. The researchers said more studies, focusing on changes in the Earth's climate over even longer periods—thousands of years—would be needed to fully resolve this important issue.

Snowball Earth. Between about 750 million and 550 million years ago—a period called the Neoproterozoic—the Earth was apparently engulfed by a series of global ice sheets and was in effect a giant snowball, according to a report published in August 1998 by geologist Paul F. Hoffman and his colleagues at Harvard University in Cambridge, Massachusetts, and at the University of Maryland. The researchers studied the carbon content of layers of glacial debris capped by layers of limestone in Namibia, in southwest Africa. They found evidence indicating that *photosynthesis* (the process by which plants produce carbon-based matter from carbon dioxide and water, using the energy of sunlight) had been severely reduced in the oceans for millions of years. This finding suggested that the oceans were once largely covered with ice that blocked sunlight.

The scientists theorized that these icy conditions developed because of a runaway *albedo effect*—the reflection of solar energy from light-colored surfaces. The ice would have formed first at the poles and then spread as the albedo effect caused global temperatures to drop.

Permian extinction. Life on Earth has experienced five major mass extinctions, the largest of which occurred near the end of the Permian Period, about 250 million years ago, when some 85 percent of marine species and many land animals went extinct. Although the reason for this enormous mass extinction has remained a mystery, an American and Chinese research team led by geologist Samuel A. Bowring of the Massachusetts Institute of Technology in Cambridge suggested a possible cause in May 1998.

Bowring and his colleagues used data on the carbon content of late Permian ocean deposits to argue that the huge extinction episode occurred in a period of less than 1 million years. They suggested that the Permian extinction was caused by either massive volcanic eruptions in Siberia or by the collision of a comet with the Earth. Either event would have filled the atmosphere with gas and dust and disrupted the global climate.

☐ Henry T. Mullins

Georgia. President Eduard Shevardnadze survived an assassination attempt on Feb. 9, 1998. Followers of former Georgian president Zviad Gamsa-khurdia, who died under mysterious circumstances after a failed 1994 *coup* (overthrow), were blamed for the attack, which resulted in the deaths of two presidential bodyguards. Shevardnadze had ousted Gamsakhurdia in 1992, following a civil war.

Shevardnadze in 1998 was unable to find a political solution agreeable to Georgia's three regions seeking independence. In May, he proposed an "asymmetric federation" in which the regions—Abkhazia, Adjaria, and South Ossetia—would be granted varying degrees of autonomy within Georgia. The proposal lacked specifics, however, and failed to calm the separatist movement in Abkhazia. In July, five Russian peacekeeping troops in Abkhazia were killed by a land mine, and violent clashes in the region continued through autumn.

Soldiers in the town of Senaki revolted on Oct. 19, 1998, seizing several armored vehicles and advancing toward Kutaisi, Georgia's second largest city. By October 20, government negotiators had persuaded the rebel troops to yield. The rebels had reportedly been led by Akaky Eliava, a former Gamsakhurdia supporter. ☐ Steven L. Solnick

See also **Asia** (Facts in brief table.)

Georgia. See **State government.**

Germany underwent a dramatic political change in 1998 when voters rejected the 16-year-old Christian Democratic government of Chancellor Helmut Kohl and elected a Social Democratic government led by Gerhard Schroeder. The election produced the first change in a German government by popular vote—rather than by shifting allegiances between political parties—since the Federal Republic was founded after World War II (1939-1945). The results reflected a desire for change at a time of high unemployment, which in January and February 1998 stood at a record 12.6 percent of the work force. The result also revealed a national weariness with Kohl, who had governed longer than any German chancellor since Otto von Bismarck in the late 1800's.

The campaign for the Sept. 27, 1998, election focused largely on economics. Schroeder, a moderate who had served as premier of the German state of Lower Saxony since 1990, promised to revitalize the country with policies that called the "New Middle." He offered somewhat vague promises of reform to generate faster economic growth and job creation while also pledging to reverse some of the welfare cutbacks enacted by Kohl's government. The Christian Democrats campaigned for welfare and labor reforms and tax cuts and urged voters to stick with Kohl as Europe's most experienced statesman.

Election result. The Social Democrats emerged from the election as the largest single party, winning 40.9 percent of the vote, up from 36.4 percent in the 1994 election. The party took 298 seats in the Bundestag, the lower house of parliament. The Christian Democrats and their Bavarian sister party, the Christian Social Union, won 245 seats, down from 294 in the previous parliament. The two parties' share of the vote dropped to 35.1 percent from 41.5 percent. Schroeder was elected as chancellor of the new parliament on Oct. 27, 1998.

The Social Democrats formed a coalition with the environmentalist Green Party, which won 6.7 percent of the vote and 47 seats. The coalition, which was the first time the Greens joined a government in Germany, forced the party to moderate or abandon some of its radical stances, such as tripling gasoline prices and withdrawing Germany from the North Atlantic Treaty Organization. The party's leader, Joschka Fischer, was named foreign minister.

Economic controversy. The new government quickly stirred controversy with its economic program, which critics believed was dictated more by the left wing of the Social Democrats than by the business-oriented moderates allied to Schroeder. The government promised to streamline Germany's complex tax system by cutting income and business taxes. It planned to finance the reduction by eliminating tax breaks and introducing new environmental taxes on business. The net effect of the package was expected to reduce the national tax burden by 1 percent, or $6.2 billion, per year. The government also convened a so-called alliance for jobs that brought business leaders and labor unions together to negotiate initiatives for fighting unemployment.

The program was immediately attacked by German industry, which claimed that the measures would increase the overall tax level on companies and reduce German competitiveness and employment. One of Schroeder's top economic advisers, computer industry executive Jost Stollmann, turned down the post of economics minister because of dissatisfaction with the program.

The government's policies also had an international impact. The Social Democrats demanded that economic policies across Europe be modified to emphasize job creation rather than the reduction of budget deficits, which most governments had been pursuing in order to launch the single European currency. Schroeder joined other leaders of the European Union (EU—an organization of 15 Western European nations) in endorsing the new policy direction at a summit meeting in Portschach, Austria, in October. Under Kohl, Germany had strongly resisted such a shift.

Firefighters search the wreckage for survivors of a train crash near Eschede, Germany, on June 3, 1998. More than 100 people died when the train derailed because of a broken wheel and then crashed into an overpass support pillar.

The Schroeder government also sparked a debate about global currency trading. Oskar Lafontaine, the new finance minister, proposed in October that Europe, the United States, and Japan agree to limit fluctuations between the euro, the dollar, and the yen. Lafontaine contended that freely floating currencies weakened economies by encouraging speculation rather than long-term investment. The proposal was opposed by U.S. officials and many central banks in Europe. They argued that fluctuation controls could be difficult to manage and could prove more damaging to their economies.

Other policies. Schroeder promised more continuity than change in foreign policy, but he also vowed to vigorously defend German interests, a change that unsettled the country's allies. He pledged to maintain German support for closer integration among EU countries and for the expansion of the EU into Eastern Europe, but he demanded a reduction of Germany's large payments to the EU budget. The government also urged NATO to agree not to be the first to use nuclear weapons in any conflict. The proposal was opposed by the United States, Great Britain, and France, which regarded nuclear weapons as essential for deterring aggression.

The government also vowed to shut down the country's nuclear power reactors, though it set no time limit for the process. It also promised to facilitate the integration of the more than 7 million immigrants living in the country. The integration included the introduction of dual citizenship, which would let immigrants' children born in Germany become citizens. In the past, citizenship was reserved for people of German ancestry.

Resurgent industry. In contrast to the continuing problem of unemployment, German business exhibited a new dynamism in 1998 with several large, foreign acquisitions. Daimler-Benz AG, the country's largest industrial company and maker of Mercedes-Benz automobiles, took over Chrysler Corp., the third-largest U.S. automaker, in November. The takeover was one of the largest in history. The new company, called Daimler-Chrysler AG, became the world's third-largest car manufacturer with sales of $130 billion a year.

German automakers Volkswagen AG and Bayerische Motoren Werke AG (BMW) battled for Rolls-Royce Motor Cars PLC, the British luxury carmaker. BMW almost concluded an agreeement to purchase Rolls-Royce, but Volkswagen outbid it. BMW managed to reopen part of the deal, however, because it had the support of Rolls-Royce PLC, the aircraft-engine maker that owns the Rolls-Royce trademark. Under a final arrangement struck in August, Volkswagen kept Rolls-Royce Motor Cars' factory and the right to produce its Bentley line. BMW got the Rolls-Royce

trademark and planned to build a new factory.

In July, Bertelsmann AG purchased Random House Inc. of New York City, the largest general-interest book publisher in the United States. The move made Bertelsmann the world's largest publisher of English-language books and the world's third-largest media company.

Deutsche Bank AG, Germany's largest bank, agreed in November to acquire Bankers Trust Corp. of New York City, the eighth-largest U.S. bank, for $10 billion. The deal, if accepted by government regulators, would become the biggest foreign takeover of a U.S. financial institution in history.

Nazi-era slave labor. The German government and major German companies began considering paying compensation to people forced into slave labor by the Nazi regime during World War II. Lawsuits on behalf of some of the 8 million people subjected to such labor were filed in German and U.S. courts in 1998, after two of Switzerland's banks agreed to pay $1.25 billion to settle a similar suit over financial dealings between Swiss banks, the Nazis, and Holocaust victims.   □ Tom Buerkle

See also **Europe** (Facts in brief table); **Europe** Special Report: **European Union; People in the news** (Schroeder, Gerhard); **Switzerland.**

Ghana. See Africa.

Golf.
Mark O'Meara was named Golfer of the Year by the Professional Golfers' Association (PGA) of America in 1998, even though David Duval took four tournaments and was the year's top money winner, with earnings of just under $2.5 million. O'Meara won only two tournament victories in 1998, but they came in two of the year's major events—the Masters and the British Open. Duval became the first three-time winner on the PGA tour on August 30, when he captured the World Series of Golf in Akron, Ohio. The $405,000 first prize enabled Duval to pass $2 million in earnings for the year faster than anyone else in history.

Eldrick (Tiger) Woods remained Number 1 in the world rankings in 1998. Woods won only one tournament during the year, but finished in the top 10 in 13 tournaments. Annika Sorenstam of Sweden, with four tournament victories, was the Player of the Year on the Ladies Professional Golf Association (LPGA) Tour and was the Tour's top money winner, with $1.1 million.

Legal challenge. The year began with a controversial legal challenge when golfer Casey Martin, 25, fought a PGA rule banning the use of carts by players in its tournaments. In December 1997, Martin—who had a congenital condition that restricted blood flow to his right leg—obtained a temporary injunction that allowed him to use a cart in PGA competition until his case was heard in

February 1998. On Jan. 11, 1998, Martin, riding a golf cart between shots, won the Lakeland Classic, a tournament on the lower-level Nike Tour, which was governed by PGA rules. On February 6, legendary golfers Arnold Palmer, Jack Nicklaus, and Ken Venturi testified on the PGA's behalf, saying that stamina and walking were an integral part of golf. On February 11, a federal judge granted Martin a permanent injunction against the PGA.

Grand Slam. O'Meara won the Masters, his first major title, on April 12 in Augusta, Georgia. It was his 15th Masters appearance. O'Meara sank a 20-foot (6.1-meter) birdie putt on the 18th hole to take the lead for the first time in the tournament. He won by one stroke, with a nine-under-par score of 279. Duval and Fred Couples tied for second place at 280. Woods, the defending champion, finished in a tie for eighth place.

The 98th U.S. Open began on June 18, 1998, at the Olympic Club in San Francisco. Lee Janzen, who trailed Paine Stewart by five strokes after three rounds, shot a 68 in the final round to take the title with an even-par total of 280. Stewart shot a 74 to finish one stroke behind on June 21.

O'Meara took the 127th British Open on July 19 in Southport, England, by beating Brian Watts by two strokes in a four-hole play-off. O'Meara made four out of six birdies on the back nine and another on the first play-off hole.

Vijay Singh, a native of Fiji, won the PGA Championship in Redmond, Washington, on August 16. Singh one-putted eight greens in the final round to record a nine-under-par 271.

Seniors. For the second straight year, Hale Irwin dominated the PGA Senior Tour, finishing no lower than fifth place in 14 tournaments. Irwin won his third PGA Senior championship in a row, along with the U.S. Senior Open, and was the top senior money winner, with $2.9 million.

Women. The LPGA's Rookie of the Year Award went to Se Ri Pak, a 20-year-old South Korean. On May 17, Pak won her first major tournament, the LPGA Championship in Wilmington, Delaware, with an 11-under-par score of 273. On July 6 in Kohler, Wisconsin, she won the longest and most dramatic U.S. Women's Open ever played, sinking an 18-foot (5.5-meter) birdie putt to beat American Jenny Chuasiriporn on the 20th play-off hole. In July, Pak shot a 61 in a tournament at Sylvania, Ohio, the lowest score ever recorded on the LPGA Tour.

Team. On Sept. 20, 1998, the United States retained the Solheim Cup, the women's version of the Ryder Cup, in a 16-12 victory over Europe at Dublin, Ohio. The victory was the Americans' fourth in five biennial competitions.   ☐ Ron Reid

See also **People in the news** (O'Meara, Mark; Pak, Se Ri).

Great Britain. See **United Kingdom.**

Mark O'Meara tees off during the Masters Tournament in Augusta, Georgia, in April 1998. O'Meara, who won the Masters and the British Open in 1998, was chosen the PGA Golfer of the Year.

Greece continued to make strides toward entering the economic mainstream of Europe in 1998. The Socialist government of Prime Minister Costas Simitis devalued the Greek currency, the drachma, and announced a fresh round of budget cuts in March to prepare the economy to join Europe's single currency, the euro, in 2001.

Economy. On March 15, 1998, the government agreed with the European Union (EU) to devalue the drachma by 14.3 percent against other European currencies and then peg the currency to Europe's exchange-rate mechanism. The mechanism obliged Greece to limit the fluctuation of the drachma and was regarded as a precursor to participating in the euro.

The devaluation was something of a reversal, coming after a year in which the government had strongly defended the value of the drachma to bring down inflation and the budget deficit. That policy succeeded as Greece's inflation rate fell to 4.8 percent in 1998 and the budget deficit declined to 2.4 percent of *gross domestic product* (the value of all goods and services produced in a country in a given year). The government hoped the devaluation would be Greece's last, setting a permanent exchange rate at which the country's economy could compete with other EU countries.

To back up the move, the government announced it would cut the budget deficit by $1.2

A man wielding a garden hose attempts to halt a fire approaching his house near Athens, Greece, in August 1998. The fire, which began on Mount Pendeli, was one of more than 3,000 wildfires that broke out in the area during the summer.

billion and reduce labor regulations. It also promised to sell off its 49 percent stakes in 11 state-owned companies, including the telephone company OTE. By reversing Greece's tradition of high public spending, inflation, and state ownership of industry, the government claimed the measures would enable Greece to meet the economic criteria for the single currency in 1999 and to adopt the euro in 2001. The measures also helped to boost the economy, which economists expected to grow by 3.4 percent in 1998. However, the budget cuts contributed to significant losses for Simitis' Socialist Party in municipal elections in October. The Socialists, who previously controlled a majority of municipalities, won control of only 372, while the conservative opposition party, New Democracy, won 423.

Relations with Turkey, Greece's Aegean neighbor and rival, were defused in December when Prime Minister Simitis persuaded the government of Cyprus, which is closely allied to Greece, not to station Russian anti-aircraft missiles on the divided island. Turkey, which invaded the island in 1974 and set up a breakaway Turkish Cypriot government on the northern third of the island, had threatened a military attack if the missiles were deployed.   □ Tom Buerkle

See also **Europe** (Facts in brief table); **Europe** Special Report: **European Union; Turkey.**

Guatemala. On April 26, 1998, Roman Catholic Bishop Juan Gerardi Conedera, 75, a human-rights leader in Guatemala, was bludgeoned to death, apparently with a concrete block. Gerardi's murder and the subsequent investigation aroused old hatreds in a country that had endured a civil war from the 1960's until 1996.

On Oct. 21, 1998, prosecutors filed murder charges against Mario Lionel Orantes Najera, a Roman Catholic priest who shared a residence with Gerardi. Church and human-rights leaders, however, suspected military involvement in the murder. Two days before his death, the bishop had issued a report, the culmination of a three-year probe, that accused the military of the majority of the human-rights violations during the civil war.

On January 16, five students from St. Mary's College in St. Mary's City, Maryland, were raped while on an educational trip in Guatemala. Near Santa Lucia Cotzumalguapa, several gunmen stopped a bus carrying St. Mary's students and teachers, robbed all of them, and raped five of the women. Four of the rape victims and others on the trip returned in April to testify against the accused attackers. The case was not yet resolved at the end of 1998.   □ Nathan A. Haverstock

See also **Latin America** (Facts in brief table); **Roman Catholic Church.**

Guinea. See Africa.

Haiti. On Dec. 17, 1998, Haiti's parliament approved Jacques-Edouard Alexis as prime minister. The decision ended a political stalemate that had left the country without a prime minister since June 1997. Without a budget or fully functional government—conditions necessary for increases in international aid—Haiti survived in 1998 largely on remittances of more than $500 million sent home by Haitians living in the United States or Canada.

On September 23, Hurricane Georges wreaked extensive damage across Haiti and left more than 145 people dead. High winds and heavy rainfall destroyed at least 30 percent of the country's mature rice crops and 60 percent of a freshly planted rice crop in the Artibonite Valley, an area that had been made productive by an agriculture reform program.

In November, the United Nations Security Council voted to keep a 300-member, multinational force in Haiti for another year to train a local police force created in 1996. An additional 300 soldiers from a U.S. military mission helped local authorities improve facilities that provide pure drinking water, sanitation, and electrical services.   ☐ Nathan A. Haverstock

See also **Latin America** (Facts in brief table).

Harness racing. See Horse racing.

Hawaii. See State government.

Health-care issues. In July 1998, the United States House of Representatives approved a bill designed, in part, to increase protections for patients who belong to managed-care plans, such as Health Maintenance Organizations (HMO's). Managed care is a form of health insurance in which costs are controlled by offering incentives to providers to practice more conservative care. Although the bill, which was supported primarily by Republicans, included a number of protective measures—including allowing women access to *obstetricians* (physicians who specialize in childbirth) and *gynecologists* (physicians who specialize in women's health) without referrals—it did not offer the public as many protections as an alternate plan supported by Democrats. A key provision of the defeated Democrat plan allowed patients to collect punitive damages from managed-care providers that denied them appropriate care. The Senate, however, failed to pass any managed-care legislation in 1998. Health-care experts predicted that Congress would take the issue up again in 1999.

Medicare managed care. In 1998, more than 6 million elderly Americans who were beneficiaries of Medicare belonged to managed-care plans. Medicare is a federal program that covers many health-care costs for people over age 65 and some disabled people. The federal government pays managed-care plans a fixed monthly fee to cover the health-care costs of Medicare beneficiaries. Many managed-care providers, however, withdrew wholly or in part from the Medicare program in 1998, claiming that they had paid more for the health care of Medicare beneficiaries than they had received from the government.

Despite the claims of managed-care providers that they were losing money on Medicare, the Health Care Financing Administration (HCFA)—the agency of the Department of Health and Human Services (HHS) that administers Medicare—announced in October that it had overpaid managed-care costs by more than 5 percent in 1997. In August 1998, the HHS Inspector General reported that HMO's had been overstating administrative costs billed to the Medicare program by more than $1 billion per year since 1994.

The HCFA announced in October 1998 that health plans would not be allowed to drop benefits or raise premiums for Medicare patients in 1999. This announcement was expected to result in the withdrawal of more managed-care providers from Medicare.

The Viagra debate. In March 1998, the U.S. Food and Drug Administration (FDA) approved the drug Viagra as a treatment for *impotence* (an inability to achieve and maintain an erection). Within the drug's first four months on the market, physicians wrote 3.6 million prescriptions for it. Viagra, however, sparked controversies over both the safety of the drug and whether insurance companies should pay for it.

In August, the FDA reported the deaths of 69 men who had used Viagra. Many of the men had a history of cardiovascular problems. Although the FDA maintained that Viagra was safe when used properly, critics claimed it was dangerous.

In July, HCFA announced that state Medicaid programs must cover the costs of Viagra. Medicaid is a federal-state program that provides medical care for many people who cannot pay for it. A number of states, including New York and Wisconsin, protested this order, claiming that the expense of Viagra took money needed for more basic services.

Some private insurance companies did provide coverage for use of the drug, which prompted health authorities to accuse the insurers of discrimination against women for not also providing coverage for contraceptive drugs and birth control devices. To address this concern, Congress considered legislation in 1998 that would require insurers to pay for prescription contraceptives. No such bill came to votes in either the House or Senate during the year.   ☐ Emily Friedman

See also **Medicine; People in the news** (Satcher, David); **Public health and safety.**

Hinduism. In March 1998, the Hindu national-ist Bharatiya Janata Party (BJP) formed a coalition government in India. In general elections, the BJP campaigned for a government strongly influenced by Hindu cultural and religious traditions. More than 80 percent of India's 846 million people were Hindu in 1998, while the minority populations were mostly Muslim, Sikh, or Christian. The BJP-led government caused concern among the minority groups and more moderate Hindus, but the BJP modified many of its Hindu-centered goals to reach an agreement with its coalition partners.

Pilgrimages. The kumbh mela pilgrimage, a rite of spiritual renewal that is held every three years, took place at the northern Indian city of Hardwar in early 1998. The destination of the pil-grimage rotates between four sites, where the de-vout believe drops of immortal nectar fell during a heavenly conflict. In June, the Indian government provided heavy security for a pilgrimage in the state of Jammu and Kashmir to the shrine of Vaishno Devi, a Hindu goddess. Muslim separatists in the region, which is claimed by both India and Pakistan, had threatened to disrupt the event.

Tragedies. A pilgrimage in August to the Kailash Temple near Lake Manasarowar in Tibet ended in tragedy. As the pilgrims returned home through the mountains in the northern Indian state of Uttar Pradesh, a mudslide buried at least 60 of them and more than 140 other people.

The 200-year-old Balaji Temple in Varanasi, Hinduism's holiest city, collapsed in October. Nine

Devout Hindus bathe in the Ganges River in 1998 during the kumbh mela pilgrimage to the city of Hardwar. An estimated 10 million pilgrims participated in the bathing ritual, an act of spiritual renewal held every three years at one of four rotating sites.

women died and at least two other people were seriously injured. Local authorities arrested the trustees of the temple for negligence.

Hindu leader honored. A 10-foot (3-meter) bronze statue of Swami Vivekananda was dedicated at the Hindu Temple of Greater Chicago in Lemont, Illinois, in July. Vivekananda (1863–1902) gained worldwide recognition in 1893 when he addressed the World's Parliament of Religions in Chicago. At the conference, he promoted religious tolerance and the beliefs of some Hindu teachers that all faiths share a common goal. He founded the monastic Ramakrishna Order; the Ramakrishna Mission, a social service organization; and the Vedanta Society, which promotes Hindu teachings primarily in Western countries.

Amartya Kumar Sen, a Hindu and native of India, was awarded the Nobel Prize for economics in October 1998. The Nobel Prize committee recognized Sen for his study of the economic conditions that lead to poverty and famine. Sen's life and economic theories were influenced by his family's participation in the progressive Hindu movement, Brahmo Samaji, which contributed to many social reforms in India and changes in Hindu practices.   □ Premen Addy

See also **India; Nobel Prizes; People in the news** (Vajpayee, Atal Bihari).

Hobbies. See Toys and games.

Hockey. One season after capturing their first National Hockey League (NHL) championship in 42 years, the Detroit Red Wings defeated the Washington Capitals, 4–1, on June 16, 1998, to retain their hold on the Stanley Cup championship. The Red Wings once again swept the finals in four games and became the first team to win consecutive championships since 1992. The last game of the final series was an emotional one, highlighted by the appearance of defenseman Vladimir Konstantinov, who joined his victorious teammates on the ice for the first time since suffering a severe head injury in a car crash in 1997.

Season. In the 82-game regular season, the Dallas Stars led the NHL with 109 points. Detroit finished 6 points behind Dallas in the Central Division. The New Jersey Devils, who led the Eastern Conference with 107 points, were the only other team to exceed 100 points. The Pittsburgh Penguins compiled 98 points to take the Northeast Division. The Colorado Avalanche finished as the Pacific Division champions, with 95 points.

Play-offs. The Capitals reached the Stanley Cup finals for the first time in the 24-year history of the franchise. Along the way, they beat Boston (4 games to 2), Ottawa (4 to 1), and Buffalo (4 to 2). Three of Washington's victories in the hard-fought Buffalo series came in overtime. Detroit returned to the final series by beating Phoenix,

National Hockey League standings

Western Conference

Central Division

	W.	L.	T.	Pts.
Dallas Stars*	49	22	11	109
Detroit Red Wings*	44	23	15	103
St. Louis Blues*	45	29	8	98
Phoenix Coyotes*	35	35	12	82
Chicago Blackhawks	30	39	13	73
Toronto Maple Leafs	30	43	9	69

Pacific Division

Colorado Avalanche*	39	26	17	95
Los Angeles Kings*	38	33	11	87
Edmonton Oilers*	35	37	10	80
San Jose Sharks*	34	38	10	78
Calgary Flames	26	41	15	67
Anaheim Mighty Ducks	26	43	13	65
Vancouver Canucks	25	43	14	64

Eastern Conference

Northeast Division

Pittsburgh Penguins*	40	24	18	98
Boston Bruins*	39	30	13	91
Buffalo Sabres*	36	29	17	89
Montreal Canadiens*	37	32	13	87
Ottawa Senators*	34	33	15	83
Carolina Hurricanes	33	41	8	74

Atlantic Division

New Jersey Devils*	48	23	11	107
Philadelphia Flyers*	42	29	11	95
Washington Capitals*	40	30	12	92
New York Islanders	30	41	11	71
New York Rangers	25	39	18	68
Florida Panthers	24	43	15	63
Tampa Bay Lightning	17	55	10	44

*Made play-offs

Stanley Cup champions—Detroit Red Wings
(defeated Washington Capitals, 4 games to 0)

Leading scorers	Games	Goals	Assists	Pts.
Jaromir Jagr, Pittsburgh	77	35	67	102
Peter Forsberg, Colorado	72	25	66	91
Pavel Bure, Vancouver	82	51	39	90
Wayne Gretzky, N.Y. Rangers	82	23	67	90
John Leclair, Philadelphia	82	51	36	87

Leading goalies (26 or more games)	Games	Goals against	Avg.
Ed Belfour, Dallas	61	112	1.88
Martin Brodeur, New Jersey	70	130	1.89
Tom Barrasso, Pittsburgh	63	122	2.07
Dominik Hasek, Buffalo	72	147	2.09
Ron Hextall, Philadelphia	46	97	2.17
Trevor Kidd, Carolina	47	97	2.17
Jamie McLennan, St. Louis	30	60	2.17

Awards

Adams Trophy (coach of the year)—Pat Burns, Boston
Calder Trophy (best rookie)—Sergei Samsonov, Boston
Hart Trophy (most valuable player)—Dominik Hasek, Buffalo
Jennings Trophy (team with fewest goals against)—Martin Brodeur, Mike Dunham, New Jersey
Lady Byng Trophy (sportsmanship)—Ron Francis, Pittsburgh
Pearson Award (best player as voted by NHL players)—Dominik Hasek, Buffalo
Masterton Trophy (perseverance, dedication to hockey)—Jamie McLennan, St. Louis
Norris Trophy (best defenseman)—Rob Blake, Los Angeles
Ross Trophy (leading scorer)—Jaromir Jagr, Pittsburgh
Selke Trophy (best defensive forward)—Jere Lehtinen, Dallas
Smythe Trophy (most valuable player in Stanley Cup)—Steve Yzerman, Detroit
Vezina Trophy (best goalkeeper)—Dominik Hasek, Buffalo

St. Louis, and Dallas, all by 4 games to 2.

Olympics. Both the United States and Canada, each a gold-medal favorite, failed to win a medal at the 1998 Winter Olympics in February in Nagano, Japan. The Czech Republic, led by goalie Dominik Hasek, the NHL's most valuable player, won the gold. Hasek made 38 saves in a 4–1 victory over the United States and stopped all five post-overtime shoot-out attempts by Canada in a 2–1 victory. He then shut out Russia, 1–0, in the gold medal game. Finland won the bronze.

A public-relations fiasco erupted at Nagano after reports surfaced that unknown members of the U.S. team had vandalized their living quarters in the athletes' village. Team captain Chris Chelios later apologized and sent a $3,000 check to Japanese officials to cover the damage.

Women's hockey made its Olympic debut at Nagano in 1998, and the first gold medal was won by the U.S. team. As expected, the United States and Canada dominated the tournament. The U.S. team, boosted by goalie Sarah Tueting's 21 saves on 22 shots , beat Canada, 3–1, for the gold. Finland beat China, 4–1, to win the bronze.

International. Sweden beat Finland in the two-game final series of the World Hockey Championships at Zurich on May 17, 1998.   □ Ron Reid

See also **Olympics** Special Report: **The 1998 Winter Olympics.**

Honduras. In late October 1998, Hurricane Mitch devastated Honduras. Torrential rains caused flooding and mudslides that destroyed entire communities and wiped out crops, roads, and communications systems. The government reported that more than 7,000 people died, another 11,000 people were injured, and more than 10,000 others were missing. Contaminated water supplies and increased mosquito populations contributed to more than 60,000 cases of respiratory diseases, malaria, diarrhea, and other illnesses.

President Carlos Flores Facusse, who had been sworn in on January 27, described the country as "a panorama of death, desolation and ruin." Foreign countries provided immediate emergency and monetary aid.

In February, a judge ruled that a 1987 amnesty agreement protected Colonel Juan Blas Salazar, who was found guilty of the 1982 attempted murder and torture of six students. Salazar was the first of 10 indicted officers from a United States-trained battalion to stand trial for the crime.

In May 1998, human-rights investigators unearthed the remains of 98 leftist guerrillas at an undisclosed location. The Honduran army allegedly captured and executed the rebels, including a former U.S. Roman Catholic priest, James Francis Carney, in 1982.   □ Nathan A. Haverstock

See also **Latin America** (Facts in brief table).

Washington goaltender Olaf Kolzig dives after a loose puck in front of Detroit right-winger Kirk Maltby in Game Four of the Stanley Cup finals. The Red Wings swept the Capitals in four games with the 4–1 victory.

Victory Gallop (foreground) wins by a nose, edging Real Quiet out of the Triple Crown in a photo finish at the Belmont Stakes on June 6, 1998.

Major horse races of 1998

Thoroughbred racing

Race	Winner	Value to Winner
Belmont Stakes	Victory Gallop	$600,000
Blue Grass Stakes	Halory Hunter	$434,000
Breeders' Cup Classic	Awesome Again	$2,662,400
Breeders' Cup Distaff	Escena	$1,040,000
Breeders' Cup Juvenile	Answer Lively	$520,000
Breeders' Cup Juvenile Fillies	Silverbulletday	$520,000
Breeders' Cup Mile	Da Hoss	$520,000
Breeders' Cup Sprint	Reraise	$572,000
Breeders' Cup Turf	Buck's Boy	$1,040,000
Buick Haskell Invitational Handicap	Coronado's Quest	$600,000
Canadian International	Royal Anthem	$630,000
Derby Stakes (United Kingdom)	High-Rise	$928,450
Dubai Cup (United Arab Emirates)	Silver Charm	$2,400,000
Hollywood Gold Cup Stakes	Skip Away	$600,000
Irish Derby (Ireland)	Dream Well	$592,567
Japan Cup (Japan)	El Condor Pasa	$1,084,248
Jim Beam Stakes	Event of the Year	$360,000
Jockey Club Gold Cup	Wagon Limit	$600,000
Kentucky Derby	Real Quiet	$700,000
Kentucky Oaks	Keeper Hill	$375,410
King George VI and Queen Elizabeth Diamond Stakes (United Kingdom)	Swain	$584,560
Massachusetts Handicap	Skip Away	$500,000
Matriarch Stakes	Squeak	$420,000
Oaklawn Handicap	Precocity	$450,000
Pacific Classic Stakes	Free House	$600,000
Pimlico Special Handicap	Skip Away	$450,000
Preakness Stakes	Real Quiet	$650,000
Prix de l'Arc de Triomphe (France)	Sagamix	$724,000
Santa Anita Derby	Indian Charlie	$450,000
Travers Stakes	Coronado's Quest	$450,000

Harness racing

Race	Winner	Value to Winner
Cane Pace	Shady Character	$379,941
Hambletonian	Muscles Yankee	$1,000,000
Little Brown Jug	Shady Character	$566,630
Meadowlands Pace	Day in a Life	$1,000,000
Messenger Stakes	Fit For Life	$387,380
Woodrow Wilson	Grinfromeartoear	$660,250

Sources: The Blood Horse Magazine and U.S. Trotting Association

Horse racing. Real Quiet, a horse purchased for only $17,000, won both the Kentucky Derby and the Preakness Stakes in 1998. He fell short of becoming history's 12th Triple Crown winner when he lost the Belmont Stakes, finishing second, by a nose, to Victory Gallop. The year was also noteworthy for the finest contingent of thoroughbreds to come along in several years and the establishment of the National Thoroughbred Racing Association (NTRA), a marketing group founded to renew fan interest in the sport.

Three-year-olds. Real Quiet, an 8-1 shot, won the 124th Kentucky Derby on May 2, 1998, at Churchill Downs in Louisville, Kentucky. Under the whip of jockey Kent Desormeaux, Real Quiet took the lead after a mile and held off the spirited challenge of Victory Gallop through the stretch. Indian Charlie, a stablemate of Real Quiet also trained by Bob Baffert, finished third.

Two weeks later, on May 16, the 1³⁄₁₆-mile 123rd Preakness Stakes was run before a record 91,122 spectators at Pimlico Race Course in Baltimore, Maryland. Two small fires at a nearby transformer knocked out much of the track's electrical power, closing down many betting windows for about 40 minutes. Real Quiet ran strong again, moving up from fifth place and taking the lead while making the turn for home, maintaining a 2¼-length lead on Victory Gallop at the finish.

The Preakness victory gave Real Quiet a chance to become the first Triple Crown winner since Affirmed in 1978. However, on June 6, 1998, at the 1½-mile Belmont Stakes in Elmont, New

York, Victory Gallop, under jockey Gary Stevens, ran true to his name, edging Real Quiet by a nose in a thrilling photo finish. The victory denied Real Quiet the $600,000 winner's purse and $5-million Triple Crown bonus.

Harness. Muscles Yankee, like Real Quiet, was in a position to win the Triple Crown for trotters after taking the Hambletonian and the Yonkers Trot. His chances disappeared, however, on October 9, in a qualifying heat loss at the Kentucky Futurity. Muscles Yankee's $1-million Hambletonian victory was the fifth in 12 seasons for driver John Campbell.

International. On March 28 in the United Arab Emirates, Silver Charm won one of the world's richest horse races, the $4-million, 1¼-mile Dubai World Cup. Silver Charm lost and regained the lead in the stretch to defeat Swain, the home favorite, and take the $2.4-million first prize, by a nose. Loup Savage of France came in third.

Earth Summit, a 7-1 favorite, won the 4½-mile Grand National in Liverpool, England, on April 4. Only 6 of 37 starters completed the 30-jump steeplechase at Aintree. Animal rights activists were outraged when three horses fell during the race. One collapsed and died, and the other two had to be destroyed due to injury. ☐ Ron Reid

Hospital. See **Health-care issues.**

Housing. See **Building and construction.**

Houston. The first African American mayor of Houston, Lee Brown, took office on Jan. 2, 1998. Brown had defeated businessman Robert Mosbacher in a runoff for the mayor's seat in December 1997. The new mayor succeeded Bob Lanier, who stepped down after three terms because of a city term-limitations law.

Brown, in his inaugural address, pledged an ethical administration that would not exclude anyone on the basis of race or sex. His election, he noted, marked the fall of a long-standing barrier. "Today, all children—black, white, Asian, and Hispanic—can point to City Hall and say, 'I, too, can be mayor,'" he said. Before running for mayor, Brown served as Houston's first African American police chief from 1982 to 1990. In 1995, he returned to Houston to teach at Rice University, after serving as New York City's police commissioner and director of the White House Office of National Drug Control Policy.

Brown's agenda. Brown, who dedicated his administration to Houston's children, joined a movement among big-city mayors to use municipal funds to aid public schools, which generally are not funded by city government. In September 1998, Brown won City Council approval to spend $466,000 on after-school programs at 42 city schools. The program was aimed, in large part, at reducing the high number of crimes committed

by and against juveniles in the after-school hours.

Brown also launched a large-scale effort to make city government more responsive and city services more accessible to residents. The concept, called Neighborhood Oriented Government, involved such city-sponsored events as town hall meetings and such activities as fostering civic groups. In addition, Houston's planning department divided the city into 88 superneighborhoods, each of which was invited to submit its own development plan.

Corruption trials. In September 1998, former city council member Ben Reyes and former Port Commissioner Betti Maldonado were tried for the second time in a Houston federal court. In December, a jury found both guilty of bribery and conspiracy. Reyes, Maldonado, lobbyist Ross Allyn, and three others had been indicted in July 1997 by a federal grand jury on charges of conspiracy and bribery. They were accused of bribing council members to help a South American company, The Cayman Group, get part of a contract to build a convention center hotel in downtown Houston. In reality, the Cayman Group was part of a sting operation by the Federal Bureau of Investigation, organized to expose suspected corruption by Reyes and others. Allyn was acquitted in a trial held earlier in 1998. Jurors had originally deadlocked on the guilt or innocence of Reyes and Maldonado.

"Big Unit," big thrills. Houston baseball fans turned out in record numbers to see the Astros win the National League (NL) Central Division championship for the second straight year. However, the Astros faltered again in the first round of the play-offs, losing three games to one to the San Diego Padres.

Slugger Moises Alou, traded to Houston by the 1997 world champion Florida Marlins, added power to the 1998 line-up for the Astros. In a July trade, Houston acquired hard-throwing left-handed pitcher Randy Johnson from the Seattle Mariners of the American League. Johnson, who at 6 feet 10 inches (2 meters) tall is nicknamed "The Big Unit," won 10 games and lost 1 as the Astros finished with a 102-60 record.

Second title for Comets. In 1998, Houstonians cheered another championship team—the Women's National Basketball Association (WNBA) Comets, which debuted in 1997. Led by Cynthia Cooper and Sheryl Swoopes, the Comets defeated the Phoenix Mercury on Sept. 1, 1998, to take their second consecutive WNBA title, two games to one. Cooper was named the WNBA's most valuable player, and Van Chancellor, the head coach of the Comets, was named the league's coach of the year, both for the second consecutive year. ☐ Burke Watson

See also **City; Dallas.**

Human rights.

In 1998, the United Nations (UN) celebrated the 50th anniversary of the Universal Declaration of Human Rights, a document that established a standard for protecting human rights throughout the world. The UN General Assembly approved the document on Dec. 10, 1948.

South Africa. On Oct. 29, 1998, South Africa's Truth and Reconciliation Commission issued its final report, alleging that the apartheid government, which was in power from 1948 to 1994, used security forces to abduct and kill citizens who sought equality. (Apartheid is an official policy of racial segregation and discrimination.) The commission also noted atrocities committed by other groups, such as the African National Congress, the party that has governed since 1994. The commission was established in 1995 to compile an accurate record of the country's violent history and to heal wounds from years of discrimination.

Switzerland's two largest banks agreed on Aug. 12, 1998, to pay $1.25 billion to settle claims filed by 31,500 individuals for assets the banks gained during World War II (1939–1945). Before the war, thousands of people, particularly Jews fearing Nazi Germany's anti-Semitic policies, deposited their assets in Swiss bank accounts. The Swiss banks also received gold that the Germans had looted from victims of the Holocaust, the Nazi persecution of Jews that resulted in the deaths of more than 6 million people. Since 1945, the banks blocked the efforts of survivors and their relatives to recover money.

A UN tribunal sentenced former Prime Minister Jean Kambanda of Rwanda to life in prison on Sept. 4, 1998, for his role in the 1994 *genocide* (extermination of a racial or ethnic group) that resulted in the death of an estimated 500,000 Tutsi and moderate Hutu. On April 24, 1998, Rwandan authorities executed 22 ethnic Hutus who had been found guilty of genocide in Rwandan courts.

Sexual harassment. The Equal Employment Opportunity Commission, a U.S. agency charged with the enforcement of nondiscrimination laws, announced two major sexual harassment settlements in 1998. In both cases, employees had complained of degrading behavior and language directed mostly by men toward women. The U.S. subsidiary of Astra AB, a Swedish drug company, agreed on February 5 to pay $9.85 million to settle claims by 79 women and 1 man who worked for the firm in Westborough, Massachusetts. Mitsubishi Motor Corporation's division in Normal, Illinois, agreed on June 11 to pay $34 million to more than 300 female employees.

Referendums. On February 10, Maine voters repealed a law that barred discrimination against homosexuals in housing, jobs, credit, and public accommodations. In 1997, the state government had added sexual orientation to its list of protected categories under the Maine Human Rights Act.

Voters in Washington state approved a measure on Nov. 3, 1998, to ban preferences based on race or sex in state or municipal hiring, admission to state colleges, and state contracts with private businesses. Washington's Initiative 200 was modeled after a 1996 California initiative.

Hate crimes. Three white men were indicted on capital murder charges for the June 9, 1998, killing of an African American man in Jasper, Texas. The three men reportedly beat 49-year-old James Byrd, Jr., and dragged him to death behind a pickup truck. The case gained national attention because of its alleged racial motivations.

Matthew Shepard, a 21-year-old, openly gay student at the University of Wyoming in Laramie died October 12 after being severely beaten. Two men allegedly attacked Shepard because of his sexual orientation. People around the United States responded to the murder by holding vigils and calling for the passage of laws that exact severe punishments for crimes motivated by hate of an individual's race, ethnicity, religion, or sexual orientation.

Church fires. A jury in South Carolina ruled on July 24 that two chapters of the Ku Klux Klan, a secret society of white people, should pay $37.8 million to the Macedonia Baptist Church for a 1995 arson attack that destroyed the church's building. The jury concluded that the Klan's message of hatred for blacks had motivated the four former Klansmen, who were convicted of the arson in 1997. In November 1998, a judge reduced the award to $21.5 million.

Revisiting the past. On August 21, a jury in Hattiesburg, Mississippi, convicted Sam H. Bowers, a former Ku Klux Klan leader, of ordering the firebombing that killed civil rights activist Vernon Dahmer, Sr., on Jan. 10, 1966. Authorities said Klan members attacked Dahmer's residence because he allowed fellow African Americans to pay their poll taxes, which were required for voting, at his store. Bowers had been tried four times before, but juries deadlocked each time, resulting in mistrials.

On March 17, 1998, Mississippi opened the files of the state's Sovereignty Commission, an agency founded in 1956, allegedly to shield the state from federal government intrusion. However, the agency's primary function was to monitor the activities of civil rights activists and to derail desegregation efforts. The Sovereignty Commission was shut down in 1973, but years of legal proceedings kept the files closed. On Jan. 13, 1998, a U.S. district court judge ordered the state to open the files.

☐ Geoffrey A. Campbell and Linda P. Campbell

See also **Crime; Human rights** Special Report: **A Common Standard—50 Years of Defending Human Rights for All; Judaism; South Africa; Switzerland; United Nations.**

All human beings are born free
and equal . . .

A Common Standard—
50 Years of Defending
Human Rights for All

. . . right to a nationality . . .

*In 1948, the United Nations General Assembly
adopted the Universal Declaration of Human
Rights, the document that launched the first
worldwide defense of human rights.*

No one shall be subjected to
torture . . .   *By Makau Wa Mutua*

. . . the right to work . . .

All are equal before the law . . .
. . . the right to own property . .

In 1998, individuals, organizations, and governments around the world celebrated the 50th anniversary of the event that initiated an international commitment to protecting human rights. On Dec. 10, 1948, the United Nations (UN) General Assembly adopted the Universal Declaration of Human Rights, the world's first comprehensive human rights document. Since its creation, the Declaration has become the standard guideline and philosophical basis for worldwide efforts to protect the rights, freedoms, and dignity of individuals. Consequently, the document has had a far-reaching impact on national policies, international law and politics, and the work of the United Nations.

The Universal Declaration of Human Rights was in many ways the direct result of the devastation and horrors of World War II (1939–1945). Determined to prevent a recurrence of the cruelties of that war, the victorious nations founded the UN in 1945 at the San Francisco Conference. The Charter of the United Nations, which established the organization's structure and aims, pledged to promote and respect human rights but did not specify what those rights included. In 1946, the UN established the Commission on Human Rights and asked it to draft a document that would establish the UN's position on human rights. Eleanor Roosevelt, the first lady of the United States from 1933 to 1945, served as the first chairperson of the commission. Less than two years later, the commission's work was approved by the UN General Assembly, beginning a 50-year legacy of promoting equality and nondiscrimination.

Creating the Declaration

The Declaration consists of a *preamble* (introduction that explains the document's purpose) and 30 articles that set forth the fundamental rights of all people. The Declaration proclaims two broad categories of human rights. The first category is civil and political rights, such as the right to life and liberty; the prohibition of slavery and torture; the right to a fair trial; and freedoms of speech, belief, and assembly. The second category encompasses economic, social, and cultural rights. These include the right to an education, to work, to an adequate standard of living, to security in the event of unemployment, and to participation in the cultural life of society. The inclusion of this second category was significant because the constitutions of many countries gave priority to civil and political rights. The Declaration presents all rights as indivisible and interdependent, meaning that one right cannot be completely fulfilled if another is denied. In addition to proclaiming the rights of individuals, the Declaration argues that each person "bears duties to the community in which alone the free and full development of his personality is possible."

While many officials participated in the UN Commission on Human Rights, a small number actually drafted the Declaration. These included Rene Cassin of France, John Humphrey of Canada, Eleanor Roosevelt, Hernan Santa Cruz of Chile, Charles Malik of Lebanon, P. C. Chang of China, and Fernand Dehousse of Belgium. Humphrey prepared the initial draft of the Declaration, drawing extensively from proposals submitted by Western organizations and individuals, and Cassin substantially revised it. His edited version was close to the one finally adopted by the UN.

The drafting of the Universal Declaration was not genuinely universal or inclusive of all major political, cultural, religious, and philosophical traditions of the world. The persons primarily responsible for drafting the document were either from Western Europe and the Americas or had a distinctly Western outlook. Chang and Malik, for instance, were both educated in the United States. The dominant influence of Western liberal thought and philosophies on the Declaration is unmistakable. For example, Article 17, which proclaims the right to own property and not to be deprived of it arbitrarily, reflects the predominance of free-market capitalism in Western democracies. No one familiar with Western traditions of liberal democracy would find the Declaration unusual. Much of the initial draft borrowed heavily from the U.S. Bill of Rights and the French Declaration of the Rights of Man and of the Citizen.

Most African and many Asian states were European colonies in the 1940's and did not participate in the drafting of the Declaration. These countries' traditions of balancing the interests and obligations of the individual with those of the community are missing from the document. Delegates from India hoped to include an article condemning discrimination against minorities and encouraging their cultural development, but the United States and Latin American countries rejected that proposal. The only departure from the Western orientation was the inclusion of economic, social, and cultural rights—revisions recommended by Latin American states, the Soviet Union, and the Eastern European socialist bloc.

The Declaration's impact

After various stages of revision, 48 member states of the UN General Assembly adopted the Declaration. Eight states—Saudi Arabia, South Africa, the Soviet Union, and its East European allies—*abstained* (chose not to vote). The document is not a treaty, which carries the force of law and is legally binding on every country that ratifies it. Instead, the Declaration, as stated in the preamble, is intended as a "common standard of achievement for all peoples and nations."

Nonetheless, during the 50 years of the Declaration's existence, certain rights outlined in its 30 articles acquired the status of customary international law. These include prohibitions against *genocide* (the extermination of a racial or ethnic group), slavery, torture, and racial discrimination. The Declaration superseded its original purpose and became an instrument that creates legal obligations for member states of the UN. It also changed the concept of the *sovereignty* (complete independence) in matters of international law. Claims of sovereignty could no longer shield a nation from external scrutiny of the way it treats its citizens. As the UN, governments, and the international community continued to rely on the Declaration as the authoritative

The author:
Makau Wa Mutua is Director of the Human Rights Center at the School of Law at the State University of New York at Buffalo.

right to education...

interpretation of human rights, it acquired a special moral and legal status that no other document of its kind possesses.

Since 1948, an impressive catalogue of human rights treaties and related documents have been adopted by the UN and ratified by governments of all political persuasions. In 1966, the UN adopted the two basic universal human rights treaties, the International Covenant on Civil and Political Rights and the International Covenant on Economic, Social and Cultural Rights. These documents clarified and expanded the rights specified in the Declaration, and they are legally binding on the UN member states that have ratified them. In 1976, both of the covenants went into force. By 1998, more than 135 states had ratified them. The covenants and the Declaration are known collectively as the International Bill of Rights. Many other legally binding agreements developed from the Declaration, addressing such issues as *apartheid* (an official policy of racial segregation and discrimination), the discrimination against women, and the rights of children.

The Universal Declaration and the agreements that followed sought to create in every nation a constitutional system of laws and a political structure that respects and guarantees individual rights. This principle requires various institutions and processes that make a government accountable to the citizen, such as free and open elections. Judicial systems must be sufficiently inde-

Eleanor Roosevelt, U.S. Ambassador to the United Nations, displays the original copy of the Universal Declaration of Human Rights for reporters in 1948. Roosevelt served as the first chairperson of the United Nations Commission on Human Rights and helped draft the Declaration.

equal in

The Declaration provides the inspiration and authority for people to challenge human rights abuses. Hong Kong citizens, *above,* hold a vigil on June 4, 1998, reminding the world of the 1989 massacre of prodemocracy protestors in Beijing, China. At South Africa's 1994 inaugural ceremony, Deputy President F. W. de Klerk, *right,* and President Nelson Mandela, *far right,* celebrate the end of official racial segregation, a change that was largely brought about by worldwide condemnation of South African policies.

pendent and strong enough to protect the rule of law and check the power of authorities. The Declaration left its imprint on almost all constitutions adopted in the last half century. These recently adopted constitutions include those of South Africa and of previously one-party Communist or military-ruled nations in Africa, Latin America, Asia, and Eastern Europe.

The Universal Declaration of Human Rights also acted as a charter for the human rights movement as a whole. Working with nongovernmental human rights organizations, governments, and regional intergovernmental organizations, the UN presided over the creation of processes and institutions that promote and protect human rights. Together these bodies established standards. They processed petitions, conducted investigations that cataloged human rights abuses, and pressured states to fulfill their human rights obligations.

Virtually every disempowered and disadvantaged group has used the principles of the Declaration as weapons against oppression. Groups involved in anticolonial struggles in Africa and Asia relied heavily on human rights language in their fight for self-determination. Civil rights movements throughout the world drew inspiration and resilience from claims made in the Declaration. The UN Fourth World Conference on Women, which was held in the People's Republic of China in 1995, was a testimony to the power of the human rights movement in the lives of women around the globe. Similarly, *indigenous* (native) peoples in the Americas, Australia, New Zealand, and elsewhere employed the language of human rights and its institutions to demand equitable treatment. Gay and lesbian groups around the world drew from the same principles to fight discrimination.

Making human rights a global concern

The Declaration laid an irreversible foundation on which the building blocks for preserving human dignity have been laid for the past 50 years. Human rights groups mushroomed everywhere. Inspired to some extent by Western organizations—such as Amnesty International in London, Human Rights Watch in New York, and the International Commission of Jurists in Geneva, Switzerland—domestic human rights organizations became an important part of civil society in many countries. Because of the work of such organizations, few nations or political groups care to be labeled as perpetrators of genocide, torture, or other human rights abuses.

In the 50 years since the UN adoption of the Declaration, an international consensus evolved that human rights abuses, wherever they occur, are the responsibility of the global community. The former apartheid government of South Africa defied worldwide standards of human rights and ultimately became the target of widespread criticism and severe economic sanctions. The genocide in Rwanda and the former republics of Yugoslavia— as well as the bloody struggles in Northern Ireland, Algeria, and the Middle East—commanded the attention of people untouched by the violence and drew condemnation from the world's community of nations.

Despite 50 years of remarkable progress, a wide gap remains between the goals of the human rights movement and the actual practices of many governments. The hundreds of thousands who have died of bullet wounds and starvation in Sudan continue to speak to the global collective conscience. The billions of people in the world who are denied the rights to health, self-determination, education, housing, water, and a sustainable environment provide a stark reminder that the standards of the Universal Declaration of Human Rights have yet to be achieved. As the UN World Conference on Human Rights affirmed in 1993 in Vienna, Austria, the empowerment of the least among us remains the challenge of the human rights movement for the next 50 years.

Hungary. The center-right Young Democrats-Civic Party won 148 of the 386 seats in Hungary's legislature in national elections held in May 1998. Their allies, the rightist Hungarian Democratic Forum, won 17 seats. The Socialist Party of Prime Minister Gyula Horn won 134 seats, and its partner in Horn's leftist coalition, the Alliance of Free Democrats, captured 24 seats. The agrarian-based Independent Smallholders' Party, which won 48 seats, was sought as a partner by both the left and right alliances. On June 24, the Smallholders formed a coalition with the Young Democrats and Democratic Forum. The government, led by Prime Minister Viktor Orban, pledged to cut taxes and stimulate the development of small and medium-sized businesses.

Economy. In January 1998, the World Bank, a United Nations agency that makes long-term loans for development to member countries, approved a $150-million loan to help reform Hungary's pension system. The World Bank also approved a $150-million loan in February to support educational reform. Economists expected Hungary's 1998 *gross domestic product* (the total value of goods and services produced by a country in a given year) to grow by 5 to 6 percent and inflation to hit 14 percent. In September, the nation's budget deficit reached $1.3 billion, and unemployment stood at 7.5 percent.

Foreign affairs. Membership talks with the European Union (EU), an organization of 15 Western European nations, began on March 30, 1998. Hungary's new leaders stressed their willingness to meet conditions for joining the EU and the North Atlantic Treaty Organization (NATO). Hungary and France signed a cooperation pact in February. In March, Hungary and Romania signed an agreement to form a joint peacekeeping unit. In April, Hungary signed a mutual peacekeeping agreement with Italy and Slovenia. Hungary joined Austria in May in opposition to the opening of the Mochovce nuclear plant in Slovakia, citing safety concerns.

Relations with Slovakia were further complicated in June by a new snag in the ongoing dispute over the Gabcikovo-Nagymaros hydroelectric project. Despite mediation efforts by the International Court of Justice in The Hague, Netherlands, Hungary's new leadership revoked a previous draft agreement with Slovakia. The agreement specified that Hungary would build half of a dam on the Danube River, which separates Hungary and Slovakia. Hungary also called on Slovakia to live up to its obligations under a Slovak-Hungarian treaty, signed in 1996, regarding ethnic Hungarians living in Slovakia. The government also expressed concern in June about the rights of ethnic Hungarians in Romania and expressed willingness to help fund a Hungarian language university in Romania. ☐ Sharon L. Wolchik

See also **Europe** (Facts in brief table); **Romania; Slovakia.**

Ice skating. Figure skating captivated the sporting world in 1998 whenever American skaters Tara Lipinski, 15, and Michelle Kwan, 17, competed against each other. The pair's ultimate showdown went to Lipinski, who scored the biggest victory of her career on Feb. 20, 1998, when she upset Kwan for the Olympic gold medal at Nagano, Japan. It was the first one-two American finish in women's figure skating since 1956. Lu Chen of China won the bronze.

Women. Kwan had reclaimed the U.S. title from Lipinski on Jan. 10, 1998, in Philadelphia, when she received a perfect 6.0 score from eight of the nine judges for her long program. But Lipinski's Olympic long-program performance hit a new high for athleticism, with seven triple jumps and a triple loop-triple loop combination. This compelled six judges to place Lipinski first, making her the youngest Olympic figure skating champion in history and the sixth American to win the gold.

On April 4, in Minneapolis, Kwan won the world championship, which Lipinski chose to pass up. On April 7, Lipinski announced that she was turning professional.

Other Olympic medalists. On February 14, Ilia Kulik gave Russia its second straight Olympic gold in men's figure skating, with a program that included a quadruple toe loop. Elvis Stojko of Canada placed second, and France's Philippe Candeloro took third. U.S. champion Todd Eldredge was fourth.

Amid considerable controversy over the consistency of the judging, Pasha Grishuk and Yevgeny Platov became the first couple to win two Olympic ice-dancing gold medals by capturing their 22nd straight competition since first winning Olympic gold in 1994. The pairs title went to Oksana Kazakova and Artur Dmitriev of Russia. Dmitriev thus became the first man to win at the Olympics with two different partners. Alexei Yagudin led a Russian men's sweep in the European championships and beat Eldredge for the world championship.

Speed skating. Thanks to a new speed-skate design called the "clap skate," new world or Olympic records were set in every long-track speedskating event at Nagano except the men's 500 meters. (Short-track speed-skaters do not use clap skates.) Led by Gianni Romme, who set world records in the 5,000 and 10,000 meters, the Netherlands won 9 of the 15 Olympic long-track speedskating medals for men. Germany's Gunda Niemann-Stirnemann took one gold and two silver medals at Nagano.   □ Ron Reid

Iceland. See Europe.
Idaho. See State government.
Illinois. See Chicago; State government.

Immigration. The U.S. Census Bureau reported in April 1998 that approximately 25.8 million U.S. residents—9.7 percent of the population—had been born in other countries. The percentage was the highest since 1930. The bureau reported that 27 percent of the foreign-born population were from Mexico, 4.4 percent were born in the Philippines, and 4.3 percent came from China and Hong Kong. The estimates were based on a March 1998 survey of legal and illegal immigrants and naturalized citizens.

Fee increases. The Immigration and Naturalization Service (INS) in January announced plans to increase 30 of the 40 fees charged for processing various citizenship applications. For example, the INS increased the fee to file an application for U.S. citizenship from $95 to $225, the fee to replace a residency permit from $75 to $110, and the fee for processing applications for legal permanent residence from $130 to $220. The INS claimed that the increases were needed to cover the cost of processing applications. Immigrant groups responded that the higher fees would penalize low-income immigrants trying to become American citizens.

Citizenship legislation defeated. The U.S. House of Representatives in February failed to pass a bill that would have created a program to check voters' citizenship by using records from the Social Security Administration and the INS.

The legislation was voted down on the same day that the House ended its investigation of the 1996 election victory of Representative Loretta Sanchez (D., California) over Robert K. Dornan, a nine-term Republican congressman. Dornan had charged that noncitizens had voted for Sanchez, allowing her to win. Sanchez had defeated Dornan by 984 votes.

A House task force on contested elections discovered that 748 votes had been cast by noncitizens in the Sanchez/Dornan election. The numbers, however, did not affect the outcome.

Benefits restored. On June 23, 1998, President Bill Clinton signed a bill that restored food stamp benefits to 250,000 of the 935,000 legal immigrants who had lost eligibility after the U.S. Congress overhauled the welfare program in 1996. The 1996 welfare bill had made all legal immigrants ineligible for food stamps.

Bilingual education defeated. California voters in June 1998 voted to end that state's bilingual educational system. Under that educational system, bilingual students learned their primary subjects in their native language while studying English. Under the new system, public schools in California must limit English-intensive classes to a single year, after which pupils must attend classes taught in English.
                    □ William J. Eaton

Figure skater Tara Lipinski of the United States performs her long program at the 1998 Winter Olympics in Nagano, Japan, in February. Lipinski upset her chief rival, Michelle Kwan, also of the United States, to win the gold medal.

India. The Bharatiya Janata Party (BJP), India's main Hindu nationalist party, took control of the government in March 1998, after assembling a coalition with smaller parties to secure the majority of seats in parliament. The new government, headed by Prime Minister Atal Bihari Vajpayee, stunned the world in May by conducting underground nuclear weapons tests.

Nationalists rise to power. The BJP had gained power only once before in India's 51-year history. In 1996, the BJP won the most seats of any party in the Lok Sabha, the lower house of parliament—a body responsible for choosing a government. Vajpayee, the BJP parliamentary leader, was named prime minister. He was forced to resign after only 13 days, however, because he was unsuccessful in gaining the support needed for a governing majority.

Many Indians were reluctant to support a BJP-led government because they regarded its nationalist philosophy as a threat to India's tradition of religious and cultural tolerance. The Hindu nationalist movement was dedicated to political supremacy for India's Hindus, a goal that alienated the country's 120 million Muslims as well as many lower-caste Hindus who were suspicious of the upper-caste Brahmins who dominated the nationalist movement.

In an effort to keep the BJP out of power, the Congress Party, which had long dominated Indian politics, supported a coalition government—the United Front—following the 1996 ouster of the nationalists. The United Front government collapsed in December 1997, leading to a tumultuous national election in March 1998.

Election strife. Campaigning was marred by violence and corruption. Politically motivated bombings killed more than 60 people during balloting in Coimbatore in southern India.

The election ended on March 7 with no clear victor and produced a parliament with 38 parties. The BJP received the highest share of the popular vote—26 percent of the 344 million voters backed the BJP, giving it 178 of the 543 seats in the Lok Sabha. The BJP abandoned much of its commitment to Hindu supremacy in an effort to win the support of other political parties. As a result, the BJP cobbled together a coalition of 18 smaller parties, gaining the majority of parliamentary seats needed to form a government. Vajpayee was named prime minister on March 19.

Vajpayee's government was weakened by the demands of its coalition partners, especially the All India Anna Dravida Munetra Kazhagam Party, which controlled 27 Lok Sabha votes. The party was headed by Jayalalitha Jayaram, a former movie actress.

Jayaram demanded that the BJP dismiss the government of Tamil Nadu, a southern state she

headed from 1991 to 1996 that was prosecuting her on charges of corruption. Vajpayee refused to dismiss the Tamil Nadu government, but in August 1998, he removed two finance ministry officials who were investigating charges against Jayaram and her associates.

The Congress Party won 140 seats in the election, maintaining its position as the second largest party in parliament. Campaign observers credited Sonia Gandhi, who became president of the Congress Party in April, with winning over many voters who had become disenchanted with the party that had led India to independence. Gandhi was the Italian-born widow of former prime minister Rajiv Gandhi.

Gandhi's election reaffirmed the family dynasty that had dominated the party since the days of Jawarharlal Nehru, India's first post-independence prime minister. Nehru was the father of Indira Gandhi and grandfather of Rajiv Gandhi, prime ministers in the 1960's, 1970's, and 1980's, who were both killed by assassins.

Sonia Gandhi was first offered the post of president of the Congress Party after her husband's death in 1991, but she refused it, saying she did not wish to expose her family to further risk. Several newspapers suggested that Gandhi became involved in politics in 1998 to head off investigations into a $1.3-billion armaments deal with a Swedish company that was approved in 1986 by Rajiv Gandhi. The deal generated millions of dollars in kickbacks to Gandhi family associates. Rajiv Gandhi had been posthumously indicted in the affair, but Sonia Gandhi denied that the family made any personal gains.

Nuclear testing. India conducted five underground nuclear tests in May 1998 at Pokhran in the Rajasthan desert of western India, where India's first nuclear test had been conducted in May 1974. India's detonation of nuclear devices in 1998 caught world security officials by surprise and brought immediate international condemnation and economic sanctions. The act also touched off a nuclear arms race with India's archrival, Pakistan, which responded by conducting its own series of nuclear tests.

India had refused in 1995 to sign the Comprehensive Test Ban Treaty, a United Nations plan that prohibited all nuclear tests. U.S. spy satellites photographed clear signs in 1995 that India was preparing for a nuclear test. The United States showed the photographs to top Indian officials and threatened to impose tough economic sanctions if India carried out its nuclear plans. India cancelled the tests, but continued to maintain mines that could be used for underground nuclear explosions.

The BJP made a campaign promise in 1998 to add nuclear weapons to India's arsenal. Defense

Atal Bihari Vajpayee enters parliament in March for the first time since being sworn in as India's prime minister. Vajpayee headed a Hindu nationalist coalition government, which took control following an election that produced no clear winners.

Minister George Fernandes hinted at India's growing interest in nuclear power in early May when he warned that China was India's "potential enemy No. 1." He accused China of stockpiling nuclear weapons in Tibet, on India's northern border.

On May 11, India conducted three underground nuclear tests and detonated two more devices on May 13. Indian officials announced that the country had between 25 and 75 nuclear warheads that could be fitted on missiles capable of reaching targets as close as Pakistan and as distant as China. The government pledged that it would not launch nuclear weapons first against another country and would halt further testing.

Economic sanctions. Several countries imposed economic sanctions on India. U.S. sanctions included a suspension of American economic aid, a ban on American bank loans to government institutions, and pressure for a cutoff of emergency loans from the International Monetary Fund, a United Nations affiliate that provides short-term credit to member nations. The United States blocked $865 million in loans from the World Bank (a United Nations agency that provides loans to countries for development) to improve India's electrical distribution system. In 1998, India's electrical system was in shambles and badly needed the loan money to offset the $2.3 billion

lost by state electricity boards in recent years. The World Bank also postponed a $130-million loan to build small hydroelectric generators throughout the country. Generators were most needed in remote villages that had no other source of power. The United States and other countries continued, however, to send food and medical aid.

Pakistan retaliates. Pakistan responded to India's nuclear tests on May 30 by conducting its own series of nuclear tests. Pakistan announced that it planned to fit nuclear warheads on a type of missile capable of striking targets across most of north and central India.

In September, Pakistan and India promised to reconsider signing the Comprehensive Test Ban Treaty. The United States agreed to lift sanctions if the countries signed the treaty.

Economic problems. The government approved large budget increases in June for India's armed forces, as well as for nuclear research and missile programs. The budget increase was among the largest ever made by India in peacetime and pushed total military outlays to more than $12 billion.

The budget reflected the BJP platform to give Indian businessmen preference over foreigners, which reversed years of effort to open the economy to international trade. As a result, the Indian currency, the rupee, plunged to a record low against the U.S. dollar, making it difficult for the country to cut interest rates to attract investors. Inflation soared and economic growth fell well short of original projections.

Conflict in Kashmir. The strained relations between India and Pakistan resulting from nuclear tests intensified tensions over Kashmir, a Himalayan region that had been at the center of a dispute between the countries since the two nations were created by partition in 1947. India and Pakistan have fought three wars, two of them over Kashmir. Each country claimed Kashmir as part of its territory.

In the 1990's, as many as 50,000 people had been killed in the Kashmir dispute, most of them victims of the struggle between Indian forces and Muslim rebels that Pakistan had armed and financed. India controlled the most populous part of Kashmir, the Srinagar Valley. Pakistan pressed for India to honor its pledge in the 1950's to allow Kashmir's people to choose between India and Pakistan.

Following the nuclear tests in 1998, artillery exchanges between Indian and Pakistani troops increased across the 550-mile (885-kilometer) "line of control" that separated the Indian and Pakistani armies. In August, Muslim rebels crossed from the Indian state of Jammu and Kashmir into the neighboring Indian state of Himachal Pradesh and opened fire on dozens of sleeping construction workers, killing 34 of the Hindu civilians.

Vajpayee met with Pakistani Prime Minister Nawaz Sharif in July to negotiate an end to both the Kashmir conflict and nuclear testing, but the effort collapsed in angry disagreement between the two leaders. In October, Indian and Pakistani diplomats agreed to restart talks about Kashmir and to negotiate ways to reduce the risk of nuclear conflict.

Disasters. A hurricane, known as a cyclone in India, hit the country's northwestern coast in early June, killing an estimated 1,200 people. Most of the people killed were salt workers living near the Arabian Sea port of Kandla.

A tornado driven by winds of up to 115 miles (185 kilometers) per hour ripped through several villages in eastern India in March, killing more than 100 people. Several children were killed when their school collapsed.

The worst heat wave in more than 50 years killed at least 2,500 people across northern India in May and June before monsoon rains fell. The rains caused flooding and landslides. Landslides in August buried villages in the northern Himalaya, killing more than 200 people.

☐ Henry S. Bradsher

See also **Asia** (Facts in brief table); **Pakistan; People in the news** (Vajpayee, Atal Bihari).

A Congress Party worker carries a cutout of Sonia Gandhi in February to campaign sites in the state of Maharashtra. Gandhi, a member of a family dynasty that had ruled India for most of its 51-year history, was named president of the party in April.

Indian, American. The Sand Creek Massacre National Historic Site Preservation Act of 1998 was signed into law by United States President Bill Clinton on October 6. The legislation, introduced by Senator Ben Nighthorse Campbell (R., Colorado), provided funds for the National Park Service to lead a project to identify, purchase, and preserve the location of a massacre of more than 200 Cheyenne and Arapaho in eastern Colorado.

A Colorado militia, led by Colonel John L. Chivington, attacked a Cheyenne-Arapaho village on Nov. 20, 1864, and mutilated the bodies of their victims, many of whom were women and children. The village leaders were in the process of negotiating a peace treaty with the U.S. government. Under the terms of the 1998 law, the former village would be designated a national historic site once researchers identified its exact location.

The U.S. Supreme Court ruled on February 25 that the Neetsaii' Gwich'in Indians, an Athabascan tribe in the remote Native Village of Venetie in Alaska, did not have the authority to levy taxes for the use of their land. In 1987, Venetie leaders imposed a 5-percent tax for the use of roads and water on a contractor whom the state had hired to build a school on Venetie land. The contractor forwarded the bill to the state, and the state refused to pay.

The Alaska Native Claims Settlement Act of 1971 was at the core of the dispute. The Supreme Court declared that while the 1971 law designated lands to Alaskan tribes, it did not give them sovereign authority over the land—an authority held by some Indian nations over reservation property in the lower 48 states. The Gwich'in tribe, therefore, had no authority to tax outside individuals or agencies. Many American Indians saw the ruling as a blow to the right of self-government for tribes throughout the United States.

Devils Tower. On April 2, 1998, District Court Judge William F. Downes in Casper, Wyoming, dismissed a suit filed by rock climbers claiming that the U.S. National Park Service's "voluntary ban" on climbing at Devils Tower National Monument was an unconstitutional endorsement of a religious practice. The ban, first issued in 1995, discouraged people from climbing Devils Tower in June out of respect for the religious beliefs of Indians.

Devils Tower, an 865-foot (264-meter) rock formation in Wyoming, has been a sacred site for more than 20 Northern Plains tribes for hundreds of years. Every June, Devils Tower is the site of religious and cultural ceremonies, including the Sun Dance, sweat lodge rites, and prayer offerings.

In 1996, the National Park Service issued a mandatory ban, but Judge Downes ruled it unconstitutional. The service then reinstated the voluntary ban and provided information about the religious significance of the site. In 1998, Downes ruled that the voluntary ban was not a government endorsement of a religion, noting that the government can and sometimes must accommodate religious practices without violating the Constitution's clause that separates church and state.

White House meeting. President Clinton met with tribal presidents at the Conference on Building Economic Self-Determination in Indian Communities in August in Washington, D.C. Clinton signed the Executive Order on American Indian and Alaska Native Education, which set goals for improving education programs and established an interagency task force to coordinate the efforts of federal, regional, and local programs. At the August conference, the president also announced several initiatives for improving health care and economic opportunities for American Indians.

Smoke Signals, the first film directed and coproduced by American Indians, opened in U.S. theaters in June. Director Chris Eyre, a Cheyenne-Arapaho, and screenwriter Sherman Alexie, a Colville, received critical acclaim for their film based on Alexie's collection of short stories, *The Lone Ranger and Tonto Fistfight in Heaven.* Many Native Americans praised the film, which tells the story of two young men on a journey of forgiveness, for capturing the modern American Indian experience.   □ Avis Little Eagle

Indiana. See **State government.**

Indonesia. Violent riots and a deepening economic crisis in 1998 led to the ouster of Suharto, who had served as president of Indonesia for 32 years. Suharto resigned on May 21, 1998. He was succeeded by Vice President Bacharuddin Jusuf Habibie.

Economic unrest. Indonesia's economy was devastated by the economic downturn touched off in 1997 by plunging stock and currency values in many Asian countries. By mid-1998, Indonesia had slid into its first recession in 30 years. The economy, which had grown by nearly 8 percent annually throughout the 1990's, contracted by more than 12 percent in 1998. Indonesia's currency, the rupiah, lost more than 80 percent of its value, and nearly one-fifth of Indonesia's workers were unemployed.

Suharto's fall. Indonesians blamed the financial crisis on a corrupt government led by Suharto, whose family and friends had become billionaires during his reign. In early 1998, protesters gathered in the capital, Jakarta, calling for Suharto's dismissal.

On March 10, the People's Consultative Assembly, a rubber-stamp group of Suharto's supporters, reelected Suharto as president until 2003. Suharto chose Habibie, a boyhood friend and the minister of research and technology, as vice president.

A Jakarta street vendor displays a May 21, 1998, newspaper with an account of the resignation of President Suharto, who had held power in Indonesia for 32 years, and his replacement by Bacharuddin Jusuf Habibie. Habibie was chosen by Suharto as his successor.

Deadly riots. On May 12, 1998, students at a private university in Jakarta staged a peaceful demonstration, which became violent when a member of the police or the military fired into the crowd, killing four people. Nearly 1,200 people died in the resulting riots, and thousands of buildings were looted, vandalized, and burned. The riots turned most of the people of Indonesia against Suharto and his government. Suharto resigned under pressure from his cabinet.

President Habibie, a 61-year-old German-trained aeronautical engineer, took office in May, saying that he hoped to satisfy "the demands for reform that have been led by students and the younger generation." He promised to rebuild the shattered economy, reduce the military's dominant role in politics, shape new electoral laws meant to lead to democracy, and investigate Suharto's wealth.

Habibie also pledged to push forward with stalled reforms demanded in 1997 by the International Monetary Fund (IMF), a United Nations affiliate that provides short-term credit to member nations. The IMF offered a $15-billion emergency aid package to Indonesia in 1997. The package included wide-ranging austerity measures, which Suharto had failed to implement.

East Timor accepted Habibie's offer in June 1998 of limited autonomy within Indonesia, but remained committed to independence. Indonesia withdrew thousands of soldiers from the territory. The military had been accused of widespread human rights abuses since it invaded East Timor, a former Portuguese colony, in 1975.

Military reform. In August 1998, Wiranto, commander of Indonesia's armed forces, discharged Prabowo Subianto, Suharto's son-in-law and a general in the Indonesian military, on charges of brutality. Prabowo had been chief of special forces, which stood accused of murder and kidnapping. Human rights groups gathered evidence that Prabowo instigated the May riots, organizing gangs to loot and destroy houses and businesses, and ordered soldiers to abduct and torture dissidents.

More riots. In November, a student protest exploded into renewed bouts of violence in the streets of Jakarta. Soldiers fired into a crowd of demonstrators, killing at least eight students and setting off a street battle between students, soldiers, and gangs. The protesters demanded aggressive reforms and called for Habibie's resignation. On November 13, the parliament adopted only modest reforms, including approval of an electoral assembly that would name a new president in August 1999.   □ Henry S. Bradsher

See also **Asia** (Facts in brief table); **Economics** Special Report: **Asian Economic Crisis; People in the news** (Habibie, Bacharuddin Jusuf).

International trade. Global trade went through severe upheavals in 1998, as the financial crisis that began in Southeast Asia in 1997 pushed many Asian nations into deep economic downturns in 1998. The crisis spread to Russia and Latin America and distorted normal trading patterns worldwide.

The United States maintained strong growth. This pulled unprecedented amounts of goods into the United States from other nations, which cost trade-sensitive U.S. jobs. The role of the United States as an engine for world growth was aided by European nations whose economies slowed, but generally remained on a growth track.

The economic shifts put a tremendous strain on exporters worldwide, in addition to U.S. and European businesses that competed in their domestic markets. By the end of 1998, a wave of trade-protection pressure was building in major consumer nations.

Shifting trade. Japan, the world's second-largest economy and an exporting powerhouse, was in the midst of a severe economic contraction in 1998, which complicated its trade situation. Japan's economic problems included declining consumer spending and a falling international value of the national currency, the yen. Economic output in Japan declined throughout the year. Efforts to stimulate the economy failed, and experts in late 1998 predicted that until Japan could stimulate its economy, most Asian nations would continue to slump and the rest of the world would continue to live under the threat of recession.

The impact of the changed economic situation was evident in the ranking of U.S. trade flows. Japan had long held the second spot in two-way trade with the United States, behind Canada. According to U.S. government trade reports released in September, however, Mexico had become the second-largest U.S. trading partner. In 1994, Canada, Mexico, and the United States created the North American Free Trade Agreement (NAFTA), which cut tariffs and other trade barriers to boost cross-border trade among the three nations.

China and Hong Kong. As trade distortions weakened many sectors within the big industrial democracies outside of Asia, many people looked to China as a source of hope. China, the world's largest Communist country and the most populous nation in the world, was a powerful exporter as well as a big consumer market for goods and services sold by major industrial nations. During 1998, China resisted pressures to devalue its own currency, the yuan. Devaluation would have made it easier to sell more Chinese goods abroad, but would most likely have also triggered the collapse of currencies in yet more countries.

The Chinese economy survived 1998 with a slowed growth pace and managed to provide an important degree of world stability. Ironically, Hong Kong, the thriving free-market trade center that China reclaimed in 1997 after 150 years of British rule, was among those economies that fell into recession by mid-1998.

Economic growth. Reacting to concern that their economies might slow too much in 1999, the United States and many European nations cut interest rates late in 1998 to spur greater growth. The U.S. Federal Reserve System (the Fed), the central bank of the United States, made the first of three, one-quarter of a percentage point cuts in its short-term interest rates in September. The initial rate cut was the first made by the Federal Reserve since 1996. Some trade barriers were lowered in Europe in 1998 in preparation of the 1999 launch of a single currency, the euro, by 11 countries of the European Union (EU)—an organization of 15 Western European nations that promotes cooperation among its members.

The United States continued to pressure Japan throughout 1998 to bail out its banking system, which was crippled by billions of dollars in bad loans. The pressure was also designed to stimulate the Japanese economy with big tax cuts and government-spending programs and to lower trade barriers to absorb more goods from the United States and goods from struggling Asian nations. By December 1998, however, Japan's economic outlook for 1999 remained unclear, as the country resisted opening its markets significantly to foreign goods.

Trade deficits. With about half the world in a recession in 1998, prices for a variety of basic commodities and finished goods fell. The deflation in raw material costs affected energy supplies, minerals, metals, forest products, and farm goods. It provided a boon to buyers but made it more difficult for sellers to make profits. It also held down prices for everything from toys to high-technology goods, like computers and cellular telephones, as deflation spread through much of the production chain. Nations whose economies suffered the most could sell their goods cheaply abroad. However, as they tried to export their way back to health, those countries increasingly took market share away from local producers in major industrial nations.

This was evident in a monthly increase in the U.S. trade deficit, which hit record levels as U.S. export markets decreased dramatically in many regions. A trade deficit is the shortfall between the value of a country's exports of goods and services and the value of its imports. The U.S. trade deficit reached $109.9 billion in the first eight months of 1998, an increase of $37.8 billion com-

pared to the same period in 1997. In August 1998, the deficit reached a record $15.9 billion, according to U.S. Department of Commerce figures. Statistics released in November revealed that the U.S. trade deficit had decreased to $14 billion in September.

Protecting domestic industries. Government agencies in major consumer nations increased efforts in late 1998 to protect domestic industries from countries that might break trade rules and sell their goods well below the cost of production. The United States threatened to impose duties, or taxes, on steel imports from Brazil, Japan, and Russia—countries that were in the midst of recessions in 1998. The nations limited shipments to prevent formal sanctions. Canada and the EU enacted similar measures against a wider range of countries over steel imports, as the EU became a net steel importer.

The United States and the EU also targeted such goods as clothing, food items, and machine tools. Such less-developed nations as those in Latin America, Africa, and Asia launched their own initiatives to prevent nations from selling items too cheaply, including U.S. goods.

☐ John D. Boyd

See also **Economics; Economics** Special Report: **Asian Economic Crisis—Global Contagion; Manufacturing.**

Internet. America Online, Inc. (AOL), of Dulles, Virginia, announced plans on Nov. 24, 1998, to purchase Internet software maker Netscape Communications Corp. of Mountain View, California, for approximately $4.2 billion in stock. The companies reported that the merger would allow them to offer improved Internet service and handle a greater share of electronic commerce, called e-commerce. In a related deal, AOL also announced a three-year agreement with Sun Microsystems Inc. of Palo Alto, California, to develop e-commerce technology.

Portals. Much of the buzz in the Internet business world in 1998 focused on the concept of "portals." Portals are Web sites that serve as easy-to-use entryways to the sometimes forbidding reaches of cyberspace by providing a sort of Internet package of search engines, E-mail, chatrooms, and other services.

The sites attracted revenue by selling advertising space, and consequently, more companies decided to get into the portal business. The success of portals appeared to be built on a less-than-solid foundation, however. According to the market research firm Forrester Research of Cambridge, Massachusetts, the top nine Internet portals—Alta Vista, America Online, Excite, Infoseek, Lycos, Microsoft, Netscape, Snap, and Yahoo!—drew almost 60 percent of all Internet advertising revenue, but these sites accounted for only about 15 percent of Internet traffic. Some analysts noted that such a discrepancy showed portals were more a fad than a sign of the Web's future.

E-commerce. The Internet continued to fulfill its promise as a new business medium as more companies set up shop online. Few businesses, however, made a profit in 1998. Nonetheless, the allure of a cybereconomy attracted an intense round of speculation from investors, and stock prices soared. Speculators eager to cash in on the Internet phenomenon pushed up the price of stocks of companies that had yet to turn a profit, such as bookseller Amazon.com and software retailer Egghead.com. When Broadcast.com, a company that offers live media and entertainment broadcasts on the Web, went public in July, the value of it shares more than tripled on opening day—the fastest such rise in the 1990's.

Clinton scandal. The Internet played a major role in the 1998 scandal regarding the relationship between President Bill Clinton and Monica Lewinsky, a former White House intern. The first report of the relationship appeared on January 17 in the Drudge Report, an independent Website. The allegations were picked up by the mainstream media.

In September, Independent Counsel Kenneth Starr delivered a report on his investigation of Clinton to the U.S. Congress. After brief debate, legislators voted to release the entire report to the public immediately via the Web.

Legislation. The U.S. Congress again tried in 1998 to pass a law that would limit certain kinds of content on the Internet. In 1996, Congress had passed the Communications Decency Act, which the Supreme Court struck down in 1997. The Child On-line Protection Act, passed on Oct. 21, 1998, was intended to protect minors from accessing Web sites with potentially offensive content by requiring Web sites offering such material to employ some form of access restriction. For example, a site could grant access only after receiving a credit card number. Civil liberties organizations filed suit against the law in November.

The surge in Internet commerce posed a threat to state and municipal governments that depend primarily on sales-tax revenue. Since the Internet is independent of geographic boundaries, online purchases usually cross state lines and are legally exempt from sales tax. In 1998, Congress passed the Internet Tax Freedom Act, which banned any new state or local taxes on Internet commerce for three years while a panel studied whether and how Internet commerce ought to be taxed.

Privacy. As greater numbers of people began using the Internet, concern over the issue of on-line privacy increased. The World Wide Web Consortium, a loose confederation of some 275 organizations that sets Web standards, formally pro-

posed a system that would screen out Web sites that did not adhere to specified privacy practices. Using the Platform for Privacy Preferences Project (P3P), users would customize their *Web browsers* (software for accessing the Web) to permit connection only to Web sites that, for example, promised not to reveal information to other parties about what a user purchased at the site or what information was requested.

Music. The Internet emerged in 1998 as a formidable medium for distributing music, a development that caused great anxiety in the music industry. Dozens of Web sites offered assortments of songs stored in a highly compressed format called MP3. Users downloaded near-perfect copies of songs as MP3 files free of charge. Much of this music was copied illegally, with no licensing or royalty fee paid to the publisher or artist.

Diamond Multimedia Systems of San Jose, California, announced in 1998 that it would sell a device called Rio, a digital personal stereo that stored up to one hour of MP3 music. The Recording Industry Association of America went to court in October 1998 to prevent Diamond from marketing the device. □ Herb Brody

See also **Computer; Newspaper** Special Report: **Tabloid Journalism—Yesterday and Today; People in the news** (Bezos, Jeff; Filo, David; Yang, Jerry).

Iowa. See State government.

Iran. Iran's conservative Islamic clerics moved against supporters of moderate President Mohammed Khatami in 1998. In June, the Iranian parliament, headed by Ali Akbar Nateq-Noori, the conservative candidate who lost the 1997 presidential election to Khatami, dismissed Interior Minister Abdullah Noori for allegedly being permissive in allowing peaceful public demonstrations. Khatami countered by reappointing Noori to his cabinet in a different position. In July, a conservative cleric convicted Gholamhossein Karabaschi, the moderate mayor of the capital, Teheran, of corruption and misuse of public money and sentenced him to five years in prison.

Many Iranians viewed the conservative moves as attacks against Khatami for his advocacy of greater political and social freedom. Some observers also speculated that conservatives may have been behind the murder of three *secular* (nonreligious) intellectuals and a dissident and his wife in November and December 1998.

U.S. relations. Khatami angered conservatives in January by inviting cultural exchanges between Iranians and Americans. U.S.-Iranian relations were frozen in 1979 after an Islamic revolution toppled Iran's monarch. In November 1998, a member of Khatami's cabinet condemned an attack by Islamic militants on a tourist bus carrying Americans in Teheran. The militants smashed

Members of the Iranian Revolutionary Guard salute Ayatollah Ali Khamenei in September 1998 as he orders Iran's armed forces to prepare for military action against the Taliban militia in Afghanistan. Taliban fighters in Afghanistan killed at least nine Iranian diplomats and one journalist in August.

the bus's windows after conservative Iranian newspapers claimed the Americans were spies.

In June, U.S. Secretary of State Madeleine Albright called on Iran to draw up a "road map" to normalize relations. She said that Iran's alleged links to terrorists, attempts to acquire weapons of mass destruction, and condemnation of Israel remained obstacles in improving relations. In September, Iranian Foreign Minister Kamal Kharrazi rejected Albright's proposal and accused the Clinton Administration of pursuing policies hostile toward Iran.

Reprieve for Rushdie. In September, Kharrazi distanced the Iranian government from the death edict that had been imposed on British author Salman Rushdie in 1989 by Ayatollah Ruhollah Khomeini. The late Iranian spiritual leader had accused Rushdie of blaspheming Islam. Great Britain restored full diplomatic relations with Iran following Kharrazi's announcement that the government would not seek Rushdie's death. More than half the members of Iran's parliament, however, signed a letter maintaining that the death sentence still stood. In addition, an Iranian religious foundation continued to offer a huge monetary reward for Rushdie's killing.

Clash with Afghanistan. Tens of thousands of Iranian troops began military exercises near the Afghanistan border in September 1998 after

approximately 50 Iranian citizens disappeared from the northern Afghanistan town of Mazar-i-Shariff. The Iranians vanished after Afghanistan's Taliban militia, which controls most of the country, captured the town from opposition forces. The Iranian government, dominated by Shiite Muslims, is opposed to the Taliban, which is composed of Sunni Muslims who believe in a very strict interpretation of Islam. Shiite and Sunni Muslims form the two major sects of Islam.

Tensions increased along the border after the Taliban admitted that "renegade units" of the militia had killed nine Iranian diplomats and one journalist. In October, Iranian reports stated that fighting along the border had resulted in heavy casualties to Taliban units. Following the October visit of a United Nations envoy to Afghanistan, the Taliban released all Iranian nationals held in the country. Despite this development, tensions between Iran and Afghanistan continued.

Economy. Khatami called for an overhaul of Iran's economy in March as declining world oil prices cast doubt that oil revenues for the Iranian new year, which began in March, would meet expectations. Khatami proposed that Iran increase nonoil exports, boost tax collection, and privatize state monopolies.   □ Christine Helms

See also **Afghanistan; Middle East** (Facts in brief table); **Saudi Arabia.**

Iraq. On December 16, 1998, United States and British forces launched four days of air and missile strikes against military and industrial sites in Iraq. United States President Bill Clinton claimed he ordered the strikes because Iraqi President Saddam Hussein had failed to cooperate with inspections of suspected weapons facilities by the United Nations (UN) Special Commission (Unscom). Unscom had attempted to account for and destroy any Iraqi chemical, biological, and nuclear capabilities, as well as Iraqi long-range missiles. The UN required an Unscom report proving that Iraq no longer possessed such capabilities before the UN would lift economic sanctions imposed on Iraq after Iraq's 1990 invasion of Kuwait. More than 60 Iraqi soldiers and 40 civilians were reportedly killed in the attack.

The crisis that led to the 1998 military action against Iraq built throughout the year. After Hussein blocked Unscom inspectors in January, UN Secretary General Kofi Annan averted threatened U.S. military action by brokering an agreement with Hussein to allow inspectors access to sites that were previously off limits. In August, Hussein again banned inspections of suspected weapons facilities, and in October, he halted all cooperation with Unscom. In the midst of a massive deployment of U.S. forces to the region in November, Hussein agreed to allow Unscom to resume its work. The December air and missile strikes were triggered by a report prepared by Unscom chairman Richard Butler, who accused Iraq of continuing to block inspectors' access to weapons sites and information.

Attack criticized. Many nations criticized the attack on Iraq because the United States acted without UN approval. France, Russia, and China were the most vocal critics among UN Security Council members. Most regional governments that were allied with the United States in its ouster of Iraqi troops from Kuwait in 1991 refused to support the U.S. action. Officials in many of these nations questioned the necessity of the bombings and said they feared that military action would inflict hardship on the Iraqi people. Some nations were also concerned about an anti-U.S. backlash.

Mistrust of Unscom and U.S. Iraqi officials expressed deep mistrust of Butler, who repeatedly accused Iraq of failing to cooperate with Unscom during 1998. They pointed to news reports that Butler received instructions from the U.S. government in preparing his report. They also noted that revelations earlier in 1998 indicated that Israel provided intelligence to Unscom.

Tariq Aziz, Iraq's deputy prime minister, announced on December 19 that Iraq would never allow Unscom to continue its work. Some UN members said they believed that Unscom's methods and role needed to be reevaluated.

Clashes over Iraq. In late December, U.S. warplanes and Iraqi air defense forces exchanged fire over regions in northern and southern Iraq patrolled by the U.S. and British military since the early 1990's. U.S. officials said a number of Iraqi missiles were destroyed. Iraqi Vice President Taha Yassin Ramadan had warned prior to the incidents that Iraq would fire at U.S. or British planes flying over Iraqi territory.

U.S. pushes opposition. In October 1998, President Clinton signed the Iraq Liberation Act, which authorized him to provide $97 million in funding for political support and weapons to opposition groups seeking to replace Hussein with democratic leadership. The act also provided funds for Radio Free Iraq, which was established in 1998. The station broadcast editorials calling for the indictment of Hussein as a war criminal.

Oil-for-food. The UN in 1998 raised the amount of oil Iraq could sell to purchase humanitarian supplies from $2 billion every six months to $5.2 billion for the six-month period beginning in June. However, Iraqi officials expected the nation to earn no more than $3 billion in oil revenues during the period because of deteriorated oil facilities and low oil prices. ☐ Christine Helms

See also **Armed Forces** Special Report: **Chemical and Biological Weapons; Middle East** (Facts in brief table); **United States, Government of the.**

Ireland. In a referendum on May 22, 1998, 94 percent of the people of Ireland who went to the polls voted to change the country's constitution to end the republic's claim to sovereignty over Northern Ireland. They voted to amend the constitution to stress that a united Ireland could only be brought about "with the consent of the majority of the people" in separate votes in Northern Ireland and the republic. The referendum was a key feature of the April 10 Belfast Agreement, which was designed to end three decades of conflict between the primarily Roman Catholic republic in the south and the British-ruled province with a Protestant majority in the north.

The Irish economy grew in 1998 at the rate of 7.5 percent, according to Department of Finance projections announced in July. In its annual review, the department predicted that 50,000 new jobs would be created, with unemployment falling to 9 percent. Inflation, however, rose to 2.7 percent in May, a three-year high. Some economists noted that labor shortages in skilled trades and a boom in housing prices were signs that suggested the economy was overheating.

Political corruption. Investigations continued in 1998 into allegations that former Taoiseach (prime minister) Charles Haughey had received Irish £1.3 million while in office between 1988 and 1992 from Ben Dunne, chairman of Ireland's largest supermarket chain. Haughey was accused of obstructing the McCracken tribunal, which in 1997 investigated payments to politicians. A second tribunal under Justice Michael Moriarty was established in December 1997 to enquire into Haughey's finances. Authorities noted that during Haughey's last term in office as prime minister, he acquired a house, an island, and a yacht.

Sports stars. Swimmer Michelle Smith de Bruin, Ireland's most successful sports star, was banned from competition for four years for tampering with a urine sample that was to be tested for drugs. On Aug. 6, 1998, the International Amateur Swimming Federation—the governing body of international swimming, known by its French acronym FINA—announced that alcohol had been found in the sample taken at de Bruin's residence in Kells, in southeastern Ireland. De Bruin, who won three gold medals and one bronze at the Atlanta Olympic Games in 1996, protested her innocence.

One of Ireland's leading Olympic equestrian figures, David Foster, was killed at age 43 when his horse fell on him while competing in trials near Dublin on April 13, 1998. □ Ian Mather

See also **Europe** (Facts in brief table); **Europe** Special Report: **European Union; Northern Ireland.**

Islam.

Islam. On Oct. 23, 1998, Sheikh Omar Abdel Rahman, the spiritual leader of the Islamic militant group al-Jamaa al-Islamiyya, called on his followers to give up the violent campaign begun in 1992 to establish Islamic rule in Egypt. Abdel Rahman issued his appeal from the United States, where he had been sentenced to life in prison in 1995 for terrorist activity. He asked his followers to seek peaceful means for advancing Islam. The announcement fell on the first anniversary, according to the Islamic calendar, of the 1997 massacre of tourists by Jamaa militants in Luxor, Egypt, which left 58 foreign tourists and 4 Egyptians dead.

In July 1998, senior Jamaa official Mohammed Mustafa al-Muqri' called for a ban on the murder of civilians and foreign tourists in the Middle East. He also denounced Islamic militants in Algeria, who had killed thousands of civilians since 1992. In a move that many political observers saw as a conciliatory gesture in response to such statements, the Egyptian government released some 4,000 Islamic militants from prison during 1998.

Pilgrimage crisis. The government of Saudi Arabia reported that 118 pilgrims were killed and more than 180 others were injured in a stampede on April 9 during the *hajj,* an annual pilgrimage to Mecca. The tragedy occurred during the "stoning of Satan," when pilgrims throw stones at pillars

that represent the temptations of Satan. At least 270 people had died in a similar stampede in 1994.

Following the 1998 incident, Saudi Arabia's Muslim clergy announced that they would consider issuing a *fatwa* (judicial opinion) to prevent similar accidents by permitting the ceremony to begin at dawn instead of midday as traditionally required. This change would allow people to avoid the afternoon heat or attend the event in smaller groups throughout the day. The Saudi clergy, who normally adhere to the strict Hanbali school of Islamic law, were willing to consider the more flexible Hanafi school of law, which is widely followed elsewhere in the Middle East and in southern Asia.

Muslims in the United States continued to export their version of Islam to the Middle East in 1998. Many Palestinian immigrants to the United States had returned to the Israeli-occupied regions of Gaza and the West Bank since the beginning of Israeli-Palestinian peace talks in 1993. In the West Bank city of Ram Allah alone, some 40,000 people, including former immigrants to the United States, had returned. Taking with them a more liberal American interpretation of Islam, many immigrants advocated a greater role for women in the religious community. The new ideas reportedly posed a significant challenge to the more conservative Palestinian clerics. □ Vincent J. Cornell

See also **Algeria; Saudi Arabia.**

Israel

Israel celebrated its 50th anniversary as a modern state in 1998. The nation, however, faced tension over Arab relations and internal dissent.

Arab-Israeli peace process. Israeli Prime Minister Benjamin Netanyahu agreed to move the Arab-Israeli peace process forward with Palestinian leader Yasir Arafat on Oct. 23, 1998, when they signed the Wye River Accord. The accord, brokered by United States President Bill Clinton, bound Israel to withdraw troops from 13 percent of the West Bank (Arab territory captured by Israel in the 1967 Six-Day War) and release hundreds of jailed Palestinians. In exchange, Arafat promised to crack down on Islamic terrorists and nullify provisions in the Palestinian charter that called for Israel's destruction. The agreement also provided for the opening of an international airport in the Gaza Strip, territory controlled by Palestinian authorities. The Arab-Israeli peace process had been stalled since early 1997, when Netanyahu, fearful of a break-up of his coalition government, refused to fulfill troop withdrawals agreed to by the previous Israeli government.

Implementation of the Wye River Accord proved to be difficult. Netanyahu's cabinet, dominated by conservatives opposed to transferring land to Palestinian control, delayed approving the accord for several days. The Knesset (Israeli parliament), however, overwhelmingly approved

U.S. President Bill Clinton (left) meets with Palestinian leader Yasir Arafat (center) and Israeli Prime Minister Benjamin Netanyahu (right) in October 1998 for discussions that led to the Wye River Accord, an agreement to move the Arab-Israeli peace process forward.

the accord in mid-November 1998. In late November, Arafat complained that most of the Palestinian prisoners released by Israel during the month were common criminals rather than the political prisoners agreed to in the Wye Accord. Nonetheless, during a December 14 visit to the Gaza Strip by President Clinton, the Palestinian National Council renounced its call for Israel's destruction.

On December 20, Netanyahu's Cabinet again suspended troop withdrawals from the West Bank. Netanyahu said Israel would not resume withdrawals until Arafat met a number of conditions, including increasing efforts to stop terrorist attacks and abandoning plans to declare an independent Palestinian state in 1999. On Dec. 21, 1998, Netanyahu, under fire from the left for suspending the peace process and from the right for signing the Wye Accord, agreed with the Knesset to hold new national elections in early 1999.

Israeli Arabs, citizens of Israel who make up 20 percent of the population, demonstrated growing dissatisfaction with the government by observing their first general strike on April 6, 1998. The strike came after clashes with police, who had razed Arab houses built without permits near a Jewish settlement in northern Israel. Israeli Arabs clashed again with police in northern Israel in September after the Israeli Army confiscated land farmed by Israeli Arabs.

Palestinian role at UN. In July, the United Nations (UN) General Assembly voted to upgrade the diplomatic status of the UN Palestinian delegation. The new status allowed Palestinians to take part in debates and cosponsor resolutions, but did not grant the delegation voting rights.

Lebanon. Netanyahu was under increasing pressure in 1998 to withdraw Israeli troops from a "security zone" in southern Lebanon used to deter attacks by militant Islamic guerrillas. Between January and December, more than 20 Israeli soldiers had been killed in the zone.

Spy. During the October peace talks that produced the Wye Accord, Netanyahu attempted to make the release of Jonathan Pollard, an American imprisoned in the United States for passing classified U.S. intelligence documents to Israel, a precondition to Israeli approval of the accord. President Clinton, however, promised only to review Pollard's case.

Mossad. The Israeli intelligence agency Mossad suffered many setbacks in 1998, including the capture of agents in Switzerland and Cyprus. In addition, Mossad's chief was forced to resign for his role in an unsuccessful assassination attempt against an Islamic leader in Jordan in 1997.
□ Christine Helms

See also **Israel** Special Report: **A Special Day in Israel; Lebanon; Middle East** (Facts in brief table).

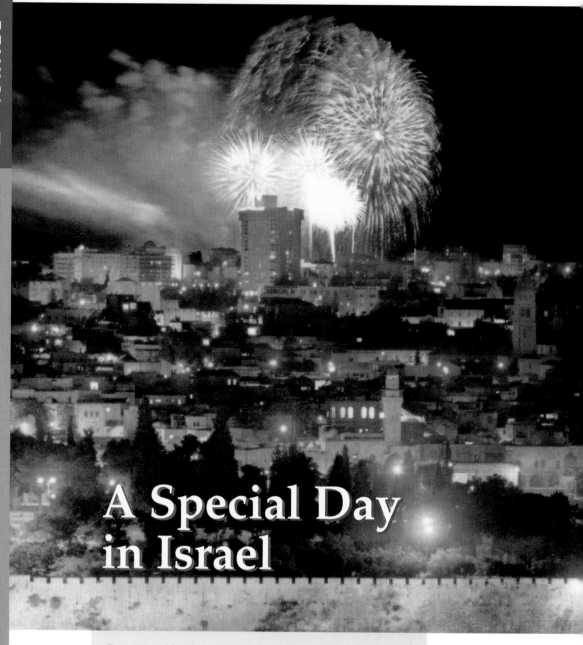

A Special Day in Israel

On April 30, 1998, Israel celebrated 50 years of existence, a half-century of both triumph and turmoil.

By Al Smuskiewicz

Israel's 50th anniversary celebration on April 30, 1998, culminates with a spectacular fireworks display over historic Jerusalem. The display highlights the walls of the ancient city and the Dome of the Rock, one of the most sacred sites of Islam.

Fireworks and air force flybys, barbecues and beach parties, somber prayer and national introspection all marked Israel's commemoration of *Yom Ha'atsma'ut* (Independence Day) on April 30, 1998. The day was the 50th anniversary (according to the Hebrew lunar calendar) of the creation of the state of Israel, as proclaimed by David Ben-Gurion on May 14, 1948.

The proclamation by Ben-Gurion, Israel's first prime minister, represented the rebirth of the ancient state from which Jews had been expelled by the Romans in A.D. 70. The modern state of Israel was born in a United Nations (UN) plan to carve up British-controlled Palestine into separate Jewish and Arab sectors. Jews embraced the plan, and millions came from around the world to settle in the tiny, Biblical land. The Arabs in Palestine rejected the plan, which led to a conflict that has continued for half a century. Despite the conflict, Israel's 50th anniversary party celebrated extraordinary accomplishments, including stunning economic and technological progress and the conversion of barren desert into rich farmland.

Three million Israelis gathered in parks, squares, forests, and beaches to mark the anniversary with picnics, reunions, and sporting events. The national celebration centered on the three-hour *Pa'amuney Hayuval* (Jubilee Bells) program, held at Jerusalem's Ramat Gan Stadium. The show featured actors, singers, musicians, and dancers commemorating Israeli history and culture. The guest of honor was United States Vice President Al Gore, representing the first nation of the world to recognize the state of Israel. The show concluded with fireworks that lit up the ancient city's many landmarks.

The people of Israel also marked their 50 years of nationhood with expressions of gratitude to their military forces, which had prevailed in five wars since 1948. Israelis visited sites of battles and memorials to fallen soldiers. The Israeli navy put on a display along the Tel Aviv beaches, and air force jets flew over the country in the pattern of a giant number 50.

Religious Jewish communities in Israel commemorated the special day with private and public prayer services that expressed their gratitude for the existence of a nation that they believe God promised them 4,000 years ago. Independence Day 1998 was the 50th anniversary of their realization of that promise.

ISRAEL

SPECIAL REPORT

1947

The United Nations (UN) recommends the partition of Palestine into a Jewish and Palestinian state, a plan that Jews accept and Arabs reject.

1948

David Ben-Gurion, *right,* proclaims the establishment of the state of Israel. Five Arab nations attack. President Harry Truman of the United States grants Israel diplomatic recognition.

1949

An armistice ends the first Arab-Israeli war. The UN admits Israel as a member.

1950

The Knesset (Israeli parliament) passes the "Law of Return," which grants all of the world's Jews the right to settle in Israel.

1956

Israel joins Great Britain and France in an invasion of Egypt after Egyptian President Gamal Abdel Nasser nationalizes the Suez Canal. The UN ends the fighting.

The Palestinians

For many Arabs living in Israel, the nation's 50th anniversary was no cause for celebration. They viewed the creation of Israel as *al nakba* (the catastrophe). In 1948, Palestine—homeland of the Palestinian Arabs—disappeared from the map of the world. On the same day that Israel proclaimed its independence, five Arab nations—Egypt, Syria, Lebanon, Iraq, and Transjordan—attacked. By the time the war ended in 1949, 700,000 Palestinians—approximately half the total Palestinian population—had emigrated or been expelled from Israel.

These *emigrants* (people who leave their own countries to settle in others) became refugees in various Middle Eastern nations or in those parts of the former Palestine that were not under Israeli control. The largest Palestinian refugee camps were on the West Bank of the Jordan River, which was held by Transjordan (now Jordan) after the war, and the Gaza Strip, which was occupied by Egypt.

The author:
Al Smuskiewicz is a staff editor with *World Book Year Book.*

In 1948, 1.4 million Arabs and 600,000 Jews lived in Palestine. In 1998, 1 million Arabs and 5 million Jews were citizens of Israel. As Arab numbers dwindled relative to Jewish numbers, many Arabs in Israel came to feel that they were treated as second-class citizens.

In 1998, almost 3 million Palestinians lived in the West Bank and Gaza Strip, which were conquered by Israeli troops in 1967 in the Six-Day War—a war prompted by Israeli fears that Arab troops were preparing to attack. Since the 1993 Oslo Accords, Israeli troops have withdrawn from most of Gaza and some West Bank towns, resulting in combined Israeli and Palestinian rule in these areas. In 1997, negotiations over additional withdrawals and the final status of the lands stalled. However, by late 1998, Israeli and Palestinian authorities had resumed negotiations, which Palestinians hoped would lead to an independent homeland in the West Bank and Gaza Strip in 1999.

An Israeli family enjoys Independence Day around a mangal, or barbecue grill, *left,* which many Israelis consider an essential part of any national holiday. A father boosts his young daughter on his shoulders, *bottom,* to give her a better view of Independence Day festivities.

1964

The Palestine Liberation Organization (PLO) is founded to establish an Arab state in Palestine.

1967

Israeli forces led by Moshe Dayan, *right,* capture the Sinai Peninsula, Gaza Strip, West Bank, East Jerusalem, and Golan Heights, before defeating Egypt, Jordan, and Syria in the Six-Day War.

1973

Israel repels an Egyptian and Syrian invasion in the Yom Kippur War.

1974

The UN recognizes the right of Palestinians to an independent homeland.

1978

Israeli Prime Minister Menachem Begin, *right,* and Egyptian President Anwar Sadat sign the Camp David Accords to end the conflict between the two countries.

1982

Israel returns the Sinai Peninsula to Egypt. Israel invades Lebanon to rout Palestinian guerrillas.

1985

Israel withdraws from most of Lebanon.

Cultural conflict

Jubilee Bells, the showpiece of Israel's 50th anniversary celebration, was marred when the world-renowned Batsheva Dance Company withdrew from the program minutes before its scheduled performance. The withdrawal was prompted by ultra-Orthodox Jewish leaders who strongly objected to a number in which performers in abbreviated costumes planned to dance to the rhythms of a Hebrew prayer. Coming as it did on Independence Day 1998, the incident drew international attention to what many Israelis have labeled the *Kulturkampf* (Yiddish for culture war), which describes the philosophical conflict that divides Jews with strict religious beliefs from those who hold more moderate views on religion or who consider themselves *secular* (nonreligious).

Of the 5 million Jews in Israel in 1998, the ultra-Orthodox numbered 480,000. The group is known for its strict adherence to the commandments in the *Torah* (the first five books of the Bible) and belief that the state should serve religious purposes. Israel was also home to 970,000 Modern Orthodox Jews. While Modern Orthodox Jews were more integrated into mainstream society than the ultra-Orthodox, they were often allied with the ultra-Orthodox. The rest of Israel's Jews considered themselves either moderately religious or secular.

Although Orthodox Jews constituted a small minority in Israel in 1998, their fellow citizens believed the Orthodox exercised political influence far beyond their numbers.

Observers saw the partnership between the Orthodox and the government of Prime Minister Benjamin Netanyahu as the key to the group's power. Orthodox political influence led the government to ban women from praying with men at the Western Wall (a remnant of Herod's Temple Mount, the ancient holy place destroyed by the Romans in A.D. 70) and to close certain market areas on the Sabbath. In addition, Orthodox rabbis continued to exercise a monopoly over certain government-related matters, including absolute authority over marriages, divorces, and religious conversions. (The lack of official recognition of conversions performed by non-Orthodox rabbis affected immigration policies guaranteeing Israeli citizenship to any person who is a Jew.)

Besides these political disputes, several acts of violence in 1997 and 1998 served to ratchet up the tension between religious and secular Jews. Ultra-Orthodox Israelis were accused of firebombing a butcher shop selling nonkosher meat and an antiquities office responsible for archaeological digs. The Orthodox claimed the digs disturbed tombs and burial sites of ancient Israelis. In turn, the Orthodox in 1998 accused secular Jews of firebombing a religious school in a predominantly secular neighborhood. Faced with increasing tension and violence, some Israelis expressed fears in 1998 that the culture war spreading throughout Israel could some day escalate into civil war.

1987

Intifada (an uprising) breaks out among Palestinians living on the Gaza Strip and West Bank.

1990

The second great wave of migration to Israel begins with the arrival of the first of more than 800,000 Russian Jews fleeing the collapsing Soviet Union.

1993

Israeli Prime Minister Yitzhak Rabin, *right,* and PLO leader Yasser Arafat sign the Oslo Accords, setting the framework for Palestinian autonomy in the West Bank and Gaza Strip.

1994

Palestinians begin self-rule in Gaza and the West Bank town of Jericho. Israel and Jordan sign a nonaggression pact.

1995

Yitzhak Rabin is assassinated by a Jewish militant.

1997

The Arab-Israeli peace process stalls following construction of Jewish settlements in Arab territory and suicide bombings by Arab militants.

1998

The peace process is revived in October with an agreement signed by Israeli and Palestinian authorities.

U.S. Vice President Al Gore joins Israeli Prime Minister Benjamin Netanyahu, *above,* on Independence Day to pay honor to the long-lasting, close ties between the two countries. Dancers surround the dove of peace, *right,* at the centerpiece of the anniversary commemoration—the Jubilee Bells program in Jerusalem.

Italy reaped the rewards of several years of budget austerity in 1998 by winning approval to participate in the launch of a single European currency, the government's paramount objective. No sooner had Italy achieved its economic goals when the government of Prime Minister Romano Prodi began to collapse.

Most economists and politicians had doubted Prodi's chances of success when he came to power in 1996 by promising to end Italy's history of profligate government spending and high inflation. But Prodi's policies paid off. The government announced in early 1998 that the deficit for 1997 had been 2.7 percent of *gross domestic product* (GDP—the value of all goods and services produced in a country in a given year) while inflation had fallen to 2.5 percent. Both figures were low enough for Italy to qualify for the single currency. Leaders of the European Union (EU—an organization of 15 Western European nations) approved Italy's participation at a May 2, 1998, meeting, when they selected 11 nations to launch the euro.

Government collapse. Shortly after the euro success, Prodi ran into difficulty with the Refounded Communists, a left-wing party that supported his coalition government. In June, the party refused to support the ratification of a treaty involving the expansion of the North Atlantic Treaty Organization into Eastern Europe. In September, the government proposed a 1999 budget that combined $7.9 billion in tax increases with substantial spending cuts. Prodi claimed the measures were needed to keep the deficit down and reduce a national debt of nearly 120 percent of GDP, almost twice as high as the debts of other countries joining the euro. The Refounded Communists refused to support the budget and demanded more public spending on employment and quicker action to introduce a 35-hour work week. The party's move coincided with increased public discontent over the impact of the government's budget policies, which slowed economic growth to only 1.7 percent in 1998 compared with an EU average of 2.9 percent. Prodi lost a vote of confidence in parliament over the budget by one vote on October 9 and then resigned. His two-and-a half-year tenure as prime minister was Italy's second longest since the end of World War II (1939–1945).

D'Alema forms government. A modified center-left coalition government was quickly rebuilt by Massimo D'Alema, leader of the Democratic Party of the Left, Italy's former Communist Party. D'Alema was sworn in as prime minister on October 21 and promised to push Prodi's budget through parliament unchanged. D'Alema also kept many key ministers from the Prodi government, including Lamberto Dini as foreign minister and Carlo Ciampi as treasury minister. However, there were doubts about the coalition's strength because the new government contained a number of old rivals, including members of the left-wing Refounded Communists and a center-right group of former Christian Democrats.

Berlusconi trials. Silvio Berlusconi, the opposition leader and former prime minister, was convicted in two trials in July of bribing tax inspectors and paying $12 million in bribes to former Prime Minister Bettino Craxi and his Socialist Party. In December 1997, Berlusconi had been convicted of fraud in a film company deal. He appealed both verdicts and was unlikely to go to prison because he was sentenced to less than three years, a term that is usually suspended under Italian law. Berlusconi was also fined $5.6 million for the Craxi bribe. Craxi, who continued to live in exile in Tunisia, was convicted in absentia, sentenced to four years in prison, and fined $11.2 million.

Cable-car disaster. Twenty people were killed at the Cavalese ski resort in northern Italy on February 3 when a U.S. Marine Corps jet flying on a training mission severed the wires of a cable car, causing it to plunge 370 feet (111 meters) to the ground. The accident sparked outrage in Italy about the use of the area for low-level military training flights. The pilot and navigator of the EA-6B Prowler surveillance jet were ordered to face a court martial in the United States on charges of involuntary manslaughter and negligent homicide, and the commander of the air squadron involved was relieved of his post.

War crimes tribunal. A group of 120 nations meeting at a United Nations conference in Rome agreed in July to establish an international court to prosecute cases of genocide, crimes against humanity, and war crimes. Supporters hoped that the court would combat the kinds of mass murder and human-rights abuses that took place in Bosnia and Rwanda in the 1990's. The court's prospects were cast in doubt when the United States refused to back the agreement out of fear that the court could bring politically motivated charges against U.S. soldiers or politicians.

Mafia. The government pulled Italian soldiers out of Sicily in June 1998, claiming that a series of arrests in recent years had damaged the power of the Mafia and restored law and order on the island. The troops had been sent to Sicily in 1992 to protect key government buildings and officials after the murder of anti-Mafia prosecutors.

Floods. More than 150 people were believed killed after torrential rains triggered landslides in the Campania region east of Naples in early May 1998.   □ Tom Buerkle

See also **Armed forces; Europe** (Facts in brief table); **Europe** Special Report: **European Union.**

Bulldozers attempt to clear the streets of Sarno, Italy, a village east of Naples, in May 1998. Mudslides unleashed by torrential rains buried a number of villages in the Campania area and resulted in the deaths of more than 150 people.

Japan. Ryutaro Hashimoto resigned as prime minister of Japan on July 13, 1998, the day after his ruling conservative Liberal Democratic Party (LDP) lost seats in elections for the upper house of parliament. Keizo Obuchi, who had been foreign minister, succeeded Hashimoto on July 30 as head of the LDP government. Obuchi was Japan's sixth prime minister in six years.

The LDP had been slow to address financial problems in Japan and unsuccessful in pulling the nation out of an economic slump that had begun in 1991. Eventually, the slump evolved into Japan's worst economic crisis in 50 years. Political analysts said that voters in the July 1998 elections sent a message to parliament that they wanted strong leadership and economic change.

A blow to the ruling party. For six consecutive years, the LDP had acquired a majority of seats in the lower house, which dominates the Diet, the Japanese parliament. In 1998, LDP leaders were optimistic that they also would win a decisive majority of upper house seats in the July elections.

The LDP, however, won only 44 out of the 126 contested seats. This was still far more seats than the 27 won by LDP's closest challenger, the Democratic Party of Japan (DPJ), but far fewer than the 61 seats the LDP held going into the election. Despite the loss of seats, the LDP maintained a majority in the Diet, which selects a government and chooses a prime minister.

Some observers attributed the LDP's loss to an unusually large turnout of Japanese voters, many of whom were dissatisfied with the government's attempts to remedy the economy. Voter turnout surged from 44 percent in the 1995 election for the upper house to 59 percent in 1998.

The weakening of the LDP power base came at a time when Japan was neither the one-party nation it used to be nor a Western-style system in which two political parties alternately hold power. The LDP had run the country for years with only token opposition. They were evicted from power in 1993, when seven smaller parties created a coalition government. The LDP returned to power in 1995, though with only a fraction of the seats it had once controlled in the Diet.

Opposition movement. The election consolidated the DPJ's role as the leading opposition party in Japan. The DPJ had been created in late 1996 as part of a realignment of Japanese politics that began in 1992, when some members of parliament defected from the LDP. The Communist Party did exceptionally well in the election as the winner of protest votes. Voters also elected independents and candidates from other parties in Japan's deeply fragmented opposition.

Hashimoto said his inability to revive the economy was responsible for the LDP's disastrous finish in the parliamentary elections. "The results are attributable to my lack of ability," he said in his resignation speech. "We could not live up to the people's expectations, and it is all my fault."

When Hashimoto became prime minister in 1996, political observers hailed him as a dynamic leader who was an expert on policy issues. Public opinion turned against him, however, after he pushed through an increase in the national sales tax from 3 percent to 5 percent—an act that tipped Japan into recession.

New prime minister. The selection of a new prime minister in Japan traditionally was handled secretly among leaders of the Diet. In 1998, however, politicians openly jockeyed to succeed Hashimoto. The upper house of parliament chose DPJ leader Naoto Kan as prime minister, but the more powerful lower house rejected Kan and selected Obuchi, who was named president of the LDP on July 25 and elected prime minister on July 30. Obuchi promised to enact swift reforms for Japan's ailing economy.

Obuchi, who had limited economic expertise, chose Kiichi Miyazawa as finance minister. Miyazawa had been finance minister from 1986 to 1988 and prime minister from 1991 to 1993 and was considered an expert in international economic negotiations. Obuchi also named Toyoo Gyohten, a famed financier noted for a tough negotiating style, as a special cabinet adviser.

LDP revival. Obuchi engineered a comeback for the LDP. In December 1998, the LDP entered a coalition with the Liberal Party. The coalition held 117 out of 252 seats in the upper house, enough to pass legislation with the help of independents.

Economy. Obuchi's government was faced with massive economic problems, including a banking system with billions of dollars in bad loans, rising unemployment, soaring bankruptcies, tumbling stock prices, and a falling international value of the national currency, the yen. Japan remained one of the world's richest countries—its economy was second only to that of the United States in size—but economists considered its deteriorating economy a threat to the health of financial markets across the world.

Japan's Economic Planning Agency reported on Aug. 11, 1998, that Japan was in a "prolonged slump." Economic output declined more than 2 percent in 1998. Unemployment reached 4.1 percent, the highest level since 1953.

Japan's economy was damaged in the late 1980's by a speculative boom that inflated property prices to nearly 20 times what they had been in 1970. By the mid-1990's, the stock market had dropped 60 percent and land prices plummeted 80 percent. Several banks still held loans in the late 1990's from people who bought property at inflated prices and could not repay the notes. Throughout the 1990's, the government attempted to bail out banks, but each plan failed to revive the economy.

Obuchi, in an address to the United Nations in September 1998, blamed previous LDP governments and the heads of Japan's financial institutions for wasting years before facing up to the crippling banking crisis and the deep recession. Obuchi's government set aside $214 billion for relief of over-extended banks. However, some economists estimated that Japanese banks held as much as $1 trillion in bad debts. In November, Obuchi outlined plans for Japan's biggest stimulus package ever, including $115 billion in public spending and income tax cuts.

Corruption. The finance minister of Japan, Hiroshi Mitsuzuka, resigned in January after taking full responsibility for a bribery scandal. The resignation came one day after officials of the ministry, the most powerful arm of the Japanese government, were arrested for accepting bribes.

In March, the head of the Bank of Japan resigned after police raided the central bank and arrested the head of the capital markets division, who was charged with leaking confidential information to commercial banks.

Military ties. The Japanese government agreed to broaden military ties with the United States in April 1998 and to offer logistical support to American troops in the event of a crisis. The agreement brought Japan a step closer to playing a larger security role beyond its immediate territory. Some Asian countries, still traumatized by Japan's invasions of its neighbors in the early 1900's, were suspicious of the measure.

Under the former Japanese-U.S. military accord set in 1978, Japan could only provide U.S. forces with nonmilitary supplies in the event of a war in the region. The 1998 plan paved the way for Japan to provide certain military supports, such as enforcing naval blockades. Japan also agreed to allow access to its airports and harbors.

Poisonings. Police arrested a middle-aged couple in October on charges that they had poisoned people at a July festival in Tokyo, where four people died and 63 were injured after eating arsenic-laced curry. The incident resulted in more than 20 copycat poisoning cases in Japan.

Ten people in northern Japan were hospitalized in August after drinking coffee and tea spiked with a toxic chemical used to inflate auto airbags. The same chemical was used in a similar incident in October, when six people in central Japan fell ill after consuming poisoned drinks.

☐ Henry S. Bradsher

See also **Asia** (Facts in brief table); **Economics** Special Report: **Asian Economic Crisis; Korea, North; People in the news** (Obuchi, Keizo).

Jordan. The Jordanian press reported in July 1998 that King Hussein, the ruler of Jordan since 1952, had lymphatic cancer. In August 1998, the king, who was undergoing chemotherapy in the United States, granted his brother and heir, Crown Prince Hassan, authority to reorganize the cabinet. The move followed public criticism of the government for announcing overly optimistic economic figures for 1998. Hassan quickly appointed Fayez al-Tarawnah, an economist and former ambassador to the United States, the new prime minister.

Relations with Israel. In October, King Hussein played a key role in Israeli-Palestinian talks held outside Washington, D.C. The talks revived the Arab-Israeli peace process, which had been stalled since early 1997. Hussein and many other Arab leaders had been frustrated with what they saw as Israel's refusal to adhere to a previously established timetable by which to move the peace process forward.

In February 1998, Hussein condemned the report of an Israeli commission that cleared the Israeli government of wrongdoing in an attempted assassination in Amman, the Jordanian capital. In September 1997, Israeli intelligence agents had tried to kill a political leader of the extremist Islamic group Hamas by poisoning him.

Many Jordanians complained in 1998 that the 1994 peace accord between Jordan and Israel had not produced the economic prosperity that the king had promised them. Unemployment in Jordan in 1998 was unofficially estimated at nearly 30 percent, and the government itself employed some 50 percent of all Jordanians. Jordanian officials believed that trade with Israel was hampered by Israeli delays and strict security checks.

Internal unrest. In February, King Hussein stunned Jordanians by ordering a weeklong military curfew on the southern city of Maan after two days of violent pro-Iraqi demonstrations. During the curfew, the army arrested more than 250 people, confiscated weapons, cut telephone lines, and disrupted electricity supplies. In May, Leith Shubeilat, an Islamic leader and prominent critic of the government, was sentenced to nine months in prison for inciting the riots. In October, however, Shubeilat was released after serving only seven months of his sentence.

The riots broke out after the United States threatened a military strike against Iraq for failing to cooperate with United Nations inspections of Iraqi weapons facilities. In mid-December, after U.S. forces launched an attack on Iraq, hundreds of pro-Iraqi demonstrators, constrained by a massive police presence, rallied in Amman.

☐ Christine Helms

See also **Iraq; Israel; Middle East** (Facts in brief table).

Judaism. Israel observed its 50th anniversary as a nation in 1998, and Jewish communities around the world held celebrations, featuring Israel's most prominent performers and dignitaries. For many Jews, the anniversary celebrations were a testament to the importance of Israel in Jewish life. Demographic projections alone reflected that importance, indicating that the Jewish population of Israel would surpass the Jewish population of the United States within 10 years, making Israel the world's largest home to Jews. In July, Israeli Prime Minister Benjamin Netanyahu pledged aid to Jewish communities around the world to support Jewish education and bolster Israel as Judaism's cultural and religious center.

Jewish leaders in the United States noted, however, that the U.S. Jewish community continued to turn inward. While a majority of the community's philanthropy once went to Israel, the major portion of its funds in 1998 was distributed in the United States. Donations helped strengthen U.S. schools, synagogues, cultural institutions, and programs aimed at Jews who were not strongly affiliated with the religious community. The growth of denominational and community-based private Jewish schools across the United States was a by-product of this change.

Several studies published in 1998 also suggested that Jewish religious identity in the United States was stronger than it had been in recent years and that synagogue attendance was rising even though the rate of intermarriage between Jews and non-Jews remained high. At the same time, studies indicated that the ethnic identity of American Jews—their sense of a shared identity within the United States and their ties to Israel and world Jewry—declined.

Ongoing tensions between Orthodox and non-Orthodox Jews partly explained the trends among U.S. Jews. The problem was well-illustrated in 1998 by the last-minute cancellation of the Batsheva Dance Company's Independence Day performance in Israel after religious Jews labeled it offensive and immodest. A number of other issues—such as conversion to Judaism, the role of women in Jewish life, the ordination of gays and lesbians, and the recognition of non-Orthodox Jewish religious movements in Israel—heightened intrareligious tensions. On the Jewish holiday of Shavuot, Reform and Conservative Jews conducted services at which men and women prayed together at Jerusalem's Western Wall in defiance of the opposition of Orthodox Jews, who separate men and women during such services.

Holocaust claims. In 1998, governments and organizations offered to settle claims for their roles in the Holocaust, Nazi Germany's persecution of Jews during World War II (1939–1945)

Workers remove debris from a *mikvah* (ritual bath) at the ruins of an ancient Jewish synagogue that was discovered near Jericho in the West Bank. Hebrew University archaeologists announced in March 1998 that the 2,000-year-old synagogue was the earliest ever found.

that resulted in the deaths of more than 6 million people. In January 1998, Germany agreed for the first time to compensate Jewish Holocaust survivors living in Eastern Europe. In September, German carmaker Volkswagen established a fund for people who had worked for the company as slave laborers during the war.

In August, two Swiss banks agreed to a $1.25-billion settlement that would compensate survivors or their relatives who had tried to retrieve money from accounts opened before or during the Holocaust. The banks had also received gold that the Nazis had looted from victims.

In March, the Roman Catholic Church released a report that repented for the failure of individual Catholics to protect Jews during the Holocaust, but the document did not assign blame to the church itself or to Pope Pius XII, the Roman Catholic leader during the war. At the end of 1998, efforts continued to resolve a dispute between Roman Catholics in Poland and Jews over the placement of crosses at Auschwitz, the most infamous of the Nazi death camps.

☐ Jonathan D. Sarna and Jonathan J. Golden
See also **Germany; Israel** Special Report: **A Special Day in Israel; Roman Catholic Church; Switzerland.**

Kampuchea. See **Cambodia.**
Kansas. See **State government.**

Kazakhstan. President Nursultan Nazarbayev proposed a series of constitutional amendments aimed at liberalizing Kazakhstan's political system in his address to parliament on Sept. 30, 1998. The proposals included privatizing some state-owned holdings, strengthening parliamentary power, and making the judicial branch more independent. Political analysts saw the measures as a bid to weaken the position of opposition candidates in parliamentary elections set for 1999.

On Oct. 8, 1998, the parliament approved constitutional changes that eliminated age and term limits on the presidency and extended the length of a term from five to seven years. The measure also moved up the presidential elections scheduled for December 2000 to January 1999. The earlier balloting date reduced the opposition's time to organize an effective campaign. Opposition legislators also claimed that the reforms would permit Nazarbayev to serve as president for the rest of his life.

In May 1998, five months after Kazakhstan relocated its capital to the remote city of Akmola, President Nazarbayev formally changed the city's name from Akmola to Astana. Akmola in the Kazak language means "white grave." Astana means "capital." ☐ Steven L. Solnick
See also **Europe** (Facts in brief table).
Kentucky. See **State government.**

Kenya. Daniel arap Moi was sworn in for his fifth and, according to Kenya's constitution, final five-year term as president of Kenya on Jan. 5, 1998. At the colorful swearing-in ceremony in Nairobi, the capital, Moi, who was reelected in December 1997, promised to dedicate his final term to eliminating poverty, rebuilding the country's crumbling infrastructure, and fighting corruption.

Economic woes. Moi, for the first time in his 20-year rule, faced open rebellion in 1998 from within his ruling Kenya African National Union (KANU). The opposition was largely fueled by Kenya's dire economic situation and rivalry for position in the race to succeed Moi.

At an economic forum held in late April, Finance Minister Simeon Nyachae, the leader of one faction within KANU, candidly admitted that Kenya was on the brink of economic collapse and that corruption was rampant. Most members of Kenya's parliament attended the forum, which was sponsored by international lending organizations and the United States. Moi accused the forum's attendees and sponsors of attempting to undermine his government.

At the forum, Nyachae blamed the country's economic problems on a bloated civil service and interest on Kenya's massive debt, which, he said, had been incurred through corrupt practices. Government attempts to cut public employment and raise taxes, however, were met with strikes and the threat of strikes. On July 15, most of Kenya's 260,000 teachers struck to press their demands for the 200-percent salary increase promised by the government in 1997. In April 1998, Nyachae had warned that the government could not afford the raises.

On September 11, Nyachae reported that Kenya's *gross national product* (the sum of all goods and services produced in a country in a year) would fall in fiscal year 1998-1999 "far below" the 2.3 percent achieved in fiscal year 1997-1998. According to Nyache, more than half of Kenya's population lived below the poverty line in 1998.

Continued ethnic violence against members of the Kikuyu tribe by the Kalenjin, Moi's tribe, in eastern Kenya aroused widespread domestic and foreign criticism. The Kikuyu had largely supported Moi's opposition in the 1997 elections, and critics accused Moi of orchestrating the violence in retaliation.

Embassy bombing. On Aug. 7, 1998, 213 people were killed and some 5,000 injured when a car bomb exploded outside the U.S. embassy in Nairobi. The United States charged Muslim extremist Osama bin Laden with masterminding the attack. ☐ Simon Baynham
See also **Africa** (Facts in brief table); **Terrorism; United States, Government of the.**

Korea, North.

The Supreme People's Assembly on Sept. 5, 1998, named Kim Chong-Il "great leader" of North Korea and chairman of an expanded National Defense Commission. North Korea also revised its constitution in September to make Kim's father, Kim Il Sung—the country's founder who died in 1994—"eternal president." The Assembly selected Kim Yong Nam, a former foreign minister, to serve as president of the presidium, the second highest position in government. Former deputy prime minister Hong Song Nam was named prime minister.

Nuclear weapons plant. In August 1998, United States intelligence agencies detected a huge underground complex near Yongbyon, North Korea, that they believed was being used to revive a nuclear weapons program. The finding alarmed U.S. officials, who feared North Korea was on the verge of breaking a 1994 agreement in which the country pledged to give up its nuclear weapons program in exchange for a $6-billion nuclear energy program financed by the United States and other countries.

North Korean officials complained early in 1998 that the United States had failed to keep its part of the agreement to provide millions of dollars in fuel shipments. In September, the United States fulfilled its commitment by providing North Korea with $15 million of fuel oil.

Missile mishap. North Korea tried to launch what they claimed to be a satellite in August 1998, an act that ignited international concern about the country's missile program. The satellite was attached to a medium-range missile that broke up over Japan. The missile firing angered Japanese officials, who initially suspected that the rocket launch was a hostile act. According to intelligence agencies, the launch suggested that North Korea had developed the technology for rockets that could reach any part of Japan.

Submarine captured. In June, South Korean officials announced that a North Korean submarine had either picked up or dropped off spies shortly before its periscope became tangled in a fishing net off the South Korean coast. The submarine contained the bodies of nine North Koreans, all dead from gunshot wounds.

Starvation. The United Nations World Food Program reported in early March that North Korea was experiencing a critical food shortage after the country announced that its official food stocks would run out by mid-March. A U.S. Congressional fact-finding team reported in August that at least 1 million North Koreans had died since 1995 of starvation. ☐ Henry S. Bradsher

See also **Asia** (Facts in brief table); **Economics** Special Report: **Asian Economic Crisis—Global Contagion; Japan; Korea, South.**

South Korean divers inspect a North Korean submarine in June 1998 after it became tangled in a fishing net. The submarine contained the bodies of nine North Koreans, whom South Korean officials believed to have been spies.

Korea, South. Kim Dae-Jung, a prodemocracy dissident, assumed the office of president of South Korea in February 1998, succeeding Kim Yong-sam. Kim Dae-Jung vowed to rebuild South Korea's ailing economy, which was in its worst recession since the Korean War (1950-1953).

South Korea, which in the 1970's through the 1990's had grown from an impoverished nation to the world's 11th largest economy, fell victim in 1997 to sharp devaluations in its currency and soaring foreign debts. In December 1997, South Korea accepted a $57-billion international loan package that would help the nation pay $150 billion in foreign debts.

In January 1998, Kim Dae-Jung told industrial leaders that South Korea was in economic trouble. "We went on a spending spree on borrowed money," he said, "and we've got only ourselves to blame for this mess." He called South Korea's once-prized economy a "house of cards" built on government corruption.

The country was burdened with huge private-industry debt, which crippled financial institutions and bankrupted leading conglomerates. Kim Dae-Jung attempted to overhaul the economy by promoting a friendly new attitude toward foreign business and restricting bailouts of failing companies.

Despite Kim Dae-Jung's restructuring efforts, South Korea remained in economic turmoil in 1998. In the first six months, economic output fell 5.3 percent, a dramatic drop from the first half of 1997 when output grew by 6.2 percent. More than 14,000 companies went out of business in 1998 as sales dropped and banks tightened loan procedures.

Unemployment rose from 2.3 percent in June 1997 to 7.7 percent in June 1998. Kim Dae-Jung, an ally of labor unions, pressed labor organizations to become more flexible. Traditionally, unions made it difficult for South Korean companies to dismiss workers, a situation underscored by a strike settlement reached in August between Hyundai Motor Company and its union. The strike, which had threatened to cripple South Korea's largest automaker, ended after Hyundai agreed to cut 277 jobs—one-fifth the number sought by management.

Prime minister. In February, Kim Dae-Jung, head of the National Congress for New Politics, named Kim Jong Pil, leader of United Liberal Democrats, prime minister. The Grand National Party, which controlled a majority of National Assembly seats, rejected Kim Jong Pil's nomination, charging that his past ties to repressive regimes made him unfit for the post.

Kim Jong Pil founded the Korean Central Intelligence Agency, which in 1973 had kidnapped Kim Dae-Jung in Japan and had planned to murder him until the United States intervened. Kim Dae-Jung and Kim Jong Pil joined forces in the 1997 election campaign, after Kim Jong Pil had been promised the post of prime minister in exchange for political support. In August 1998, the National Assembly narrowly approved the nomination of Kim Jong Pil.

Amnesty. South Korea approved the most sweeping amnesty in its history in March, clearing the police records of 5.5 million people. Kim Dae-Jung also approved the release of more than 2,300 political prisoners, some of whom had spent more than 20 years in jail.

Officials of North Korea and South Korea met for the first time in four years in April. North Korea, which experienced severe shortages of food in 1998, asked the South to provide 100 million tons (91 million metric tons) of chemical fertilizers. The South Koreans hoped to end North Korean aggression and arrange for the reunion of aging family members split by the 1945 partition of the Korean peninsula. The talks collapsed just days after they began, but Kim Dae-Jung called for another summit meeting with North Korea and promised large-scale food aid to the impoverished country.　　　□ Henry S. Bradsher

See also **Asia** (Facts in brief table); **Economics** Special Report: **Asian Economic Crisis; Korea, North; People in the news** (Kim Dae-Jung).

Labor and employment. The United States economy remained relatively stable in 1998, a year in which many other countries sank into recession. The U.S Bureau of Labor Statistics (BLS) reported that in November the country's unemployment rate was 4.4 percent. Despite the low unemployment, which often triggers price inflation, the BLS reported that consumer prices had increased only 0.2 percent in October. The economy created more than 2 million jobs by the end of 1998, according to the report.

In September, the low U.S. unemployment rate reflected good economic times. Unemployment rates were 2 percent or lower in Nebraska, North Dakota, and South Dakota. States with unemployment rates between 5 percent and 7 percent included California, Hawaii, Louisiana, Mississippi, New Mexico, and New York.

General Motors strike. General Motors Corporation (GM) and the United Automobile Workers (UAW) continued to battle over local plant issues of efficiency, staffing, and job security during 1998. On June 5, approximately 3,400 UAW members at a GM metal-stamping plant in Flint, Michigan, went on strike. The plant made fenders, hoods, and steel engine cradles for GM vehicles.

Approximately 5,800 UAW workers at a second GM plant in Flint joined the strike on June

11. The factory produced air filters, dashboard instrument panels, and spark plugs.

The strikes led to a nationwide halt of GM's North American operations and a massive layoff that cost the automaker more than $2 billion. The key issues in the strike involved staffing, safety, and subcontracting. As the strikes continued, GM temporarily shut down plants.

GM filed a lawsuit against the UAW in July, alleging that the strikes focused on issues of a national scope, such as downsizing, and were not matters for which employees could strike under existing labor agreements. However, on July 29, both sides agreed to settle the strike. Among the provisions of the settlement, GM agreed to invest $300 million in the Flint metal-stamping plant by 2001, promised not to sell the Flint parts factory before the end of 1999, and withdrew its grievance that the strikes were illegal. GM also agreed to pay the laid-off workers four days of holiday pay because the strike had dragged through Independence Day.

The UAW agreed to adopt new efficiency standards to make the metal center more productive. Members of the striking union ratified the agreement by a 9-to-1 margin at the metal fabricating center and by a 3-to-1 margin at the parts plant. Because supplies were completely depleted, it took GM several weeks to return the plants to full production. Negotiations between GM and the UAW for a new national contract were scheduled to begin in 1999.

Trucking industry. The International Brotherhood of Teamsters and four major trucking companies in the United States announced on February 9 a tentative five-year pact covering more than 72,000 truckers. Among the provisions was a $1.40-an-hour wage increase by the end of the five-year deal, with the maximum hourly pay set at $19.86. Union members approved the new contract in April 1998.

On December 5, members of the International Brotherhood of Teamsters elected James P. Hoffa president of the union. Hoffa is the son of James R. Hoffa, who led the union from 1957 to 1971 and who mysteriously disappeared in 1975.

The younger Hoffa defeated Tom Leedham, head of the union's warehouse division, and John Metz, a St. Louis, Missouri, teamsters leader. Hoffa narrowly lost a bid to lead the teamsters in 1996, when he was defeated by then-President Ron Carey. A federal election official in 1997 overturned the 1996 election, citing a controversy over campaign finance irregularities. A court-appointed monitor in 1997 barred Carey from running for election to the post. The monitor ruled that Carey had illegally funneled union money to his campaign. Carey appealed the decision and took an unpaid leave of absence as president. He

was later expelled from the union. Hoffa served the remaining three years of Carey's five-year term.

Hoffa withstood an investigation in 1998 of his own 1996 election finance activities. In April, a federal monitor announced that while Hoffa had engaged in improprieties in the 1996 union election, he was eligible to remain a candidate in the 1998 election.

Airline industry. Settlements between various unions and major airlines took place in mid-1998. Members of the Air Line Pilots Association ratified a four-year contract with Trans World Airlines, Inc. (TWA), in August. Under terms of the agreement, six pay increases through 2002 would boost the salaries of TWA's 2,300 pilots to 90 percent of the industry average. The agreement, which had been reached in July 1998, took 14 months of talks and provided the first pay increase for the airline's pilots in 12 years.

In late August, approximately 6,200 pilots at Northwest Airlines went on strike following two years of negotiations. The airline invited federal government intervention on grounds of national emergency. The federal government declined the request, although officials urged both parties to continue bargaining. Both sides were divided over such issues as wage increases, job protections in a changing industry, pensions, and profit sharing. During the course of the strike, Northwest Airlines laid off approximately 31,000 nonstriking ground workers and other staff members.

On September 12, the Air Line Pilots Association ratified a four-year agreement that ended the 15-day strike. The association agreed to a 12 percent wage increase over the course of the contract. The pilots also received stock options and profit sharing. Job protections were included against possible mergers or alliances that might cost jobs. Under the agreement, the wage scale of new pilots would be increased over a five-year period.

Telephone industry. Ameritech Corporation and the Communications Workers of America (CWA) agreed on the terms of a new contract in June 1998, two months before the existing contract was scheduled to expire. The union ratified the agreement in July by a 4-to-1 margin. Under the agreement, base wages would rise more than 11 percent over a 32-month period. The contract also provided pension and other benefits.

The contract contained job protection language related to a proposed merger of Ameritech and SBC Corporation, Inc., of San Antonio. SBC announced plans in May 1998 to acquire Ameritech in a stock transaction worth more than $56 billion. SBC was a local-telephone service provider in seven states, including California

Members of the United Auto Workers rally outside a General Motors plant in Flint, Michigan, in June 1998. A series of local strikes forced the automaker to shut down its North American operation.

Changes in the United States labor force

	1997	1998*
Civilian labor force	136,297,000	138,075,000
Total employment	129,558,000	131,765,000
Unemployment	6,739,000	6,310,000
Unemployment rate	4.9%	4.6%
Change in real weekly earnings of production and nonsupervisory workers (private nonfarm sector)†	2.2%	2.7%
Change in output per employee hour (private nonfarm sector)	1.4%	2.0%

*All 1998 data is through the third quarter of 1998 (preliminary data).
†Real weekly earnings are adjusted for inflation by using constant 1982 dollars.
Source: U.S. Bureau of Labor Statistics.

and Texas. Ameritech was the primary local telephone company in five Midwestern states.

Both the CWA and the International Brotherhood of Electrical Workers (IBEW) ratified new four-year contracts with AT&T Corporation in July. The contracts called for wage boosts totaling more than 14 percent. Union members received two $500 bonuses—one for settling the strike and another for ratifying the contract.

Bell Atlantic and the CWA were unable to reach a contract agreement, and union employees went on strike on August 9. Job security was a primary issue. An agreement, reached on August 11, reduced outside contracting of work and provided wage increases of 7.8 percent over the two-year term of the contract. Bell Atlantic North, formerly the NYNEX Corporation, agreed to similar terms.

The CWA reached agreements with the remaining Bell Corporations, with the exception of U.S. West, without resorting to strikes. The two-week CWA strike against U.S. West ended in an agreement in August 1998.

Detroit newspaper strike. The National Labor Relations Board (NLRB) in September 1998 ordered *The Detroit News* and *Detroit Free Press* to rehire hundreds of workers who went on strike in 1995. The workers had not been rehired when the 19-month strike ended in 1997. The NLRB in 1998 upheld a judge's earlier decision that the two newspapers had committed unfair labor practices and must rehire all workers who offered

unconditionally to return to work. The papers were ordered to dismiss replacement workers if necessary and pay back wages to the employees who had not returned to work. In September, the newspapers appealed the order.

Contract agreements. The United Automobile Workers union in March ratified a six-year agreement with Caterpillar Corporation of Peoria, Illinois, after union members rejected a pact in February. The agreement ended a six-year labor dispute that had been marked by returns to work, agreements, rejected agreements, and federal mediation. The contract increased wages between 2 percent and 4 percent, depending on the worker's pay grade. Cost-of-living boosts were also included. Wages were to increase from a top level of $19 to $22.70 an hour

The United Parcel Service and its pilots settled on a new pact in January. The pilots had rejected an earlier settlement in 1997. Under the new pact, which was approved in March 1998, salaries for senior pilots would increase from $137,000 to

$170,000 over the seven-year contract.

The Communications Workers of America and the International Brotherhood of Electrical Workers, in separate votes in June, agreed on tentative five-year agreements with Lucent Technologies Inc., a telecommunications equipment maker in Murray Hill, New Jersey. The pact, which covered approximately 44,000 workers, increased wages 19 percent. The agreement was reached after Lucent withdrew a demand that workers share more health-care costs.

Union membership in the United States declined slightly in 1997 (the most recent year for which data are available), falling to 14.1 percent from 14.5 percent in 1996. Approximately 16.1 million people belonged to U.S. unions in 1997.

Unemployment rates. Many of the world's industrialized countries continued to experience higher unemployment than the United States in 1998, as nations struggled to emerge from recessionary and industrial restructuring difficulties.

According to the Organization for Economic Cooperation and Development (OECD), a Paris-based multinational association working to promote economic and social welfare, the jobless rate in September 1998 averaged 6.9 percent for the 21 OECD nations supplying data and 9.9 percent in the European Union (EU), an organization of 15 Western European countries. According to OECD data, the highest rates were in Spain, which reported an unemployment rate of 18.5 percent; France, which reported just under 12 percent unemployment; and Finland, which reported 11.2 percent unemployment.

Unemployment in the seven major industrialized countries—Canada, France, Germany, Italy, Japan, the United Kingdom, and the United States—averaged 6.5 percent in September 1998. In the United States, preliminary data from the BLS showed that unemployment fell to 4.4 percent. Unemployment rates in 1998 also fell in Belgium, Canada, Finland, Ireland, Luxembourg, Portugal, Spain, and Sweden. In the other nations, the jobless rates were essentially unchanged or rose slightly.

During 1998, severe international and domestic financial difficulties struck Japan and other Asian nations, including South Korea and Indonesia. Japan's troubles stemmed mainly from its domestic banking situation, in which large numbers of bad loans depressed economic activity and forced the nation's jobless rate to increase. Japan's unemployment rate averaged just over 2 percent in 1992. By September 1998, the rate rose to 4.3 percent.   □ Robert W. Fisher

See also **Economics; Economics** Special Report: **Asian Economic Crisis; Manufacturing.**
Laos. See Asia.

Latin America

Devastating weather struck Latin America in 1998 from one end of the region to the other. In the first half of the year, the northeastern third of the South Amer-ican continent was in the grip of a prolonged drought. In northeast Brazil, where more than 10 million people live by subsistence farming, the drought was the worst in 15 years. Dry conditions withered crops in areas of neighboring Colombia and Venezuela and extended north into Central America and southern Mexico.

By late February, runoff of water into the Panama Canal was so low that authorities restricted the weight of ships to keep them from running aground in the canal. The dry weather also fueled unprecedented fires in the normally lush areas of Latin America's rain forests. There were more than 50 large fires in Panama's Darien region alone, an area normally drenched by tropical downpours throughout the year.

Excessive rainfall elsewhere in Latin America in the first months of 1998 caused severe floods. In the Parana River basin, floods killed more than 70 people and wreaked havoc on cattle and crops in southern Brazil, northern Argentina, Paraguay, and Uruguay. In the coastal areas of Peru and Ecuador, nearly 500 people died when torrential rainfalls caused landslides that buried whole communities and devastated croplands.

People in Tegucigalpa, Honduras, witness the raging flood waters of the Choluteca River in October 1998. Torrential rains from Hurricane Mitch caused widespread flooding and landslides in Central America and left more than 10,000 people dead.

In September, Hurricane Georges swept across the Caribbean, leaving more than 500 people dead, primarily in Haiti and the Dominican Republic. In late October, Hurricane Mitch stalled over Central America, unleashing downpours that killed at least 10,000 people in Nicaragua and Honduras. When the rim of a water-filled volcano in Nicaragua collapsed, several villages were completely buried. So numerous were the disasters in 1998 that international relief agencies and local governments struggled to care for survivors.

Troubled economy. Latin American nations posted a modest average growth rate, estimated at 2.8 percent, in 1998. Most economists, however, regarded the growth as something of a tribute to the region's resilience in the face of economic uncertainties that, for the most part, were the result of external influences. The Asian eco-

Country	Population	Government	Monetary unit*	Foreign trade (million U.S.$) Exports†	Imports†
Antigua and Barbuda	67,000	Governor General James B. Carlisle; Prime Minister Lester Bird	dollar (2.70 = $1)	40	246
Argentina	35,805,000	President Carlos Saul Menem	peso (1.00 = $1)	25,516	30,349
Bahamas	287,000	Governor General Orville Turnquest; Prime Minister Hubert Ingraham	dollar (1.00 = $1)	202	1,262
Barbados	266,000	Governor General Sir Clifford Husbands; Prime Minister Owen Arthur	dollar (2.01 = $1)	281	987
Belize	232,000	Governor General Sir Colville Young; Prime Minister Said Musa	dollar (2.00 = $1)	177	286
Bolivia	7,944,000	President Hugo Banzer Suarez	boliviano (5.60 = $1)	1,128	1,810
Brazil	169,430,000	President Fernando Henrique Cardoso	real (1.19 = $1)	52,987	65,007
Chile	14,878,000	President Eduardo Frei Ruiz-Tagle	peso (467.67= $1)	16,875	19,860
Colombia	36,694,000	President Andres Pastrana	peso (1,564.50= $1)	11,522	15,378
Costa Rica	3,641,000	President Miguel Angel Rodriguez	colon (266.70 = $1)	3,281	4,088
Cuba	11,244,000	President Fidel Castro	peso (23.00 = $1)	2,015	3,205
Dominica	71,000	President Crispin Anselm Sorhaindo; Prime Minister Edison James	dollar (2.70 = $1)	53	134
Dominican Republic	8,217,000	President Leonel Fernandez Reyna	peso (15.80 = $1)	882	4,120
Ecuador	12,151,000	President Jamil Mahuad	sucre (6,620.00 = $1)	5,214	4,945
El Salvador	6,150,000	President Armando Calderon Sol	colon (8.76 = $1)	1,359	2,973
Grenada	93,000	Governor General Daniel Williams; Prime Minister Keith Mitchell	dollar (2.70 = $1)	21	152
Guatemala	11,542,000	President Alvaro Arzu Irigoyen	quetzal (6.60 = $1)	2,149	3,467
Guyana	864,000	President Janet Jagan	dollar (149.30 = $1)	455	528
Haiti	7,633,000	President Rene Preval; Prime Minister Jacques-Edouard Alexis	gourde (16.59 = $1)	119	647
Honduras	6,133,000	President Carlos Roberto Flores Facusse	lempira (13.78 = $1)	1,443	2,048
Jamaica	2,504,000	Governor General Sir Howard Cooke; Prime Minister P. J. Patterson	dollar (35.75 = $1)	1,351	3,021
Mexico	98,766,000	President Ernesto Zedillo Ponce de Leon	new peso (9.96 = $1)	59,072	61,179
Nicaragua	4,854,000	President Arnoldo Aleman Lacayo	gold cordoba (11.00 = $1)	629	1,211
Panama	2,763,000	President Ernesto Perez Balladares	balboa (1.00 = $1)	623	2,780
Paraguay	5,337,000	President Raul Cubas Grau	guarani (2,830.00 = $1)	919	3,144
Peru	25,124,000	President Alberto K. Fujimori	new sol (3.08 = $1)	6,754	10,282
Puerto Rico	3,522,000	Governor Pedro Rossello	U.S. dollar	22,900	19,100
St. Kitts and Nevis	41,000	Governor General Cuthbert Montraville Sebastian; Prime Minister Denzil Douglas	dollar (2.70 = $1)	27	118
St. Lucia	148,000	Governor General Perlette Louisy; Prime Minister Kenny Anthony	dollar (2.70 = $1)	123	313
St. Vincent and the Grenadines	115,000	Governor General David Jack; Prime Minister James F. Mitchell	dollar (2.70 = $1)	46	132
Suriname	437,000	President Jules Wijdenbosch	guilder (401.00 = $1)	472	472
Trinidad and Tobago	1,349,000	President Arthur Napoleon Raymond Robinson; Prime Minister Basdeo Panday	dollar (6.25 = $1)	2,543	2,991
Uruguay	3,239,000	President Julio Maria Sanguinetti	peso (10.68 = $1)	2,730	3,716
Venezuela	23,195,000	President Rafael Caldera Rodríguez	bolivar (568.50 = $1)	23,054	9,814

*Exchange rates as of Nov. 6, 1998, or latest available data.   †Latest available data.

nomic crisis that began in 1997 prompted many foreign investors to pull out of emerging markets around the world. As part of a global chain reaction, Latin America in 1998 lost many international and domestic sources of credit to feed economic growth and provide jobs.

The economic pains were especially severe in large countries, such as Argentina, Brazil, and Mexico, which had sizable stakes in the global economy. Many midsized countries—such as Chile, Colombia, Ecuador, and Venezuela—also felt the impact. These nations, with economies and government budgets dependent on petroleum and mineral exports, felt the pinch of low prices on global markets for their export products.

Crisis of confidence. Economic doomsayers prevailed for most of 1998. By September, the crisis of confidence in Latin America's economic prospects peaked, and investors had withdrawn $851 million, about 63 percent of total assets, from Latin American mutual funds. The value of Latin American stock exchanges had fallen by an average of 45 percent. Venezuela's stocks had fallen more than 70 percent.

The newly inaugurated administrations in Colombia and Ecuador were forced to devalue their national currencies in September. Consequently, the values of people's savings were diminished overnight by 15 to 25 percent. In Mexico, the value of the peso dropped by more than 20 percent against the U.S. dollar. The decreased value made it difficult for Mexicans to buy such products as household appliances from the United States and Canada—purchases to which they had grown accustomed since the three nations began a free trade agreement in 1994.

Economists and investors monitored the impact of global economic conditions most closely in Brazil. By 1998, the country had a roaring economy that was ranked the ninth largest in the world. Brazil single-handedly accounted for 30 percent of all of Latin America's production. Moreover, Brazil's economy was tied up with those of some of its neighbors through a common market arrangement known as Mercosur, which promotes economic cooperation and trade among Argentina, Bolivia, Brazil, Chile, Paraguay, and Uruguay.

Throughout 1998, the Mercosur nations feared that Brazil would not be able to cope with its 8-percent unemployment rate, a nearly bankrupt social security system, and an oversized civil service. Before national elections in October, the administration of President Fernando Henrique Cardoso spent money to appease the electorate. At the same time, the government promised foreign interests—including U.S. banks, which had more than $27 billion invested in Brazil—that the government would continue economic reforms. These promises were necessary for Brazil to secure a

$41.5-billion bailout package in November from the International Monetary Fund, a United Nations agency located in Washington, D.C., that provides credit to member nations.

By late 1998, Latin American leaders were fighting back, attacking a global financial system that, in their opinion, was penalizing them unfairly. "It has nothing to do with Mexico," declared Mexican Finance Minister Jose Angel Gurria on September 2. Most Latin American leaders had imposed harsh and unpopular austerity programs in recent years to stabilize their economies and attract investors from more developed nations. Mexico, for example, had trimmed $3.7 billion from its national budget in 1998. Nonetheless, Latin Americans found themselves caught up in global turmoil, which Gurria blamed on "an enormous vacuum of leadership worldwide."

Positive developments. Despite an abundance of bad news, there were several encouraging economic developments in 1998. Among them was an event billed as "the largest privatization in Latin American history." In July, the Brazilian government sold its controlling share in Telecommunicacoes Brasileiras, or Telebras, to foreign companies for more than $19 billion.

Also in 1998, the Atlantic LNG Company of Trinidad and Tobago completed a $1-billion natural gas processing plant on the island of Trinidad. The project marked the largest single industrial investment ever made in a Caribbean nation. A five-year boom in natural gas investment had resulted in a dramatic increase in the country's per capita income and economic stability.

Hemisphere summit. At a meeting on April 19 and 20 in Santiago, Chile, leaders from 34 Western Hemisphere nations—all but Cuba—reiterated their support for creating the Free Trade Area of the Americas (FTAA), the world's largest free trade zone, by 2005. At the summit, Latin American leaders lamented the unwillingness of the U.S. Congress to grant the U.S. president "fast-track" authority, which would allow the president to negotiate trade agreements that cannot be amended by Congress. Most Latin American leaders saw the "fast-track" authority as crucial to advancing plans for the FTAA.

International volunteers were involved in an unprecedented number of ways in Latin America in 1998. International nongovernmental organizations monitored everything from environmental degradation and endangered species to human-rights violations and government corruption. They also used the Internet, the worldwide computer network, to convey their findings to an estimated 6 million Latin Americans who had Internet access in 1998—a figure expected to reach 34 million by 2000.

In 1998, human rights activists from Belgium,

Canada, France, Germany, Italy, and the United States descended on the rebellion-torn State of Chiapas in southern Mexico, where the Zapatista National Liberation Army had first staged an uprising in 1994. The volunteers acted as human-rights observers and buffers between government troops and Maya Indians and peasants who sympathized with the Zapatistas. Mexican leaders criticized the activists, however, for interfering with government business. In May, after a group of Italian activists defied orders not to visit a town in Chiapas, the Mexican immigration service issued new rules that set restrictions on human rights observers.

The National Coordinating Office for Refugees and Displaced of Guatemala, a nonprofit organization based in Washington, D.C., sent human-rights observers to Guatemala to help people who had returned home since the end of the country's civil war in 1996. Erica Lepp of St. Paul, Minnesota, acted as an observer in Santa Elena, a village of about 250 Maya Indians. Armed with a cellular phone, her responsibility was to report human-rights violations or conflicts to volunteers in Santa Elena's "sister city" of Oberlin, Ohio. Such networks helped ensure that the reintegration of displaced persons into Guatemalan society remained under international scrutiny.

Suriname forests. In June 1998, Conservation International, based in Washington, D.C., reached an agreement with the government of Suriname to set aside 4 million acres (1.6 million hectares) of tropical forest, about one-tenth of the country's land, for the Central Suriname Wilderness Nature Reserve. The agency managing the reserve was expected to be funded by the sale of nontimber forest products, such as resins; environmentally conscious tourism; and *bioprospecting* (searching for plants from which medicines can be made).

Astronomers observed light from outer space in May through the first of a series of telescopes under construction at the European Southern Observatory in the Atacama Desert of Chile. The governments of Belgium, Denmark, France, Germany, Italy, the Netherlands, Sweden, and Switzerland sponsored the project. The so-called Very Large Telescope, scheduled for completion in 2003, was to be comprised of four 27-foot (8.2-meter) telescopes and three 6-foot (1.8-meter) telescopes. The instruments were designed to create computer-generated composite images of greater clarity than that achieved by any single telescope in use in 1998.

Drug sting. In May, U.S. law-enforcement authorities indicted more than 100 people—as well as Mexican and Venezuelan banks and Mexican branches of Italian, Spanish, and U.S. banks—for laundering profits from drug trafficking. The indictments were the result of a three-year undercover sting, code-named "Operation Casablanca."

The U.S. Customs Service, which led the investigation, seized more than $100 million in assets.

Restitution. On June 12, the U.S. government reached a settlement with some 1,200 plaintiffs who sought compensation for internment during World War II (1939–1945). After Japan attacked the United States in December 1941, the U.S. government interned Japanese Americans and arrested 2,264 Latin Americans of Japanese descent and brought them to the United States for internment. In the 1998 settlement, each Latin American internee of Japanese descent was to receive $5,000. Japanese Americans were granted $20,000 compensations in 1988.

Journalists at risk. In March 1998, the Organization of American States, an association of 35 American countries, created the position of special monitor at the urging of U.S. authorities to protect the interests of journalists in Latin America. Nearly 200 journalists had died in Latin America since 1988, according to Thomas F. McLarty, U.S. President Bill Clinton's special envoy for the Americas. Thousands more had been threatened, imprisoned, or censored.

J. Jesus Blancornelas, editor of the weekly newspaper *Zeta* in Tijuana, Mexico, was awarded a Maria Moors Cabot Prize by New York City's Columbia University on Oct. 22, 1998, for his role in uncovering corruption and drug trafficking. The award is given to individuals who promote freedom of the press and the mutual understanding of regional matters in the Americas. In November 1997, Blancornelas was shot by drug traffickers. He returned to work in March 1998.

Gift to the Met. "The most important gift ever" of modern art, Philippe de Montebello, director of New York City's Metropolitan Museum of Art, said of a bequest to the museum of 85 works by such artists as Henri Matisse, Pablo Picasso, Georges Braque, Balthus, and Amedeo Modigliani. The collection belonged to the late Jacques Gelman and Natasha Gelman, who died on May 2 at her residence in Cuernavaca, Mexico. Jacques Gelman had made his fortune producing the films of the Mexican entertainer Mario Moreno (better known as Cantinflas). Natasha Gelman, who immigrated to Mexico in the 1930's from Moravia (now the Czech Republic), left her collection of Mexican art, including works by Frida Kahlo and Diego Rivera, to a Mexican museum.

Baseball star. Dominican Sammy Sosa of the Chicago Cubs hit 66 home runs in 1998, surpassing Roger Maris's 1961 single-season record of 61 home runs. Sosa was one of 88 major league baseball players in 1998 from the Dominican Republic.   □ Nathan A. Haverstock

See also articles on the individual nations; **Art; Baseball; Economics** Special Report: **Asian Economic Crisis—Global Contagion.**

Latvia. Tensions with Russia over the status of Russians in Latvia escalated in early 1998. Relations with Russia had been strained since 1994, when a controversial law effectively denied Latvian citizenship to some 700,000 ethnic Russians still living in Latvia after the 1991 breakup of the Soviet Union. On March 3, 1998, police in Riga, the Latvian capital, used force to break up a demonstration by Russian pensioners. In April, a blast damaged the Russian embassy in Riga and the city's only synagogue was bombed.

Under international pressure, the Latvian parliament in June 1998 amended the citizenship law. The changes granted citizenship to all residents born since Latvia's independence in 1991, eliminated quotas and language requirements for citizenship, and ended other restrictions.

In parliamentary elections in October 1998, the People's Party of former Prime Minister Andris Skele led the balloting with 21 percent of the vote. Five other parties also won seats, forcing all parties to seek coalition partners. The parties deadlocked for weeks over the formation of a government until Latvia's Way party leader Vilis Kristopans formed a three-party minority coalition in late November.   □ Steven L. Solnick

See also **Europe** (Facts in brief table).

Law. See Civil rights; Courts; Supreme Court of the United States.

Lebanon. Lebanese President Emile Lahoud named Salim Hoss, a United States-trained economist, as prime minister in December 1998 after Prime Minister Rafiq al-Hariri suddenly resigned. Analysts said Hariri appeared to have lost to Lahoud in a power struggle, though Hariri denied this was the case.

Hariri, who had launched the reconstruction of Lebanon after its 1975-1990 civil war, was blamed by many Lebanese in recent years for the nation's economic difficulties. Hariri's government had run large budget deficits each year since assuming office in 1992 and had struggled with the parliament in 1998 over reducing public expenditures. Lebanon also faced a large national debt and widespread corruption.

Lahoud, who had been Lebanon's army chief, was elected to succeed Elias Hrawi as president in October. Lahoud's candidacy was supported by Syria, the main power broker in Lebanon. Economists hoped Lahoud would aggressively tackle the country's economic problems, but noted in October that Hariri and the parliament wielded greater power. Lebanese were encouraged by Hoss's replacement of Hariri, because both Hoss, who had previously served as prime minister, and Lahoud had reputations as reformers.

Elections. Lebanon's first municipal elections in 35 years were held between late May and mid-

June to elect some 650 municipal councils and 2,000 mayors. Analysts interpreted the results as a challenge to Lebanon's pro-Syrian authorities.

Israel. In March, Prime Minister Hariri rejected Israeli Prime Minister Benjamin Netanyahu's proposal to withdraw Israeli forces from southern Lebanon. Israeli troops maintained a "security zone" in southern Lebanon as a buffer against attacks by guerrillas belonging to the militant Islamic group Hezbollah. Hariri said it would be impossible to meet Israel's demand that Lebanon guarantee the security of northern Israel from the Hezbollah guerrillas, who have tried to dislodge the Israelis since 1982. Hariri also said an agreement on Israeli security was dependent on a comprehensive peace between Israel and all of its Arab neighbors—including Syria, which maintained 35,000 troops in Lebanon.

International pressure on Israel to end its occupation of southern Lebanon increased in 1998, the 20th anniversary of a UN resolution calling for Israel's withdrawal from Lebanon. Israel invaded southern Lebanon in 1978 to quash Palestinian guerrillas. Hostilities between Israeli forces and Hezbollah guerrillas continued in the security zone throughout 1998.   □ Christine Helms

See also **Israel; Middle East** (Facts in brief table); **Syria.**

Lesotho. See Africa.

Library. In April 1998, the British Library opened its new $843-million complex in London after moving half of its 12 million books from the British Museum, which had been the library's home for 151 years. Although architecture critics gave the library mixed reviews, readers praised the light-filled rooms, private reading areas, access to the Internet, and speedy delivery of reading materials. Library officials expected the 200 miles (322 kilometers) of shelves to be filled with the remainder of the library's books by early 1999. Budget cuts by the British government forced library officials to consider charging readers a fee for the first time in the library's history.

Library user surveys. A survey released in April 1998 by the Benton Foundation, a Washington, D.C.-based organization that promotes the value of communications technologies for solving social problems, revealed that although library users wanted access to computers and the Internet, they also valued books and traditional library services. According to the survey, readers valued children's services above all other library functions.

In June, a Gallup Poll commissioned by the American Library Association (ALA), a Chicago-based organization that works to promote and improve library services and librarianship, found that 64 percent of people in the United States vis-

The Humanities Reading Room is one of 11 public reading rooms in the new $843-million British Library in London, which opens to the public in April 1998. The library moved from historic, 151-year-old facilities at the British Museum.

ited a public library at least once in 1997. This figure was up from 51 percent in 1978. The poll also found that two out of every three Americans had a library card, and 1 in 10 visited a library 25 times or more in 1997. Eighty-one percent of the library visitors surveyed said they borrowed books, 51 percent used reference materials, and 17 percent used the Internet. Sixty-five percent of visitors consulted a librarian. Nine out of 10 people surveyed said they believed that libraries would continue to exist in the age of electronic information.

The Gates Library Foundation sent teams of technicians to libraries in low-income parts of the United States in 1998 to wire computers for access to the Internet and train library staffs in using computer technology. The foundation was established in 1997 by William H. Gates, chief executive officer of the computer software giant Microsoft Corporation of Redmond, Washington. The foundation, created to connect libraries across the country to the Internet, invested $2.7 million in the state of Alabama in 1998, connecting 257 libraries and training more than 1,000 librarians. Similar projects were planned for the states of Arkansas, Kentucky, Louisiana, Mississippi, New Mexico, and West Virginia.

ALA Internet services. The ALA in 1998 launched "700+ Great Sites," a Web site providing links to ALA-recommended material on the Internet for children and offering advice and safety tips for parents. Other Internet sites sponsored by the ALA included "Teen Hoopla," which provided links to educational Web sites for young adults, and "KidsConnect," which offered assistance to children with homework questions.

In September, the ALA and several local libraries began a yearlong public education campaign called "America Links Up." The campaign was designed to educate parents, children, and other interested people about the Internet.

Internet filters. The U.S. Congress in 1998 debated, but failed to pass, legislation requiring every library accepting federal funds to have "filters" on computers used by the public to access the Internet. Filters are software programs designed to prevent children or other people from viewing objectionable material, such as sexually explicit Web sites. The ALA opposed the legislation, maintaining that filters were faulty and decisions about Internet access should be made locally.

In November, a federal judge ruled that libraries in Loudoun County, Virginia, could not install Internet filters to protect children. The judge objected to the fact that the filters also deprived adults of their right to view certain Web sites. □ Peggy Barber

Libya. In August 1998, the United Nations (UN) Security Council approved a resolution, offered by the United States and Great Britain, that would suspend sanctions imposed on Libya once two suspected Libyan terrorists arrived in the Netherlands for trial. The two men were wanted by the United States and Great Britain for the 1988 bombing of Pan Am flight 103 over Lockerbie, Scotland. Libyan leader Muammar Muhammad al-Qadhafi, who had previously offered to turn the suspects over for trial to a neutral, third-party country, said he would not give up the suspects unless he had a guarantee that, if convicted, they would serve their sentences in Libya. United States and British officials, however, insisted that any prison sentences be served in Scotland. In December 1998, UN Secretary General Kofi Annan met with Qadhafi in Libya, but failed to resolve the dispute.

The UN had imposed sanctions on Libya in 1992 to pressure Libya into turning the suspects over to either the United States or Great Britain. The sanctions included a ban on sales to Libya of certain equipment needed for that country's oil industry, a freeze on some overseas Libyan assets, and a ban on flights to and from Libya.

Pressure to lift sanctions. In March 1998, Arab and African delegations to the UN argued before the Security Council that the sanctions caused unfair suffering for the Libyan people. In June, the Organization of African Unity (OAU), an association of more than 50 African nations, announced that its members had agreed to ignore the UN air ban for flights that were related to humanitarian, religious, or OAU affairs. Several African leaders flew to Libya in 1998 in violation of the sanctions.

In October, Qadhafi said he was abandoning his long-standing efforts to promote Arab unity in favor of working for greater African unity. In September, the Arab League, an association of more than 20 Arab states dedicated to promoting closer relations among members, had called for sanctions to be lifted from Libya as soon as a final agreement was reached to bring the two bombing suspects to trial. However, Qadhafi said he was disappointed that Arab nations, unlike African countries, had not violated the UN air ban.

Qadhafi's surgery. On July 6, Qadhafi underwent surgery after he broke his hip while exercising. Libya's official news service denied rumors prompted by the surgery that Qadhafi had been wounded in an assassination attempt, and state television broadcast a graphic video of the procedure. □ Christine Helms

See also **Africa** (Facts in brief table).

Liechtenstein. See **Europe** (Facts in brief table).

Literature for children.

A wide variety of picture books and much realistic fiction appeared in 1998. Some of the outstanding children's books of 1998 included the following:

Picture Books. *Scarecrow* by Cynthia Rylant, illustrated by Lauren Stringer (Harcourt Brace). A scarecrow lovingly tells of all the wonderful things he sees and experiences. All ages.

Look-Alikes by Joan Steiner (Little, Brown). Challenging pictures contain more than 100 objects from mousetraps to dominoes. All ages.

My Friend Gorilla by Atsuko Morozumi (Farrar, Straus & Giroux). A young boy befriends a gorilla that his father brings home from a closed zoo. The son remembers the gorilla fondly after it is sent to live in Africa. Ages 4 to 8.

The Old Woman and the Wave by Shelley Jackson (DK Ink). A huge wave hovers over the house of an old woman, who always complains about it dripping. A set of circumstances causes her to see the wave differently. Ages 4 to 8.

Nothing by Mick Inkpen (Orchard Books/Watts). An old stuffed animal, left behind in the attic when the family moves, begins a search for his identity. Ages 4 to 7.

Just a Minute! by Anke Kranendonk, illustrated by Jung-Hee Spetter (Front Street/Lemniscaat). Piggy wants his mother to read him a story and gets into all sorts of mischief because she is too busy. Ages 3 to 6.

Telling Time with Big Mama Cat by Dan Harper, illustrated by Barry and Cara Moser (Harcourt Brace). A clock with hands that can move helps the reader learn to tell time. Ages 3 to 6.

Fa Mulan: The Story of a Woman Warrior by Robert D. San Souci, illustrated by Jean and Mou-Sien Tseng (Hyperion). Mulan takes her father's place disguised as a male warrior and earns an enviable reputation and glory. Ages 5 to 8.

Celia and the Sweet, Sweet Water by Katherine Paterson, illustrated by Vladimir Vagin (Clarion). Celia helps strangers as she seeks the water that will save her dying mother. Ages 4 to 8.

No, David! by David Shannon (Blue Sky/Scholastic). Hilarious scenes depict many situations for which young children get scolded. Ages 3 to 6.

Fiction. *The Dark Light* by Mette Newth, translated by Faith Ingwersen (Farrar, Straus & Giroux). In the early 1800's in Norway, 13-year-old Tora's leprosy is discovered, and her family must send her to a lepers' hospital. Ages 12 and up.

Go and Come Back: A Novel by Joan Abelove (DK Ink). A Peruvian girl shares her thoughts about two United States anthropologists who visit her jungle village. Her humorous account reveals what they learn from one another. Ages 12 and up.

The Storyteller's Beads by Jane Kurtz (Gulliver/Harcourt Brace). When Sayah and her uncle flee civil strife and drought in Ethiopia, they join forces with Rahel and her brother, Ethiopian Jews, on an inspiring journey. Ages 12 and up.

The Wreckers by Iain Lawrence (Delacorte). John survives a shipwreck along the English coast in 1799 and encounters the dangerous villagers who lured the ship to its doom. Ages 10 to 14.

Whirligig by Paul Fleischman (Henry Holt). In a drunken-driving accident, Brent kills a girl. His unusual punishment changes his life and the lives of others. Ages 10 to 14.

Love Among the Walnuts by Jean Ferris (Harcourt Brace). In this funny melodrama, Sandy and a family servant must protect the family's estate from evil uncles. Ages 12 and up.

Soldier's Heart by Gary Paulsen (Delacorte). At age 15, Charlie enlists in the Union army during the Civil War, but its horrors, not adventure, are etched in his mind forever. Ages 12 and up.

Bat 6 by Virginia Euwer Wolff (Scholastic). The girls on two opposing softball teams in 1949 reveal their personalities and feelings. Ages 9 to 12.

Holes by Louis Sachar (Farrar, Straus & Giroux). Stanley is sent to a juvenile correctional camp where he must dig holes and where he finds an intriguing mystery. Ages 12 and up.

Trouble's Daughter by Katherine Kirkpatrick (Doubleday). In 1643, Native Americans capture Susanna Hutchinson. The fascinating account follows her struggle to adapt to a new life and eventually return to colonial society. Ages 10 to 14.

Joey Pigza Swallowed the Key by Jack Gantos (Farrar, Straus, Giroux). Joey, who has attention-deficit/hyperactivity disorder, tells his story, which is both funny and educational. Ages 8 to 12.

Poetry. *Insectlopedia: Poems and Paintings* by Douglas Florian (Harcourt Brace). Fine paintings and poems capture the essence and activities of insects. All ages.

This Land Is Your Land by Woody Guthrie, illustrated by Kathy Jakobsen (Little, Brown). The well-known song is illustrated with pictures that capture the many faces of the United States. All ages.

Touching the Distance: Native American Riddle Poems by Brian Swann, illustrated by Maria Rendon (Browndeer/Harcourt Brace). Each illustration offers a hint of the answer to the riddles from various tribes. Answers are included. All ages.

Boshblobberbosh: Runcible Poems for Mr. Lear by J. Patrick Lewis, illustrated by Gary Kelley (Creative Editions/Harcourt Brace). Fine illustrations accompany nonsense poems about and for Edward Lear (1812–1888), a British writer known for such works as "The Owl and the Pussy-Cat." All ages.

The Disappearing Alphabet by Richard Wilbur, illustrated by David Diaz (Harcourt Brace). Imaginative verses show what might happen if our alphabet were to disappear gradually. All ages.

Fantasy. *Clockwork* by Philip Pullman, illustrated by Leonid Gore (Arthur A. Levine/Scholastic). Karl, an apprentice clockmaker, makes a pact with dark forces in order to complete his masterpiece. Ages 12 and up.

The Secret of Platform 13 by Eva Ibbotson, illustrated by Sue Porter (Dutton). A prince from a magical island has been kidnapped when a secret passage between the island and London opens. His rescuers have one chance to find him nine years later. Ages 10 and up.

Harry Potter and the Sorcerer's Stone by J. K. Rowling (Arthur A. Levine/Scholastic). In this British award-winner, Harry learns that he is a wizard and goes to a magic school. Then the delightful adventures begin. Ages 12 and up.

The Heavenward Path by Kara Dalkey (Harcourt Brace). In this sequel to *Little Sister*, Mitsuko becomes ensnared by a ghost and has numerous adventures with characters from Buddhist and Shinto folklore. Ages 12 and up.

Informational books. *From Slave Ship to Freedom Road* by Julius Lester, illustrated by Rod Brown (Dial). Stunning paintings and comments on the slave experience in the United States present challenging questions for today. All ages.

National Audubon Society First Field Guide: Birds by Scott Weidensaul and *First Field Guide: Wildflowers* by Susan Hood (Scholastic). Superb color photos and clear information make these two books first-rate. All ages.

A Brilliant Streak: The Making of Mark Twain by Kathryn Lasky, illustrated by Barry Moser (Harcourt Brace). Twain's varied life and personality come vividly alive. Ages 9 to 13.

Lives of the Presidents: Fame, Shame (and What the Neighbors Thought) by Kathleen Krull, illustrated by Kathryn Hewitt (Harcourt Brace). Fun facts enliven brief, but informative biographical sketches of U.S. presidents. Ages 10 and up.

Shipwreck at the Bottom of the World by Jennifer Armstrong (Crown). This survival story is a riveting account of a disaster under life-threatening conditions in the Antarctic. Ages 10 and up.

Down to Earth by Michael J. Rosen (Harcourt Brace). Forty-one authors and illustrators describe their favorite fruit or vegetable, with recipes and ideas for growing your own. Ages 8 and up.

No Pretty Pictures: A Child of War by Anita Lobel (Greenwillow). Lobel's Roman Catholic nanny helps Anita and her brother, who are Jewish, to hide from Nazis, but eventually they must endure German concentration camps. Ages 12 and up.

The 1998 Newberry Medal went to Karen Hesse for *Out of the Dust*. The award is given by the American Library Association (ALA) for "the most distinguished contribution to children's literature" published the previous year. The ALA's Caldecott Medal for "the most distinguished American picture book" was awarded to Paul O. Zelinsky for *Rapunzel*.   □ Marilyn Fain Apseloff

Literature, American. For books, as for films, 1998 was the year of the list. In July, just after the American Film Institute published a list of the 100 greatest movies, a list of the 100 greatest English-language novels of the 1900's was released by Modern Library, a division of Random House publishers in New York City. The list, headed by Irish writer James Joyce's *Ulysses* (1922) and American writer F. Scott Fitzgerald's *The Great Gatsby* (1925), was intended more as a marketing tool than as a literary judgment. However, the list immediately bred alternate lists and criticism for including too few women (only nine titles) and too few nonwhite writers (only six titles). Nonetheless, the list created a stir for serious literature and briefly propelled Joyce's famously difficult novel onto American best-seller lists.

The 1998 National Book Award in fiction went to Alice McDermott's *Charming Billy,* a quiet novel about an Irish American whose life is haunted by lost love. *Charming Billy* tells the tragic story of Billy Lynch, who becomes engaged to an Irish girl. He works two jobs to save the money to bring her to the United States but learns that she has died. The truth is that she has married someone else. A heartbroken Billy drifts listlessly through life and a loveless marriage.

There were four other nominations for the fiction award. *A Man in Full,* Tom Wolfe's first novel in 11 years, is an epic tale of politics and class in Atlanta, Georgia. The story revolves around a black football star who is accused of raping a white woman. The crime shatters the already tense racial atmosphere of Atlanta. Robert Stone's *Damascus Gate,* set in Jerusalem, details a plot to blow up the Muslim shrines on the Temple Mount and build a new temple that will hasten the Second Coming of Christ. The book is both a conspiracy-laden thriller and a deeply serious novel probing the idea of faith and religion. Allegra Goodman's *Kaaterskill Falls* examines the lives of three Orthodox Jewish families, followers of Rav Kirshner, who live during the summer in the upstate New York community of Kaaterskill. Goodman's story is full of the details of their daily life and religious practices. *The Healing,* Gayl Jones's first book in more than 20 years, is the story of Harlan Jane Eagleton, an itinerant faith healer whose reminiscences are captured by Jones's eye for detail and ear for dialogue.

The National Book Foundation awarded novelist John Updike the 1998 National Book Foundation Medal for Distinguished Contribution to American Letters, which carries a cash award of $10,000. Updike has published more than 40 books during a 40-year career, including his latest novel, *Bech at Bay,* in 1998. It is the third volume of stories about Henry Bech, a New York City novelist suffering an epic case of writer's block.

Other notable fiction. A number of major novelists brought out new works in 1998. Philip Roth's *I Married a Communist* returns to the early 1950's, ground he covered in his first work, *Good-bye, Columbus*. This time, Roth details the marriage of Ira Ringold and Eve Frame. Ringold, a former leftist activist, becomes a radio actor and marries Frame, a film star. When she discovers his infidelity, she pens a vindictive memoir accusing him of being a Russian spy. With the United States caught up in investigations of Communist activity led by Senator Joseph McCarthy, Ringold's career is finished.

Toni Morrison's *Paradise* creates the entire history of a fictional all-black town. Ruby, Oklahoma, is founded in the 1800's by 158 freed slaves with the conviction that they can be self-sufficient and prosperous. Ruby develops into such an absolutely independent town that eventually even death passes it by. All begins to come apart during the 1960's, when even Ruby is struck by the nation's political and cultural upheaval.

Other important works of fiction published in 1998 included T. Coraghessan Boyle's *Riven Rock,* a recreation of the life of Stanley McCormick, the mad son of millionaire Cyrus McCormick. Russell Banks's *Cloudsplitter* recreates the life of John Brown, a leader of the U.S. *abolitionist* (antislavery) movement, in biblical proportions. John Irving's *A Widow for One Year* is a complex comedy about how four writers turn reality into fiction. Gore Vidal's *The Smithsonian Institution* is another of his complex and satirical examinations of history. It tells the story of a 13-year-old boy who discovers that the exhibits at the Smithsonian in Washington, D.C., come to life when the museum is not open. After glimpsing his future death in World War II (1939–1945), the boy goes on a quest to change the course of history. Lorrie Moore uses comedy to portray the difficulty of relationships, love, and family in contemporary America in the short-story colleciton *Birds of America*.

Definitive collections. The Library of America, a nonprofit organization in New York City that publishes American classics, continued its service to American literature in 1998. In addition to editions of the works of Gertrude Stein (1874–1946), Eudora Welty, and James Baldwin (1924–1987), the project published three novels by Charles Brockden Brown (1771–1810), whose works from the late 1700's are among America's foremost *Gothic writings,* romantic literature that explores the supernatural. The project continued to challenge the idea of what types of writing have contributed to American literature with the publication of a new anthology, *Reporting Vietnam: American Journalism 1959–1975*. The two-volume anthology includes articles from more than 80 journalists who covered the Vietnam War.

The collection documents the role journalism played in shaping the war and displays the power and literary worth of these nonfiction writers.

The National Book Award for nonfiction was given to Edward Ball's first book, *Slaves in the Family*. The book grew out of his decision to find out what happened to his ancestor's slaves and their descendants. From documents about the plantation and interviews with descendants of owners and slaves, Ball constructed a narrative about the cultural impact of slavery.

Harold Bloom's *Shakespeare: The Invention of the Human* was one of the most talked-about nonfiction nominees of 1998. Bloom argues that William Shakespeare's immense popularity is the result of the playwright's creation of the first characters with convincing inner selves. In this massive volume, Bloom writes about each of Shakespeare's plays and places particular emphasis on two characters, Hamlet and Falstaff.

Three other books were nominated for the nonfiction award. Yaffa Eliach's *There Once Was a World: A 900-Year Chronicle of the Shtetl of Eishyshok* documents the life of a Jewish community in Lithuania. The author, one of the few Jews in the town who escaped a Nazi massacre in 1941, spent 17 years recreating "nearly a millennium of vibrant Jewish life [that] had been reduced to stark images of victimization and death." Henry Mayer's *All on Fire: William Lloyd Garrison and the Abolition of American Slavery* is a comprehensive biography of a key figure in the abolitionist movement and a portrait of the United States before the Civil War (1861–1865). Beth Kephart's *A Slant of Sun: One Child's Courage* is the story of the author's struggle to help her young son Jeremy, who has a developmental disorder. The book describes Kephart's struggle first to get a diagnosis and then find ways to help Jeremy.

Literary memoirs. The year was notable for memoirs that attempted to change perceptions of famous literary men. During the summer, two separate memoirs of *The New Yorker* magazine's famed editor William Shawn were published. Shawn had gone down in history as a reserved and tactful man, whose editorial skill and insight made *The New Yorker* into one of the most important U.S. literary magazines. Ved Mehta was one of the staff writers closest to Shawn. In *Remembering Mr. Shawn's New Yorker: The Invisible Art of Editing,* Mehta presents Shawn as presiding lovingly over both the magazine and his family at home. A startlingly different picture is presented in Lillian Ross's *Here But Not Here: A Love Story,* which details her 40-year relationship with Shawn. In her portrait, Shawn is a man trapped in a marriage as well as a job that he despises.

Another tell-all memoir is Joyce Maynard's *At Home in the World,* an account of her relationship with J. D. Salinger, the notoriously reclusive author of *The Catcher in the Rye*. In 1972, after seeing a piece of the Yale freshman's writing, Salinger invites her to his house for the weekend. Their relationship ends abruptly a year later. The memoir is essentially a tale of opposing characters. Maynard is interested in documenting her life, while Salinger opposes using his own life in his fiction.

Summer of Deliverance is Christopher Dickey's memoir of his father, James Dickey (1923–1997). It is the tale of a writer of great talent, consumed by alcoholism and troubled relationships. Christopher Dickey relates the story of his father's life with sadness, but without anger.

Two notable anniversaries. In 1998, *The Hudson Review* celebrated its 50th anniversary and *The New York Review of Books* its 35th. *The Hudson Review*, founded in 1948 by Joseph Bennett and Frederick Morgan, published some of the greatest writers of the century—including Wallace Stevens (1879–1955), T. S. Eliot (1888–1965), and Saul Bellow. Morgan stepped down in 1998 after 50 years as editor. *The New York Review* was founded in 1963, after a printer's strike put the book pages of the daily newspapers on hold. It quickly became, and remained, one of the most influential literary journals in the United States.   □ Robert Messenger

See also **Literature, World; Poetry.**

Literature, World.
The 1998 Nobel Prize for literature was awarded to Jose Saramago, the first Portuguese writer to be so honored. His most recent novel in English translation, *Blindness*, is a complex political and social allegory, which critics often compared to *1984* by British writer George Orwell (1903–1950) and *The Plague* by French writer Albert Camus (1913–1960).

The United Kingdom and Ireland. British poet laureate Ted Hughes won the 1997 Whitbread Book of the Year Award in January 1998 for *Tales from Ovid*, loose translations of *Metamorphoses*, the ancient Greek poet's stories of gods and heroes. (The Whitbread awards recognize works published in the United Kingdom or Ireland.) Hughes also published the controversial, often touching *Birthday Letters*, a series of poems written to his late wife, American poet Sylvia Plath, who committed suicide in 1963. Many feminist critics had blamed him for her severe depression and death. Hughes died on Oct. 28, 1998.

Pauline Melville's lush and sensual novel, *The Ventriloquist's Tale*, won the 1997 Whitbread First Novel Award. The story relates the consequences of a love affair between a brother and sister in Guyana. The Whitbread Novel of the Year Award went to Jim Crace's comparably passionate and hallucinatory *Quarantine*, an unusual account of Jesus Christ's 40 days of fasting in the wilderness.

Ian McEwan's *Amsterdam,* which won the 1998 Booker Prize, is a satire about a composer trying to finish a "Millennial Symphony" and a journalist trying to decide whether to expose the sexual indiscretions of a politician. Critics noted that *Amsterdam*'s smoothness and wit recall the work of British satirist Evelyn Waugh (1903–1966). (The Booker Prize recognizes writers from the Commonwealth and other former British colonies.) Other highly regarded English novels included Beryl Bainbridge's *Master Georgie*, an elegant account of a photographer and his entourage confronting the violence of the Crimean War (1853–1856) and Rose Tremain's *The Way I Found Her,* in which a young English boy in Paris is drawn to the sensuality of a Russian immigrant novelist.

Scottish writer Irvine Welsh followed up his controversial *Trainspotting* (1993) with *Filth,* a black-humored novel about a degenerate policeman. Booker-nominated *The Restraint of Beasts* by Scottish writer Magnus Mills follows the misadventures of a trio of fence builders. This first novel by a former bus driver earned praise from American novelist Thomas Pynchon, who called it a "demented, deadpan-comic wonder." From Ireland, renowned writer Seamus Heaney brought out *Opened Ground: Poems 1966–1996.*

Other English-language writers. Among the year's most unusual and beautifully written novels was Murray Bail's *Eucalyptus.* Set in his native Australia, this exquisitely composed novel creates a fairy-tale atmosphere. A reclusive father agrees to marry off his beautiful daughter to the man who can identify the 200 or so species of eucalyptus on his property. Canada's leading short-story writer, Alice Munro, published a new collection, *The Love of a Good Woman.* Courtship and love, as well as loss and stoicism, lie at the heart of the stories that take up the relations between daughters and fathers, the inner life of a grandmother, and even the death of a small-town optometrist. With this latest collection, many critics heralded Munro for being at the top of her form.

Translations of past writers. The Library of Latin America, a series published by Oxford University Press, had in recent years brought out translations of works by Brazil's witty and ironic novelist Joachim Maria Machado de Assis (1839–1908). A new edition of *Quincas Borba,* translated by Gregory Rabassa, was added to the collection in 1998. In the novel, a mad philosopher dies, leaving his dog to a friend who soon inherits a fortune, falls in love with a married woman, and ends by thinking he is the French emperor Napoleon III.

The works of Argentina's Jorge Luis Borges (1899–1986) also began to be freshly translated into English in 1998. The first volume, *Collected Fictions,* gathers fairy tales and fantasies. In "Tlon, Uqbar, Orbis Tertius," Borges invents a fictional

Anne Frank (third from right), whose famous diary recorded her family's attempt to hide from the Nazis during World War II (1939–1945), became the focus of fierce debate in 1998. Newly discovered pages revealing her attitude toward her parents' strained relationship changed the tone of the work.

encyclopedia that leads to a body of literature describing another world. Critics frequently liken Borges to Czech writer Franz Kafka (1883–1924). Two of Kafka's greatest novels, *The Castle* and *The Trial,* also received fresh, careful translations in 1998—the former by Mark Harman and the latter by Breon Mitchell.

Eugenio Montale: Collected Poems 1920–1954, translated by Jonathan Galassi, is a hefty, definitive anthology of works by the Italian poet Montale (1896–1981). The edition includes facing-page Italian versions of each poem and an essay and clarifying notes by Galassi.

Martin McLaughlin revised a translation of *The Path to the Spider's Nests,* a novel by Italo Calvino (1923–1985), one of Italy's greatest modern writers. New translations of the works by French writer Georges Perec (1936–1982), Calvino's close friend, were published in 1998 in the United States, where Perec's work is highly valued by critics and readers alike. John Sturrock edited and translated Perec's *Species of Spaces and Other Pieces,* which includes the winsome "Some of the Things I Really Must Do Before I Die" and "Brief Notes on the Art and Manner of Arranging One's Books."

Michael Hofmann offered a new translation of *The Tale of the 1002nd Night,* the last novel of Austrian Joseph Roth (1894–1939). The story of a woman given a rope of pearls by the visiting

Shah of Persia gradually becomes a fable about the decline of civilization before the rise of totalitarian governments in Europe in the 1930's.

Translations of modern works. Umberto Eco brought out the genial *Serendipities: Language and Lunacy,* a series of essays about how "unanticipated truths" can emerge from mistaken beliefs. Michel Tournier, arguably France's finest living novelist, published a collection of essays, *The Mirror of Ideas,* reflections on opposites and pairs, such as the fork and the spoon, derision and celebration. Spain's Julian Rios, known for demanding, pun-filled novels, combined the essay with the romance in *Loves That Bind,* a playful book in which 26 letters from a painter to his girlfriend celebrate such heroines of fiction as the title character of Raymond Queneau's *Zazie* (1959) and Daisy Buchanan from F. Scott Fitzgerald's *The Great Gatsby* (1925).

Israeli writer Savyon Liebrecht's superb *Apples from the Desert* collects a dozen stories about the conflict between generations in modern-day Israel concerning the legacy of the Holocaust, Nazi Germany's persecution and extermination of Jews during World War II (1939–1945). Israeli novelist Aharon Appelfeld, in *The Conversion,* imagines how a young Jew in the early 1900's in Austria chooses to convert to Christianity, with hopes for social acceptance and professional success. Instead, he finds an unexpected resurgence of his Judaism in the face of anti-Jewish laws and sentiments.

Alexander Solzhenitsyn, the Russian writer best known for revealing the harsh realities of the Soviet Union, continued his "Red Wheel" series with *November 1916: The Second Knot of the Red Wheel.* Many critics noted that in his continued exploration of Russian society before the 1917 Communist revolution, Soltzhenitsyn could no longer escape the frequent charges of being too wordy.

Anne Frank revisited. In 1998, a heated debate arose over five previously unpublished pages from the diary of Anne Frank (1929–1945), a Jewish girl who chronicled her family's effort to hide in Amsterdam from the Nazis. Her father, the only member of the family to survive the Holocaust, published her diary in 1947. He reportedly removed pages that contain an unflattering account of her parents' relationship, and he later gave those pages to a friend. In *Anne Frank: The Biography,* a 1998 publication, the author Melissa Muller paraphrased the entries, and in August, a Dutch newspaper printed excerpts from them. A controversy over who could legally print the texts sparked a debate over whether the memory of the young Holocaust victim was being exploited.

☐ Michael Dirda

See also **Literature for children; Literature, American; Nobel Prizes; Poetry.**

Lithuania.
On Jan. 4, 1998, Lithuanian voters narrowly elected Valdas Adamkus, a Lithuanian-American, as their new president. Adamkus defeated Arturas Paulauskas, who was supported by Lithuania's Communists, by just over 10,000 votes. Paulauskas had won the first round of voting on Dec. 21, 1997, with 45 percent of the vote, just 5 percent short of outright victory. Adamkus was able to close the gap by winning the support of parliamentary speaker Vytautas Landsbergis, who had finished third in the balloting, while Paulauskas proved unable to broaden his support.

Adamkus, 71, took office on Feb. 26, 1998. He asked Gediminas Vagnorius to remain in office as prime minister, but reduced the number of cabinet ministries from 17 to 14. In July, Adamkus refused to sign into law a measure that would have barred former Soviet-era KGB agents from holding government posts. (The KGB was the secret police agency of the Soviet Union, of which Lithuania was a republic from 1940 to 1991.) Adamkus called the law unconstitutional and urged Lithuanians to set aside the lingering mistrust and resentment created by 50 years of Soviet rule. Parliamentary leaders agreed to postpone enactment of the legislation until 1999 in the hopes of reaching a compromise.

☐ Steven L. Solnick

See also **People in the news** (Adamkus, Valdas).

Los Angeles.
On May 26, 1998, the Los Angeles City Council approved a $4.1-billion budget. The budget included additional funds for the city's fire department and the city attorney's office. For the first time since 1993, the city provided no extra funding for hiring additional police officers. On June 29, 1998, the Los Angeles County Board of Supervisors approved a $13.2-billion budget that included the addition of about 2,700 new county jobs.

Population growth. A study released in May 1998 by the Southern California Association of Governments projected that the population of Los Angeles would increase 34 percent to nearly 5 million residents by 2020. The study projected a population of 22.35 million people, a 43-percent increase, in the same time period in the southern California counties of Imperial, Los Angeles, Orange, Riverside, San Bernardino, and Ventura. The most dramatic population increase was projected for Los Angeles County, which is expected to grow to 12.24 million people by 2020.

Construction projects. Ground was broken in March 1998 for a new downtown sports arena and entertainment center. The $300-million Staples Center was projected to open in late 1999. Organizers claimed the center would be used for more than 200 sports and entertainment events annually, including Los Angeles Lakers basketball games, Los Angeles Kings hockey games, concerts, the Grammy Awards, and national political conventions.

Groundbreaking for a second highly anticipated construction project was postponed in mid-1998. In August, organizers of the Frank O. Gehry-designed Walt Disney Concert Hall in downtown Los Angeles announced that construction would be delayed six months, partly due to new building codes requiring structures to be more earthquake resistant. Completion of the concert hall, which is to be part of a reinvigorated downtown, was expected in 2002.

Los Angeles subway system. The Los Angeles County Metropolitan Transportation Authority (MTA) in January 1998 suspended plans to extend the existing 6.5-mile (10.4-kilometer) long subway service 3.7 miles (5.9 kilometers) east of the city into East Los Angeles and 2.3 miles (3.7 kilometers) farther west of the downtown area.

Meanwhile, construction continued in 1998 on two other subway extension projects. A 4.6-mile (7.4-kilometer) extension from downtown Los Angeles to Hollywood was scheduled to open in 1999. A 6.3-mile (10-kilometer) extension from Hollywood to the San Fernando Valley was scheduled to open in 2000.

The MTA reported in late 1998 that the cost of the subway project was $4.503 billion, 12.3 percent over the original budget of 4.007 billion.

Trade. A decrease in exports, spurred by the Asian economic crisis, was expected to adversely affect southern California's international business sector in 1998. The Los Angeles Economic Development Corporation projected in May that the total value of two-way trade at the Los Angeles Customs District, which includes all the ports and airports in the Los Angeles metropolitan area, would increase 2.3 percent to $190 billion. Imports were estimated to increase 8.5 percent to $121.3 billion, while exports were projected to decrease 7.5 percent to $68.7 billion. The projected decline was only the third since 1980.

Ex-mayors die. Sam Yorty, who was elected mayor in 1961 and served three terms, died on June 5, 1998. He was considered a driving force behind the Los Angeles Convention Center. In 1972, he staged an unsuccessful bid for the Democratic nomination for president.

Thomas Bradley, who defeated Yorty for mayor in 1973, died on Sept. 29, 1998. He was the first African American mayor of Los Angeles and the only Los Angeles mayor ever elected five times. Bradley was widely viewed as a national force in politics, but lost both his 1982 and 1986 attempts at the California governorship. In 1993, Bradley left office after declining to seek a sixth term. □ Margaret A. Kilgore

See also **City.**

Magazine. Magazines aimed at specialized interests dominated the market in new titles and fueled the boom in magazine publishing, according to a March 1998 report on the United States magazine industry. The report, by journalism professor Samir A. Husni of the University of Mississippi, noted that most of the 852 magazines that debuted in 1997 were publications tailored to a narrow audience. Sex was the most popular focus of the new magazines, with 110 titles.

In 1998, readers could choose from almost 5,200 U.S. magazines, more than twice the number available in the late 1980's. Magazine advertising revenues in 1997 jumped 13 percent, the biggest increase since 1984, according to the Magazine Publishers of America, a trade group in New York City. Despite the boom, Husni noted, half of all new magazines failed within one year because of low consumer interest and sales.

Brill's Content debuted in June 1998 to considerable publicity. Founded by Steven Brill, originator of the Court TV cable television channel, the new publication was a behind-the-scenes guide to the news media. The first issue included an interview in which Kenneth Starr, the independent counsel investigating President Bill Clinton, admitted leaking information to reporters. Even more controversial was a report cataloging alleged errors by newspapers and networks in

their initial coverage of the Monica Lewinsky story. The story, which surfaced in the media in January, concerned allegations about the nature of Clinton's relationship with Lewinsky, a former White House intern. Other journalists accused Brill of dishonesty and attacked him for identifying anonymous sources quoted in their reports.

American Family Publishers (AFP), a magazine subscription service based in Tampa, Florida, agreed in March to pay $2 million to settle charges by 32 states and the District of Columbia that AFP used deceptive practices in selling subscriptions. The company also agreed to stop telling people that they had won AFP's sweepstakes unless they had actually done so. State officials had charged that AFP's promotional material led people to believe that buying a magazine raised their chances of winning the sweepstakes. In November, the state of Florida filed similar charges against AFP and included media giant Time Warner, which owns half of AFP, in the suit.

Staff changes. Tina Brown, editor-in-chief of *The New Yorker* magazine for six years, resigned in July. She became chairman of a new media company. David Remnick, a writer for *The New Yorker* since 1992 and a 1994 Pulitzer Prize winner, succeeded Brown. □ Michael Woods

Maine. See **State government.**

Malawi. See **Africa.**

Malaysia struggled in 1998 with economic turmoil and political scandal. A power struggle over economic reforms led to the ouster of Deputy Prime Minister Anwar Ibrahim.

Malaysia sank into its first recession in 13 years in 1998 after the country's economy contracted for a second consecutive quarter. The country's *gross domestic product* (the value of all goods and services produced in a country during a given year) shrank 6.8 percent from 1997. For most of the 1990's, Malaysia's gross domestic product had expanded at an annual rate of 8 percent.

The contraction came as a surprise to economists, who had expected an economic slowdown but not recession. The construction sector—a key barometer of economic health—was down by 22 percent in the second quarter of 1998. It had grown 12 percent during the same time in 1997. During that same period, Malaysia's currency, the ringgit, lost 40 percent of its value against the dollar, and the stock market lost 75 percent of its total worth.

Political ouster. Prime Minister Mahathir bin Mohammad resisted efforts by his deputy prime minister and finance minister, Anwar Ibrahim, to cut government costs and restructure the economy. Mahathir favored isolating Malaysia's economy from the pressures of international finance

Illegal Indonesian immigrants are deported in March 1998 from Malaysia, which had relied on foreign workers before its economy faltered in late 1997. Malaysia announced that it would not renew work permits for as many as 850,000 foreign workers.

and boosting government spending on expensive projects. Anwar, however, advocated tight fiscal policies and courted foreign investors.

The relationship between Mahathir and Anwar, who had been widely regarded as the prime minister's successor, deteriorated as the Asian financial crisis devastated Malaysia's economy. In June, Mahathir appointed former finance minister Daim Zainuddin as a special economic adviser. On September 2, Mahathir dismissed Anwar, saying that he was unfit to be leader of Malaysia. Two weeks later, Anwar was arrested on corruption and morals charges.

Protests. Anwar's arrest touched off massive protests against the government. Tens of thousands of people marched through the streets of Kuala Lumpur, the capital, in October calling for the resignation of Mahathir. World leaders denounced Mahathir's treatment of Anwar, who went on trial in November.

Human rights. In August, Lim Guan Eng, an opposition member of parliament, was imprisoned after questioning the government's decision not to press rape charges against a politician. Human rights groups criticized Malaysia's use of laws to intimidate those who expressed dissenting opinions.   □ Henry S. Bradsher

See also **Asia** (Facts in brief table); **Economics** Special Report: **Asian Economic Crisis.**

Manufacturing. A worldwide economic crisis threatened the strength of factories in the United States in 1998. U.S. manufacturing, which posted strong gains in early 1998, was weakened by the global economic contagion late in the year.

United States exporters lost business in foreign markets due to severe turmoil in many Asian economies. Increasingly, U.S. manufacturers were forced to compete with Asian businesses that were producing inexpensive products for the U.S. market. As a result, U.S. manufacturers experienced a slowdown in output of goods, including chemicals, computer parts, and steel. Orders for farm machinery fell, as a decrease in foreign demand left the U.S. farm sector with surplus crops and livestock, which in turn cut farm earnings.

The economic downturns spread to cover half the world's population. The crisis deeply affected emerging-market nations, as well as Japan, the world's second-largest economy and a major competitor to U.S. factories. The economic distress threatened to engulf remaining industrialized nations in Europe and North America.

Monetary union. Some experts in 1998 predicted that the creation of a single European currency, called the euro, in 1999 would create new market opportunities. The euro replaced other forms of currency circulated in individual European Union (EU) nations on Jan. 1, 1999. The EU is an organization of 15 Western Europe nations that promotes cooperation among its members.

Y2K dilemma. Manufacturers scrambled to protect their computer systems from a potentially devastating situation known as the Year 2000 (Y2K) problem. Many older computers used in businesses and government in 1998 were originally programmed to read only the last two digits of a year. As a result, these computers might misread 2000 as 1900 and not function properly. Companies worldwide in 1998 continued work to head off the risk that crucial computer systems could fail on Jan. 1, 2000. Experts maintained that such a failure would interfere with all types of businesses.

Fighting the Y2K problem cost U.S. manufacturers billions of dollars in 1998. Some businesses hired computer programmers to rewrite millions of lines of command code and install new software. Others bought new computer systems. Both solutions spurred high-technology manufacturing and left upgraded buyers with improvements that could help them run their businesses more efficiently for many years.

Manufacturer's survey. A widely watched index of industrial activity showed that the U.S. factory sector slumped in 1998. The National Association of Purchasing Management (NAPM) polls more than 300 U.S. manufacturers monthly about new orders, employment, cost of materials, delivery problems, and other factors. Index values about 50 percent mean a growing economy. Values below 50 percent indicate that the factory sector is contracting. In January, the NAPM index reading was 52.4. The NAPM index reached a high of 54.8 in March before dropping to 46.8 in November.

The broader U.S. economy grew solidly for most of 1998, propelled by consumer spending and growth in the service sector. The NAPM data, however, implied that more consumer purchases during the year were for goods made overseas rather than by U.S. factories.

Gross domestic product. The U.S. gross domestic product (GDP)—the total value of goods and services produced in the United States in a year—grew at a rate of 5.5 percent in the January-March quarter of 1998. Part of that growth, however, was a buildup of extra inventories as factories produced more products than consumers purchased. With extra inventory, slumping exports, and import competition, the GDP slowed to just a 1.8-percent growth pace in the April-June quarter. The economy improved to a 3.3-percent growth rate in the July-September quarter, but industrial output fell in four of five months from June through October, as manufacturing continued to weaken. The U.S. govern-

ment reported that usage of industrial capacity in October fell to its lowest level since 1992.

Yearlong problems. Workers at General Motors (GM), the largest automaker in North America, went on strike in June 1998. The 54-day strike by members of the United Auto Workers union stopped production at GM plants across North America.

In other job markets in the United States, oil prices plummeted during 1998, resulting in high savings for energy consumers. The decrease weakened an industry that responded to dwindling profits by cutting back on oil drilling. Prices fell for farm, forestry, and mining products. Prices also dipped for secondary materials, including leather, plywood, and steel, making it harder for producers to pay bills or order more equipment.

A severe drought in the South in spring and early summer touched off fires that burned out of control in Florida, devastating vast acres of farmland, and destroying cotton fields and livestock in Texas. The harsh weather cycle brought tornadoes, hurricanes, and floods to many states, reducing the income of many people, especially in agricultural markets.

Cigarette settlement. Tobacco manufacturers in the United States and the attorneys general of 46 states agreed to a deal in November that settled lawsuits against the various U.S. tobacco companies. Those companies agreed to pay the 46 states a total of $206 billion over a 25-year period, beginning in 2000. Throughout 1998, several states had settled individual lawsuits to recover state health-care costs related to smoking. The U.S. Congress in 1998 had failed to pass a 25-year, $368-billion national tobacco settlement proposed in 1997.

Computer lawsuit. The U.S. Justice Department and attorneys general of 20 states launched a federal trial on Oct. 19, 1998, to determine whether Microsoft Corporation of Redmond, Washington, had violated antitrust laws by trying to gain complete control over the computer marketplace by hampering competition. Attorneys for Microsoft, a leading maker of computer software, denied the allegations.

The Justice Department and attorneys general filed a lawsuit in May alleging that Microsoft had violated antitrust laws designed to prevent a business from developing too much power over competitors. If the court ruled against Microsoft, it could lead to a partial break-up of one of the biggest manufacturers in history.

☐ John D. Boyd

See also **Economics; Economics** Special Report: **Asian Economic Crisis; International Trade.**

Maryland. See **State government.**

Massachusetts. See **State government.**

Mauritania. See **Africa.**

Mauritius. The ruling Labor Party on April 5, 1998, won a special parliamentary election viewed as the first test of that party's popularity since its overwhelming victory in general elections in 1995. In a contest to fill a vacant seat in the National Assembly, Labor candidate Satish Faugoo collected 41.5 percent of the vote, compared with 37.1 percent for former Prime Minister Sir Aneerood Jugnauth of the Militant Socialist Movement (MSM).

The election also served as a test of Labor's ability to win votes without the support of the Mauritian Militant Movement, with which it was allied in the 1995 election. The alliance collapsed in June 1997. Although Mauritian Prime Minister Navinchandra Ramgoolam declared Labor's satisfaction with the April 1998 election results, independent analysts pointed out that the Labor Party's support in that district was down from the 63 percent it had received in 1995.

Economic growth. In May 1998, the African Development Bank (AfDB) praised Mauritius for its success in adapting its manufacturing industry to ensure sustained economic growth well into the 2000's. The AfDB is an international lending and investment organization composed mainly of African states. In an attempt to minimize its dependence on agricultural exports, especially sugar, Mauritius has focused on such manufactured exports as textiles, clothing, canned fish, and watches. However, competition from cheaper Asian goods in the world market slowed the country's economic momentum in late 1998. In September, the United Nations' annual Human Development Index, which ranks countries on the basis of life expectancy, income, and education, ranked Mauritius 61st, ahead of such countries as China, Saudi Arabia, and South Africa.

Foreign affairs. Mauritius raised the issue of the ownership of the Chagos Archipelago, an island group in the Indian Ocean northeast of Mauritius, at an annual summit of ministers from African, Caribbean, and Pacific nations and the European Union held in April in Mauritius. Officially known as the British Indian Ocean Territory (BIOT), the islands, which were annexed by the United Kingdom in 1810, were claimed by Mauritius at the meeting.

In 1966, the British government leased one of the islands, Diego Garcia, to the United States for 50 years for use as a military base. Under the terms of the lease, all residents of the BIOT were forced from their houses. Many of the exiles settled in Mauritius. The United Kingdom said it would give the BIOT to Mauritius if the United States, which refuses to allow resettlement anywhere in the archipelago, chooses not to renew its lease in 2016. ☐ Simon Baynham

See also **Africa** (Facts in brief table).

Medicine. In April 1998, scientists at the National Cancer Institute (NCI), an agency of the National Institutes of Health in Bethesda, Maryland, announced the first strong evidence that breast cancer can be prevented in women at high risk for the disease. The encouraging evidence came from a six-year study involving the drug tamoxifen and 13,388 healthy but high-risk women, including those with a family history of breast cancer and those who had previously been diagnosed with precancerous breast tissue. Because breast cancer is most common in women over age 60, such women were also included in the study. Approximately half the women were given tamoxifen. The other half received a *placebo* (an inactive substance).

The researchers concluded that tamoxifen reduced the risk of breast cancer in susceptible women by 45 percent. They also found that the drug reduced the risk of bone fractures of the hip, wrist, and spine. This evidence helped prompt the U.S. Food and Drug Administration in October to approve the use of tamoxifen to prevent breast cancer.

Despite the encouraging news about tamoxifen, experts cautioned that the drug might cause serious side effects in some women. The NCI study found that tamoxifen increased the risk of three rare but potentially life-threatening health problems—*endometrial cancer* (cancer of the lining of the uterus), *pulmonary embolism* (blood clots in the lungs), and blood clots in major veins.

Heart disease. Two teams of scientists reported in 1998 that new treatments can stimulate the growth of blood vessels to the heart in patients with blocked coronary arteries. Such blockages, caused by the build-up of cholesterol and other material, are the underlying cause of most heart attacks. Growing new blood vessels would increase blood supply to the heart and provide an alternative to such major surgical procedures as coronary bypass surgery.

In February, scientists at the Fulda Medical Center in Fulda, Germany, announced that a genetically engineered protein, FGF-1, injected directly into the heart, grew new blood vessels to bypass blocked vessels in all 20 patients on which it was tried. In addition, all the patients were alive and in better health three years after the procedure. FGF-1 is a type of "growth factor" that instructs body cells to multiply.

In April, a research team at Hennepin County Medical Center in Minneapolis, Minnesota, reported that injections of another growth factor, VEGF, into the heart stimulated new coronary blood vessels to grow in 15 patients. In addition, 13 of the patients reported less *angina* (chest pain that occurs when blocked coronary arteries cannot carry enough blood to the heart).

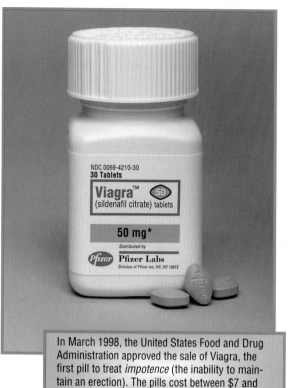

In March 1998, the United States Food and Drug Administration approved the sale of Viagra, the first pill to treat *impotence* (the inability to maintain an erection). The pills cost between $7 and $10 per tablet.

of genetic information) of *Mycobacterium tuberculosis,* the microbe that causes about 3 million deaths each year from tuberculosis. The tuberculosis bacterium was the most deadly of a number of disease-causing microbes that have had their genomes sequenced since 1995. The decoding of the tuberculosis genome could eventually result in new drugs and vaccines for the disease.

Human genome. In May 1998, the Institute for Genomic Research (TIGR), a genetics research organization in Rockville, Maryland, and Perkin-Elmer Corporation, a scientific instrument company in Norwalk, Connecticut, announced a joint project to sequence virtually the entire human genome within three years at a cost of approximately $200 million. The schedule was faster and cheaper than the U.S. government's program, begun in 1990, to decipher all the human genes by 2005 for a cost of $3 billion. In September 1998, the government announced a revised schedule to finish its sequencing effort by 2003.

TIGR and Perkin-Elmer officials said the project would use new scientific approaches and a new generation of sequencing machines developed by Perkin-Elmer. Drug companies were anxious to learn the make-up of disease-causing genes to help them design drugs to fight these diseases. □ Michael Woods

See also **Drugs; Public health and safety.**

Mental health. People who are discharged from psychiatric hospitals and who do not abuse alcohol or drugs are no more likely than other members of their communities to behave violently, according to a study published in May 1998. Researchers led by sociologist Henry J. Steadman from Policy Research Associates in Delmar, New York, conducted the study to clarify decades of confusion about alleged violence among discharged mental-health patients.

In the 1950's and 1960's, many researchers had concluded that patients discharged from psychiatric hospitals were no more violence-prone than other people. Studies in the 1970's and 1980's, however, concluded that such patients were more likely to behave violently. The latter findings were central to ongoing debates about whether transitional living arrangements for discharged mental patients posed risks for communities.

Steadman's research team monitored the behavior of 1,136 patients for a year after being discharged from psychiatric hospitals in Pittsburgh, Pennsylvania; Kansas City, Missouri; and Worcester, Massachusetts. Every 10 weeks, researchers checked police and hospital records and interviewed the former patients, family members, friends, or other people in regular contact with the former patients. The researchers found that alcohol and drug abuse was a significant factor in

Growing tissue replacements. Researchers at the University of Wisconsin at Madison and Johns Hopkins University in Baltimore independently announced in November that they had for the first time isolated human primordial stem cells and grown them in the laboratory. Primordial stem cells are unspecialized cells that have the ability to produce any of the different types of specialized cells that make up the body. The researchers harvested the stem cells from human *embryos* (organisms at an early stage of development before birth). The embryos were obtained from fertility clinics with the consent of the couples who donated them to the clinics.

The scientists said that by adding certain hormones and chemicals to the stem cells in laboratory cultures, they believed they would be able to direct the cells to grow any kind of human cell, including brain, heart, liver, and kidney cells. These specialized cells, in turn, could be used to replace damaged or diseased tissue in the various organs of the body. The scientists cautioned that practical applications of their research would be several years away.

TB genome. In June, an international collaboration led by scientists at the Sanger Centre near Cambridge, England, and the Pasteur Institute in Paris, France, said they had *sequenced* (decoded) the complete *genome* (total amount

predicting violent behavior. In fact, former patients who did abuse such substances were more violence-prone than other nonpatients who also had chemical abuse problems. Steadman said that the newly identified role of substance abuse made an important distinction that should enable health-care workers to determine the risks of violent behaviors in mental health patients.

Schizophrenia. Fewer than half of the individuals diagnosed with schizophrenia receive adequate doses of medication or other treatment to help control their symptoms, according to a March 1998 report. The findings were announced by the Schizophrenia Patient Outcomes Research Team (PORT), a panel of mental health experts convened in 1992 by the National Institute of Mental Health (NIMH), a federal research organization in Bethesda, Maryland, and the U.S. Agency for Health Care Policy and Research in Washington, D.C.

Schizophrenia is a severe form of mental illness that includes such symptoms as confusing thought patterns, hallucinations, and delusions. In PORT's 1998 study, the specialists published recommendations for treatment of schizophrenia based on an exhaustive review of published research. The group then conducted interviews with more than 700 patients with the disorder and reviewed their medical records. PORT concluded that actual treatment falls short of their recommendations, particularly in such areas as psychological and vocational counseling.

Mental distress. The U.S. Centers for Disease Control and Prevention (CDC) in Atlanta, Georgia, reported in May that almost 9 percent of people in the United States consider themselves to be in poor mental health for 14 or more days each month. In the study, CDC researchers analyzed data from 436,107 people contacted in a three-year telephone survey. The study revealed particularly high levels of distress among women in New York, Nevada, Colorado, and Kentucky. Mental distress levels were highest in all locations among people who made less than $15,000 annually or were 18 to 24 years old, unemployed, or separated or divorced.

PMS. In April, researchers at Allegheny University of the Health Sciences in Philadelphia published information on the biochemical process that can cause the anxiety, depression, and mood swings of premenstrual syndrome (PMS). PMS is a common disorder with a variety of symptoms that affects many women three to five days before the beginning of their menstrual cycle.

The Allegheny team, led by microbiologist Sheryl S. Smith, reported that the biochemical changes that cause PMS are similar to those that cause withdrawal symptoms in people with a dependence on alcohol or other substances. During most of the second half of the menstrual cycle, levels of the hormone progesterone are very high. Allopregnanolone, a chemical that the body creates from progesterone, interacts with certain cells in the brain to cause a sedating effect. At the end of the menstrual cycle, the levels of progesterone and allopregnanolone plummet.

In their experiments, Smith's team interfered with the chemical interactions in the brains of rats to recreate the rapid chemical changes associated with menstruation. They concluded that the symptoms of PMS are a kind of withdrawal anxiety. They also noted that the same biochemical changes occur after childbirth and may account for the withdrawal-like symptoms referred to as postpartum depression. The scientists said their research could lead to better treatment for PMS.

The more homework students get and complete, especially in grades 6 through 12, the better they do in school, researchers reported in March. In a study led by psychologist Harris Cooper of the University of Missouri in Columbia, researchers collected the data from more than 700 groups, each consisting of a teacher, a student, and at least one parent. Cooper's team found that the students who received and completed the most homework generally had higher grades and better scores on standardized tests.

☐ Michael Woods

Mexico. The gubernatorial elections in Mexico in 1998 provided evidence that the country was making progress in opening its political process to competition among three major parties. The long-dominant Institutional Revolutionary Party (PRI) continued to control 23 of Mexico's 31 governorships, but observers noted changes within the party. Many PRI gubernatorial candidates openly addressed the need to enact reforms. In some instances, PRI candidates were selected in primary elections, rather than being picked by party bosses. Moreover, the PRI showed increased sensitivity to public demands. In 1998, the party replaced its own governors in two states, Chiapas and Morelos, in response to allegations that the leaders had condoned police brutality.

Election results. In July, the Democratic Revolutionary Party (PRD) won the state house—its first gubernatorial victory—in Zacatecas. The victory added to the national powerbase of the left-wing party of Cuauhtemoc Cardenas Solorzano, the mayor of Mexico City, the capital. In another first, the candidate for the right-wing National Action Party (PAN) was elected governor of Aguascalientes. In November, a candidate representing a coalition of three opposition parties—the PRD, the Mexican Green Ecology Party, and the Worker's Party—was elected governor of Tlaxcala.

In January 1998, tens of thousands of people gather at the Plaza de la Constitucion in Mexico City to protest the December 1997 massacre of 45 Tzotzil Indians, allegedly by progovernment paramilitary troops in the Mexican state of Chiapas.

PRI candidates won in the remaining six gubernatorial elections of 1998. Oaxaca was the only state where an election was seriously challenged. PRD leaders alleged that a faulty computer allowed the PRI to rob the opposition party of votes.

Massacre. The December 1997 killing of 45 Tzotzil Indians in the village of Acteal, Chiapas, proved to be a lightning rod for dissent in 1998. Chiapas was the site of a bloody 1994 uprising of the Zapatista National Liberation Army (EZLN), which brought global attention to the long-standing grievances of Mexico's Indians. In January 1998, a report on the 1997 massacre blamed the attack on right-wing paramilitary forces that had been armed by local government authorities.

Some 100,000 people responded to the report by taking to the streets of Mexico City on Jan. 12, 1998, to demand the withdrawal of government troops from Chiapas. At a smaller protest in the Chiapas town of Ocosingo, police opened fire on demonstrators, killing an Indian woman and injuring her 2-year-old daughter and 17-year-old son. The shooting was videotaped.

Deportations. Many human rights groups accused Mexican authorities of making scapegoats of foreigners by blaming them for stirring up political unrest. In February, three Americans, including a member of a nonviolent organization called Pastors for Peace, were expelled from Chiapas.

The government also deported a French Roman Catholic priest who had worked in the country for 32 years, mostly in Acteal. In April, 12 human-rights observers from Belgium, Canada, Germany, Spain, and the United States were expelled as "threats to national security" after they witnessed 500 state and federal police officers raid a farming cooperative where Zapatista leaders had set up a local government. In May, 40 people from a group of 134 Italian human-rights observers were deported after they crossed a government checkpoint en route to the same farming cooperative. On May 11, the Mexican government tightened visa requirements for foreign observers, limiting the size of groups to 10 people and the length of their stay in Mexico to 10 days.

Drug sting. On May 18, U.S. authorities announced the indictment of three Mexican banks, scores of bankers, and several drug traffickers on money-laundering charges. A number of the Mexican citizens were arrested in Las Vegas, Nevada, where undercover agents had invited them to a party. The indictments were the culmination of a three-year undercover investigation, code-named "Operation Casablanca."

More than 100 people were arrested, including employees of 12 of Mexico's largest banks, employees of foreign banks, and operatives of Mexican and Colombian drug cartels. The U.S.

Federal Reserve Board responded to the indictments by suspending four Mexican banks and the Mexican branch of a Spanish bank from doing business in the United States, pending the adoption of stricter rules to deter money laundering.

On May 21, Mexican Attorney General Jorge Madrazo Cuellar protested the indictments, accusing the United States of violating Mexican sovereignty by failing to inform the Mexican government about the operation. United States officials, including President Bill Clinton, reassured the Mexican government that Operation Casablanca was not an indictment of Mexico itself or its entire banking system.

Swiss investigators issued a report in September that highlighted the role of Raul Salinas in protecting the flow of cocaine into the United States. Salinas, the older brother of former Mexican President Carlos Salinas de Gortari, reportedly made a fortune in protection money paid by drug traffickers. The Swiss also alleged that Raul Salinas channeled drug money into his brother's presidential campaign. As head of a federal food distribution agency, Raul Salinas reportedly commandeered government trucks and railroad cars to haul cocaine north without fear of interdiction by Mexico's army, coast guard, or federal police.

□ Nathan A. Haverstock

See also **Latin America** (Facts in brief table).

Miami. A state appeals court in Miami removed Mayor Xavier Suarez from office on March 11, 1998, and restored Joe Carollo to the position of mayor of Miami. Carollo, who became mayor upon winning a 1996 special election, won the majority of votes cast in the Nov. 4, 1997, election against Suarez, who had served as mayor from 1985 to 1993. However, a runoff election became necessary after absentee ballots reduced Carollo's vote share to under 50 percent. Suarez won the Nov. 13, 1997, runoff and took over as mayor two days later.

The appeals court ruled in March 1998 that thousands of absentee ballots cast for Suarez in the 1997 election had been fraudulent. The court declared Carollo the legitimate mayor, overturning an earlier circuit court ruling that had called for a new election. Carollo was sworn in for a four-year term on March 12. In November, Suarez filed a citizen's petition with the City Commission in an attempt to force a new election. The Miami-Dade County supervisor of elections ruled the petition invalid, however, saying that a large number of signatures on the petition were by people who did not live in Miami.

While in office, Suarez at times had displayed behavior that had led some observers to dub him "Mayor Loco." In one incident, he phoned the *Miami Herald* threatening to remove city adver-

Flamingos at Miami's MetroZoo take shelter against Hurricane Georges in one of the zoo's restrooms in September 1998. Zookeepers herded the birds into the building to protect them from the storm's high winds and heavy rains.

tisements from the newspaper unless the *Herald's* president was "a lot nicer to me, my people, my citizens, and my city." He later said the phone call "was mostly in jest."

Other government turmoil. The mayoral dispute was only one of several cases of government turmoil that rocked Miami in 1998. In January, James Burke, a commissioner of Miami-Dade County, was indicted on federal bribery and money-laundering charges. He was accused of directing county bond business to Calvin Grigsby, owner of a crane-operating firm at the Port of Miami, in return for bribes. In June, former Miami port director Carmen Lunetta, Grigsby, and a second businessman were charged in a federal court with diverting more than $1 million of port money to personal use.

Mayor Carollo fired Jose Garcia-Pedrosa, city manager for Miami, in June. Pedrosa, who had been appointed by former Mayor Suarez, was Miami's fourth city manager in seven months. In August, Miami City Commissioner Humberto Hernandez, an ally of Suarez, was sentenced to up to one year in prison for covering up vote fraud in the November 1997 elections.

Publishing giant moves. In April 1998, Knight Ridder Incorporated, the second-largest newspaper publisher in the United States, announced that it was moving its corporate headquarters from Miami to San Jose, California. Miami officials, who were trying to promote Miami as an important center for international business, viewed the company's move as a major blow to the city's prestige. Knight Ridder continued to own the *Miami Herald* and *El Nuevo Herald,* a Spanish-language daily in Miami.

Gay victory. The Miami-Dade County Commission in December passed a law that banned discrimination against homosexuals in housing and employment. The law was similar to one that had been repealed by county voters in 1977 after a campaign led by singer Anita Bryant.

Baseball disappointment. Florida baseball fans were disappointed in 1998 when the Miami-based Florida Marlins, the 1997 World Series champions, ended the season in the cellar of the National League Eastern Division—52 games behind the division-winning Atlanta Braves. The Marlins' 54-108 win-loss record was the poorest finish ever for a defending World Series champion. Fans blamed team owner H. Wayne Huizenga for the dismal season. Huizenga, claiming that the team had lost $34 million in 1997, sold or traded most of the Marlins' highly paid star players after the 1997 season. In November 1998, Huizenga sold the team to commodities trader John Henry for $150 million.   □ Al Smuskiewicz

See also **City.**

Michigan. See **Detroit; State government.**

Middle East

Throughout 1998 there were a number of stand-offs between Iraqi President Saddam Hussein and United Nations (UN) arms inspectors, ending with military action against Iraq in December. The stalled Arab-Israeli peace process was revived in October but encountered serious new trouble before the end of the year. Meanwhile, Iran and Afghanistan almost went to war.

Attack on Iraq. On December 16, United States and British forces launched four days of air and missile strikes against Iraqi military and industrial sites after Richard Butler, chairman of the UN Special Commission (Unscom), accused Iraq of failing to cooperate with Unscom inspections of suspected weapons facilities. Unscom had attempted to account for and destroy any Iraqi chemical, biological, and nuclear capabilities, as well as Iraqi long-range missiles. The UN required Unscom to verify that Iraq was not capable of manufacturing long-range missiles or chemical, biological, or nuclear weapons before the UN would lift economic sanctions imposed on Iraq after Iraq's 1990 invasion of Kuwait.

The attack came after similar crises had been resolved in February and November 1998. Unscom inspections were halted in January after Iraqi authorities blocked the work of an Unscom team headed by William Scott Ridder, an American who Hussein accused of being a spy for the United States and Israel. That crisis was resolved peacefully in February 1998 when UN Secretary General Kofi Annan negotiated an agreement with Hussein that allowed inspections to resume. A new crisis arose in August when Hussein once again blocked Unscom inspections. In October, Hussein broke off all dealings with Unscom. In mid-November, in the face of a buildup of U.S. forces in the region, Hussein agreed to permit Unscom to proceed with its inspection and monitoring activities.

In December, Butler claimed that Iraqi authorities yet again blocked Unscom's work and refused to turn over important documents. Hussein had been warned in November that such a negative report would trigger military action, and the U.S. and British strikes fulfilled that warning.

Kuwait and Oman allowed U.S. aircraft to use their territory to launch air strikes. Other regional governments, including those that were allied with the United States in its ouster of Iraqi troops from Kuwait in 1991, were critical of the attack. Officials in many of these nations questioned the need for the attack and feared an anti-U.S. backlash from it.

In February 1998, Palestinian students carry a huge Iraqi flag through the streets of Bethlehem, a city turned over to Palestinian authorities by Israel in 1995, to demonstrate their opposition to a planned U.S. military attack against Iraq.

Arab-Israeli peace process. On Oct. 23, 1998, Israeli Prime Minister Benjamin Netanyahu and Palestinian leader Yasir Arafat signed an agreement in Washington, D.C., to move the stalled Arab-Israeli peace process forward. King Hussein of Jordan, who was in the United States undergoing treatment for cancer, joined Netanyahu and Arafat at the peace talks, held at the Wye River Plantation outside Washington, D.C. The agreement, called the Wye River Accord, was brokered by President Clinton. Earlier in 1998, Arabs had accused the United States of failing to pressure Israel to make concessions to revive the peace process.

The peace process had been stalled since March 1997 when Netanyahu's government re-sisted fulfilling an agreement signed by the previous Israeli government. The Oslo Accords, signed by Arafat and former Israeli Prime Minister Yitzhak Rabin in 1993, stipulated that Israel was to have completed three troop withdrawals from the West Bank (Arab territory captured by Israel in the 1967 Six-Day War) by May 1999.

The Wye River Accord called for Israeli troops to withdraw from 13 percent of the West Bank over a 12-week period. In exchange, Arafat agreed to increase efforts to arrest Islamic extremists and confiscate their weapons, as well as to nullify provisions in the Palestinian charter that called for Israel's destruction.

Both Arafat and Netanyahu faced strong opposition to the agreement. In late October 1998,

Country	Population	Government	Monetary unit*	Foreign trade (million U.S.$) Exports[†]	Imports[†]
Bahrain	604,000	Amir Isa bin Salman Al Khalifa; Prime Minister Khalifa bin Salman Al Khalifa	dinar (0.38 = $1)	4,602	4,093
Cyprus	762,000	President Glafcos Clerides (Turkish Republic of Northern Cyprus: President Rauf R. Denktash)	pound (0.49 = $1)	1,104	3,695
Egypt	66,547,000	President Hosni Mubarak; Prime Minister Kamal Ahmed al-Ganzouri	pound (3.40 = $1)	3,921	13,210
Iran	71,569,000	Leader of the Islamic Revolution Ali Hoseini-Khamenei; President Mohammad Khatami-Ardakani	rial (3,000.00 = $1)	21,300	13,300
Iraq	22,345,000	President Saddam Hussein	dinar (0.31 = $1)	no statistics available	
Israel	5,883,000	President Ezer Weizman; Prime Minister Benjamin Netanyahu	new shekel (4.31 = $1)	22,502	30,783
Jordan	4,480,000	King Hussein I; Prime Minister Fayez al-Tarawnah	dinar (0.71 = $1)	1,817	4,293
Kuwait	1,702,000	Amir Jabir al-Ahmad al-Jabir Al Sabah; Prime Minister & Crown Prince Saad al-Abdallah al-Salim Al Sabah	dinar (0.30 = $1)	14,889	8,374
Lebanon	3,173,000	President Ilyas Harawi;** Prime Minister Rafiq al-Hariri[††]	pound (1,508.50 = $1)	717	7,469
Oman	2,425,000	Sultan Qaboos bin Said Al Said	rial (0.39 = $1)	7,630	5,026
Qatar	582,000	Amir Hamad bin Khalifa Al Thani; Prime Minister Abdallah bin Khalifa Al Thani	riyal (3.64 = $1)	3,181	1,891
Saudi Arabia	19,801,000	King & Prime Minister Fahd bin Abd al-Aziz Al Saud	riyal (3.75 = $1)	50,040	28,091
Sudan	30,392,000	President Umar Hasan Ahmad al-Bashir	pound (1,826.00 = $1)	556	1,185
Syria	16,180,000	President Hafez al-Assad; Prime Minister Mahmud Zubi	pound (46.25 = $1)	3,916	4,028
Turkey	65,331,000	President Suleyman Demirel; Prime Minister Mesut Yilmaz	lira (290,771.50 = $1)	23,075	42,931
United Arab Emirates	2,022,000	President Zayid bin Sultan Al Nuhayyan; Prime Minister Maktum bin Rashid al-Maktum	dirham (3.67 = $1)	31,300	22,300
Yemen	15,957,000	President Ali Abdallah Salih; Prime Minister Abd al-Karim Iryani	rial (136.66 = $1)	934	2,087

*Exchange rates as of Nov. 6, 1998, or latest available data.
[†]Latest available data.

**Succeeded by Emile Lahoud on November 24.
[††]Resigned on November 30; replaced by Salim Hoss.

Arafat arrested more than 100 members of the militant Islamic group Hamas, including senior figures, after a suicide bomber tried to blow up two Israeli school buses. In early November, an Islamic suicide bombing wounded more than 20 Israelis in a Jerusalem market, leading to an appearance by Arafat on Israeli television in which he appealed for peace. Netanyahu's Cabinet and the Israeli Knesset (parliament) approved the Wye accord in November despite the opposition of conservatives, who objected to turning over any land to the Palestinians. On December 14, the Palestinian National Council renounced its call for Israel's destruction.

Israeli troops began the scheduled withdraw-als in mid-November. However, on December 20, Netanyahu's Cabinet voted to suspend implementation of the Wye accord. Observers said Netanyahu hoped the Cabinet's move would revive support for his government among conservative religious parties. But diminishing support for Netanyahu's government led the Knesset to schedule new parliamentary elections for early 1999.

Iran-U.S. relations. In September 1998, Iranian Foreign Minister Kamal Kharrazi rebuffed a U.S. offer to establish a political dialogue. U.S. Secretary of State Madeleine Albright made the offer in a June speech in which she asked Iran to help draw up a "road map" to normalize relations between the two countries. Relations had been frozen since 1979, when an Islamic revolution toppled Iran's pro-U.S. monarch. Kharrazi responded that there was no incentive for a dialogue as long as the United States continued to pursue such anti-Iran policies as maintaining U.S. economic sanctions against Iran, funding an Iranian-opposition radio station, and blocking oil and gas export routes from passing through Iran.

The long-running U.S. policy to isolate Iran suffered setbacks in 1998. U.S. ally Saudi Arabia hosted a high-level Iranian delegation in February—the first official Iranian visit to Saudi Arabia since the 1979 revolution. In May 1998, President Clinton, fearing a trade war, was forced to waive U.S. sanctions against a consortium of French, Russian, and Malaysian companies helping to develop an Iranian gas field. U.S. law empowers the president to sanction foreign companies that invest more than $20 million a year in oil or gas operations in Iran or Libya, which the United States accuses of supporting terrorism. In September, Great Britain established full diplomatic relations with Iran after Kharrazi said his government did not support a death decree against British author Salman Rushdie. The late Iranian spiritual leader Ayatollah Ruhollah Khomeini had issued a decree for Rushdie's death in 1989 for writing *The Satanic Verses,* a book the Ayatollah condemned as blasphemous to Islam.

Iran and Afghanistan. Iran and Afghanistan almost went to war in September 1998 after approximately 50 Iranian citizens disappeared from northern Afghanistan. Iranian officials blamed the disappearances on the Taliban militia, which controlled most of Afghanistan. The Iranian government, dominated by the Shiite sect of Islam, is opposed to the Taliban, which is composed of Muslims who believe in a very strict version of the Sunni Islamic sect. Iran massed 200,000 troops along the Afghan-Iran border to face-off against 20,000 Taliban troops.

Tensions increased when the Taliban admitted that it had killed nine Iranian diplomats and one journalist. Iranian reports in October claimed that border skirmishes had resulted in heavy casualties to Taliban units. The threat of war decreased when an October UN mission to Afghanistan persuaded the Taliban to return the bodies of the killed Iranians and return captive Iranians to Iran.

War on terrorism. In August, President Clinton announced in a television address that the United States was committed to a "long, ongoing struggle . . . between the rule of law and terrorism." His address came after U.S. forces bombed an alleged chemical-weapons factory in Sudan and reputed terrorist-training camps in Afghanistan. Clinton said U.S. intelligence information had linked the sites to Osama bin Laden, a wealthy Saudi who U.S. officials claimed was responsible for funding numerous acts of terrorism against the United States and its allies. Clinton said bin Laden was behind the August bombings of U.S. embassies in Kenya and Tanzania that killed more than 200 people.

Many Arabs criticized the U.S. attack on the Sudanese factory, which officials in Sudan maintained produced only medicine. A number of weapons experts also questioned U.S. claims that the factory produced VX nerve gas. United States officials deflected the criticism by claiming the factory's destruction was justified because Iraqi weapons experts had links to the plant. This allegation also remained unverified.

In September, former U.S. President Jimmy Carter called for an independent investigation of the Sudanese incident. The United States, however, blocked UN efforts to open such an inquiry.

□ Christine Helms

See also **Afghanistan; Iraq; Iran; Israel; United Nations;** and the various Middle Eastern country articles.

Mining. See Energy supply.

Minnesota. See State government.

Mississippi. See State government.

Missouri. See State government.

Moldova. See Europe.

Mongolia. See Asia.

Montana. See State government.

Montreal and surrounding communities were plunged into darkness, cold, and near-chaos when a deadly ice storm struck on Jan. 5, 1998. The storm—the worst natural disaster in modern Canadian history—covered most of eastern Canada with up to 4 inches (10 centimeters) of freezing rain and high winds and caused billions of dollars in damage. The storm was blamed for the death of 25 people.

On the night of January 8, only one of five high-voltage transmission lines serving Montreal remained standing, forcing tens of thousands of Montreal residents in search of light and heat into hotels, emergency shelters, or the houses of family and friends. Although electricity was restored to some residents within a day, others were without power for more than one month. In the wake of the catastrophe, Hydro-Quebec, the province-owned utility, announced plans to spend $650 million to build new power lines and reinforce existing lines.

Mayor Pierre Bourque made a political comeback by winning a landslide reelection victory in municipal elections held on November 1. Bourque's first term had been plagued by numerous defections from his Vision Montreal Party and charges of financial irregularities in city expenditures. By spring 1998, Bourque ranked last among the four declared mayoral candidates.

During the summer and fall, however, Bourque campaigned more energetically than his opponents. Presenting himself as the candidate most interested in the people's everyday problems, he promised to freeze property taxes and improve city services. Bourque won 44 percent of the vote, gathering support across socio-economic and linguistic lines. His nearest rival won 26 percent.

Bourque also regained command of Montreal's City Council, with Vision Party candidates winning 39 of 51 council seats. With the July 1997 defection of the 15th Vision councillor, Bourque had become the first Montreal mayor since 1954 to head a minority council.

Minority count. More than 400,000 of Montreal's 1,016,000 inhabitants were members of a visible minority group, according to a 1996 census report on Montreal's racial makeup, released in February 1998. Canada's 1996 census marked the first time that the race of those surveyed was asked. According to the census, blacks ranked first, with 122,000 residents; Arabs and West Indians were second, with 74,000. The findings were welcomed by black community leaders, who said recognition of blacks as the city's largest visible minority would give them leverage in efforts to win equality in employment. Other community leaders expressed concern that Canadian cities such as Toronto and Vancouver were attracting more immigrants, as well as more investments and business expertise.

Casino strike. The Montreal Casino, one of the city's most popular tourist attractions, was hit with its second labor dispute in five years when 1,800 unionized employees walked off the job on June 3, 1998. Employees returned to work on July 15, after accepting a new five-year contract. The strike cost the Quebec government, which operates the gambling facility, an estimated $40 million in revenues.

New projects. On June 4, the government of Quebec approved funds for a planned $185-million expansion of Montreal's downtown convention center. Doubling the size of the center was expected to create an estimated 1,000 jobs and bring in up to $6 million per year in city taxes and an estimated $800 million in new development.

On May 22, the City Council approved a joint agreement with the provincial government to build a $75-million megalibrary in downtown Montreal. The new library would house the main branch of the city's library along with the collection of the Bibliotheque Nationale du Quebec, the provincial library. Some residents feared the cost of maintaining the facility, to be borne by the city, would drain funds from Montreal's more heavily used branch libraries.   □ Mike King

See also **Canada; Canadian provinces; City.**

Morocco. See Middle East.

Motion pictures. Filmmakers found huge success in 1998 with a new wave of movies that focused attention on historical events, including infamous war battles and sinking luxury liners. Many stars returned to the types of characters that made them famous, while others assumed roles unfamiliar to the public. Some audiences in 1998 immersed themselves in fantasy as their on-screen heroes combated giant lizards or disaster from outer space. Fans also revisited some of the greatest films of the past century, enjoyed a few new artistic and appealing films, and witnessed a resurgence of animation.

World War II revisited. Director Steven Spielberg's *Saving Private Ryan* captured rave reviews and large audiences in 1998. The combat film, set in World War II (1939–1945), began with a graphic recreation of the Allied D-Day invasion at Normandy, France, on June 6, 1944. Critics agreed that the opening scene paid tribute to the bloody sacrifices made by infantrymen in the Normandy landing and that the film's vast public acceptance raised the country's appreciation of war veterans.

Saving Private Ryan, starring Academy Award-winning actor Tom Hanks as a humane Army captain, focused on the efforts of a small squadron of men sent behind enemy lines to find an American soldier. Despite its success, some critics said that the film consisted of a weak screenplay with dramatic cliches and stock characters.

The year's second look at World War II, Terence Malick's *The Thin Red Line,* opened to critical acclaim in December 1998. The film was based on James Jones's novel set during the Battle of Guadalcanal, the first U.S. ground offensive during World War II. The movie starred Sean Penn, John Travolta, Nick Nolte, George Clooney, and an ensemble of young actors.

Audiences eagerly anticipated the release of *The Thin Red Line,* Malick's first film in 20 years. His previous features, *Badlands* (1973) and *Days of Heaven* (1978), were critically acclaimed. But Malick, who was regarded by many as a gifted and visually imaginative director, largely dropped out of sight in the 1980's and 1990's.

***Titanic* success.** Director James Cameron's film *Titanic,* released in December 1997, dominated the motion-picture scene for much of 1998. By the end of 1998, the film had made more than $600 million in the United States and $1.2 billion overseas. *Titanic,* about the 1912 sinking of the luxury liner, received 14 Academy Award nominations by the Motion Picture Academy of Arts and Sciences. It won 11 Academy Awards, or Oscars, including best picture. The film tied the record for most Oscars set by *Ben Hur* (1959).

Many fans were disappointed that *Titanic*'s lead actor, Leonardo DiCaprio, was not nominated for an Oscar for his portrayal of a selfless artist. Many

Young stars competed against veteran actors and actresses for movie audiences and Academy Awards in 1998.

Leonardo DiCaprio and Kate Winslet starred in *Titanic,* which won 11 Academy Awards in 1998, including best picture, and became the biggest box-office success in motion-picture history.

Helen Hunt and Jack Nicholson win Academy Awards for best actress and best actor on March 23, 1998, for their performances in *As Good As It Gets*.

Ben Affleck (left) and Matt Damon, win the 1998 Academy Award for the best original screenplay for *Good Will Hunting*.

people phoned, e-mailed, and sent letters to the Motion Picture Academy of Arts and Sciences in protest.

Role-playing. Jim Carrey, whose exaggerated antics in slapstick comedy were popular in previous film ventures, turned relatively serious in Peter Weir's well-received movie, *The Truman Show.* Carrey played a trusting man who slowly realizes that his entire life is being broadcast as a television show. Although some audiences found *The Truman Show* less than believable, many critics said that the film made telling comments about media manipulation, the influence of television, and the lack of privacy in everyday lives.

Brad Pitt returned to the romantic format that made him a star, playing a lovesick embodiment of Death in *Meet Joe Black.* Meryl Streep, who had found success in characters with ethnic backgrounds, added an Irish brogue to her list of accents in *Dancing at Lughnasa.* Streep played the eldest of five unmarried sisters in a small village in Ireland. Talk-show host Oprah Winfrey found success in the role of a woman haunted by the horrors she experienced during years of slavery in director Jonathan Demme's adaptation of Toni Morrison's novel, *Beloved.*

Summer hits and misses. One of the summer's eagerly anticipated box office hopefuls was the lavish remake of *Godzilla,* the saga of the giant lizard introduced in a 1954 Japanese film. Preceded by much media hype, *Godzilla* was expected to be a summer blockbuster. After a strong opening over Memorial Day weekend, the film fizzled in the United States, but audience reaction to the film was more favorable overseas.

In contrast, *There's Something About Mary* opened with little fanfare in the United States and became one of 1998's biggest hits. The comedy concentrated on a love triangle between Cameron Diaz, Ben Stiller, and Matt Dillon and combined humor with uplifting romance. The film propelled Diaz into prominence as one of the year's most successful young actresses.

Many critics agreed that the disappointment of *Godzilla* and the popularity of *There's Something About Mary* at the box office reminded both filmmakers and studio executives that word of mouth can be more powerful than hype.

Space clutter. The Earth faced catastrophes from outer space debris in two summer spectacles. The stars of *Deep Impact,* including Robert Duvall, Tea Leoni, and Morgan Freeman, attempted to avoid collision with a meteoroid. The stars of *Armageddon,* including Bruce Willis, Ben Affleck, and Liv Tyler, attempted a similar feat with an asteroid. Both films were popular with audiences but not critics, who found the films predictable.

Money makers. Despite many poor reviews, *Armageddon* became the summer's most successful film. It earned $188 million between Memorial Day and Labor Day. Overall, summer film receipts totaled $2.5 billion.

Top American films. In June 1998, the American Film Institute (AFI) unveiled its list of the 100 greatest American films in celebration of the 100th anniversary of American cinema. The AFI compiled a list of the top 400 films, based on the recommendations of a 1,500-member panel of experts and film industry figures. A group of filmmakers, scholars, historians, and journalists then used that list to select their choices of the top 100 movies.

Making the AFI top-10 list were *Citizen Kane* (1941); *Casablanca* (1942); *The Godfather* (1972); *Gone With the Wind* (1939); *Lawrence of Arabia* (1962); *The Wizard of Oz* (1939); *The Graduate* (1967); *On the Waterfront* (1954); *Schindler's List* (1993); and *Singin' in the Rain* (1952).

The AFI list sparked much debate. Some critics argued that the list included too many newer films, including *Fargo* (1996) and *Unforgiven* (1992), but no movies featuring Greta Garbo or the duo of Fred Astaire and Ginger Rogers. Others criticized the list's dismissal of silent films and films with African American themes.

Academy Award winners in 1998

The following winners of the 1997 Academy Awards were announced in March 1998:

Best Picture, *Titanic*
Best Actor, Jack Nicholson, *As Good As It Gets*
Best Actress, Helen Hunt, *As Good As It Gets*
Best Supporting Actor, Robin Williams, *Good Will Hunting*
Best Supporting Actress, Kim Basinger, *L.A. Confidential*
Best Director, James Cameron, *Titanic*
Best Original Screenplay, Ben Affleck and Matt Damon, *Good Will Hunting*
Best Screenplay Adaptation, Brian Helgeland and Curtis Hanson, *L.A. Confidential*
Best Cinematography, Russell Carpenter, *Titanic*
Best Film Editing, Conrad Buff, James Cameron, and Richard A. Harris, *Titanic*
Best Original Dramatic Score, James Horner, *Titanic*
Best Original Music or Comedy Score, Anne Dudley, *The Full Monty*
Best Original Song, James Horner and Will Jennings, "My Heart Will Go On" from *Titanic*
Best Foreign-Language Film, *Character* (the Netherlands)
Best Art Direction, Peter Lamont, *Titanic*
Best Costume Design, Deborah L. Scott, *Titanic*
Best Sound, Gary Rydstrom, Tom Johnson, Gary Summers, and Mark Ulano, *Titanic*
Best Sound Effects Editing, Tom Bellfort and Christopher Boyes, *Titanic*
Best Makeup, Rick Baker and David LeRoy Anderson, *Men in Black*
Best Visual Effects, *Titanic*
Best Animated Short Film, *Geri's Game*
Best Live-Action Short Film, *Visas and Virtue*
Best Feature Documentary, *The Long Way Home*
Best Short Subject Documentary, *A Story of Healing*

The list did lead to major reissues of many classic movies, including *Citizen Kane, The Wizard of Oz,* and *Gone With the Wind,* in their original screen formats. The availability of such films on cable networks and in video stores, however, kept them from performing strongly at national box offices.

Critical hits. Stanley Tucci and Oliver Platt scored strong reviews for their performances as unemployed actors onboard a luxury liner during the 1930's in the comedy *The Impostors.* Equally well-received was Italian director and comic actor Roberto Benigni's World War II-era film *Life Is Beautiful.* The film portrayed a man trying to protect his young son from the horrors of the Holocaust—the systematic extermination of some 6 million persons by Nazi Germany during World War II—by pretending that their life in a concentration camp is an elaborate game.

Happiness, directed by Todd Solondz, took a harsh look at suburbia. The film's subject matter, including murder, rape, obscene phone calls, and pedophilia, sharply divided both audiences and critics. Some viewed the film as a masterpiece, while others considered it "trash."

Cult-director John Waters, famous for such unconventional dark comedies as *Pink Flamingos* (1972), *Polyester* (1981), and *Hairspray* (1988), was criticized for making *Pecker,* a film considered too light for his audiences. *Pecker* told the story of a young photographer lured to the trendy New York art crowd.

Comedian Bill Murray drew rave reviews for his performance as a tycoon who becomes a mentor and friend to an underachieving but visionary high school student in director Wes Anderson's film *Rushmore.*

Celebrity, a comedy about fame and notoriety directed by Woody Allen, provided audiences with another view of urban angst. Reviewed by some critics as one of Allen's weakest efforts, others considered *Celebrity* as one of Allen's most provocative works.

Animation reemerged in peak form during 1998. *Mulan,* based on the Chinese legend of a young woman who disguises herself as a man in order to take her ailing father's place in combat, proved to be the Disney Studio's most acclaimed animated feature in years. Since the tale was not widely known outside China, industry observers predicted that *Mulan* would not have the impact of previous Disney films. But the public responded with warm enthusiasm.

DreamWorks Studios brought animation to a new level of complexity with *The Prince of Egypt,* an animated version of the biblical story of Moses. Some critics claimed the film was on par with the Cecil B. DeMille classic version of the same story, *The Ten Commandments* (1956).

The insect world received Hollywood treatment through two films in 1998. DreamWorks Studios' *Antz* featured the voice of Woody Allen as a nonconformist worker ant who falls in love with the ant princess, voiced by Sharon Stone. Allen's and Stone's animated venture received better reviews than some of their recent live-action appearances. Disney Studio's *A Bug's Life* also gave audiences an inside look at the insect world, but did not capture the same level of praise from critics or audiences as did *Antz.*

Foreign success. The film industries of several countries realized substantial gains in 1998, even as the nations' economies remained fragile. Despite economic recession, Japan's film industry did well during 1998. The country's largest film company, Toho, reported record profits. Most of the company's success was credited to the release of the animated film *Princess Mononoke,* which made more than $150 million in Japan.

Polish-produced films released in 1998 also captured their largest audiences of the 1990's. *Killer,* a comedy starring Cesary Pazura as a hitman, became the most successful Polish film in that country's history, selling approximately 2.2 million tickets.   □ Philip Wuntch

See also **People in the news** (Cameron, James).

Mozambique. See Africa.

Music. See Classical music; Popular music.

Myanmar. The National League for Democracy (NLD), which had won a 1990 parliamentary election in Myanmar, then known as Burma, struggled in 1998 to wrest power from the governing *junta* (military group that holds power after a coup or revolution). The junta—the State Peace and Development Council—had refused to recognize the 1990 election results and had never allowed the NLD to convene a parliament.

The NLD, led by Daw Aung San Suu Kyi, announced in September 1998 that it would act as the country's legitimate parliament and declared all laws and proclamations issued by the junta null and void. The junta responded by arresting approximately 900 NLD members, including nearly 200 elected representatives.

Thousands of students protested with demonstrations in September that resulted in the largest number of arrests since 1996, when the junta reacted to student riots by closing all universities.

Forced labor. The International Labor Organization, a United Nations affiliate, reported in August 1998 that the junta ran a system of forced labor in "a systematic manner with total disregard for human dignity, safety and health and the basic needs of the people." It accused the regime of torture, rape, and murder.

□ Henry S. Bradsher

See also **Asia** (Facts in brief table).

Netherlands. The center-left coalition government of Prime Minister Wim Kok won a second, four-year mandate from Dutch voters in 1998. The coalition promised to continue its economic policy of wage restraint, job creation, and modest increases in social spending. It emerged from the May election with a majority of 97 seats in the 150-seat parliament, a gain of five seats from the previous parliament. Kok's Labor Party remained the biggest party, winning 45 seats, a gain of eight. The Liberal Party won seven more seats, for a total of 38. The third coalition party, the centrist Democrats '66, won 14 seats, a loss of 10. Its founder and leader, Hans van Mierlo, retired after the election, giving up the post of foreign minister to Jozias van Aartsen, a Liberal.

The election dealt a further setback to the main opposition party, the Christian Democrats. The party won only 30 seats in the new parliament, a decline of four. The government's legislative program, presented to parliament by Queen Beatrix in September 1998, promised to increase social spending by 2.5 billion guilders ($1.2 billion), mainly on education, health care, and child care. The government announced that it would finance part of its plans with tax increases, rather than through deficit spending, in order to bring down the national debt and prevent the economy from growing too quickly.

The economy remained one of Europe's strongest. Output was forecast to grow by nearly 4 percent in 1998, and unemployment to fall below 4 percent, a level not seen since 1980 and the lowest rate of any major European economy. The Dutch succeeded in lowering unemployment through an agreement between unions and employers that limits wage increases in return for extra jobs and the promotion of part-time work.

Philips Electronics NV, a Dutch maker of consumer electronics products that is Europe's largest, agreed in May 1998 to sell PolyGram NV, a music and film company, to Seagram Co. of Canada, a distilling company that is expanding into the entertainment industry, for $10.4 billion. Philips, which owned 75 percent of PolyGram, said it wanted to concentrate on its core electronics business. PolyGram was the world's largest music company.   □ Tom Buerkle

See also **Europe** (Facts in brief table); **Europe** Special Report: **European Union.**

Nevada. See State government.

New Brunswick. See Canadian provinces.

New Hampshire. See State government.

New Jersey. See State government.

New Mexico. See State government.

New York. See New York City; State government.

Police officers guard massive portraits of Queen Beatrix of the Netherlands before the Royal Palace in Amsterdam in January 1998. The pictures were part of a three-day celebration of the queen's 60th birthday.

Engineers inspect a 48-story construction elevator tower that collapsed at a building site in midtown Manhattan on July 21, 1998. Steel rods crashed through the roof of a nearby hotel, killing an elderly woman. The accident and cleanup closed a section of the Times Square area for weeks.

New York City. In 1998, the administration of Mayor Rudolph W. Giuliani proposed that new baseball stadiums be built for the Yankees and the Mets, New York City's two professional baseball teams. A new Yankee stadium on Manhattan's West Side, projected to cost $1.1 billion, was proposed to replace Yankee Stadium in the Bronx, the team's home since 1923. In April 1998, a 500-pound beam in the aging structure fell, luckily while the stadium was empty. Two baseball games had to be canceled during repairs. The Yankees' lease on the stadium was due to expire in 2002.

Despite a record season for the Yankees, which included a four-game World Series sweep of the San Diego Padres, opposition to a new stadium was intense. Attorneys in the mayor's office suc-

cessfully blocked a referendum that was scheduled for Nov. 3, 1998, regarding the use of public funds to build a stadium. Two polls showed that more than 70 percent of voters were against the new stadium and against the club leaving the Bronx. Although the team drew a record 2.95 million fans in the regular season, principal owner George Steinbrenner demanded a modern stadium as his price to keep the Yankees in New York City.

The proposed Mets plan called for a $600-million multipurpose stadium with a retractable roof next to Shea Stadium, the ballpark in the borough of Queens where the team has played since 1964. The Mets' management said the new field would be modeled after Ebbets Field, the Brooklyn home of the Dodgers until 1958.

Blueprint for civility. Mayor Giuliani was sworn in Jan. 1, 1998, for a second and final four-year term. In a speech to city officials on February 25, he announced a broad campaign to further the "quality of life" in New York City. In time, his civility campaign came to include crackdowns on litterbugs, rude civil service workers, jaywalkers, reckless bicycle messengers, blaring car alarms, vendors who clog sidewalks, and drivers who ignore the speed limit of 30 miles (48 kilometers) per hour on city streets. The mayor also pressed for policies requiring not only that public school pupils wear uniforms and take classes in civics, but that teachers adhere to a dress code.

The city's 12,187 Yellow Cab drivers became a particular quality-of-life target in the mayor's civility campaign. Citing riders' complaints and increasing taxi accidents, the mayor urged the Taxi and Limousine Commission to toughen licensing standards and require higher insurance coverage. Cab drivers responded to the stiff penalties proposed by City Hall by staying off the job for 24 hours, causing major inconveniences.

Grand Central Terminal, a *Beaux-Arts* (architectural style based on the teachings of the Ecole de Beaux Arts in Paris) cathedral for commuters since 1913, was rededicated on Oct. 1, 1998, after undergoing a $200-million restoration. The terminal came close to being demolished in the 1970's to make room for an office tower. A campaign by preservationists to block demolition, spearheaded by the late Jacqueline Kennedy Onassis, was upheld by the United States Supreme Court in 1978. A plaque honoring Onassis was installed in the main concourse.

The project included a restored ceiling replicating a blue-green sky with twinkling stars, refurbished and new marble stairways, and space for a number of upscale shops and restaurants. Nearly 500,000 commuters passed through the terminal each day in 1998.

Economy. Merrill Lynch, the nation's largest brokerage house and one of New York City's biggest employers, announced the layoff of 3,400 employees on Oct. 13, 1998, in response to wide-spread economic troubles in Asia and Russia. Despite cutbacks by Wall Street firms and a sharp decline in stocks, New York City's economy remained resilient in 1998.

Tourism also remained strong with an estimated 34 million visitors in 1998. According to the city's Convention and Visitors Bureau, the city's five most popular tourist attractions were Central Park, the upscale shopping area on Madison Avenue, the Times Square theater district, the Statue of Liberty, and the Empire State Building.   □ Owen Moritz

See also **City; Theater** Special Report: **A New Broadway Takes Center Stage.**

New Zealand. New Zealand's coalition government, consisting of the National Party and the New Zealand First Party, collapsed on Aug. 12, 1998. The crisis occurred when members of the New Zealand First Party walked out of a Cabinet meeting during a dispute over whether to sell the government's share of an airport to an investment group. The coalition government had been formed in December 1996 under rules requiring that political parties be represented in the government in proportion to their share of election votes.

On Aug. 21, 1998, Prime Minister Jenny Shipley, leader of the National Party, dismissed Deputy Prime Minister and Treasurer Winston Peters, a member of the New Zealand First Party, from both posts. The National Party continued to rule as a minority government in 1998 with the support of two smaller political parties and several independent Parliament members.

Shipley on September 8 won a parliamentary vote of confidence for her minority coalition government. The prime minister had requested the vote to prove to the public that her minority government had the support of a majority in Parliament. Another confidence-vote victory on November 19 regarding a new tax bill confirmed that her government would remain in power into 2000.

Economy. In 1998, New Zealand felt the effects of an economic crisis in Asia that had begun in 1997. New Zealand's forest industry was hit especially hard as timber exports to Japan and South Korea dropped more than 25 percent. Exports to Indonesia, Malaysia, and Taiwan also dropped significantly. A recession in Russia affected New Zealand's foreign trade, especially of dairy products. The loss of exports was offset partially by expansion into new markets and increased sales to non-Asian countries, including the United States.

New Zealand Finance Minister Bill Birch predicted in September 1998 that the Asian financial crisis would cause New Zealand's economic growth rate in fiscal year 1998 to decline by 0.5 percent. In April, the government had projected growth of 2.7 percent.

A power blackout struck the central business district of Auckland, New Zealand's largest city, in February when all four of the city's major electrical power cables failed. The outage left a 1-square-mile (2.6-square-kilometer) area without power for five weeks. The outage led many of the area's 5,000 residents to voluntarily evacuate, reduced many businesses to skeleton staffs, and forced the relocation of some financial institutions. Inadequate maintenance of electrical cables allegedly caused the blackout.   □ Gavin Ellis

See also **Pacific Islands** (Facts in brief table).

Newfoundland. See **Canadian provinces.**

■ News bytes

Selected news from 1998:

Saving "Willy." On Sept. 9, 1998, Keiko, the 10,000-pound (4,540-kilogram) killer whale famous for his title role in the motion picture *Free Willy* (1993), was flown from Newport, Oregon, to Iceland, returning to the waters from which he was captured in 1979. Keiko had made news headlines around the world in 1996, when it was learned that the performing whale was kept in a cramped, overheated tank in a Mexico City amusement park. Concerned activists responded by forming the Save Willy-Keiko Foundation and arranged to have Keiko brought to the Oregon Coast Aquarium in Newport, where he could regain his health and be taught how to survive in the wild.

Keiko's new home in Iceland was a 250-foot (76-meter) pen in a bay just off Vestmannaeyjar, one of the Westmann Islands, not far from Reykjavik, the capital. Unlike his previous quarters, the new pen was not opened to visitors. The ultimate goal of the foundation was to end the 21-year-old animal's dependence on human beings after spending most of his life in captivity.

Cleopatra's palace found. In October 1998, a team of French archaeologists, led by Franck Goddio, located what they believed to be Cleopatra's palace on the lost island of Antirhodos in the Mediterranean Sea off the Egyptian coast near Alexandria. The island and palace sank into the sea more than 1,600 years ago as a result of a series of devastating earthquakes. The team also found a well-preserved shipwreck, dating from between 90 B.C. and A.D. 130, which contained remains of food, jewelry, and pottery. Among other relics found by divers in the 17-foot (5.2-meter) waters was a sphinx bearing the likeness of King Ptolemy XII of Egypt, Cleopatra's father.

The explorers used satellites and global positioning equipment to map the sunken island as well as the location and layout of the palace. A three-dimensional computer model of the site made from these measurements precisely matched details from two documented episodes from Cleopatra's past. Julius Caesar, the Roman general with whom Cleopatra had formed an alliance, had written of his feet being burned while he was taking refuge in Cleopatra's palace. The computer model revealed that the region's intense sunlight shining through the palace windows might have made the palace's stone floors very hot. In another tale, Cleopatra was said to have chided Mark Antony, another Roman general with whom she was allied, while she was in the palace and he was fishing. The story made little sense until the explorers discovered that the palace was situated on a platform by the sea.

Down to earth, again. Chicago millionaire and adventurer Steve Fossett began his fourth attempt to fly around the world in a balloon on

Divers retrieve an ancient sphinx from the Mediterranean Sea near Alexandria, Egypt, in October 1998. French archaeologists believe the sphinx and other artifacts are relics from a palace kept by the Egyptian queen Cleopatra on the island of Antirhodos, which sank 1,600 years ago.

Aug. 7, 1998. His previous attempt ended on January 5, when a cabin heater malfunctioned, and frigid temperatures forced him to set his balloon down in southern Russia. However, the journey did set a world distance record for travel in a balloon, 15,200 miles (24,462 kilometers).

On the fourth try, Fossett took off on the *Solo Spirit* from Mendoza, Argentina, the first time an around-the-world flight had been attempted in the Southern Hemisphere. On August 16, Fossett ran into rough weather. A violent downdraft struck the balloon, causing it to fall into the ocean about 575 miles (925 kilometers) east of the Australian coast. Fossett escaped from the wreckage and got himself into a life raft. A French reconnaissance plane tracking Fossett's distress beacon located the raft several hours later. The balloonist was subsequently rescued by a privately owned Australian sailboat.

Fossett then joined forces with a rival balloonist, British tycoon Richard Branson, and veteran balloonist Per Lindstrand for another attempt. They launched their balloon on December 18 from Morocco and reached speeds of 200 miles (320 kilometers) per hour as they crossed North Africa, Asia, and the Pacific Ocean. On December 25, however, unfavorable winds forced them to land near Oahu in the Hawaiian Islands, where they were rescued by the U.S. Coast Guard.

Oprah beef settled. On Feb. 26, 1998, a federal jury in Amarillo, Texas, cleared television talk-show host Oprah Winfrey of slander in a $12-million lawsuit filed against her by a group of cattle ranchers. The suit stemmed from an April 1996 segment of "The Oprah Winfrey Show" that focused on the topic of "mad cow disease." In March 1996, researchers had found a link between mad cow disease in British beef cattle and a rise in cases of Creutzfeldt-Jakob disease, a degenerative, fatal brain disease that had claimed the lives of 23 people in Great Britain. A panelist on Winfrey's show commented that many U.S. cattle were routinely fed ground-up animal parts, a practice that had been blamed for the spread of mad cow disease in Britain. The panelist said that a similar outbreak was likely in the United States. In response, Winfrey exclaimed "It has just stopped me cold from eating another burger! I'm stopped!" The day after the program aired, the price of cattle futures on U.S. commodity markets plunged 10 percent. Some industry analysts pointed out, however, that futures prices had dropped generally that day.

The cattlemen's suit claimed Winfrey and the show's producers had favored the viewpoints of guests opposed to the beef industry. On the witness stand, Winfrey asserted that her viewers understood that her statements on eating beef had been a personal opinion, not a matter of fact. Winfrey's attorney argued that his client's expression of an opinion was protected by the First Amendment of the U.S. Constitution, which guarantees freedom of speech and of the press. Emerging from the courthouse after being exonerated, Win-

Russian artists line up in March 1998 for a slice of cake shaped in the likeness of the preserved body of Soviet leader V. I. Lenin, which has been on display in Moscow's Red Square since 1924. The artists consumed the life-sized cake as a performance-art piece representing Russia's departure from Lenin's legacy.

Libertad, an Argentinian frigate (foreground) joins in a parade of ships to celebrate the 200th anniversary of the maiden voyage of the U.S.S. *Constitution* on July 23, 1998. The *Constitution,* the nation's oldest commissioned warship, was recently restored and made seaworthy.

Koko, a 26-year-old lowland gorilla taught to communicate using sign language, participates in an Internet "cyberchat" on April 27, 1998. Subscribers to the Internet service America Online asked Koko questions, which were relayed between Koko and a typist by a sign-language interpreter.

frey was greeted by hundreds of cheering supporters. "Free speech not only lives," Winfrey said to reporters, "it rocks!"

Woodstock revisited. A three-day concert on the 29th anniversary of the Woodstock Festival of 1969 was staged in August 1998 on the same site where the original festival had helped shape the spirit of the 1960's hippie counterculture. The site of the event, Max Yasgur's former farm near Bethel, New York, was transformed for the 1998 event, which was billed as "A Day in the Garden." The latest event did not use the name "Woodstock" because it was not affiliated with Woodstock Ventures, which staged the original festival and holds the rights to the name. A developer had bought the famous site and nearly 2,000 acres (800 hectares) of surrounding land with plans to develop it into a music-themed attraction. The 1998 event was the first step in his plan.

Unlike the original festival, which drew some 400,000 young people, the 1998 event drew a smaller but more diverse audience, including families with children. There were also no traffic jams or shortages of bathroom facilities or food. At least one Woodstock tradition held true, however—rain soaked the crowd while the lead act, singer Stevie Nicks, performed.

Swimmer crosses the Atlantic. Frenchman Benoit Lecomte, 31, made history on Sept. 25, 1998, by becoming the first person to swim across the Atlantic Ocean. Lecomte began his quest in Hyannis, Massachusetts, on July 16 and completed the 3,395-mile (5,464-kilometer) journey 72 days later in Brittany, France.

Lecomte swam in two-hour blocks, six to eight hours a day, and stopped to eat and rest in a boat that accompanied him along the way. He wore a wet suit, swim fins, and a custom-made snorkel and was surrounded by a mild electrical field that repelled predators, including sharks.

Lecomte, an American marketing executive, who was born and raised in France, told reporters that he took on the challenge in memory of his father, who died of colon cancer in 1991. The feat raised about $175,000 for cancer research.

Paraplegic swims channel. Australian John MacLean on Aug. 31, 1998, became the first paraplegic to swim the English Channel. MacLean, 32, completed the 21-mile (34-kilometer) swim from Dover, England, to Calais, France, in 12 hours, 55

Workers unveil the completed face of Crazy Horse in June 1998. The statue of the Lakota warrior, which will be the world's largest sculpture when completed, is being carved from a mountain in South Dakota's Black Hills by the family of sculptor Korczak Ziolkowski, who began work on the memorial in 1948.

Microsoft chairman Bill Gates is struck by a pie while visiting Brussels, Belgium, in February. The attack was reportedly instigated by Noel Godin, who is well-known in Belgium as an *entarteur*—a person who throws pies in peoples' faces as a gesture of disrespect.

minutes. Despite losing the use of his legs in an accident 10 years before, MacLean in 1995 became the first wheelchair athlete permitted to participate in the Hawaiian Ironman competition, a one-day event that is widely considered the toughest endurance event in the world. The competition includes a 2.4-mile (3.8-kilometer) swim, a 112-mile (180-kilometer) bicycle ride, and a full 26.2-mile (42.2-kilometer) marathon. MacLean competed in the event again in 1996 and in 1997.

Star Wars mania returns, early. The long-anticipated fourth installment of the *Star Wars* saga thrilled movie audiences in November 1998, half a year before its scheduled release. A trailer, or "coming attractions" preview, of *Star Wars: Episode I—The Phantom Menace* was shown in 75 theaters nationwide on November 17. The official *Star Wars* site on the World Wide Web tipped off fans to the appearance of the trailer before its official debut on November 20. According to reports from several cities, thousands of movie-goers paid the full price of admission—an average of $7 to $9—during the ensuing weekend to see the two-minute clip. After the trailer ended, most *Star Wars* fans left theaters without seeing the feature film.

In addition to the theatrical screenings, the movie's producer, Lucasfilm Ltd., made the trailer available on the *Star Wars* Web site. In the days following the trailer's debut, the site reportedly averaged an incredible 350 *hits* (requests for Web pages) per second. □ Peter Uremovic

Newspaper. Patricia Smith, a columnist with *The Boston Globe,* resigned on June 18, 1998, after her editors determined that people and quotations described as real in some of her columns were fictional. On August 19, the paper's best-known columnist, Mike Barnicle, also resigned. The resignation came amid suspicions that Barnicle had *plagiarized* (taken as one's own the writing of another) jokes published in a book by comedian George Carlin and made up a 1995 column that he claimed to be true.

Newspaper apology. *The Cincinnati Enquirer* was forced to publish a front-page apology on June 28, 1998, to Chiquita Brands International, retracting an 18-page article published in May that had questioned the Cincinnati-based fruit company's business practices. *The Enquirer* also paid more than $10 million to avoid legal actions.

In its apology, the newspaper's publisher and editor wrote that the story's reporter may have illegally removed voice-mail tapes from Chiquita. The newspaper fired the reporter, Mike Gallagher, in June. Gallagher pleaded guilty on September 24 to unlawful interception of communication and unauthorized access to computer systems.

Photographer problems. On October 1, California became the first state to pass a law that strengthened privacy rights against *paparazzi* (aggressive free-lance photographers). The law, scheduled to go into effect on Jan. 1, 1999, defined invasion of privacy as trespassing with the intent to capture audio or video images of a celebrity or crime victim "engaging in a personal or family activity in circumstances where they had a reasonable expectation of privacy."

Newspaper closings. *The Nashville* (Tennessee) *Banner* shut down on Feb. 20, 1998, after 122 years of publication. Like many afternoon newspapers, *The Banner* had experienced declining circulation for several years. The publisher of *The Evansville* (Indiana) *Press,* another afternoon newspaper, announced in September that the paper would close on December 31 after 92 years.

Labor decision upheld. The National Labor Relations Board in September 1998 ordered *The Detroit News* and *Detroit Free Press* to rehire hundreds of workers who went on strike in 1995 and had not been rehired when the strike ended in 1997. The board upheld a judge's decision that the 19-month strike at the two papers was caused by unfair labor practices by the newspapers. The board also ordered the papers to pay back wages to the employees who had not returned to work. Newspaper representatives in September 1998 appealed the order.

□ Mark Fitzgerald

See also **Newspaper** Special Report: **Tabloid Journalism—Yesterday and Today**.

ZOLA'S "WIFE

NIGHT
SPECIAL.
NEW Y

NEW Y

NO. 5,566—P. M.

EXTRA

ALLOWS $605,237 FOR THE TEACHERS.

LIGHT ON

BABIES

Board of Estimate Fixes the Amount
for Salaries and Other Expenses
for January.

DREYFUS

The Board of Estimate and Apportion-
ment this afternoon allowed $605,237 for
the Board of Education, covering expenses
and salaries for January.

KILLED

The Board heard Colonel Kearny on a
proposition to renovate the brownstone
building in City Hall Park for the use of
the City Court. He agreed to put in new
floors and elevators and to make other improvements for $13,000.
The bid was accepted.

PLOTTIN

BY SCORE

THE DE LOME QUESTION

Colonel Picquart Tells
Disregarded Evidence
Against Esterhazy.

Washington, Feb. 11. — Will
Hale sail?

HANDWRITING RECOGNI

Twenty Bodies Have Been
Recently Found in the
Streets of Harlem.

BELIEVED TO BE
TROLLEY ROBBERS.

Zola Feelingly Replies to a
flection of General Pellie
Amid Great Excitement

RTILLON DISCOVE

Colonel Picquart,
dor of the Assis
a witness in the
d an immense sen
had decided to d
sistry in the m
sequences to his
ter
haft at Zola.
who was the firs
ified that G

TABLOID JOURNALISM

Yesterday *and* Today

PUBLIC CONFIDENCE IN THE RELIABILITY OF

NEWS REPORTING DECLINED IN 1998, ECHOING

THE STATE OF JOURNALISM OF 100 YEARS AGO.

By Tom Rosenstiel

A credibility crisis afflicted American journalism in the
late 1990's. Public confidence in the reliability of news
reporting was in decline.
   A poll conducted in mid-1998 for *Newsweek* magazine by
Princeton Survey Research Associates, an attitude and opinion
research company located in Princeton, New Jersey, revealed
that 53 percent of adult Americans surveyed characterized news
reporting in the United States as "often inaccurate." The poll
also revealed that 77 percent of those surveyed believed that
journalists of the 1990's were more likely than journalists of the
1890's to allow media owners to slant or sensationalize the news

in order to boost ratings, influence politics, or increase corporate profits. Media critics noted that competition among radio and television news programs and newspapers had become so intense that *The New York Times,* often considered the newspaper of record in the United States, had published information on its front page that was attributed to the *National Enquirer,* the nation's largest supermarket tabloid.

The trouble for the media in 1998 began in January, when information about a possible relationship between U.S. President Bill Clinton and a former White House intern, Monica Lewinsky, was reported in an Internet gossip column. The story immediately spread to television and newspapers. Soon, the airwaves and newspapers were blanketed with it, driving nearly all other news—including a papal visit to Cuba and an important meeting between President Clinton and Israeli Prime Minister Benjamin Netanyahu—off newscasts and front pages. Because media coverage of the Lewinsky scandal often raced ahead of the facts, major news organizations were forced, eventually, to retract unproven accounts. In the wake of the scandal, the U.S. news media discovered that the Lewinsky story, apparently, had damaged the president's standing with the public far less than it had sullied the public's image of the press.

The nation's news media continued to be battered throughout the year. Editors at *The New Republic,* a weekly magazine, and *The Boston Globe,* a daily newspaper, fired writers for allegedly inventing characters and quotes in their news stories. In June, another major newspaper, *The Cincinnati Enquirer,* fired a reporter for a serious breach of journalistic ethics. The reporter's allegations of illegal business practices at Chiquita Brands International Inc. had been based on employee voice mail tapes, which the reporter had obtained illegally. The paper retracted the reporter's series of stories on Chiquita and paid the Cincinnati-based fruit company a $10-million settlement. In July, Cable News Network (CNN) was forced to retract a report that accused the U.S. military of using nerve gas to kill suspected American deserters in Laos during the Vietnam War (1957-1975). *Time* magazine, which had reported the same story, was also forced to issue a retraction.

Some media experts saw evidence of a growing trend in these dismissals and retractions. They cited the inaccuracies and lapses in ethics as indications that American journalism had entered a new era of sensationalism, a time in which the news was designed to entertain or shock, rather than provide facts. They dubbed the new era the "age of infotainment"—a time in which information and entertainment were combined.

The era of yellow journalism

News as entertainment is not new. In the 1880's and 1890's, American journalism was dominated by a type of sensationalism that became known as "yellow" or "tabloid" journalism. The term yellow journalism refers to "The Yellow Kid," a popular comic strip that appeared in the late 1800's in two New York

The author

Tom Rosenstiel is the director of the Project for Excellence in Journalism in Washington, D.C.

City newspapers that specialized in sensationalism. The word "tabloid" became associated with sensationalism because many of the newspapers that published these kinds of stories were printed in a tabloid format, which is approximately half the size of a broadsheet-formatted paper. The working class, which was the target audience, found the smaller trim size of the tabloid easier to handle on public transportation.

Tabloid journalism was largely invented by two New York City publishers, Joseph Pulitzer, who owned the *New York World*, and William Randolph Hearst, who owned the *New York Journal*. Both men also owned papers in other cities. Pulitzer and Hearst created a journalistic recipe that exhibited certain common traits. The stories in Pulitzer and Hearst's papers contained heavy doses of crime, scandal, disasters, and the goings on of high society. Their papers were filled with lurid tales of the frightening, startling, and bizarre aspects of American city life, in part, because such city life was new and sensational to the many immigrants who came from rural Europe. So sensationalism flourished in American cities with large immigrant populations, such as New York, Chicago, and Philadelphia. While the journalists of the tabloid press did attempt to bring realism, or a kind of accuracy, to their reporting, they did not yet worry about objectivity or fairness, as journalists did in the 1900's. The result was newspapers that lacked balance and proportion.

Pulitzer, who was copied by Hearst, also put the most important news on the front page, organized it according to significance, and invented leads that concentrated vital information in the first paragraph. He added political cartoons, front-page crusades, stories of scientific oddities, illustrations, color, and comic strips. Many of these journalistic innovations became standard among American newspapers.

Circulation wars

Tabloid journalism was largely fueled by new technology. In the 30 years following the American Civil War (1861-1865), the price of *newsprint* (coarse paper on which newspapers are printed) dropped by 50 percent every 10 years, in large part because of innovations that allowed the paper to be made of boiled tree pulp. The innovation allowed newspaper publishers to add pages, increase the number of copies they printed, and still drop prices. The ability to cut price without losing money fostered intense competition that resulted in circulation wars among newspapers published in the same markets. To lure readers, publishers raided each other's staffs for the most popular reporters, columnists, and cartoonists. Hearst hired the creator of "The Yellow Kid" away from Pulitzer during one such circulation war. Publishers also hired street toughs, usually members of urban gangs, to threaten newspaper vendors who stocked rival publications, a practice

"The Yellow Kid," Richard Felton Outcault's very popular cartoon strip of the 1890's, lent its name to the highly sensationalized journalism of the day.

that often resulted in violence between rival street gangs. Above all else, the intense competition drove the reporters and editors on such papers to greater and greater heights of sensationalism.

Even though publishers such as Pulitzer and Hearst fought ruthlessly over circulation, tabloid journalism was not entirely about competition or money. It also evolved in response to existing social trends, such as political corruption and the working and living conditions of the immigrants that flooded major American cities at the time. Both Pulitzer and Hearst, as well as other publishers of tabloid newspapers, launched many reform campaigns to hunt out and expose corruption in business and government and to improve urban conditions.

Pulitzer used screaming headlines; front-page cartoons; drawings; and simple words, subject matter, and sentence structure to appeal to the working class and particularly the immigrant.

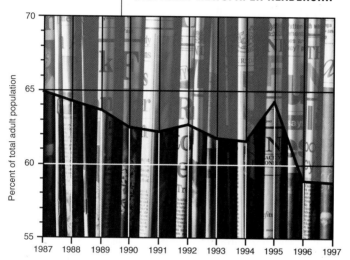

U.S. DAILY NEWSPAPER READERSHIP

Percent of total adult population

70 — 65 — 60 — 55

1987 1988 1989 1990 1991 1992 1993 1994 1995 1996 1997

Sources: W. R. Simmons & Associates Research Inc; Simmons Market Research Bureau Inc.; Scarborough Reports–Top 50 DMA Markets.

The percentage of adults in the United States who reported reading a newspaper daily declined dramatically in the middle to late-1990's.

While his wild front pages lured readers, his editorial pages—designed specifically to instruct new immigrants on how to be good Americans—were meant to be civic minded. Pulitzer's newspapers, according to Pulitzer, were "a daily schoolhouse and a daily forum—both a daily teacher and a daily tribune."

Nearly all of the newspapers that practiced tabloid journalism were serious about democratizing an America changed by massive immigration. The *Boston Herald* was "A Newspaper Made for All." The *Chicago Tribune*, not yet the "World's Greatest Newspaper," was "The People's Paper." Edward W. Scripps, who built the first newspaper chain in the United States, instructed his editors "to serve that class of people and only that class of people from whom you cannot hope to derive any other income than the one cent a day they pay you for your paper."

Fall from grace

Gradually, the excesses of yellow journalism fell out of fashion. By the early 1900's, many Americans had grown tired of sensationalized stories, and editors and reporters strove to make newspapers more professional, scientific, and objective. Starting in the 1890's, Adolph Ochs, owner of *The New York Times*, marketed his newspaper as an alternative to the tabloid papers by claiming to publish only "the news that's fit to print." Ochs avoid lurid and sensational stories and instructed his editors to publish news that was as free from prejudice as possible.

At the same time, the children of the great wave of immigrants in the 1890's were reaching adulthood. Lurid tales of the city were no novelty to a generation of people who had grown up in city streets. Educated in the public school systems of such cities, the new generation developed tastes that differed markedly from their parents. They wanted news that was reliable and rejected such papers as the *World* and the *Journal* for publications that were considered respectable by the establishment of the day, such as Ochs's *The New York Times*.

Advertising also played a major role in the decline of the tabloid press. Big advertisers, such as department stores, gravitated toward newspapers that appealed to middle- and upper-class readers. When newspaper publishers came to realize that profits from advertising were far greater than profits from circulation, Pulitzer and Hearst's tabloid journalism was doomed by its own success. Big advertisers were uninterested in reaching people with little or no disposable income.

By the end of World War I (1914-1918), the worst excesses of tabloid journalism were largely over, and a movement, which was never wholly successful, was underway to make journalism a profession akin to medicine and law. Pulitzer, who died in 1911, bequeathed $2 million to New York City's Columbia University to establish a graduate school of journalism. He also left money to fund the Pulitzer Prizes, annual awards that recognize excellence in journalism.

A new era of sensationalism

The sensationalism of the 1990's, like its counterpart in the 1890's, was born of technological change and reared in an atmosphere of intense competition. In the early 1990's, cable television, which delivers television signals via cable rather than over airwaves, expanded the number of TV channels available to most American viewers from 6 or 7 to nearly 100. As a result, the three major networks—the American Broadcasting Companies (ABC), National Broadcasting Company (NBC), and CBS Inc.—lost their dominance over the industry. In the 1970's and early 1980's, these national networks shared more than 90 percent of television's American audience. By the beginning of the 1990's, they had lost more than 40 percent of that audience.

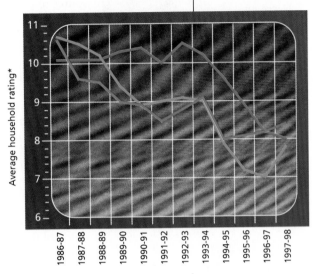

EARLY EVENING NEWS RATINGS

ABC
CBS
NBC

*One rating point represents 1 percent of the total U.S. households with a television.
Source: Nielsen Media Research.

Ratings for evening news broadcasts at each of the three major U.S. television networks began to decline in the mid-1990's.

Studies conducted in the 1990's by the Pew Research Center for the People and the Press concluded that the television audience in the United States had become so segmented that no regularly scheduled program drew more than 20 percent of the population. The Pew Research Center is a Washington, D.C.-based polling operation that studies public attitudes toward the press. This splintering of the audience, combined with a general decline in the number of people watching television, seriously eroded advertising revenues, the networks' primary source of profit.

During approximately the same period, all three networks were sold. In 1986, General Electric Company merged with the RCA Corporation, the parent corporation of NBC; Westinghouse Electric Corporation became the largest broadcasting company in the United States with the acquisition of CBS in 1995; and Walt Disney Company purchased Capital Cities/ABC Incorporated, the company that owned ABC, in 1996. Faced with declining revenues from advertisers, the new owners demanded that news departments produce profits. Before this time, television executives did not expect the news to make money. News programs, whether daily, weekly, or specials, were produced to enhance the reputation of the network as well as to satisfy Federal Communications Commission (FCC) requirements that networks provide a certain amount of programming in the public interest. In the 1980's, the federal government systematically deregulated television. The deregulation all but eliminated public interest requirements.

A changing political landscape

The rise of cable television also overlapped with the end of the *Cold War* (the intense rivalry that existed between the former Soviet Union and the United States between approximately 1945 and 1991). With its constant threat of nuclear attack and retaliation, the Cold War had provided journalists with stories of enormous importance. It also provided a yardstick against which the importance of all other news could be measured. While the divorce and remarriage of a film star was capable of generating a great deal of media attention in the early 1960's, its importance compared with the Cuban Missile Crisis was never in question. The 1991 collapse of the Soviet Union greatly diminished the threat of nuclear war. Without that threat, the importance accorded the news, by both journalists and their audiences, also diminished.

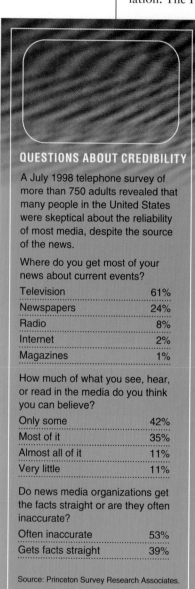

QUESTIONS ABOUT CREDIBILITY

A July 1998 telephone survey of more than 750 adults revealed that many people in the United States were skeptical about the reliability of most media, despite the source of the news.

Where do you get most of your news about current events?

Television	61%
Newspapers	24%
Radio	8%
Internet	2%
Magazines	1%

How much of what you see, hear, or read in the media do you think you can believe?

Only some	42%
Most of it	35%
Almost all of it	11%
Very little	11%

Do news media organizations get the facts straight or are they often inaccurate?

Often inaccurate	53%
Gets facts straight	39%

Source: Princeton Survey Research Associates.

Covering the rich and famous

Journalists in the 1990's refocused their attention from the international scene to those subjects that had fueled the tabloid press a century earlier—crime, scandal, disasters, and the goings on of the rich and famous. Nancy Kerrigan, a top U.S. figure-skater, became one of the earliest subjects of that focus. In 1994, an attacker struck Kerrigan on the knee as she was leaving the ice during a skating competition. One of the men connected to the attack turned out to be the former husband of one of Kerrigan's rivals, Tonya Harding. The media gave the story the coverage usually reserved for wars and political assassinations.

When the Harding-Kerrigan story wound down, networks and local TV news programs nationwide searched for other high-profile stories. The most spectacular was the 1995 trial of former football star and sports commentator O. J. Simpson, who was accused of the 1994 murder of his former wife, Nicole Brown Simpson, and her friend, Ronald Goldman. Experts label media events like the Simpson trial "crossover stories," because their appeal cuts across a number of core audience groups. In the case of the Simpson trial, these included fans of sports, movie and Hollywood gossip, crime, and courtroom dramas.

When the O. J. Simpson case began, CNN, the all-news cable network launched in 1980, was losing audience share in much the same way as the networks. CNN's audience had declined by nearly 25 percent in 1993 alone. Believing that the Simpson trial would become a crossover story that could boost audience size above that 20 percent threshold, CNN converted itself into a virtual "all O. J." network for the two years, covering every aspect of the trial and subsequent civil suits. While audience ratings for the Simpson trial were high, they were not overwhelming. They were, however, higher than CNN had been getting before the trial.

Executives at news organizations began to believe that big, sensational stories, like the Kerrigan attack and the Simpson trial, would provide the larger audiences that would boost profits. They also recognized other economic aspects of such sensational fare. Such stories were relatively inexpensive to cover. Sending a news crew to Los Angeles to cover a murder trial cost considerably less then dispatching

---

Location: `http://www.info`

What's New?   What's Co[

REPORTS OF BOB HOPE'S DEATH WERE GREATLY EXAGGERATED

Journalists in the late-1990's are faced with increasing pressures from outside the traditional media of television, radio, and newspapers to report news first. The availability of unreliable or unverified facts on the Internet helped spread misinformation. A prime example occurred in June 1998, when news of Bob Hope's death appeared on the Internet.

A technical error resulted in the Associated Press (AP) placing comedian Bob Hope's advance obituary on its Web site.

House Majority Leader Dick Armey (R., Texas) saw a copy of the AP story, handed it to Representative Bob Stump (R., Arizona), and asked him to announce Hope's death on the House floor.

The announcement, broadcast live on the cable television channel C-SPAN, became the source for other news organizations. Several NBC affiliates and ABC News Radio, were soon reporting that Hope had died. Reporters cited Stump's tribute on the House floor.

Within minutes of the initial announcement, a family spokesman notified the media that Hope had not died, but was eating breakfast at his California home.

foreign correspondents to Bosnia-Herzegovina to cover a civil war. The Harding-Kerrigan story also demonstrated the profitability of the magazine-format program in prime time. While such programs as "Prime Time Live" and "Dateline" did not necessarily attract big audiences, they were inexpensive to produce, costing approximately half what a traditional entertainment program costs. They filled expensive, prime television time cheaply, turning a profit for networks and for news divisions.

After the Simpson trial, journalists found other sensational stories, such as the JonBenet Ramsey murder case; the murder of Ennis Cosby, the son of comedian Bill Cosby; the death of Diana, Princess of Wales; and then Monica Lewinsky. The Lewinsky story helped define the new era of infotainment because it was political scandal that had all branches of the media cross-fertilizing each other's journalism in their intense competition for a daily exclusive.

The Internet and journalism

The Lewinsky story was also the first time in which the Internet competed with traditional news sources to play a major role in the development of a major news story. After *Newsweek* magazine concluded in early January 1998 that certain parts of their article on Lewinsky's relationship with the president could not be verified and should not, therefore, be printed, a gossip columnist broke the story on the Internet. Within a few days it was confirmed and picked up by all of the media, including both the tabloid press and the mainstream press.

As competition increased, many reputable news organizations increasingly began republishing stories they had not independently checked for accuracy or verified with sources. *The Dallas Morning News* published a story in January on its Website that claimed a Secret Service agent had seen the president and Lewinsky in "a compromising position." The story appeared on the front pages of newspapers the following day. One of the article's sources later said that the story was inaccurate. In February, *The Wall Street Journal* ran a story on its Website about an employee in the White House who had reportedly testified before a grand jury that he saw the president and Lewinsky alone together. The following day, the story appeared on websites and in newspapers. *Journal* editors retracted it after other sources reported that the account of the testimony was inaccurate.

Many media critics cited such cross-fertilization between news organizations and news media as a demonstration of tabloid journalism's negative effect on the industry. They argued that the news organizations with the lowest standards, those publishing or broadcasting gossip as fact, were pulling down the standards of the rest of the media.

Decreasing audiences

Even as the news became more and more sensationalized in the late 1990's, media experts were concluding that infotainment in the long run had not generated a larger audience. Despite crossover stories and political scandals, network news audiences continued to shrink. According to Nielsen Media Research, a New York City-based agency that tracks television viewership, early evening news programs during the 1997-1998 television season received an average of 8 ratings points. (A rating point represents 1 percent of all the nation's estimated residences with a television in that season.) During the 1987-1988 television season, nightly news programs had received an average of 10 ratings points, a 20 percent decline.

Continuing challenges

There were also signs of public backlash. During the late 1990's, the National Enquirer lost a third of its readers, roughly a million people. Public opinion surveys suggested a simmering public anger toward the more moderate or mainstream press over sensationalism. While approximately 25 percent of the American public followed the Simpson trial closely, 75 percent of the American public was angry that the story so dominated the news, according to studies by the Pew Research Center. By 1997, sensationalism and hype had become the major source of public dissatisfaction with the press, up substantially from 1994 when political bias topped the list.

A second backlash against infotainment began in the newsroom, which led to the formation of organizations like the Committee of Concerned Journalists, a group of writers, correspondents, producers, and editors taking a stand for excellence. During the same period, the American Society of Newspaper Editors undertook a three-year study on ways to enhance media credibility with the public.

Various factors killed tabloid journalism in the late 1800's, including dissatisfaction among the public and within the industry. Then *The New York Times* came up with a new model of journalistic excellence that offered readers and advertisers an alternative to the tabloid newspapers. Public and professional dissatisfaction with tabloid journalism also existed in the late 1990's. The still-missing ingredient to journalistic reform for the 2000's was a new model of economic success for others to follow.

QUESTIONS ABOUT REPORTING

A July 1998 telephone survey of more than 750 adults revealed that many people in the United States blame outside pressures for moving reporting toward entertainment and away from hard news.

In competition for ratings and profits, have the news media gone too far in the direction of entertainment and away from traditional reporting?

Yes, gone too far	76 %
No, not too far	20 %

Compared with the past, is journalists' reporting today more likely, less likely, or about as likely to be influenced by: (percentage saying more likely)

Pressure from media owners and news executives for higher ratings and profits	77 %
Competitive pressure from other journalists for a story	71 %
A desire to become a celebrity or make money from personal fame	70 %
A desire to report the news fairly and accurately	33 %

Are cases of media inaccuracy isolated incidents, or do they make you less likely to trust the media's reporting?

Isolated incidents	62 %
Less likely to trust the media	30 %

Source: Princeton Survey Research Associates.

Nicaragua. In late October 1998, torrential rains from Hurricane Mitch left more than 4,000 people dead and at least 1,300 others missing in Nicaragua. In western Nicaragua near the Honduran border, the wall of the water-filled crater of the Casita Volcano gave way, burying entire villages near the city of Polsotega and killing at least 1,500 people.

In March, Zoilamerica Narvaez Murillo, the 30-year-old stepdaughter of former President Daniel Ortega Saavedra, accused him of sexually abusing and harassing her since she was 11 years old. Despite the ensuing controversy, Ortega was re-elected secretary general of the Sandinista National Liberation Front on May 23. On May 27, Narvaez filed charges against Ortega, who claimed immunity to prosecution as a member of the National Assembly.

On May 5, President Arnoldo Aleman Lacayo suspended seven government officials after learning that he and other Nicaraguan leaders had flown, unknowingly, aboard a stolen jet aircraft loaded with cocaine. Allegedly, Jose Francisco Guasch, a Cuban American, offered his plane for presidential flights to avoid regular inspections of his cargo. Several officials faced criminal charges. ☐ Nathan A. Haverstock

See also **Latin America** (Facts in brief table).

Niger. See Africa.

Nigeria. The death of military dictator General Sani Abacha on June 8, 1998, reportedly from a heart attack, provided a window of opportunity for democratic reform in Nigeria. After a tentative start, Abacha's successor, General Abdul-salam Abubakar, instituted a plan aimed at restoring civilian government in May 1999.

More of the same. In early 1998, Abacha had come under growing domestic and foreign criticism for plotting to break his promise to end military rule by October. At the urging of Nigeria's prodemocracy organizations, 90 percent of the country's voters boycotted legislative elections held on April 25. The elections were criticized as a sham because all official candidates represented parties supported by Abacha's regime. In addition, all the parties had endorsed Abacha as their candidate for a presidential election scheduled for August.

Plans for democracy. Much to the dismay of Nigeria's prodemocracy groups, Abubakar initially pledged only to follow Abacha's widely criticized program for restoring democracy. On July 20, however, Abubakar promised national elections within the first three months of 1999 and a return to civilian rule on May 29, 1999. Abubakar also nullified the results of the April 1998 elections and announced the release of all the country's political prisoners.

Nigerian dictator General Sani Abacha reviews troops during a visit to Freetown, Sierra Leone, in early 1998. Abacha's death on June 8 paved the way for his successor, General Abdul-salam Abubakar, to institute plans to return the Nigerian government to civilian control in 1999.

Abiola's death. Abubakar's transition plan was overshadowed by the sudden death of Moshood Abiola on July 7. Abiola, widely believed to have won a 1993 presidential election that was annulled by the military, died of a heart attack just hours before his expected release from four years in detention. The timing of his death led to violent protests on July 7 and 8, 1998, in which about 60 people were killed. An independent investigation by an international team of pathologists confirmed in August that Abiola had died of natural causes and not foul play, as some, including members of his family, had suspected.

Soyinka returns. Exiled Nigerian author Wole Soyinka, one of the most outspoken critics of Abacha's military regime, returned home on October 14, at Abubakar's invitation. Soyinka, winner of the 1986 Nobel Prize for literature, had fled Nigeria in 1994 under threat of arrest. In 1997, he had been charged with treason.

Pipeline blast. At least 700 people died on Oct. 17, 1998, when fire engulfed a gasoline pipeline punctured by thieves near the southern town of Warri. Many of the victims had been scavenging fuel from the pipeline. Although Nigeria is a major oil-producing state, corruption and mismanagement have resulted in gasoline shortages. ☐ Simon Baynham

See also **Africa** (Facts in brief table).

Nobel Prizes in literature, peace, the sciences, and economics were awarded in October 1998 by the Norwegian *Storting* (parliament) in Oslo and by the Royal Swedish Academy of Sciences, the Karolinska Institute, and the Swedish Academy in Stockholm. Each prize was worth about $978,000.

The 1998 Nobel Prize for literature went to Portuguese writer José Saramago. The Swedish Academy noted that "with parables sustained by imagination, compassion, and irony," Saramago's work illuminates the often baffling reality of the human condition. In his 1995 novel *Blindness,* the narrator witnesses the rest of humanity going blind. In his 1989 novel, *The History of the Siege of Lisbon,* a proofreader of a history book changes world events by inserting the word "not" into a sentence. One of his most successful novels, *The Year of the Death of Ricardo Reis,* is a fictional account of war-torn Portugal in 1936. Saramago, who was born in 1922, began his professional writing career when he was 60 years old.

The 1998 Nobel Peace Prize was shared by David Trimble and John Hume "for their efforts to find a peaceful solution to the conflict in Northern Ireland." Trimble, Northern Ireland's first minister, is leader of the Ulster Unionist Party, a Protestant pro-British group. He set the framework for 1998 peace agreements by meeting with leaders of the Republic of Ireland. John Hume, a Roman Catholic leader who had been nominated twice before for the peace prize, worked for more than 30 years to resolve the social, religious, and political problems in Northern Ireland. Hume ensured that the peace talks included the separatist Sinn Fein party and Protestant paramilitary groups. Trimble and Hume were the primary creators of the Belfast, or Good Friday, Agreement, a peace settlement signed on April 10, 1998.

The 1998 Nobel Prize for physiology or medicine was given to three pharmacologists from the United States, Robert Furchgott of the State University of New York at Brooklyn, Louis Ignarro of the University of California at Los Angeles, and Ferid Murad of the University of Texas Medical School at Houston. They were recognized for their discoveries, primarily during the 1980's, of the role of nitric oxide in the human body.

Nitric oxide is most commonly known as a pollutant produced by burning fossil fuels. The researchers learned, however, that the gas also acts as a *signal molecule* (biological messenger) that initiates functions in the immune, nervous, and cardiovascular systems. The Nobel winners were cited, in particular, for their research on how nitric oxide affects the expansion of blood vessels. Their insights led to treatments for high blood pressure, heart disease, and *impotence* (the inability to achieve or maintain a penile erection).

The 1998 Nobel Prize for economics went to Amartya Sen of India, a professor at Trinity College, Cambridge University, in Cambridge, England. He was cited for his contributions to *welfare economics,* the study of the cause and impact of poverty and hunger in developing nations. Some of his most important studies showed that famines "occurred even when the supply of food was not significantly lower than during previous years" and that such catastrophes had more to do with inadequate incomes among the poorest people. Sen, a native of India, stated that he was gratified to win the prize because his theories affect the lives of ordinary people.

The 1998 Nobel Prize for chemistry was awarded to Walter Kohn of the University of California at Santa Barbara and John Pople of Northwestern University in Evanston, Illinois, for their contributions to quantum chemistry. This field of study applies *quantum mechanics,* the branch of physics dealing with the behavior of atoms and subatomic particles, to the study of molecules.

Since the early 1900's, chemists had hoped to describe how bonds between atoms in molecules function, but researchers were limited by the complexity of the mathematical computations necessary to describe such quantum behavior. Kohn and Pople, whose work in this field began in the 1960's, advanced the research dramatically. Kohn developed a sort of atomic averaging method that simplified computations for studying molecules. Pople developed computational methods for studying molecules, their properties, and changes in their properties during chemical reactions.

The 1998 Nobel Prize for physics was shared by Robert Laughlin of Stanford University in Stanford, California, Horst Stormer of Columbia University in New York City, and Daniel Tsui of Princeton University in Princeton, New Jersey, for the discovery of a phenomenon known as the fractional quantum Hall effect. In 1982, Stormer and Tsui observed that when *electrons* (negatively charged subatomic particles) are exposed to extremely cold temperatures and strong magnetic fields, the electrons appear to break up into identical pieces with charges that can be measured as fractions of their original charges. These "quasiparticles" make up a kind of quantum fluid that can conduct electricity without any resistance.

Laughlin developed a theory that successfully explained the observations of the two other physicists. Although the practical application of the discovery remained undetermined, the Nobel committee offered an explanation of the importance of this discovery. "The events in a drop of quantum fluid can afford more profound insights into the general inner structure and dynamics of matter."
□ Brian Bouldrey

See also **Hinduism; Northern Ireland.**

Children in Belfast rejoice in May 1998 when voters in the Republic of Ireland and Northern Ireland overwhelmingly approved the Belfast—or Good Friday—Agreement. The British and Irish initiative was intended to end years of violence.

Northern Ireland. An agreement to end years of conflict between Northern Ireland, Ireland, and Great Britain was signed on April 10, 1998. The Belfast—or Good Friday—Agreement was the most significant initiative between unionists and nationalists since the 1921 Anglo-Irish treaty. Unionists favored the union of Northern Ireland with Great Britain; nationalists favored the reunion of Northern Ireland with Ireland. The Anglo-Irish treaty divided Ireland into a British-ruled province with a Protestant majority in the north and an independent, primarily Roman Catholic republic in the south.

The 1998 Belfast Agreement stated that Northern Ireland was to remain part of the United Kingdom unless a majority of Northern Ireland's people voted for a change. However, the Republic of Ireland was to play a role in the north's affairs by sending representatives to a newly created, 108-member Northern Ireland Assembly. The assembly can pass laws on such issues as health and education, but not security. The assembly was to set up a North-South Ministerial Council in which Northern Ireland and Ireland were to cooperate on such issues as economic development, tourism, and fisheries. As part of the agreement, most of Northern Ireland's more than 500 convicted terrorists were to be released within two years. Unofficial military groups, including the Irish Republican Army (IRA)—which sought to unite Northern Ireland with Ireland—were to surrender their weapons within two years.

Referendum. In May, 71 percent of the voters in Northern Ireland approved the agreement, and 94 percent of voters in the Republic of Ireland agreed to drop the republic's claim to the north. In elections for the Northern Ireland Assembly in June, the Ulster Unionist Party (UUP)—Northern Ireland's largest political party—took the most seats, 28. The Assembly elected UUP leader David Trimble as first minister.

More troubles. Annual summer marches by members of the Orange Order, a 200-year-old Protestant organization, through Catholic neighborhoods threatened the agreement in July. However, the deaths of three Catholic boys in an arson attack believed to have been staged by Protestants incited public outrage, and the Orangemen dispersed. The agreement was threatened again in August when a bomb exploded in the town of Omagh in western Northern Ireland, killing 29 people. An IRA splinter group that opposed the peace agreement claimed responsibility. In the wave of revulsion that followed, the group declared a cease-fire. ☐ Ian Mather

See also **Ireland; United Kingdom**.

Northwest territories. See **Canadian territories**.

Norway. Prime Minister Kjell Magne Bondevik took a leave of absence in September 1998 after his physician reported that he was suffering from depression caused by overwork and the stress of holding together Norway's minority, center-right government. Bondevik's Christian People's Party and its coalition partners, the Center and the Liberal parties, controlled only 42 of the 165 seats in the Storting (parliament).

Bondevik's health problems coincided with growing pressures that threatened the health of Norway's economy. After five years of strong growth, the economy was at risk for an outbreak of inflation. The economy was forecast to grow by 3.4 percent in 1998, with inflation rising to 3.5 percent and unemployment falling to 3.2 percent. However, the sharp drop in global oil prices reduced 1998 revenues from Norway's North Sea oil and gas industry and depressed the value of the Norwegian crown. In October, the government proposed a \$1.7-billion package of spending cuts and tax increases in its 1999 budget to slow the economy and ease the threat of inflation.   □ Tom Buerkle

See also **Europe** (Facts in brief table); **Europe Special Report: European Union.**

Nova Scotia. See Canadian provinces.
Nuclear energy. See Energy supply.
Nutrition. See Food.

Ocean. In 1998, *El Nino,* a warming of the eastern tropical Pacific waters that disrupts global weather patterns every three to seven years, became a staple of television news and was blamed, rightly or wrongly, for nearly every unusual weather condition worldwide. The El Nino of late 1997 and early 1998 was the most intense yet recorded. Pacific Ocean water temperatures peaked in December 1997 at more than 8 °F (4.5 °C) above normal. In May 1998, these temperatures began a steep decline, and by July, they dropped to about 4 °F (2 °C) below normal.

The westward spread of the cooling in August signaled the beginning of a cold episode known as La Nina. La Nina's effects, which scientists predicted in 1998 would last through the spring of 1999, are generally the opposite of those of El Nino. For example, in contrast to El Nino, La Nina causes more hurricanes in the western Atlantic and fewer in the eastern Pacific.

Ocean programs progress. Three ocean-research programs—the Joint Global Ocean Fluxes Study (JGOFS), the World Ocean Circulation Experiment (WOCE), and the Climate Variability and Predictability Program (CLIVAR)—achieved major milestones in 1998. JGOFS, a 32-nation program begun in 1988 by an international group of scientists called the Scientific Committee for Ocean Research, completed the most detailed survey to date of dissolved carbon and chemical nutrients in the world's oceans. The JGOFS scientists hoped their data would help them better understand how the oceans moderate the greenhouse effect by removing carbon dioxide from the atmosphere. The greenhouse effect is a warming of the atmosphere that results from the trapping of heat rays by certain atmospheric gases. Many scientists believe that carbon dioxide produced by the burning of fossil fuels increases this atmospheric warming.

In May 1998, 400 scientists from 28 countries affiliated with WOCE, a major component of the intergovernmental World Climate Research Program (WCRP), marked the end of their eight-year survey of the world's oceans by holding a conference in Halifax, Nova Scotia. In an early and striking conclusion drawn from the data, the scientists noted that the circulation of ocean waters is much more complicated than previously thought.

In December, scientists with CLIVAR, an international project to improve long-term climate prediction through better computer models, presented their "first implementation plan" at a conference in Paris. The plan included a set of guiding principles that government agencies might implement to improve the observation, modeling, and analysis of factors, including ocean conditions, that influence climate.

New ocean program. The Global Ocean Data Assimilation Experiment (GODAE), an international project funded partly by the U.S. National Oceanic and Atmospheric Administration, was launched in 1998 to demonstrate the benefits of an integrated worldwide ocean observation system. Scientists began preparing research proposals for the experiment, which was scheduled to be carried out from 2003 to 2005. Once implemented, GODAE was to include a network of some 3,000 floats with sensors that are to gather a constant stream of data on temperature, *salinity* (saltiness), and currents from all the world's oceans. Such a reporting network has long been a dream of ocean scientists.

Microbes found beneath sea floor. In August 1998, researchers with the international Ocean Drilling Program, which was established in 1985 by 22 countries to conduct sea-floor research, completed their investigation of one of the world's most active fault zones in a region off the coast of Papua New Guinea. The scientists discovered bacteria in sedimentary rock collected from more than 2,700 feet (800 meters) below the sea floor. The discovery extended the known limit of the *biosphere* (the region around Earth that can support life).   □ Arthur G. Alexiou

Ohio. See State government.
Oklahoma. See State government.
Old age. See Social security.

Tara Lipinski, United States, Women's Figure Skating

THE 1998 WINTER
OLYMPICS

By Peter Uremovic

New records,
career milestones,
and individual
triumphs
highlighted
the 28th Olympic
Winter Games
in February 1998.

The opening ceremonies on Feb. 7, 1998, of the XVIII Winter Olympics, in Nagano, Japan, kicked off a two-week winter sports showcase, which many observers would later describe as the best organized Olympics in the event's modern history. Athletes from 72 nations participated in the games, many of them achieving career milestones and setting new Olympic records. In the final medal tally, Germany came away with 29 medals, 12 of them gold, followed by Norway with 25 medals, 10 of which were gold. Russian athletes captured 18 total medals with 9 golds. And Japanese athletes thrilled local fans with their best showing in a Winter Olympics, winning 10 medals, of which 5 were gold. Canada also reached a historic high, taking 15 medals, 6 of which were gold.

The debut of a new skate design in Olympic competition was chiefly responsible for an avalanche of broken speedskating records at Nagano. The "clap skate," a new speed skate design legalized by the International Skating Union in June 1997, features a blade that is not attached to the skater's heel. This allows the blade to remain in contact with the ice slightly longer as the skater pushes off, resulting in a more powerful forward stroke. A total of five Olympic and six world long-track speed-skating records were broken at the 1998 games. (Short-track speed skaters do not use clap skates.) The only long-track Olympic record set prior to the introduction of clap skates that remained unbroken after Nagano was the men's 500 meters.

The greatest drama for Alpine skiing fans centered around Austria's Hermann Maier, a long time star on the Alpine skiing circuit and a gold-medal favorite at Nagano. Treacherous conditions during the men's downhill event caused crashes that eliminated 15 competitors from contention. Among them was Maier, who lost control and cartwheeled violently down the mountainside, coming to rest only after crashing through a protective barrier. However, Maier suffered no serious injuries and returned to the slopes to win gold medals in the giant slalom and super giant slalom within the week.

Cross-country skiing veteran Bjorn Daehlie also won two gold medals at Nagano. His gold in the men's 50 kilometers was the eighth Olympic gold medal of his distinguished career, a record for the winter games. In addition, Daehlie's performance at Nagano lifted his career Olympic medal tally to 12, surpassing the previous record of 10 held by Russian cross-country skier Raisa Smetanina.

The Winter Olympics at Nagano featured the debut of women's hockey as a medal sport. As expected, the United States and Canada squared off in the gold-medal game, which the Americans won, 3-1. For North American hockey fans, the women's tournament provided an emotional boost after the highly touted Canadian and U.S. men's teams failed to even reach the medal round of their tournament. The Czech Republic won the gold in men's hockey, upsetting Russia by a score of 1-0.

Of all the events at the Winter Olympics, women's figure skating received the lion's share of attention, fueled by the ongoing rivalry between Americans Michelle Kwan and Tara Lipinski. At age 15, Lipinski became the youngest figure-skater ever to win Olympic gold. Following her impressive long-program routine, she sprinted to center ice to take her bows in an exuberant display of joy and triumph. Lipinski's upset victory over Kwan and Kwan's graciousness in defeat provided one of the chief highlights of the Nagano games.

The highlight of the closing ceremonies on February 22 was a haunting, twilight tribute to the Olympic tradition. In the gathering darkness, the lighting systems of Nagano Sports Park were turned off, and on cue, spectators switched on battery-operated lanterns to transform the stadium into a sea of soft, glowing light. As a giant video monitor showed highlights from past winter games, the spectators in the stadium fell silent until a barrage of fireworks filled the skies to the crowd's cheers. The Olympic flag was then lowered and passed on to the mayor of Salt Lake City, Utah, host city of the XIX Winter Games in 2002.

The author:
Peter Uremovic is a staff editor with *World Book Year Book.*

Biathlon

Men's 10 Kilometers
GOLD	Ole Einar Bjoerndalen, Norway
SILVER	Frode Andresen, Norway
BRONZE	Ville Raikkonen, Finland

Men's 20 Kilometers
GOLD	Halvard Hanevold, Norway
SILVER	Pier Alberto Carrara, Italy
BRONZE	Aleksei Aidarov, Belarus

Men's 4x7.5-Kilometer Relay
GOLD	Germany
SILVER	Norway
BRONZE	Russia

Women's 7.5 Kilometers
GOLD	Galina Koukleva, Russia
SILVER	Ursula Disl, Germany
BRONZE	Katrin Apel, Germany

Women's 15 Kilometers
GOLD	Ekaterina Dafovska, Bulgaria
SILVER	Elena Petrova, Ukraine
BRONZE	Ursula Disl, Germany

Women's 4x7.5-Kilometer Relay
GOLD	Germany
SILVER	Russia
BRONZE	Norway

Pierre Lueders and David MacEachern, Canada, Two-man Bobsled

Bobsled

Two-Man
GOLD (TIE)	Canada I (Pierre Lueders, David MacEachern)
	Italy I (Guenther Huber, Antonio Tartaglia)
BRONZE	Germany I (Christoph Langen, Markus Zimmermann)

Four-Man
GOLD	Germany II (Christoph Langen, Markus Zimmermann, Marco Jakobs, Olaf Hampel)
SILVER	Switzerland I (Marcel Rohner, Markus Nuessli, Markus Wasser, Beat Seitz)
BRONZE (TIE)	Great Britain I (Sean Olsson, Dean Martin Ward, Orville Rumbolt, Paul Jason Attwood)
	France (Bruno Mingeon, Emmanuel Hostache, Eric Le Chanony, Max Robert)

Curling

Men's
GOLD	Switzerland
SILVER	Canada
BRONZE	Norway

Women's
GOLD	Canada
SILVER	Denmark
BRONZE	Sweden

Figure Skating

Men's
GOLD	Ilia Kulik, Russia
SILVER	Elvis Stojko, Canada
BRONZE	Philippe Candeloro, France

Women's
GOLD	Tara Lipinski, United States
SILVER	Michelle Kwan, United States
BRONZE	Lu Chen, China

Pair's

GOLD Oksana Kazakova, Artur Dmitriev,
Russia

SILVER Elena Berezhnaya, Anton Sikharulidze,
Russia

BRONZE Mandy Woetzel, Ingo Steuer,
Germany

Ice Dancing

GOLD Pasha Grishuk, Evgeny Platov,
Russia

SILVER Anjelika Krylova, Oleg Ovsyannikov,
Russia

BRONZE Marina Anissina, Gwendal Peizerat,
France

Ice Hockey

Men's
GOLD Czech Republic
SILVER Russia
BRONZE Finland

Women's
GOLD United States
SILVER Canada
BRONZE Finland

Pasha Grishuk and Evgeny Platov, Russia,
Ice Dancing

United States Women's Hockey Team

Luge

Men's Singles
GOLD Georg Hackl, Germany
SILVER Armin Zoeggeler, Italy
BRONZE Jens Mueller, Germany

Men's Doubles
GOLD Stefan Krausse, Jan Behrendt,
Germany
SILVER Chris Thorpe, Gordy Sheer,
United States
BRONZE Mark Grimmette, Brian Martin,
United States

Women's Singles
GOLD Silke Kraushaar, Germany
SILVER Barbara Niedernhuber, Germany
BRONZE Angelika Neuner, Austria

Skiing

Alpine

Men's Combined
GOLD	Mario Reiter, Austria
SILVER	Lasse Kjus, Norway
BRONZE	Christian Mayer, Austria

Men's Downhill
GOLD	Jean-Luc Cretier, France
SILVER	Lasse Kjus, Norway
BRONZE	Hannes Trinkl, Austria

Men's Super Giant Slalom
GOLD	Hermann Maier, Austria
SILVER (TIE)	Didier Cuche, Switzerland
	Hans Knauss, Austria

Men's Giant Slalom
GOLD	Hermann Maier, Austria
SILVER	Stefan Eberharter, Austria
BRONZE	Michael Von Gruenigen, Switzerland

Men's Slalom
GOLD	Hans-Petter Buraas, Norway
SILVER	Ole Christian Furuseth, Norway
BRONZE	Thomas Sykora, Austria

Women's Combined
GOLD	Katja Seizinger, Germany
SILVER	Martina Ertl, Germany
BRONZE	Hilde Gerg, Germany

Women's Downhill
GOLD	Katja Seizinger, Germany
SILVER	Pernilla Wiberg, Sweden
BRONZE	Florence Masnada, France

Women's Super Giant Slalom
GOLD	Picabo Street, United States
SILVER	Michaela Dorfmeister, Austria
BRONZE	Alexandra Meissnitzer, Austria

Women's Giant Slalom
GOLD	Deborah Compagnoni, Italy
SILVER	Alexandra Meissnitzer, Austria
BRONZE	Katja Seizinger, Germany

Women's Slalom
GOLD	Hilde Gerg, Germany
SILVER	Deborah Compagnoni, Italy
BRONZE	Zali Steggall, Australia

Hermann Maier, Austria,
Men's Giant Slalom and Super Giant Slalom

Freestyle

Men's Moguls
GOLD	Jonny Moseley, United States
SILVER	Janne Lahtela, Finland
BRONZE	Sami Mustonen, Finland

Men's Aerials
GOLD	Eric Bergoust, United States
SILVER	Sebastien Foucras, France
BRONZE	Dmitri Daschinsky, Belarus

Women's Moguls
GOLD	Tae Satoya, Japan
SILVER	Tatjana Mittermayer, Germany
BRONZE	Kari Traa, Norway

Women's Aerials
GOLD	Nikki Stone, United States
SILVER	Xu Nannan, China
BRONZE	Colette Brand, Switzerland

Nordic (Cross-Country)

Men's 10 Kilometers
GOLD	Bjorn Daehlie, Norway
SILVER	Markus Gandler, Austria
BRONZE	Mika Myllylae, Finland

Men's 15 Kilometers Combined Pursuit
GOLD	Thomas Alsgaard, Norway
SILVER	Bjorn Daehlie, Norway
BRONZE	Vladimir Smirnov, Kazakhstan

Men's 30 Kilometers

GOLD	Mika Myllylae, Finland
SILVER	Erling Jevne, Norway
BRONZE	Silvio Fauner, Italy

Men's 50 Kilometers

GOLD	Bjorn Daehlie, Norway
SILVER	Niklas Jonsson, Sweden
BRONZE	Christian Hoffmann, Austria

Men's 4x10-Kilometer Relay

GOLD	Norway
SILVER	Italy
BRONZE	Finland

Women's 5 Kilometers

GOLD	Larissa Lazutina, Russia
SILVER	Katerina Neumannova, Czech Republic
BRONZE	Bente Martinsen, Norway

Women's 10 Kilometers Combined Pursuit

GOLD	Larissa Lazutina, Russia
SILVER	Olga Danilova, Russia
BRONZE	Katerina Neumannova, Czech Republic

Women's 15 Kilometers

GOLD	Olga Danilova, Russia
SILVER	Larissa Lazutina, Russia
BRONZE	Anita Moen-Guidon, Norway

Women's 30 Kilometers

GOLD	Julija Tchepalova, Russia
SILVER	Stefania Belmondo, Italy
BRONZE	Larissa Lazutina, Russia

Women's 4x5-Kilometer Relay

GOLD	Russia
SILVER	Norway
BRONZE	Italy

Nordic Combined

Individual

GOLD	Bjarte Engen Vik, Norway
SILVER	Samppa Lajunen, Finland
BRONZE	Valery Stolyarov, Russia

Team

GOLD	Norway
SILVER	Finland
BRONZE	France

Markus Gandler, Austria; Bjorn Daehlie, Norway; Mika Myllylae, Finland, Men's 10-kilometer Nordic (cross-country) skiing

Ross Rebagliati, Canada, Men's Giant Slalom Snowboarding

Ski Jumping

Normal (90-meter) Hill
GOLD   Jani Soininen, Finland
SILVER   Kazuyoshi Funaki, Japan
BRONZE   Andreas Widhoelzl, Austria

Large (120-meter) Hill
GOLD   Kazuyoshi Funaki, Japan
SILVER   Jani Soininen, Finland
BRONZE   Masahiko Harada, Japan

Team
GOLD   Japan
SILVER   Germany
BRONZE   Austria

Snowboarding

Men's Halfpipe
GOLD   Gian Simmen, Switzerland
SILVER   Daniel Franck, Norway
BRONZE   Ross Powers, United States

Men's Giant Slalom
GOLD   Ross Rebagliati, Canada
SILVER   Thomas Prugger, Italy
BRONZE   Ueli Kestenholz, Switzerland

Women's Halfpipe
GOLD   Nicola Thost, Germany
SILVER   Stine Brun Kjeldaas, Norway
BRONZE   Shannon Dunn, United States

Women's Giant Slalom
GOLD   Karine Ruby, France
SILVER   Heidi Renoth, Germany
BRONZE   Brigitte Koeck, Austria

Speedskating

Men's 500 Meters
GOLD   Hiroyasu Shimizu, Japan, 1:11.35†
SILVER   Jeremy Wotherspoon, Canada
BRONZE   Kevin Overland, Canada

Men's 1,000 Meters
GOLD   Ids Postma, Netherlands, 1:10.64†
SILVER   Jan Bos, Netherlands
BRONZE   Hiroyasu Shimizu, Japan

Men's 1,500 Meters
GOLD   Adne Sondral, Norway, 1:47.87*
SILVER   Ids Postma, Netherlands
BRONZE   Rintje Ritsma, Netherlands

Men's 5,000 Meters
GOLD   Gianni Romme, Netherlands, 6:22.20*
SILVER   Rintje Ritsma, Netherlands
BRONZE   Bart Veldkamp, Belgium

Men's 10,000 Meters
GOLD   Gianni Romme, Netherlands, 13:15.33*
SILVER   Bob de Jong, Netherlands
BRONZE   Rintje Ritsma, Netherlands

Women's 500 Meters
GOLD   Catriona LeMay Doan, Canada, 1:16.60†
SILVER   Susan Auch, Canada
BRONZE   Tomomi Okazaki, Japan

*=World record
†=Olympic record

Hiroyasu Shimizu, Japan, Men's 500-meter Speedskating

Women's 1,000 Meters
GOLD   Marianne Timmer,
              Netherlands, 1:16.51†
SILVER   Chris Witty, United States
BRONZE   Catriona LeMay Doan, Canada

Women's 1,500 Meters
GOLD   Marianne Timmer,
              Netherlands, 1:57.58*
SILVER   Gunda Niemann-Stirnemann,
              Germany
BRONZE   Chris Witty, United States

Women's 3,000 Meters
GOLD   Gunda Niemann-Stirnemann,
              Germany, 4:07.29†
SILVER   Claudia Pechstein, Germany
BRONZE   Anna Friesinger, Germany

Women's 5,000 Meters
GOLD   Claudia Pechstein,
              Germany, 6:59.61*
SILVER   Gunda Niemann-Stirnemann,
              Germany
BRONZE   Lyudmila Prokasheva, Kazakhstan

Short-Track Speedskating

Men's 500 Meters
GOLD   Takafumi Nishitani, Japan
SILVER   An Yulong, China
BRONZE   Hitoshi Uematsu, Japan

Men's 1,000 Meters
GOLD   Kim Dong-Sung, South Korea
SILVER   Li Jiajun, China
BRONZE   Eric Bedard, Canada

Men's 5,000-Meter Relay
GOLD   Canada
SILVER   South Korea
BRONZE   China

Women's 500 Meters
GOLD   Annie Perreault, Canada
SILVER   Yang S. Yang, China
BRONZE   Chun Lee-Kyung, South Korea

Women's 1,000 Meters
GOLD   Chun Lee-Kyung, South Korea
SILVER   Yang S. Yang, China
BRONZE   Won Hye Kyung, South Korea

Women's 3,000-Meter Relay
GOLD   South Korea, 4:16.260*
SILVER   China
BRONZE   Canada

Country	Population	Government	Monetary unit*	Foreign trade (million U.S.$) Exports[†]	Imports[†]
Australia	18,758,000	Governor General William Deane; Prime Minister John Howard	dollar (1.59 = $1)	62,901	65,910
Fiji	820,000	President Ratu Sir Kamisese Mara; Prime Minister Sitiveni Rabuka	dollar (1.96 = $1)	748	984
Kiribati	84,000	President Teburoro Tito	Australian dollar	7	34
Marshall Islands	59,000	President Imata Kabua	U.S. dollar	21	70
Micronesia, Federated States of	135,000	President Jacob Nena	U.S. dollar	29	141
Nauru	12,000	President Bernard Dowiyogo	Australian dollar	25	21
New Zealand	3,683,000	Governor General Sir Michael Hardie-Boys; Prime Minister Jennifer Shipley	dollar (1.86 = $1)	14,052	14,520
Palau	18,000	President Kuniwo Nakamura	U.S. dollar	1	25
Papua New Guinea	4,596,000	Governor General Sir Silas Atopare; Prime Minister William Skate	kina (2.14 = $1)	2,137	1,696
Samoa	180,000	Head of State Malietoa Tanumafili II; Prime Minister Tofilau Eti Alesana	tala (2.97 = $1)	15	97
Solomon Islands	416,000	Governor General Sir Moses Pitakaka; Prime Minister Bartholomew Ulufa'alu	dollar (3.26 = $1)	168	154
Tonga	104,000	King Taufa'ahau Tupou IV; Prime Minister Baron Vaea	pa'anga (1.59 = $1)	11	75
Tuvalu	10,000	Governor General Sir Tomasi Puaqua; Prime Minister Bikenibeu Paeniu	Australian dollar	1	4
Vanuatu	182,000	President Jean Marie Leye; Prime Minister Donald Kalpokas	vatu (127.75 = $1)	30	97

*Exchange rates as of Nov. 6, 1998, or latest available data.
†Latest available data.

Pacific Islands.

A series of *tsunamis* (enormous waves triggered either by earthquakes or landslides on the ocean floor) struck Papua New Guinea's northern coast on July 17, 1998. The deadly waves washed over 22 miles (35 kilometers) of coastline in West Sepik Province, wiping out seven villages and severely damaging several others. More than 3,000 people died, including most of the children in those villages.

International aid organizations met immediate relief needs, but the government faced the difficult task of rebuilding communities and developing a warning system that could prevent a similar disaster.

Cease-fire agreement. On April 30, leaders of a rebel movement on the Papua New Guinea island of Bougainville signed a cease-fire agreement with the central government. The agreement ended a decade of armed conflict that resulted in the deaths of as many as 15,000 people. The conflict had begun in 1988 when Bou-

gainville residents demanded assistance from the Papua New Guinea government to help settle disputes over property rights and environmental pollution at a copper mine, which was the nation's most important source of export income. The protests eventually led to demands for Bougainville independence. Conflicts escalated when the Bougainville rebels split into various factions.

The 1998 cease-fire agreement included the installation of a United Nations (UN) force, called the Peace Monitoring Group. Australia, the UN, and some European countries pledged financial assistance to help restore order to what had been one of the most prosperous provinces in Papua New Guinea.

Vanuatu. On March 30, Donald Kalpokas was elected prime minister of Vanuatu. He headed a coalition government composed of his own party, Vanua'aku Pati, and the National United Party. In April, Kalpokas reached an agreement with the Asian Development Bank to borrow

$20 million to fund a comprehensive financial reform program. In a surprise move in October, Kalpokas dropped his coalition partner and formed a new coalition government with the Union of Moderate Parties.

Tuvalu. In August, Prime Minister Bikenibeu Paeniu of Tuvalu announced a business deal with Information.ca Corporation of Toronto, Canada, that was expected to provide the nation of 10,000 people with an annual income of more than $60 million. The government's budgets in the 1990's were approximately $5 million.

Tuvalu sold the Canadian company the marketing rights to the country's "domain suffix" on the Internet, the international computer network. Every domain name, or Internet address, in the world (except for those from the United States) has a suffix at the end that identifies the country. Tuvalu's suffix is "tv"—the common abbreviation for television. As the new owner of "tv," Information.ca began selling domain names, for example, www.sitcom.tv, to companies that feature television-related content on their Internet sites.

According to the agreement, Tuvalu receives a 65-percent share of profits from the sale of "tv" domain names. Paeniu promised to manage the nation's anticipated wealth prudently, with priorities given to such projects as health care, education, and global-warming research. (Many scientists have predicted that rising ocean levels caused by global warming could threaten Tuvalu's low-lying islands.)

Solomon Islands. In July, the Solomon Islands observed the 20th anniversary of its independence from Great Britain with a four-day holiday. The festivities coincided with the first Melanesian Arts Festival, held in the capital city, Honiara. (Melanesia is a group of Pacific Islands stretching from eastern Indonesia to Fiji.) People from all of Solomon Islands' provinces and other Melanesian nations presented music, dance, and visual arts.

Palau hosted the Micronesian Games, which attracted more than 1,600 athletes from nine other countries. (Micronesia is the northwestern group of Pacific Island nations.) The host country won the greatest number of medals, but Nauru won the most gold medals and dominated the weightlifting competition.   □ Eugene Ogan

Painting. See Art.

A survivor inspects Sissano, Papua New Guinea, one of seven towns destroyed on July 17, 1998, by powerful *tsunamis,* enormous waves that were triggered by underwater earthquakes.

Pakistan. Prime Minister Nawaz Sharif declared Pakistan a nuclear power in May 1998, after the government conducted the first underground nuclear tests in the country's 51-year history. The tests came two weeks after India—Pakistan's neighbor and archrival—tested its own nuclear weapons.

Pakistan announced that it planned to fit nuclear warheads on a type of missile capable of striking targets across most of north and central India. Pakistan and India, whose military is twice the size of Pakistan's, had raced to develop a nuclear weapons program since India first tested a nuclear device in 1974.

Pleas for restraint. After India conducted tests in early May 1998, world leaders asked Pakistan not to test weapons in retaliation, but the government ignored pleas for restraint. Sharif declared that India "had radically altered the strategic balance in our region," and Pakistan needed its own nuclear weapons to restore the balance.

Sanctions. The tests set off widespread alarm around the world, with statements of condemnation from Russia, China, and Great Britain. The United States reacted by imposing the same package of economic sanctions on Pakistan that it had applied to India after its tests. The sanctions included a suspension of U.S. economic aid, a ban on U.S. bank loans to government institutions,

and pressure for a cutoff of emergency loans from the International Monetary Fund, a United Nations economic agency.

In September, Pakistan and India promised to sign the Comprehensive Test Ban Treaty, which bans nuclear testing. In November, the United States lifted some sanctions, but Pakistan's debt-laden economy was on the edge of bankruptcy. Industrial output in Pakistan fell, inflation rose, and exports declined.

Kashmir. Pakistan and India agreed in October to resume talks on their dispute over Kashmir, a Himalayan region that had been at the center of a dispute between the countries since the two nations were created by partition in 1947. India and Pakistan have fought three wars, two of them over Kashmir. Each country claimed the state as part of its territory.

New president. Mohammad Rafiq Tarar, Sharif's friend and political ally, became president on Jan. 1, 1998. Tarar, a former Supreme Court judge, succeeded Farooq Leghari, who had resigned the presidency in December 1997.

Political feuds. The government placed Pakistan's largest city, Karachi, under military control in late October 1998, after political feuds resulted in the deaths of more than 700 people.

☐ Henry S. Bradsher

See also **Asia** (Facts in brief table); **India.**

A Pakistani child stands in a mosque among adults bowed in a prayer of thanksgiving in May 1998, after Pakistan successfully detonated nuclear weapons. The nuclear tests were the first conducted by Pakistan and came only weeks after India tested its own nuclear bombs.

Paleontology.

In February 1998, two teams of researchers announced that they had separately found microscopic fossils of *embryos* (animals in an early stage of development) in 570- to 580-million-year-old phosphate deposits in southern China. These finds demonstrated that well-preserved fossils of animals at a very early stage of development could be recovered and that complex, multicellular animals lived tens of millions of years earlier than previously thought.

A research team led by paleontologist Chia-Wei Li of National Tsing Hua University in Taiwan recovered not only fossilized embryos of the oldest known *sponges* (simple marine animals) but also embryos of animals that appear to be *bilaterally symmetrical* (having definite left and right sides). Bilaterally symmetrical animals, which include organisms ranging from worms to human beings, are more complex and evolutionarily advanced than such *radially symmetrical* (having a body arranged around a central axis) animals as sponges and corals.

The second group of scientists, headed by paleontologists Shuhia Xiao and Andrew Knoll of Harvard University in Cambridge, Massachusetts, documented fossilized embryos preserved in various stages of cell division, ranging from 2 cells to 64 cells. From the distinctive patterns of cell division, the researchers determined that these embryos also belonged to the bilaterally symmetrical group of animals. The scientists said that some of the patterns indicated a relationship to *crustaceans* (the animal class that includes lobsters, shrimp, and crabs).

Ancient animal traces? Although the fossils from China confirmed the existence of multicellular animals more than half a billion years ago, a discovery announced in October would double that range if verified. Paleontologists led by Adolf Seilacher of Yale University in New Haven, Connecticut, reported finding narrow, wiggly furrows preserved on the surfaces of sandstone layers in central India. The paleontologists interpreted these structures as tunnels made by wormlike animals that lived beneath a sandy sea floor. Scientists had previously dated the sandstone rocks containing the burrows to 1.1 billion years ago, indicating that the fossils were also of that age.

Some scientists doubted that the structures were made by animals. They suggested that the furrows were produced by the *contraction* of sediment or some other geological process. Other researchers doubted the age of the structures, noting that fossil shells in limestone beds directly above the sandstone probably date to less than 540 million years ago.

An age of 1.1 billion years was in line with calculations of molecular biologists who believe that, based on the rate of molecular changes in genetic material, a common ancestor of all animals lived more than 1.2 billion years ago.

Data from dung. Two studies published in 1998 proved that *coprolites* (fossilized feces) are an important storehouse of information about the life habits of extinct animals. The first study, reported in June by paleontologist Karen Chin of the United States Geological Survey and her associates, described a large coprolite, 17 inches (43 centimeters) long by 6 inches (15 centimeters) wide, found in southwestern Saskatchewan. The size, location, and age (66 million to 70 million years old) of the fossil, as well as the abundant dinosaur bone fragments inside it, led scientists to conclude that it was likely left by the huge predatory dinosaur *Tyrannosaurus rex*.

The highly pulverized condition of the bones within the coprolite indicated that *T. rex* chewed its food considerably before swallowing. This came as a surprise to paleontologists, who had assumed that dinosaurs, like crocodiles, gulped chunks of meat with little or no chewing.

In July, a research team headed by molecular biologist Hendrik Poinar and geneticist Svante Paabo of the University of Munich in Germany described their analysis of deoxyribonucleic acid (DNA), the molecule that makes up genes, from a 20,000-year-old dropping preserved by *desiccation* (drying) in Gypsum Cave near Las Vegas, Nevada. Some of the DNA, believed to be from intestinal cells shed with the feces, matched well with DNA that had previously been extracted from the desiccated fossil remains of a giant ground sloth, an animal that became extinct 10,000 years ago. The DNA match indicated that a giant ground sloth produced the coprolite. The scientists also identified DNA from various plants that had been a part of the sloth's diet.

Scientists said if DNA can be extracted and analyzed from coprolite specimens of different ages, it might provide a record of changing vegetation, which reflects changes in climate. Such a record might reveal clues to clarify the suspected relationship between climatic change and animal extinctions over the ages.

Feathered dinosaurs. The case for an evolutionary link between birds and dinosaurs was strengthened in 1998 by the discovery of feathers on two fossils believed to be of small predatory dinosaurs. In June, paleontologists led by Ji Qiang of the National Geological Museum of China in Beijing described two feathered dinosaurs—*Protarchaeopteryx robusta* and *Caudipteryx zoui*—found in a volcanic ash deposit in northeastern China. The specimens are of turkey-sized animals with both downy and shafted types of feathers, including a fanlike plume of feathers at the ends of their tails. Despite the presence of feathers, details of the skeletal structure, particu-

FOCUS ON PALEONTOLOGY

A life-sized model of a baby dinosaur called *Scipionyx samniticus, right,* is based on a fossil described by Italian paleontologists in March 1998. The fossil, *below*—the first dinosaur ever found in Italy—contains well-preserved organs, including the animal's liver, intestines, and windpipe.

Paleontologists in 1998 reported finding highly detailed evidence of soft structures, including organs and feathers, in a number of dinosaur fossils.

A model of *Caudipteryx zoui, right,* one of two feathered dinosaurs described by Chinese paleontologists in June 1998 from fossils found in northeastern China, has long feathers on its arms and tail. Although *C. zoui* and other species appeared very birdlike in life, details of their skeletal structure convinced the paleontologists that the creatures were dinosaurs, not birds.

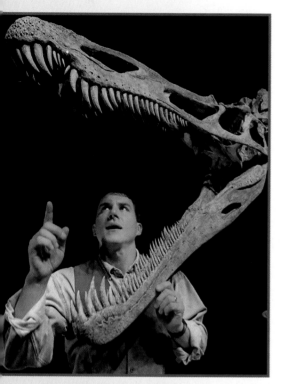

In November 1998, paleontologist Paul Sereno points out features of the teeth of a fish-eating dinosaur, *Suchomimus tenerensis*, which he discovered in the Sahara Desert in late 1997. It was only the third fish-eating dinosaur to be unearthed and was as large as a *Tyrannosaurus rex*.

larly the pelvis, which resembled those found in *theropods* (small carnivorous dinosaurs), convinced most paleontologists that the new finds were dinosaurs.

The specimens came from *strata* (layers of sedimentary rock) dated at between 120 million to 135 million years ago. This age range placed the feathered dinosaurs in a period more recent than the earliest known bird, *Archaeopteryx*, which lived 140 million years ago. These dinosaurs evidently survived alongside early birds. In addition, paleontologists speculated that since neither dinosaur appeared to have had functional wings, feathers probably evolved not for flight but for insulation, camouflage, or sexual displays.

Dinosaur scales. In November 1998, scientists at the American Museum of Natural History in New York City and the Carmen Funes Museum in Argentina announced they had discovered fossilized embryos of dinosaurs showing impressions of the embryos' skin. The scientists said the scale patterns on the 70- to 90-million-year-old fossils, found in Argentina, resembled patterns seen on the skin of modern lizards.   ☐ Carlton E. Brett

Panama was the scene of heated political debates and intrigue in 1998 as the country prepared for May 1999 elections. Many Panamanians worried about who would be in power on Dec. 31, 1999, when the United States turns over complete control of the Panama Canal and $3.5 billion worth of real estate within the Canal Zone.

On Aug. 30, 1998, Panamanians rejected a constitutional amendment by a two-to-one margin that would have allowed President Ernesto Perez Balladares to run for a second consecutive term. Balladares's 1997 appointments of relatives and political allies to the board that would manage the canal after the handover had angered many voters.

During the 1998 campaigning, Panamanian politicians faulted the United States for not doing more to remove unexploded bombs and munitions within the Canal Zone. The U.S. military reportedly had also failed to clean up sites where dangerous nerve, mustard, and phosgene gases had been stored since as early as the 1940's. Popular anger on the issue jeopardized an arrangement allowing the United States to station about 2,000 troops at an antinarcotics center in Panama after the handover.   ☐ Nathan A. Haverstock

See also **Latin America** (Facts in brief table).

Papua New Guinea. See Asia; Pacific Islands.

Paraguay. Raul Cubas Grau, a member of the Colorado Party, was sworn in on Aug. 15, 1998, to a five-year term as president of Paraguay. The new president, an engineer and businessman by profession, pledged to fight against crime, drug trafficking, and government corruption, which he claimed had cost Paraguay some $2 billion since 1996.

Grau stirred up resentment within Paraguay's congress almost immediately after his inauguration by releasing from prison General Lino Cesar Oviedo. In March 1998, a military tribunal had convicted Oviedo, the original Colorado Party presidential candidate, of attempting a *coup d'etat* (takeover) in 1996 that was intended to overthrow a reportedly corrupt administration. The general was sentenced to 10 years in prison, and an electoral tribunal barred him from running for president. Grau, originally Oviedo's running mate, became the new Colorado Party candidate.

Paraguay's congress, which had been controlled by the president's own party since 1954, sought various legal means to reverse Grau's release of Oviedo. Some members of congress threatened to seek Grau's impeachment.

☐ Nathan A. Haverstock

See also **Latin America** (Facts in brief table).

Pennsylvania. See Philadelphia; State government.

■ People in the news

in 1998 included those listed below, who were all Americans unless otherwise indicated.

Adamkus, Valdas (1926–), was elected president of Lithuania on Jan. 4, 1998, in a narrow victory over incumbent Communist President Arturas Paulauskas. Adamkus had spent most of the 50 previous years of his life in the United States.

Adamkus was born on Nov. 3, 1926, in Kaunas, Lithuania. During most of World War II (1939–1945), when the country was occupied either by the Soviet Union or Germany, Adamkus, his parents, sister, and brother lived as refugees in Germany. Adamkus joined the Lithuanian resistance movement and fought in the 1944 battle of Seda, at which the Soviet army defeated the Lithuanians and installed a Communist government. Adamkus returned to Germany where he attended a Lithuanian secondary school and began studies at the University of Munich.

The family immigrated to the United States in 1949, and Adamkus married his wife Alma in 1951. After taking a degree in civil engineering in 1960 at Illinois Institute of Technology in Chicago, he began working for the U.S. Environmental Protection Agency (EPA). In 1981, he was appointed regional administrator for the EPA's Great Lakes Region based in Chicago. During his years in the United States, he remained active in the Lithuanian American community, organizing protests against the Soviet Union's control of Lithuania, which ended in 1991.

Before Adamkus took office as Lithuania's president on Feb. 26, 1998, he relinquished his U.S. citizenship. In response, President Bill Clinton sent Adamkus a letter thanking him for his outstanding service to the United States.

See also **Lithuania**.

Bezos, Jeff (1964–), made headlines in 1998 when his on-line bookstore, Amazon.com, based in Seattle, Washington, became the top retail site on the Internet, the worldwide computer network. The founder and CEO of Amazon.com, Bezos built a company that offered more than 1 million books in 1998. The success of the company, which is marketed as "the Earth's biggest bookstore," drew attention to the promise of the Internet for retail markets and criticism from the company's competitors. The nationwide retailer Barnes & Noble sued Amazon.com in 1998 for false advertising, claiming that Barnes & Noble was a larger store.

Bezos graduated from Princeton University in Princeton, New Jersey, in 1986 with a bachelor's degree in electrical engineering and computer science. He joined FITEL, a high-tech company in New York City and completed an M.B.A. degree in 1988 at Harvard University in Cambridge, Massachusetts. Bezos was hired by Bankers Trust Company of New York City in 1988 to develop a computer system that managed more than $250 billion in assets. Later that same year, he became the youngest vice president of Bankers Trust. From 1990 to 1994, Bezos created one of the most successful and technically complex investment funds for D. E. Shaw & Company of New York City. He became the company's youngest senior vice president in 1992.

Recognizing the possibilities of the Internet, Bezos made a list of products in 1994 that would be well-suited for sales on the Internet, and books topped the list. After the initial successes of Amazon.com, the company's Web site expanded to CD music sales. With future plans of expansion into other markets, Bezos, worth an estimated $1.6 bil-

Valdas Adamkus,
president of Lithuania

Gro Harlem Brundtland, director general of the World Health Organization

lion, was expected to acquire many other on-line sales avenues, especially in the area of software and information-rich commodities.

Brundtland, Gro Harlem (1940–), was appointed in January 1998 to serve as director general of the World Health Organization (WHO), a United Nations agency based in Geneva, Switzerland. Brundtland, the first woman to lead WHO, had served three separate terms as Norway's prime minister, representing the Labor Party—in 1981, from 1986 to 1989, and from 1990 to 1996.

Brundtland graduated from Harvard's School of Public Health in 1965 and worked in maternal and child health care for the Norwegian health care system. She entered the Norwegian government in 1974, serving as environment minister. In 1981, she was elected prime minister, becoming at 41 the youngest Norwegian to hold this office. She also became the first woman to lead a Scandinavian government. During her terms as prime minister, she was heralded by her supporters as a populist leader with an iron-willed style. Many political observers considered her a left-wing version of Margaret Thatcher, Great Britain's conservative prime minister from 1979 to 1990.

Brundtland also received international recognition as the chairperson of the United Nations World Commission on Environment and Development from 1984 to 1987. The commission's 1987 study called "Our Common Future," or better known as the "Brundtland Report," led to the first Earth Summit in 1992, an international conference on global environmental issues. She resigned from her third term as prime minister to spend more time with her family and briefly stayed away from the public arena.

A long-time champion of women's rights as well as environmental issues, Brundtland returned to her first profession as a physician with her appointment at WHO. She pledged to make international public health policy more scientifically based and to pressure world leaders to make health-care issues a top priority.

Cameron, James (1954–), directed *Titanic,* the monumental motion picture that won 11 Academy Awards in 1998, including best director and best picture. The film, which told a fictionalized account of the sinking of the luxury liner *Titantic* in 1912, broke most standing box-office records and became the highest grossing film of all time, earning more than $500 million in its initial release.

Cameron was born on Aug. 16, 1954, in Kapuskasing, Canada, and immigrated to Brea, California, at the age of 17. He studied physics at California State University at Fullerton, but dropped out before completing a degree. His interest in special effects in the motion picture industry led him to begin making special-effects models for New World Pictures in Beverly Hills, California. He married Gale Anne Hurd, his second of four wives, in 1984. They coproduced several successful films —including *The Terminator* (1984), *Aliens* (1986), *The Abyss* (1989), and *Terminator 2* (1991)—even after their divorce in 1989.

While filming *Titanic,* Cameron was criticized by Hollywood executives for spending too much money, allegedly violating health and safety standards on the film set, and running behind schedule. To prove his commitment to and confidence in the quality of his film, Cameron agreed to give up his $8-million director's salary and his share of the film's profits. However, due to the unprecedented success of the film, Paramount and Fox studios, joint funders of the film, gave him a $50-million bonus. Cameron announced plans in 1998 for several film projects, including a remake of *Planet of the Apes* (1968) and a live-action version of the comic book character Spiderman.

See also **Motion pictures.**

Duisenberg, Wim (1936–), of the Netherlands in May 1998 was named the first head of the European Central Bank, the monetary branch of the European Union (EU), an organization of 15 European nations. Duisenberg oversaw the Jan. 1, 1999, launch of the EU's new currency, the euro, in 11 EU countries.

Duisenberg served as finance minister for the Netherlands' socialist government from 1973 to 1977, seeing the country through the global oil cri-

David Filo (left) and Jerry Yang, creators of Yahoo!, an Internet directory

sis of the 1970's. His left-leaning approach, according to economic analysts, was tempered by the constraints of various economic problems. In 1982, when Duisenberg began his 15-year term as governor of the Bank of the Netherlands, he locked the value of the Dutch guilder to the German mark—a move that was considered conservative because it suggested that the Dutch economy was dependent on the more powerful German economic system. However, it was his combination of conservatism and socialism that led EU representatives to elect Duisenberg to lead the Central Bank.

Duisenberg's nomination hit a snag in November 1997 when French Prime Minister Jacques Chirac insisted that the head of the Central Bank be French. Chirac nominated Jean-Claude Trichet, the governor of the Bank of France. Although the other EU countries backed Duisenberg's nomination, the unanimous agreement of all 11 participating EU nations was needed to fill the post. Duisenberg ended a heated debate by voluntarily agreeing to share the position's eight-year term. He was expected to direct the bank until 2003, when Trichet would assume the duties.

See also **Europe** Special Report: **European Union.**

Estrada, Joseph (1937–), a former movie star, was elected the 13th president of the Philippines on May 11, 1998. His six-year term began on June 30, during celebrations of the 100th anniversary of Philippine independence from Spain.

Estrada was born on April 19, 1937, with the name Joseph Ejercito. Following in his father's footsteps, he studied engineering at Mapua Institute of Technology in Manila. During his third year, he left school to become an actor. His parents were so displeased with his decision to drop

out of college that they forbade him to use his family name. He adopted Estrada, Spanish for *road,* as a screen name. He played the lead role in more than 100 movies and produced more than 70 films.

Estrada ran for mayor of the Philippine city of San Juan in 1968, in his first attempt for public office. He was proclaimed mayor in 1969 after his opponent was investigated for election fraud. Estrada served as San Juan's mayor until 1986. He was elected to the senate in 1987 and became vice president in 1992. Calling himself a man of the people. Estrada reportedly developed his political views through the parts he played in the movies, characters who were uneducated and poor, but persevering.

Estrada succeeded former President Fidel Ramos, who was credited with bringing economic stability to the Philippines. Estrada planned to move forward with many of Ramos's programs but faced the challenge of the financial crisis that had begun to sweep across Asia in 1997.

See also **Economics** Special Report: **Asian Economic Crisis—Global Contagion; Philippines.**

Filo, David (1966–), cofounder of Yahoo! Inc. of Santa Clara, California, was identified by *Forbes* magazine in October 1998 as one of the 400 wealthiest persons in the United States, with a net worth of $840 million. Yahoo! provides a directory of sites on the Internet, the worldwide computer network.

Born in Mountain View, California, Filo received an undergraduate degree at Tulane University in New Orleans, Louisiana, and a master's degree at Stanford University in Stanford, California. While at Stanford, he met Yahoo! cofounder Jerry Yang. They began compiling lists of favorite sites on the Internet as a hobby.

In 1994, Filo and Yang turned their hobby into an organizational directory that provided a kind of telephone book for the Internet. After naming their navigational tool "Yahoo!," the partners offered their service, which was funded with commercial advertising, to Internet users. In April 1996, on the first day Yahoo! was traded as a public stock, the company was valued at nearly $1 billion. By 1998, Yahoo! was the largest and most profitable search tool on the Internet.

Because of the success of the company, Filo put his doctoral studies at Stanford on hold. But the Yahoo! partners did endow the university with a $2-million chair in 1997—the Yahoo! Founders Professor of the Stanford School of Engineering.

Habibie, Bacharuddin Jusuf (1936–), became president of Indonesia in May 1998, replacing President Suharto, who had held power for 32 years. Suharto had resigned after widespread protests over his troubled economic policies became increasingly violent.

Habibie promised many reforms, including an end to political corruption, freedom for political prisoners, and an intolerance of racism. During the weeks of protests and rioting before Suharto's resignation, many native Indonesians had targeted the country's ethnic Chinese, who have frequently been blamed for the country's economic turmoil. Habibie also promised to hold free national elections before his term expired in 2003 and perhaps as early as mid-1999. Indonesians had voted in only one free election since the country declared its independence from the Netherlands in 1945.

Born on June 25, 1936, to a wealthy and well-connected family, Habibie grew up as a neighbor of former President Suharto on the Indonesian island of Sulawesi. During the 1960's and early 1970's, Habibie lived in Germany, where he rose to the rank of vice president for Messerschmitt-Bolkow-Blohm, an aircraft manufacturer.

In 1974, Suharto brought Habibie back to Indonesia to develop a domestic aerospace industry and to become a principal leader in an effort to make Indonesia into a high-tech country. Habibie served as minister of research and technology until Suharto appointed him vice president in February 1998. A devout Muslim, Habibie founded the Indonesian Association of Muslim Intellectuals in 1990 and led the organization until 1998.

See also **Economics** Special Report: **Asian Economic Crisis—Global Contagion; Indonesia.**

Hunt, Helen (1963–), captured both the Academy Award and the Golden Globe Award for best actress in 1998 for her role in the film *As Good As It Gets.* In the dramatic comedy, Hunt played the role of a strong, compassionate woman who befriends a difficult man with obsessive-compulsive disorder and his troubled gay neighbor.

Hunt was born in Culver City, California, on June 15, 1963, and at the age of 10 got her first role in the television movie *Pioneer Woman.* While in high school, she studied acting during summers at Interlochen Arts Academy in Interlochen, Michigan, and at the Goodman Theatre in Chicago. Hunt played many children's roles in the 1970's on such television series as "The Mary Tyler Moore Show" and "Swiss Family Robinson."

In 1992, Hunt premiered the role of Jamie Buchman on the situation comedy "Mad About You." Her father, Gordon Hunt, a film director, occasionally directed his daughter in the series, which she also coproduced. Hunt also played notable roles in the films *The Waterdance, Project X,* and *Twister* and on the television shows "The Hitchhiker" and "St. Elsewhere." She made stage appearances in *Our Town* on Broadway in 1989 and New York City's Shakespeare in the Park production of *The Taming of the Shrew* in 1990.

Hunt received Emmy awards in 1996, 1997, and 1998 for best actress in a comedy series for her role in "Mad About You." She has also won three additional Golden Globe Awards (1994, 1995, 1997), a Screen Actors Guild Award in 1994, and the Blockbuster Entertainment Award in 1997.

See also **Motion pictures.**

Kim Dae-jung (1925–) was sworn in as the president of South Korea on Feb. 25, 1998. His inauguration marked South Korea's first transfer of power from the ruling party to an opposition leader. Kim and his party, the National Congress for New Politics, assumed leadership during South Korea's worst economic crisis since the 1950's. The recession had forced the country to seek a $57-billion international bailout package in 1997 to help pay foreign debts.

Kim Dae-jung, or "DJ" as he is called by his supporters, first ran for president in 1971. He lost to military strongman Park Chung Hee in an election that was reportedly fraudulent. The South Korean Central Intelligence Agency arrest-

South Korean President Kim Dae-jung

ed Kim in 1973 for subversive political activity and threatened to execute him. The United States and Japan pressured the South Korean government into commuting the sentence. In 1980, he was again sentenced to death on sedition charges for prodemocracy demonstrations. The sentence was also later commuted. In 1982, he was exiled for two years to the United States

In 1987, Kim was allowed to run again for president of South Korea. Kim and another opposition candidate, Kim Young Sam, split the opposition vote, which gave the victory to the ruling party candidate. Kim Dae-jung lost again in the 1992 elections. Kim's clean reputation was tarnished on the eve of the 1997 presidential elections when one of his sons was jailed for allegedly taking bribes for political gain. When Kim took office in 1998, the country faced severe labor unrest, continued economic problems, and troubled relations with North Korea.

See also **Economics** Special Report: **Asian Economic Crisis—Global Contagion; Korea, South.**

McGwire, Mark (1963–), first baseman for Major League Baseball's St. Louis Cardinals, made history in 1998 when he hit 70 home runs during the regular season, breaking Roger Maris's 1961 record of 61 home runs in a single season.

Born on Oct. 1, 1963, in Pomona, California, McGwire started his baseball career as a pitcher in high school in Claremont, California. He was drafted by the Montreal Expos in 1981 but chose to attend the University of Southern California (USC) in Los Angeles, where he set the Pacific 10 conference single-season record with 32 home runs in his junior year. He also played on the 1984 U.S. Olympic baseball team.

McGwire pitched in college and had a best earned-run average of 2.78. When he participated in the Alaska Summer League during his sophomore year, he changed positions on the field because of a shortage of first basemen. At that point, he decided to concentrate on hitting rather than pitching when he returned to USC.

In 1984, he was selected by the Oakland Athletics in the first round of the free-agent draft. He was traded to St. Louis in July 1997. The right-handed batter had several career highlights prior to the 1998 season. He hit 52 home runs in 1996 and 58 in 1997.

McGwire's record-breaking home run streak was closely matched by Sammy Sosa of the Chicago Cubs, who also exceeded Maris's record with 66 home runs in 1998. McGwire's historic 62nd home-run ball was placed in the Baseball Hall of Fame in Cooperstown, New York.

See also **Baseball.**

O'Meara, Mark (1957–), won both the British Open and U.S. Masters golf tournaments in 1998—only the third golfer in history to win both championships in the same year. Born in Goldsboro, North Carolina, on Jan. 13, 1957, O'Meara attended California State University at Long Beach, where he was named an All-American after winning the Californian, Mexican, and U.S. amateur golf tours. He turned to professional competition in 1980 and was named by the Professional Golfers' Association of America (PGA) as the PGA Tour's 1981 Rookie of the Year. Between 1984 and 1992, O'Meara regularly appeared among the top 30 money-winning players.

O'Meara won 16 PGA Tour victories after turning professional, as well as championships in the Buick Invitational in 1997, France's Trophee Lancome in 1997, the Argentine Open in 1994, and Japan's Tokia Classic in 1992.

On April 13, 1998, O'Meara won the Masters Tournament in Augusta, Georgia, after making a 25-foot (7.6-meter) putt on the final hole, winning the tournament by one stroke and ending his 18-year campaign to win a major title. Defending Masters champion Tiger

Home-run champion
Mark McGwire

Woods handed over the symbolic green jacket of victory to O'Meara, his friend and adviser.

O'Meara took the British Open on July 18 at Royal Birkdale golf course in Southport, England, a difficult course known for its unpredictable weather. His narrow win over another American champion, Brian Watts, came after the two men finished at even par after 72 holes. O'Meara was the victor after a four-hole playoff.

See also **Golf**.

Obuchi, Keizo (1937–), of the Liberal Democratic Party, became the new prime minister of Japan on July 30, 1998. The 61-year-old Obuchi, known in Japanese politics as "Mr. Ordinary," replaced Prime Minister Ryutaro Hashimoto, who resigned in the face of a glaring economic crisis, including a record 4.1-percent unemployment rate and a banking system loaded down with an estimated $1 trillion in bad loans. Obuchi, the country's 84th prime minister, inherited the worst recession Japan has experienced since the end of World War II (1939–1945).

Obuchi was born on June 25, 1937, in Naka-nojo, Japan. At 26, he became the youngest person to win election to the Japanese parliament, representing his father's district upon his father's death in 1963. Obuchi held that seat until the Liberal Democratic Party elected him secretary-general of the party in 1993. In 1997, he became foreign minister in Hashimoto's cabinet, where he was noted for his sharp negotiating skills and for forging compromises among competing political groups. Many political observers saw his 1998 nomination for prime minister as symbolic of the older power brokers of the Liberal Democratic Party prevailing over younger politicians calling for more dynamic leadership.

Obuchi spent the first months of his premiership dealing with the troubled economy and quelling the political turmoil surrounding several unpopular party officials. He promised large tax cuts and government spending to restart economic growth.

See also **Economics** Special Report: **Asian Economic Crisis—Global Contagion; Japan**.

Pak, Se Ri (1977–), a rookie on the Ladies Professional Golf Association (LPGA) Tour, won two of the four major United States tournaments in 1998. In May, she won the McDonald's LPGA Championship in Wilmington, Delaware, with an 11-under-par score of 273. In July, she also won the U.S. Women's Open in Kohler, Wisconsin, in a sudden-death playoff. Winning two other tournaments on the tour, Pak ranked second for most wins for a rookie in the history of the LPGA. In August, she also took the $100,000 first place

Se Ri Pak, pro golf champion

prize in the Mercury LPGA Series Bonus Pool, an award divided among the top 10 players in a series of seven tournaments.

Born in Daejeon, South Korea, on Sept. 28, 1977, Se Ri Pak started playing golf at age 14. She won 30 tournaments as an amateur golfer in Korea and became a professional player in 1996. In 1997, she relocated to Orlando, Florida. With the sponsorship of South Korea-based Samsung Corporation, Pak took on high-profile golf coach David Leadbetter. In spite of her success on the 1998 tour, Pak suffered some setbacks, but she declared her intention to continue playing and improving. "I have just started," Pak stated. "I want to play for a long, long time and become like the great players."

See also **Golf**.

Pastrana, Andres (1954–), was sworn in as president of Colombia on Aug. 7, 1998. Pastrana, a member of the Conservative Party, faced numerous problems, the legacy of the previous Liberal Party administration and the guerrilla warfare that had plagued the country since the 1960's.

U.S. Secretary of Energy Bill Richardson

Andres Pastrana Arango was born on Aug. 17, 1954. The son of a former Colombian president, he was the first popularly elected mayor of Bogota, the capital, in 1988. In 1994, he was narrowly defeated for the presidency by Liberal Party leader Ernesto Samper. Pastrana revealed soon after the election that his rival's campaign had been funded partly by donations from drug barons. While Samper was cleared of wrongdoing, more than a dozen congressional members, the defense minister, and an attorney general were convicted of charges in the fund-raising scandal. The controversy weakened Samper's leadership and contributed to his defeat in 1998.

Pastrana ran his 1998 presidential campaign under a single-word slogan—*change.* He promised to fight poverty, eliminate government corruption, and invest in agricultural regions, where farmers were dependent on growing crops, such as coca, for illegal drug trade. He also pledged to include more women in his cabinet. Many political observers saw this move as a gesture of solidarity with the independent presidential candidate, Noemi Sanin, who won unexpectedly large support in the first round of elections in January.

Pastrana's top priority was to begin peace talks with left-wing guerrilla groups. In July, he met with the country's largest rebel group, the Revolutionary Armed Forces of Colombia. Pastrana promised to demilitarize some areas of Colombia as a condition for launching peace talks. After taking office, he also appointed new military leaders, who had no known ties to paramilitary groups that had carried out attacks against rebels and civilians.

See also **Colombia.**

Primakov, Yevgeny (1929–), was confirmed as the prime minister of Russia on Sept. 11, 1998, by the *Duma* (the lower house of Russia's parliament). He had been nominated by President Boris Yeltsin in the midst of a deep economic crisis.

Primakov was born in October 1929 in Kiev, Ukraine, which was then a part of the former Soviet Union. A member of the Communist Party for more than 30 years, he served as deputy head of the state committee for radio and television from 1956 to 1988. Primakov was also a Middle East correspondent for *Pravda,* the Communist Party newspaper, in the 1960's. From 1989 to 1990, he served as an alternate member of the Politburo, the core body of the Communist Party. During the reform period of the early 1990's that was headed by Soviet President Mikhail Gorbachev, Primakov became special adviser for foreign policy issues. He was the only close aide to Gorbachev to survive the change of government in Russia when the Soviet Union collapsed in 1991.

Primakov then headed Russia's Federal Security Service and was named foreign minister in 1996. His close alliance with Iraqi leader Saddam Hussein led Primakov to attempt to avert the Persian Gulf War in 1991 and United States bomb strikes on Baghdad in 1996. Primakov also played a key role in preventing hostilities between U.S.-led allies and Iraq in early 1998. Primakov's new government faced profound economic challenges as well as ongoing foreign-relations issues.

See also **Russia.**

Richardson, Bill (1947–), was nominated United States secretary of energy in June 1998 by President Bill Clinton. The Senate approved his appointment in July.

Richardson was born on Nov. 15, 1947, in Pasadena, California, but grew up primarily in Mexico's capital, Mexico City. He earned his undergraduate degree from Tufts University in Medford, Massachusetts, and a master's degree from Tuft's Fletcher School of Law and Diplomacy. Later he moved to New Mexico, where from 1983 to 1997, he served in the U.S. Congress, representing one of the most ethnically diverse U.S. districts. During his congressional tenure, he gained a reputation for introducing progressive legislation, including many bills related to health, foreign policy, energy, Native Americans, and the environment.

After being sent on several sensitive diplomatic missions by President Clinton, Richardson was widely recognized as an effective diplomat. He helped free hostages in several countries and in 1996 met with Cuban leader Fidel Castro to negotiate the release of three political prisoners. Richardson was nominated twice for the Nobel Peace Prize, most recently in 1997.

In December 1996, President Clinton nominated Richardson as U.S. Permanent Representative to the United Nations (UN), and Richardson took office in February 1997. He served in the UN for 16 months and dealt with several diplomatic crises, such as negotiating with the leaders of Congo (Kinshasa) to allow UN personnel to investigate alleged human-rights abuses.

See also **Cabinet, U.S.**

Satcher, David (1941–), was sworn in on Feb. 13, 1998, as the 16th surgeon general of the United States and the assistant secretary of the U.S. Department of Health and Human Services (HHS). Satcher—a physician, medical researcher, and lifelong pubic health advocate—had served as the Director of the U.S. Centers for Disease Control and Prevention (CDC), a public health agency in Atlanta, Georgia. During his tenure with the CDC, he created programs to increase childhood immunization and set up plans for the Early Warning System to detect and prevent illnesses from contaminated agricultural products.

Satcher , who was born March 2, 1941, in Armistan, Alabama, graduated from Morehouse College in Atlanta in 1963 and received his M.D. and Ph.D. degrees from Case Western Reserve University in Cleveland in 1970. From 1977 to 1979, he served as dean of family medicine at the King/Drew Medical Center in Los Angeles and served as director of the facility's Sickle Cell Center from 1976 to 1982. He was president of Meharry Medical College in Nashville, Tennessee, from 1982 to 1993.

During his career, Satcher received many awards, including *Ebony* magazine's American Black Achievement Award in Business and the Professions in 1994. In 1996, he received the Dr. Nathan B. Davis Award, the American Medical Association's most prestigious honor, which is given in recognition of outstanding service to public health.

In 1997, HHS Secretary Donna E. Shalala, speaking at a ceremony celebrating the lowest level of vaccine-preventable childhood illnesses in U.S. history, called Satcher one of the CDC's "immunization heroes." Satcher's own battle with childhood whooping cough had inspired him to become a scientist and physician.

Schroeder, Gerhard (1944–), was sworn in as the new chancellor of Germany on Oct. 27, 1998. He replaced Helmut Kohl, who had led the country for 16 years, seeing it through the tumultuous reunification of the East and West in 1990.

Schroeder was born on April 7, 1944, in Mossenberg in the province of Lower Saxony. His father, drafted into the German army, died in combat in Romania in the same year. His mother cleaned houses to feed her five children. Schroeder worked at numerous jobs while studying law. He married his fourth wife, journalist Doris Koepf, in 1997.

Schroeder, the leader of the Social Democratic Party (SPD), became active in the party's radical left wing in the 1970's. Over time, he moderated his political positions. In the 1998 election, Schroeder asked his party, which traditionally represented labor, to promote business interests. He called his platform the "New Middle." Political observers often compared him with left-of-center moderates, like British Prime Minister Tony Blair and United States President Bill Clinton.

Schroeder represented Lower Saxony in the *Bundestag* (Germany's lower house of parliament) from 1980 to 1986. He became head of the politi-

German Chancellor Gerhard Schroeder

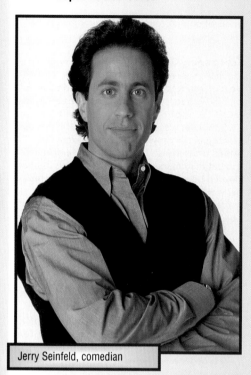

Jerry Seinfeld, comedian

cal opposition in Lower Saxony in 1986 and premier of the province in 1990. Under Schroeder's leadership in 1998, the Social Democratic Party announced plans to work closely with Germany's environmentally concerned Green Party. Schroeder's administration led the country into the 1999 introduction of the euro, the common currency launched by 11 of the 15 member nations of the European Union in January 1999. His government also faced high unemployment, tax reform proposals, and ongoing reunification challenges.

See also **Europe** Special Report: **European Union; Germany.**

Seinfeld, Jerry (1954–), a prominent comedian, ended a highly successful and long-running television comedy series, "Seinfeld," in 1998. As the star, creator, and producer of the critically acclaimed nine-year series, Seinfeld and his program garnered many top industry honors.

Seinfeld was born on April 29, 1954, in New York City. At the age of eight, he became fascinated with comedians while watching them on television. While studying at Queens College in Flushing, New York, he developed his own stand-up comedy routines while working as a light bulb salesman and jewelry street vendor. He claimed to be heavily influenced by the routines of Bud Abbott and Lou Costello, a comedy duo that rose to fame in the 1930's.

In 1987, Seinfeld starred in his own special, "Jerry Seinfeld's Stand-up Confidential" for HBO and began making regular appearances on "The Tonight Show" with Jay Leno and David Letterman's "Late Show." Seinfeld's 1993 publication *SeinLanguage* sold more than 1 million copies and remained on *The New York Times* best-seller list for 33 weeks.

In 1993, "Seinfeld" won the Emmy award for outstanding comedy series, and during the series' run, Seinfeld garnered three Emmy nominations for outstanding actor in a comedy category. Other awards included the 1993 Golden Globe for best actor in a television comedy and the 1993 Screen Actors Guild Award for best ensemble in a comedy. With the close of his television series, Seinfeld worked on a one-man show on Broadway in 1998 and made plans for additional live stand-up comedy performances.

See also **Television.**

Starr, Kenneth (1946–), the independent counsel who investigated the political, business, and personal lives of President Bill Clinton and First Lady Hillary Rodham Clinton, made news throughout 1998. In July, Starr subpoenaed Clinton to testify before a grand jury about his relationship with former White House intern Monica Lewinski. In September, Starr issued a 445-page report that identified 11 alleged grounds for impeachment of the president. Starr also testified about his investigation before the U.S. House Judiciary Committee on November 19.

Starr was born in Vernon, Texas, on July 21, 1946, the son of a Church of Christ minister. He received degrees at George Washington University in Washington, D.C., in 1968 and Brown University in Providence, Rhode Island, in 1969. He earned his law degree at Duke University School of Law in 1973.

From 1975 to 1977, Starr served as clerk to former U.S. Supreme Court Justice Warren Burger. He worked in a private law practice until 1981 and then served as assistant to U.S. Attorney General William French Smith until 1983. Under Smith, Starr helped draft the Reagan Administration's opposition to the law that created the position of independent counsel to investigate the improprieties in the executive branch of the U.S. government.

Starr was appointed judge in 1983 for the U.S. Court of Appeals in Washington, D.C., and served as the U.S. Solicitor General from 1989 to 1993. He accepted the job of independent counsel in 1994 to investigate the Whitewater affair, a failed Arkansas real estate venture in which the future president and first lady had invested.

See also **Congress of the United States; United States, Government of the; United States, President of the.**

Taymor, Julie (1953–), captured two Antoinette Perry (Tony) Awards in 1998 for best director of a musical and best costume design for the Walt Disney Company's production of *The Lion King.* The musical, based on Disney's animated film by the same name, won a total of six Tony Awards, including best musical. Noted for her use of puppetry, masks, and low-tech theater craft, Taymor was highly regarded in the theater industry for her original and stylized stagings.

Taymor started acting at the age of 11. She studied in Paris at the age of 16 with mime artist Jacques LeCoq and later studied mythology and folklore at Oberlin College in Oberlin, Ohio. She moved to Japan in 1975 to study puppetry. A few months later, in a decision that came to define her theatrical vision, she moved to Indonesia to study non-Western theater. She worked and studied throughout the Indonesian islands for four years.

In 1979, she returned to the United States and designed sets for the Joseph Papp Public Theater in New York City. She received high marks for her staging of *King Stag,* an Italian fairy tale, in 1984 and the fablelike Uruguayan story *Juan Darien: A Carnival Mass* in 1988. Other notable productions include *The Green Bird* (1996) and *Titus Andronicus* (1994) and several opera designs, including *Salome* (1993) and *The Flying Dutchman* (1995).

Taymor and her partner, composer Elliot Goldenthal, frequently collaborate on productions, including the original musical *Liberty's Taken* (1985) and *King Stag.* Taymor has received many awards and grants, including a Guggenheim Fellowship, the Dorothy B. Chandler award in theater, the Brandeis Creative Arts Award, and the prestigious MacArthur Foundation "genius grant."

See also **Theater; Theater** Special Report: **A New Broadway Takes Center Stage.**

Vajpayee, Atal Bihari (1926–), of the Bharatiya Janata Party (BJP), took office as India's prime minister in March 1998. Vajpayee had been elected prime minister once before in 1996, but his administration lasted for only about two weeks because he could not muster a majority vote of confidence in India's parliament.

Vajpayee was born on Dec. 25, 1926, in Gwalior, a town in the Indian province of Madhya Pradesh. As a young man, he was active in the movement that led to India's independence from Great Britain in 1947. He was educated at Victoria College (now called Laximbai College) in Gwalior and DAV College in Kanpur, India. Throughout the 1950's and 1960's, Vajpayee was employed as a social worker and journalist. He has published collections of poetry as well as several volumes of his political speeches.

Vajpayee helped found the hard-line Hindu nationalist party Jana Sangh in 1951 and first became a member of parliament in 1957. He later served as a leader in other Hindu nationalist parties. From 1977 to 1980, Vajpayee served as the External Affairs Minister as a member of the more centrist Janata Party. He served as president of the BJP from its founding in 1980 until 1986.

Although most BJP members considered Vajpayee a moderate and he promised to respect the freedoms of all Indians, many members of the country's diverse religious and ethnic minority groups voiced concern over the new government. Political analysts noted, however, that the BJP's need to work with coalition partners in parliament would keep Hindu nationalist goals in check.

Soon after Vajpayee took office, he was involved in a struggle of nuclear brinkmanship with the Muslim government of neighboring Pakistan. After Pakistan tested a missile in April, the Indian government responded with a series of five underground tests of nuclear weapons. Pakistan tested its own nuclear weapons in turn, but both governments backed off after intense international pressure.

See also **Hinduism; India.**

Independent Counsel Kenneth Starr

Yang, Jerry (1968-), cofounder of Yahoo! Inc. of Santa Clara, California, was ranked by *Forbes* magazine in October 1998 among the 400 wealthiest people in the United States, with a net worth of $830 million. Yahoo! provides a directory of sites on the Internet, the worldwide computer network.

Yang and his family immigrated from Taiwan to San Jose, California, when he was 10 years old. He received a bachelor's degree from the Wharton School at the University of Pennsylvania in Philadelphia and entered Stanford University in 1990 to work toward a Ph.D. in electrical engineering.

While at Stanford, he met Yahoo! cofounder David Filo. They began compiling lists of favorite sites on the Internet as a hobby. In 1994, Filo and Yang turned their hobby into an organizational directory that provided a kind of telephone book for the Internet. The partners named their navigational tool Yahoo!, which stands for "Yet another hierarchical officious oracle." They began offering Yahoo! to Internet users and funded the service with commercial advertising. In April 1996, on the first day Yahoo! was traded as a public stock, the company's value shot up to nearly $1 billion. By the end of 1998, the value had risen to about $6 billion. ☐ Brian Bouldrey

Julie Taymor, stage director

Peru. On Oct. 26, 1998, Peru and Ecuador signed a treaty that provided a peaceful resolution to a bitter territorial dispute along their common border. The conflict, dating to 1830, had led to repeated armed clashes, including a brief war in 1995.

On Aug. 7, 1998, Prime Minister Javier Valle Riestra of Peru resigned just two months after being appointed by President Alberto K. Fujimori. Valle Riestra claimed that the administration was dominated by a "totalitarian spirit." He attacked the political maneuvers of the past two years that would make it possible for Fujimori to run for a third term in 2000. He also criticized the imprisonment of Lori Helene Berenson, a U.S. citizen who was convicted by a secret Peruvian military court in 1996 for allegedly collaborating with leftist rebels.

On June 8, 1998, Peruvians mourned the loss of Maria Reiche, 95, the self-appointed guardian for more the 50 years of the ancient Nazca lines. These enormous images of animals, plants, and geometric designs were carved into the desert plateaus of southern Peru by the Nazca people, who lived from about 100 B.C. to A.D. 800. Reiche, who immigrated from Germany in the 1940's, mapped the designs and protected them from intruders. ☐ Nathan A. Haverstock

See also **Latin America** (Facts in brief table).

Petroleum and gas. See **Energy supply.**

Philadelphia. In April 1998, Philadelphia's last large locally owned bank was purchased by First Union Corporation, of Charlotte, North Carolina. The United States Federal Reserve, an independent agency of the U.S. government that oversees the nation's banking system, gave First Union permission to take over Philadelphia's CoreStates Financial Corporation for $19 billion. The acquisition made First Union the dominant bank in the Philadelphia region and the sixth largest in the nation, with assets of $220 billion.

Transport strike. Members of the Philadelphia Transport Workers Union, who operate the city's buses, streetcars, and subways, walked off their jobs on June 1 and did not return to work until a tentative agreement for a new job contract was reached on July 10.

In October, the union and the transit system's management, Southeastern Pennsylvania Transportation Authority, ratified a formal contract. The three-year contract provided for an annual 3-percent wage increase for the union's 5,500 members. In addition, the agreement stipulated that the top salary would rise from $38,000 to $42,000 but take 18 additional months to go into effect. Under the terms of the contract, the average employee's pension benefits would increase by approximately 32 percent, and workers' compensation benefits would also be hiked.

The contract also included a zero-tolerance drug and alcohol policy, an attendance and discipline program, and work rules giving managers greater flexibility to handle transportation needs.

New police commissioner. In March, John F. Timoney was sworn in as Philadelphia's police commissioner. Timoney, 49, was formerly second in command at New York City's police department, where he had served as a policeman for 29 years. After taking over in Philadelphia, Timoney reshuffled the department's command structure by filling the top tier with longtime police veterans. The Philadelphia Police Department had been criticized by many observers for ineffectiveness and corruption.

In June, Timoney launched Operation Sunrise, a police program to reclaim the city's most drug-infested streets. Over the summer, police arrested hundreds of drug dealers. As part of the operation, city crews sealed buildings that were drug houses, cleared trash-strewn vacant lots, and towed abandoned cars from the streets. Counselors intervened to get addicts off the streets and into drug programs.

Police claimed many of the streets targeted by Operation Sunrise were attracting suburbanites and out-of-towners who made drug deals through car windows. Families who lived in the drug-infested neighborhoods said they lived in fear of the gun violence that frequently accompanied the competition for narcotics sales.

Health-care bankruptcy. In July, eight hospitals, a medical school, and several physician practices in the Philadelphia area declared bankruptcy. The declarations amounted to one of the largest groups of health-care bankruptcies ever in a U.S. city. The institutions were owned by the Allegheny Health, Education, and Research Foundation, a not-for-profit health-care system based in Pittsburgh, Pennsylvania. Allegheny had debts of $1.3 billion. After filing for bankruptcy on the Philadelphia health-care operations, Allegheny sold the properties to the for-profit Tenet Health-care Corporation of Santa Barbara, California.

Arts venues. Philadelphia officials broke ground in November for the $255-million Regional Performing Arts Center. Scheduled to be completed in 2001, the center will include a 2,500-seat concert hall, which will be the future home of the Philadelphia Orchestra.

Renovation continued throughout the summer of 1998 on the 141-year-old Academy of Music, the current home of the Philadelphia Orchestra, the Pennsylvania Ballet, and the Opera Company of Philadelphia. When the renovation project is complete, the academy will house the ballet and opera companies and touring Broadway plays.   □ Howard S. Shapiro

See also **City.**

Philippines. Joseph Estrada was elected president on May 11, 1998, with 40 percent of the vote, and began a six-year term on June 30. His nearest rival among 10 candidates, House Speaker Jose de Venecia, who was backed by retiring President Fidel V. Ramos, won only 16 percent of the vote. Estrada's vice presidential candidate, Edgardo Angara, lost to Gloria Macapagal-Arroyo, who was supported by Ramos.

Estrada, known as Erap (Filipino slang for "buddy"), gained a devoted following during his career as a star of Philippine action films. He used his movie fame to cultivate a political career—first as mayor of a Manila suburb, then as a senator. In 1992, he was elected vice president.

Estrada emphasized his break with the nation's English-speaking elite by giving his inaugural address in the national language, Filipino. In his address, Estrada pledged to focus on helping the poor and developing the country's agricultural industry. He also vowed to solve the Philippines' severe crime problem and crack down on official corruption, estimating that 40 percent of the national budget was lost through corruption.

Business supporters. Estrada's candidacy initially alarmed businessmen, who feared he would halt economic reforms begun by Ramos. Estrada eventually attracted the support of some of the nation's top business tycoons by vowing to continue most of Ramos's policies.

Estrada's supporters included business leaders who had grown rich during the dictatorship of the late Ferdinand E. Marcos. One of these tycoons, Eduardo Cojuangco, headed Estrada's political party, Laban ng Masang Pilipino (Fight of the Filipino Masses). Cojuangco, who had fled the Philippines with Marcos when Marcos was overthrown in 1986, ran for president in 1992, placing third in the elections.

Other former Marcos supporters helped finance Estrada's campaign in 1998 and advised him on economic issues. Ramos warned that Estrada's association with "Marcos's cronies" would frighten off foreign investors.

Estrada also reached out to supporters of Marcos's wife, Imelda. He agreed to allow Imelda to bury Marcos—whose body had been in cold storage since his death in 1989—in the military's Heroes' Cemetery. After much public protest, however, Imelda announced that she would postpone the burial indefinitely.

Economic problems. In early 1998, some economists predicted that the Philippines would be the first country to emerge from the crisis that had rocked Asian financial markets since 1997. However, the Philippine economy continued to deteriorate in late 1998. The country's *gross domestic product* (the value of all goods and services produced in a country during a given period) declined at an annual rate of 1.2 percent in the second quarter of 1998. The economy had expanded at an annual pace of 1.6 percent in the first quarter and 5.6 percent in the second quarter of 1997.

A severe drought in 1998, attributed to the effects of *El Nino* (a periodic warming of tropical eastern Pacific waters that affects weather patterns worldwide), caused the worst decline in Philippine farm output in three decades. Agriculture accounts for 20 percent of the Philippines' economic production and employs 40 percent of its work force. Increased industrial exports helped offset financial losses caused by the drought.

Guerrilla warfare continued in the southern Philippines, where a Muslim group, the Moro Islamic Liberation Front (MILF), sought to establish an Islamic state. The MILF dominated part of Mindanao Island plus several smaller islands. Estrada promised to resolve the conflict.

Disasters. A passenger ferry carrying 430 people sank near Manila on September 18, killing at least 60. Typhoon Babs hit the Philippines in late October, killing more than 180 people and leaving some 320,000 homeless.

☐ Henry S. Bradsher

See also **Asia** (Facts in brief table); **China; Economics** Special Report: **Asian Economic Crisis; People in the news** (Estrada, Joseph).

Physics. Evidence that subatomic particles called neutrinos have mass was presented in June 1998 by a team of 120 physicists from 23 institutions in the United States and Japan. The physicists, headed by Yoji Totsuka of the University of Tokyo, reported that their findings indicated that neutrinos could make up much of the universe's mass and play a critical role in determining the ultimate fate of the universe.

Neutrinos are subatomic particles occurring throughout the universe that pass constantly through everything on Earth, including human beings, at or near the speed of light. Although neutrinos normally pass through objects unhindered, a neutrino occasionally collides with an *atomic nucleus* (the center part of an atom). In such a collision, a neutrino, which is uncharged, is transformed into one of three types of charged particle—an electron, a muon, or a tau. The type of charged particle a neutrino changes into depends on the neutrino. Different types of neutrinos are predisposed toward being transformed into different particle types. Scientists cannot detect neutrinos directly, so they look for those three types of charged particles with special particle detectors.

Super K. A huge underground device known as the "Super-Kamiokande," or "Super-K," supplied the data underlying the argument that neu-

If a black hole with the mass of Saturn stood between the Smithsonian Institution, *left*, and an observer, a phenomenon known as gravitational lensing would make the building appear distorted, *right*. Gravitational lensing, which scientists found evidence of in space in 1998, is a phenomenon in which the gravity of a massive object, such as a black hole, causes light from a more distant object, such as a galaxy, to appear as a ring around the first object.

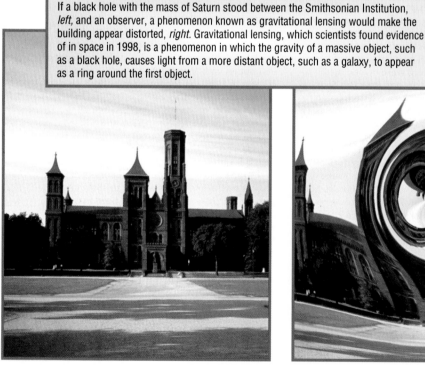

trinos have mass. Located 2,000 feet (610 meters) below the surface in a mine in western Japan, the Super-K consists of a tank containing 55,000 tons (50,000 metric tons) of ultrapure water monitored by 13,000 electronic detectors. The detectors measure the timing and pattern of brief flashes of blue light generated in the tank when neutrinos collide with the atomic nuclei of water molecules. The patterns indicate the types of particles the neutrinos are transformed into.

Approximately half of the transformations detected by the scientists resulted in electrons. The physicists working on the project had expected that two-thirds of the transformations would result in muons. These expectations were based on the fact that the neutrinos in this study originated in the upper atmosphere, where radiation from space was known to cause chemical reactions that produce roughly two neutrinos predisposed to become muons for every electron-neutrino. The reactions in the upper atmosphere also produce an occasional tau-neutrino.

Neutrino oscillation. The physicists explained that the larger-than-expected number of electrons and fewer-than-expected muons resulted from *neutrino oscillation* (a process in which a neutrino *oscillates* [varies] from one state to another). Through neutrino oscillation, some muon-neutrinos were transformed into tau-neutrinos. According to *quantum mechanics* (the branch of physics dealing with the behavior of subatomic particles), there must be a difference in mass between two oscillating states to effect such a transformation. The muon-neutrinos or tau-neutrinos (or both) involved in the oscillation, therefore, must have mass. The scientists, however, were unable to measure actual neutrino masses.

Implications. The Super-K results, if confirmed, have implications for theories about "dark matter." Through observations of the motions of stars undergoing gravitational attraction, astronomers believe that there is more mass in the universe than can be seen. That invisible mass is called "dark matter." If neutrinos do have mass, that mass could shed light on what unseen mass produces additional gravitational attraction.

The existence of neutrino mass also has enormous implications for the fate of the universe. Physicists believe that the universe has been expanding since its creation 10 to 15 billion years ago. They are not sure if the expansion will continue forever or ultimately be reversed. If there is enough mass in the universe, the force of gravity will eventually overcome the momentum of expansion and the universe will contract. If there is not enough mass, the universe will expand forever. Scientists expected that a future accurate measurement of neutrino mass will help resolve this uncertainty. ☐ Robert H. March

Poetry. Fine works by American poets in 1998 were largely overshadowed by British poet Ted Hughes's collection, *Birthday Letters,* poems addressed to his former wife, Sylvia Plath. Plath, one of the most famous modern American poets, committed suicide in 1963 shortly after Hughes had left her. He was often blamed for her death, particularly by feminist critics. Hughes rose to become Great Britain's poet laureate. He was generally private about his feelings for Plath, but *Birthday Letters* tenderly evokes the youthful and passionate couple, dreaming of literary success, but increasingly troubled by Plath's self-destructive mood swings. Hughes died on Oct. 28, 1998.

In U.S. poetry, one of the most exciting books of 1998 was *The Collected Poems of Robert Penn Warren,* superbly edited by John Burt. According to American critic Harold Bloom, Warren (1905– 1989) was probably the most multitalented American writer of the century—a leading literary critic, a novelist, an influential teacher, and the author of "much the best poetry composed" from 1966 to 1986. *Collected Poems* is filled with stories of the old South, memories of boyhood, reflections on age, and memorable lines: "In the momentary silence of the cicada, / I can hear the appalling speed, / In space beyond stars, of / Light. It is / A sound like wind."

John Ashbery—heralded by critics as either the greatest living poet or the worst—released *Wakefulness* in 1998. The poems mix great musical quality with seemingly strained sounds, as in "Many Colors": "There is a chastening to it, / a hymnlike hemline. / Hyperbole in another disguise. / Dainty foresters walk through it. / On the splashed polyester walls / a tooth fairy held court . . ." For some critics, however, the poems' gorgeous textures mask ideas that almost border on nonsense.

Kenneth Koch, who can also compose exquisite verbal music, offers wit and geniality. In *Straits,* he composes songs for plays that did not exist and comments on the nature of poetry. In "Spring," a meditation on the seasons in homage to the Scottish poet James Thomson (1700–1748), Koch writes: "Now pizza units open up, and froth / Steams forth on beers in many a frolic bar . . ."

W. S. Merwin's *The Folding Cliffs* is an epic poem about Hawaii and the destruction of native culture. Written in one-page sections, the poem resembles chants that echo native storytelling: "It was when the still days of summer were gone and the light / at every hour held the reflection of something never / visible as the glaze does in the eyes of someone / remembering a time not there."

In *Blizzard of One,* Mark Strand typically mingles wit with philosophy. "In Memory of Joseph Brodsky," the modern Russian poet who died in 1996, Strand alternates between a sense of loss and a playfulness that Brodsky himself would

Before his death in October 1998, British poet Ted Hughes published *Birthday Letters,* poems addressed to his wife, American poet Sylvia Plath, who committed suicide in 1963. Hughes's poetry revealed the romance and troubles of their relationship.

have cherished: "What remains of the self unwinds / Beyond us, for whom time is only a measure of meanwhile / And the future no more than et cetera et cetera . . . but fast and forever."

Virginia Hamilton Adair, at age 83, published her first poetry collection, *Ant on the Melon* in 1996 and received immediate acclaim. In her second book, *Beliefs and Blasphemies,* published in 1998, Adair focuses her wit and grace on the theme of religion. "Goddesses First" opens "From the beginning, they must have been miles ahead of the men, / fleet as fawns, nimbly evading those heavy hulks lumbering after / giving apelike yells to establish mastery . . ."

Short takes. William Logan's *Vain Empires* is learned and witty. "The Advent of Common Law in Littoral Pursuits" deftly plays with sounds: "From marshy ditch to ruined copse / to ruined corpse, trained arguments confuse / police with politesse." August Kleinzahler's *Green Sees Things in Waves* explores the contemporary urban environment in verse that is hip, edgy, and fun: "The sopressata fee outside of Calfasso's / with the swept-back 'do and blood on her smock / grabs a quick smoke on the sidewalk, / tosses it in the gutter then sucks back her lips, / till they smack, getting her lipstick right." □ Michael Dirda

See also **Literature, American; Literature, World.**

Poland. The Polish parliament on Jan. 8, 1998, approved by a large majority a treaty with the Vatican. The treaty, which formally set down relations between the predominantly Catholic country and the Roman Catholic Church, was signed by President Aleksander Kwasniewski and Pope John Paul II on February 23. Poland's former Solidarity-led government had signed the same treaty in July 1993, but ratification stalled after national elections put former Communists in control of the government two months later. A new Solidarity-led coalition won a parliamentary majority in September 1997.

Government. Polish legislators struggled with the issue of administrative reform in 1998. In July, President Kwasniewski signed into law a measure to consolidate Poland's 49 provinces into 16 units. The reform, which went into effect Jan. 1, 1999, was designed to eliminate the centralized Communist-era administration and shift power to local governments. The parliament also passed legislation in July 1998 designed to reform Poland's health-care and judicial systems.

In March, miners and factory workers protested the government's plans to privatize large factories and mines and to close nearly half of the nation's 65 coal mines by 2002. After the protests, officials softened some provisions of the plan. Approximately 15,000 leftist union workers staged a demonstration in Warsaw in March 1998, demanding that the government speed reform of health, education, and pension policies.

Economy. Analysts expected Poland's *gross domestic product* (the total value of goods and services produced by a country in a given period) to grow by 5.6 percent in 1998 and the inflation rate to drop to 10.9 percent. Unemployment was expected to fall to 9.5 percent. Direct foreign investment in Poland exceeded $6 billion in the first nine months of 1998.

Foreign affairs. Negotiations regarding Poland's entry into the European Union (EU) began in March. In May, EU officials cut $36 million from an aid program due to mismanagement of previous funds. The program was designed to help Poland meet certain economic standards that are a prerequisite for EU membership.

New Polish visa regulations that require travelers from Russia and Belarus to show proof of the ability to support themselves while in Poland strained relations with those countries in 1998. Russia retaliated with similar measures against Polish tourists. Travel restrictions and increased waiting times to cross the borders led to a protest in Poland by more than 1,500 small traders, who depend on tourist business. □ Sharon L. Wolchik

See also **Belarus; Europe** (Facts in brief table).

Pollution. See Environmental pollution.

Popular music.

The popularity of rock music eroded in 1998 as public acceptance of rap music widened. While mainstream popular music continued to focus on younger fans, many young people, particularly in the United States, also became interested in an old style of popular music.

Rap wave. Rock music's hold on young music fans lost some of its grip in 1998 as rap music continued to gain acceptance with a mainstream audience. Rap music, the dominant form of black popular music since its emergence in the 1980's, consists of words spoken over a strong rhythm track. The lyrics are often a commentary on such social issues as racism and poverty. Many critics have argued that some rap lyrics deal too graphically with sex and violence.

The record industry reported in 1998 that the majority of rap music sold in 1997 was purchased by white consumers. Many white teen-agers embraced rap music because it represented an alternative to mainstream culture and the values of their parents—much in the same way that an earlier generation of teen-agers embraced rock-and-roll music.

Rap music offered audiences new rhythms, new artists, and new styles without as much promotion by radio and the rock media. Such independence from the mainstream media allowed rap to retain a reputation as an "underground"

form of music, even as it achieved popular acceptance. As 1998 progressed, rap coverage became more prominent in magazines catering to the interest of rock and pop music, which reflected the changes in the musical climate. Rap music in 1998 was dominated by such artists as DMX, Jay-Z, Method Man, Missy Elliott, Master P, and Puff Daddy. Many of the most successful rappers also produced the albums of other artists or owned their own record labels, which allowed them to retain greater control over their musical product, compared to most rock acts.

Rap's influence in 1998 was also reflected in other forms of popular music. Such aggressive rock acts as Korn and Rage Against the Machine maintained their popularity by incorporating rap into their musical mix. Even Bruce Springsteen, one of the most influential rock musicians, had reportedly been working on an album that featured a rap influence.

Pop music. Despite rap music's domination of record sales during 1998, most major radio stations in the United States continued to saturate the airwaves with mainstream popular rock music. Much of this music was primarily targeted at preteen girls.

The Spice Girls, the British quintet that first gained popularity in 1997, continued their success in the music scene in 1998. Their first American tour, which started in June, attracted sell-out crowds and received largely positive reviews from fans and critics.

The group made headlines away from the stage in May, when Geri Halliwell, who was also known as Ginger Spice, announced that she had left the band due to unspecified "differences." The remaining Spice Girls—Victoria Adams, Melanie Brown, Emma Bunton, and Melanie Chisholm—announced that they would continue as a foursome. Halliwell's departure and the reported pregnancies of two other members of the group left many critics and fans in late 1998 wondering whether the Spice Girls would run out of flavor. In 1998, the Spice Girls shared the youthful appeal in popular music with such young artists and groups as Brandy, the Backstreet Boys, and 'N Sync.

Breakthrough artist. Lauryn Hill, lead singer of the rap group the Fugees, fused contemporary rap with classic rhythm and blues in 1998 and established herself as one of the year's most popular artists. Her first solo album, *The Miseducation of Lauryn Hill,* was reviewed by many critics as one of the year's best releases.

Country music continued to lose popular momentum in 1998 as both record sales and radio ratings declined. However, two prominent names continued to breathe life into the country music scene.

The Spice Girls—(left to right) Melanie Brown, Melanie Chisholm, Emma Bunton, Geri Halliwell, and Victoria Adams—made news in May 1998 after Halliwell, also known as Ginger Spice, announced that she was leaving the group due to "differences."

Shania Twain, a Canadian-born singer whose album, *Come On Over,* topped country album charts for more than four months in 1998, promoted the album with her first world tour. Her failure to tour after the release of her two previous albums led to some suspicions that her singing voice required much studio enhancement and that it was too weak for a live performance.

Although her concerts received mixed reviews from critics, who claimed that her popularity had more to do with her attractive looks, outfits, and pop-oriented material than with talent, Twain's pop music and country music fans both responded enthusiastically.

Garth Brooks, one of the most popular country artists of the 1990's, released a live concert recording entitled *Double Live* on Nov. 17, 1998. To promote the album, Brooks gave an hour-long concert that was beamed exclusively to more than 2,000 Wal-Mart stores in the United States and Canada. The new album sold more than 1 million copies in its first week of availability.

Let's swing. One of the more popular musical trends of 1998 was the revival of swing music, which found both bands and fans looking to the sophistication of the 1940's for inspiration. Swing music is a type of jazz music that developed in the 1930's and highlights brass instruments.

In 1998, such bands as the Squirrel Nut Zippers, Royal Crown Revue, the Brian Setzer Orchestra, and the Cherry Poppin' Daddies led the swing-music revival, drawing heavily upon the dance styles and clothing fashions of the swing era and mixing it with jump blues and up-tempo dance tunes.

While the new era of swing lacked the improvising musicianship of Count Basie, Duke Ellington, and Benny Goodman, the new wave provided a sophisticated alternative for many people who believed that they had outgrown traditional rock music. The resulting popularity in swing music also led to a boom throughout the United States in swing-dancing lessons.

Rock archives. Music labels in late 1998 released boxed sets of old recordings and previously unreleased material by some of the most influential artists in rock-and-roll history.

Tracks, Bruce Springsteen's four-disc boxed set, was dominated by material that he had recorded with the E Street Band. The release, which mainly contained previously unreleased material, spanned Springsteen's career from the early 1970's through the mid-1990's.

John Lennon's four-disc *Anthology* box included home recordings, alternate versions of popular songs, and live performances from his solo career after the break up of the Beatles in 1970.

The two-disc set *Live 1966: The Royal Albert Hall Concert* by Bob Dylan documented Dylan's first tour of England with an electric band. The archival recording, which included one solo acoustic disc and one with a band, was hailed as one of the finest recordings of 1998 and of Dylan's long career.

Industry merger. Seagram Company, a Canadian-based liquor company, announced on May 21 that it planned to purchase the PolyGram Company of the Netherlands for $10.4 billion. Industry analysts described the consolidation of Seagram's record labels, including MCA, Geffen Records, and Interscope, with such PolyGram's record labels as A&M, Decca, Motown, and Verve, as the most massive restructuring in the history of the music industry. Critics predicted that the newly merged company, named the Universal Music Group, would become the leading corporation in American music.

Sinatra dies. On May 14, 1998, Frank Sinatra, whom many critics consider to be the greatest singer in American pop history, died at age 82 at a Los Angeles hospital. Critics credited Sinatra with elevating popular song to an art form through his flexible baritone and trademark style. Sinatra appeared in more than 50 films, including *The Manchurian Candidate,* and recorded more than 2,000 songs, including such standards as "All or Nothing at All," "Angel Eyes," "I Get a Kick Out of You," "I've Got You Under My Skin," and "One for My Baby." □ Don McLeese

See also **Popular music** Special Report: **Frank Sinatra—"The Voice"—(1915-1998).**

Grammy Award winners in 1998

Record of the Year, "Sunny Came Home," Shawn Colvin

Album of the Year, "Time Out of Mind," Bob Dylan

Song of the Year, "Sunny Came Home," Shawn Colvin and John Leventhal

New Artist, Paula Cole

Pop Vocal Performance, Female, "Building a Mystery," Sarah McLachlan

Pop Vocal Performance, Male, "Candle in the Wind 1997," Elton John

Pop Performance by a Duo or Group with Vocal, "Virtual Insanity," Jamiroquai

Traditional Pop Vocal Performance, "Don't Look Back," John Lee Hooker with Van Morrison

Pop Instrumental Performance, "Last Dance," Sarah McLachlan

Rock Vocal Performance, Female, "Criminal," Fiona Apple

Rock Vocal Performance, Male, "Cold Irons Bound," Bob Dylan

Rock Performance by a Duo or Group with Vocal, "One Headlight," The Wallflowers

Hard Rock Performance, "The End Is the Beginning Is the End," Smashing Pumpkins

Metal Performance, "Aenema," Tool

Rock Instrumental Performance, "Block Rockin' Beats," The Chemical Brothers

Rock Song, "One Headlight," Jakob Dylan

Alternative Music Performance, "OK Computer," Radiohead

Rhythm-and-Blues Vocal Performance, Female, "On and On," Erykah Badu

Rhythm-and-Blues Vocal Performance, Male, "I Believe I Can Fly," R. Kelly

Rhythm-and-Blues Performance by a Duo or Group with Vocal, "No Diggity," Blackstreet

Rhythm-and-Blues Song, "I Believe I Can Fly," R. Kelly

Rap Solo Performance, "Men In Black," Will Smith

Rap Performance by a Duo or Group, "I'll Be Missing You," Puff Daddy and Faith Evans featuring 112

New-Age Album, "Oracle," Michael Hedges

Contemporary Jazz Performance, "Into the Sun," Randy Brecker

Jazz Vocal Performance, "Dear Ella," Dee Dee Bridgewater

Jazz Instrumental, Solo, "Stardust," Doc Cheatham and Nicholas Payton

Jazz Instrumental Performance, Individual or Group, "Beyond the Missouri Sky," Charlie Haden and Pat Metheny

Large Jazz Ensemble Performance, "Joe Henderson Big Band," Joe Henderson Big Band

Latin Jazz Performance, "Habana," Roy Hargrove's Crisol

Country Album, "Unchained," Johnny Cash

Country Vocal Performance, Female, "How Do I Live," Trisha Yearwood

Country Vocal Performance, Male, "Pretty Little Adriana," Vince Gill

Country Performance by a Duo or Group with Vocal, "Looking In the Eyes of Love," Alison Kraus and Union Station

Country Vocal Collaboration, "In Another's Eyes," Trisha Yearwood and Garth Brooks

Country Instrumental Performance, "Little Liza Jane," Alison Kraus and Union Station

Bluegrass Album, "So Long So Wrong," Alison Kraus and Union Station

Country Song, "Butterfly Kisses," Bob Carlisle, Jeff Carson, and the Raybon Brothers

Frank Sinatra: "The Voice"— (1915-1998)

Sinatra, a singer legendary for his professional artistry and colorful personal life, died in 1998 at age 82.

By Jennifer Parello

"Get that! His name is Sinatra, and he considers himself the greatest vocalist in the business," bandleader Harry James said in 1939, shortly before hiring Frank Sinatra to sing with his band. "No one's ever heard of him! He's never had a hit record, and he looks like a wet rag, but he says he's the greatest!" Years later, many music critics did, in fact, consider Sinatra, who died on May 14, 1998 at age 82, the greatest singer in American pop history. Critics credited Sinatra with elevating popular song to an art form.

"Frank Sinatra was a true original," said jazz singer Mel Torme. "He held the patent, the original blueprint on singing the popular song, a man who would have thousands of imita-

tors but who, himself, would never be influenced by a single,
solitary person."

"I'd never heard a popular singer with such fluidity and
style," said songwriter Sammy Cahn. "Or one with his incredible breath control . . . He actually gasped, and his whole being
seemed to explode, to release itself. I'd never seen or heard anything like it."

From his earliest fame as America's first pop superstar to his
final performance at age 79, Sinatra's captivated the public with
his ability to mine the emotional core of a song and convey the
human condition through music. Sinatra used his flexible baritone and trademark style—characterized by masterful phrasing

The author
Jennifer Parello is a
managing editor with
World Book Annuals.

Sinatra escorts Ava Gardner to the 1951 premiere of *Show Boat,* a film that featured Gardner in a starring role. The couple married in November 1951. Their stormy relationship contributed to problems that almost destroyed Sinatra's career.

and an intimacy with his audience—to leave his imprint on more than 2,000 songs, including such standards as "Angel Eyes," "All or Nothing at All," "I Get a Kick Out of You," "I've Got You Under My Skin," "One for My Baby," and "All the Way."

"One grew up, fell in love, fell out of love, all to the sound of his voice," said actress Angela Lansbury, who co-starred with Sinatra in *The Manchurian Candidate* (1962), one of the more than 50 films he appeared in.

Sinatra's professional artistry was at times overshadowed—and often influenced—by his colorful private life. Tales of his romances, association with gangsters, and brawls with reporters were grist for the gossip columns. Yet, he was also known for his generosity and loyalty to family and friends.

Sinatra started his career in the 1930's as a romantic crooner. By the late 1940's, personal and professional troubles caused his career to nose dive, leaving him all but finished as an entertainer. Then, in the early 1950's, Sinatra made one of the most phenomenal career comebacks in show business history, landing a small, but choice role in an important film, which won him an Academy Award. He also launched the second phase of his musical career—virtually reinventing popular music in the process. By the late 1950's, he had transformed himself into the quintessential middle-aged playboy for whom life was a perpetual party, and Las Vegas was a favorite playground. In the 1980's and 1990's, long after his voice was in decay, Sinatra continued to draw sell-out crowds and record hit albums.

A singer is born

Francis Albert Sinatra was born in Hoboken, New Jersey, on Dec. 12, 1915, the only child of Martin, a fireman and tavern owner, and Natalie. Sinatra was about 9 years old when he first realized that he wanted to be a singer. The young Sinatra, whose brooding renditions of love ballads would later earn him acclaim as America's premier "saloon singer," would sit atop a piano in his father's bar and sing the popular songs of the early 1900's. "One day, somebody gave me a nickel or a dime after a song," Sinatra recalled. "And I said, 'This is the racket! This is what I gotta be doing!' The seed began there. And I never forgot it."

At age 15, Sinatra told his parents that he was dropping out of high school to become a singer. His mother, who had wanted him to attend college and become a civil engineer, threw a shoe at him. His father refused to speak to him for a year.

In 1939, Sinatra landed his first important engagement, per-

forming at the Rustic Cabin, a popular
New Jersey nightclub. His act caught the
attention of Harry James, a trumpet player
who had recently formed his own band.
James hired Sinatra in spite of concerns
about Sinatra's romantic appeal. Sinatra
was so thin at the time that one comic said
Sinatra could walk through an olive without disturbing the pimento.

The same year he joined James, Sinatra
married Nancy Barbato. They had three
children—Nancy, who was born in 1940;
Frank Jr., born in 1944; and Christina,
born in 1948.

The rise and fall of America's first pop superstar

Six months after he signed with Harry James, bandleader Tommy Dorsey invited Sinatra to join his orchestra, which was one of
the most popular big bands in the United States. In 1940, while
singing with the Dorsey orchestra, Sinatra scored his first No. 1
hit with the ballad "I'll Never Smile Again."

Sinatra's dreamy interpretation of love songs, and his frail,
underfed appearance, appealed to millions of women in the
1940's. Some of Sinatra's fans, many of whom were teen-aged
girls known as bobby-soxers, would swoon, or faint, when they
heard "The Voice"—Sinatra's nickname at the time.

In 1942, Sinatra, at age 27, left Dorsey's band determined to
be the first singer since Bing Crosby to have a successful solo career. He signed contracts with Columbia Records, R.K.O. Pictures, and the radio program "Your Hit Parade." His first concert
as a solo artist was at the Paramount Theater in New York City.
Thousands of bobby-soxers mobbed the theater, creating pande-
monium in the streets. At his return engagement at the Paramount
in 1944, more than 30,000 fans crowded outside the theater.

"It was the war years and there was great loneliness," said

Sinatra as Maggio,
above left, in *From
Here to Eternity*
(1953), dies in the
arms of Prewitt, played
by Montgomery Clift.
The role won Sinatra
an Academy Award in
1953 and relaunched
his career. "The Rat
Pack"—Sinatra, Dean
Martin, Sammy Davis
Jr., Peter Lawford, and
Joey Bishop—pose
outside the Sands
Hotel in Las Vegas,
above, where the
friends performed
together in the 1960's.

Sinatra. "I was the boy in every corner drugstore who'd gone off, drafted to war." A punctured eardrum kept Sinatra out of military service during World War II (1939-1945). Yet, in many of his early movie roles, he appeared in uniform—most often in a sailor suit.

Sinatra's popularity began to slide after 1946, the year in which he had 15 hit singles on the pop charts. Only four Sinatra songs made the Top 10 charts in 1947, and Sinatra recorded only one hit single in 1948. This professional decline coincided with increasing tensions between Sinatra and Columbia Records. Desperate to find a hit song for Sinatra, Columbia urged him to record several inferior songs, including "Mama Will Bark," which features Sinatra accompanied by a man performing dog imitations.

Sinatra's personal life was also unraveling in the late 1940's. In 1949, while married to Nancy, he began a highly publicized relationship with movie star Ava Gardner. After a stormy courtship marked by public battles, suicide attempts, and shoving matches with photographers, Sinatra and Gardner married in 1951. They separated in 1953.

The relationship with Gardner shattered Sinatra's legendary self-confidence, but added emotional depth to his singing. "I think being jilted is one of life's most painful experiences," Sinatra said. "It takes a long time to heal a broken heart. It's happened to all of us and never gets any easier. I understand, however, that playing one of my albums can help."

Career comeback

In 1952, Sinatra pleaded with Columbia Studios to cast him as Maggio, the feisty Italian-American soldier who is ultimately beaten to death, in *From Here to Eternity*. His role in the film, which was based on James Jones's best-selling novel about American soldiers in Hawaii on the eve of the Japanese attack on Pearl Harbor, won Sinatra the Academy Award for best-supporting actor in 1953, and relaunched his career.

In April 1953, Sinatra signed with Capitol Records, where he teamed with Nelson Riddle, a music arranger known for his sophisticated swing music. Music critics have credited Sinatra and Riddle with reshaping popular music, in part, by pioneering the *concept album*, a long-playing record that focused on one idea or theme.

Most critics agree that Sinatra and Riddle hit their artistic peak with three albums released between 1955 and 1958. *In the Wee Small Hours*, released in 1955, featured Sinatra's mournful interpretation of classic torch songs. *Songs for Swinging Lovers*, released in 1956, defined Sinatra's urbane "swinger" style. The album contains what many critics consider Sinatra's greatest recorded performance: Cole Porter's "I've Got You Under My Skin." In 1958, Sinatra and Riddle released *Only the Lonely*, a jazzy, world-weary look at lost love.

Sinatra's movie career boomed in the mid-1950's in such films as *Suddenly* (1954), *Guys and Dolls* (1955), *Pal Joey* (1957), and *The Joker Is Wild* (1957). His performance as a heroin addict in the 1955 film *The Man with the Golden Arm* won him an Academy Award nomination for best actor.

In the 1960's, Sinatra appeared mainly in films that critics judged to be mediocre, including several movies co-starring Dean Martin, Sammy Davis Jr., Peter Lawford, and Joey Bishop—a group of friends known as "The Rat Pack." In addition to making movies, the men performed together in Las Vegas, where Sinatra was a pioneer entertainer.

Sinatra's recording career entered a new phase in 1961, when he left Capitol Records and formed his own record company, Reprise. Over the next 20 years he would make more than 30 albums for Reprise. Although most critics agree that Sinatra made his best albums at Capitol, he recorded several of his signature songs on the Reprise label, including "Strangers in the Night" (1966), "My Way" (1969), and "New York, New York" (1980).

In 1966, Sinatra married actress Mia Farrow, who at age 21 was 30 years his junior. They divorced in 1968. He married Barbara Blakeley Marx in 1976, a union that lasted until his death.

Although his recordings and films became less frequent in the 1980's and 1990's, Sinatra continued to perform in concert. He toured the world in 1989 with Sammy Davis, Jr., and Liza Minnelli and, in 1992, he toured with Shirley MacLaine. His last performance was in 1995.

In 1993, at the age of 77, Sinatra made another career comeback with the release of *Duets*, a collection of standards rerecorded with such singers as Aretha Franklin, Tony Bennett, Barbra Streisand, and Bono from the Irish rock group U2, who called Sinatra "the big bang of pop." The recording was a huge success and led to the release of *Duets II* in 1994.

Shortly before Sinatra's death, a biographer asked him to reveal the secret of his success. Sinatra responded, "I do remember being described in one simple word that I agree with. The writer said that when the music began and I started to sing, I was 'honest.' That says it as I feel it."

Population. In October 1998, the United Nations Population Fund (UNFPA) estimated that the world population had grown by about 78 million people in 1997. The rate of increase in the population was a slight drop from the average annual increase of 81 million in the mid-1990's. The UNFPA also reported that the total world population in mid-1998 stood at about 5.9 billion and estimated that the population would exceed 6 billion by October 1999.

The State of the World Population Report, issued by the UNFPA on Sept. 2, 1998, noted that more than 1 billion people in the world in 1998 were between the ages of 15 and 24. The large number of young people, the result of high fertility rates in the past decades, was unprecedented in the history of world population. Because these people were in their childbearing years, the UNFPA anticipated that the population could continue to grow significantly for several years.

The UNFPA also noted that the great number of people reaching their prime working age, most of whom lived in developing countries, could provide "a demographic bonus" for some nations. For example, the UN noted that people in this age group had contributed to the economic boom in East Asia in the first half of the 1990's. In order to capitalize on the resources of a large working population, the UNFPA called upon countries to invest in education, training, long-term economic development, and political systems that ensured the human rights of its citizens. Governments would also have to provide better information about reproductive health so that young people could plan the size of their families and avoid sexually transmitted diseases.

The world's elderly population also grew at an unprecedented rate in the late 1990's. The number of people 65 years of age and older grew by about 9 million from 1997 to 1998 to reach a record number of 400 million worldwide. The UNFPA estimated that the elderly population would grow annually at a rate of 4.5 million by 2010 and at a rate of 21 million by 2050.

People in both developing and industrialized countries were living longer and healthier lives. From 1950 to 1998, the percentage of elderly people increased from 8 percent of the total population to 14 percent. Life expectancy was still much higher—by as much as 25 years—in industrialized nations, compared with the rates in the least-developed countries. The UNFPA predicted that over the next 35 years, the elderly would constitute at least 30 percent of the population in Japan, Germany, and Italy. The report warned that governments needed to improve programs to assist the social, medical, and financial needs of this group. □ J. Tuyet Nguyen

See also **AIDS; City.**

Portugal enjoyed one of the strongest economies in Europe in 1998. The government of Prime Minister Antonio Guterres continued its policies of reducing the budget deficit and privatizing state-owned companies. Those policies helped interest rates and inflation decline toward the low levels prevailing in most northern European countries, creating a climate that fostered a fifth straight year of economic growth.

The European Commission, the administrative arm of the European Union (EU), forecast that the Portuguese economy would grow by 4.2 percent during 1998, one of the strongest growth rates in Europe, and that unemployment would fall to 5.7 percent, the lowest of any southern European country. The commission expected the budget deficit to decline to 2.3 percent of *gross domestic product* (the value of all goods and services produced in a country in a year) and inflation to run at 2.6 percent. EU leaders in May selected Portugal along with 10 other EU countries to participate in the launch of the euro, the single European currency, in January 1999.

The economy also benefitted from several large construction projects. In March, the $1-billion Vasco da Gama Bridge opened. The 11-mile (18-kilometer) bridge spans the Tagus River. Work also continued in 1998 on an expansion of the Lisbon Metro system. In addition, the econo-

Flame-throwing cranes move around a giant, inflatable, egg-shaped globe during the nightly sound and light show at Expo '98 in Lisbon. The world's fair, held from May through September 1998, was Portugal's first international exposition.

my got a boost from tourists visiting the world's fair, Expo '98.

Expo '98. Portugal held its first international exposition from May through September 1998. The theme of Expo '98 was preservation of the world's oceans, and the centerpiece was Europe's largest aquarium. The event also highlighted the dramatic steps the country had taken to modernize its economy and raise its people's standard of living toward the level of other European countries. Built along the Tagus River in Lisbon, the exposition cost $2 billion and attracted more than 10 million visitors.

Abortion. Portuguese voters failed to pass a referendum legalizing abortion, leaving Portugal one of the few countries in Europe where abortions remain illegal. Only 32 percent of voters cast ballots in the June 28 referendum, well below the 50 percent required for passage. Of those voting, 51 percent rejected the proposal.

Nobel Prize. In October 1998, Jose Saramago, a 75-year-old novelist and poet, became the first Portuguese-language writer to win the Nobel Prize for literature. Saramago received critical acclaim for works that blended Portuguese history with fantasy and criticized political repression and poverty. □ Tom Buerkle

See also **Europe** (Facts in brief table); **Europe** Special Report: **European Union.**

Prison. The adult prison population in the United States grew by 5.2 percent in 1997, according to a U.S. Department of Justice Bureau of Justice Statistics (BJS) report released in August 1998. The BJS reported that there were 1,244,554 inmates in state and federal prisons in 1997. The increase over the 1996 prison population was the equivalent of adding 1,177 inmates a week. The BJS also reported that as of June 30, 1997, an additional 567,076 inmates were incarcerated in jails, which hold people who are awaiting trial or serving sentences of one year or less.

Women in prison. According to the BJS's 1997 figures, the female population in prison increased more rapidly than the male population. Between Dec. 31, 1996, and Dec. 31, 1997, the number of female prisoners increased by 6.2 percent to 79,624. The number of male prisoners increased 5.2 percent during that same period. Female prisoners still represented a small minority —6.4 percent—of all state and federal prisoners.

Racial inconsistencies continued among U.S. prisoners during 1996, according to BJS statistics released in August 1998. Although white Americans accounted for 73 percent of the U.S. population in 1996, they comprised 47.9 percent of all U.S. prisoners as of Dec. 31, 1996. However, African Americans, who comprised about 12 percent of the U.S. population, made up 49.4 percent of prisoners at the end of 1996. The contrasts between white and black prison populations were starker when those populations were broken down by gender and age. According to the BJS statistics, nearly 7 percent of black males in their 20's and 30's were in prison in 1996, compared with less than 1 percent of white men in the same age group. More than 8 percent of all black men between the ages of 25 and 29 in the United States in 1996 were in federal or state prisons.

Drug and alcohol dependence among prisoners was on the rise, according to a survey conducted by the BJS between October 1995 and March 1996. According to the survey results, released in April 1998, more than 50 percent of all convicted inmates reported having used drugs in the month prior to committing their crime, compared to 44 percent who responded to a similar survey in 1989.

The BJS also reported that 63 percent of convicted males and 50 percent of convicted females reported having used alcohol regularly prior to their convictions. The study revealed that 60 percent of the inmates reported using drugs, alcohol, or both at the time of the offense for which they were imprisoned. □ Michael Tonry

See also **Courts** Special Report: **Marking Time on Death Row; Crime.**

Prizes. See Nobel Prizes; Pulitzer Prizes.

Protestantism. In June 1998, the Lutheran World Federation, an international communion representing some 57 million Lutherans, reached an agreement with the Roman Catholic Church about a theological controversy that led to the founding of the Protestant faith in the 1500's. The conflict was over the doctrine of justification, the means by which an individual receives salvation. Martin Luther, the leader of the religious movement that led to Protestantism, taught that a person was justified by faith in God. Roman Catholic theology taught that justification depended, in part, on good works.

The new agreement, "The Joint Declaration on the Doctrine of Justification," states that by "grace alone" are people accepted by God, who equips them to do good works. Believers must, in turn, respond in faith. Although some Catholic leaders did not agree with other aspects of the document, most Lutherans celebrated the declaration as an act of reconciliation.

Husband-wife relations. In June 1998, the Southern Baptist Convention, the largest Protestant body in the United States, added to its statement of beliefs a declaration that a wife should "submit herself graciously to the servant leadership of her husband." Based on an interpretation of biblical texts, the statement was approved at an annual gathering that took place in Salt Lake City, Utah. While Baptists are not required to follow such statements of faith, the new ruling is considered central to Southern Baptist teaching.

Anglican bishops attended the once-a-decade international Lambeth Conference in Canterbury, England, in August 1998. For the first time in the history of the Anglican Communion, the majority of bishops came from Africa and Asia, rather than from churches in Great Britain, Australia, Canada, New Zealand, and the United States. Anglican churches in Africa and Asia grew rapidly in the past 10 years, while the sizes of congregations in Western countries declined.

Homosexuality remained a controversial issue among many Protestants in 1998. In August, the Anglican bishops at the Lambeth Conference approved a resolution that proclaimed homosexual activity "incompatible with Scripture." The resolution, passed by a vote of 526 to 70, was a statement of general agreement rather than a church law. The document also advised against the ordination of noncelibate homosexuals and the blessing of same-sex unions.

Also in August, the highest court of the United Methodist Church in the United States ruled that the church's *Book of Discipline* forbade, rather than recommended against, blessing ceremonies for gay couples. The judgment overturned the decision of a church jury in Omaha,

Anglican bishops attend the 1998 Lambeth Conference in Canterbury, England, an international gathering held every 10 years. Reflecting changes in the membership of the Anglican Communion, the majority of bishops were, for the first time, from Africa and Asia.

Nebraska, that Jimmy Creech, a Methodist minister, was permitted to conduct such a ceremony.

On July 13, a coalition of 15 conservative Christian groups in the United States launched an advertising campaign that claimed God could help homosexuals overcome their sexual orientation. The campaign gave support to organizations that counsel homosexuals who want to change.

Religious persecution. The Freedom from Religious Persecution Act of 1998 passed in the U.S. House of Representatives by a vote of 375 to 41. Conservative Protestant organizations, working with some Jewish and Catholic groups, spearheaded support for the bill, which would require the U.S. government to withhold aid from countries that engage in religious persecution. A version of the bill in the U.S. Senate remained in committee at the end of 1998.

Henry Lyons, president of the National Baptist Convention U.S.A. (NBC), one of the largest African American churches, was indicted on July 2 by a federal grand jury in Tampa, Florida, on charges of fraud, money laundering, tax evasion, and conspiracy. He had been indicted in February on similar charges by the state of Florida. Although many NBC members criticized Lyons, the church's board of directors announced its support of him on September 8.   □ Martin E. Marty

Psychology. See Mental health.

Public health and safety. The Institute of Medicine (IOM), an agency of the National Academy of Sciences in Washington, D.C., recommended in April 1998 that women who might become pregnant should take 400 micrograms of folic acid per day to reduce the risks of neural tube defects. The neural tube is a structure in a fetus that develops into the brain, spinal cord, and related tissues. Folic acid reduces the risk of problems in this development.

The IOM noted that most men and women do not get adequate amounts of folic acid, a B vitamin. The report emphasized the importance of folic acid for women of childbearing age, because neural tube defects occur in the first months of pregnancy when women often do not know they are pregnant. Folic acid is found in dark-green leafy vegetables, some citrus fruits, and enriched grain products. The IOM recommended that women also take folic acid supplements.

Hepatitis C. In March, the U.S. Department of Health and Human Services (HHS) announced a plan to notify many Americans who received blood transfusions before 1992 that they may be infected with hepatitis C, a virus that causes irreversible liver damage. Hepatitis C is most often transmitted by infected blood and shared intravenous needles. Although an estimated 4 million Americans are infected, many do not know it, be-

cause symptoms often do not appear for years.

HHS warning letters were to go to people who received blood from donors who later tested positive for the virus. HHS expected the blood recipients to have a 40 to 70 percent chance of being infected. (By mid-1992, a test that screens donated blood for the hepatitis C virus had essentially eliminated the risk of contracting the disease through the transfusion of tainted blood.)

Flu vaccine. The National Institutes of Health (NIH), a U.S. government agency located in Bethesda, Maryland, announced in May 1998 that an experimental influenza vaccine, administered as a nasal spray, was effective in preventing both flu and flu-related ear infections in children. Children catch the flu as much as 10 times more often than adults. However, standard flu shots are not recommended for children.

In clinical trials with more than 1,600 children, the new flu vaccine was 93 percent effective in producing immunity against three strains of flu virus. It was 98 percent effective in preventing *otitis media,* a middle ear infection that is a common complication of flu in children. The NIH expected the vaccine to be ready for use by 1999.

Food safety. In April 1998, the U.S. Food and Drug Administration (FDA) proposed hazard-control programs to prevent the contamination of fruit and vegetable juices. The programs would require manufacturers to use stringent cleaning methods to reduce levels of harmful microbes and contaminants prior to processing. The FDA also proposed warning labels for juices that are not *pasteurized* (heated to kill bacteria). By the end of 1998, only one proposal was put into effect—labels for nonpasteurized apple juice and cider.

In May, the U.S. General Accounting Office (GAO), an investigative agency of Congress, warned that federal food inspection programs could not assure the safety of imported fruits and vegetables. The GAO reported that the FDA inspects about 1.7 percent of the 2.7 million annual shipments of imported food. Of the 46,395 total inspections, only 16,000 included laboratory analysis for disease-causing microbes.

Rollover warnings. In April, the U.S. National Highway Traffic Safety Administration (NHTSA), a regulatory agency in Washington, D.C., announced a plan requiring manufacturers to use more visible warning labels on sports-utility vehicles (SUV's) at risk of rolling over. Because SUV's stand high off the ground, they have a high center of gravity, putting some at risk of tipping over when turning at high speeds. SUV warning labels in use since 1986 had text only. The NHTSA planned to add bright colors and a drawing that depicts a rollover.   □ Michael Woods

See also **AIDS; Drugs; Medicine; Mental health; People in the news** (Brundtland; Satcher).

Puerto Rico. On Dec. 13, 1998, the citizens of the U.S. Commonwealth of Puerto Rico voted on a nonbinding referendum that was intended to send a message to the U.S. government about how Puerto Ricans want to define their political status. Most political observers noted that the impact of the vote was unclear, however, because the terms of the referendum were reportedly flawed. While more than 46.5 percent of the voters chose U.S. statehood, more than 50 percent chose the referendum's "none of the above" selection. The rest of the electorate was split over three other choices—independence, commonwealth status, and "free association," a loosely defined autonomy without complete independence.

The ongoing debate over Puerto Rico's future was particularly intense in 1998, because the year marked the 100th anniversary of the United States acquisition of Puerto Rico at the end of the Spanish-American War. In 1952, the U.S. Congress granted Puerto Rico commonwealth status, which provided Puerto Ricans with U.S. citizenship but did not allow them to vote for president or congressional representatives.

Proponents of the commonwealth status argued that the definition of *commonwealth* in the 1998 referendum was unclear and implied that Puerto Ricans would lose their U.S. citizenship. The procommonwealth leaders claimed that a vote for "none of the above" should be interpreted as a vote for the current status. Prostatehood Governor Pedro J. Rossello saw the vote as somewhat of a victory since the majority of those who voted for change preferred statehood.

Telephone company sale. On June 24, Rossello approved the sale of the commonwealth-owned Puerto Rico Telephone Company (PRTC) for about $1.9 billion to a group of private investors led by the GTE Corporation, based in Stamford, Connecticut. The sale was unpopular with most Puerto Ricans and proved to be a lightning rod for protests during 1998.

On June 18, more than 6,000 PRTC employees walked off the job in protest of the anticipated sale. On July 7, hundreds of thousands of people, in a display of solidarity with telephone workers, began a 48-hour general strike. Commerce and transportation were brought to a virtual halt. More militant protestors caused an estimated $2.59 million worth of damage to telephone company property.

Aftermath of sale. Facing sustained and damaging labor unrest, Governor Rossello promised to use proceeds from the sale to fund PRTC employees' retirement and health-care benefits. He also pledged $1 billion for public works, including much-needed sewage-treatment and water-distribution systems.   □ Nathan A. Haverstock

See also **Latin America** (Facts in brief table).

Pulitzer Prizes in journalism, letters, and music were awarded on April 14, 1998, by Columbia University in New York City on the recommendation of the Pulitzer Prize Board.

Journalism. The *Grand Forks* (North Dakota) *Herald* won the public service award for coverage of the floods, blizzard, and fire that devastated the city in 1997. The *Los Angeles Times* staff received the breaking news award with its report of a bank robbery and police shoot-out. Gary Cohn and Will Englund of *The Baltimore Sun* took the investigative reporting award for a series on the hazards of dismantling ships. The prize for explanatory journalism went to Paul Salopek of the *Chicago Tribune* for a profile of the Human Genome Diversity Project.

Linda Greenhouse of *The New York Times* won the award for beat reporting for her coverage of the United States Supreme Court. Russell Carollo and Jeff Nesmith of the *Dayton* (Ohio) *Daily News* took the national reporting award for their series on mismanagement in the military health-care system. *The New York Times* staff received the prize in international reporting for articles about drug trafficking in Mexico.

Mike McAlary of the New York City *Daily News* received the prize for commentary for his coverage of police brutality toward a Haitian immigrant. The editorial prize went to Bernard L. Stein of *The Riverdale Press* in New York City. The prize for criticism went to book reviewer Michiko Kakutani of *The New York Times.*

Clarence Williams of the *Los Angeles Times* won the prize for feature photography for his work documenting children with parents addicted to alcohol and drugs. The prize for spot news photography went to Martha Rial of the *Pittsburgh* (Pennsylvania) *Post-Gazette* for portraits of Rwanda and Burundi civil war survivors. Stephen P. Breen of the *Asbury Park Press* in Neptune, New Jersey, won the prize for editorial cartoons.

Letters and music. Philip Roth won the fiction prize for *American Pastoral.* The drama prize went to Paula Vogel for *How I Learned to Drive.* Edward J. Larson received the history prize for *Summer for the Gods: The Scopes Trial and America's Continuing Debate Over Science and Religion.* The biography prize was awarded to Katharine Graham for her autobiography, *Personal History.* Charles Wright won the prize for poetry for his collection *Black Zodiac.* Jared Diamond earned the general nonfiction prize for *Guns, Germs, and Steel: The Fates of Human Societies.*

Aaron Jay Kernis won the music prize for String Quartet No. 2 *(Musica Instrumentalis).* A special award was given to George Gershwin (1898–1937), commemorating the 100th anniversary of his birth.   □ Brian Bouldrey

Quebec. See **Canadian provinces.**

Radio. The explosive growth of big radio companies continued in 1998 to be the most important trend in the United States radio industry. Companies that had begun to buy stations following the passage of the Telecommunications Reform Act of 1996 continued to acquire stations in their effort to become dominant in the country's 268 radio markets. Before the passage of the Telecommunications Act, which removed most restrictions on radio ownership, no single company was allowed to own more than eight stations in a single market. By late 1998, four companies owned 1,259 of the 12,300 U.S. radio stations.

Radio's large chains operated on the theory that controlling a cluster of stations in a market allowed them to boost ratings for all cluster stations and cut operating expenses. Ratings—the number of listeners a station attracts—largely determine the amount stations can charge advertisers. Stations in clusters commonly offer package deals to advertisers, promote one another, and share office and studio space as well as personnel, particularly news staffs.

Becoming number one. The largest radio deal of 1998 was announced in October, when Clear Channel Communications, a San Antonio media company, agreed to buy Jacor Communications of Covington, Kentucky, for $2.8 billion in stock. If approved by the Federal Communications Commission (FCC), the combined company would have 454 stations in 101 markets, and it would rank second among U.S. radio chains, with annual revenues of about $1 billion.

The second-largest acquisition of 1998 was announced in August, when Chancellor Media Corporation of Dallas, the largest independent U.S. radio broadcaster, said it would merge with Capstar Broadcasting Corporation of Austin, Texas. The $4.1-billion merger would create the largest U.S. radio chain, with 474 stations in 105 markets and annual revenues of $1.5 billion. The merger was widely predicted because both Chancellor and Capstar were controlled by the Dallas-based investment firm of Hicks, Muse, Tate & Furst, Inc.

In June, CBS Corporation, the highest-grossing U.S. radio chain, announced its $2.6-billion acquisition of 90-station American Radio Systems Incorporated of Boston. The acquisition, along with subsequent purchases, gave CBS—renamed Infinity Broadcasting—160 stations and clusters in some of the country's biggest cities. The combined company had assets of about $21 billion with annual revenues of about $1.5 billion.

Concentration debate. On May 29, FCC Commissioners Susan Ness and Gloria Tristani touched off a fresh debate about the growing concentration of radio ownership. The commissioners questioned the FCC Mass Media Bureau's approval of the sale of four stations in Redding, California, to Regent Communications Inc. of Covington. The acquisition gave Regent control over 6 of 13 stations in Redding and 64 percent of that market's radio advertising revenue. The sale also gave Regent and a three-station company, McCarthy Wireless, Inc., of Redding, control over 99 percent of the radio advertising dollars in that market. In August and September, the FCC solicited public comment about station sales if that would allow one company to control at least 50 percent of the radio advertising dollars in a market or two companies to control at least 70 percent of a market's revenues.

Talk and sports talk. News/talk stations remained the most popular U.S. radio format for the fourth consecutive year, attracting about 16 percent of the audience, according to the Arbitron Company, a media ratings firm. Conservative talk show host Rush Limbaugh and advice counselor Laura Schlessinger continued to attract some 18 million listeners at least once a week. All-sports stations, which offered sports talk and live sports broadcasts, continued to grow explosively. In 1998, about 600 stations classified themselves as sports stations, an increase of about 25 percent over 1997 and a 60 percent increase from 1995.   □ Gregory Paeth

See also **Telecommunications; Television.**

Republican Party. The Republican Party was jolted by the results of the Nov. 3, 1998, congressional election. The GOP (for Grand Old Party) lost five seats in the House and failed to make gains in the Senate. Speaker of the House Newt Gingrich (R., Georgia), under mounting criticism for Republican losses in elections, announced in November that he would resign from the speakership and from the United States Congress in early 1999.

Senate races. Republicans maintained the same 55 to 45 majority in the Senate following the November 1998 election. Both the Republicans and Democrats gained three seats, but lost three others. The loss of Alfonse M. D'Amato's (R., New York) Senate seat to Democrat Charles E. Schumer, who had served in the House, and the defeat of Senator Lauch Faircloth of North Carolina by Democrat John Edwards, a political newcomer, were viewed as major blows to the GOP.

The Republicans, however, did enjoy some important victories in the November 3 congressional elections. In Illinois, Republican state Senator Peter Fitzgerald defeated Democratic Senator Carol Moseley-Braun in her bid for a second term. Republican George V. Voinovich of Ohio captured the seat of retiring Senator John H. Glenn, Jr., a Democrat.

House races. The November election shrank

In November 1998, Republicans in the House of Representatives elect (left to right) Robert L. Livingston as speaker, Richard K. Armey as majority leader, and J. C. Watts as Republican Conference chairman for the 106th Congress, which begins in 1999. Livingston resigned the speakership on December 19.

the Republican majority in the House from 223 to 218, with one independent who usually voted with the Democrats. While only a few Republicans lost reelection bids, Democratic victories in open races and in reelection campaigns surprised political experts who had predicted major Republican gains. Republicans who lost reelection bids included representatives Bill Redmond of New Mexico, Vince Snowbarger of Kansas, and Jon Fox of Pennsylvania.

Gingrich resigns. In the wake of Republican defeats in Congress in the November election, Speaker of the House Gingrich announced on November 6 that he would step down as leader of the House and resign from Congress. Gingrich had been elected to the House in 1979. During the 1994 congressional election campaign, he had led a Republican movement that included calls for cuts in government spending to achieve a balanced federal budget. Analysts credited the strategy with giving the GOP control of the House for the first time in 40 years. In 1998, GOP leaders and members of Congress blamed Gingrich for allowing Democratic gains in the House.

GOP leadership. House Republicans unanimously selected Representative Robert L. Livingston of Louisiana on November 18 as their nominee for House Speaker. The full House was scheduled to vote on the nomination in January 1999. Represen-

tative Richard K. Armey (R., Texas) fought off challenges by representatives Jennifer Dunn of Washington, Steve Largent of Oklahoma, and J. Dennis Hastert of Illinois to remain House majority leader. Representative J. C. Watts of Oklahoma defeated Representative John A. Boehner of Ohio for the chairmanship of the Republican Conference. Representative Thomas Davis, III, of Virginia replaced Representative John Linder of Georgia as chairman of the National Republican Congressional Committee. Representative Tom DeLay of Texas retained his position as Republican Whip. The new leadership announced that the party's priorities in the 106th Congress would focus on tax cuts.

On Dec. 19, 1998, Livingston stunned the House by announcing that he would not run for the speakership and instead would resign from Congress.

Gubernatorial elections. Republicans won 23 of the 36 open governor's seats in the November 1998 election. The GOP had held 24 of those governorships before the election.

Two sons of former U.S. President George H. W. Bush won gubernatorial bids. Voters reelected Texas Governor George Bush to a second term by a wide margin. He was the first GOP governor in Texas history to win reelection. Florida voters elected Jeb Bush governor. The former president's younger son ran unsuccessfully for the office in 1994. In Colorado, Bill Owens was the first Republican elected governor since the 1970's. Governor Fob James, Jr., of Alabama and Governor David M. Beasley of South Carolina were both defeated by Democratic challengers.

Fund-raising report. The Federal Election Commission (FEC) in September 1998 reported that Republican national, state, and local committees had raised $193 million in contributions in the first six months of 1998, compared with $108 million raised by the Democratic Party. The Republicans raised $71.8 million in soft money, compared with $53 million raised by the Democrats. Soft money refers to individual contributions to political parties that are not subject to the same stringent restrictions placed on contributions to candidates. The FEC reported that the GOP soft money donations accounted for 27 percent of their $265-million total. The Democrats' soft-money donations accounted for approximately 33 percent of the $161-million total.

Proposal blocked. The Republican National Committee, at its winter meeting in January 1998, blocked a proposal that would have barred the party from contributing funds to candidates who were not opposed to a type of late-term abortion procedure.   □ William J. Eaton

See also **Congress of the United States; Democratic Party; Elections; State government; United States, President of the.**

Rhode Island. See **State government.**

Roman Catholic Church. Pope John Paul II began a five-day visit to Cuba on Jan. 21, 1998, that was significant for both the Roman Catholic Church and the government of President Fidel Castro. Since Cuba's Communist revolution in 1959, Cuba's Catholic Church had faced numerous restrictions. On the pope's first visit to Cuba, however, Castro allowed the pontiff to travel relatively freely and meet the country's estimated 4.5 million Roman Catholics.

The pope noted the strengths and weaknesses of both Cuba and its political rivals. At a welcoming ceremony with Castro, the pope stated, "May Cuba, with all its magnificent potential, open itself up to the world, and may the world open itself up to Cuba." He later called upon the United States to end its nearly 40-year-old economic embargo against Cuba.

Papal statements. On Oct. 15, 1998, the eve of the 20th anniversary of his papacy, John Paul II issued a statement entitled "Faith and Reason." The pope denounced modern philosophers for abandoning a search for truth and questioning people's ability to know anything for sure. Alternatively, he argued that faith and reason are "two modes of knowledge" that "lead to truth in all its fullness." Many Roman Catholic leaders viewed the statement as a culmination of the pope's theological and philosophical teachings.

Roman Catholics pay homage to the Shroud of Turin, a relic traditionally believed to be the burial cloth of Jesus. The cloth, which bears the mysterious image of a crucified man, was displayed in Turin, Italy, over Easter 1998 for the first time since carbon dating experiments, conducted in 1988, suggested the cloth dated from the 1200's or 1300's.

In a June 1998 letter titled "To Defend the Faith," the pope inserted into official Roman Catholic Church law three paragraphs intended to end dissent in the church ranks. The pope's letter raised certain "definitively held" teachings to the level of unquestionable doctrine and called for penalties as severe as excommunication for defying such doctrines. The changes in church law were expected to affect many theologians at Roman Catholic universities and many American Catholics who had engaged in debates about matters such as the ordination of women, the validity of ordinations in the Anglican church, and the ethics of sexual relations outside of marriage.

Sainthood. On Oct. 11, 1998, the pope proclaimed Edith Stein, a Roman Catholic nun who had been born a Jew, a saint and martyr of the church. Born in Germany in 1891, Stein converted to Roman Catholicism in 1922 and entered a convent in 1933. In 1938, she fled to the Netherlands to escape Nazi persecution. When Dutch bishops denounced the deportation of Jews to German concentration camps, the Nazis began deporting those Roman Catholic converts who had been born Jews. Previously, such converts had been spared. Stein died at Auschwitz on Aug. 9, 1942.

Many Jews criticized the *canonization* (proclamation of sainthood) of Stein as insensitive. They argued that she was killed because she was a Jew, rather than a martyr to the Christian faith. The Roman Catholic Church claimed that the Germans had killed Jewish converts to punish the Dutch church for speaking out against the deportations.

Roman Catholic bishops from Asia gathered in Rome on April 19, 1998, for a month-long synod, a meeting of bishops to advise the pope. The synod focused on what evangelization, or the church's ministry, means in the context of Asian cultures. Vatican leaders said evangelization inherently means proclaiming Jesus Christ as savior to the world and seeking converts to the faith. Most of the Asian bishops, however, said that evangelization should primarily be about maintaining a dialogue with people of other faiths in Asia—mainly Buddhists, Hindus, and Muslims—and working with them to meet the needs of the poor and disadvantaged.

Bishop Juan Gerardi Conedera, a human rights leader in Guatemala, was beaten to death on April 26. Two days earlier, Gerardi had delivered a report about human rights abuses during the country's 36-year civil war, which ended in 1996. The report blamed the Guatemalan military for most of the violence, including the deaths of about 150,000 people and the unexplained disappearances of 50,000 others. Many Roman Catholic officials criticized police investigations of the murders and suspected that military personnel were involved.　□ Thomas C. Fox

Romania. Conflict within Romania's four-party governing coalition threatened to paralyze the government in early 1998. On March 30, Prime Minister Victor Ciorbea resigned under heavy pressure from the coalition's junior partners, who had criticized Ciorbea for moving too slowly in implementing economic reforms. Radu Vasile became prime minister in April.

Leaders of the Hungarian Democratic Union of Romania party threatened to leave the governing coalition in June unless the government moved to reestablish a Hungarian-language university in the city of Cluj. In October, after parliament approved a compromise plan to establish a Hungarian-German university, party leaders agreed to remain in the coalition.

Communist legacy. In June, the Senate voted not to publish the files of the Securitate, Romania's Communist-era secret police, but passed a measure that would permit individual citizens to view their own secret personal files. The bill needed to pass parliament's lower house before becoming law. Health Minister Francisc Baranyi was dismissed by Prime Minister Vasile on June 25, after admitting that he had signed a commitment to work for the Securitate in 1961.

Economy. Romania in 1998 attempted to renegotiate the terms of a 1997 loan agreement with the International Monetary Fund (IMF), a United Nations affiliate that provides credit to member nations. IMF officials, critical of the slow pace and poor organization of Romania's privatization program, in February 1998 halted the third part of the $430-million loan. In September, Romania's finance minister was ousted. The privatization minister resigned in October.

Romanian health-care workers went on strike in February for higher wages. In August, about 28,000 miners staged a one-day warning strike to protest layoffs and unpaid salaries. In October, approximately 200,000 teachers and professors struck to protest low wages and budget cuts planned for education.

Romania's *gross domestic product* (the total value of goods and services produced by a country in a given year) dropped 9.4 percent in the first half of 1998. Inflation for the year was forecast to be about 40 percent. Unemployment stood at 8.8 percent in June.

Foreign affairs. Relations with Ukraine were strained after authorities in the Odessa region of Ukraine, a region inhabited by many ethnic Romanians, decided in August to ban the study of the Romanian language and literature. In September, Romania signed an agreement with Greece and Bulgaria to work together to fight organized crime.　□ Sharon L. Wolchik

See also **Europe** (Facts in brief table); **Ukraine.**

Rowing. See **Sports.**

Rugby football. In Rugby Union, South Africa triumphed for the first time in the Annual Tri-Nations Series, and France went undefeated in the European Five Nations Championship for the second successive season. In February 1998, Rugby Union officials announced that, beginning in 2000, Italy was expected to join France, England, Wales, Scotland, and Ireland in the European Championship, creating a Six Nations Tournament. In Rugby League, Australia retained its supremacy in the international arena by defeating New Zealand in the Super League Series.

International Rugby Union (RU). France won the 1997-1998 Five Nations championship, which is played annually between France, England, Wales, Scotland, and Ireland, for the second consecutive season. On April 5, France completed its second straight *Grand Slam* (twice defeating all four opposing teams) by dismantling Wales, 51-0, in the final. England won the *Triple Crown* (an unofficial side challenge among the four English-speaking nations) for the fourth straight season.

South Africa won the third annual Tri-Nations competition, a six-match series played on a home-and-away basis in July and August between Australia, New Zealand, and South Africa. In their two Tri-Nations encounters, Australia and New Zealand also contested the Bledisloe Cup, which Australia won, 2 games to 0. Australia also defeated New Zealand, 33-26, in the final of the International Rugby Sevens in Paris on May 17.

In the championship game of the Super 12 Series, contested by 12 provincial teams from three Southern Hemisphere countries, the Canterbury Crusaders defeated the reigning champion Auckland Blues, 20-13, on May 30 in New Zealand. Canada won its third straight Pacific Rim Rugby Championship, which also featured the United States, Japan, and Hong Kong, in May and June 1998. The Japan Rugby Football Union announced in 1998 that the Pacific Rim series will be expanded to seven teams—with the addition of Fiji, Tonga, and Samoa—in 1999.

RU national competitions. In the Heineken European Cup Final, Bath narrowly defeated Brive, the reigning champion, 19-18, in Bordeaux on Jan. 31, 1998. On June 6, Stade Francais captured the French club championship for the first time since 1908, beating Perpignan, 34-7.

In England, the Saracens defeated the Wasps, 48-18, to win the Tetley's Bitter Cup for the first time, on May 9, 1998, at Twickenham. Gloucester won the inaugural Cheltenham and Gloucester Cup with a 33-25 victory over Bedford at Northampton on April 3. In the Tetley's Bitter County Championship Final on April 18, Cheshire beat Cornwall, 21-14. Newcastle won the Allied Dunbar Premiership, 44-20, over the Harlequins on May 17.

Watsonians became the Scottish Rugby Union (SRU) First Division champions on points only, despite a May 2 loss to defending champion Melrose, 37-17. The Glasgow Hawks defeated Kelso, 36-14, to win the SRU Tennents Velvet Cup on May 9. Gala routed Selkirk, 31-0, to win the Bank of Scotland Border League trophy.

The AIB All-Ireland League was won by Shannon for the fourth consecutive season, and Munster became the first winner of the new-style Guinness interprovincial championship by defeating Leinster, 25-10, on October 23.

On October 31, the Blue Bulls defeated defending Western Province, 24-20, in South Africa's Currie Cup Final in Pretoria. In May, Griqualand West won the Vodacom Cup with a victory over the Golden Lions, 57-0.

In New Zealand, Waikato retained the Ranfurly Shield after defeating Canterbury 29-23 but lost the National Provincial Championship Final to Otago by 49-20.

In Australia, New South Wales won the 1998 State of the Union Series, comprising two matches each between Queensland, New South Wales, and Australian Capital Territories. Gordon was the winner in the First Grade Grand Final.

International Rugby League (RL). Great Britain met New Zealand for a three-test series in October and November 1998. New Zealand won the series with victories in the first two matches, 22-16 at Huddersfield and 36-16 at Bolton. Great Britain, however, managed a 23-23 draw in the final test, at Watford on November 14.

In the Super League International Series, New Zealand defeated Australia, 22-16, in Auckland on April 24. But Australia won the title with consecutive victories, 30-12 in Brisbane on October 9, and 36-16 on October 16 in Auckland.

RL national competitions. In England, the Sheffield Eagles upset Wigan, 17-8, to win the Silk Cut Challenge Cup Final, in London's Wembley Stadium on May 2. In the Super League Grand Final in Manchester on October 24, Wigan defeated Leeds, 10-4. Wakefield Trinity took the First Division Grand Final at Huddersfield on September 26 by defeating the Featherstone Rovers, 24-22.

The Australian Rugby League (ARL) and Australian Super League (ASL), which operated independently in 1997, merged in 1998 to form the National Rugby League (NRL). The ASL had split from the ARL in 1996.

In Australia, Queensland won the three-match State of Origin series against New South Wales in May and June 1998. In the NRL Grand Final, the Brisbane Broncos defeated the Canterbury Bankstown Bulldogs, 38-12, on September 27 in Sydney. In New Zealand, Glenora defeated Mangere East, 35-6, to win the Auckland Grand Final in Auckland on September 6.   □ David Duckham

Russia began 1998 with low inflation, political compromise, and the best opportunity for economic growth since the 1991 collapse of the Soviet Union. However, by September 1998, the country was mired in a grave financial crisis. As the Russian economy disintegrated, political conflict toppled three successive governments, and President Boris Yeltsin's repeated illnesses raised speculation that his role had dwindled to that of a figurehead.

Government changes. Yeltsin reshuffled his cabinet on Feb. 28, 1998, under persistent pressure by the Communist-led Duma (lower house of parliament), which criticized the government's lack of progress in improving the Russian economy. Yeltsin had publicly warned that he intended to remove the officials responsible for the country's poor economic state. However, he left in place the cabinet ministers blamed for the economic problems, including deputy prime ministers Anatoly Chubais and Boris Nemtsov. Yeltsin vowed to keep these reformers in his cabinet until the end of his term in 2000.

On March 23, 1998, however, Yeltsin abruptly dismissed Prime Minister Viktor Chernomyrdin and the rest of his cabinet, explaining the surprise move as "an effort to make economic reforms more energetic and effective." On March 27, Yeltsin nominated as prime minister Sergei Kiriyenko, an obscure 35-year-old banker who had become the nation's fuel and energy minister just four months earlier. Kiriyenko's nomination was soundly rejected in April by the Duma in two successive votes. Parliamentary leaders, especially Communist Party chief Gennady Zyuganov, criticized him for being young, inexperienced, and too fond of free-market reforms.

Refusing to yield, Yeltsin nominated Kiriyenko a third time. Under the Russian Constitution, if a presidential nominee for prime minister is rejected three times by the Duma, the president may dissolve the legislature and call for new elections. Faced with the prospect of losing their seats in a new election, the lawmakers relented. Communist leader Zyuganov and liberal opposition leader Grigory Yavlinskiy both instructed their supporters to boycott the confirmation vote on April 24, but enough of the 450 lawmakers defied the boycott to confirm Kiriyenko.

Kiriyenko moved quickly to appoint a new cabinet, which retained many of Chernomyrdin's ministers. Kiriyenko's cabinet, however was considered free of strong ties to the national financial or industrial lobbies that had dominated the Russian political landscape during Chernomyrdin's administration.

Tax problems addressed. On May 29, 1998, Yeltsin named former Finance Minister Boris Fyodorov as his new chief of the national tax service.

The problem of poor tax collection was at the heart of Russia's fiscal and economic woes. Many Russian firms, undercapitalized since the fall of the Soviet Union, paid suppliers and workers in goods and promissory notes. These kinds of transactions, which by some accounts represented up to 70 percent of Russia's economy, were virtually impossible for the government to tax. In addition, many regional governments had gained control over local branches of the tax service and finance ministry, making it especially difficult for the federal government to collect money. Analysts believed that by 1998 the federal government was spending two *rubles* (Russian currency units) for every one collected in taxes.

Fyodorov attempted in June to address these problems by ordering tax inspectors to target Russia's richest citizens for audits. He also began an aggressive campaign against Gazprom, the Russian natural gas monopoly, which owed nearly $2 billion in accumulated taxes. Fyodorov threatened to begin seizing Gazprom's property unless it accelerated payment of its tax debts.

Financial crisis erupts. Russia's chronic financial problems had forced the government to seek other sources of funding. Beginning in 1995, the government began issuing short-term treasury notes to finance its budget deficit. These notes—known by their Russian acronym GKO—allowed the government to borrow rubles at high interest rates for periods of up to a year. The interest on these notes was as high as 30 or 40 percent, forcing Russian officials to borrow ever greater amounts just to cover their mounting interest payments. By the summer of 1998, the government had accumulated more than $70 billion in outstanding short-term notes, one-third of which were in the hands of foreign investors.

In July, the foundations of this pyramid of debt began to crack. The collapse of currencies and stock markets in Asia prompted worried international investors to withdraw their money from developing markets around the globe, including Russia. Russian officials were forced to offer interest rates as high as 150 percent to keep investors from demanding full and immediate repayment of principal. A dramatic drop in the price of oil, Russia's most lucrative export, severely restricted the nation's export earnings in 1998, and by July, the government was running out of money.

Devaluation of the ruble. The stability of the ruble had been one of the few economic successes of Yeltsin's presidency, and he vowed to defend it at all costs. By July, the Russian Central Bank was spending as much as $1 billion of its foreign reserves each week to shore up the ruble's value. When reserve currency levels dropped below $10 billion, Russia appealed to the Interna-

Mourners attend the funeral of Czar Nicholas II, the last imperial ruler of Russia, on July 17, 1998. The remains of the czar, his wife, and three of their five children were entombed at the Saints Peter and Paul Cathedral in St. Petersburg. The family was executed and secretly buried by the Bolsheviks in 1918, during the Russian Revolution.

tional Monetary Fund (IMF) for assistance. The IMF is a United Nations-affiliated organization that provides short-term credit to member nations. The United States strongly lobbied the IMF to help Russia avoid a financial collapse. On July 20, IMF officials agreed to give Russia $11.2 billion in loans as part of a $22.6-billion bailout package assembled from a wide range of international lenders.

The international rescue package proved to be too little, too late. When the Duma balked at implementing tax and budget reforms sought by the IMF and promised by Kiriyenko, many foreign investors resumed pulling capital from Russian markets. With interest rates prohibitively high, tax receipts still weak, and the stock market in

another downward slide, Russia's commitment to preserving the value of the ruble seemed increasingly unrealistic.

On August 13, Russian banks began defaulting on debts they owed to other banks, signaling the impending collapse of the entire Russian banking system. Many Russian banks had borrowed heavily to purchase stocks and GKO's, and the collapse of the stock market had left them insolvent. Using all their funds to pay foreign creditors, the banks were, therefore, unable to meet the withdrawal demands of their own depositors. The Russian Central Bank began making loans to prevent the collapse of the banking system. However, even with the IMF's assistance, the Central Bank could not both defend the value of the ruble and keep Russia's banking system solvent.

Black Monday. On Monday, August 17, Kiriyenko announced that the Russian government would allow the exchange rate of the ruble to "float" within a specified range and would suspend payments on GKO's pending a restructuring plan. While the move slashed the value of the government's GKO debt, it also left many Russian banks unable to pay their debts to foreign lenders. The government, therefore, simultaneously decreed a 90-day moratorium on all foreign interest payments by banks, commercial firms, and regional governments. In effect, Russia had simultaneously devalued its currency and defaulted on its debt.

The move triggered turmoil in global stock and bond markets as investors began to assess their losses. The ruble fell from under 6 rubles per U.S. dollar, to over 15 in less than two weeks. The banking system froze, unable to pay depositors or make simple transfers. Over half the operating banks in Russia found themselves bankrupt. Consumer prices jumped more than 40 percent in the first two weeks.

In the face of mounting economic chaos, the IMF suspended payments of its $22.6-billion loan package. Yeltsin dismissed Kiriyenko and his government on August 25 and reappointed Viktor

Chernomyrdin as prime minister. Again, the Duma resisted, complaining that Chernomyrdin's fiscal policies had set the stage for the summer's collapse. Duma leaders rejected Chernomyrdin twice and vowed to do so a third time even if the rejection triggered new elections.

Yeltsin, who appeared to be increasingly ill and out of touch with day-to-day affairs, realized that the economic crisis would offer his political opponents great campaign leverage. On September 10, he withdrew his nomination of Chernomyrdin. The move was Yeltsin's most serious concession to the parliament in his eight years as president, and it signaled to many political analysts that his power was finally on the wane. In place of Chernomyrdin, Yeltsin nominated Yevgeny Primakov, 68, the foreign minister, whose name had been proposed by several parliamentary leaders.

Primakov's government. The Duma overwhelmingly confirmed Primakov as prime minister on September 11. Despite the paralysis of Russia's economy, he took more than six weeks to form a cabinet. Ultimately, he selected ministers from many political parties who shared no common philosophy. Several of his economic advisers had previously served under Mikhail Gorbachev, the last leader of the Soviet Union.

On Oct. 20, 1998, President Yeltsin confirmed

A striking miner, blocking a railway line in southern Russia in May 1998, rests in the shade of an umbrella. Disgruntled Russian miners staged railway blockades in various parts of the country for several days in May to demand the payment of back wages.

reports that he would not seek reelection when his term expired in mid-2000. On October 28, a spokesman announced that Yeltsin would turn over his day-to-day responsibilities to Primakov and focus on constitutional issues related to choosing a successor at the end of his term. The announcement fueled increasing speculation about Yeltsin's health and his ability to govern.

In December 1998, government leaders continued to work out a budget plan for 1999. IMF officials insisted that Russia adopt and begin implementing a sound economic program—including repayment of its debts—before aid package payments, which had been frozen since August 1998, would resume.

Food shortage danger. In November 1998, the United Nations Food and Agriculture Organization (FAO) announced that Russia's grain harvest was down 43 percent from the previous year. At the same time, prices for imported food skyrocketed as a result of the devaluation of the ruble. Fearing that food shortages could arise during the coming winter, the United States and the European Union, an organization of 15 Western European nations, pledged to send 1 billion dollars in aid to Russia.   □ Steven L. Solnick

See also **Economics** Special Report: **Asian Economic Crisis—Global Contagion; People in the news** (Primakov, Yevgeny).

Rwanda. Rwanda's Tutsi minority and Hutu majority remained bitterly divided in 1998, four years after the slaughter of an estimated 500,000 people, mostly Tutsi, by Hutu extremists. During the year, Rwanda's Tutsi-dominated government, which seized power in 1994, battled a growing Hutu rebellion led by armed militias loyal to the Hutu regime that had orchestrated the killings.

Executions. On April 24, 1998, 22 people found guilty of organizing and leading the 1994 *genocide* (extermination of a racial or ethnic group) were executed by firing squad. Those executed were the first Rwandans punished for their role in the massacres. President Pasteur Bizimungu had rejected an appeal for pardons, drawing widespread international condemnation. During 1998, some 130,000 other genocide suspects, mostly Hutus, remained in jail awaiting trial.

An international criminal tribunal on the Rwandan genocide, established in 1996 by the United Nations (UN), sentenced former Rwandan Prime Minister Jean Kambanda to life imprisonment on Sept. 4, 1998, for his role in the massacres. Kambanda, a Hutu extremist, was the first person sentenced by a world court for genocide.

UN Secretary General Kofi Annan received a frigid reception from Rwandans on his visit there in early May. Many Rwandans remained bitter at the UN for not only failing to use peacekeeping troops stationed in the country in 1994 to halt the slaughter but also withdrawing those troops as the carnage mounted. Annan, head of UN peacekeeping operations at the time, came under attack for allegedly ignoring an advance warning of the Rwandan government's genocidal plans from the commander of the UN forces.

Civil war continues. Meanwhile, militant Hutus continued to massacre civilians and battle government troops in northwest Rwanda. According to Amnesty International, a London-based human-rights group, government forces were also responsible for indiscriminate attacks on civilians during their attempts at crushing the insurgency.

Foreign policy. Rwanda's relations with the Democratic Republic of the Congo (formerly Zaire) deteriorated rapidly from mid-1998, after Rwanda decided to back rebels fighting to oust Congo's President Laurent Kabila. Rwanda had helped Kabila seize power in 1997 from the Zairian government, which had allowed Hutu militants to use eastern Zaire as a staging ground for attacks on Rwanda. Rwanda, however, accused Kabila of doing little to stop the raids or to protect ethnic Tutsi in Congo. □ Simon Baynham

See also **Africa** (Facts in brief table); **Congo (Kinshasa).**

Sailing. See Boating.

San Francisco. In 1998, continuing population increases, soaring housing costs, and transportation problems soured San Francisco's economic boom and the mood of city residents. The population of the Bay Area—San Francisco and the suburbs and towns ringing San Francisco Bay—was expected to grow by 1.4 million people by 2017, according to a report by the Association of Bay Area Governments issued in late 1997.

Fueling the economic boom and contributing to San Francisco's congestion problems was a shift in the Bay Area's economic base. Beginning in the 1980's, computer industries in the region south of the city known as Silicon Valley began replacing tourism and entertainment as the area's chief source of wealth.

Housing. The influx of workers to Silicon Valley—many of whom moved to San Francisco for its cultural and entertainment resources—boosted the demand for housing and sent home prices and apartment rents skyrocketing. In September 1998, the National Association of Home Builders, a trade organization, ranked San Francisco as the least affordable housing market in the United States. A median-priced house in San Francisco in 1998 was valued at $343,210. Median rent for a one-bedroom apartment in the city jumped from $800 in 1994 to $1,245 in 1998.

Apartments in San Francisco's lower-income

neighborhoods increasingly grew too expensive for the working-class, minority, and immigrant families that traditionally had lived there. In 1998, fewer than one-third of the people who lived in the city's Mission District in 1990 could have afforded the median rent on a vacant apartment anywhere in San Francisco, according to data from the U.S. Census Bureau. A 1998 survey by the San Francisco Tenants Union revealed that 50 percent of city tenants who had moved within the previous year had left the city entirely.

Proposition G, a measure that restricted so-called owner move-in evictions, was passed by San Francisco voters in November. In such evictions, landlords or their family members moved into a building, displacing tenants who often had paid lower than average rents. Although some evictions were ordered by owners who wished to occupy the buildings themselves, others were ordered by investors who wanted to rent the apartments at higher rates or sell the building. From 1996 to 1998, the number of owner move-in evictions rose from 439 to at least 1,250. In September, San Francisco's Board of Supervisors temporarily halted such evictions of seniors, extremely ill people, or the disabled who were long-term tenants of their building. Proposition G and other provisions extended owner move-in eviction protection to all tenants and required evicting landlords or their relatives to move into the building within three months of the eviction and to live there for at least three years. Opponents of the measure said it would prevent families with an average income from buying a home in the city.

Transportation challenges. The San Francisco Municipal Railway (Muni), the city's public transportation system, suffered crisis after crisis in 1998. On August 22, Muni's $70-million automated train control system for the underground portion of the railway went on-line, two years behind schedule. For months, however, the new system was plagued with breakdowns and long delays caused by defective parts, inadequately trained staff, and faulty computer installations.

School battle. A decision by the San Francisco Unified School District in June to privatize one of the city's worst schools became the chief issue in elections to the city's Board of Education in November. The board handed over the administration of the Thomas Edison Elementary School in south-central San Francisco to the for-profit Edison Project, a company that was already running 25 U.S. schools. Opponents of the decision accused the board of dismantling public education for the benefit of middle-class families, while supporters argued that such a drastic step was necessary to save the school.   □ Brian Bouldrey

See also **City.**

Saskatchewan. See **Canadian provinces.**

Saudi Arabia. Serious tensions emerged in 1998 between the United States and Saudi Arabia, the major U.S. ally in the Persian Gulf. The Saudi government repeatedly refused to allow U.S. forces to use Saudi territory for air strikes against Iraq. The United States had threatened such strikes in February and November after Iraq blocked United Nations (UN) inspections of Iraqi weapons facilities. In December, the United States launched air strikes without the cooperation of Saudi Arabia. The Saudi refusal undercut U.S. claims that it had the support of Gulf Arabs in the confrontation with Iraq.

The nations of the Persian Gulf states also refused to help pay the $1.5-billion cost of the U.S. military build-up to the region undertaken in early 1998. Analysts noted that many Gulf Arabs, who had supported the U.S.-led war against Iraq in 1991, had by 1998 become concerned about the plight of the Iraqi people under economic sanctions imposed after the war. Some Arabs also believed that repeated U.S. warnings about the threat of Iraq were an excuse for keeping large numbers of U.S. forces in the region.

Dhahran bombing investigation. Saudi cooperation with the U.S. Federal Bureau of Investigation (FBI) over the 1996 bombing of a U.S. airbase in Dhahran fell apart in 1998. The bombing killed 19 U.S. military personnel and wounded 380 other people. The FBI had been investigating links between the bombing and Iran. But in May 1998, Saudi Interior Minister Prince Nayef said that Saudi dissidents were solely responsible for the bombing. Some observers suggested that the Saudis no longer wanted to implicate Iran, with which they were trying to improve relations.

Relations with Iran. In February, former Iranian President Ali Akbar Hashemi Rafsanjani became the first Iranian leader to head an official delegation to Saudi Arabia since the 1979 Islamic revolution in Iran. During the 10-day visit, Saudi and Iranian officials discussed greater cooperation concerning the world oil market, regional security, and trade.

The Saudi royal family, Sunni Muslims who regard themselves as protectors of the holiest sites in the Muslim world, had viewed Iran's radical Shiite Muslim revolution, which toppled a pro-U.S. monarchy, with suspicion. (Sunni and Shiite Muslims form the two major divisions of Islam.) Improved relations between Saudi Arabia and Iran began after the 1997 election of a more moderate Iranian government. Relations between the two countries were also influenced by growing Muslim anger with the United States for failing to pressure Israel to make concessions in the stalled Arab-Israeli peace process.

Economy. In May 1998, the Saudi government enacted new austerity measures after world oil prices fell to their lowest level in a decade. The measures included a stoppage of new government projects, spending cuts, and a hiring freeze. The kingdom, which relies on oil for more than 75 percent of its income, expected oil export earnings in 1998 to be more than $15 billion below 1997 oil revenues, which were estimated at approximately $45 billion. Although Saudi Arabia took the lead among the world's major oil producers in cutting production to shore up prices in 1998, the oil market failed to recover.

A stampede during the annual *hajj* (the pilgrimage to Mecca and other holy sites of Islam in Saudi Arabia) killed more than 100 people on April 9. More than 2.3 million Muslims from 100 countries attended the pilgrimage.

Diplomatic crisis. In May, King Fahd freed two British nurses convicted in 1997 for the 1996 murder of an Australian colleague. The sentence of beheading against one of the nurses, Deborah Parry, had raised an international outcry. Parry claimed after her release that Saudi investigators had tortured her to force her to confess to the killing. The nurses raised another controversy when it was reported that they had each sold their stories to British tabloids for sums of more than $100,000. □ Christine Helms

See also **Iran; Iraq; Middle East** (Facts in brief table); **Yemen.**

Sierra Leone. The democratically elected government of Sierra Leone was forcibly restored in early 1998 after the military regime that had overthrown it in May 1997 was ousted. However, the return of President Ahmed Tejan Kabbah on March 10, 1998, failed to end fierce resistance from rebel fighters in the war-ravaged countryside or to improve the grave economic situation. Sierra Leone's condition was so dire that it was ranked last in the United Nations' (UN) 1998 Human Development Index, which measures prosperity in 174 countries in terms of income, literacy, and life expectancy. In Sierra Leone in 1998, adult life expectancy averaged 34.7 years.

Kabbah restored. The military regime of Major Johnny Paul Koromah was ousted in February, after an assault on Freetown, Sierra Leone's capital, by Nigerian-led troops from a peacekeeping force organized by the Economic Community of West African States (ECOWAS). ECOWAS troops attacked after Koromah reneged on a Nigerian-sponsored plan to restore Kabbah's government by April 22. Kabbah, whose 1996 election was part of a peace settlement that ended a five-year civil war, was overthrown by military officers led by Koromah and allied with the rebel Revolutionary United Front (RUF). In June 1997, the Organization of African Unity, an association of more than 50 African nations, had authorized

Sierra Leonians brutalized by supporters of the former military regime, ousted in February 1998, await treatment at a Freetown hospital in May. The regime's supporters terrorized civilians by cutting off hands and legs in an attempt to regain power over the West African country.

the use of "appropriate" action to reinstate Sierra Leone's civilian government.

Civil war continues. Although Kabbah's 1998 return to Sierra Leone was greeted with jubilation by thousands of citizens, fighting continued between ECOWAS forces and militia loyal to the former *junta* (military government). Most of the conflict occurred in Sierra Leone's diamond-rich northeastern region. In addition, thousands of civilians in rural areas were subjected to attacks by RUF forces and allied groups. In April, the UN Commission for Refugees reported that more than 50,000 Sierra Leoneans had fled to neighboring Guinea. In an effort to end the terror, the government offered the guerrillas an amnesty in April, but the offer was refused. In August, Nigeria returned RUF leader Foday Sankoh to Sierra Leone for trial. He had been arrested in Nigeria in 1997 after arriving to buy arms.

The Sandline affair. In April 1998, the British government launched an investigation into allegations that the British ambassador to Sierra Leone had aided a British mercenary force that had smuggled planeloads of arms to Kabbah's forces in violation of a UN arms embargo. Kabbah reportedly paid the force, known as Sandline International, $10 million to arm and train his supporters.   □ Simon Baynham

See also **Africa** (Facts in brief table).

Sikhism. In May 1998, a former member of the Indian parliament, Amarjeet Kaur, apologized for supporting military action in 1984 against Sikhs demanding an independent state in India. Kaur had defended the army's entry into the precincts of the Golden Temple in Amritsar, India, where independence advocates had sought refuge. Leaders of the Akal Takht, Sikhism's highest seat of authority, pardoned Kaur, but required her to perform religious service, such as sweeping *gurdwaras* (temples).

Ranjit Singh, a leader of the Akal Takht, excommunicated seven Canadian Sikhs in 1998 for disputing a *hukamnama* (religious directive) that prohibited the use of tables and chairs at *langars* (community meals). Over the years, many Sikhs had abandoned the custom of sitting on the floor, which was a sign of equality and humility.

In April 1998, Gurcharan Singh Tohra, the president of the Shiromani Gurdwara Parbandhak Committee, Sikhism's highest elected authoritative body, was accused of violating a 1978 hukamnama that forbids Sikhs to associate with Sant Nirankaris, a religious group that departs from traditional Sikh practices. In February 1998, Tohra allegedly sought Sant Nirankaris's votes for a political candidate in the Indian state of Punjab. The Akal Takht leaders did not take any disciplinary action.   □ Eleanor M. Nesbitt

Singapore. Asia's financial crisis pulled Singapore into a recession in late 1998. The raging economic crisis eroded Singapore's manufacturing output, electronic production, and tourist trade. The rate of domestic growth in Singapore retracted to between 0.5 and 1.5 percent, a dramatic drop from 7.8 percent in 1997.

In March 1998, Parliament approved an 11.4 percent increase in Singapore's military budget, a move that drew criticism from people concerned that Singapore was facing a budget deficit for the first time in 10 years. Defense Minister Tony Tan defended the increase in defense spending, calling it a premium on a "national insurance policy."

Conflict with Malaysia. In January, Singapore Prime Minister Goh Chok Tong and Malaysian Prime Minister Mahathir bin Mohamad opened a bridge that provided a second vehicular link between the two countries. Mahathir called the bridge "an important milestone in Malaysia-Singapore relations."

However, relations between the two countries soured in August, when Singapore relocated its railroad immigration and customs facility for passengers crossing the Malaysia-Singapore border. The relocation caused hardship for thousands of commuters who were forced to disembark twice for immigration checks. In retaliation, Malaysia threatened to break an agreement that allowed Singapore to purchase Malaysian drinking water.

In 1998, Singapore consumed 280 million gallons (1.06 billion liters) of water per day, more than half of which was provided by Malaysia. In August, Singapore began negotiations with Indonesia for a long-term water supply contract.

Crackdown on immigrants. Singapore enacted tougher laws on illegal immigrants in September, making illegal entry into the country punishable by imprisonment and *caning* (beating with a rattan stick). The laws were passed by Parliament amid fears of an influx of economic refugees from Indonesia and other Asian countries hard hit by financial crisis.

Aid to Indonesia. Singapore announced in July that it was sending nearly $7 million in humanitarian aid to Indonesia. Earlier in 1998, Indonesia had reported that its food and medical supplies had dwindled to dangerously low levels.

Joss sticks banned. In February 1998, Singapore banned the burning of giant joss sticks at religious rituals in an effort to minimize air pollution. Joss sticks are made of fragrant tinder mixed with clay. They are burned as incense during religious festivals. Before the ban, joss sticks were often made dozens of feet in length and burned for 24 hours.   □ Pauline Khng

See also **Asia** (Facts in brief table); **Economics** Special Report: **Asian Economic Crisis.**

Japanese ski jumper Masahiko Harada celebrates his team's gold-medal victory in team ski jumping at the 1998 Winter Olympics in Nagano, Japan, in February.

Skiing. Hermann Maier of Austria dominated World Cup and Olympic Alpine skiing throughout 1998. At the 1998 Olympic men's downhill event on February 12, he also gave the sport one of the year's spectacular moments. Maier went airborne off a turn, spun out of control high above the ground, and crashed hard on his left shoulder. He tumbled down the slope and smashed through a fence before landing, unhurt, in a bank of deep powder snow. Maier came back within the week to win gold medals in the giant slalom and super giant slalom (super G).

World Cup. Maier finished the World Cup season in first place with 1,685 points—571 points ahead of Andreas Schifferer, his Austrian teammate, who finished second. Maier also led the giant slalom and super G standings and finished second to Schifferer in the downhill. Austrian skiers also placed second, third, and fifth in the overall standings and took seven of the top 10 places. In addition, Austria won the Nation's Cup team competition, more than doubling the score of runner-up Germany. Italy finished third.

Katja Seizinger of Germany was dominant in women's World Cup racing. Early in the season, she won her sixth straight World Cup race, tying a record set by Jean-Claude Killy in 1967. At the end of the season, Seizinger held first place in the overall standings with 1,655 points and was ranked first in both the downhill and super G.

The World Cup season did not end well for American skier Picabo Street. On March 13, 1998, in the final women's downhill run of the season at Crans Montana, Switzerland, Street missed a turn and crashed, fracturing her left leg in four places and rupturing a ligament in her right knee. Both injuries required surgery.

Olympics. Ski competition at the Nagano winter Olympics suffered, ironically, from too much winter weather. Heavy snowfalls forced repeated postponements of the men's downhill and the women's super G events. France's Jean-Luc Cretier won the downhill gold medal, and Norway's Hans-Peter Buraas captured the slalom. Seizinger struck gold twice in the women's competition, in the downhill and combined events. Street won what may have been the most thrilling race at Nagano when she captured the women's super G by just 0.01 second.

Bjorn Daehlie, the legendary Norwegian cross-country skier, took two gold medals at the Nagano games to raise his career total to a record 12 Olympic medals, 8 of them gold, also a record. Kazuyoshi Funaki of Japan won individual gold and silver medals at Nagano. In January 1998, just prior to the Olympics, Funaki had taken first place in the ski-flying world championships at Oberstdorf, Germany.   □ Ron Reid

Slovakia. The prospect of parliamentary elections in September dominated political developments in Slovakia during 1998. After President Michal Kovac's term expired in March, several attempts to elect a successor failed when no candidate received the required approval of three-fifths of the deputies in parliament. Under the terms of Slovakia's constitution, most presidential powers temporarily reverted to Prime Minister Vladimir Meciar and his Cabinet. Representatives of Western governments and institutions had been critical of Meciar's authoritarian rule and his poor record on human rights. Except for seven months in 1994, Meciar had ruled Slovakia since his Movement for a Democratic Slovakia (HZDS) came to power in 1992.

Election. HZDS took 27 percent of the vote in the elections on Sept. 26 and 27, 1998, but was unable to gather enough support to form a government when the party's previous coalition partners won only 9 percent of the vote. In all, opposition to HZDS captured 93 of 150 parliamentary seats. On October 30, a four-party coalition headed by the Slovak Democratic Coalition party, which received a combined 58 percent of the vote, took control of the government, naming Mikulas Dzurinda prime minister.

Dzurinda announced that his government would make Slovakia's integration into Western European systems and institutions a top priority. Toward this end, he pledged to restart serious economic reforms and restore respect for human rights and democratic liberties. Coalition leaders also said they would change Slovakia's constitution to have the country's future presidents elected directly by the people.

Economic trends in Slovakia continued to be favorable in the first half of 1998. However, high budget deficits threatened economic performance. Slovakia's foreign debt also grew, reaching $11.3 billion in May. Inflation in September stood at 5.9 percent. The unemployment rate in 1998 averaged 13.5 percent through September. Experts predicted that Slovakia's currency would be devalued to ease the balance of payments problem. The government announced that it would halt privatization measures temporarily in order to ensure that the process occurred fairly.

Foreign affairs. Slovakia's relations with Hungary continued to be complicated by the status of the ethnic Hungarian minority in Slovakia and the 15-year dispute over construction of the Gabcikovo-Nagymaros Dam on the Danube River. In September, Slovak leaders turned to the International Court of Justice after Hungary's newly elected leaders backed out of the partial agreement on the project that the two sides had reached in February. □ Sharon L. Wolchik

See also **Europe** (Facts in brief table); **Hungary.**

Soccer. The World Cup finals tournament, held in France in June and July, highlighted international soccer in 1998. In the championship match, the host country defeated the reigning champ and strong favorite, Brazil, 3-0. In Major League Soccer, the North American professional league, D.C. United, was defeated in the MLS Cup final, 2-0, by the Chicago Fire, a new franchise playing its first season. The European Champions Cup final, hosted by the Union of European Football Associations (UEFA), also provided a surprise, when Real Madrid of Spain beat Italy's Juventus of Turin, 1-0.

World Cup. The 16th World Cup competition, which is held every four years, was staged in France from June 10 to July 12, 1998. The United States, making its sixth appearance, was eliminated in the first round after losing three straight matches. While the team was not disgraced by its poor performance, head coach Steve Sampson, heavily criticized by several of his players, subsequently resigned. The post remained vacant until D.C. United coach Bruce Arena, 47, who led D.C. to MLS championships in 1996 and 1997, was named the new coach on Oct. 27, 1998.

Federation Internationale de Football Association (FIFA) introduced a new rule regarding "serious foul play" at the start of the World Cup. The rule specified that a player making a tackle from behind that "endangers the safety of an opponent" was to receive a red card, meaning he is removed from the game. Another change, known as the "golden goal" rule, called for a sudden-death overtime period of 30 minutes if a match is tied after 90 minutes of regulation play.

Annual rule changes normally take effect on July 1. However, in 1998 FIFA put them into effect for the World Cup finals, which began on June 10. This proved to be a controversial decision. Neither players, coaches, nor referees were given the chance to get used to the new ruling regarding tackles from behind. This led to a record 22 ejections in World Cup matches.

The 1998 World Cup was the last tournament to be presided over by the Brazilian Joao Havelange, who had served as president of FIFA since 1974. Havelange turned over the reins of office on July 9, after the World Cup semifinals, to FIFA's general secretary, Joseph S. Blatter of Switzerland.

FIFA's World Player of the Year (1997), was named at a gala held near Paris on Jan. 12, 1998. The award, voted on by 121 national coaches, went to Brazilian striker Ronaldo for the second year running. He received 480 points, a landslide victory. Brazilian left back Roberto Carlos received 65 points. Striker Dennis Bergkamp of The Netherlands and French midfielder Zinedine Zidane tied for third place, with 62 points each.

International tournaments. The United States hosted the 1998 CONCACAF Gold Cup, the championship for North and Central American and Caribbean countries. In a February 10 semifinal match in Los Angeles, the U.S. team won a historic first victory over Brazil, the invited guest team. The U.S. won, 1-0, on a goal by substitute Preki Radosavljevic. It was the first goal scored by the U.S team against the four-time world champions in nine meetings going back 68 years. The United States then met Mexico in the final match, which was played at the Los Angeles Coliseum on February 15. Luis Hernandez dashed U.S. hopes with a 43rd-minute goal to give Mexico the 1-0 victory, its third straight win in this competition.

The 1998 African Nations' Cup was won by Egypt, which beat the reigning champion, South Africa, 2-0, in the final on February 28.

New Zealand upset Australia, 1-0, in the final of the Oceania Nations' Cup, held in Brisbane on October 4.

Brazil remained at the top of the FIFA world rankings, with France in second place, and Germany in third. The United States, ranked 26th in 1997, moved up to 23rd at the end of 1998.

International club competition. The 1998 European Champions Cup was won by Real Madrid for a record seventh time. It was the Spanish club's first European championship since 1966. Real Madrid had once dominated the international club competition, winning the first five championships (1956–1960). Real Madrid beat Italy's Juventus of Turin, 1-0, in the 1998 final in Amsterdam on May 20. The only goal was scored by Predrag Mijatovic in the 67th minute.

English club Chelsea won the European Cup-Winners' Cup, beating Germany's VfB Stuttgart, 1-0, in Stockholm on May 13. The UEFA Cup final, held in Paris on May 6, was not staged in its customary home-and-away, two-legged format. Instead, it was held for the first time as a one-off match. Two Italian clubs met in the final, which ended with InterMilan beating Rome's Lazio, 3-0.

The Brazilian team Vasco Da Gama won the major South American club trophy, the Copa de los Libertadores, beating Barcelona of Ecuador, 4-1, on aggregate over two legs. It won the first leg, 2-0, in Rio de Janeiro on August 12. Two weeks later, Vasco won its away leg, 2-1, in Guayaquil, Ecuador.

Vasco Da Gama played D.C. United over two legs for the InterAmerican Cup. D.C. United, the first team from the United States to play in this annual championship between the CONCACAF and South American club champions, lost the first leg, 1-0, at Washington, D.C.'s RFK Stadium on November 14. In the second game, played in Ft. Lauderdale, Florida, on December 5, United upset Vasco, 2-0, winning the InterAmerican Cup by an aggregate of 2 goals to 1 over both legs.

On December 1, Vasco went down to Real Madrid, 2-1, in the final of the 1998 World Club Championship for the Toyota Cup, played in Tokyo. Real's Raul Gonzalez tallied the game-winning goal in the 83rd minute of the match.

Major League Soccer. In the MLS's third season, two-time champion D.C. United again reached the final, but this time suffered a surprising defeat by the Chicago Fire. The Fire was one of two new franchises that expanded MLS to 12 teams in 1998. In the play-offs, the Fire beat the Colorado Rapids in the semifinals, then won the Western Conference title against the favored Los Angeles Galaxy. D.C. United eliminated the Miami Fusion in the semifinals and the Columbus Crew in the Eastern Conference final, which was decided four days before the MLS Cup final. This meant that Chicago had five more days than D.C. to rest and prepare for the game. Even so, Chicago's 2-0 victory was arguably the biggest shock in MLS's short history.

The Fire, using a defensive style of play, stifled the champions with tight man-for-man coverage and benefited from some controversial decisions by the referee. Two first-half goals, by Jerzy Podbrozny and Diego Gutierrez, sealed D.C.'s fate. The game was played before a crowd of 51,000 at the Rose Bowl in Pasadena, California, on October 25.

D.C.'s defeat was all the more surprising because, in August, it had won the CONCACAF Champions Cup. Playing on its home ground, D.C. flew the flag for MLS, beating two strong Mexican teams, Leon (2-0) in the semifinal and Toluca (1-0) in the final. At the end of August, MLS appointed its first women referees, Sandra Hunt and Nancy Lay.

Women's soccer. The U.S. women's team continued to win international tournaments in 1998, beginning in January with 3-0 victories over both Sweden and Norway to take the International Women's Tournament in Guangzhou, China. However, at the Algarve Cup tournament in Portugal, the U.S. team suffered its worst defeat ever, losing to Norway, 4-1, in the semifinals on March 19.

The U.S. team won the gold medal at the Goodwill Games tournament at Uniondale, New York, in July and took the U.S. Women's Cup in September with three consecutive shut-out victories over Mexico (9-0), Russia (4-0), and Brazil (3-0). Michelle Akers, the U.S. team's most prolific striker, received the FIFA Order of Merit at the FIFA Congress held in Paris in June. The award is normally reserved for the top personalities of men's soccer. ☐ Norman Barrett

See also **Soccer** Special Report: **The 1998 World Cup.**

THE 1998 WORLD CUP

French striker Zine-dine Zidane scores the first of his two goals against Brazil in the championship match of 1998 World Cup finals.

By Norman Barrett

The top soccer players from 32 nations met in France from June 10 to July 12, 1998, to compete in the World Cup, the 16th tournament since the first was staged in 1930. For the first time in its history, the World Cup in 1998 was expanded to include 32 teams, which required organizers to schedule games over a period of nearly five weeks at 10 venues across France. As always, the host country, France, and the reigning champion, Brazil, qualified automatically for the tournament. The other 30 finalists were pared down from a field of 170 teams, who competed in World Cup qualifying matches that had begun more than two years earlier. This is why the championship tournament is often referred to as the World Cup finals.

For the sixth time in World Cup history, the host country won. The French defeated Brazil by a score of 3-0 in the final match, which was the greatest winning margin since Brazil beat Italy, 4-1, in the 1970 final. An estimated 1.7 billion people watched the 1998 final, which was broadcast live on television worldwide. Croatia, competing in its first World Cup as an independent nation, upset the Netherlands to take third place.

There were few major upsets in the 1998 World Cup finals, an indication that the competitive gap between teams from Europe

France, playing on their home turf, defeated Brazil, 3-0—the greatest margin since 1970—to win their first World Cup title.

and South America—regions where soccer is extremely popular—and teams from other parts of the world was narrowing. Only two teams, the United States and Japan, failed to gain at least one victory or *draw* (tie) in the first round, but neither was greatly outclassed in matches against much stronger opponents.

World Cup history

International soccer (or football, as it is known mainly outside the United States) began in the United Kingdom in 1872, but it was 1904 before the Federation Internationale de Football Association (FIFA) was founded. FIFA is the international body that governs soccer. The sport, however, did not enjoy worldwide exposure until the 1924 Olympic Games in Paris, where a crowd of 60,000 watched Uruguay beat Switzerland, 3-0, for the gold medal. After a disappointing tournament at the 1928 Olympics in Amsterdam, FIFA members decided to organize their own tournament, the World Cup. However, unlike the Olympics, which was restricted to amateur players, FIFA decided that the World Cup would be a professional tournament. Like the Olympic Games, the World Cup finals are held every four years and are hosted by a different country each time. The first World Cup tournament took place in Uruguay in 1930. Thirteen teams, nine of which were from the Americas, competed, and Uruguay took the first championship, defeating Argentina, 4-2, in the final.

Teams invited to the World Cup finals are determined by a series of qualifying matches sanctioned by FIFA and organized by the continental governing bodies. For the first round of the finals, the qualifying countries are divided into groups, with the top-ranking teams seeded. Teams within each group play each other once, and the top two teams from each group advance to the second round. For the first time, the 1998 World Cup finals invited 32 teams, which were organized into eight groups of four, designated by the letters A through H. Brazil was assigned to Group A and France to Group C.

The 1998 final

FIFA introduced two new features in the 1998 finals. The first was the so-called "golden goal" rule, which calls for a sudden-death overtime period in cases where the score is tied at the end of regulation play. The first team to score in the overtime period wins. If

The author:

Norman Barrett, a former World Book editor, is the author of numerous books on soccer and other sports.

Croatia's Davor Suker, *left,* celebrates a teammate's goal over German goalkeeper Andreas Kopke during Croatia's quarterfinal match with Germany, which Croatia won, 3-0. Suker, who scored a total of six goals in the 1998 World Cup, was the top scorer of the tournament.

Nigeria's Taribo West, *below left,* and Denmark's Peter Moeller battle for control of the ball during their second-round match. Nigeria, the reigning Olympic champion, was considered a strong contender, but was ousted by Denmark, 4-1.

no goal is scored in overtime, a "shoot-out" series of five penalty kicks by each team—and, if necessary, single penalty kicks after that—determines the winner. Previously, matches tied at the end of regulation and 30 minutes of overtime were decided by penalty kicks alone. The second innovation was a board displayed by an official at each half of the playing field to show the *stoppage time* (time to be added by the referee for interruptions in play).

FIFA also instituted a rule change in 1998—a new interpretation of the rule governing tackling—that caused substantial controversy. The change required referees to punish all tackles from behind that endangered "the safety of an opponent" with a *red card* (ejection). As a result, a record 22 red cards were issued during the 1998 tournament. Sixteen players were red-carded in the first round alone, including five each from groups C and E. All of the Group C dismissals occurred on June 18, the day referees were reminded to get tough with dangerous foul play. Three players were sent off in the second half of the 1-1 draw between South Africa and Denmark, equaling the record for the most dismissals in a World Cup match. In that day's other Group C match, France's 4-0 victory over Saudi Arabia was soured when their influential playmaker Zinedine Zidane earned a two-match suspension for stepping on Saudi captain Fuad Amin. Cameroon, in its crucial Group B game against Chile, had two players ejected and so finished the game with only nine men on the field. Cameroon still managed a 1-1 draw, but this was not enough to prevent Chile from advancing to the second round instead of Cameroon.

The first round

Brazil opened the tournament with a hard-fought 2-1 victory over Scotland that sent them on the way to winning Group A. France and Argentina were the only two undefeated teams in the first round, with France scoring the most goals (9) and Argentina allowing the fewest (0). Most of the other traditional favorites also reached the second round. Italy, the Netherlands, and Germany won their respective groups, and England advanced behind Romania in Group G. However, Spain was eliminated despite winning its last first-round match, 6-1, over Bulgaria in Group D. Instead, Paraguay took the second slot in Group D by beating Nigeria, 3-1.

A new technique was introduced by Mexican winger Cuauhtemoc Blanco, who twice split South Korea's defense by wedging the ball between his feet and jumping with it between two defenders. The trick was promptly dubbed the "Blanco bounce" by commentators.

The "knockout round"

Sixteen teams advanced to the second round, which is known as the "knockout round" because losing means elimination from the tournament. Only two countries from outside the traditional soccer powerhouses of Europe and South America reached the second round, Mexico and Nigeria, and neither progressed any further. Reigning champion Brazil scored a resounding 4-1 win over Chile. France, playing without Zidane, struggled to a 0-0 draw against Paraguay at the end of 90 minutes. In the ensuing overtime period, French defender Laurent Blanc made World Cup history by scoring the first "golden goal," ending the match in the 24th minute of extra time. Nigeria, the 1996 Olympic champion, was considered a strong contender after earning first-round victories over Spain

Brazilian goalkeeper Taffarel dives after a penalty kick by midfielder Ronald de Boer of the Netherlands. Taffarel blocked the shot, sending Brazil to the World Cup championship match for the second time in a row.

1998 WORLD CUP (FIRST ROUND)

W Win **L** Loss **T** Tie **PTS** Points **GF** Goals (For) **GA** Goals (Against) **+/-** Goals differential **x** Advanced to second round

Group A	W	L	T	PTS	GF	GA	+/-
x Brazil	2	1	0	6	6	3	+3
x Norway	1	0	2	5	5	4	+1
Morocco	1	1	1	4	5	5	0
Scotland	0	2	1	1	2	6	-4

Group B	W	L	T	PTS	GF	GA	+/-
x Italy	2	0	1	7	7	3	+4
x Chile	0	0	3	3	4	4	0
Austria	0	1	2	2	3	4	-1
Cameroon	0	1	2	2	2	5	-3

Group C	W	L	T	PTS	GF	GA	+/-
x France	3	0	0	9	9	1	+8
x Denmark	1	1	1	4	3	3	0
South Africa	0	1	2	2	3	6	-3
Saudi Arabia	0	2	1	1	2	7	-5

Group D	W	L	T	PTS	GF	GA	+/-
x Nigeria	2	1	0	6	5	5	0
x Paraguay	1	0	2	5	3	1	+2
Spain	1	1	1	4	8	4	+4
Bulgaria	0	2	1	1	1	7	-6

Group E	W	L	T	PTS	GF	GA	+/-
x Netherlands	1	0	2	5	7	2	+5
x Mexico	1	0	2	5	7	5	+2
Belgium	0	0	3	3	3	3	0
South Korea	0	2	1	1	2	9	-7

Group F	W	L	T	PTS	GF	GA	+/-
x Germany	2	0	1	7	6	2	+4
x Yugoslavia	2	0	1	7	4	2	+2
Iran	1	2	0	3	2	4	-2
United States	0	3	0	0	1	5	-4

Group G	W	L	T	PTS	GF	GA	+/-
x Romania	2	0	1	7	4	2	+2
x England	2	1	0	6	5	2	+3
Colombia	1	2	0	3	1	3	-2
Tunisia	0	2	1	1	1	4	-3

Group H	W	L	T	PTS	GF	GA	+/-
x Argentina	3	0	0	9	7	0	+7
x Croatia	2	1	0	6	4	2	+2
Jamaica	1	2	0	3	3	9	-6
Japan	0	3	0	0	1	4	-

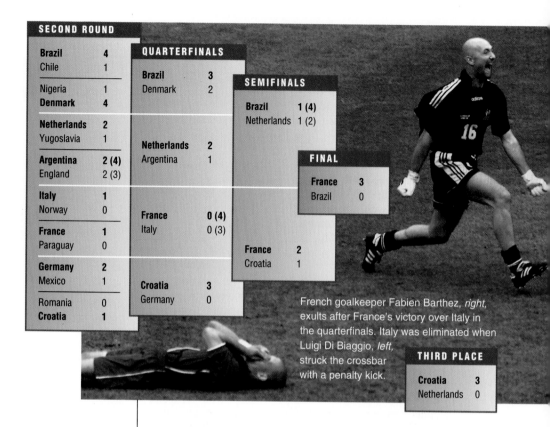

SECOND ROUND		QUARTERFINALS		SEMIFINALS		FINAL	
Brazil	4						
Chile	1	**Brazil**	3				
Nigeria	1	Denmark	2	**Brazil**	1 (4)		
Denmark	4			Netherlands	1 (2)		
Netherlands	2						
Yugoslavia	1	**Netherlands**	2			**France**	3
Argentina	2 (4)	Argentina	1			Brazil	0
England	2 (3)						
Italy	1						
Norway	0	**France**	0 (4)				
France	1	Italy	0 (3)	**France**	2		
Paraguay	0			Croatia	1		
Germany	2						
Mexico	1	**Croatia**	3				
Romania	0	Germany	0				
Croatia	1						

French goalkeeper Fabien Barthez, *right,* exults after France's victory over Italy in the quarterfinals. Italy was eliminated when Luigi Di Biaggio, *left,* struck the crossbar with a penalty kick.

THIRD PLACE	
Croatia	3
Netherlands	0

and Bulgaria. But the Nigerians lost, 4-1, to Denmark, who thereby advanced to the quarterfinals for the first time.

The last of the second-round matches, England versus Argentina, proved to be one of the most dramatic games of the tournament, with two penalty kicks in the first 10 minutes of the game. Gabriel Batistuta put Argentina ahead in the game's sixth minute, but England's Alan Shearer answered soon after with a penalty kick of his own. A few minutes after Shearer's goal, 18-year-old striker Michael Owen electrified the crowd with a breakaway goal that gave England the lead. Then, just before half-time, Javier Zanetti evened the score with a beautifully worked free kick. At the start of the second half, English midfielder David Beckham was red-carded. Left with 10 players for the rest of the half and through the overtime period, the English more than held their own, but Argentina prevailed by winning the penalty shoot-out, 4 goals to 3.

Quarterfinals and semifinals

The eight surviving teams faced each other in the quarterfinals. After playing to a scoreless draw through the overtime period, France defeated Italy on penalty kicks in a disappointing first quarterfinal match. But the clash between Brazil and Denmark resulted in plenty of exciting play, including five goals. In the second half, Rivaldo, normally a playmaker, turned goal scorer, hitting his second goal of the match to give Brazil the victory, 3-2. (Many soccer professionals in Brazil customarily adopt one-word names.)

In the quarterfinal match between the Netherlands and Argentina, each side scored early in the first half, and each had a man sent off in the second. Dutch striker Dennis Bergkamp scored a last-minute winner with what was arguably the finest goal of the tournament. Bergkamp ran under a lofted pass from his own half, trapped the ball with one touch, used the sole of his boot to turn it inside a defender, and volleyed it past Argentinian goalkeeper Carlos Roa. The aging German team, handicapped by the ejection of defender Christian Worms in the game's 40th minute, was beaten 3-0 by Croatia. It was Germany's worst World Cup defeat in 40 years.

Now down to four teams, the tournament entered the semifinal round. In the first semifinal match, Ronaldo caught the Dutch defense napping early in the second half to put Brazil ahead, but Dutch striker Patrick Kluivert equalized in the 87th minute. Brazil reached the final thanks to their goalkeeper, Taffarel, who turned away two penalty shots in the shoot-out. In the second semifinal match, France's Lilian Thuram scored both goals in their 2-1 victory over Croatia. It was, however, a bittersweet win for France, whose stalwart central defender Laurent Blanc earned a red card that disqualified him from the final. The losing teams in the semifinals, Croatia and the Netherlands, met in the third-place match, from which Croatia emerged with a 2-1 victory. Davor Suker's game-winning goal, his sixth of the tournament, put him alone atop of the list of leading scorers.

The final

The drama of the July 12 final match between Brazil and France began even before the match kicked off, when reporters were stunned to notice that the name of Ronaldo, Brazil's star striker and World Player of the Year, was missing from Brazil's announced line-up. The mystery deepened when the Brazilians failed to take the field for their customary prematch warm-up. But at the last minute, Ronaldo was reinstated and took the field with the rest of the team. However, Ronaldo's play was noticeably lackluster, and the rest of the Brazilian team seemed to lack their usual spirit and inventiveness. Ronaldo's poor showing led to rumors of injury, illness, a visit to a hospital, and even poisoning. An official explanation was not given.

France completely outplayed the defending champions in the final. Their strikers missed several scoring chances until Zidane, usually a playmaker, took matters into his own hands, steering two corner kicks into the net with his head in the first half. Even after defender Marcel Desailly was red-carded in the 68th minute, France retained the upper hand. Finally, midfielder Emmanuel Petit, having been dropped back to play defense, ran through and scored on a spectacular breakaway. The result, 3-0, was Brazil's worst World Cup defeat and France's first taste of triumph in soccer's premiere international competition.

A jubilant Zinedine Zidane hoists the FIFA World Cup after France defeated Brazil in the 1998 World Cup.

President Bill Clinton discusses the Social Security Trust Fund during a national forum on social security held on April 7, 1998, at Penn Valley Community College in Kansas City, Missouri. The president championed saving federal budget surpluses to pay for social security.

Social security. President Bill Clinton opened a national debate on the soundness of the social security system in his State of the Union Address to Congress on Jan. 27, 1998. The president said that Congress should not spend any federal budget surpluses until new laws could be passed to keep the system strong when the 76-million member *baby boom generation* (people born in the United States from 1946 to 1964) reach retirement age over the next 20 years.

The president also called for a major change in Medicare, the federal program that pays for health care for elderly Americans. President Clinton proposed expanding Medicare coverage to people aged 55 to 64. He said this could be done without adding to the federal deficit.

Life spans extended. Trustees of the Social Security Trust Fund reported in April 1998 that higher-than-expected economic growth, low inflation, and low unemployment had improved the financial outlook for social security. The trustees reported that social security funds would not run out until 2032, three years later than had been predicted

The trustees also reported that changes made as part of the 1997 balanced-budget agreement in the Medicare Hospital Insurance Trust Fund would allow the fund to remain solvent until 2008.

☐ William J. Eaton

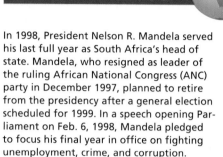

South Africa

In 1998, President Nelson R. Mandela served his last full year as South Africa's head of state. Mandela, who resigned as leader of the ruling African National Congress (ANC) party in December 1997, planned to retire from the presidency after a general election scheduled for 1999. In a speech opening Parliament on Feb. 6, 1998, Mandela pledged to focus his final year in office on fighting unemployment, crime, and corruption. Opposition politicians criticized the speech, saying Mandela had made the same promises in his four previous state-of-the-nation addresses.

Mandela and the ANC also came under attack for South Africa's sluggish economy, which economists predicted would grow by only about 1 percent in 1998. Between June and July, the value of the rand, South Africa's currency, dropped by 20 percent, triggering fears of an economic recession. Unemployment in 1998 ranged from 30 to 40 percent.

Political rivalry. A new multiracial party led by two former political enemies emerged in 1998 to challenge the ANC, which has dominated the government since South Africa's first all-race parliamentary elections in 1994. The United Democratic Movement (UDM) elected black politician Bantu Holomisa as its president and white politician Roelf Meyer as its deputy president at its first party congress in June 1998.

Holomisa previously ruled as dictator of the Transkei, one of the black "homelands" established by South Africa's former white supremacist government. The ANC expelled him from the party in 1996 on charges of insubordination. Meyer, formerly a top official in the National Party (NP), which created South Africa's system of *apartheid* (rigid racial separation), resigned from the NP in 1997 following his dismissal from a key party post. The goals of the UDM included fighting crime and enriching South Africa's poor without impoverishing the wealthy.

In July 1998, the rivalry between the UDM, the ANC, and the Inkatha Freedom Party (IFP), the ANC's strongest rival, exploded into violence in the IFP stronghold of KwaZulu-Natal province. At least 40 people were murdered in or near the city of Richmond. In mid-July, the government dispatched security forces to the province to maintain order after talks between the three parties broke down. The violence raised fears of a revival of the widespread fighting that rocked the province in the late 1980's and early 1990's. Some 20,000 people had died in violence that became a virtual civil war between the ANC and the IFP.

Sports both united and divided South Africa in 1998. The national soccer team, Bafana Bafana, had strong multiracial support as it advanced to the final round of the African Nations Cup, ultimately losing 2-0 to Egypt on February 28.

On May 11, the president of the South African Rugby Football Union (SARFU) resigned in the wake of a government investigation into alleged corruption and racism in SARFU. The conflict had begun in February 1997 when Sports Minister Steve Tshwete ordered a judicial commission to investigate accusations of bribery and embezzlement leveled against SARFU President Louis Luyt. The accusations had been made by the president of a SARFU member team. SARFU responded to the investigation by taking the government to court, arguing that the ANC was persecuting SARFU because it was controlled by whites.

The dispute escalated in February 1998 with the publication of the transcript of a conversation in which the coach of the 1997 Springboks team, South Africa's national rugby team, repeatedly used an insulting term for blacks. Tshwete then charged SARFU with

In March 1998, United States President Bill Clinton and South African President Nelson R. Mandela gaze through the bars of the cell that Mandela occupied for 18 years as a prisoner of South Africa's apartheid government. Clinton was the first U.S. president ever to pay a state visit to South Africa.

racism and failing to promote rugby among blacks. Tshwete pointed out that the Springboks team, which was made up of the top 15 players in the country, was all white, while only 4 of the 121 players at the next level were nonwhites.

The judge hearing the SARFU case forced President Mandela to testify in court in March 1998 about his decision to appoint the investigative commission. The development infuriated many South Africans. Mandela became the first sitting president of South Africa ever required to defend his actions before a judge. In April, the judge found in favor of SARFU, ruling that Mandela had failed to act deliberatively in appointing the commission by merely rubber-stamping Tshwete's actions. Despite SARFU's victory, Luyt, who had repeatedly resisted demands for his resignation, finally stepped down after the National Sports Council, South Africa's governing body for sports, called for an international boycott of South African rugby.

Truth and Reconciliation Commission. Controversy dogged the procedures and revelations of the Truth and Reconciliation Commission (TRC), a body set up in 1995 to shed light on the human rights abuses of the apartheid era and to grant *amnesties* (pardons) to those who willingly confessed their crimes. The commission's authority, which was set to expire on July 31, 1998, was extended to October because of a backlog of 7,000 applications for amnesty.

In January, the Truth and Reconciliation Commission acknowledged that it might have erred in granting blanket amnesties to 37 ANC leaders, including Deputy President Thabo Mbeki, in December 1997. Unlike other applicants who received amnesties, the ANC leaders, who were active in the struggle against apartheid, were not required to appear before the commission or to confess any crimes.

On Jan. 23, 1998, P. W. Botha, prime minister of South Africa from 1978 to 1989, appeared in court charged with contempt of the TRC. Botha, who had ignored three orders to appear before the commission, called the TRC "a circus" and refused to acknowledge responsibility for illegal or immoral acts committed during his premiership.

Throughout 1998, the commission heard testimony about the apartheid-era government's extensive chemical and biological weapons program. According to some scientists who had been employed at a secret research laboratory run by South Africa's military intelligence, the program included production of the bacteria that cause anthrax,

a deadly infectious disease. The scientists also testified that they had searched for chemical agents that would kill black people without affecting white South Africans. Scientists also testified about a plot by white leaders to poison Mandela and damage his brain before releasing him from prison in 1986. Most of the allegations were denied by Wouter Basson, director of the weapons program, who admitted that toxins were produced at the facility but only as part of a defensive chemical warfare program.

In a final report of its findings, released on Oct. 29, 1998, the TRC charged South Africa's

The Ministry of South Africa*

Nelson R. Mandela—president

Thabo Mbeki—executive deputy president

Derek Hanekom—minister of agriculture and land affairs

L. P. Mtshali—minister of arts, culture, science and technology

S. E. Mzimela—minister of correctional services

Joe Modise—minister of defence

S. M. Bengu—minister of education

Z. P. Jordan—minister of environmental affairs and tourism

Trevor Manuel—minister of finance

Alfred Nzo—minister of foreign affairs

N. C. Zuma—minister for health

M. G. Buthelezi—minister of home affairs

S. D. Mthembi-Mahanyele—minister of housing

Dullah Omar—minister of justice

T. T. Mboweni—minister of labour

Penuell Maduna—minister of minerals and energy

J. Naidoo—minister for posts, telecommunications and broadcasting

M. V. Moosa—minister for provincial affairs and constitutional development

S. N. Sigcau—minister for public enterprises

Z. S. Skweyiya—minister for the public service and administration

J. T. Radebe—minister of public works

F. S. Mufamadi—minister for safety and security

S. V. Tshwete—minister of sport and recreation

A. Erwin—minister of trade and industry

S. R. Maharaj—minister of transport

A. K. Asmal—minister of water affairs and forestry

G. J. Fraser-Moleketi—minister for welfare and population development

*As of Dec. 31, 1998.

apartheid-era government with institutionalizing violence in its fight against racial equality. The report also criticized the ANC for the murder of informers and the killing of civilians during military operations. All South Africa's political parties boycotted the ceremony at which the report was presented to President Mandela. Many observers believed that the TRC's hearings into human-rights abuses contributed to racial disharmony, rather than to a spirit of national reconciliation. A survey published in July revealed that a majority of South Africans thought that race relations had worsened during the TRC's hearings.

International affairs. President Bill Clinton, the first president of the United States to visit South Africa, arrived in Cape Town, the legislative capital, with First Lady Hillary Rodham Clinton on March 26. Previously, U.S. leaders had avoided South Africa in an attempt to pressure the white government to abandon its system of apartheid. In a speech to Parliament, Clinton stressed the two countries' bond in trying to forge a multiracial society. He also stated that the United States should have a "trade, not aid" policy with Africa—an idea criticized by Deputy President Mbeki, who said that Africa needed both trade and aid.

Despite the warm welcome given Clinton, South Africa pursued an independent course in foreign relations. On August 2, the government announced its intention to establish full diplomatic relations with Iraq and North Korea, countries considered hostile by the United States. The actions were taken as South Africa prepared to host a September summit of the Nonaligned Movement, an organization of developing countries and other political groups, to which all three countries belong.

Coup plot. Clinton's visit to South Africa followed what some people believed was an attempt to destabilize Mandela's government. On February 5, General Georg Meiring, chief of the South African National Defence Force (SANDF), personally delivered to Mandela a report describing a conspiracy by black generals working with Winnie Madikizela-Mandela, Mandela's former wife, and dissident ANC officials to overthrow Mandela's government.

Mandela dismissed the claims as "ludicrous" and said that the report was a hoax by conservative, white military officers who intended to spread confusion in government circles. Three senior judges, ordered by Mandela to investigate the report, also dismissed it as "inherently fantastic." As a result, Meiring was forced to resign his post on April 6. Lieutenant General Siphiwe Nyanda, one of the "plotters" identified in the report and the first

black chief of the SANDF, was named as his successor.

Crime remained a major concern in South Africa in 1998. The country had the world's highest death rate from violence, with an average of 50 murders a day during 1998. Violence resulted in the hospitalization of another 2,000 people daily. Nevertheless, South Africa's crime rate continued on a downward trend that began in 1997, according to Safety and Security Minister Sydney Mufamadi. In May 1998, Mufamadi said that analyses of crime statistics by two independent organizations showed that public skepticism over the statistics was misplaced. However, some observers charged that a high proportion of criminal activity was never reported because of police corruption and low public confidence in the crime-fighting ability of the police.

The significant underreporting of crime was compounded by another major defect in South Africa's criminal justice system—a very low rate of prosecutions and convictions. On May 26, Mufamadi admitted that only 205 (1.6 percent) of the 12,895 car thefts reported in 1997 had resulted in convictions.

☐ Simon Baynham

See also **Africa** (Facts in brief table); **South Africa, President of.**

South Africa, President of. President Nelson R. Mandela opened his last full Parliament on Feb. 6, 1998, by appealing to all South Africans to eliminate the country's greatest challenges, which he said were unemployment, poverty, budgetary reform, and crime and corruption. Mandela planned to retire from the presidency after elections scheduled for 1999.

From March 26 to March 28, 1998, Mandela hosted President Bill Clinton of the United States. The visit was the first to South Africa by a U.S. president. The two leaders toured Robben Island, in the South Atlantic Ocean near Cape Town, where Mandela spent 18 of his 27 years imprisoned under *apartheid* (government policy of racial separation).

In June, Mandela attended the European Union (EU) summit in Cardiff, Wales, becoming one of only a few heads of state from outside the EU ever invited to that annual meeting. Mandela celebrated his 80th birthday on July 18 by marrying children's rights activist Graca Machel. Machel is the widow of former Mozambican President Samora Machel, who was killed in a plane crash in 1986. Mandela paid a traditional bride price for his new wife.   ☐ Simon Baynham

South America. See Latin America.
South Carolina. See State government.
South Dakota. See State government.

Space exploration.

The United States and Russia, after more than a decade of preparation, began building an international space station in 1998. The U.S. space shuttle flew five missions during the year, including one with John H. Glenn, Jr., the first American to orbit Earth and the oldest person to ever fly in space. In 1998, spacecraft were launched to study the moon, an asteroid, and Mars, and a new type of communication system was placed into orbit.

Missions to Mir. The space shuttle Endeavour was launched by the National Aeronautics and Space Administration (NASA) for a mission to the Russian space station Mir on January 22. The nine-day flight carried supplies and a crew of six, which included astronaut Andrew S. W. Thomas. Thomas replaced David A. Wolf, who left Mir and returned to Earth after 128 days in space.

On June 2, Discovery flew what may have been the last U.S. shuttle mission to Mir. Although Russia wanted to maintain its aging space station while a new international space station was built, NASA did not plan to send more astronauts to Mir. Discovery's crew of six included a Russian cosmonaut, Valery Ryumin. Thomas, the last U.S. astronaut to stay aboard Mir, returned to Earth on the shuttle after spending 130 days on Mir.

Glenn returns to space. On October 29, former astronaut and U.S. Senator John Glenn returned to space 36 years after he became the first American to orbit Earth in 1962. Glenn had been one of the original seven U.S. astronauts selected in 1959.

Glenn had left NASA in 1964 to launch a career in politics. As he neared retirement from the Senate, he lobbied NASA to include him on another mission so that scientists could study the effects of space on the aging process. During his first flight, Glenn, alone in a Mercury capsule named Friendship 7, orbited Earth three times. During his second trip, the 77-year-old Glenn spent nine days aboard Discovery and orbited Earth 134 times. Glenn's six crewmates aboard the shuttle included the first Spaniard in space—Pedro Duque—and Chiaki Mukai, who had been the first Japanese woman in space and was making her second flight.

Spacelab mission. On April 17, 1998, Columbia began a 16-day Spacelab mission to study the effects of very low gravity on the brain and nervous system. The crew of seven, which included Canadian physician Dafydd Rhys Williams, performed experiments on themselves and on more than 2,000 animals, including fish, snails, mice, and rats. The crew dissected some of the rodents to see how their nervous systems changed under near weightless conditions.

The international space station. The last shuttle mission of 1998 was also the first in a series of shuttle flights to be made during the construction of the new international space station. The first section of the station, a Russian-built control module named Zarya ("sunrise" in Russian), was launched on a Proton rocket from the Baikonur Cosmodrome in Kazakstan on November 20. On December 4, Endeavour lifted off from the Kennedy Space Center in Florida with a crew of six and the second station component, Unity. Unity, a "node" used to connect various larger station modules, was lifted from Endeavour's cargo bay by the shuttle's Canadian-built manipulator arm. In three space walks spread over six days, astronauts Jerry L. Ross and James H. Newman connected the node to Zarya as they orbited 240 miles (386 kilometers) above Earth.

NASA had long hoped to build a space station and had begun the project in 1984, with Japan, Canada, and the European Space Agency as partners. However, the station had to be redesigned several times before construction began. The United States accepted Russia as a partner in 1993. By 1998, 16 nations were participating in the creation of the station, which was expected to weigh some 470 tons (425 metric tons) and sprawl over an area the size of two football fields. When the station was completed—about 2004—as many as seven astronauts at a time were to live and work on the station.

Work on the project, however, did not progress smoothly. Even before the first unit was placed into orbit, the planned launch of the third unit, the service module, was delayed in 1998 until at least July 1999. The service module was to be funded by and built in Russia. However, funds dried up in the wake of Russia's 1998 economic crisis. NASA proposed giving Russia money to finish the work, and the agency began building backup hardware. U.S. President Bill Clinton voiced support for the station and for helping the Russians. At the end of 1998, however, Congress had not yet acted on the NASA plan.

Planetary science. On January 7, an Athena rocket launched NASA's low-cost Lunar Prospector spacecraft to the Moon. The project was a triumph in the agency's drive to build simpler, less expensive spacecraft. Equipment aboard Prospector, which was in lunar orbit in early 1998, gathered strong evidence that water exists on the moon in the form of polar ice.

Japan launched its Planet B (later named

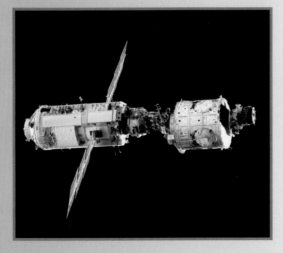

The international space station, *above,* appears in an artist's rendering as it will look upon completion, in about 2004. It will be the size of approximately two football fields. U.S. astronaut James H. Newman, *left,* connects the first two modules of the station in December 1998. Newman worked from the space shuttle Endeavour.

After being connected, the first modules of the international space station orbit Earth in December 1998. Zarya (left), a Russian-built unit financed by the United States, will serve as a control module. Unity (right) a U.S.-built node, will function as a passageway to other, larger units.

A Titan 4A rocket, *above*, explodes 40 seconds after its launch from Cape Canaveral, Florida, in August 1998. The Air Force rocket was carrying a satellite for monitoring air-defense radar networks and tracking missile tests.

Commander of the U.S. space shuttle Discovery, Charles Precourt (left), says good-bye to Talgat Musabayev, commander of space station Mir, in June 1998. Discovery was expected to be the last U.S. space shuttle to visit the aging Russian space station.

Nozomi—Japanese for "hope") spacecraft to Mars on July 4. Nozomi was scheduled to reach Mars in October 1999 and gather information about the planet's atmosphere and the moons Phobos and Deimos.

On Dec. 10, 1998, NASA launched the first of a pair of spacecraft also due to arrive at Mars in 1999. The Mars Climate Orbiter was to study the planet's atmosphere and provide a communications link for the second spacecraft, the Mars Polar Lander, which was scheduled for launch in early January 1999.

NASA launched Deep Space 1, the first low-cost spacecraft in its New Millennium program, on Oct. 24, 1998. The spacecraft was bound for an encounter with an asteroid in July 1999. The flight's primary mission was to test advanced technologies, especially systems of autonomous navigation and a novel form of propulsion. The spacecraft's electric engine accelerated very slowly, by *ionizing* (separating into ions) the element xenon. Ionizing produced minute thrust but used the xenon fuel very efficiently.

Galileo, which many experts have labeled the last of the big, expensive planetary spacecraft, continued to produce important data about and pictures of Jupiter and its moons. Galileo began orbiting Jupiter in 1995 and was scheduled for termination in 1997. In 1998, NASA extended the spacecraft's mission to 1999.

New launch vehicles. The first flight of a new U.S. launch vehicle, the Delta 3, ended in failure on Aug. 26, 1998. The rocket exploded 71 seconds after take-off because the steering system failed.

Ariane 5, a large launch vehicle developed by the European Space Agency (ESA), made its first successful flight on October 21. The rocket was launched from Kourou, French Guiana. The first launch of Ariane 5, made in 1996, exploded seconds after liftoff. The second flight, in 1997, placed a test satellite in too low an orbit. Ariane 5 will be used to launch commercial satellites. The ESA hoped it also would be used to carry supplies and astronauts to the international space station.

Going mobile. A constellation of a new type of communications satellite, Iridium, was completed in orbit in November 1998 and was considered a landmark in commerical space endeavors. A network of 66 satellites in low Earth orbits, Iridium allowed users of special mobile telephones to make and receive calls from any point on the planet. The small satellites were launched in batches by Chinese, European, Russian, and U.S. rockets.

☐ James R. Asker

See also **Astronomy.**

Spain. The country's economy continued to perform strongly in 1998, helping Spain to qualify for participation in the launch of a single currency, the euro, with 10 other European countries at the start of 1999. Economists forecast that economic output would expand by 3.8 percent during 1998, the fastest growth rate of any major European Union (EU) country. The performance reflected the success of economic policies instituted by the conservative government of Prime Minister Jose Maria Aznar since taking power in 1996. Aznar's government cut public spending and increased taxes to reduce the budget deficit, allowing interest rates to decline sharply and boosting the confidence of consumers and businesses alike. The government also reformed labor laws, a move that was expected to generate more than 300,000 new jobs in 1998, reducing the unemployment rate to below 19 percent.

Basque separatism. Hope grew during 1998 for an end to 30 years of terrorism by a guerrilla group seeking independence for the Basque region of northern Spain. The group, ETA, whose initials stand for Basque Homeland and Freedom in the Basque language, declared a cease-fire in September. The move—the first unlimited cease-fire ever offered by ETA—appeared to be inspired by the peace agreement in Northern Ireland. Aznar, who escaped assassination in a 1995 ETA bomb attack, responded warily to the declaration, authorizing the government to contact ETA directly for the first time in November 1998.

The ETA claimed responsibility for six killings in 1998, and authorities announced in May they had broken up a plot to kill King Juan Carlos during a visit to the Basque region. Some 800 people died in the violence since it began in 1968.

Past efforts to combat the terrorists continued to influence Spanish politics. In July 1998, the supreme court found a former interior minister and his director of state security guilty of involvement in a "dirty war" against the ETA in the mid-1980's. The men were sentenced to 10 years in prison and ordered to pay $200,000 for kidnapping a businessman they mistook for a terrorist. The convictions undermined former Prime Minister Felipe Gonzalez Marquez's campaign to become president of the European Commission, the executive arm of the EU, in 1999. Although Gonzalez was not charged in the case, he was suspected of knowing about the death squads.

Royalty. The first grandson of King Juan Carlos and Queen Sofia was born on July 17, 1998. The king's daughter, Princess Elena, gave birth to Felipe Juan Froilan de Todos los Santos, the 11th generation of the Spanish Bourbon dynasty.

☐ Tom Buerkle

See also **Europe** (Facts in brief table); **Europe** Special Report: **European Union; Northern Ireland.**

Sports. The 1998 sports year was highlighted by the setting of new baseball milestones, including a spectacular home-run record. But the year was also marred by several incidents of athletes using performance-enhancing drugs. One incident nearly stopped the Tour de France cycling race before it reached the halfway mark. Legal troubles affecting collegiate sports also made headlines during the year.

Drug use. The corrupting influence of performance-enhancing drugs on sports was nowhere more visible in 1998 than during the 85th Tour de France. Rocked by a drug scandal that resulted in the ouster of one team and the withdrawal of six others, the world's most prestigious cycling event degenerated into a war of attrition. By the time the cyclists rolled across the Paris finish line on the Champs Elysees on August 2, only about half of the original 189 riders were still in the race.

The controversy began on July 8, three days before the Tour started, when more than 400 capsules and vials of performance-enhancing drugs were found by border guards in the car of Willy Voet, a masseur for the world's top-ranked Festina team from France. Voet later admitted that the drugs were intended for team use. On July 17, the Festina team was expelled from the Tour by director Jean-Marie Leblanc, after Festina team director Bruno Roussel admitted to supplying drugs to his riders to improve their performances.

On July 23, the director and physician of the Dutch team TVM also were questioned. On July 28, police searched the hotel rooms of TVM team members. Four TVM riders were taken to a hospital for drug tests. To protest the treatment of the TVM riders, cyclists still competing in the Tour de France removed the numbers from their jerseys on July 29, forcing organizers to nullify the stage. On July 30, three more teams dropped out, and Italy's Rodolfo Massi, the Tour's leading hill-climber, failed to start after being taken into police custody. TVM dropped out on July 31, leaving only 14 of the original 21 teams that had started the Tour on July 11. In the aftermath, Leblanc announced that the Tour would adopt a code of conduct and ethics that teams will have to abide by in the future.

The issue of performance-enhancing drugs also surfaced in August 1998, when a State Court in Berlin, Germany, convicted and fined two former East German swimming coaches and two team physicians on charges of "inflicting grievous bodily harm" by supplying steroids and other performance-enhancing hormones to female East German swimmers between 1978 and 1989. Nearly all of the swimmers subsequently suffered physical problems that were believed to be caused by steroid use.

Romanian gymnast Simona Amanar competes in the vault at the World Cup gymnastics finals in Sabae, Japan, on May 30, 1998. Amanar placed first in the vault and in the floor exercise in Sabae on May 31.

Legal troubles. In May 1998, a federal jury in Kansas City, Kansas, ordered the National Collegiate Athletic Association (NCAA) to pay almost $67 million in damages to assistant coaches whose salaries had been capped by the NCAA in violation of federal antitrust laws. The $22.3-million jury award was tripled because antitrust laws were violated. The NCAA, which was also held liable for an estimated $10 million in legal fees, appealed the verdict. On October 5, the NCAA's appeal failed when the U.S. Supreme Court allowed the lower court ruling to stand without comment.

Notre Dame's reputation was tarnished in 1998 by an age-discrimination lawsuit filed by Joe Moore, 66, a former assistant football coach who had been dismissed by head coach Bob Davie. During the course of the trial in July, testimony and depositions revealed incidents of physical abuse of players by coaches and bitter infighting between the Notre Dame football staff. Davie testified that he had fired Moore because Moore had abused players and frequently used obscene language. A federal jury of five women and three men awarded Moore almost $86,000 in damages on July 15, 1998, after deciding that he had been fired, in part, because of his age. Notre Dame was also ordered to pay all court costs and attorneys' fees.

Milestones. The race by Mark McGwire of the St. Louis Cardinals and Sammy Sosa of the Chicago Cubs to break Roger Maris's 1961 single-season record of 61 home runs captivated rabid and casual baseball fans alike. The Cardinals slugger tied Maris first, on Sept. 7, 1998, blasting his 61st homer off Cubs pitcher Mike Morgan before a sellout crowd in St. Louis, Missouri. McGwire broke the record one night later, with an uncharacteristically short 341-foot (104-meter) line drive off Cubs pitcher Steve Trachsel, which barely cleared the left field fence.

On September 13, Sosa tied Maris when he sent a pitch by the Milwaukee Brewers's Bronswell Patrick 480 feet (146 meters) into the street beyond left field at Wrigley Field in Chicago. Sosa hit another homer in the same game, passing Maris and briefly catching McGwire at 62.

McGwire closed out his season on an extraordinary note, blasting two homers in each of his last two games for a season total of 70. Sosa finished with 66 home runs.

Cal Ripken, Jr., the Baltimore Orioles infielder who had appeared in 2,632 consecutive Major League baseball games, reached another milestone when he voluntarily called an end to his record-breaking streak on September 20. When the Orioles took to the field for their final home game of the 1998 season, Ripken watched from the dugout for the first time in 16 years.

Awards. Haile Gebrselassie, the world and Olympic champion distance runner from Ethiopia, received the Jesse Owens International Trophy Award on Feb. 25, 1998, for athletic excellence and global good will. Gebrselassie, 25, broke world records at 5,000 and 10,000 meters during 1998. Marion Jones, the U.S. and world champion sprinter, and Wilson Kipketer, the Kenyan 800-meter runner who competed for Denmark, were the other finalists for the award. The 1998 Sullivan Award for athletic achievement, leadership, and character in amateur sports was presented to Peyton Manning, the University of Tennessee's star quarterback, on February 25.

Jackie Joyner-Kersee retired from track and field competition in July 1998 at the age of 36. In a career that spanned 18 years, Joyner-Kersee won six Olympic medals, four world championships, set the heptathlon world record, and was recognized as one of the greatest female athletes of all time.

Among the winners in 1998 were—

Cycling. Marco Pantani of Italy unseated Germany's Jan Ullrich as champion of the Tour de France, cycling's premiere event, on Aug. 2, 1998. The Tour, which started in Ireland for the first time in its 85-year-history, covered 2,392 miles (3,850 kilometers) over 21 stages. Pantani fought off numerous distractions to win in 92 hours, 49 minutes, and 46 seconds. Ullrich came in second by a 3-minute, 21-second margin. Bobby Julich, an American riding for the French team Cofidis, took third place. Surprisingly, he trailed the winner by only 4 minutes and 8 seconds. Lance Armstrong turned in one of the most heart-warming cycling performances of 1998. The American champion, who returned to competition after a two-year recovery from testicular cancer, finished fourth in the Tour of Spain in September.

Diving. At the U.S. championships in August 1998, Mark Ruiz of Orlando, Florida, won both the men's 1-meter springboard and 10-meter platform titles and shared the synchronized platform diving medal. David Pichler of Ft. Lauderdale, Florida, took the 3-meter championship. The team of Chris Mantilla and Bryan Gilooly were first in synchronized, 3-meter springboard diving. In women's competition, Katie Beth Bryant of Chatham, Illinois, took the 1-meter springboard title, Michelle Davison of Columbia, South Carolina, won the 3-meter springboard title, and Kathy Pesek of Houston was the 10-meter platform champion.

Gymnastics. The United States won both the men's and women's senior division gymnastics titles at the International Team championships held in Knoxville, Tennessee, in March 1998. Led by two-time national champion Blaine Wilson, the U.S. men held off China, the defending world champion, for the gold medal. The competition was tight until the fifth rotation, when China scored poorly on the high bar and the United States came through with a winning performance in the floor exercise. Romania won the bronze medal. Wilson posted the highest individual scores in four of the six events—and tied for first in a fifth—to top the all-around scoring. The U.S. women also received a strong closing effort from Kristin Maloney to hold off Romania and China, which settled for the silver and bronze medals, respectively.

The Goodwill Games, the second major international gymnastics competition of 1998, ended on a note of tragedy when Sang Lan, a 17-year-old Chinese gymnast, was paralyzed after a neck fracture damaged her spinal cord. The accident occurred during warmups for the women's vault. All-around champions Ivan Ivankov of Belarus and Dominique Moceanu of the United States were the leading performers of games. Alexsei Bondarenko of Russia finished with the men's silver medal, and Blaine Wilson of the United States won the bronze. Maria Olaru and Simona Amanar, both of Romania, took the silver and bronze medals, respectively, in the women's all-around.

Marathon. Brazilian distance runner Ronaldo da Costa, 28, surprised the running world by shattering the 10-year-old world record for the 26-mile, 385-yard (42.2-kilometer) race. Da Costa finished the Berlin Marathon, only the second marathon of his career, in 2 hours, 6 minutes, 5 seconds, lowering the previous world mark by 45 seconds. Belayneh Densimo of Ethiopia had set the previous record in Rotterdam in 1988.

Moses Tanui gave Kenya its eighth straight victory in the Boston Marathon on April 20, 1998, completing the course in 2 hours, 7 minutes, and 34 seconds. With four miles to go, Tanui was so far behind he could not see the race leaders, but he maintained his powerful pace well enough to claim the laurel wreath, which he first won in 1996. Fellow Kenyan Joseph Chebet was second. Fatuma Roba, the Ethiopian Olympic champion, won the women's race for the second straight year.

On Nov. 1, 1998, Kenya's John Kagwe won his second New York City marathon, finishing in 2 hours, 8 minutes, and 45 seconds. Italy's Franca Fiaccon, the winner among women, finished in 2 hours, 25 minutes, 17 seconds.

Rowing. The United States and Romania successfully defended their eights titles on Sept. 13, 1998, at the world championships at Cologne, Germany. The U.S. men held off a late challenge by the Germans, who had thousands of fans cheering along the 2,000-meter course. But the Americans prevailed, finishing in 5 minutes, 38.78 seconds, to become the first U.S. boat in any rowing event to defend a world championship. Steven Redgrave won a record eighth career title as part of Great Britain's four without coxswain. Germany led the medal standings for the second straight year, with 5 golds and 5 silvers. Romania, the reigning Olympic champion in the women's eights, surged to the finish line in 6:14.62.

In the Henley Royal Regatta in Great Britain, the Harvard University women defeated a combined Cambridge University and Star Club crew by 1½ lengths, and the U.S. defeated Marlowe and Thames of Great Britain in the invitational eights. In the 144th rowing of The Boat Race in England, Cambridge University shattered the 4¼-mile (7.2-kilometer) course record on its way to beating Oxford University by 19 seconds. Cambridge was timed at 16 minutes, 19 seconds—26 seconds faster than the former record, which had been set by Oxford 14 years earlier.

Other champions

Equestrian. World Equestrian Games individual champions: show jumping, Rodrigo Pessoa, Brazil; driving, Ulrich Werner, Switzerland.

Lacrosse. World champions: United States (defeated Canada, 15-14, in overtime).

Modern Pentathlon. World champions: men, Mexico; women, Poland.

Motorcycle racing. FIM Grand Prix 500-cc champion, Mick Doohan, Australia.

Sled Dog racing. Jeff King won the 26th Iditarod Trail Sled Dog Race from Anchorage to Nome for the third time in six years. His team covered the 1,150-mile (1,851-kilometer) Alaska race in 9 days, 5 hours, and 52 minutes.

Soap Box Derby. Masters champion, James Marsh, Cleveland.

Triathlon. World Cup champions: men, Hamish Carter, New Zealand; women, Michellie Jones, Australia.

Volleyball. World League men's champion, Cuba.

Weightlifting. World Champions: men, over 105 kilograms (231 pounds), Andrei Tchemerkine, Russia; women, over 75 kilograms (165 pounds), Tang Gonghong, China.

□ Ron Reid

See also **Baseball; People in the news** (McGwire, Mark); **Soccer; Soccer** Special Report: **The 1998 World Cup.**

Sri Lanka. Three suicide bombers crashed a truck through the gates of Sri Lanka's holiest Buddhist temple on Jan. 25, 1998, killing themselves and 13 other people. The act set off ethnic riots. The nation, which is mostly Sinhalese Buddhist, reacted with outrage upon hearing news of the blast, which damaged the Temple of the Tooth in Kandy. The temple houses a tooth that the faithful believe belonged to the Buddha. The tooth was not harmed in the attack.

Sri Lanka officials attributed the attack to the Liberation Tigers of Tamil Eelam (LTTE), a guerrilla group fighting to carve out an ethnic Tamil homeland in northern and northeastern Sri Lanka. The LTTE claimed that Tamils were discriminated against by the Sinhalese, who controlled the government and the military. In 1983, the LTTE launched a civil war, which had resulted in the death of an estimated 50,000 people by late 1998 and directly affected approximately 2 million people in Sri Lanka.

On January 26, the government of President Chandrika Kumaratunga reacted to the temple attack by formally outlawing the LTTE and halting efforts to negotiate an end to the civil war. Before the attack, the government had proposed granting extensive powers to regional councils in Tamil areas, a measure that the LTTE rejected. On January 29, the main opposition to Kumaratunga's governing Sri Lanka Freedom Party—the United National Party (UNP)—withdrew support for any compromise with the LTTE.

Police search through the rubble at the Temple of the Tooth, Sri Lanka's holiest Buddhist site, in January 1998, after an attack by three suicide bombers. The temple houses a tooth, unharmed in the explosion, that the faithful venerate as having belonged to the Buddha.

In March, the LTTE bombed a bus in the capital, Colombo, killing 38 people. In August, the government arrested 50 LTTE members suspected of planning bombings and killings.

Fighting flared between government soldiers and the LTTE along a strategic highway that links Colombo, in the south, with the government-held town of Jaffna, at the country's northern tip. The worst fighting in 1998 took place in late September, when more than 1,300 people were killed in a week-long campaign by the government to recapture the highway.

Terrorist funding. The Center for the Study of International Terrorism at St. Andrews University in Edinburgh, in Scotland, reported in 1998 that the LTTE was among the most well-funded and well-armed terrorist groups in the world. According to some estimates, the LTTE collected $1 million a month, mostly from hundreds of thousands of Tamil refugees who had fled Sri Lanka since the civil war began.

Sri Lanka's economy remained stable despite the cost of the civil war. The income of the government's 120,000 soldiers supported an estimated 720,000 people in poorer parts of the country, and security firms that guarded private businesses from suicide bombers employed some 150,000 people.   □ Henry S. Bradsher

See also **Asia** (Facts in brief table).

State government.

Several popular Republican governors retained their offices following the November 1998 elections. Democrats, who had feared a backlash in the wake of controversy surrounding a relationship between President Bill Clinton and a White House intern, still managed major victories. Of the 36 open governors' seats on the November 3 ballot, 24 had been held by Republicans, 11 by Democrats, and 1 by an independent. In the election, 23 were won by Republicans, 11 by Democrats, and 2 by independent candidates. Political experts considered the 1998 gubernatorial elections especially important because those governors will participate in the redistricting of state legislatures and United States congressional seats after the 2000 census.

Sons of former President George Bush captured victories in the 1998 election. Voters reelected Republican Texas Governor George W. Bush by a wide margin. Florida voters elected Republican Jeb Bush, who had been defeated in a run for the same office in 1994. The victories meant that two brothers would serve simultaneously as governors for the first time since 1967, when Nelson A. Rockefeller was governor of New York and his brother, Winthrop Rockefeller, was governor of Arkansas.

Bill Owens became the first Republican governor of Colorado since the 1970's by defeating Democratic challenger Gail Schoettler in a close race. Senator Dirk Kempthorne (R., Idaho) won a landslide victory for governor of Idaho. Voters in Illinois elected Republican Secretary of State George H. Ryan governor. Also winning first gubernatorial terms were Mike Johanns of Nebraska; Kenny Guinn of Nevada; and Secretary of State Robert Taft of Ohio. Taft is the great-grandson of President William Howard Taft.

Republican governors reelected in 1998 included Jane Dee Hull of Arizona; Mike Huckabee of Arkansas; John Rowland of Connecticut; Bill Graves of Kansas; Paul Cellucci of Massachusetts; John Engler of Michigan; Gary E. Johnson of New Mexico; George E. Pataki of New York; Frank Keating of Oklahoma; Tom J. Ridge of Pennsylvania; Lincoln C. Almond of Rhode Island; William J. Janklow of South Dakota; Don Sundquist of Tennessee; Tommy G. Thompson of Wisconsin; and Jim Geringer of Wyoming.

Democrats won what was considered a major victory in California when Lieutenant Governor Gray Davis defeated State Attorney General Dan Lungren. California had not elected a Democratic governor since Jerry Brown in 1978. In Alabama, Democrat Don Siegelman defeated incumbent Governor Fob James, Jr., and in Alaska, Tony Knowles became the first governor to win reelection to a second term since 1978.

Voters elected Democrats Roy Barnes of Georgia; Tom Vilsack of Iowa; and Jim Hodges of South Carolina to first terms as governor. Democratic governors winning reelection included Benjamin J. Cayetano of Hawaii; Parris N. Glendening of Maryland; Jeanne Shaheen of New Hampshire; John Kitzhaber of Oregon; and Howard Dean of Vermont.

In a stunning upset in Minnesota, Reform Party candidate Jesse Ventura, a former professional wrestler, shocked fellow candidates Democrat Hubert H. Humphrey III and Republican Norm Coleman by winning that state's governorship. Maine Governor Angus S. King, the nation's other independent governor, easily won reelection.

Budget surpluses. Many states ended fiscal 1998 on June 30 with higher-than-expected financial balances. Nationwide, states recorded a combined surplus of nearly $40 billion, according to a National Conference of State Legislatures (NCSL) report issued in October. The NCSL noted that 19 states had cut taxes, 16 had increased spending in such areas as education and prisons, 16 financed new one-time projects such as roads, and 23 had saved the funds to handle a future economic downturn.

More than half of the tax breaks in 1998 were in personal income taxes. California approved a $1.4-billion cut, and New York passed $711 mil-

Selected statistics on state governments

State	Resident population*	Governor†	Legislature† House (D)	(R)	Senate (D)	(R)	State tax revenue‡	Tax revenue per capita‡	Public school expenditure per pupil§
Alabama	4,319,154	Don Siegelman (D)	69	36	23	12	$ 14,008,000,000	$ 3,240	$ 5,110
Alaska	609,311	Tony Knowles (D)	16	24	5	15	9,439,000,000	15,500	10,650
Arizona	4,554,966	Jane Dee Hull (R)	20	40	14	16	13,692,000,000	3,010	4,940
Arkansas	2,522,819	Mike Huckabee (R)	77	23	29	6	8,844,000,000	3,510	5,220
California	32,268,301	Joseph Graham (Gray) Davis (D)	48	32	25	15	131,099,000,000	4,060	5,350
Colorado	3,892,644	Bill F. Owens (R)	25	40	15	20	12,780,000,000	3,280	5,700
Connecticut	3,269,858	John G. Rowland (R)	96	55	19	17	14,520,000,000	4,440	9,220
Delaware	731,581	Tom Carper (D)	15	26	13	8	4,211,000,000	5,750	8,580
Florida	14,653,945	Jeb Bush (R)	47	73	15	25	41,432,000,000	2,830	6,140
Georgia	7,486,242	Roy Barnes (D)	102	78	33	23	24,028,000,000	3,210	6,180
Hawaii	1,186,602	Benjamin J. Cayetano (D)	39	12	23	2	6,701,000,000	5,640	6,130
Idaho	1,210,232	Dirk Kempthorne (R)	12	58	4	31	4,289,000,000	3,540	4,970
Illinois	11,895,849	George H. Ryan (R)	62	56	27	32	39,038,000,000	3,280	6,360
Indiana	5,864,108	Frank L. O'Bannon (D)	53	47	19	31	17,537,000,000	2,990	6,640
Iowa	2,852,423	Tom Vilsack (D)	44	56	20	30	9,509,000,000	3,330	5,710
Kansas	2,594,840	Bill Graves (R)	48	77	13	27	7,950,000,000	3,060	6,350
Kentucky	3,908,124	Paul E. Patton (D)	66	34	20	18	15,033,000,000	3,850	6,280
Louisiana	4,351,769	Murphy J. (Mike) Foster (R)	78	27	25	14	15,929,000,000	3,660	5,190
Maine	1,242,051	Angus S. King, Jr. (I)	#79	71	#20	14	5,215,000,000	4,200	7,110
Maryland	5,094,289	Parris N. Glendening (D)	106	35	32	15	20,128,000,000	3,950	7,380
Massachusetts	6,117,520	Paul Cellucci (R)	#131	28	33	7	26,538,000,000	4,340	7,860
Michigan	9,773,892	John Engler (R)	52	58	15	23	45,509,000,000	4,660	7,670
Minnesota	4,685,549	Jesse Ventura (Reform)	63	71	#42	24	22,882,000,000	4,880	6,730
Mississippi	2,730,501	Kirk Fordice (R)	**83	36	34	18	9,400,000,000	3,440	4,730
Missouri	5,402,058	Mel Carnahan (D)	#86	76	18	16	16,601,000,000	3,070	5,600
Montana	878,810	Marc Racicot (R)	41	59	18	32	3,524,000,000	4,010	6,240
Nebraska	1,656,870	Mike Johanns (R)	unicameral (49 nonpartisan)				5,537,000,000	3,340	5,850
Nevada	1,676,809	Kenny Guinn (R)	28	14	9	12	6,494,000,000	3,870	5,600
New Hampshire	1,172,709	Jeanne Shaheen (D)	#154	245	13	11	3,561,000,000	3,040	6,560
New Jersey	8,052,849	Christine Todd Whitman (R)	32	48	16	24	36,087,000,000	4,480	10,430
New Mexico	1,729,751	Gary E. Johnson (R)	40	30	25	17	8,188,000,000	4,730	5,870
New York	18,137,226	George E. Pataki (R)	98	52	26	35	95,442,000,000	5,260	9,810
North Carolina	7,425,183	James B. Hunt, Jr. (D)	65	55	35	15	25,527,000,000	3,440	5,830
North Dakota	640,883	Edward T. Shafer (R)	34	64	18	31	2,818,000,000	4,400	4,980
Ohio	11,186,331	Robert Taft (R)	40	59	12	21	45,250,000,000	4,050	6,540
Oklahoma	3,317,091	Frank Keating (R)	61	40	33	15	11,328,000,000	3,420	4,630
Oregon	3,243,487	John Kitzhaber (D)	25	34	#12	17	15,004,000,000	4,630	6,720
Pennsylvania	12,019,661	Tom J. Ridge (R)	100	103	20	30	49,318,000,000	4,100	7,750
Rhode Island	987,429	Lincoln C. Almond (R)	86	13	42	8	4,229,000,000	4,290	6,430
South Carolina	3,760,181	Jim Hodges (D)	56	68	26	20	13,805,000,000	3,670	5,560
South Dakota	737,973	William J. Janklow (R)	18	51	13	22	2,316,000,000	3,140	5,170
Tennessee	5,368,198	Don Sundquist (R)	59	40	18	15	15,696,000,000	2,920	5,590
Texas	19,439,337	George W. Bush, (R)	79	71	15	16	63,864,000,000	3,290	6,290
Utah	2,059,148	Michael O. Leavitt (R)	21	54	11	18	7,724,000,000	3,750	3,900
Vermont	588,978	Howard Dean (D)	††77	67	17	13	2,370,000,000	4,020	7,930
Virginia	6,733,996	James S. Gilmore III (R)	#50	49	19	21	24,322,000,000	3,610	6,570
Washington	5,610,362	Gary Locke (D)	49	49	28	21	26,841,000,000	4,780	6,490
West Virginia	1,815,787	Cecil H. Underwood (R)	75	25	29	5	7,467,000,000	4,110	7,110
Wisconsin	5,169,677	Tommy G. Thompson (R)	44	55	17	16	23,859,000,000	4,610	7,270
Wyoming	479,743	Jim Geringer (R)	17	43	10	20	2,559,000,000	5,330	6,310

*July 1, 1997, estimates. Source: U.S. Bureau of the Census.
†As of December 1998. Source: National Governors' Association;
 National Conference of State Legislatures; state government officials.
‡1997 figures. Source: U.S. Bureau of the Census.
§1997-1998 figures for elementary and secondary students in average
 daily attendance. Source: National Education Association.

#One independent.
**Three independents.
††Two independents; four progressives.
‡‡Two independents.

lion in tax cuts. Massachusetts reduced taxes by a total of $1 billion. Kansas cut taxes, including property taxes, by $252 million. The Ohio legislature approved a 9-percent, one-time income tax reduction for 1999. Georgia approved a $205-million income tax break, and Virginia reduced its tax on cars.

Oklahoma lawmakers, however, rejected deep tax cuts proposed by the governor. The South Carolina legislature also rejected the governor's proposed cut in property taxes on cars. Indiana legislators, despite a large surplus, deferred acting on tax relief. In Florida, the governor vetoed $50 tax rebates to property owners that had been passed by the legislature.

Transportation. States benefited financially in May 1998 when the U.S. Congress approved the final version of the Transportation Equity Act for the 21st Century (TEA 21). The federal transportation funding act provides $217 billion over six years for road construction and transportation projects in all 50 states.

Tobacco settlement. A number of states in 1998 pursued individual lawsuits to recover state health-care costs related to smoking, when Congress failed to pass a 25-year, $368-billion national tobacco settlement proposed in 1997. Tobacco companies in May 1998 agreed to pay Minnesota $6.1 billion over a 25-year period. In July, Texas officials finalized a $17.6-billion settlement with the tobacco industry. The settlement was to be paid over a 26-year period. Washington state officials agreed in October to a $2-million settlement with two tobacco industry defendants. In November, the attorneys general of 46 states settled their lawsuits against various U.S. tobacco companies. The companies agreed to pay the states a total of $206 billion over a 25-year period, beginning in 2000.

Education. The New Jersey Supreme Court in May 1998 approved Governor Christine Todd Whitman's plan to improve education in low-income, urban school districts. The state had agreed in 1997 to spend $248 million on urban schools to close a spending gap between high-income and low-income school districts.

In July 1998, the Arizona Supreme Court approved a plan to allow the state to finance the construction, equipping, and repair of public schools. The justices ruled that a previous plan allowing each school district to issue bonds gave wealthier districts the advantage of offering better education to students than poorer districts.

The Wisconsin Supreme Court ruled in June that state funds could be used to send students in Milwaukee to private religious schools. The court ruled that a 1995 state measure expanding the use of government-sponsored vouchers to help low-income children pay for parochial schooling did not violate the principle of separation of church and state. The decision allowed up to 15,000 Milwaukee students to apply for vouchers from the state to pay for private education.

Charter schools gained further acceptance in 1998. Georgia, Idaho, Utah, and Virginia approved legislation allowing the creation of such schools. Charter schools are typically created and run by parents, teachers, or other groups outside of a school district's authority.

Microsoft lawsuit. Attorneys general from 20 states, the District of Columbia, and the U.S. Department of Justice filed an antitrust lawsuit on May 18 charging the Microsoft Corporation of Redmond, Washington, with illegally hampering competition in the computer software industry. Microsoft's attorneys denied the allegations.

Florida Governor Lawton Chiles died on Dec. 12, 1998, less than one month before he was to leave office. Chiles, a Democrat, served 12 years in the Florida state legislature, 18 years as a U.S. senator, and 8 years as governor of Florida. State law prohibited Chiles from running for a third term. Lieutenant Governor Buddy MacKay was sworn in on December 13 to complete Chiles's term.   □ Elaine Stuart

See also **Courts; Democratic Party; Education; Elections; Health-care issues; Puerto Rico; Republican Party; Transportation; Welfare.**

Stocks and bonds. Stock market investors in the United States took a quick, somewhat scary round trip in 1998. Fears of global recession drove major stock indexes down 20 percent from their all-time highs between mid-July and the end of August. Three rounds of interest rate cuts by the Federal Reserve Board (the Fed), the U.S. central bank, between September and November soothed investor fears and led stocks to new highs in late November.

The Dow Jones Industrial Average—a composite of the stock prices of 30 major companies traded on the New York Stock Exchange—rallied sharply for the first four months of 1998, as investors predicted that an economic crisis that had erupted in Asia in 1997 would not seriously harm corporate profits in the United States.

The Dow closed at a record high 9337.97 on July 17, 1998. The closing was a 15-percent increase from the 7908.25 close at the beginning of 1998. In late July, however, investors began to sell their stocks after Fed Chairman Alan Greenspan warned of inflationary pressures in the economy and of instability in Asian economies.

In August, Russia froze payments on several billion dollars worth of its debts after its currency, the ruble, plunged to approximately half its former value. Despite a relatively small economy, Russia's decision sparked fears of loan defaults

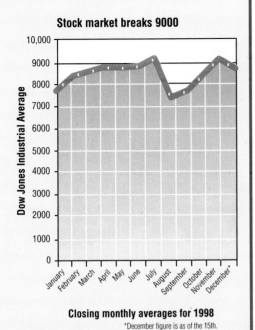

Stock market breaks 9000

Dow Jones Industrial Average

Closing monthly averages for 1998
*December figure is as of the 15th.

The Dow Jones Industrial Average broke 9000 for the first time in July 1998, only to plunge a record 512 points on August 31. The Dow later rebounded, climbing to a new record high on November 23.

and currency devaluations throughout Asia and Latin America. Financial markets worldwide faced gridlock. The sell-offs were capped on August 31, when the Dow plunged 512 points—a 19 percent drop from the record that had been set on July 17.

The stock market attempted to rally in September, but stalled after Long Term Capital Management, a Greenwich, Connecticut-based private investment fund, disclosed massive losses. The fund, run by prominent money managers and two Nobel Prize-winning economists, had borrowed heavily from major New York City banks to make what managers had thought were sure bets on minor moves in stock and bond prices. When the bets came up losers, the Federal Reserve Bank of New York convened a meeting of bankers to arrange a bailout. A group of commercial banks and investment firms on September 23 agreed to loan the fund $3.5 billion. Damage to the stock market, however, lingered throughout the rest of 1998 as investors and lenders worldwide became uncharacteristically averse to risk. Several banks tightened lending requirements to other investment funds, raising fears of a possible credit shortage.

The Fed cut *short-term interest rates*, the rates banks charge each other for loans, in September, October, and November. The rates dropped from

5.5 percent to 4.75 percent in November. The rate cut was the first made by the Fed since 1996. The reduction injected money into the nation's banking system. Central banks in other countries, including Canada and Great Britain, also put money into their national banking systems.

The Dow climbed to another record high on Nov. 23, 1998, when it closed at 9374.27, up 18.5 percent for the year. The increase in the price of stocks furthered a recovery that some economists had considered impossible following September declines.

Broader market indexes also rebounded. The Standard & Poor's 500 index of 500 large company stocks hit an all-time high, up 22 percent for the year. The Nasdaq Composite Index of all stocks traded on the electronic Nasdaq Stock Market, operated by the National Association of Securities Dealers, rallied to an all-time closing high of 2016.44, up 28 percent for the year. The Russell 2000 index of small-company stocks rebounded from early October lows, but did not break through its April all-time high.

The Federal Reserve's action on interest rates in late September pushed long-term Treasury bond yields lower. Mortgage rates, in turn, fell for most of the year, helping home buyers and homeowners seeking to refinance mortgages. The yield on the benchmark 30-year Treasury bond fell to nearly 5 percent in early December 1998 from 5.92 percent in December 1997.

Winners and losers. The restoration of confidence in global financial markets in 1998 rekindled an investor mania for the stocks of companies offering products and services in connection with the burgeoning Internet. Among the weaker sectors were the stocks of oil drilling equipment makers, health maintenance organizations, real estate investment trusts, heavy machinery manufacturers, and shipbuilders.

International stock markets. Instability in the economies of Southeast Asia caused Asian stock markets to experience sharp swings in 1998. Those markets recovered to stand essentially unchanged from the end of 1997. The Nikkei 225 index of major stocks on the Tokyo Stock Exchange sank to 12,788 in 1998 but rebounded to 14,884 at the end of November, down 2 percent for the year. Latin American stocks made a slow recovery. The Bovespa index of stocks on the Brazil Stock Exchange traded as low as 4576 but rebounded to 8815 at the end of November, down 13 percent for the year. The main German stock index, the DAX index, traded at just over 5000 at the end of November 1998, up 18 percent from the end of 1997.   ☐ Bill Barnhart

See also **Economics** Special Report: **Asian Economic Crisis—Global Contagion.**

In August 1998, U.S. missiles reduced a factory in Khartoum, Sudan, to rubble in retaliation for the terrorist bombing of U.S. embassies in East Africa. U.S. officials claimed the factory had ties to the terrorists and was involved in the manufacture of chemical weapons.

Sudan. Sudanese authorities demanded a United Nations (UN) inquiry after United States missiles destroyed the El Shifa Pharmaceutical Industries factory in Khartoum, the Sudanese capital, on Aug. 20, 1998. U.S. officials claimed that traces of Empta, a chemical used to make VX nerve gas, had been found in soil outside the factory, indicating that the plant was involved in the manufacture of chemical weapons. Sudanese officials, however, maintained that the factory produced only medicine. The U.S. attack was in retaliation for terrorist bombings of U.S. embassies in Tanzania and Kenya on August 7. Immediately after the attack, U.S. officials said that Osama bin Laden, the alleged leader of a terrorist group that was suspected of being responsible for the embassy bombings, had financial interests in the factory. This and a subsequent U.S. claim linking Iraq to the plant remained unverified.

Many arms experts said the United States offered insufficient proof that the factory produced Empta or chemical weapons. In September, former U.S. President Jimmy Carter joined the call for an independent investigation of the attack, citing widespread doubts about the justification for the U.S. missile strikes. The United States blocked efforts at such an investigation.

Civil war. Peace talks to end the civil war between Sudan's government and the southern rebel group Sudan People's Liberation Army (SPLA) ended inconclusively in May. The rebels, mainly black Christians and *animists* (those believing that souls are present in all parts of nature), have sought autonomy from the Arab- and Muslim-dominated north since 1983. Although the government agreed in 1997 to allow a referendum on southern self-determination, government and rebel negotiators failed to agree on a timetable for the referendum or on the boundaries of the area to be polled. In addition, the rebels, who demanded a *secular* (nonreligious) government, objected to new Sudanese constitutional reforms, which they said instilled Islamic ideals of governance.

Famine and flood. In February 1998, some 100,000 people fled the southern Sudanese state of Bahr el-Ghazal to avoid intense fighting in the region. Many of the refugees, who had already suffered two years of drought, starved to death. In July, UN officials estimated that famine, caused mainly by food shortages resulting from the civil war, threatened 1.2 million lives in Sudan.

In September, UN relief agencies reported that hundreds of thousands of people had been left homeless by the worst flooding of the Nile River in Sudan in 10 years.   □ Christine Helms

See also **Middle East** (Facts in brief table); **Terrorism.**

Supreme Court of the United States.

In 1998, the U.S. Supreme Court provided clearer rules on sexual harassment in the workplace and in public schools through several key rulings. The justices canceled the president's power to veto individual items from spending bills and expanded protections from discrimination covered by the Americans With Disabilities Act (ADA).

Sexual harassment. The court on June 26 issued two decisions clarifying the law against sexual harassment in the workplace. Both decisions came on 7-to-2 votes and involved Title VII of the Civil Rights Act of 1964, which bars discrimination based on a person's gender.

In the first decision, the justices ruled that employers are responsible for sexual harassment committed by managers toward their subordinates. The decision involved a case in which a former lifeguard sued the city of Boca Raton, Florida, claiming that her supervisors made inappropriate remarks and gestures. The justices ruled that the city did not inform its employees about policies against sexual harassment and did not monitor supervisors' conduct.

In a second ruling, the court decided that an Illinois woman could sue Burlington Industries, Inc., for sexual harassment, even though the woman did not formally complain to company officials about comments made by a supervisor and did not suffer adverse job consequences. The court determined that an employee may sue a company for sexual harassment without having to prove job-related harm. The court also determined that a company may defend itself by showing it has adequate procedures for workers to complain about illegal behavior and a victim did not use the procedures.

Same-sex harassment. In another sex discrimination case, the court ruled unanimously on March 4, 1998, that an employee can sue an employer for having been sexually harassed at the workplace by co-workers of the same sex. The court determined that such conduct would violate the law if it was so severe that it made the workplace hostile or abusive. The decision upheld a lawsuit filed by an oil rig worker against his employer and three members of the all-male crew with whom he worked. The man claimed that his co-workers improperly touched and threatened him.

Teacher misconduct. The court ruled on June 22 that public school districts cannot be held responsible when a teacher sexually harasses a student if school administrators were unaware of the conduct. In a 5-to-4 vote, the court determined that school districts may be held liable only when an administrator is aware of the harassment and does nothing to stop it.

The ruling did not affect the right of a harassed student to recover monetary damages from a guilty teacher or from a school district under separate state laws. The decision left open the possibility that Congress could amend the law to place more responsibility on school officials to stop teacher misconduct.

Attorney-client privilege. On June 25, the court ruled that a lawyer cannot be forced to reveal a client's confidential statements even after the client is dead. By a 6-to-3 vote, the court blocked Independent Counsel Kenneth Starr from obtaining a lawyer's notes of a meeting with presidential aide Vincent W. Foster, Jr., shortly before Foster committed suicide in 1993. Starr was investigating the political, business, and private lives of President Bill Clinton and First Lady Hillary Rodham Clinton.

HIV discrimination. In a 5-to-4 decision, the court ruled on June 25, 1998, that the Americans With Disabilities Act (ADA) prevents unequal treatment of people with human immunodeficiency virus (HIV), the virus that causes AIDS, even if the person shows no symptoms of the disease. Adopted in 1990, the ADA bars discrimination against anyone with a physical problem that limits a major life activity. The court's ruling came in the case of a Maine woman with HIV who sued her dentist after he refused to perform a procedure in his office rather than at a hospital.

The arts. The court voted 8 to 1 on June 25, 1998, to uphold a government limit on federal grants to artists whose work is considered indecent. The court determined that a 1990 federal law does not violate artists' rights of free speech by directing the National Endowment for the Arts (NEA) to take into account standards of decency and respect for diverse beliefs and values when awarding grants. The NEA is a federal agency that grants financial support to state art programs, symphonies, and museums to encourage development of the arts.

Four performance artists had challenged the constitutionality of the 1990 law, and lower courts had blocked its enforcement since 1992. Critics of the Supreme Court's 1998 ruling feared it might have a negative effect on artistic creativity and freedom of expression.

Line-item veto. The justices on June 25 struck down the line-item veto power that the U.S. Congress granted the president in 1996. The line-item veto gave the president power to cancel individual items of federal spending from budget and tax bills without vetoing the entire measure. It was passed as a way to trim budgets.

Voting 6-to-3, the court ruled that the U.S. Constitution specifies the means for enacting laws and does not give the president the power to cancel portions or to amend them. President Clinton used the line-item veto power 11 times in 1997 to eliminate 82 individual items from various spending bills.

Justices of the Supreme Court of the United States join the procession from a church in Richmond, Virginia, following the funeral of former Supreme Court Justice Lewis F. Powell, Jr., on Aug. 31, 1998.

Ellis Island. The justices on May 26, 1998, settled a 160-year-old dispute between the states of New Jersey and New York over Ellis Island, located in New York Harbor. From 1892 to 1954, Ellis Island was the nation's chief immigration center, where 12 million immigrants first entered the United States. In a 6-to-3 decision, the court ruled that most of the 27.5-acre (11-hectare) island is located in New Jersey under an 1834 border agreement between the two states. That agreement gave New York jurisdiction over the island, which at the time covered only three acres (1.2 hectares). It gave New Jersey jurisdiction over the surrounding water and underwater land. The federal government later used landfill to expand the island's size to 27.5 acres.

Although the island is owned by the federal government, New Jersey and New York officials argued over the power to collect sales taxes and control future development. The court's ruling left New York with 3.3 acres (1.3 hectares) and New Jersey with 24.2 acres (9.8 hectares).

Police chases. In a unanimous ruling on May 26, 1998, the justices gave police officers more protection from federal lawsuits when high-speed chases kill or injure someone. The court ruled that police do not violate a person's constitutional right to life unless an officer intends to hurt someone. The ruling does not prevent injured parties or their relatives from suing police officers under state laws. The court ruled that an officer's actions must show a "reckless disregard for life" before anyone injured in a crash, including bystanders, can sue.

Powell dies. Former Supreme Court Justice Lewis F. Powell, Jr., died on Aug. 25, 1998. He was 90 years old. Powell, who generally held conservative views, was considered an important moderate on a court that had become *polarized* (split) between liberal and conservative justices.

Powell was born in Suffolk, Virginia, and practiced law in Richmond, Virginia, until President Richard M. Nixon appointed him to the high court in 1972. Powell served until 1987. In 1978, Powell cast the deciding vote in controversial decision regarding college affirmative-action programs. In *University of California Regents v. Bakke,* the court ruled 5 to 4 that state universities may not use racial quotas in admissions. However, a separate 5-to-4 majority ruled that college and university officials may consider a student's race as a factor in the admissions process. Powell cast the deciding vote in both parts of the ruling.

□ Geoffrey A. Campbell and Linda P. Campbell
See also **Courts; Courts** Special Report: **Marking Time on Death Row; People in the news** (Starr, Kenneth); **United States, President of the.**

Surgery. See Medicine.
Suriname. See Latin America.
Swaziland. See Africa.

Sweden. The government of Prime Minister Goran Persson won a narrow reelection victory in 1998 after a campaign that focused on the future of Sweden's welfare system. Persson's Social Democratic Party promised to protect benefits and spend an additional $1.1 billion on health care, child care, and the elderly. The center-right opposition parties campaigned on a pledge to reduce unemployment by cutting Swedish income tax rates, which are among the highest in the developed world. They promised to finance tax cuts by reducing welfare payments and other government spending.

Election. The Social Democrats scored their worst election result in decades, winning 36 percent of the vote in the September 20 election and taking 131 seats in the 349-seat Riksdag (parliament). In 1994, the party took 45 percent of the vote and 161 seats. However, the Moderate Party, the largest opposition party, failed in 1998 to make significant gains. It won 23 percent of the vote and 82 seats, a gain of only 2 seats from the previous parliament. Persson's Social Democrats formed a minority government with the Left Party, the former Communists, which doubled its share of the vote to 12 percent, and the smaller Green Party, which won 5 percent of the vote.

Economic policies. At the opening session of the new parliament in October, Persson promised to continue the same economic course for the next four years, including running a budget surplus. The 1998 budget surplus ran approximately 0.5 percent of *gross domestic product* (GDP—the value of all goods and services produced in a country in a given year), compared with a deficit of 0.8 percent of GDP the previous year. The surplus was designed to keep interest rates low and the Swedish krona (the state currency) stable while the country remained outside Europe's single currency, which 11 other European Union (EU) countries were to launch in January 1999. The government left open the possibility of Sweden's eventually joining the single currency.

Lower interest rates helped the economy to pick up in 1998. The European Commission, the executive arm of the EU, forecast in October that Sweden's 1998 growth would accelerate to 3.0 percent from 1.8 percent in 1997. However, unemployment remained at around 8 percent, stubbornly high by Swedish standards.

Deadly fire. A fire swept through a discotheque in a Macedonian cultural center in the southern city of Gothenberg on the night of Oct. 30, 1998, killing 63 people who were attending a Halloween party. It was one of the worst fires in Swedish history.   □ Tom Buerkle
See also **Europe** (Facts in brief table); **Europe** Special Report: **European Union.**

Swimming. Athletes from the United States took 14 gold medals—their best showing in 20 years—at the World Swimming Championships in Perth, Australia, Jan. 7 to 18, 1998. The U.S. team won the most medals—24. Australia was second with 20 medals, 7 of them gold.

The Americans were led by Jenny Thompson of Palo Alto, California. A five-time Olympic champion in relay events, Thompson captured individual gold medals in the 100-meter freestyle and 100-meter butterfly and won two more golds with the 400-meter freestyle and 400-meter medley relay teams. Bill Pilczuk of Cape May Point, New Jersey, upset Russia's Aleksandr Popov in the men's 50-meter freestyle. Pilczuk's win ended Popov's unbeaten streak in both the 50- and 100-meter freestyle events, which the Russian had held since the 1992 Summer Olympics in Barcelona. Michael Klim of Australia set the short-course world record for the 100-meter butterfly at 51.07 seconds. Klim was also the top individual performer at Perth, winning four gold medals, two silvers, and a bronze.

Drugs. The world championships were clouded by a drug scandal that began when an Australian customs officer discovered Somatotropin in the luggage of the female Chinese swimmer Yuan Yuan. The performance-enhancing drug is banned by the Federation Internationale de

Natation Amateur (FINA), which governs amateur aquatic sports. FINA suspended Yuan, a silver medalist in the 1994 World Championships, from competition for four years. On Jan. 14, 1998, four additional female Chinese swimmers were disqualified from the world championships after testing positive for a substance used as a masking agent for performance-enhancing drugs. FINA suspended each of the swimmers for two years.

Ireland's Michelle de Bruin, triple gold-medalist at the 1996 Summer Olympics, received a four-year suspension on Aug. 6, 1998, for tampering with her own urine sample before it could be tested for drugs. Accusations of performance-enhancing drug use had shadowed de Bruin since the 1996 games. On Aug. 20, 1998, Mexico's Erendira Villegas was suspended for four years, after testing positive for drugs at the Central American Games. Her victories in that competition were annulled.

Records fall. On February 2, at a meet in Beijing, China's Hu Xiaowen set a world record for the women's 100-meter individual medley of 1:00.60. At a meet in Paris in March, Russia's Andrei Korneev set a 200-meter breaststroke mark of 2:07.79; Germany's Mark Warnecke swam the 50-meter breaststroke in 26.97 seconds; and James Hickman of Great Britain completed the 200-meter butterfly in 1:51.76. □ Ron Reid

Switzerland.

The country's largest banks agreed in 1998 to settle legal claims that they and the Swiss government had profited from gold dealings with Nazi Germany during World War II (1939-1945). The agreement ended two years of negotiations with Jewish organizations and averted the threat of sanctions against the banks' activities in the United States.

The dispute began in 1996, when the British government opened wartime archives that indicated Swiss banks had received gold looted by the Nazis. The disclosure led Jewish groups and Holocaust survivors to sue the country and its banks for compensation. The banks began negotiating with the groups in 1997, with U.S. officials acting as mediators.

In May 1998, the Swiss government and the Swiss National Bank, the central bank that handled the bulk of the wartime gold trade, declared they would not join any settlement. The government based its decision on a report by a group of historians who found that the central bank had bought $2.8 billion in Nazi gold but had not acted improperly, given Switzerland's neutrality during the war. On August 12, the country's two largest banks, UBS AG and Credit Suisse Group, agreed to pay $1.25 billion over three years to settle all claims against the banks, the Swiss government, and the Swiss National Bank.

Switzerland's first woman president— Ruth Dreifuss—was elected by the federal parliament in December 1998. The country's presidency rotates among a seven-member Federal Council.

UBS AG, created in 1998 by the merger of Union Bank of Switzerland and Swiss Bank Corporation, suffered an early setback. The bank lost $700 million on its investment in Long Term Capital Management Ltd., a U.S. investment fund that nearly failed because of turmoil in global financial markets in September. The chairman of UBS, Mathis Cabiallavetta, and three other executives took responsibility for the loss and resigned.

Switzerland's economy enjoyed a modest recovery in 1998 as a result of low interest rates and improved business and consumer confidence. However, a strong Swiss franc slowed growth. International investment flowed into the franc during 1998 because of concerns about the performance of the euro, the single currency to be launched by 11 European Union countries in 1999, and because of the weakness of the U.S. dollar. Economists forecast that the Swiss economy would grow by 1.5 percent in 1998, a welcome change from the country's 1990 fall into recession. Unemployment fell below 5 percent.

□ Tom Buerkle

See also **Europe** (Facts in brief table); **Europe** Special Report: **European Union.**

Syria.

Syrian President Hafiz al-Assad took several steps in 1998 to reduce his country's international isolation. In July, Assad traveled to France, which, with Egypt, had announced its support in May for an international summit on the Arab-Israeli peace process as a means of pressuring Israel into making concessions in negotiations, which had been stalled since early 1997. The trip was Assad's first visit to France in 22 years. The United States opposed the summit despite Syrian Foreign Minister Farouk al-Sharaa's warning in January 1998 that the stalemated peace talks would damage U.S. relations with Arab states. Increasingly in 1998, Arab countries accused the United States of bias toward Israel. U.S.-sponsored talks between Israeli and Palestinian officials in October finally led to a break in the stalemate.

Other international outreach. In March, Syria's health minister led a delegation bearing humanitarian aid to Iraq. He was the first Syrian minister to visit Iraq in 20 years. In July, Syria announced it would reopen the Iraqi-Syrian oil pipeline, which it had closed when the Iran-Iraq war began in 1980. Also in July 1998, Syria allowed British naval vessels to dock in a Syrian port for the first time in 48 years.

Economic woes. Economic analysts predicted that Syria's *gross domestic product* (the value of all goods and services produced in a country in a given year) would grow only 3 percent in 1998, down from a high of 6.7 percent in 1993.

Crude-oil production, which accounted for more than 50 percent of Syria's export earnings, dropped from 600,000 barrels per day in 1996 to 560,000 barrels per day in 1998. The decline in production, coupled with depressed oil prices, which fell to a 10-year low in 1998, severely cut Syria's revenues. Energy industry analysts predicted that unless Syria discovers new oil reserves, its oil production might cease by 2010.

Domestic politics. In February 1998, Assad announced the dismissal of his brother Rifaat from the post of vice president for national security affairs. Rifaat, who many observers once thought might succeed Assad, had seen his power steadily erode in recent years. In July, Assad released more than 225 political prisoners. At least 500 political prisoners reportedly remained in jail.

Death of a poet. Thousands of Syrians attended the funeral of Nizar Kabani, the Arab world's most renowned, modern love poet, in the Syrian city of Damascus on May 4. Kabani died in London on April 30 at age 75. His 1954 collection of poems, *Childhood of a Breast,* dispensed with the conservative traditions of Arab verse.

□ Christine Helms

See also **Israel; Lebanon; Middle East** (Facts in brief table); **Turkey.**

Taiwan. The financial crisis that devastated many Asian countries in 1998 failed to drag down Taiwan's resilient economy. Taiwan's economic growth increased by approximately 5 percent, while other countries in the region sank into recession. Taiwan's ability to maintain a solid economy led one economist to call the island nation "the model of Asian capitalism."

According to economists, Taiwan kept its economy buoyant by limiting subsidies to failing businesses, regulating banks, and maintaining low foreign debt. It also welcomed businesses that produced high-tech products, such as computer parts, which helped its export trade.

Since the early 1990's, the structure of Taiwan's exports changed dramatically. In 1990, according to the finance ministry, electronics and other high-tech products accounted for only 2.5 percent of manufacturing. In 1997, about 37.5 percent of the total value of Taiwan's manufacturing came from these products.

In 1998, the gloomy regional economy weakened Taiwan's trade to neighboring countries. As a result, exports declined by about 8 percent.

Talks with China. In October, a senior member of Taiwan's ruling Kuomintang (KMT) Party, Koo Chen-fu, met China's President Jiang Zemin to discuss reunification of China and Taiwan. The leaders, however, failed to resolve the issue,

Supporters of Taiwanese independence march in June 1998 through the capital, Taipei, with banners reading "Resolutely Defend Taiwan" in response to a veiled Chinese threat to attack if Taiwan refused to agree to reunify with the mainland.

though Jiang did promise Taiwan some autonomy. The island had separated from China in 1949, but China still regarded Taiwan as its province.

Tensions escalated between Taiwan and China in June 1998, when U.S. President Bill Clinton said that he did not support Taiwanese independence. In July, China reiterated a long-standing threat to attack Taiwan if it declared formal independence. The Taiwanese government responded by releasing results of a poll that showed only 18 percent of its citizens supported reunification.

Elections. The ruling KMT, which was committed to eventual reunification with China, reasserted itself across much of Taiwan in December 5 elections. KMT challenger Ma Ying-jeou unseated Chen Shui-bian, a member of the Democratic Progressive Party (DPP), as mayor of Taipei. In elections for the national legislature, which included 225 representatives, the KMT won a commanding 124 seats.

The elections were a major setback for the DPP, which cautiously advocated independence from China. Many observers said the elections served as a referendum on whether citizens wanted to risk seeking independence from China.

□ Henry S. Bradsher

See also **Asia** (Facts in brief table); **China; Economics** Special Report: **Asian Economic Crisis.**

Tajikistan. The government of Emomali Rahmonov and the United Tajik Opposition (UTO), led by Said Abdullah Nuri, struggled during 1998 to keep the 1997 peace accord—ending five years of civil war—from unraveling. In January 1998, the UTO withdrew from the National Reconciliation Commission, which Nuri chaired, to protest Rahmonov's reluctance to implement provisions of the peace pact. The UTO returned in February, after Rahmonov began to appoint UTO members to senior cabinet posts.

Ongoing violence underscored the government's uncertain control in Tajikistan. Muslim rebels took more than 100 government police and soldiers hostage in central Tajikistan in late March and held them for more than a week. In July, four members of a United Nations observer mission were murdered. In August, rebels opposed to the peace process killed five people in the western city of Tursunzade, including the mayor. The violence peaked in November, when some 1,000 rebels led by Mahmoud Khodabardiyev, a former Tajik army general opposed to the 1997 peace accord, staged a revolt in the northern province of Leninabad. An estimated 120 rebels and 100 government troops were killed during the six-day revolt.   □ Steven L. Solnick

See also **Asia** (Facts in brief table).

Tanzania. See Africa.

Taxation. The United States Congress joined with President Bill Clinton to reform the Internal Revenue Service (IRS) in 1998. The overhaul was an attempt to promote efficiency in the tax agency and make it more taxpayer-friendly. President Clinton signed the IRS makeover into law on July 22, following approval by the U.S. House of Representatives and the U.S. Senate.

The legislation created 74 new rights for taxpayers, such as easing penalties and interest payments and shifting the burden of proof from the taxpayer to the IRS on disputes that go to court. The law also placed restrictions on some IRS collection methods; made it more difficult for the federal government to seize a person's property; required the IRS to explain to taxpayers why it had denied a refund and to provide the phone number of the agency employee handling the case; and reduced from 18 months to 12 months the time period in which investments must be held to qualify for the minimum tax rate on *capital gains* (profit on the sale of assets).

In addition, the legislation created a nine-member board to supervise the IRS. Members include six private citizens, the secretary of the treasury, the IRS commissioner, and an IRS employee representative.

The changes were expected to reduce federal revenues by approximately $12.9 billion by 2008. Senate Finance Committee hearings in 1997 on the abuse and harassment of some taxpayers by the IRS paved the way for swift passage of the legislation. Defenders of the IRS argued that the hearings had presented isolated cases of abuse.

Tax cut. The House on Sept. 26, 1998, approved an $80-billion tax reduction bill, despite the fact that the measure had little chance of passage in the Senate. The House bill would have provided tax relief for married couples, self-employed persons, small business owners, and farmers. The $80-billion tax cut stalled in the Senate and was never presented for debate.

President Clinton argued that the tax cut would reduce the projected $1.6-trillion budget surplus through 2008. He asked that the surplus be set aside until Congress adopts a plan to prevent the social security system from running out of money in the early 2000's.

Tax code. The House on June 17, 1998, voted to abolish the entire federal tax system by 2002 and replace it with a new, simpler code. Many experts viewed the vote as a symbolic gesture, since the legislation did not specify how the tax code should be rewritten to replace revenue generated by the U.S. income tax and other federal taxes. It also did not specify what would happen if Congress failed to enact a new tax code in time.

□ William J. Eaton

Telecommunications. The three-year trend toward the merging of long-distance and local-service telephone companies in the United States continued through 1998. The Telecommunications Reform Act of 1996 had been legislated to boost competition in both local and long-distance service. Instead, the act—and a booming stock market—encouraged some of the biggest corporate marriages in U.S. history and little new competition. As a result, some lawmakers and government regulators began to question whether such mergers warranted greater scrutiny.

Merger momentum. The first big merger after the passage of the Telecommunications Act involved the purchase of the long-distance company MCI Communications Corp. of Washington, D.C., by a Jackson, Mississippi-based telecommunications company, WorldCom Inc. The $37-billion merger, announced in October 1997, was approved by the Federal Communications Commission (FCC) in September 1998. The combined MCI WorldCom Inc. ranked as one of the world's largest telecommunications companies.

In May, SBC Communications Inc., the major local-service telephone company in seven western states, agreed to purchase Ameritech Corp. for $56.18 billion in a stock swap. Ameritech was the dominant local-service provider in five Midwestern states. If approved by the FCC, the enlarged SBC would be the largest U.S. local-service provider, controlling about one-third of the country's 178 million local access lines, including half of all business lines.

Bell goes long distance. One-third of all local access lines would fall under the control of a single company if a proposed $52.8-billion merger announced on July 28 between Bell Atlantic Corp. of New York City and GTE Corp. of Stamford, Connecticut, won FCC approval. In 1998, Bell Atlantic was the largest U.S. local-service provider. GTE, which controlled 21 million local lines in 28 states, had 2.2 million long-distance customers. In addition to creating the second-largest U.S. telephone company, the merger would give Bell Atlantic, a "Baby Bell" created at the 1984 breakup of the American Telephone and Telegraph Company, entry into the long-distance business.

AT&T goes local. A proposed merger between long-distance giant AT&T Corp. and cable giant Tele-Communications Inc. (TCI) of Englewood, Colorado, announced in June 1998, provided the first major evidence of the technology convergence promoted by the Telecommunications Act. Technology convergence describes the process by which telephone companies and cable operators cross over into one another's business. Both AT&T and TCI ranked first in their industries in number of subscribers.

If approved by federal regulators, the $37.3-billion deal would give AT&T the ability to offer local as well as long-distance service to TCI's 13.5 million subscribers. In the process, AT&T would be able to avoid paying substantial access fees to local-service providers, which own the lines used by long-distance carriers. Using TCI's cable transmission lines, AT&T could also offer high-speed access to the Internet, which cable and telephone companies view as a fast-growing and profitable enterprise.

Telecommunications Act reconsidered. The failure of the Telecommunications Act to stimulate competition for local telephone or cable service forced the U.S. Congress and the FCC to reconsider the act. After congressional hearings on the telecommunications industry in September, some lawmakers called on the FCC to withhold approval of the Ameritech-SBC and the Bell Atlantic-GTE mergers until the FCC had established means of enforcing the companies' promises to compete for local-service customers in areas dominated by other providers. The Telecommunications Act banned a local-service provider from entering the long-distance market until other local-service providers were free to compete in the areas it dominated.

☐ Tim Jones

See also **Internet; Radio; Television.**

Television networks in 1998 attempted to hold their share of the dwindling U.S. television audience by spending vast sums of money to retain control of popular programs. In January, the National Broadcasting Company (NBC) agreed to pay Warner Brothers, the company that created the series "E.R.," a record $13 million per episode over the next three years to keep the hospital-based drama from moving to another network. The fee surpassed the prior cost of $2 million per "E.R." episode.

Other networks poured money into sports programming. The American Broadcasting Companies (ABC) agreed on January 13 to pay the National Football League (NFL) $550 million a year as part of an eight-year deal to retain "Monday Night Football." CBS Inc. agreed on January 12 to pay the NFL $500 million per year for eight years for the rights for Sunday afternoon American Football Conference games. On January 13, cable network ESPN signed an eight-year contract to pay $600 million a year for exclusive cable rights to air Sunday night NFL games.

Winter Olympics. The television ratings for the XVIII Winter Olympics, in Nagano, Japan, were the lowest for any Olympic competition since the 1968 games in Grenoble, France. Only 16 percent of U.S. households with television sets watched the Nagano games, which were broad-

"Frasier," starring (left to right) Kelsey Grammer, John Mahoney, Jane Leeves, David Hyde Pierce, and Peri Gilpin, on Sept. 13, 1998, won its fifth consecutive Emmy Award for outstanding comedy series.

cast on CBS between Feb. 7 and Feb. 22, 1998.

The network blamed the low ratings on several factors, including snowstorm-caused delays and the poor performance of American teams. Viewers were more frustrated by having to watch taped versions of major events caused by a 14-hour time difference between Nagano, Japan, and the United States. As a result, most people learned the outcome of events from news sources and did not tune in to the competition.

News magazines. The number of nights featuring newsmagazine shows, whose low production costs made them highly profitable programs for networks, continued to increase in 1998. NBC aired "Dateline" five times a week, while ABC showed its news program "20/20" three times a week. In July, CBS announced plans to add another edition of "60 Minutes," called "60 Minutes II," to its 1999 lineup.

In June 1998, Cable News Network (CNN) launched "NewsStand," produced in conjunction with *Time* magazine. The production ran into difficulties with its first show when an investigative report alleged that the United States military used nerve gas to kill suspected American deserters in Laos in 1970. The story was later proven to be untrue, and both CNN and *Time* retracted the story and apologized to the public. CNN also dismissed staff members responsible for the report.

Comedic farewells. Several successful *sit-coms* (situation comedies) ended their runs in

Emmy Award winners in 1998

Comedy

Best Series: "Frasier"
Lead Actress: Helen Hunt, "Mad About You"
Lead Actor: Kelsey Grammer, "Frasier"
Supporting Actress: Lisa Kudrow, "Friends"
Supporting Actor: David Hyde Pierce, "Frasier"

Drama

Best Series: "The Practice"
Lead Actress: Christine Lahti, "Chicago Hope"
Lead Actor: Andre Braugher, "Homicide: Life on the Street"
Supporting Actress: Camryn Manheim, "The Practice"
Supporting Actor: Gordon Clapp, "N.Y.P.D. Blue"

Other awards

Drama or Comedy Miniseries or Special:
From the Earth to the Moon
Variety, Music, or Comedy Series: "Late Show with David Letterman"
Made for Television Movie: *Don King: Only in America*
Lead Actress in a Miniseries or Special:
Ellen Barkin, *Before Women Had Wings*
Lead Actor in a Miniseries or Special:
Gary Sinise, *George Wallace*
Supporting Actress in a Miniseries or Special:
Mare Winningham, *George Wallace*
Supporting Actor in a Miniseries or Special:
George C. Scott, *12 Angry Men*

1998. Media attention was focused on the final episode of "Seinfeld," which was broadcast on May 14, when NBC turned the nine-year-old show's departure into a major event. An estimated 76 million viewers watched the finale of the series starring Jerry Seinfeld. The final episode, which was preceded by a retrospective of past shows, was the third-most-watched such episode in television history. In an unusual move, NBC rebroadcast the episode and retrospective a week later.

The critically acclaimed series "The Larry Sanders Show," comedian Garry Shandling's satiric backstage look at a talk show, ended its six-year run on Home Box Office (HBO), a cable station, in May 1998. In September, Shandling and Peter Tolan won an Emmy Award for best writers in a comedy series for the show.

Two often-controversial series also departed the airwaves in 1998. In April, ABC announced that it had canceled "Ellen" after five years. "Ellen" was the subject of national debate in 1997 when its main character, Ellen, and the actress playing her, Ellen DeGeneres, "came out" as a homosexual. The CBS comedy "Murphy Brown," starring Candice Bergen, ended its 10-year run in May.

Lackluster debuts. The 1998 fall line-up contained few runaway hits, with most of the excite-

Top-rated U.S. television series

The following were among the most-watched television series for the 1997-1998 regular season, which ran from Sept. 22, 1997, to May 20, 1998.

1. "Seinfeld" (NBC)
2. "E.R." (NBC)
3. "Veronica's Closet" (NBC)
4. "Friends" (NBC)
5. "NFL Monday Night Football" (ABC)
6. "Touched by an Angel" (CBS)
7. "60 Minutes" (CBS)
8. "Union Square" (NBC)
9. "CBS Sunday Night Movie" (CBS)
10. (tie) "Frasier" (NBC)
    "Home Improvement" (ABC)
    "Just Shoot Me" (NBC)
13. "Dateline NBC (Tuesday)" (NBC)
14. "Dateline NBC (Monday)" (NBC)
15. (tie) "Drew Carey Show" (ABC)
    "Fox NFL Sunday Post Game" (FOX)
17. "20/20 (Friday)" (ABC)
18. (tie) "N.Y.P.D. Blue" (ABC)
    "Prime Time Live" (ABC)
    "The X-Files" (FOX)
21. "Law and Order" (NBC)
22. "20/20 (Monday)" (ABC)
23. "Diagnosis Murder" (CBS)
24. "Mad About You" (NBC)
25. "Cosby" (CBS)

"The Practice," featuring (left to right) Dylan McDermott, Kelli Williams, Steve Harris, Camryn Manheim, Michael Badalucco, Lara Flynn Boyle, and Lisa Gay Hamilton, captured an Emmy Award for outstanding drama series in 1998.

ment generated by "Felicity," a program airing on Time Warner's WB network. "Felicity" focused on the love life of a college freshman.

The program garnered media attention in October when it was revealed that Riley Weston, a 32-year-old woman, had claimed to be 19 years old when she secured a job as a staff writer on the show. Weston denied any purposeful deception and argued that many actresses lied in Hollywood about their age in order to land roles.

Despite the controversy, "Felicity" remained a hit with viewers and critics. Many critics viewed the show as being on a par with another WB success, "Dawson's Creek," a drama about the lives of a group of small-town teen-agers.

Another highly acclaimed newcomer was ABC's "Sports Night," which blended comedy and drama in a behind-the-scenes look at a sports TV show. Two NBC comedies, "Will and Grace" and "Jesse," also received positive reviews from critics and audiences.

Among dramatic series, "L.A. Doctors" depicted physicians in private practice, trying to maintain their medical ideals amidst demanding patients. "Martial Law" was a cops-and-robbers action show with a twist. The hero was a paunchy Chinese detective barely conversant in English. Both series aired on CBS.

The revival of series from the 1970's, with new casts and slightly updated concepts, became something of a trend in 1998. The United Paramount Network (UPN) offered viewers "Love Boat: The Next Wave," starring Robert Urich as the captain of a cruise ship. ABC revived "Fantasy Island," one of its hits from the 1970's. The new version starred Malcolm McDowell as the mysterious Mr. Roarke, host of a tropical island where visitors' dreams are fulfilled.

Top daytime serial. The CBS daytime drama "The Young and the Restless" made television history on July 30, 1998, when it marked its 500th week as the top-rated daytime serial. The program, which focused on the lives and loves of the residents of fictional Genoa City, had first gained the top spot on Dec. 26, 1988.

Children's programming. "Teletubbies," a British import, made its American debut on Public Broadcasting System (PBS) stations in April 1998. The series, which featured four plump and colorful live-action characters who engaged in simple adventures, used the constant repetition of words and actions to build language skills in children. Critics of the program complained that the target audience, which ranged from 1 year olds up, was too young. The program, however, still proved to be successful with children.

A long-established PBS children's television show celebrated its 30th anniversary in 1998. "Mister Rogers' Neighborhood," starring Fred

Rogers, was first aired in February 1968.

Successful miniseries in 1998 included documentaries that focused on historical events. Actor Tom Hanks was host and executive producer of *From the Earth to the Moon*, a 12-part docudrama about the National Aeronautics and Space Administration (NASA) space program of the 1960's and 1970's. *From the Earth to the Moon* first aired on cable's HBO beginning in April 1998. Hanks also starred in and directed an episode of the docudrama. *From the Earth to the Moon* won the 1998 Emmy Award for best miniseries.

In September, CNN launched *Cold War*, a 24-part series that traced the history of the intense rivalry that existed between the United States and the former Soviet Union between 1945 and 1991. Actor Kenneth Branagh narrated the program, which featured previously unscreened newsreel footage from the era. Most critics considered the series to be of historical significance.

In October 1998, PBS focused audience attention on slavery in the United States from the 1600's through the Civil War (1861-1865) in the documentary *Africans in America*. Critics hailed the four-part program as a provocative and moving series. □ Troy Segal

See also **People in the news** (Seinfeld, Jerry).

Tennessee. See State government.

Tennis. Four women and four men won Grand Slam tennis titles in 1998. The year was characterized by stiffer competition in the women's professional tour, which created an upsurge of fan interest, while interest in men's tennis, particularly in the United States, continued to decline. Swiss teen-ager Martina Hingis again held the top ranking for women and topped the earnings list at $2.6 million. American Pete Sampras was again the top-ranked men's player, earning almost $4 million.

Women. Hingis began the season with a significant victory when she easily took the Australian Open on Jan. 31, 1998, in Melbourne for the second straight year. The youngest player ever to defend a Grand Slam title, Hingis, 17, required only 86 minutes to beat Conchita Martinez of Spain, 6-3, 6-3, in the women's singles finals. It was the fourth Grand Slam title of Hingis's career and made her the youngest player ever to hit $5 million in career earnings.

While Hingis won three Grand Slam titles in 1997, the Australian Open was her only title of 1998, as overall competition on the women's tour grew more intense. In the French Open semifinals on June 4, Hingis was ousted, 6-3, 6-2, by Monica Seles of the United States, who entered the tournament soon after the loss of her father, Karolj, to cancer. Seles's courageous bid for a fourth

French Open title failed, however, when she lost to Spain's Arantxa Sanchez Vicario, 7-6 (7-5), 0-6, 6-2, in the final.

The depth of talent on the women's tour was evident at the All England Tennis Championship at Wimbledon, England, on July 1, 1998, when Seles, Venus Williams, and Lindsay Davenport were eliminated by the unseeded Natasha Zvereva and Jana Novotna of the Czech Republic, and Nathalie Tauziat of France. Novotna beat Hingis in the semifinals, 6-4, 6-4, and went on to win her first Wimbledon title on July 4, defeating Tauziat, 6-4, 7-6.

Davenport, a power-hitting American, beat Hingis, 6-3, 7-5, to win the U.S. Open on September 12 in New York City. It was the first Grand Slam title for Davenport, the reigning U.S. Olympic champion, and the first U.S. Open victory by an American woman since Chris Evert in 1982. It was also Davenport's 20th victory in 21 matches since Wimbledon and her third in four 1998 finals match-ups against Hingis.

Men. Petr Korda of the Czech Republic won his first Grand Slam title at the age of 30 on Feb. 1, 1998, defeating ninth-seeded Marcelo Rios, 22, of Chile, in the Australian Open. Korda took the final, 6-2, 6-2, 6-2, to become the oldest Grand Slam champion since 1990.

For the second straight year, upsets prevailed at the French Open in Paris, where Korda and Andre Agassi were eliminated in the first round by qualifiers, and Sampras fell in the second round. The war of attrition ended on June 7, 1998, when Carlos Moya beat fellow Spaniard, Alex Corretja, 6-3, 7-5, 6-3, for the French Open title.

Once again, Sampras achieved his lone Grand Slam success at Wimbledon, where he won for the fifth time in six years on July 5, in a five-set match with two tie-breakers against Goran Ivanisevic of Croatia. Sampras's 6-7 (2-7), 7-6 (11-9), 6-4, 3-6, 6-2 victory brought him his 11th Grand Slam title and left him tied with Bjorn Borg and Rod Laver on the all-time Grand Slam win list, one place behind Roy Emerson's record 12 titles.

Sampras's grass court success, however, failed to carry over into the U.S. Open. Patrick Rafter of Australia, the defending champion, ousted Sampras in the semifinals, 6-7, 6-4, 2-6, 6-4, 6-3, after Sampras pulled his left quadriceps, which hurt his mobility. On September 13, Rafter won his second U.S. Open, with a 6-3, 3-6, 6-2, 6-0 victory over fellow Australian Mark Philippoussis.

Davis Cup. On Sept. 27, 1998, an unusually weak U.S. team was beaten by Italy, 4-1, in the semifinals in Milwaukee, Wisconsin, and Sweden ousted Spain, 4-1, in Stockholm. In the final match in December, Sweden defeated Italy to win its second straight Davis Cup title. □ Ron Reid

Pete Sampras of the United States was the top-ranked men's tennis player for the sixth consecutive year in 1998. His achievement broke the record held by Jimmy Connors, who captured the top ranking annually from 1974 to 1978.

Terrorism. While many people hoped that peace negotiations would resolve longstanding conflicts in the Middle East, Northern Ireland, and Spain, terrorist attacks by militant religious and nationalist groups continued in 1998. Unfortunately, negotiations themselves provoked terrorism, as groups used violence to disrupt the peace process.

Kenya and Tanzania. On Aug. 7, 1998, U.S. embassies in Nairobi, Kenya, and Dar es Salaam, Tanzania, were allegedly bombed by a militant Islamic group led by Osama bin Laden, an exiled Saudi Arabian . At least 224 people died and more than 5,000 others were injured. Bin Laden's organization, the World Islamic Front for *Jihad* (holy war) Against Jews and Crusaders, is opposed to American and Israeli interests everywhere.

The United States retaliated for the bombings on August 20 by launching at least 75 Tomahawk cruise missiles at a suspected World Islamic Front training camp in Afghanistan and at a pharmaceutical factory in Khartoum, Sudan. United States authorities believed that the factory, in which bin Laden had a financial interest, was a manufacturing site for chemical weapons. By the end of 1998, the United States had extradited and arrested several suspects in the embassy attacks.

Leaders of Northern Ireland, the Republic of Ireland, and Great Britain approved on April 10 the Belfast, or Good Friday, Agreement, which was drafted to end years of terrorist violence between militant Roman Catholic and Protestant groups. Former U.S. Senator George S. Mitchell mediated the talks leading to the agreement.

A splinter group from the Irish Republican Army (IRA), calling itself "The Real IRA," attempted to derail the peace process on August 15 by detonating a car bomb that killed 29 people and wounded more than 200 others in Omagh, Northern Ireland. The bombing and other regional violence shocked the public and strengthened support for peace. Two of the principal signers of the Good Friday Agreement, Protestant leader David Trimble and Roman Catholic leader John Hume, were awarded the Nobel Prize for Peace in October. Noting that many obstacles to peace remained, Trimble stated that he hoped the prize was not awarded prematurely.

Israel. In October, Israeli Prime Minister Benjamin Netanyahu and Palestine Liberation Organization (PLO) leader Yasir Arafat met for talks with U.S. President Bill Clinton in Maryland. After days of negotiations, they agreed that Israel would transfer some territory in the West Bank to the PLO in exchange for Palestinian commitments to curtail terrorist activity by militant Islamic organizations, such as Hamas.

On October 19, a Palestinian militant attempted to scuttle the negotiations by lobbing hand grenades at a bus terminal in Beersheba, Israel. More than 60 people suffered

Osama bin Laden, an exiled Saudi Arabian who is the alleged head of an Islamic terrorist group, addresses followers in Afghanistan in 1998. U.S. authorities accused bin Laden of masterminding the August bombings of U.S. embassies in Kenya and Tanzania, which killed at least 224 people.

injuries. On October 28, an Israeli soldier died as he and other soldiers stopped a Hamas suicide bomber from destroying an Israeli school bus in the Israeli-occupied area of Gaza. After two Palestinian suicide bombers injured more than 20 people in Jerusalem on November 6, the fate of the peace process in the Middle East was once again uncertain.

Other peace talks. The Basque Homeland and Liberty movement, a group that seeks an independent state for the Basque people of northern Spain, declared a cease-fire on September 17. In the last 30 years, the independence movement had led to the deaths of approximately 800 people in terrorist and counterterrorist attacks. In November, Spanish Prime Minister Jose Maria Aznar announced that the government would begin talks with the separatist group.

In Colombia, President Andres Pastrana agreed to hold peace talks with two Marxist guerrilla organizations, the Revolutionary Armed Forces of Colombia and the National Liberation Army. After Pastrana's announcement, both groups struck police stations and antinarcotics army bases to gain additional leverage before serious talks began.   □ Richard E. Rubenstein

See also **Colombia; Israel; Kenya; Northern Ireland; Spain; United States, Government of the.**

Texas. See Dallas; Houston; State government.

Thailand. After many years of rapid growth, Thailand's depressed economy staggered from crisis to crisis in 1998. The country experienced widespread unemployment and bankruptcies as economic growth plummeted and the government instituted austerity measures.

The Thai economy had crashed in 1997, after the government devalued its currency, the baht, in an attempt to shore up the country's faltering economy. The move caused foreign investors to lose confidence in the country and made it harder for the government to repay loans and borrow from abroad. The devaluation also triggered a financial crisis throughout Asia.

Thailand's economy fell approximately 8 percent in 1998, and the Thai stock market dropped to 10 percent of its 1995 value. The baht remained weak in 1998 against foreign currencies. In January, the baht dropped 50 percent against the U.S. dollar, a record decline.

Financial reforms. In May, Chaiyawat Wibulswasdi, the chief of Thailand's central bank, resigned after a government panel linked him to mistakes that had led to the plunge in the baht. The panel criticized the central bank for losing billions of dollars in loans to debt-ridden finance companies.

The Thai government approved a $1.2-billion spending plan in June to stimulate the economy,

and in August, it approved a rescue program for its financial system. Under the plan, devised in conjunction with the International Monetary Fund, a United Nations affiliate that provides short-term credit to member nations, the government gained control of half of the nation's 16 commercial banks. The package allowed banks to dispose of bad loans.

Unemployment in Thailand rose as many businesses closed. The National Statistics Office estimated in mid-1998 that 2.8 million people—or 8.8 percent of the work force—were without work. In mid-1997, only 1.2 million people were unemployed. Many of the unemployed were people who had left rural regions of Thailand to seek jobs in Bangkok, the capital and center of industrial activity.

Chuan Leekpai, who became prime minister in November 1997, added a seventh party to his coalition government in October 1998. The addition of the Chart Pattana party gave Chuan support from 257 of the 389 members of parliament.

New army commander. In September, Chuan appointed General Surayud Chulanont commander of the army. Surayud announced plans to reduce the army by 170,000 people.

□ Henry S. Bradsher

See also **Asia** (Facts in brief table); **Economics Special Report: Asian Economic Crisis.**

Theater. The 1997-1998 theater season was vibrant on both sides of the Atlantic. Broadway enjoyed its most financially successful year in history, with theaters bringing in more revenue to New York than all the city's sports teams combined. In London, three powerhouse nonprofit companies—the Royal Court, Almeida, and Donmar Warehouse—produced a number of hits that transferred to either the West End, London's commercial theater district, or Broadway.

A big year for women. The 1997-1998 season could have been named the "year of the woman" in American theater. Before 1998, not a single woman had won an Antoinette Perry (Tony) Award, Broadway's highest honor, for directing. In June, two women earned best-director Tonys—Julie Taymor for the blockbuster Walt Disney musical *The Lion King* and Garry Hynes, an Irish director, for the play *The Beauty Queen of Leenane*.

The 1998 Pulitzer Prize for drama also went to a woman—Paula Vogel for *How I Learned to Drive,* a bittersweet and disturbing story about adolescence and incest. After a highly acclaimed and extended off-Broadway run during the 1997-1998 season, *How I Learned to Drive* was set to become one of the most-performed plays in the 1998-1999 regional theater circuit around the United States. International productions of Vogel's play were also being planned.

Newcomers on Broadway. Perhaps the most significant event in the 1997-1998 theater season was the advent of the corporate theatrical producer, whose business power fueled the success of musicals such as Disney's *The Lion King* and *Ragtime*, produced by Livent Inc., based in Toronto, Canada. The influx of capital and energy spurred a strong year overall on Broadway, with more productions clamoring for theaters than there were spaces to accommodate them.

A renaissance in Irish culture also added vitality to New York and London theater. One of the most talked about plays of the year was *The Beauty Queen of Leenane,* a tightly plotted family thriller written by Martin McDonagh, a 27-year-old Londoner of Irish descent. *Beauty Queen,* one of a trilogy of plays set in the barren Connemara region of western Ireland, tells the story of a lonely woman whose manipulative mother interferes with the daughter's one chance at a happy relationship with a man—with tragic results. The play started its life at the tiny Druid Theatre in Galway, Ireland, in 1996. Its success led to runs in London, an off-Broadway theater, and then Broadway's Walter Kerr Theatre in 1998.

Other Irish offerings included McDonagh's *The Cripple of Inishmaan,* which received mixed reviews off-Broadway at the Public Theatre. The play examines the lives of Irish villagers during the filming of the 1934 documentary film *Man of Aran. St. Nicholas,* a one-man show written and directed by young Dubliner Conor McPherson, reveals the life of a troubled theater critic. The show's success at the off-Broadway Primary Stages paved the way for McPherson's expected Broadway debut in 1999 with *The Weir.* This moving drama set in an Irish country pub received high praise in its London and Dublin runs in 1997 and 1998.

Another big Tony winner in 1998 was also an import. The winner in the best play category was *Art,* a satire on the fine arts world by Parisian playwright Yasmina Reza. The play, translated by Christopher Hampton, came to New York via London's West End.

The Roundabout Theatre, a large nonprofit company in New York City, had an unusually successful—and unusually troubled—year in 1998. The Roundabout, which had built a strong reputation throughout the 1990's for its high-quality productions of classics and new plays, produced two high-profile, Tony Award-winning revivals—Arthur Miller's *A View from the Bridge* (1955) and the musical *Cabaret* (1966), which was presented in a renovated nightclub made to look like the 1930's Berlin cabaret where the show is set. Later in the year, the company scored another hit with *Side Man,* a sentimental drama by Warren Leight about a young man's memory of

his childhood with his traveling jazz-musician parents. The Roundabout moved the show from a small off-Broadway theater to the company's main stage in June, and the play transferred to a commercial Broadway theater in November.

During the summer of 1998, however, the Roundabout suffered two serious blows. On July 21, the collapse of an elevator tower at a construction site in midtown Manhattan temporarily closed three Roundabout productions. The company lost an estimated $1.7 million in ticket sales. In September, the theater's long-time and highly regarded artistic director, Todd Haimes, announced that he would become the artistic director of Livent Inc., which faced serious financial troubles in 1998. Haimes agreed to stay on at the Roundabout during the 1998-1999 season.

Controversial play. Another noteworthy event in 1998 was the furor over the premiere of Tony-winning playwright Terrence McNally's *Corpus Christi,* a retelling of the story of Jesus Christ with the main character and his disciples portrayed as gay men. Several conservative Christian organizations had criticized the play before it opened at the Manhattan Theatre Club (MTC). In May, after the MTC received threats of violence, the company canceled the production. A flurry of headline-making protests from liberal groups and individuals ensued. South African playwright Athol Fugard

---

Tony Award winners in 1998

Best Play, *Art* by Yasmina Reza
Best Musical, *The Lion King*
Best Play Revival, *A View from the Bridge*
Best Musical Revival, *Cabaret*
Leading Actor in a Play, Anthony LaPaglia, *A View from the Bridge*
Leading Actress in a Play, Marie Mullen, *The Beauty Queen of Leenane*
Leading Actor in a Musical, Alan Cumming, *Cabaret*
Leading Actress in a Musical, Natasha Richardson, *Cabaret*
Featured Actor in a Play, Tom Murphy, *The Beauty Queen of Leenane*
Featured Actress in a Play, Anna Manahan, *The Beauty Queen of Leenane*
Featured Actor in a Musical, Ron Rifkin, *Cabaret*
Featured Actress in a Musical, Audra McDonald, *Ragtime*
Direction of a Play, Garry Hynes, *The Beauty Queen of Leenane*
Direction of a Musical, Julie Taymor, *The Lion King*
Book of a Musical, Terrence McNally, *Ragtime*
Original Musical Score, Stephen Flaherty and Lynn Ahrens, *Ragtime*
Orchestration, William David Brohn, *Ragtime*
Scenic Design, Richard Hudson, *The Lion King*
Costume Design, Julie Taymor, *The Lion King*
Lighting Design, Donald Holder, *The Lion King*
Choreography, Garth Fagan, *The Lion King*
Regional Theater, Denver Center Theatre Company, Colorado

withdrew his latest play from the theater's production schedule because of the cancellation. MTC then reversed its decision and opened the play in October. Ironically, it received devastating reviews. Critics and audiences alike found the play less shocking than dull. Nonetheless, all the controversy ensured that the play's limited run was sold out.

Off-Broadway energy. A series of unexpected hit shows at off-Broadway theaters gave heartening proof that a youthful audience for theater existed. John Cameron Mitchell and Stephen Trask's *Hedwig and the Angry Inch* enjoyed a successful downtown run that played to young and enthusiastic audiences. The small-scale musical tells the story of a transsexual rock singer from Germany who finds herself trapped in a new life in the American Midwest.

Following a hit world premiere production off-Broadway, John C. Russell's *Stupid Kids,* which explored the psyches of American high school youth, was picked up for a commercial run by the established Shubert Organization in August. Perhaps most spectacular was *Villa Villa,* a combination of theater, carnival, and dance staged by the Argentine troupe De la Guarda. The show drew packed houses of nontraditional theatergoers to its hit off-Broadway run at the Daryl Roth Theater.

London calling. One of the biggest stories in British theater in 1998 was the success of three small theater companies in London. The Donmar Warehouse, the Almeida, and the Royal Court theaters enjoyed an influence over London and international stages that far outweighed their diminutive sizes. The three theaters had budgets of only $3.7 million, $2.57 million, and $3.9 million, respectively, in 1998. But thanks to their excellent reputations for artistic quality and adventurousness, they all attracted some big-name talent, including Liam Neeson, Kevin Spacey, Dame Diana Rigg, and Nicole Kidman.

All three companies produced shows that fed the West End theaters through the 1997-1998 season. Some shows, such as the Royal Court's world premiere of *The Weir,* transferred to the commercial district after opening on the company's own stage. Other shows, such as Almeida's production of David Hare's *The Judas Kiss,* opened directly in a commercial theater. *The Judas Kiss,* which featured Liam Neeson playing the role of Oscar Wilde, also transferred to Broadway in 1998. The success of the three theater companies contributed to a lively buzz in the West End, which earned a record $369.15 million in box-office revenues in 1998. □ Karen Fricker

See also **People in the news** (Taymore, Julie); **Theater** Special Report: **A New Broadway Takes Center Stage.**

Togo. See **Africa.**

Anna Manahan (left), Brian F. O'Byrne, and Marie Mullen play lonely people living in a desolate region of Ireland in Martin McDonagh's *The Beauty Queen of Leenane.* Manahan and Mullen won the 1998 Tony Awards for best featured actress and best leading actress, respectively.

A New Broadway Takes Center Stage

A new behind-the-scenes player on Broadway—the corporate producer—restores luster to New York City's theater industry and redefines the business of the stage.

By
Karen Fricker

Two musicals opened on Broadway during New York City's 1997-1998 theater season that quite possibly changed the face of American theater forever. It was not just that they were ambitious, high-quality productions that won rave reviews and dueled for the coveted Antoinette Perry (Tony) Award for best musical. It was not just that they were both huge audience hits that played to capacity crowds for eight performances a week. What was history-making about these musicals—*The Lion King* and *Ragtime*—was the business power behind them.

Both shows were produced by publicly owned companies—*The Lion King* by The Walt Disney Company of Burbank, California, and *Ragtime* by Livent Inc. of Toronto, Canada. And both musicals opened in historic Broadway theaters that the producers had renovated especially for their own productions. The most obvious influence of the corporate players on Broadway was their crucial role in improving the appearance of New York City's commercial theater district. The productions also revealed how the business of Broadway had changed over the century of its existence and how those changes might affect all aspects of Broadway theater in the future.

A typical week's offering of shows gives a general impression of the state of Broadway in 1998. During the week of June 15, the 28 productions included 4 long-running megamusicals, 10 new musicals, 6 new plays, 3 musical revivals, 4 revivals of plays, and a dance revue. The variety of productions represented one of the healthiest environments in commercial New York theater for several decades. After a creative slump in the late 1980's and early 1990's, Broadway was booming again, with more productions in need of performance spaces than there were theaters to go around. The reasons for this were many, including an influx of work from Great Britain and nonprofit theaters. But the theater community agreed that a significant reason for this boom was the entry of Disney and Livent on the Broadway scene.

The business of Broadway in the past

In order to understand the importance of these corporate producers on Broadway, it is necessary to look at how Broadway shows were produced in the past. Between about 1900 and 1930, some 80 theaters were built in a region of midtown Manhattan around the intersection of Broadway and Seventh Avenue. The productions that filled these new theaters were, for the first 60 or so years of Broadway's existence, the work of independent producers. The producer provided the business force behind any production and had enormous influence over its artistic outcome. The producer found or commissioned a new play or musical, hired the creative staff, rented the theater, hired the business personnel, supervised the rehearsal process and marketing, and saw the show through to opening night and beyond.

One of the producer's biggest jobs, of course, was raising money. In the early days of Broadway, the producer called on small-scale investors, commonly known as "angels" in the theater industry, to contribute money to cover production costs in exchange for a percentage of any profits. If a production was a particular success in New York City, the producer would launch a national tour. Touring, or "the road," was and continues to be a potentially enormous profit-maker.

This method of production led Broadway theater through its heyday, about 1943 to 1965. Well-known musicals from this era include *Oklahoma!* (1943), *Guys and Dolls* (1950), *My Fair Lady* (1956), *West Side Story* (1957), and *Gypsy* (1959). When the artists who fueled this golden age began to disappear from the scene, another power in American theater was on the rise—the off-Broadway and regional theater company. Off-Broadway the-

Opposite page:
Puppets created by director and designer Julie Taymor bring the wildlife of Africa to the Broadway stage in Walt Disney Company's 1997 production of *The Lion King.*

aters, those located outside the central commercial theater district of New York City, and regional theaters, those located throughout the United States, created a platform for innovative theater.

These groups could take risks with new works that were financially unfeasible on Broadway. Costs of Broadway productions skyrocketed after the 1950's, due to inflation, corruption, and the growing extravagance of Broadway productions. In 1925, a particularly expensive play might cost $25,000 to mount. In 1950, the average one-set play cost about $60,000 and the average musical more than $200,000. By the mid-1990's, the cost to mount a one-set play could run to $850,000. The budget for *The Lion King* topped $20 million.

Big business on Broadway

Rising costs eventually led to more profitable ways of doing business on Broadway. By the 1980's, the most important force in shaping the American theater scene was not American at all, but a string of megamusicals from Great Britain. Most of them were written by composer Andrew Lloyd Webber and produced by Cameron Mackintosh. Megamusicals can best be described as pop operas. The music is lush and romantic, and the shows feature dazzling sets and special effects.

The primary significance of megamusicals lay not in their artistic achievements but in the way they were produced. When the initial production of a show began making money—usually at a London theater—Mackintosh would use the revenue to mount identical versions of the show simultaneously around the world. A smart, easily recognized logo for each musical helped him market the shows internationally. These musicals were enormously popular with audiences worldwide and proved that theater productions could generate dependable, long-term revenue. They also demonstrated that, unlike many musical productions of the past, the producer did not have to rely on casting theater stars in leading roles in order to draw crowds. By 1998, Lloyd Webber's *Cats* (1981) had grossed an estimated $2 billion and *Phantom of the Opera* (1988) an estimated $2.7 billion.

The megamusical led to the demise of the independent American producer. One Broadway producer working with a few angels could not compete with the new business style and power created by Mackintosh or Lloyd Webber. Another reason for the demise of old-style independent producing was the rising importance of Broadway's theater owners as producers. Rather than simply renting their houses to independent producers, the owners were mounting their own productions. By the early 1990's, the "big-three" theater owners—the Shubert Organization, the Nederlander Organization, and Jujamcyn Theaters—were the dominant domestic Broadway theater producers.

In the 1990's, the British megamusical boom began to wane. *Phantom of the Opera* and *Cats* continued to play on Broadway and elsewhere in 1998, as did Mackintosh's productions of *Les Miserables* (1985) and *Miss Saigon* (1989), musicals by the French team of Alain Boublil and Claude-Michel Schonberg. But

The author:
Karen Fricker, an American theater critic living in Dublin, Ireland, writes about Irish theater for *Variety.* Formerly, she was director of publications at the Public Theater in New York City.

My Fair Lady

My Fair Lady, a musical adapted from the play *Pygmalion* by George Bernard Shaw, debuted on Broadway on March 15, 1956.

- **Producer:** Herman Levin
- **Cost to mount show:** $360,000
- **Star power on stage:** Rex Harrison, Stanley Holloway, and Julie Andrews (after opening night)
- **Venue:** Mark Hellinger Theater, a Broadway theater then owned by Nederlander Organization, a large theater management firm
- **Path to Broadway:** One week in New Haven, Connecticut, and four weeks in Philadelphia

Ragtime

Ragtime, a musical adapted from the E. L. Doctorow novel by the same title, debuted on Broadway on January 18, 1998.

- **Producer:** Livent Inc.
- **Cost to mount show:** $10,000,000
- **Star power on stage:** None
- **Venue:** Ford Center for the Performing Arts, a Broadway theater operated by Livent for its own productions
- **Path to Broadway:** More than 9 months with the future Broadway cast in Toronto, Canada, and more than 10 months with a separate cast in Los Angeles

Mackintosh had not produced a new show in New York City since the early 1990's, and Lloyd Webber's spectacular *Sunset Boulevard* (1993) closed in 1997 without earning back its initial investment. In the megamusical's place, a new producing power was on the rise.

Corporations debut on Broadway

The Walt Disney Company entered the theater arena in 1994 with a stage version of its animated film *Beauty and the Beast.* Although most theater experts agreed that the production was not particularly innovative—it was basically a literal staging of the film—it proved to be massively popular with audiences. In 1998, *Beauty and the Beast* was still playing on Broadway and in several cities worldwide. Its success convinced Disney to expand its theatrical operations, and to do so, the company decided to find a home base—its own Broadway theater.

My Fair Lady (1956) and *Ragtime* (1998) both achieved commercial success after they debuted on Broadway. A comparison of their histories demonstrates significant changes in the business of Broadway theater since the mid-1900's.

Livent Inc.'s Ford Center for the Performing Arts, *below and right,* the venue for the company's musical *Ragtime,* is one of several newly renovated theaters on New York City's 42nd Street.

Disney's search coincided with the long-awaited revitalization of 42nd Street, the thoroughfare that had been the heart of the Broadway theater district in the early part of the century. Since the 1950's, 42nd Street had been in decline. By the 1970's, most of the theaters were deserted, and the street had become a haven for vice and pornography. In 1990, the city and state governments of New York formed a nonprofit organization, The New 42nd Street Inc., to operate seven of the street's theaters and to bring life and respectability back to the area. The organization's first visible success came in 1995 when it reopened the Victory Theater as the New Victory, the city's only theater devoted exclusively to year-round programming for children.

In 1995, Disney signed a lease on the New Amsterdam Theater, one of the nonprofit organization's seven theaters. With a $28-million, low-interest loan from the city and state of New York, Disney spent $34 million to renovate the theater. The New Amsterdam reopened in late 1997 with the world premiere of *The Lion King.* Disney's presence on the block encouraged other producers to start up operations there as well. The Ford Center for the Performing Arts, Livent's New York home also leased from The New 42nd Street Inc., was actually two historic theaters gutted and rebuilt as a single theater with more than 1,800 seats. *Ragtime* inaugurated the Ford Center in January 1998.

The impact of big business

Beneath the surface of this new face on Broadway were a series of changes in the theater industry that had evolved since the 1960's. As production costs escalated, ticket prices also shot up. A ticket to a Broadway musical averaged $3 in 1925 and $10 in 1965. By 1996, the price of a ticket for a Broadway musical topped out at $75. In response to such trends, the selling of Broadway shows became a sophisticated business.

Before the 1970's, theater advertising and marketing was fairly predictable. Advertisements in the major newspapers and a few billboards around New York were all that was necessary to attract audiences. In the 1990's, however, Broadway producers devoted approximately 10 to 15 percent of any show's initial budget and more than 20 percent of its weekly running costs to marketing and advertising. Long before tickets go on sale, producers create an eagerness for a show through the selection of a memorable logo, local and national advertising, cast albums (often recorded before rehearsals even begin), and tie-ins with corporations (such as "official airline" schemes).

Stephen Sondheim: A Man Outside the System

Most theater critics agree that no artist since the golden age of the American musical has contributed more to the art form than Stephen Sondheim. His entry on the scene began favorably in 1957, when at age 27, he wrote the lyrics for *West Side Story.*

The first full-length musical for which he wrote music and lyrics was *A Funny Thing Happened on the Way to the Forum,* which won six Tony Awards in 1963. Since that time, Sondheim's work has won countless awards, including the 1985 Pulitzer Prize for drama for *Sunday in the Park with George.*

Sondheim is a constant experimenter who has refused to settle into any one form or subject matter. Critics and audiences have lauded him as one of the most brilliant lyricists of the American musical. His scores are noted for integrating songs into the storytelling and character development.

Because of his uncompromising standards and roving imagination, however, Sondheim has never found a secure place in the Broadway system, particularly since the 1980's with rising production costs and audience expectations for spectacle. Sondheim's *Sunday in the Park, Into the Woods* (1987), and *Passion* (1994) all had award-winning Broadway runs, but closed before making a profit. *Assassins* (1991) opened off-Broadway but was never transferred to Broadway.

With the rise of corporate producers in the 1990's, original and challenging shows, such as Sondheim's, were likely to face an even more uncertain future.

■ Karen Fricker

The producers of the British musical hits of the 1980's used memorable logos, *below,* to market their productions around the world. The popular and commercially successful shows, often called megamusicals, changed the business practices of the theater industry. Once a musical proved to be successful, the producers mounted simultaneous productions of the show in other cities. The familiar logo helped generate interest in a musical before each new opening.

Merchandising—the sale of associated products such as T-shirts, posters, and CD's—also became an important part of theater marketing and a significant source of revenue. The New Amsterdam, for example, is connected to a huge Disney Store, through which the audience exits the theater after every performance of *The Lion King.* Livent, too, built a large retail area in the lobby of the Ford Center to sell its merchandise.

The high production costs have also influenced what kinds of shows appear on Broadway. Since new material presents a major financial risk, producers have frequently turned to tried-and-true products—successful musicals and plays from the past—that are likely to draw crowds. Revivals of classic musicals have always been an important part of the Broadway environment, but a new, commercially successful trend developed in the 1990's.

In the past, revivals had been fueled primarily by nostalgia and brought little originality to the former box-office hits. But the musical revivals of recent years—dubbed "revisals"—were often praised by critics for blowing the dust off the original products and helping audiences see them anew. The first major example of this trend was a 1994 revival by the Royal National Theatre in London of *Carousel,* the 1945 musical by Richard Rodgers and Oscar Hammerstein II. Director Nicholas Hytner, who also directed *Miss Saigon,* and designer Bob Crowley approached the material seriously and without sentimentality, revealing ground-breaking, timely, and even disturbing themes that had not been explored in past productions. The show eventually transferred to Broadway, where it won five Tony Awards in 1995, and toured the United States. Other successful revivals included a concert-style version of the 1975 musical *Chicago* and a 1997 production of the 1966 musical *Cabaret.*

New paths to Broadway

The high price tags and financial risks of commercial theater have also resulted in a variety of paths that productions, particularly musicals, take before landing on a Broadway stage. In the past, the producing history of every Broadway musical was pretty much the same. The artistic team developed the show in New York City, the producer launched a brief tryout tour in one or two East Coast cities, and then the production opened in a Broadway theater. Over the years, that path diversified enormously. By the 1990's, there were almost as many routes to Broadway as there were musicals that opened there.

Some productions continued to have a brief one-city, out-of-town tryout before opening in New York. Other commercial productions opened directly on Broadway, since the expense of a tryout could be a greater risk than opening to demanding New York audiences and critics. Increasingly, however, producers such as Livent started up and ran more than one company of the same musical at approximately the same time before moving to New York, thus maximizing the profit potential for the producer. *Ragtime,* for example, began a long run in Toronto in December 1996. Before it closed, another company opened in Los Angeles in June 1997 and ran for almost a year. It was not until January 1998 that the original Toronto cast opened on Broadway. Therefore, regardless of the critical or financial success of the show on Broadway, the producer enjoyed long, successful out-of-town runs.

Also during the 1990's, commercial and nonprofit producers of musicals developed closer relationships, ushering in another path to Broadway. At first this relationship was simple. Essentially, the nonprofit theaters took the artistic and financial risks, and the commercial producers "shopped" for promising shows that could be transferred to Broadway theaters for profitable runs.

Commercial producers also began looking for other ways to help start up shows at nonprofit theaters, which are experienced at developing new, innovative projects. In some cases, the producers funded a certain theater or a particular play or musical that could lead to commercial success. In others, the producer essentially handed over one of its own promising projects to the nonprofit theater company, allowing them to develop a show that the commercial producer hoped to eventually take to Broadway. This was the scenario behind Disney's *Elaborate Lives,* a pop musical version of Guiseppe Verdi's opera *Aida* that opened in October 1998 at the Alliance Theatre in Atlanta, Georgia.

Corporate producers and creative risks

The various changes in the production of Broadway shows clearly revitalized the commercial theater scene in New York City by the end of the 1990's. But the changes also raised concerns about how the new production methods would affect the quality and type of productions themselves. New plays, in particular, have become an endangered species on Broadway, because producers rarely take chances on a new play unless it has a star name attached to it.

For musicals, however, the future seemed more hopeful in 1998. Although *Beauty and the Beast* was of questionable artistic quality, *The Lion King* represented a major creative leap for Disney. The company's risky choice of Julie Taymor as director and designer paid off. Taymor, an industry veteran known for her experimental work, used elaborate costumes, puppets, and stagecraft to bring the animal kingdom to life on stage. Critics and audiences alike welcomed the musical as one of the most visually inventive

Broadway productions in history. It won the 1998 Tony Award for best musical, and Taymor won for best director. Livent, as well, continued to show a commitment to producing original work. *Ragtime,* a new musical based on E. L. Doctorow's novel about America in the early 1900's, earned rave reviews and four Tony Awards, including best book of a musical.

Both Disney and Livent, then, had become creative producers, corporate versions of the independent producers of yesteryear. They had indicated that they were committed to high-quality and ambitious musical theater, and they had given work to numerous talented theater professionals. All of this seemed to be good news for the industry, but there were some signs that the corporate presence on Broadway might also have some drawbacks.

Hollywood in New York City

Disney's theatrical producing style is heavily influenced by the way the company produces films and, therefore, involves elements that are new to Broadway. First, Disney is less interested in the bottom line of each individual production than on the overall revenue that its theater productions can eventually generate. That is, it does not matter to Disney if the Broadway productions of *Beauty and the Beast* and *The Lion King* ever make a profit (and they are unlikely to do so), because the company stands to make an overall profit on the related merchandise and future American and foreign productions.

The way that Disney hires personnel is equally film-influenced. Rather than giving artists—such as directors, writers, and designers—a fee and a cut of the potential profits of the production, as is the norm in theater, Disney pays its artists in installments throughout the creative process. The company does not share its

Imaginative sets by Bob Crowley helped bring new life to the critically acclaimed 1994 revival of *Carousel,* the 1945 musical by Richard Rodgers and Oscar Hammerstein II. Revivals that offer new interpretations of old Broadway favorites offer commercial theater producers fewer financial risks than new shows.

profits. Thus, the people who have put their creative work into the production do not share in the show's ownership.

By the end of 1998, it was still too early to know whether Livent would handle its finances similarly. In mid-1998, after reporting a loss of some $30.8 million dollars in 1997, Livent suspended its chairman, Garth Drabinsky. The company replaced him with Michael Ovitz, a former Hollywood talent agent and former Disney president. Since Ovitz had no experience in theater, the industry viewed his appointment with some reservations and expected his Hollywood background to influence the financial practices of Livent.

In November 1998, Livent filed for bankruptcy protection, a step that would allow the company to withhold payments to creditors while it refinanced its debts. The company also formally dismissed Drabinsky, amid accusations that he and a business partner had manipulated financial statements to hide what company executives considered extravagant spending on recent productions. In spite of the financial turmoil, Livent intended to keep most current productions running.

Jonathan Larson's rock opera *Rent,* which won the 1996 Tony award for best musical, was a surprise off-Broadway hit that made a successful transfer to Broadway. Many people in the theater industry question whether large corporate producers will inhibit such creativity in commercial theater.

Broadway in the next century

Regardless of the future of Livent, its influence on Broadway in 1998, along with that of Disney, was expected to have far reaching effects on the commercial theater scene into the next century. Concerns focused on their impact on the creativity of Broadway theater. One of the hallmarks of a healthy artistic environment is variety, and the more that large corporations expand their theatrical operations, the more the New York theater industry will shrink to a small number of producers who can compete with their corporate might.

A comparison of two recent theater seasons—the one dominated by Disney and Livent in 1997-1998 and the 1995-1996 season—revealed the delicate balance in which Broadway found itself as it approached the year 2000. The Tony Award nominations in 1996 were dominated by the noisy rock-and-roll musicals *Rent* (1996) and *Bring in 'Da Noise, Bring in 'Da Funk* (1995), both of which began as off-Broadway productions. These shows received high praise from the critics and attracted fresh, young audiences to the theater. Also, the productions—at least initially—were not driven by the promises of commercial success, but by the artistic aspirations of artists who were hardly household names such as Walt Disney. At the close of the 1998 season, many members of the theater community questioned whether the corporate domination would allow room for the innovation, artistic risks, and undiscovered talents that remain essential to American theater.

Toronto. On Jan. 2, 1998, the new unified City of Toronto was born. Court challenges, opposition in Ontario's provincial legislature, and vehement citizen protests had failed to halt the creation of Canada's most populous city.

New Toronto, popularly known as Megacity, encompassed the six municipalities of what had been Metropolitan Toronto—Toronto, Scarborough, York, Etobicoke, North York, and East York—with a combined population of 2.4 million. The unification of Metro Toronto, approved by the provincial legislature in April 1997, was a major element in a massive restructuring of government financing and services in Ontario undertaken in 1997 by Premier Mike Harris and his Progressive Conservative Party government. According to Harris, the consolidation of Metro Toronto would slash government spending and streamline the delivery of public services.

A new 56-member Toronto City Council replaced Metro Toronto's six city councils and the regionwide Metropolitan Council. Many of the new councilors, elected in November 1997, were members of Metro Toronto's defunct city councils and had opposed the creation of Megacity. In the election, voters chose Mel Lastman, mayor of North York since 1972, as new Toronto's first mayor. Lastman and the new councilors—elected to three-year terms—were sworn in on Jan. 2, 1998. In his inaugural speech, Lastman promised to create jobs, provide affordable rental housing, and develop a strategy for helping the homeless.

Getting to work. Although the council was predominantly conservative, Lastman appointed leftist New Democrats (social democrats) to several key administrative positions, including the chair of the powerful Toronto Transit Commission and the new post of Children's Advocate. By April, the council had passed new Toronto's first budget, a $5.9-billion plan. The councilors supported Lastman's pledge not to raise taxes.

Education. In return for shifting provincial responsibilities to municipalities, the Harris government took greater control of regulating and funding education. Toronto's six public school boards were combined into one citywide body, and the number of locally elected school boards in Ontario was reduced from 129 to 72. The local boards also lost the right to levy taxes.

Property taxes. In July, the City Council voted to phase in the provincial government's controversial new property tax system based on "current value assessment." Under the old system, many properties in Toronto had not been *reassessed* (reevaluated for their tax value) since the 1950's. Under the new system, many property owners, particularly owners of small businesses, faced huge property tax increases or large decreases. The City Council decided to cap changes to commercial taxes at 2.5 percent for three years and to phase in changes to the residential property tax over five years.

Festivities. On June 8, 1998, Mayor Lastman and his wife, Marilyn, held a Ball for the Arts to raise $500,000 for the Toronto Arts Council Foundation, a funding organization for local artists and art organizations. As part of his continuing efforts to bring together diverse communities in the new city, Lastman rode in Toronto's Gay Pride parade and was widely praised for doing so. Following July 1 Canada Day celebrations, Lastman closed sections of Yonge Street, Toronto's main thoroughfare, for a street festival to celebrate the new city. The music, food, and performers drew more than 400,000 people.

Sports. In April, the Toronto Maple Leafs of the National Hockey League acquired the Toronto Raptors of the National Basketball Association for an estimated $500 million. The owners of the Leafs also bought the Raptors' new sports arena, the Air Canada Centre, scheduled for completion in February 1999, but left in question the future of Maple Leaf Gardens, the historic home of the hockey team. The purchase of the Centre ended three years of negotiations over whether the teams would build a shared arena or separate spaces.   □ David Lewis Stein

See also **Canadian provinces; City.**

Toys and games. Retail toy sales in the United States in 1998 rose about 5 percent over 1997 sales. Low interest rates, job growth, low unemployment, and rising home ownership boosted consumer confidence, despite stock market adjustments in late summer and the yearlong Asian economic crisis.

The growth of on-line retailing continued in 1998, with consumers spending an estimated $13 million on toy purchases via the World Wide Web. Both Toys "R" Us of Paramus, New Jersey, and K-B Toys of Pittsfield, Massachusetts, the nation's two largest toy retailing chains, launched online shopping Web sites in 1998.

High-tech toys were at the forefront of the holiday toy-buying season, which normally accounts for 53 percent of all sales. In early October, Furby, a fuzzy interactive toy, became the runaway hit of 1998. The toy was manufactured by Tiger Electronics Ltd. of Vernon Hills, Illinois. Furby had sensors that allowed it to react to human sounds or the sounds of other Furbies by winking, giggling, or speaking in a half-English, half-imaginary language called Furbish.

A doll named Amazing Amy also combined technology with tradition. Introduced in 1998 by Playmates Toys, Inc. of Costa Mesa, California, Amy, programmed by an internal clock, announced what she wanted at particular times of

The Teletubbies, from a British television show, speak in the voices of toddlers and show video clips on their television tummies. Tinky Winky (purple), Dipsy (green), Po (red), and Laa Laa (yellow) were popular in 1998 with children as young as 12 months.

Furbies, interactive stuffed toys, were the hit of the 1998 holiday shopping season. They react to human sounds—and the sounds of other Furbies—with giggles, winks, and Furbish, a half-English, half-imaginary language.

the day or night using her vocabulary of 10,000 phrases.

The LEGO Co. of Enfield, Connecticut, took construction toys to a new level in 1998 with its LEGO Mindstorms Robotics Invention System. Developed in cooperation with the Massachusetts Institute of Technology's Media Lab, Mindstorms allowed children to design and program robots on a personal computer and then build them.

Reel life. Television, movie, and videocassette characters provided the inspiration for some of the toy industry's biggest hits in 1998. The popular children's cable TV series "Blue's Clues" sparked Sing Along Blue, an electronic stuffed animal from Fisher-Price Inc. of East Aurora, New York. The plush, talking versions of the four Teletubbies, made by the Playskool division of Hasbro, Inc. of Pawtucket, Rhode Island, were based on public broadcasting's Teletubby characters.

Other best-selling toys of 1998 were tied into movies, such as Hasbro's Small Soldiers action figures and *A Bug's Life* creature characters from Mattel, Inc. of El Segundo, California. Tigger, a character from the *Winnie the Pooh* video and book series, bounded out of toy stores as the electronic Bounce Around Tigger. Mattel's stuffed toy bounced, emitting a "boing, boing" sound, and proclaimed "bouncing's what Tiggers do best."

World on a string. The yo-yo made a comeback in 1998, with an estimated $80 million in sales of a toy that was first introduced in the United States in the late 1920's. Products from the Duncan Toys Company of Middlefield, Ohio—the largest producer of yo-yos in the United States—and What's Next Manufacturing Inc. of Arcade, New York—manufacturers of wooden yo-yos—were particularly popular. The X-Brain yo-yo made by the Yomega Corp. of Fall River, Massachusetts, was a top seller during the holiday season. The toy featured an automatic clutch that "climbed" the yo-yo up the string, helping beginning yo-yoists master difficult tricks.

A time for heroes. Collector dolls with the faces of American heroes reflected a growing hobby among adults and children in 1998. To honor astronaut John H. Glenn, Jr.'s, return to space after 36 years, Mattel premiered a special set from its Hot Wheels line that featured action figures of Glenn as a space shuttle crew member, Mercury astronaut, and senator. The set also included a space shuttle Discovery vehicle and a Mercury Friendship 7 capsule. Hasbro added action figures bearing the likenesses of Colin L. Powell, former chairman of the Joint Chiefs of Staff, and comedian Bob Hope, who frequently entertained U.S. troops, to its G.I. Joe Classic Collection. □ Diane P. Cardinale

Track and field. Sprint champion Marion Jones of the United States, middle-distance star Hicham El Guerrouj of Morocco, and long-distance runner Haile Gebrselassie of Ethiopia were the outstanding track and field athletes of 1998. The three athletes shared $1 million in prize money after going undefeated in Golden League competition in Europe and winning their respective events at the Grand Prix final in Moscow.

Marion Jones had a remarkable season in 1998. She excelled in sprint, long jump, and relay events and remained undefeated through 37 finals. As she had vowed, Jones won the 100 meters, 200 meters, and long jump in the U.S. outdoor championships at New Orleans. Jones took the women's 100 meters on June 20, with temperatures on the track above 100 °F (38 °C). She reached the finish line in 10.72 seconds, the seventh-fastest time in history. She won the long jump on the same day with a wind-aided leap of 23 feet, 8 inches (7.21 meters) and ran a 200-meter qualifying heat in 22.46 seconds, the second-fastest time to date. On June 21, Jones took the 200-meter final in 22.24 seconds to complete the first triple victory at the U.S. championships in 50 years.

Jones set two meet records at the Goodwill Games, which took place July 19 through August 2, in New York City and Uniondale, New York. She won the 100 meters in 10.90 seconds, on a soft track and into a slight headwind on July 19. A day later, she powered through the 200 meters in 21.80 seconds. She also won the 100 meters and the long jump at the Grand Prix final on September 5 in Moscow.

At the World Cup final in Johannesburg, South Africa, on September 11, Jones won the 200 meters in a meet-record 21.62 seconds. But her winning streak ended two nights later, when Heike Drechsler of Germany bested her in the long jump. Jones's prize money at Johannesburg pushed her total earnings for the 1998 outdoor season above $850,000.

Hicham El Guerrouj. On July 14 at Rome, El Guerrouj ran the 1,500 meters in 3 minutes 26 seconds, knocking more than a second off the world record. After breaking Noureddine Morceli's 1995 record of 3:27.37, El Guerrouj fell to the ground and kissed the track. Two nights after his record-breaking performance—the equivalent of a 3:42.5 mile—El Guerrouj went after the mile standard in a Grand Prix meet in Nice, France. His time, 3:44.60, missed breaking Morceli's 1993 record by only 0.21 seconds.

Haile Gebrselassie broke two world records in June 1998. On June 1 in Hengelo, Netherlands, he cut five seconds off the world record for the 10,000 meters, completing the race in 26 minutes,

World outdoor track and field records established in 1998

Men

Event	Holder	Country	Where set	Date	Record
1,500 meters	Hicham El Guerrouj	Morocco	Rome	July 14	3:26.00
5,000 meters	Haile Gebrselassie	Ethiopia	Helsinki	June 13	12:39.36
10,000 meters	Haile Gebrselassie	Ethiopia	Hengelo, Netherlands	June 1	26:22.75
4x400 relay	Jerome Young Antonio Pettigrew Tyree Washington Michael Johnson	USA	Uniondale, New York	July 22	2:54.20
Half mararthon	Paul Tergat	Kenya	Milan	April 4	59.17
Marathon	Ronaldo da Costa	Brazil	Berlin	Sept. 20	2:06.05

Women

Event	Holder	Country	Where set	Date	Record
Marathon	Tegla Loroupe	Kenya	Rotterdam	April 19	2:20.47
Pole Vault	Emma George	Australia	Brisbane	March 21	15' ¾" (4.59m)
Hammer throw	Michaela Melinte	Romania	Poiana Brasov, Romania	July 16	239' 11" (73.14m)

m = meters
Source: International Amateur Athletic Foundation (IAAF), USA Track & Field.

22.75 seconds. It was the third time in Gebrselassie's career that he had broken the 10,000-meter world record. The former record, 26:27.85, was set by Kenya's Paul Tergat in August 1997. On June 13, 1998, Gebrselassie set his 14th world record when he completed the 5,000 meters in 12 minutes 39.36 seconds in Helsinki, Finland. He ran each of his final two laps in under 59 seconds.

Goodwill Games. On July 22, a brilliant performance at the Goodwill Games by the U.S. team of Jerome Young, Antonio Pettigrew, Tyree Washington, and Michael Johnson, lowered the world record for the 4x400-meter relay to 2:54.20 . The old record, 2:54.29, was set by Andrew Valmon, Quincy Watts, Butch Reynolds, and Michael Johnson of the United States at the 1993 World Championships.

Jackie Joyner-Kersee won the final heptathlon of her career at the Goodwill Games. She remained the women's world record holder in the event when she retired on July 25, 1998, at a farewell meet in her honor in Edwardsville, Illinois.

"Flo Jo" dies. Florence Griffith Joyner, the three-time gold medalist at the 1988 Olympics and holder of the women's world records in the 100-meter and 200-meter dash, died suddenly on Sept. 21, 1998, at the age of 38.

☐ Ron Reid

Transit. See Transportation.

Transportation. On June 3, 1998, more than 100 people died in Western Europe's worst train accident in more than 10 years. Traveling at 125 miles (200 kilometers) per hour, a German Inter-City Express derailed near Eschede in northern Germany and demolished a bridge, which collapsed on 2 of the train's 12 passenger cars. After experts determined that faulty materials in the wheels caused the accident, all trains of the same type were withdrawn for examination.

Driverless subway trains. In October, Metro, the Paris subway system, opened the first wholly automated subway train service. The driverless trains reached speeds of 50 miles (80 kilometers) per hour on a new 4.3-mile (7-kilometer) route that crossed beneath the Seine River. The subway platforms on the line have plastic barriers separating the commuters from the tracks. When a train stops, doors open on the barriers and train cars. Four people at a command center can monitor as many as 13 trains running on the line.

Channel Tunnel. In January, a coalition of banks signed a refinancing agreement with Eurotunnel, the company that operates the 30-mile (50-kilometer) Channel Tunnel, an undersea rail service that links France and Great Britain. Restructuring of the company's debt was made possible by a 1997 agreement between the British and French governments to extend Eurotunnel's

The Grand Princess, the largest cruise ship ever built, makes its maiden voyage in May 1998 from Southampton, England, to Istanbul, Turkey. The 2,600 passengers aboard the 18-deck luxury liner enjoyed a nightclub, five pools, and a 748-seat theater.

contract to operate the service from 65 to 99 years. In spite of the company's troubled past, Eurotunnel reported in February 1998 that it showed an operating profit in 1997 for the first time.

Railway purchases. In July 1998, the U.S. Surface Transportation Board approved the purchase of Philadelphia-based Conrail Incorporated by two companies—Norfolk Southern Corporation of Norfolk, Virginia, and CSX Transportation Corporation of Jacksonville, Florida. The decision ended a long bidding war that began in 1997.

Conrail was formed in 1976 as part of a federal bailout of bankrupt railroads in the Northeast. Eleven years later, it was sold to the public at $14 a share. The new owners purchased the company for $115 a share and were expected to split Conrail's assets officially in early 1999. The transaction reintroduced competition in the railroad industry to parts of the Northeast.

Canadian National Railway of Montreal announced in February 1998 that it would purchase the Chicago-based Illinois Central Railroad for $2.4 billion. If the acquisition receives U.S. regulatory approval, the combined railroad would become the seventh largest in North America, providing transcontinental service in Canada and north-south service in the United States.

Union Pacific, based in Omaha, Nebraska, announced in August that it would divide its management into three separate regions in order to deal with major backlogs in delivering goods. The company's operational problems were largely the result of its acquisition of the Chicago & North Western Railroad in 1995 and the Southern Pacific Railroad in 1996. The complexity of operating a large, widespread system resulted in a shortage of locomotives, freight cars, and crews—and consequently, delays in providing service to grain shippers and other customers. A 1997 U.S. government order that allowed rival railroads to operate over Union Pacific tracks in order to relieve the backlog remained in effect in 1998.

Transportation bill. In June, President Bill Clinton signed the Transportation Equity Act for the 21st Century (TEA-21). The $217-billion bill, passed by Congress in May, provided a 40-percent increase in spending over the Intermodal Surface Transportation Efficiency Act of 1991, which expired in 1997. TEA-21 provided funds for road construction and repair and for expansion of mass transit services over a six-year period. Critics noted that TEA-21 exceeded spending limits set by the balanced-budget agreement. They also accused lawmakers of spending money on projects in their congressional districts and states in order to attract votes in the November 1998 elections.

Drunken driving. U.S. Transportation Secretary Rodney B. Slater announced in August that alcohol-related traffic deaths in the United States had dropped to 16,189 in 1997, an all-time low. The number represented less than 40 percent of all traffic deaths nationwide. In 1982, nearly 60 percent of traffic deaths resulted from drunken driving. Slater credited the decrease to tougher laws and a change in public attitudes toward drinking and driving.

Distracted drivers. In January 1998, the National Highway Traffic and Safety Administration (NHTSA), an agency of the Department of Transportation, issued a report warning that the use of cellular telephones while driving was a "growing factor in crashes." In a review of accident statistics from several U.S. states, the NHTSA found that in accidents involving cellular phones, drivers were most often talking on the phone rather than dialing at the time of the crash. The report listed other common distractions, such as navigational systems, fax machines, and small computers. Nonetheless, the NHTSA noted the value of having some electronic devices in automobiles, particularly the benefit of cellular phones for calling emergency services.   □ Ian Savage

See also **Automobile; Aviation; Germany.**

Trinidad and Tobago. See **West Indies.**

Tunisia. See **Middle East.**

Turkey. In November 1998, the coalition government of Turkish Prime Minister Mesut Yilmaz collapsed after losing a no-confidence vote in the parliament. Opposition lawmakers accused Yilmaz of corruption, including helping organized-crime figures purchase a state-owned bank. Yilmaz denied the charges.

The allegations against Yilmaz were among many such charges of government links to organized-crime figures made in 1998. In January, Yilmaz confirmed Turkish newspaper reports that a government investigation had found that corrupt security officials had used right-wing gangs to kill supporters of Turkey's Marxist Kurdish Workers' Party (PKK) from 1993 to 1996. In exchange for killing PKK supporters, the gangs were allowed to engage in drug trafficking and arms trading and to launder their profits through licensed casinos. (The PKK launched a war of independence from Turkey in 1984.) Fears about government-condoned right-wing death squads increased in May 1998 when six men were arrested for the attempted murder of prominent Turkish human-rights activist Akin Birdal. Some of the men allegedly had links to government security groups.

On December 21, Bulent Ecevit, whom Turkish President Suleyman Demirel had given the task of forming a new government, said he would be unable to do so because of factional rivalries in the Turkish parliament. Ecevit warned that the power vacuum would help Virtue, an Islamic opposition

Women medical students at Istanbul University in February 1998 protest a university ban on the wearing of Islamic headscarves. The dress code was one of a number of laws instituted by the military-backed secular government to discourage Turkey's growing Islamic fundamentalist movement.

party, in elections scheduled for April 1999. On Dec. 23, 1998, Demirel asked Industry and Trade Minister Yalim Erez, the only independent in his Cabinet, to form a government.

Islamists. Turkey's Supreme Court banned the Welfare (Refah) Party in January after ruling that the party's goals to change the state from a *secular* (nonreligious) government to an Islamic system were unconstitutional. The court also banned seven Welfare leaders, including party head and former Prime Minister Necmettin Erbakan, from political activity for five years. In February, more than 100 of Welfare's 150 members in the 550-seat parliament joined Virtue.

In March, the Turkish National Security Council demanded that Prime Minister Yilmaz enforce a long list of anti-Islamic demands, including curbs on Islamic dress, Islamic officials, religious schools, the media, and efforts to reestablish the Welfare Party. By early April, several Islamic mayors had been removed from their posts. On April 20, police arrested 16 businessmen for allegedly laundering money for Islamic groups. Security authorities also detained 130 people during April on the grounds that they belonged to the armed Islamic group Hezbollah (Party of God), which was blamed for a number of violent attacks in southeast Turkey.

In September, the Supreme Court upheld a 10-month jail sentence for the popular mayor of Istanbul, Recep Tayyip Erdogan, a former leader of Welfare. A security court had convicted and sentenced Erdogan in April for inciting unrest during a 1997 speech.

Military chief resigns. Hard-line military Chief of Staff Ismail Hakki Karadayi resigned in August 1998. During Karadayi's five-year term, the military began its crusade against the influence of Islam in politics and intensified the military campaign against the PKK. Most analysts viewed Karadayi's successor, Huseyin Kivrikoglu, as more moderate than Karadayi.

Kurds. Open hostilities between Turkey and Syria were averted in October when Syria agreed to end its support for the PKK. In November, PKK leader Abdullah Ocalan sought political asylum, first in Russia and then in Italy, after Syria, which had been sheltering Ocalan, expelled him. Italian authorities refused Turkish demands that they turn Ocalan over to Turkey to face terrorism and murder charges. Also in November, Turkish troops launched an offensive into Iraq against some 500 PKK rebels who had fled there from Syria. In April, Turkish commandos in Iraq had captured Semdin Sakik, who was formerly the PKK's second-in-command.   ☐ Christine Helms

See also **Cyprus; Iraq; Middle East** (Facts in brief table).

Turkmenistan. See Asia.

Ukraine. Voters in Ukraine selected a new parliament on March 29, 1998, after a campaign that had been marked by assaults on candidates and the bombing of newspaper offices. The election, which was peaceful, resulted in the retention of the existing government and slight gains for Communists, who oppose the government.

Under Ukrainian election law, half of the seats in the 450-seat legislature are filled by direct elections in 225 national districts. The rest are filled in proportion to each party's share of the national vote. The Communist Party, with 25 percent of the vote, ended up with 123 seats in parliament, well ahead of the progovernment People's Democratic Party (PDP). The PDP won 5 percent, earning 17 seats from the proportional voting. However, the PDP retained the loyalty of an additional 73 deputies elected in district races. Many of these candidates were local officials who had run as independents in the district elections.

Parliamentary stand-off. The poor showing of progovernment parties was a blow to President Leonid Kuchma, who faced reelection in October 1999. Because the Communists and their allies fell short of a clear parliamentary majority, political analysts expected the stand-off between Kuchma and the legislature to continue. This became apparent when the legislature took 19 ballots over two months to elect a new speaker of parliament. The deputies finally chose Oleksandr Tkachenko, a member of the minority Peasants Party, in July 1998. Tkachenko had been minister of agriculture under Ukraine's Soviet regime.

Economy. In February, the outgoing legislature lifted a suspension of privatization activities imposed the previous November, but continued to forbid the sale of farmland. In August, the Cabinet, faced with a looming financial crisis, approved a sharply reduced budget for 1999 without waiting for parliamentary approval. This helped Ukraine secure a loan from the International Monetary Fund, a United Nations-affiliated organization that provides short-term credit to member nations. The $2.2-billion deal enabled Ukraine to stabilize the value of its currency as the Russian ruble was collapsing in late summer.

An explosion at the Skachinskoho coal mine in Donetsk killed 63 miners and injured 45 others on April 4, 1998. It was the worst mining accident in Ukraine since 1985. Investigators blamed poor safety precautions for a build-up of methane gas that probably was ignited by a spark. The number of mining fatalities in Ukraine had risen in recent years because of a lack of funds needed to maintain safety. More than 300 miners were killed in Ukraine in 1998.   ☐ Steven L. Solnick

See also **Europe** (Facts in brief table).

Unemployment. See Labor and employment.

The Labour Party in 1998 continued its program of reforms, ranging from cut-backs in welfare programs (which cost $160 billion annually) to dramatic changes to the British constitution, giving more powers to Scotland, Wales, and Northern Ireland. Conservatives expressed frustration with the reforms, claiming that "New Labour," as Prime Minister Tony Blair's party had begun to call itself, had taken over many of the Conservatives' ideas. Labour came to power in mid-1997 in the biggest political landslide of the century.

Welfare reforms. Blair began his reform program with the announcement that he planned to cut welfare benefits for those not in dire need. Under the "cradle-to-grave" system of welfare implemented in Great Britain after World War II (1939–1945), many benefits were universal, paid to rich and poor alike. The Labour Party had traditionally been the defender of that system.

In March 1998, Labour unveiled a *green paper* (legislative proposal) that extolled work as the best defense against poverty. Welfare reform minister Frank Field said that the government sought to replace the cycle of dependency and insecurity with the ethics of work and savings. Field insisted that the government would continue to pay a basic state pension, though plans were being considered to make contributions to a second, private pension compulsory. Field also promised a crackdown on welfare fraud, including a way of testing whether the sick and disabled who receive benefits are in financial need.

The House of Lords. Labour's campaign promise to abolish the right of *hereditary peers* (nobles who have inherited their title) to sit in the House of Lords—the upper chamber of the British Parliament—increased as the overwhelmingly conservative chamber continued to delay government bills. By mid-1998, the end of the first year of Labour rule, the Lords had rejected an unprecedented 29 bills. (Rejection by the upper chamber has the power to slow, but not kill, legislation.) At a conference in June, Ivor Richard, leader of the House of Lords at that time, said that the government planned to remove the voting rights of hereditary peers and create an "interim chamber" of about 600 *life peers* (persons of achievement given titles of nobility for their lifetime). Opposition leader William Hague said that Conservative hereditary peers would strongly oppose the government's attempts without a clear, long-term plan for the Lords.

New parliaments. Planning continued in 1998 for the first meeting of a Scottish Parliament in 300 years, following approval for such a body in a referendum held in September 1997. British Foreign Secretary Robin Cook announced in January 1998 that he would not run for the position of first minister of the new Parliament, seen by many Scots as the equivalent of being prime minister of an *autonomous* (independent) administration. Cook's announcement left the way open for Donald Dewar, the Scottish secretary, to run as the Labour Party candidate.

But concern grew among Labour Party members about the increase in popularity of the Scottish National Party (SNP). A surge in support for Scottish nationalism led the SNP to hope that it would be the majority party in the Scottish Parliament after the first elections, planned for May 1999. A SNP majority, Labour leaders feared, could lead to demands for full independence for Scotland from the United Kingdom.

Wales also moved ahead with plans to establish a Welsh parliament. Welsh Secretary Ron Davies was chosen in September 1998 to represent the Labour Party in May 1999 elections for the position of prime minister of the new Parliament. In Northern Ireland, a ground-breaking peace agreement, signed in April 1998 and approved by a majority of Irish and Northern Irish voters in May, led to the establishment of a new Northern Ireland Assembly.

A mayor for London. The government took steps in 1998 to give London an elected mayor for the first time in its history. The decision was approved by 72 percent of Londoners in a vote in May. The mayor, to be elected in 1999 or 2000, was to be responsible for a $5.5-billion budget to cover such services as police, transportation, and fire protection, as well as economic development and tourism.

Government scandals brought the Labour Party—which had emphasized Conservative breaches of ethics in its 1997 election campaign—its share of embarrassment in 1998. Many problems centered on Robin Cook, who promised that British foreign policy would become more "ethical" when he became foreign secretary. In January 1998, Cook publicly admitted to engaging in a relationship with his assistant, Gaynor Regan. Cook and Regan were married in April after Cook obtained a divorce from his wife of 28 years.

Cook became involved in a bigger crisis when it was discovered that Sandline International, a British arms company, had supplied weapons to deposed President Ahmad Tejan Kabbah of Sierra Leone, despite a United Nations (UN) arms embargo to the country. In May, Cook denied that any Foreign Office ministers or officials had known about the arms shipments. Sandline then produced a letter it had sent to Cook naming the Foreign Office and Ministry of Defence officials who had allegedly colluded with the company. Prime Minister Blair, forced to amend an answer he had made to Parliament, stated that officials had not "deliberately" breached UN sanctions. Blair argued that the regime that had overthrown Kabbah's democratically elected government had been a brutal dictatorship that did not deserve to survive.

Blair's image was further tarnished when a London newspaper claimed on July 5 that former government aides were selling their contacts with ministers. According to *The Observer*, two former advisers to Blair—Chancellor of the Exchequer (treasury secretary) Gordon Brown and minister without portfolio Peter Mandelson—admitted to having passed confidential government information to large corporations. The most embarrassing allegation for Blair was the claim that Roger Liddle, a senior member of his policy unit, appeared to have close ties to Derek Draper. Draper, a former Mandelson aide, had become a director of GPC Market Access, a firm of lobbyists. While attending a party, Liddle allegedly offered his and Draper's help to put businessmen in touch with policymakers. Draper denied having made such promises but was fired from the GPC.

Mandelson made headlines again in November when London newspapers focused public attention on the sexual orientation of some members of the government. Cabinet Secretary for Wales Ron Davies resigned after being beaten and robbed in a park known as a gathering place for homosexuals. Agriculture Minister Nick Brown announced that he was a homosexual after the publication of an interview with a man with whom Brown once had a relationship. A *Times* of London reporter claimed that Mandelson, who had never discussed his sexual orientation in public, was a homosexual. *The Sun,* one of Britain's most popular dailies and one that had aggressively reported the stories, announced in response to a surge of complaints by readers a new editorial policy of not revealing the sexual orientation of any individual unless the matter was of "overwhelming public interest."

Age of consent. The government was forced to temporarily abandon a measure to lower the age of homosexual consent from 18 to 16 after the House of Lords rejected the reform on July 22. The measure had been passed in the House of Commons by a massive majority of 207 with the backing of the leaders of Britain's three main political parties. The measure was opposed by an alliance of Conservative peers and Church of England bishops led by the Archbishop of Canterbury, George Carey. Home Secretary Jack Straw announced that the measure was being withdrawn because it had formed part of a crime and disorder bill, and the government did not want to lose the entire bill.

Land mine treaty. The House of Commons rushed into law a ban on land mines on July 10, in time for the first anniversary of the death of Diana, Princess of Wales, on August 31. Diana's campaign against land mines, which included a visit to Angola in January 1997, had embarrassed the previous Conservative government and helped to put the issue before the public.

The bill, which was passed by unanimous acclamation, imposed prison sentences of up to 14 years on anyone who used, developed, produced, bought, owned, or transferred a land mine. A controversial clause provided a defense for British soldiers who might take part in joint exercises involving land mines with allied forces—notably those of the United States, which had not signed the Ottawa Convention banning land mines.

A museum dedicated to Diana was opened by her brother, Earl Spencer, at Diana's birthplace, Althorp House, Northamptonshire, on July 1, 1998. The day would have been her 37th birthday. For about $16, visitors viewed the dress Diana had worn at her wedding; personal effects from her childhood, such as a school uniform; report cards; tap shoes; and family photographs and home movies. The public was allowed to view, but not visit, the island where Diana was buried—in an ornamental lake on the grounds of the estate.

The Diana, Princess of Wales, Memorial Fund, launched a number of court cases in 1998 to try to stop "unauthorized" exploitation of her memory. The fund was established after Diana's death to support some of her favorite charitable causes. In July 1998, the British Patent Office ruled that the fund could not register the Princess's face and name as trademarks. However, lawyers acting for the fund in Los Angeles started proceedings in May against the Franklin Mint, a U.S. corporation that produces commemorative products. According to the fund, the company was marketing unauthorized dolls.

The fund was the object of a legal complaint in August brought by the Bradford Exchange, an Illinois-based souvenir company. The fund demanded that the company stop selling commemorative musical plates. The Bradford Exchange claimed that it had a legal right to produce Diana memorabilia without obtaining a license from the fund. Trustees of the fund expressed concern that, if the complaint were to be upheld, the fund could lose millions in licensing revenues as manufacturers swamped the market with Diana memorabilia.

Visitors gather before a memorial to Diana, Princess of Wales at the Spencer family estate, Althorp, on the memorial's opening day, July 1, 1998. Admission included access to a museum and views across an ornamental lake to the island (above left) on which the princess was buried.

The investigation into Diana's death continued in 1998. Diana had been killed on Aug. 31, 1997, in an auto accident after leaving the Ritz Hotel in Paris with her friend Emad (Dodi) Fayed. In early 1998, Mohamed Al Fayed, Dodi's father, claimed that a "conspiracy" by people opposed to his son's friendship with Diana had brought about her death. In August, Fayed blamed two bodyguards, Trevor Rees-Jones, who was himself seriously injured in the accident, and Kes Wingfield. However, a report in November on the Mercedes in which Diana was riding at the time of the accident indicated no signs of malfunction or tampering with the auto. But a report on the blood of driver Henri Paul indicated that Paul was legally drunk at the time of the accident. By the end of the year, the Paris court conducting the investigation had not issued a final report.

Nurses freed. Two British nurses who had spent 17 months in prison in Saudi Arabia for the murder of an Australian colleague were freed on the orders of King Fahd on May 20 after the personal intervention of Prime Minister Blair. Deborah Parry and Lucille McLaughlan had been arrested in 1996 after the body of Yvonne Gilford was found stabbed and suffocated in her room at the King Fahd medical complex in Dhahran, where all three worked. McLaughlan was convicted as an accessory to murder and sentenced to eight years imprisonment and 500 lashes. Parry was sentenced to death but escaped possible execution when Gil-

Members of the British House of Commons

Queen Elizabeth II opened the 1998-1999 session of Parliament on Nov. 24, 1998. When it convened, the House of Commons consisted of the following members: 417 Labour Party, 162 Conservative Party, 46 Liberal Democrats, 10 Ulster Unionists, 6 Scottish National Party, 4 Plaid Cymru, 3 Social Democratic and Labour Party, 2 Ulster Democratic Unionist Party, 2 Sinn Fein, 1 United Kingdom Unionist, 1 Independent, and 1 Scottish Labour. In addition, an unaffiliated speaker and 3 deputies attend sessions but do not vote. This table shows each legislator and party affiliation. An asterisk (*) denotes those who served in the Parliament at some time before the 1997 general election.

A
Diane Abbot, Lab.*
Gerry Adams, S.F.*
Irene Adams, Lab.*
Nick Ainger, Lab.*
Peter Ainsworth, Con.*
Robert Ainsworth, Lab.*
Douglas Alexander, Lab.
Richard Allan, L.Dem
Graham Allen, Lab.*
David Amess, Con.*
Michael Ancram, Con.*
Donald Anderson, Lab.*
Janet Anderson, Lab.*
James Arbuthnot, Con.*
Hilary Armstrong, Lab.*
Paddy Ashdown, L.Dem.*
Joe Ashton, Lab.*
Candy Atherton, Lab.
Charlotte Atkins, Lab.
David Atkinson, Con.*
Peter Atkinson, Con.*
John Austin, Lab.*
B
Norman Baker, L.Dem.
Tony Baldry, Con.*
Jackie Ballard, L.Dem.
Tony Banks, Lab.*
Harry Barnes, Lab.*
Kevin Barron, Lab.*
John Battle, Lab.*
Hugh Bayley, Lab.*
Nigel Beard, Lab.
Margaret Beckett, Lab.*
Anne Begg, Lab.
Roy Beggs, U.U.*
Alan Beith, L.Dem.*
Martin Bell, Ind.
Stuart Bell, Lab.*
Tony Benn, Lab.*
Andrew Bennett, Lab.*
Joe Benton, Lab.*
John Bercow, Con.
Sir Paul Beresford, Con.*
Gerald Bermingham, Lab.*
Roger Berry, Lab.*
Harold Best, Lab.
Clive Betts, Lab.*
Liz Blackman, Lab.
Tony Blair, Lab.*
Hazel Blears, Lab.
Bob Blizzard, Lab.
David Blunkett, Lab.*
Crispin Blunt, Con.
Paul Boateng, Lab.*
Sir Richard Body, Con.*
Betty Boothroyd, Speaker*
David Borrow, Lab.
Tim Boswell, Con.*
Peter Bottomley, Con.*
Virginia Bottomley, Con.*
Keith Bradley, Lab.*
Peter Bradley, Lab.
Ben Bradshaw, Lab.
Graham Brady, Con.
Tom Brake, L.Dem.
Peter Brand, L.Dem.
Julian Brazier, Con.*
Colin Breed, L.Dem.
Helen Brinton, Lab.
Peter Brooke, Con.*
Gordon Brown, Lab.*
Nick Brown, Lab.*
Russell Brown, Lab.
Desmond Browne, Lab.
Angela Browning, Con.*
Ian Bruce, Con.*
Malcolm Bruce, L.Dem.*
Karen Buck, Lab.
Richard Burden, Lab.*
Colin Burgon, Lab.
John Burnett, L.Dem.

Simon Burns, Con.*
Paul Burstow, L.Dem.
Christine Butler, Lab.
John Butterfill, Con.*
Stephen Byers, Lab.*
C
Vincent Cable, L.Dem.
Richard Caborn, Lab.*
Alan Campbell, Lab.
Anne Campbell, Lab.*
Menzies Campbell, L.Dem.*
Ronnie Campbell, Lab.*
Dale Campbell-Savours, Lab.*
Dennis Canavan, Lab.*
Jamie Cann, Lab.*
Ivor Caplin, Lab.
Roger Casale, Lab.
William Cash, Con.*
Martin Caton, Lab.
Ian Cawsey, Lab.
Ben Chapman, Lab.*
Sir Sydney Chapman, Con.*
David Chaytor, Lab.
David Chidgey, L.Dem.*
Malcolm Chisholm, Lab.*
Christopher Chope, Con.*
Judith Church, Lab.*
Michael Clapham, Lab.*
James Clappison, Con.*
Alan Clark, Con.
David Clark, Lab.*
Lynda Clark, Lab.
Michael Clark, Con.*
Paul Clark, Lab.
Charles Clarke, Lab.
Eric Clarke, Lab.*
Kenneth Clarke, Con.*
Tom Clarke, Lab.*
Tony Clarke, Lab.
David Clelland, Lab.*
Geoffrey Clifton-Brown, Con.*
Ann Clwyd, Lab.*
Vernon Coaker, Lab.
Ann Coffey, Lab.*
Harry Cohen, Lab*
Iain Coleman, Lab.
Tim Collins, Con.
Tony Colman, Lab.
Michael Colvin, Con.*
Michael Connarty, Lab.*
Frank Cook, Lab.*
Robin Cook, Lab.*
Yvette Cooper, Lab.
Robin Corbett, Lab.*
Jeremy Corbyn, Lab.*
Sir Patrick Cormack, Con.*
Jean Corston, Lab.*
Brian Cotter, L.Dem.
Jim Cousins, Lab.*
Tom Cox, Lab.*
James Cran, Con.*
Ross Cranston, Lab.
David Crausby, Lab.
Ann Cryer, Lab.
John Cryer, Lab.
John Cummings, Lab.*
Lawrence Cunliffe, Lab.*
Jack Cunningham, Lab.*
Jim Cunningham, Lab.*
Roseanna Cunningham, S.N.P.
David Curry, Con.*
Clare Curtis-Thomas, Lab.
D
Cynog Dafis, P.C.*
Tam Dalyell, Lab.*
Alistair Darling, Lab.*
Keith Darvill, Lab.
Edward Davey, L. Dem.
Valerie Davey, Lab.
Ian Davidson, Lab.*
Denzil Davies, Lab.*
Geraint Davies, Lab.

Quentin Davies, Con.*
Ronald Davies, Lab.*
David Davis, Con.*
Terry Davis, Lab.*
Hilton Dawson, Lab.
Stephen Day, Con.*
Janet Dean, Lab.
John Denham, Lab.*
Donald Dewar, Lab.*
Andrew Dismore, Lab.
Jim Dobbin, Lab.
Frank Dobson, Lab.*
Jeffrey Donaldson, U.U.
Brian H. Donohoe, Lab.*
Doran Frank, Lab.
Stephen Dorrell, Con.*
Jim Dowd, Lab.*
David Drew, Lab.
Julia Drown, Lab.
Alan Duncan, Con.*
Iain Duncan Smith, Con.*
Gwyneth Dunwoody, Lab.*
E
Angela Eagle, Lab.*
Maria Eagle, Lab.
Huw Edwards, Lab.*
Clive Efford, Lab.
Louise Ellman, Lab.
Sir Peter Emery, Con.*
Jeff Ennis, Lab.*
Bill Etherington, Lab.*
Nigel Evans, Con.*
Margaret Ewing, S.N.P.
F
David Faber, Con.*
Michael Fabricant, Con.*
Michael Fallon, Con.*
Derek Fatchett, Lab.*
Ronnie Fearn, L.Dem.*
Frank Field, Lab.*
Mark Fisher, Lab.*
Jim Fltzpatrick, Lab.
Lorna Fitzsimons, Lab.
Howard Flight, Con.
Caroline Flint, Lab.
Paul Flynn, Lab.*
Barbara Follett, Lab.
Clifford Forsythe, U.U.*
Eric Forth, Con.*
Derek Foster, Lab.*
Don Foster, L.Dem.*
Michael Foster, Lab.
Michael J. Foster, Lab.
George Foulkes, Lab.*
Sir Norman Fowler, Con.*
Liam Fox, Con.*
Christopher Fraser, Con.
Maria Fyfe, Lab.*
G
Sam Galbraith, Lab.*
Roger Gale, Con.*
George Galloway, Lab.*
Mike Gapes, Lab.*
Barry Gardiner, Lab.
Edward Garnier, Con.*
Andrew George, L.Dem.
Bruce George, Lab.*
Neil Garrard, Lab.*
Nick Gibb, Con.
Ian Gibson, Lab.
Christopher Gill, Con.*
Cheryl Gillan, Con.*
Linda Gilroy, Lab.
Norman A. Godman, Lab.
Roger Godsiff, Lab.*
Paul Goggins, Lab.
Llin Golding, Lab.*
Alistair Goodlad, Con.*
Eileen Gordon, Lab.
Teresa Gorman, Con.*
Donald Gorrie, L.Dem.
Thomas Graham, S.Lab.*

Bernie Grant, Lab.*
James Gray, Con.
Damian Green, Con.
John Greenway, Con.*
Dominic Grieve, Con.
Jane Griffiths, Lab.
Nigel Griffiths, Lab.*
Win Griffiths, Lab.*
Bruce Grocott, Lab.*
John Grogan, Lab.
John Gummer, Con.*
John Gunnell, Lab.*
H
William Hague, Con.*
Peter Hain, Lab.*
Mike Hall, Lab.*
Patrick Hall, Lab.
Sir Archie Hamilton, Con.*
Fabian Hamilton, Lab.
Philip Hammond, Con.
Mike Hancock, L.Dem.*
David Hanson, Lab.*
Harriet Harman, Lab.*
Evan Harris, L.Dem.
Nick Harvey, L.Dem.*
Sir Alan Haselhurst, Deputy*
Nick Hawkins, Con.*
John Hayes, Con.
Sylvia Heal, Lab.*
Oliver Heald, Con.*
John Healey, Lab.
David Heath, L.Dem.
Sir Edward Heath, Con.*
David Heathcoat-Amory, Con.*
Doug Henderson, Lab.*
Ivan Henderson, Lab.
Stephen Hepburn, Lab.
John Heppell, Lab.*
Michael Heseltine, Con.*
Stephen Hesford, Lab.
Patricia Hewitt, Lab.
Keith Hill, Lab.*
David Hinchcliffe, Lab.*
Margaret Hodge, Lab.*
Kate Hoey, Lab.*
Douglas Hogg, Con.*
John Home Robertson, Lab.*
Jimmy Hood, Lab.*
Geoffrey Hoon, Lab.*
Phil Hope, Lab.
Kelvin Hopkins, Lab.
John Horam, Con.*
Michael Howard, Con.*
Alan Howarth, Lab.*
George Howarth, Lab.*
Gerald Howarth, Con.*
Kim Howells, Lab.*
Lindsay Hoyle, Lab.*
Beverley Hughes, Lab.
Kevin Hughes, Lab.*
Simon Hughes, L.Dem.*
Joan Humble, Lab.
John Hume, S.D.L.P.*
Andrew Hunter, Con.*
Alan Hurst, Lab.
John Hutton, Lab.*
I
Brian Iddon, Lab.
Eric Illsley, Lab.*
Adam Ingram, Lab.*
J
Michael Jack, Con.*
Glenda Jackson, Lab.*
Helen Jackson, Lab.*
Robert Jackson, Con.*
David Jamieson, Lab.*
Bernard Jenkin, Con.*
Brian Jenkins, Lab.*
Alan Johnson, Lab.
Melanie Johnson, Lab.
Sir Geoffrey Johnson Smith, Con.*
Barry Jones, Lab.*

Fiona Jones, Lab.*
Helen Jones, Lab.*
Ieuan Wyn Jones, P.C.*
Jenny Jones, Lab.
Jon Owen Jones, Lab.*
Lynne Jones, Lab.*
Martin Jones, Lab.*
Nigel Jones, L.Dem.*
Tessa Jowell, Lab.*

K
Gerald Kaufman, Lab.*
Sally Keeble, Lab.
Alan Keen, Lab.*
Ann Keen, Lab.
Paul Keetch, L.Dem.
Ruth Kelly, Lab.
Fraser Kemp, Lab.
Charles Kennedy, L.Dem.*
Jane Kennedy, Lab.*
Robert Key, Con.*
Piara S. Khabra, Lab.*
David Kidney, Lab.
Peter Kilfoyle, Lab.*
Andrew King, Lab.
Oona King, Lab.
Tom King, Con.*
Tess Kingham, Lab.*
Julie Kirkbride, Con.
Archy Kirkwood, L.Dem.
Ashok Kumar, Lab.*

L
Stephen Ladyman, Lab.
Eleanor Laing, Con.
Jacqui Lait, Con.*
Andrew Lansley, Con.
Jackie Lawrence, Lab.
Bob Laxton, Lab.
Edward Leigh, Con.*
David Lepper, Lab.
Christopher Leslie, Lab.
Oliver Letwin, Con.
Tom Levitt, Lab.
Ivan Lewis, Lab.
Julian Lewis, Con.
Terry Lewis, Lab.*
Helen Liddell, Lab.*
David Lidington, Con.*
Peter Lilley, Con.*
Martin Linton, Lab.
Ken Livingstone, Lab.*
Richard Livsey, L.Dem.*
Sir Peter Lloyd, Con.*
Tony Lloyd, Lab.*
Elfyn Llwyd, P.C.*
David Lock, Lab.
Michael Lord, Deputy*
Tim Loughton, Con.
Andrew Love, Lab.
Peter Luff, Con.*
Sir Nicholas Lyell, Con.*

M
John McAllion, Lab.*
Thomas McAvoy, Lab.*
Steve McCabe, Lab.
Chris McCafferty, Lab.
Ian McCartney, Lab.*
Robert McCartney, U.K.U.*
Siobhain McDonagh, Lab.
Calum MacDonald, Lab.*
John McDonnell, Lab.
John McFall, Lab.*
Eddie McGrady, S.D.L.P.*
John MacGregor, Con.*
Martin McGuinness, S.F.
Anne McGuire, Lab.
Anne McIntosh, Con.
Shona McIsaac, Lab.
Andrew Mackay, Con.*
Rosemary McKenna, Lab.
Andrew Mackinlay, Lab.*
David MacLean, Con.*
Henry B. McLeish, Lab.*
Robert Maclennan, L.Dem.*
Patrick McLoughlin, Con.*
Kevin McNamara, Lab.*
Tony McNulty, Lab.
Denis MacShane, Lab.*
Fiona Mactaggart, Lab.

Tony McWalter, Lab.
John McWilliam, Lab.*
Sir David Madel, Con.*
Ken Maginnis, U.U.*
Alice Mahon, Lab.*
John Major, Con.*
Humfrey Malins, Con.*
Judy Mallaber, Lab.
Seamus Mallon, S.D.L.P.*
Peter Mandelson, Lab.*
John Maples, Con.*
John Marek, Lab.*
Gordon Marsden, Lab.
Paul Marsden, Lab.
David Marshall, Lab.*
Jim Marshall, Lab.*
Robert Marshall-Andrews, Lab.
Michael Martin, Deputy*
Eric Martlew, Lab.*
Michael Mates, Con.*
John Maxton, Lab.*
Theresa May, Con.
Michael Meacher, Lab.*
Alan Meale, Lab.*
Gillian Merron, Lab.
Alun Michael, Lab.*
Bill Michie, Lab.*
Ray Michie, L.Dem.*
Alan Milburn, Lab.*
Andrew Miller, Lab.*
Austin Mitchell, Lab.*
Laura Moffatt, Lab.
Lewis Moonie, Lab.*
Michael Moore, L.Dem.
Margaret Moran, Lab.
Alasdair Morgan, S.N.P.
Julie Morgan, Lab.
Rhodri Morgan, Lab.*
Elliot Morley, Lab.*
Estelle Morris, Lab.*
John Morris, Lab.*
Malcolm Moss, Con.*
Kali Mountford, Lab.
Marjorie Mowlam, Lab.*
George Mudie, Lab.*
Chris Mullin, Lab.*
Denis Murphy, Lab.
Jim Murphy, Lab.
Paul Murphy, Lab.*

N
Douglas Naysmith, Lab.
Patrick Nicholls, Con.*
Archie Norman, Con.
Dan Norris, Lab.

O
Mark Oaten, L.Dem.
Bill O'Brien, Lab.*
Mike O'Brien, Lab.*
Eddie O'Hara, Lab.*
Bill Olner, Lab.*
Martin O'Neill, Lab.*
Lembit Opik, L.Dem.
Diana Organ, Lab.
Sandra Osborne, Lab.*
Richard Ottaway, Con.*

P
Richard Page, Con.*
James Paice, Con.*
Ian Paisley, U.D.U.P.*
Nick Palmer, Lab.
Owen Paterson, Con.
Ian Pearson, Lab.
Tom Pendry, Lab.*
Linda Perham, Lab.
Eric Pickles, Con.*
Colin Pickthall, Lab.*
Peter Pike, Lab.*
James Plaskitt, Lab.
Kerry Pollard, Lab.
Chris Pond, Lab.
Greg Pope, Lab.*
Stephen Pound, Lab.
Sir Raymond Powell, Lab.*
Bridget Prentice, Lab.*
Gordon Prentice, Lab.*
John Prescott, Lab.*
Dawn Primarolo, Lab.*
David Prior, Con.

Gwyn Prosser, Lab.
Ken Purchase, Lab.*

Q
Joyce Quin, Lab.*
Lawrie Quinn, Lab.

R
Giles Radice, Lab.*
Bill Rammell, Lab.
John Randall, Con.
Syd Rapson, Lab.
Nick Raynsford, Lab.*
John Redwood, Con.*
Andrew Reed, Lab.
John Reid, Lab.*
David Rendel, L.Dem.*
Andrew Robathan, Con.*
George Robertson, Lab.*
Laurence Robertson, Con.
Geoffrey Robinson, Lab.*
Peter Robinson, U.D.U.P.*
Barbara Roche, Lab.*
Marion Roe, Con.*
Allan Rogers, Lab.*
Jeff Rooker, Lab.*
Terry Rooney, Lab.*
Ernie Ross, Lab.*
William Ross, U.U.*
Andrew Rowe, Con.*
Ted Rowlands, Lab.*
Frank Roy, Lab.
Chris Ruane, Lab.
Joan Ruddock, Lab.*
David Ruffley, Con.
Bob Russell, L.Dem.*
Christine Russell, Lab.
Joan Ryan, Lab.

S
Nick St. Aubyn, Con.
Alex Salmond, S.N.P.*
Martin Salter, Lab.
Adrian Sanders, L.Dem.
Mohammad Sarwar, Lab.
Malcolm Savidge, Lab.
Phil Sawford, Lab.
Jonathan Sayeed, Con.*
Brian Sedgemore, Lab.*
Jonathon Shaw, Lab.
Barry Sheerman, Lab.*
Robert Sheldon, Lab.*
Gillian Shephard, Con.*
Richard Shepherd, Con.*
Debra Shipley, Lab.
Clare Short, Lab.*
Alan Simpson, Lab.*
Keith Simpson, Con.
Marsha Singh, Lab.*
Dennis Skinner, Lab.*
Andrew Smith, Lab*
Angela Smith, Lab.
Chris Smith, Lab.*
Geraldine Smith, Lab.
Jacqui Smith, Lab.
John Smith, Lab.*
Llew Smith, Lab.*
Sir Robert Smith, L.Dem.*
W. Martin Smyth, U.U.*
Peter Snape, Lab.*
Nicholas Soames, Con.*
Clive Soley, Lab.*
Helen Southworth, Lab.
John Spellar, Lab.*
Caroline Spelman, Con.
Sir Michael Spicer, Con.*
Richard Spring, Con.*
Rachel Squire, Lab.*
Sir John Stanley, Con.*
Phyllis Starkey, Lab.
Anthony Steen, Con.*
Gerry Steinberg, Lab.*
George Stevenson, Lab.*
David Stewart, Lab.
Ian Stewart, Lab.
Paul Stinchcombe, Lab.
Howard Stoate, Lab.
Roger Stott, Lab.*
Gavin Strang, Lab.*
Jack Straw, Lab.*
Gary Streeter, Con.*

Graham Stringer, Lab.
Gisela Stuart, Lab.
Andrew Stunell, L.Dem.
Gerry Sutcliffe, Lab.*
Desmond Swayne, Con.
John Swinney, S.N.P.
Robert Syms, Con.

T
Sir Peter Tapsell, Con.*
Ann Taylor, Lab.*
Dari Taylor, Lab.
David Taylor, Lab.
Ian Taylor, Con.*
John D. Taylor, U.U.*
John M. Taylor, Con.*
Matthew Taylor, L.Dem.*
Sir Teddy Taylor, Con.*
Peter Temple-Morris, Lab.*
Gareth Thomas, Lab.
Gareth R. Thomas, Lab.
William Thompson, U.U.
Stephen Timms, Lab.*
Paddy Tipping, Lab.*
Mark Todd, Lab.
Jenny Tonge, L.Dem.
Don Touhig, Lab.*
John Townend, Con.*
David Tredinnick, Con.*
Michael CBE Trend, Con.*
Jon Trickett, Lab.*
David Trimble, U.U.*
Paul Truswell, Lab.
Dennis Turner, Lab.*
Desmond Turner, Lab.
George Turner, Lab.
Derek Twigg, Lab.
Stephen Twigg, Lab.
Paul Tyler, L.Dem.*
Andrew Tyrie, Con.

V
Keith Vaz, Lab.*
Peter Viggers, Con.*
Rudi Vis, Lab.

W
Cecil Walker, U.U.*
Jim Wallace, L.Dem.*
Joan Walley, Lab.*
Robert Walter, Con.
Claire Ward, Lab.
Charles Wardle, Con.
Robert Wareing, Lab.*
Nigel Waterson, Con.*
Dave Watts, Lab.
Steven Webb, L.Dem.
Bowen Wells, Con.*
Andrew Welsh, S.N.P.*
Brian White, Lab.*
Alan Whitehead, Lab.
Sir Raymond Whitney, Con.*
John Whittingdale, Con.*
Malcolm Wicks, Lab.*
Ann Widdecombe, Con.*
Dafydd Wigley, P.C.*
John Wilkinson, Con.*
David Willetts, Con.*
Alan Williams, Lab.*
Alan W. Williams, Lab.*
Betty Williams, Lab.
Phil Willis, L.Dem.
Michael Wills, Lab.
David Wilshire, Con.*
Brian Wilson, Lab.*
David Winnick, Lab.*
Ann Winterton, Con.*
Nicholas Winterton, Con.*
Rosie Winterton, Lab.
Audrey Wise, Lab.*
Mike Wood, Lab.
Shaun Woodward, Con.
Phil Woolas, Lab.
Tony Worthington, Lab.*
James Wray, Lab.
Tony Wright, Lab.*
Tony Wright, Lab.*
Derek Wyatt, Lab

Y
Tim Yeo, Con.*
Sir George Young, Con.*

The Cabinet of the United Kingdom*

Tony Blair—prime minister; first lord of the treasury; minister for the civil service

John Prescott—deputy prime minister; secretary of state for the environment, transport, and the regions

Gordon Brown—chancellor of the exchequer

Robin Cook—secretary of state for foreign and Commonwealth affairs

Lord Irvine of Lairg—lord chancellor

Jack Straw—secretary of state for the home department

David Blunkett—secretary of state for education and employment

Margaret Beckett—president of the Privy Council and leader of the House of Commons

Jack Cunningham—minister for the cabinet office; chancellor of the Duchy of Lancaster

Donald Dewar—secretary of state for Scotland

George Robertson—secretary of state for defence

Frank Dobson—secretary of state for health

Ann Taylor—chief whip

Chris Smith—secretary of state for culture, media, and sport

Marjorie Mowlam—secretary of state for Northern Ireland

Alun Michael—secretary of state for Wales

Clare Short—secretary of state for international development

Alistair Darling—secretary of state for social security

Nick Brown—minister of agriculture, fisheries, and food

Baroness Jay of Paddington—lord privy seal; leader of the House of Lords; minister for women

Peter Mandelson—secretary of state for trade and industry

Stephen Byers—chief secretary to the treasury

*As of Dec. 1, 1998.

ford's brother waived his right under Islamic law to demand her death and accepted $1.2 million in "blood money" instead, part of which was to go to charity. British firms with economic interests in Saudi Arabia were thought to have put up most of the money.

Au pair freed. Louise Woodward, a British *au pair* (nanny), was freed by a court in the United States and returned to Great Britain in June 1998. She had been convicted of manslaughter in the death of Matthew Eappen, an 8-month-old American baby who had been in her care. In October 1997, Woodward was found guilty of the second-degree murder of Matthew, whom prosecutors claimed she had shaken furiously. The verdict carried a mandatory life sentence. But in November, Judge Hiller Zobel downgraded the murder verdict to manslaughter. He imposed a prison sentence of 279 days, the exact time Woodward had already been incarcerated. In June 1998, Zobel's decision was upheld by the Massachusetts Supreme Judicial Court. Woodward returned to her home village of Elton, Cheshire, where neighbors had mounted a fund to finance her defense.

☐ Ian Mather

See also **Europe** (Facts in brief table); **Europe Special Report: European Union; Northern Ireland; Saudi Arabia.**

United Kingdom, Prime Minister of.

Prime Minister Tony Blair's (1953-) unprecedented popularity in the opinion polls continued throughout much of 1998. A poll on May 1, the first anniversary of the Labour Party's victory, showed that 72 percent of the British people approved his performance, making him the most popular prime minister of the 1900's. By September 1998, however, public support had fallen to 60 percent. In addition, Blair's rating for being "more honest than most politicians" had fallen from 54 percent to 34 percent in the wake of several government scandals.

With a huge majority in the House of Commons, Blair pursued many Conservative policies that Margaret Thatcher had imposed during her market-oriented revolution. Some commentators ironically described Blair as the best Conservative prime minister Britain had ever had. Blair denied he had betrayed Labour's traditional socialist values, claiming to have found a "third way"—a market economy with social responsibility.

The high point of Blair's year was the Belfast Agreement to bring peace to Northern Ireland. Blair was criticized during 1997 for his reliance on "spin doctors" and his insistence that Labour Party members speak with a single voice, which gave rise to criticism that he was establishing a U.S.-style presidential system. ☐ Ian Mather

See also **Northern Ireland.**

United Nations.

An ongoing conflict between the United Nations (UN) and Iraq culminated on Dec. 16, 1998, when the United States and the United Kingdom launched a four-day attack against Iraqi military sites. British Prime Minister Tony Blair and U.S. President Bill Clinton made their decision to strike after the chief UN weapons inspector, Richard Butler, reported that Iraqi leaders had repeatedly failed to cooperate. The clash continued late in December, when U.S. warplanes and Iraqi air defense forces exchanged fire in areas of northern and southern Iraq that were routinely patrolled by the U.S. and British military.

In 1991, the UN Security Council, the highest political body of the UN, had charged weapons inspectors from the UN Special Commission and the UN's International Atomic Energy Agency to demonstrate that Iraq could no longer manufacture long-range missiles and biological, chemical, and nuclear weapons. The elimination of such military capability was the condition for ending UN economic sanctions that were imposed after Iraqi military forces invaded Kuwait in August 1990.

The conflicts with Iraq in 1998 began in January, when Iraqi President Saddam Hussein blocked UN inspectors' work. With Iraq facing threats of U.S. and British air strikes, UN Secretary General Kofi Annan and Iraqi Deputy Prime Minister Tariq Aziz signed a memorandum of understanding on

February 23. Iraq pledged to cooperate fully with inspectors to allow "immediate, unconditional and unrestricted access" to all sites. But Iraq suspended all inspections of new sites in August and threatened to halt the monitoring of activities at known military sites in September. On September 3, the Security Council, in turn, canceled all reviews of its economic sanctions until Iraq cooperated again. Unsuccessful talks staged between Aziz and Annan led to a crisis on October 31, when Iraqi leaders ceased all cooperation with UN weapons inspectors. Annan's last-minute warnings avoided air strikes again and led Iraq on November 15 to agree to fully cooperate with weapons inspectors. According to Butler's report in December, however, Iraq failed to meet its obligations. UN Security Council members were divided over whether the U.S. and British strikes were justified.

Drugs. Representatives of more than 150 countries at a UN General Assembly session in June adopted a declaration calling for global programs to reduce the supply of and demand for illicit drugs. The declaration set 2003 as the target date for governments to have legislation and programs in place to combat money laundering. It set 2008 as a target for legislation to drastically reduce the traffic in such drugs as cocaine and opium.

Land mines. On Sept. 16, 1998, Burkina Faso became the 40th country to ratify the Convention of the Prohibition of the Use, Stockpiling, Production and Transfer of Anti-Personnel Mines and on their Destruction. The 40th ratification guaranteed that the international agreement, also known as the Ottawa Convention, would become a binding international law on March 1, 1999, for those countries that ratified it. Thousands of people around the world are maimed annually by mines, which can remain functional for years.

War crimes. Representatives from several nations and scores of nongovernmental human rights organizations met in Rome from June 15 to July 17, 1998, for a UN diplomatic conference to establish an International Criminal Court. The conference adopted a statute for a permanent court to try cases of *genocide* (the extermination of a racial or ethnic group), war crimes, and crimes against humanity. The agreement indicated that the court was to be established at The Hague, Netherlands, after 60 countries ratify the statute.

On September 4, the UN International Criminal Tribunal for Rwanda, based in Arusha, Tanzania, sentenced former Prime Minister Jean Kambanda of Rwanda to life imprisonment after finding him guilty of the genocide of ethnic Tutsi. On October 2, the tribunal also sentenced Jean-Paul Akayesu, the former mayor of Taba, Rwanda, to life imprisonment for genocide, crimes against humanity, and rape. An estimated 500,000 Rwandans were massacred during ethnic conflicts in 1994.

The UN General Assembly opened its 53rd session on Sept. 9, 1998, with the election of Uruguay's Foreign Minister Didier Opertti as president. At the opening session, Secretary General Annan reported that the UN's "single greatest impediment to good performance is the financial straitjacket within which we operate." By the end of October, the UN membership owed $2.2 billion to the administrative and peacekeeping budgets. The United States alone owed $1.2 billion.

On October 8, the General Assembly elected Canada, the Netherlands, Malaysia, Namibia, and Argentina to two-year terms on the Security Council. In 1999, the council was composed of the newly elected countries plus Bahrain, Brazil, Gabon, Gambia, and Slovenia. China, France, Russia, the United Kingdom, and the United States are permanent members of the council.

Human rights. In 1998, the UN celebrated the 50th anniversary of the Universal Declaration of Human Rights, a document that established the UN's commitment to defending human rights. The UN General Assembly adopted the Declaration on Dec. 10, 1948.   □ J. Tuyet Nguyen

See also **Armed forces** Special Report: **Chemical and Biological Weapons; Human rights** Special Report: **A Common Standard—50 Years of Defending Human Rights for All; Iraq; People in the news** (Brundtland, Gro Harlem); **Rwanda.**

United States, Government of the.

The U.S. House of Representatives voted 228 to 206 on Dec. 19, 1998, to impeach President Bill Clinton on one charge of perjury. Representatives voted 221 to 212 to impeach the president on a charge of obstruction of justice. The House rejected a second charge of perjury and a charge of abuse of power. At issue was whether President Clinton had lied or obstructed justice in trying to conceal a relationship with Monica Lewinsky, a former White House intern. The charges were made by Independent Counsel Kenneth Starr in a 445-page report delivered to the leaders of the House of Representatives in September 1998. The report, which culminated a four-year, $40-million investigation into the personal, political, and business affairs of President Clinton and Hillary Rodham Clinton, contained 11 alleged impeachable offenses.

Several leading Democrats criticized the president's behavior, but few supported the president's removal from office. Many Republicans insisted that lying under oath to a grand jury, as alleged in Starr's report, justified impeachment.

Attack on Iraq. The United States and Great Britain launched a series of air strikes on Iraq on December 16. The attacks followed a United Nations (UN) report that UN inspectors had been denied full access to suspected chemical and biological weapons sites.

Budget surplus. The U.S. government ended nearly three decades of deficit spending in 1998, with a budget surplus of $70 billion for fiscal year 1998, which ended on September 30. For the first time since 1969, the federal government spent less money than it took in from taxes and fees. Both Democratic and Republican leaders in Congress claimed credit for the surplus. Most economists, however, agreed that the surplus was the result of such factors as low unemployment and high economic growth, rather than the efforts of either political party.

Political battles erupted over how to use the surplus funds. President Clinton and most Democrats favored using the money to keep the Social Security system solvent past 2032, the year experts predicted funds would run out. Republicans favored a major tax cut.

Spending bill. President Clinton in October 1998 signed a $520-billion spending bill for fiscal year 1999, which began on Oct. 1, 1998. The bill accounted for approximately one-third of the government's $1.7-trillion budget. The spending bill included emergency funding for agriculture and added educational spending.

Interest rates. The Federal Reserve System (the Fed), the nation's central bank, moved to avert a possible recession by reducing key short-term interest rates in September, October, and November.

The reductions were the first since 1996 and followed a long period of stability in money markets. As a result, the rate that banks charge each other for loans dropped from 5.5 percent to 4.75 percent in November 1998.

Terrorism. Terrorists targeted two U.S. government installations overseas in 1998. American embassies in Kenya and Tanzania were bombed by suspected terrorists on August 7. The bombings killed 224 people, including 12 Americans.

President Clinton on August 20 ordered missile attacks against targets in Sudan and Afghanistan in retaliation for the bombings. President Clinton said that the attacks, launched from U.S. naval vessels in the Red Sea and Arabian Sea, targeted terrorist and suspected chemical weapons sites. United States officials claimed that the targets were funded by Osama bin Laden, an exiled Saudi Arabian living in Afghanistan. Officials believed that bin Laden was the head of a terrorist network and had been involved in several previous terrorist attacks against U.S. facilities.

Human-rights issues. The U.S. State Department issued its annual human-rights report in January 1998. The report surveyed personal, political, and religious rights violations in 194 countries. The state department concluded that China, which had been criticized in a 1997 report for human-rights abuses, had become "somewhat more tolerant"

Federal spending
United States budget for fiscal 1998*

Billions of dollars	
National defense	270.4
International affairs	13.1
General science, space, technology	19.6
Energy	1.4
Natural resources and environment	21.9
Agriculture	14.3
Commerce and housing credit	0.9
Transportation	36.6
Community and regional development	10.4
Education, training, employment, and social services	52.2
Health	131.0
Social security	379.2
Medicare	192.6
Income security	232.9
Veterans' benefits and services	41.8
Administration of justice	22.6
General government	13.9
Interest	243.4
Undistributed offsetting receipts	–47.2
Total budget outlays	**1,651.0**

*Oct. 1, 1997, to Sept. 30, 1998.
Source: U.S. Department of the Treasury.

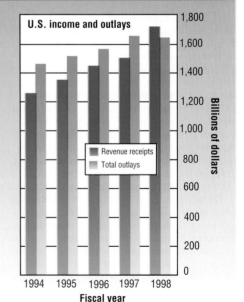

U.S. income and outlays

Revenue receipts
Total outlays

Billions of dollars

Fiscal year
Source: U.S. Department of the Treasury.

The remains of 10 victims killed in the August 7, 1998, terrorist bombings of U.S. embassies in Kenya and Tanzania are escorted by a military honor guard on their return to the United States. The bombings killed at least 224 people, including 12 Americans.

Selected agencies and bureaus of the U.S. government*

Executive Office of the President
President, Bill Clinton
 Vice President, Albert Gore, Jr.
 White House Chief of Staff, John D. Podesta
 Presidential Press Secretary, Joe Lockhart
 Assistant to the President for Domestic Policy, Bruce N. Reed
 Assistant to the President for National Security Affairs,
  Samuel R. Berger
 Assistant to the President for Science and Technology,
  Neal F. Lane
 Council of Economic Advisers—Janet L. Yellen, Chairperson
 Office of Management and Budget—Jacob J. Lew, Director
 Office of National Drug Control Policy—
  Barry R. McCaffrey, Director
 U.S. Trade Representative, Charlene Barshefsky

Department of Agriculture
Secretary of Agriculture, Daniel R. Glickman

Department of Commerce
Secretary of Commerce, William M. Daley
 Bureau of Economic Analysis—J. Steven Landefeld, Director
 Bureau of the Census—Kenneth Prewitt, Director

Department of Defense
Secretary of Defense, William S. Cohen
 Secretary of the Air Force, F. Whitten Peters (acting)
 Secretary of the Army, Louis Caldera
 Secretary of the Navy, Richard J. Danzig
 Joint Chiefs of Staff—
  General Henry H. Shelton, Chairman
  General Michael E. Ryan, Chief of Staff, Air Force
  General Dennis J. Reimer, Chief of Staff, Army
  Admiral Jay L. Johnson, Chief of Naval Operations
  General Charles C. Krulak, Commandant, Marine Corps

Department of Education
Secretary of Education, Richard W. Riley

Department of Energy
Secretary of Energy, Bill Richardson

Department of Health and Human Services
Secretary of Health and Human Services, Donna E. Shalala
 Office of Public Health and Science—
  David Satcher, Assistant Secretary
 Centers for Disease Control and Prevention—
  Claire V. Broome, Director (acting)
 Food and Drug Administration—
  Jane E. Henney, Commissioner
 National Institutes of Health—Harold Varmus, Director
 Surgeon General of the United States, David Satcher

Department of Housing and Urban Development
Secretary of Housing and Urban Development,
  Andrew M. Cuomo

Department of the Interior
Secretary of the Interior, Bruce Babbitt

Department of Justice
Attorney General, Janet Reno
 Bureau of Prisons—Kathleen Hawk Sawyer, Director
 Drug Enforcement Administration—
  Thomas A. Constantine, Administrator
 Federal Bureau of Investigation—Louis J. Freeh, Director
 Immigration and Naturalization Service—
  Doris M. Meissner, Commissioner
 Solicitor General, Seth P. Waxman

Department of Labor
Secretary of Labor, Alexis M. Herman

Department of State
Secretary of State, Madeleine K. Albright
 U.S. Ambassador to the United Nations, vacant

Department of Transportation
Secretary of Transportation, Rodney E. Slater
 Federal Aviation Administration—
  Jane F. Garvey, Administrator
 U.S. Coast Guard—Admiral James M. Loy, Commandant

Department of the Treasury
Secretary of the Treasury, Robert E. Rubin
 Internal Revenue Service—Charles O. Rossotti, Commissioner
 Treasurer of the United States, Mary Ellen Withrow
 U.S. Secret Service—Lewis C. Merletti, Director
 Office of Thrift Supervision—Ellen S. Seidman

Department of Veterans Affairs
Secretary of Veterans Affairs, Togo D. West, Jr.

Supreme Court of the United States
Chief Justice of the United States, William H. Rehnquist
 Associate Justices—
  John Paul Stevens   David H. Souter
  Sandra Day O'Connor   Clarence Thomas
  Antonin Scalia   Ruth Bader Ginsburg
  Anthony M. Kennedy   Stephen G. Breyer

Congressional officials
President of the Senate pro tempore, Strom Thurmond
 Senate Majority Leader, Trent Lott
 Senate Minority Leader, Thomas A. Daschle
 Speaker of the House, Newt Gingrich
 House Majority Leader, Richard K. Armey
 House Minority Leader, Richard A. Gephardt
 Congressional Budget Office—June E. O'Neill, Director
 General Accounting Office—James F. Hinchman, Comptroller
  General of the United States (acting)
 Library of Congress—James H. Billington, Librarian of Congress

Independent agencies
Central Intelligence Agency—George J. Tenet, Director
Commission on Civil Rights—Mary Frances Berry, Chairperson
Commission of Fine Arts—J. Carter Brown, Chairman
Consumer Product Safety Commission—
  Ann Winkelman Brown, Chairman
Corporation for National Service—
  Harris Wofford, Chief Executive Officer
Environmental Protection Agency—
  Carol M. Browner, Administrator
Equal Employment Opportunity Commission—
  Ida L. Castro, Chairwoman
Federal Communications Commission—William E. Kennard, Chairman
Federal Deposit Insurance Corporation—
  Donna A. Tanoue, Chairman
Federal Election Commission—Darryl R. Wold, Chairman
Federal Emergency Management Agency—James Lee Witt, Director
Federal Reserve System Board of Governors—
  Alan Greenspan, Chairman
Federal Trade Commission—Robert Pitofsky, Chairman
General Services Administration—David J. Barram, Administrator
International Development Cooperation Agency—
  J. Brian Atwood, Director (acting)
National Aeronautics and Space Administration—
  Daniel S. Goldin, Administrator
National Endowment for the Arts—William J. Ivey, Chairman
National Endowment for the Humanities—
  William R. Ferris, Chairman
National Labor Relations Board—vacant
National Railroad Passenger Corporation (Amtrak)—
  George D. Warrington, President & CEO (acting)
National Science Foundation—Rita R. Colwell, Director
National Transportation Safety Board—James E. Hall, Chairman
Nuclear Regulatory Commission—Shirley A. Jackson, Chair
Peace Corps—Mark D. Gearan, Director
Securities and Exchange Commission—Arthur Levitt, Jr., Chairman
Selective Service System—Gil Coronado, Director
Small Business Administration—Aida Alvarez, Administrator
Smithsonian Institution—I. Michael Heyman, Secretary
Social Security Administration—Kenneth S. Apfel, Commissioner
U.S. Arms Control and Disarmament Agency—
  John D. Holum, Director
U.S. Information Agency—Joseph D. Duffey, Director
U.S. Postal Service—William J. Henderson, Postmaster General

*As of Dec. 31, 1998.

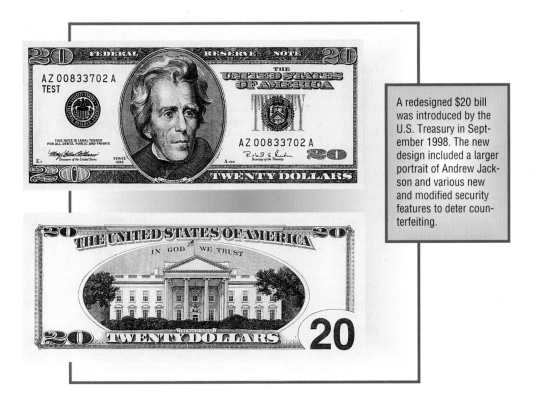

A redesigned $20 bill was introduced by the U.S. Treasury in September 1998. The new design included a larger portrait of Andrew Jackson and various new and modified security features to deter counterfeiting.

toward political dissidents and had taken steps to restore some personal freedoms. The report was more critical of Iraq, accusing that nation of creating a climate of "intimidation and fear." It also criticized Cambodia, Cuba, Indonesia, Libya, Mexico, Myanmar, Nigeria, Pakistan, Saudi Arabia, Sudan, Turkey, and Vietnam for human-rights inadequacies.

Foreign policy. The Clinton Administration on Feb. 26, 1998, certified that Mexico was cooperating in antidrug efforts, despite U.S. Drug Enforcement Administration complaints of wide-spread corruption in Mexican law enforcement. The same certification was denied to Afghanistan, Iran, Myanmar, and Nigeria. The United States also found Cambodia, Colombia, Pakistan, and Paraguay uncooperative in the war on drugs, but nevertheless issued national interest waivers, allowing the countries to continue to receive aid.

President Clinton met with Chinese leader Jiang Zemin in Beijing on June 27, as part of a summit meeting. It was the first visit a U.S. president had made to China since the 1989 crackdown on prodemocracy demonstrators in Tiananmen Square, in which hundreds of Chinese dissidents were killed. The meeting resulted in symbolic agreements on military issues, but failed to reach agreements on such issues as trade or human rights.

Military spending. President Clinton in October 1998 signed a $250-billion defense spending bill for fiscal year 1999. The legislation provided funds for new weapons programs and peacekeeping operations.

Aircraft accident. A low-flying U.S. Marine Corps EA-6B Prowler surveillance aircraft cut the cable of a ski gondola near Cavalese, Italy, in February 1998, causing it to plunge to the ground. All 20 persons in the gondola were killed. Investigators alleged that the aircraft flew under the gondola cable, severing it. Courts-martial proceedings against the aircraft pilot, Captain Richard Ashby, and Captain Joseph Schweitzer, the navigator, were postponed in October until 1999. Both officers had been charged with 20 counts of involuntary manslaughter and negligent homicide, as well as dereliction of duty and damage to military and private property.

Court-martial verdict. A military court in March 1998 convicted former Sergeant Major of the Army Gene McKinney of one count of obstructing justice. He was acquitted on 18 charges of obstructing justice and sexual misconduct with five female soldiers and a Navy enlisted woman.

McKinney, who had been the Army's highest-ranking enlisted soldier, had been reduced in rank in 1997 to command sergeant major after he was first charged. The military court in March 1998 reduced his rank an additional grade, to master sergeant, but allowed McKinney to retire from the service with full retirement pay.

Bay of Pigs report. A secret internal report by the U.S. Central Intelligence Agency (CIA) on the 1961 invasion of Cuba, known as the Bay of Pigs Invasion, was made public in February 1998. The report, written in 1961, blamed the CIA for the failed U.S.-backed invasion.

Former President John F. Kennedy had approved the April 1961 invasion by Cuban exiles at the Bay of Pigs on Cuba's south coast. The military action had been designed to bring about the overthrow of Cuba's president, Fidel Castro. However, the attack had been poorly planned by the CIA, and about 200 Cuban exiles were killed and more than 1,000 others captured.

Microsoft lawsuit. The Justice Department, attorneys general from 20 states, and the District of Columbia on May 18, 1998, filed a federal lawsuit against Redmond, Washington-based Microsoft Corp. The lawsuit alleged that Microsoft, the world's largest maker of computer software, violated antitrust laws by requiring buyers of Microsoft's popular Windows *operating system* (the master control program that coordinates the operations of a computer) to also purchase its Internet Explorer *browser* (a program that enables computers to access the World Wide Web). Microsoft's attorneys denied the allegations.

Campaign fund-raising. Attorney General Janet Reno announced on November 24 that she would not appoint an independent counsel to examine whether Vice President Al Gore lied to Department of Justice officials in 1997 during an investigation of fund-raising phone calls made for the Democratic National Committee from the vice president's government office. Reno reported that she found no reasonable grounds that the vice president misled investigators examining alleged fund-raising abuses in the 1996 election.

Reno announced on Dec. 7, 1998, that she would not seek a special prosecutor to investigate President Clinton's involvement in campaign advertising during the 1996 election.

Espy verdict. A federal jury on Dec. 3, 1998, acquitted former U.S. Agriculture Secretary Mike Espy on corruption charges. The jury determined that Espy had not illegally accepted gifts from companies he was supposed to regulate.

Line-item veto. The Supreme Court of the United States on June 25, 1998, struck down the line-item veto, which had allowed the president to delete specific items in spending bills without rejecting the entire legislation. Congress in 1996 passed the legislation granting the president the line-item veto. The justices voted that such a veto upset the balance of power between the branches of government as specified in the U.S. Constitution.

Unabomber sentenced. Theodore J. Kaczynski, an antitechnology fanatic known as the "Unabomber," pleaded guilty on Jan. 22, 1998, to 13 federal charges stemming from four mail-bombings that killed three people and injured more than 20 others during a 17-year bombing spree. A federal judge on May 4 sentenced Kaczynski to four life terms in prison plus 30 years.

Terrorist convictions. A federal judge on Jan. 8, 1998, sentenced Ramzi Ahmed Yousef to life in prison plus 240 years for the 1993 bombing of the World Trade Center in New York City and for a 1994 bombing of a Philippine airliner. The World Trade Center bombing killed six people and injured more than 1,000 others. One passenger was killed in the airliner bombing.

A U.S. District Court judge on June 4, 1998, sentenced Terry L. Nichols to life in prison for his role in the 1995 bombing of the Alfred P. Murrah Federal Building in Oklahoma City, Oklahoma. The judge also sentenced Nichols to six years in prison for each of eight involuntary manslaughter convictions in connection with the deaths of eight federal law enforcement officers killed in the bombing.   ☐ William J. Eaton

See also **Congress of the United States; Democratic Party; Elections; People in the news** (Starr, Kenneth); **Republican Party; State government; Terrorism; United States, President of the.**

United States, President of the.

The U.S. House of Representatives on Dec. 19, 1998, voted to impeach President Bill Clinton on charges of perjury and obstruction of justice. The House voted 228 to 206 on the charge of perjury and 221 to 212 on the charge of obstruction of justice. The House rejected a second charge of perjury and an abuse of power charge.

On Jan. 17, 1998, the president had denied that he had a sexual relationship with Monica Lewinsky, a former White House intern. The denial was made in a deposition in a sexual harassment lawsuit filed by Paula Jones, a former Arkansas state employee. On August 17, President Clinton admitted during a live television broadcast that he had misled his family and the nation when he denied a relationship with Lewinsky. As Republicans demanded his ouster, opinion polls indicated that the majority of the American public opposed impeachment and approved of Clinton's performance as president.

The charges arose from evidence presented by Independent Counsel Kenneth Starr in a 445-page report delivered to the leaders of the House of Representatives in September. The report was part of a four-year, $40-million investigation into the personal, political, and business affairs of President Clinton and First Lady Hillary Rodham Clinton. On October 8, the House voted 258 to

President Bill Clinton admits his involvement with a former White House intern on a live television broadcast on Aug. 17, 1998.

176 to proceed with an impeachment inquiry by the Judiciary Committee. On December 11 and 12, the committee voted to send four articles of impeachment to the full House for a vote.

Highlights. President Clinton shared credit with the U.S. Congress after the government ended fiscal year 1998 with a $70-billion surplus. In October, President Clinton helped broker the Wye River Accord. The agreement called for Israel to withdraw troops from 13 percent of the West Bank and release hundreds of jailed Palestinians. In return, the Palestinians agreed to crack down on terrorism and nullify the part of their charter that called for Israel's destruction.

Trips. On March 23, President Clinton began a 12-day, 6-nation tour of Africa. He became the first U.S. president to visit South Africa, where he met with South African President Nelson R. Mandela on March 26.

On June 25, the president began a 9-day, 5-city visit to China. On June 27, the president met with Chinese President Jiang Zemin. It was the first visit by a U.S. president to China since the 1989 crackdown on prodemocracy demonstrators in Tiananmen Square. ☐ William J. Eaton

See also **China; Democratic Party; Middle East; People in the news** (Starr, Kenneth).

Uruguay. See **Latin America**.

Utah. See **State government**.

Uzbekistan. President Islam Karimov consolidated his power base and signaled a new offensive against Islamic fundamentalism in 1998. In the fall, Karimov dismissed a series of ministers linked to powerful Uzbek clan groups, including Kayim Khakulov, the head of the national oil and gas company. The moves increased Karimov's independence from the regional clan bosses who dominated the political landscape in Central Asia. Khakulov had tolerated widespread corruption in the oil sector, and foreign companies operating in Uzbekistan generally welcomed his departure.

In May 1998, the government began a series of high-profile trials of Islamic fundamentalists accused of carrying out terrorist bombings in Uzbekistan in December 1997. Karimov used the trials to launch a new campaign against Wahhabism, a conservative Islamic sect with roots in Saudi Arabia. Karimov argued that Muslim extremists originating in Afghanistan and Tajikistan were trying to topple the government in Uzbekistan and establish an Islamic state. In response to this alleged threat, the Uzbek parliament passed a law in May that required all religious groups and activities to be approved by the government. Human rights groups condemned the new law, which went into effect during the summer. ☐ Steven L. Solnick

See also **Asia** (Facts in brief table).

Vanuatu. See **Pacific Islands**.

Venezuela. Hugo Chavez Frias, 44, a retired army colonel, was elected president of Venezuela on Dec. 6, 1998. Chavez, a leftist leader, was imprisoned from 1992 to 1994 after attempting a military overthrow of the government. In his presidential campaign, Chavez promised to review the concessions granted to foreign oil companies, delay the privatization of state-owned assets, and possibly withhold repayments on foreign debts, which consumed more than 30 percent of the national budget in 1998.

The Venezuelan economy was in disarray through much of 1998. By mid-year, earnings from oil exports, which financed nearly 45 percent of the annual national budget, stood at approximately half the mid-1997 levels. The Venezuelan stock market lost more than 70 percent of its value during 1998. According to economic analysts, the preelection threat of a political shift to the left spurred the flight of capital and discouraged new foreign investment.

In May, U.S. authorities in Los Angeles indicted four Venezuelan bank officials and an attorney on charges of laundering profits derived from drug trafficking. The charges were the result of a widespread investigation called Operation Casablanca.   ☐ Nathan A. Haverstock
    See also **Latin America** (Facts in brief table).

Vermont. See State government.

Vietnam. The ruling Communist Party fought political corruption in 1998 and struggled to keep the country's economy afloat. Le Kha Phieu, who had been appointed general secretary of the Communist Party on Dec. 29, 1997, called corruption the greatest threat to Vietnam's social stability.

Phieu, a two-star general, succeeded Do Muoi as the country's top leader. Muoi had steered Vietnam through an economic transformation in the 1990's. The changes opened markets and encouraged free enterprise while maintaining the Communist Party's grip on political and economic affairs.

Western diplomats described Phieu as an ideological hard-liner with no formal economic training. Phieu emphasized the "leading role" of large government-controlled enterprises, which Western economists claimed were one of Vietnam's chief hindrances to economic growth.

Corruption charges. Tran Do, a retired general and former party boss, appealed to the Communist Party in 1998 to implement political reforms. Do and 10 other party members charged that political appointees used corruption and intimidation to control access to land in the capital, Hanoi. A letter that Do sent to the party leadership in May focused on corruption charges against Pham The Duyet, who had been promoted in 1997 to the party's most elite group—a five-member standing committee of the politburo.

Amnesty. Vietnamese officials announced in August 1998 that the country would release 5,219 prisoners as part of a general amnesty. The prisoners included two dissidents, Doan Viet Hoat, an academic, and Nguyen Dan Que, a physician.

Hoat and Que had been arrested in 1975 for advocating greater political and individual freedoms after the Communists had captured Saigon and gained control of South Vietnam. The Vietnamese government agreed to release Hoat and Que on the condition that they leave Vietnam and move to the United States.

Economy. Vietnam's economy weakened in 1998, though it was not hit as hard by the Asian financial crisis as those of some of its neighbors. In September, Premier Phan Van Khai said that economic growth had been declining since 1996. He warned that economic losses in 1998 threatened national stability and development.

The financial crisis in Asia reduced business in Vietnam by major investors, such as South Korea, Singapore, and Taiwan. It also threatened Vietnam's competitiveness with the devalued currencies of the region.   ☐ Henry S. Bradsher
    See also **Asia** (Facts in brief table); **Economics** Special Report: **Asian Economic Crisis.**

Washington. See State government.

Washington, D.C. The city government of Washington, D.C., showed significant improvements in 1998. Audits of 1997 finances revealed that the city had a budget surplus for the first time since 1993. While a financial control board appointed by the United States Congress in 1995 continued to oversee city finances in 1998, that responsibility was expected to return to the mayor after three additional years of balanced budgets.

A new mayor. In May, Marion S. Barry, Jr., mayor of Washington, D.C., for 16 of the past 20 years, announced that he would not seek reelection. Although Barry had been widely blamed for the District's woes, some federal officials still considered him capable of winning a fifth term. Barry's announcement set off an intense race for the job of mayor. In a city where Democrats outnumber Republicans 10 to 1, the real contest was for the Democratic nomination.

On November 3, Democrat Anthony Williams, who had held the position of chief financial officer (CFO) of the District since 1995, won the mayoral race. As the city's CFO, he had slashed spending, cut payrolls, and produced a balanced budget. Shortly after the election, the financial control board began discussing what responsibilities they would turn over to the new mayor.

Williams faced serious challenges. According to most political observers, the District needed to re-

Workers position concrete barriers around the Washington Monument on Aug. 22, 1998, after the U.S. military attacked alleged terrorist sites in Afghanistan and Sudan in retaliation for the bombings of U.S. embassies in Kenya and Tanzania.

store its relationship with the U.S. Congress, which oversees the city and controls the money it receives from the federal government. Crime still remained a problem, as did corruption in the police force. The city's schools and infrastructure needed immediate attention, and the city needed to attract middle-class residents, whose flight to the suburbs had robbed the city of much of its tax base.

Other leadership changes. In June, Andrew Brimmer, the chairman of Washington, D.C.'s financial control board, resigned. Although the board had been generally credited with turning the city around, several officials criticized Brimmer for an allegedly authoritarian management style. He announced his retirement after *The Washington Post* reported that three of the

board's five members planned to resign. Alice Rivlin—vice chairman of the U.S. Federal Reserve System, which oversees the nation's banks—took Brimmer's place.

In April, the city council approved Charles H. Ramsey as chief of police. His predecessor, Larry D. Soulsby, had resigned in 1997 in the wake of a corruption scandal. Ramsey, who had been the deputy superintendent of police in Chicago, vowed to crack down on police corruption and to raise morale.

In June 1998, Arlene Ackerman succeeded Julius W. Becton, Jr., as superintendent of the District of Columbia Public Schools. In 1996, Becton had taken on the task of revitalizing a school system that critics had called one of the worst in the nation. Becton's administration had focused on various crises involving school funds and unsafe buildings. He turned over the task of improving academic performance to Ackerman, the District's chief academic officer.

Ronald Reagan in 1998 joined the roster of former presidents of the United States commemorated in Washington, D.C. On February 6, Reagan's 87th birthday, President Bill Clinton signed into law a bill renaming the National Airport the Ronald Reagan Washington National Airport. In May, the Ronald Reagan Building and International Trade Center opened. Designed by American architect James Ingo Freed, the Ronald Reagan Building completes the Federal Triangle, an enormous three-sided block of federal office buildings begun in the 1930's. The new building, the federal government's second-largest structure after the Pentagon, houses small government agencies and nongovernment businesses and organizations.

The cultural event of 1998 in Washington, D.C., was an exhibition of works by the Dutch artist Vincent van Gogh (1853–1890) at the National Gallery of Art. "Van Gogh's Van Goghs," which opened in October 1998, displayed 72 paintings, 70 of them from the Van Gogh Museum in Amsterdam, the Netherlands.   □ Robert Messenger
See also **City.**

Weather.

The year 1998 was the warmest since record-keeping began in 1880, with an average temperature over the Earth's surface during the first 10 months of 1.25 °F (0.7 °C) above normal. Many atmospheric scientists suggested that the very strong *El Nino* (a periodic warming of central and eastern equatorial Pacific Ocean waters) during the first half of 1998 contributed to the unusually warm conditions.

Climate abnormalities consistent with strong El Nino conditions were evident around the world. Drought led to wildfires in Indonesia, Brazil, and Central America and caused crop losses in southeastern Africa. Potent winter storms contributed to record rains in parts of the southern United States. Exceptionally mild weather gave much of Canada the warmest spring on record.

One of the most significant weather phenomena of the year was Hurricane Mitch, which ravaged Central America in October 1998. Government officials called Mitch the worst natural disaster to ever strike Latin America.

January dawned stormy across the eastern United States. Between January 5 and 9, moisture from the Gulf of Mexico brought heavy rain to portions of the southern Appalachians and interior Northeast. Sections of western North Carolina and eastern Tennessee were inundated with more than 12 inches (30 centimeters) of rain.

Twelve deaths were attributed to the flooding.

A catastrophic ice storm ravaged portions of Canada and the northeastern United States in January, as moist air covered a layer of subfreezing air along the ground. Ice accumulations from January 5 to January 9 measured 2 inches (5.1 centimeters) thick in much of the southern St. Lawrence River Valley, with greater than 3-inch (7.6-centimeter) ice depths reported in several locations. The weight of the ice toppled hundreds of thousands of trees and electric utility lines from Ontario to New Brunswick and from northern New York to interior Maine. At the height of the storm, more than 80 percent of Maine's residents were without electricity. In Canada, conditions were worse, with Ottawa and Montreal particularly hard hit. A total of 3 million Canadians lost power, compared with 500,000 people in the United States. Total losses from the ice storm were estimated at billions of dollars in Canada and $400 million in the United States.

February floods and tornadoes. Two powerful Pacific storms lashed central and southern California in February. On February 2 and 3, heavy rain and winds of 90 miles (145 kilometers) per hour caused power outages and mud slides throughout the state. On February 23 and 24, a second storm caused more heavy rain and flooding. San Francisco recorded its wettest February, with 14.89 inches (37.82 centimeters) of rain.

In Florida, severe thunderstorms erupted along a cold front on the night of February 22, spawning at least seven tornadoes in the central part of the state. The tornadoes caused 42 deaths and over 200 injuries. More than 20 deaths occurred in Kissimmee near Walt Disney World.

A state snowfall record was set in Lead, South Dakota, when 115 inches (292 centimeters) of snow fell over a six-day period ending March 2. From March 6 to 9, a blizzard in the eastern Plains and upper Midwest produced 12-foot (3.7-meter) snowdrifts in central Iowa.

Record-breaking warmth and rain. January and February 1998 combined were the warmest and wettest such period in the United States since record-keeping began. Tampa, Florida, received 31 inches (79 centimeters) of rain during the winter—four times the normal amount. California's 1997-1998 rainy season, from fall to spring, was the wettest on record in many locations, including Los Angeles, where 31 inches of rain fell at the airport. In the Midwest, Lake Erie remained ice-free throughout the winter for only the third time in the 1900's.

Early spring brought tornadoes to the Southeast. On April 8 and 9, 1998, tornadoes ripped through parts of Alabama, Georgia, and Mississippi, killing at least 40 people and injuring hundreds. A tornado hit the suburbs of Birming-

A child in Nicaragua salvages belongings from the floodwaters caused by Hurricane Mitch in October 1998. Mitch—the deadliest natural disaster to ever hit Latin America—caused the deaths of between 10,000 and 20,000 people and destroyed 70 percent of the infrastructure in Honduras and Nicaragua.

The year 1998 was the warmest on record throughout the world, and an El Nino caused deadly winds, wildfires, and floods.

Mobil homes rest on their sides by a swimming pool near Kissimmee, Florida, after a deadly tornado tore through the area on February 23. The twister was one of at least seven that hit the central part of Florida, causing more than 20 deaths and over 200 injuries.

A fireman battles wildfires between Daytona Beach and De Land, Florida, in May 1998. By July 4, the fires had burned nearly 500,000 acres (202,000 hectares), affecting all of Florida's 67 counties. Meteorologists attributed the fires to weather conditions brought about by El Nino.

Houses in Laguna Niguel, California, slide down a rain-soaked hillside in March 1998. Torrential rains in February caused by powerful Pacific storms broke records in central and southern California, including San Francisco's record for its wettest February with 14.89 inches (37.82 centimemeters) of rain.

Walkers along the breakwater at Brighton, England, *above,* brace themselves against the wind in January 1998. Storms brought high winds and hail to much of Western Europe. Members of the U.S. Army Corps of Engineers, *left,* install a new high-water marker at Hamburg, Iowa, in June 1998. The rising waters of the Nishnabotna River forced the evacuation of the town.

A resident of Lexington, Kentucky, blows snow out of a driveway on February 4. Rain and snow across much of the United States in February contributed to making the first 10 months of 1998 the wettest such period the country has experienced since record-keeping began.

ham, Alabama, narrowly missing the downtown area. On April 16, a twister in the business district of Nashville, Tennessee, damaged many large structures, but no one was killed.

Spring drought and fires in areas bordering the Gulf of Mexico followed the unusually wet winter. April, May, and June were the driest months in 104 years of record-keeping in Florida, Texas, and Louisiana. In May, brushfires in Central America, resulting from a drought, sent thick smoke across parts of Mexico, Texas, and the Southeast coast.

In Florida, the drought produced record heat and dryness in May and June. At Melbourne, Florida, temperatures exceeded 95 °F (35 °C) for more than 20 consecutive days in June. Average state temperatures in the May-June period were the hottest on record.

The abundant growth of brush during the mild, wet winter fueled devastating wildfires in northern Florida from May through July. More than 120,000 people were forced to evacuate, including all of the residents of Flagler County. The fires ultimately burned nearly 500,000 acres (202,000 hectares) and destroyed $500 million in property, including 300 houses and businesses.

Tornadoes in late May and early June, spawned by severe thunderstorms, struck regions from the northern Plains to the Northeast. More than 370 tornadoes occurred across the nation during June—nearly 200 more than average. At the end of the first six months of 1998, 124 people had died as a result of tornadoes, the most since 1974. On May 30, 1998, a powerful tornado hit Spencer, South Dakota, killing 6 people and destroying 90 percent of the town.

Summer brought blistering heat to the southern Plains. July was the hottest month ever recorded in Shreveport, Louisiana, and San Antonio, Texas. In Dallas, temperatures of 100 °F (38 °C) or higher occurred on 29 consecutive days.

The Atlantic tropical storm and hurricane season began on July 29 with the christening of Tropical Storm Alex. Alex formed off the western coast of Africa but quickly dissipated. A more formidable storm, Bonnie, was born near the Windward Islands. On August 25, Bonnie made landfall near Cape Fear, North Carolina, with central winds near 100 miles (161 kilometers) per hour. A weak tropical storm named Charley brought relief from the drought in southern Texas in late August. Nearly 22 inches (56 centimeters) of rain fell on Del Rio, Texas, in a single day. The resulting flash flood claimed 9 lives.

Hurricane Georges formed in the eastern Atlantic, reaching hurricane status on September 17. The storm moved through the northern Windward Islands and then across the Greater Antilles, with winds as high as 115 miles (185 kilo-

meters) per hour. Georges was the worst storm to hit Puerto Rico since 1932 and caused over $2 billion in damages. More than 500 people were killed in the Dominican Republic, Haiti, and Cuba. A weakened Georges swept over the Florida Keys before making final landfall near Pascagoula, Mississippi, on September 28. The storm flooded coastal regions from Mississippi to the Florida panhandle, which recorded 10 to 25 inches (25 to 64 centimeters) of rain.

Hurricane Mitch, the worst storm—and the deadliest natural disaster—to ever strike Latin America, formed in the Caribbean on October 22. Mitch made landfall at Honduras, where incessant rain caused tremendous floods and mud slides. On October 30, in neighboring Nicaragua, the cone of dormant volcano Casita—which had filled with water—collapsed, burying entire villages in mud. Mitch was believed to have caused the deaths of 10,000 to 20,000 people in Honduras, Nicaragua, El Salvador, and Guatemala.

A deadly cold wave struck Eastern and Central Europe from November 22 through December 7. More than 180 people died, most of them in Poland and Romania. On November 22, temperatures in Poland plummeted to -4 °F (-20 °C).

☐ Todd Miner and Fred Gadomski

See also **Disasters; Latin America.**

Weightlifting. See Sports.

Welfare. President Bill Clinton announced in May 1998 that the number of people receiving welfare benefits in the United States dropped from 12.2 million to 8.9 million people since the federal welfare system was overhauled in 1996. Some political analysts credited a strong economy and the availability of more jobs as reasons for the decrease.

The president credited some of the decrease to the Welfare to Work Partnership, a 1997 program designed to place welfare recipients in jobs. He said that 5,000 participating companies had hired 135,000 former welfare recipients.

Executives of several companies participating in the program said that employees who had been receiving welfare stayed on the job longer than employees who had not received welfare benefits. Some critics of the program, however, argued that many welfare recipients were too unskilled or unaccustomed to working full-time jobs to make the Welfare to Work Partnership a long-term success.

Government jobs. Vice President Al Gore announced in April 1998 that 31 federal departments and agencies had hired 3,688 welfare recipients since 1997. President Clinton had set a goal in 1997 to reduce the number of people on welfare by hiring 10,000 welfare recipients for U.S. government jobs by 2000.

Food stamps restored. President Clinton signed legislation on June 23, 1998, restoring food stamp benefits to about 250,000 of the 935,000 legal immigrants who had lost eligibility when the welfare system was revised in 1996. The legislation, which was part of a $1.9-billion agriculture bill that included expanding agricultural research programs, provided $818 million through 2003 to restore food stamps for immigrants who were in the United States legally when welfare legislation was signed in 1996. The 1996 welfare bill had made all legal immigrants ineligible for food stamps.

Income gap. The Economic Report of the President, presented to the United States Congress in February 1998, revealed that the economic gap between African Americans and white Americans narrowed during the economic boom of the 1990's.

The economic report showed that the median income of black families rose 13.4 percent between 1993 and 1996, compared with a 5 percent increase in the median income of white families. The percentage of African American families below the poverty line fell to 26.1 percent, according to the report. However, analysts noted that the figure was still more than three times the 8.6 percent of white families below the poverty line.

☐ William J. Eaton

West Indies. The Atlantic LNG Company of Trinidad and Tobago completed a $1-billion natural gas processing plant at Point Fortin in southern Trinidad in 1998. The plant represented the largest single industrial investment ever made in a Caribbean nation. (LNG stands for liquefied natural gas.)

The Atlantic LNG project was the fifth natural gas plant built in the two-island nation since 1993. During that time, 50 American companies invested more than $4 billion to tap Trinidad's natural gas reserves, which were estimated in 1998 at approximately 75 trillion cubic feet (2.1 trillion cubic meters).

By 1998, Trinidad and Tobago ranked as the world's second-largest exporter of ammonia and methanol, by-products of natural gas. Moreover, according to 1998 reports, the natural gas investments from 1993 to 1997 had helped raise the nation's annual per capita income from $3,920 to $4,290. During this same period, inflation dropped from 13 to 3.8 percent.

Hurricane Georges swept through the Caribbean in September 1998, leaving more than 500 people dead and more than 100,000 others homeless. Most of the deaths and destruction occurred on the island of Hispaniola, which is shared by the Dominican Republic and Haiti. Dominican President Leonel Fernandez Reyna re-

ported that the storm had destroyed 90 percent of his country's crops.

Elections. In midterm elections on May 17 in the Dominican Republic, the opposition Dominican Revolutionary Party (PRD) won a sweeping victory, taking 24 of 30 seats in the Senate and 83 of 149 seats in the Chamber of Deputies. Analysts attributed the victory partly to sympathy for 61-year-old Jose Pena Gomez, one of Latin America's foremost black politicians, who died on May 10. Filling in for Pena Gomez as the PRD candidate for mayor of Santo Domingo, the capital city, popular singer Johnny Ventura easily won the mayoral election.

General elections in the Netherlands Antilles on January 30 failed to produce a clear winner. After a 5-month stalemate, six parties agreed to form a coalition government. Suzy Camelia-Romer of the People's National Party was sworn in as prime minister on June 1.

St. Kitts and Nevis. On August 10, voters on the island of Nevis narrowly defeated a referendum on its independence from St. Christopher (commonly called St. Kitts), the larger partner in the two-island nation. ☐ Nathan A. Haverstock

See also **Latin America** (Facts in brief table).

West Virginia. See **State government.**

Wisconsin. See **State government.**

Wyoming. See **State government.**

Yemen. Acts of violence and growing tensions with Saudi Arabia during 1998 threatened to derail the Yemeni government's efforts to restore economic and political stability after the devastating 1994 civil war.

In June 1998, at least 21 soldiers and 30 civilians were killed in Yemeni cities, including the capital, Sana, in violent protests that followed steep price increases for gasoline, cooking gas, wheat, and flour. The government implemented the price increases at the urging of the International Monetary Fund and the World Bank, two United Nations agencies that provide credit to member states, in the hope that the economic reforms would stabilize Yemen's inflation and reduce its dependence on oil export revenues.

Problems with Saudi Arabia. Yemen's relations with Saudi Arabia deteriorated in July when at least 5 Yemeni and 10 Saudi troops were killed in territorial clashes on the island of al-Duwaima in the Red Sea and on the eastern border of Yemen's Marah province. The two countries have contested their mutual borders for six decades. Negotiations between Saudi and Yemeni officials in 1998 failed to resolve the border disputes.

In September, the Yemeni government accused opposition groups funded by "foreign parties" of carrying out a series of bombings in the southern port city of Aden. Western diplomats said the Yemeni government believed these foreign parties to be Saudis.

Saudi Arabia's backing of Eritrea in that country's dispute with Yemen over ownership of the Hanish Islands in the Red Sea further complicated relations. In October, an international arbitration committee in London ruled that Yemen and Eritrea were to share sovereignty over the Hanish Islands. Yemen, Eritrea, and Saudi Arabia supported the ruling.

Kidnappings. On December 29, four Western tourists were reportedly killed when Yemeni security forces stormed the hideout near the southern town of Mawdiyah where Islamic militants were holding 16 British, Australian, and American tourists. The militants had seized the tourists the previous day and demanded the release of imprisoned colleagues.

More than 100 foreigners, mainly diplomats and oil company employees, have been kidnapped in Yemen since 1992. Most of the abductions have been carried out by disgruntled tribesmen hoping to earn government concessions for their regions. In August 1998, Yemeni President Ali Abdallah Salih approved a law that imposed the death penalty for kidnapping, looting, hijacking, and highway robbery.   □ Christine Helms

See also **Middle East** (Facts in brief table); **Saudi Arabia.**

Yugoslavia.
Violence and ethnic cleansing erupted in the Serbian province of Kosovo in 1998. Kosovo, where 90 percent of the 2.2 million people are ethnic Albanians, enjoyed limited autonomy under Serbia until 1990. (Yugoslavia has been comprised of two republics, Serbia and Montenegro, since 1992.) In January 1998, the Kosovo Liberation Army (KLA), which seeks independence for Kosovo, announced its intention to unify Kosovo with Albania. By March, heavily armed Serbian police and Yugoslav Army forces began massive crackdowns against demonstrators and armed KLA units, which resulted in at least 80 deaths. Serbian forces began a campaign of ethnic cleansing in Kosovo, burning villages and preventing relief workers from aiding Albanian refugees driven from their homes.

Kosovo violence escalates. On March 2, 1998, a clash between Serb police and ethnic Albanians resulted in the death of 16 rioters and 4 police officers. This led to an intensification of the army's offensive against the KLA. On March 18, Serb police opened fire on protesters in Pristina, the Kosovar capital. One person was killed, and several were wounded.

Yugoslav President Slobodan Milosevic largely ignored the warnings of the international community to end the violence and ethnic cleansing. On March 21, the European Union (EU), a political and economic alliance of 15 European nations, imposed economic sanctions and an arms embargo on Yugoslavia. On March 31, the United Nations (UN) imposed its own arms embargo. In July, the International Criminal Tribunal for the Former Yugoslavia, which meets in The Hague, Netherlands, announced that it would include Kosovo in its investigations of war crimes. Despite threats of military force by the North Atlantic Treaty Organization (NATO), Serb police and army units attacked pockets of KLA resistance through August and September and destroyed many villages. In late September, Serb forces massacred 18 civilians, mainly women and children, in Gornje Obrinje, near Pristina.

By September, an estimated 300,000 residents of Kosovo had been driven from their homes. More than 40,000 had fled to Montenegro, which eventually closed its borders. Albania, which had already taken in 10,000 to 20,000 refugees, accepted another 3,000 people. UN representatives labeled the situation a humanitarian disaster.

The threat of NATO air strikes led Milosevic to agree in October to withdraw all military and security forces that had not been in Kosovo prior to February, when the offensive against the KLA began. He also allowed 2,000 international monitors into Kosovo. Sporadic violence continued, however. On December 24, Serb forces launched an offensive against KLA strongholds after a number of Serbs, including a policeman, were gunned down. Days of heavy fighting followed.

Montenegro. Milo Djukanovic was sworn in as president of Montenegro in January 1998, replacing Milosevic's ally, Momir Bulatovic. Djukanovic supported economic reform and criticized Milosevic's actions in Kosovo. In May, Yugoslavia's federal parliament, packed with Milosevic supporters, elected Bulatovic prime minister. Djukanovic's coalition won a majority in Montenegro's parliament and control of local governing bodies in May. Djukanovic's government broke off high-level ministerial contact with Bulatovic's federal government of Yugoslavia in July.

Economy. Yugoslavia's inflation rate rose to double digits early in 1998, and economists estimated that it would reach 50 percent for the year. The government devalued the national currency, the dinar, in March. To ease food shortages and the sharp increase in prices of essential goods, the government instituted bread, milk, and cooking oil subsidies. The trade deficit reached $1.5 billion in July. Analysts estimated that the unemployment rate in Yugoslavia in October was 50 percent, with some 1 million people on leave from businesses closed due to sanctions.

□ Sharon L. Wolchik

See also **Albania; Europe** (Facts in brief table).

Yukon Territory.
See **Canadian territories.**

Ethnic Albanian Muslims pray at a funeral for men killed in April 1998 by Yugoslav troops in Kosovo, a province of Serbia. Through much of 1998, Serbian police and the Yugoslav army fought to suppress an armed separatist movement among Kosovo's ethnic Albanian population.

Zambia. President Frederick Chiluba on March 17, 1998, lifted a national state of emergency imposed on Oct. 29, 1997, one day after a group of junior army officers unsuccessfully attempted to seize control of Zambia's government. The emergency law had given the government sweeping powers, including the right of detention without trial. Chiluba's decision to impose emergency rule was criticized by Western countries, which cut off about $800 million in aid.

Kaunda charged. Among the approximately 90 people arrested on charges of participating in the plot was Kenneth Kaunda, who had ruled Zambia for 27 years and had been defeated by Chiluba in 1991 in Zambia's first democratic elections. Kaunda was charged in January 1998 with concealing knowledge of the plot from the government. The government also accused him and two other politicians of financing and supporting the attempted overthrow.

Kaunda had left Zambia shortly before the attempted overthrow, warning of imminent civil disorder. Officers who had implicated Kaunda in the plot, however, testified in court that they had made the accusation under threat of torture. Kaunda's arrest triggered an outcry from a number of African leaders, the United States, and the United Kingdom.

Zambia's supreme court freed Kaunda on June 1 after the government dropped all charges against him. On June 9, 77 soldiers and 2 politicians accused of involvement in the plot went on trial. On July 9, Kaunda resigned as leader of the United National Independence Party, a condition of his release.

The economy. In May, the African Development Bank, an international lending agency, reported that Zambia's *gross domestic product* (the total value of all goods and services produced by a country in a year) was expected to grow by 4 percent in 1998 after a decline in 1997. The decline had resulted mainly from agricultural problems, particularly drought. Fueling the increase were mining operations and gains from *privatization* (the sale of government-owned companies to private investors). Although the bank reported that Zambia's medium-term growth prospects were encouraging, about 80 percent of Zambians lived below the bank's official poverty line.

Regional relations. On Jan. 15, 1998, Zambia and its northern neighbor, the Democratic Republic of the Congo (formerly Zaire), announced a 15-point agreement covering, among other areas, trade, communications, and security. As part of the pact, the two countries agreed to develop a hydroelectric power station to supply both countries with electricity.   □ Simon Baynham

See also **Africa** (Facts in brief table); **Congo (Kinshasa).**

Zimbabwe. President Robert Mugabe in 1998 faced his worst political and economic problems since taking office in 1980, when Zimbabwe gained its independence. A 50-percent unemployment rate, a 40-percent inflation rate, a deteriorating currency, and growing public discontent with official corruption led to civil unrest and nationwide strikes. Several senior officials of Mugabe's ruling party called for his resignation.

Food riots. In January 1998, Mugabe was forced to deploy 30,000 troops on the streets of Harare, the capital, to quell rioting triggered by price hikes of up to 45 percent for basic foods. At least eight people were killed in the three-day protest. In response to the riot, the government rescinded part of the price increase and imposed price controls on food.

In March and August, the Zimbabwe Congress of Trade Unions staged several short nationwide strikes that virtually paralyzed Zimbabwe's economy. The strikes forced the cancellation of tax increases that the union said were being used to fund luxuries for Mugabe's political allies. In November, thousands of people staged violent demonstrations in Harare in protest against the doubling of fuel prices and Mugabe's decision to send troops to the Congo.

The land question. A government plan, announced in November 1997, to confiscate about 840 large commercial farms owned by whites aroused considerable controversy in 1998. Under the plan, about 162,000 landless black families were to be settled on 13.6 million acres (5.5 million hectares), which comprised about half of all commercial acreage in Zimbabwe and about 70 percent of the country's prime farmland.

In January 1998, the Commercial Farmers' Union, a trade organization, concluded that the redistribution would cut Zimbabwe's agricultural exports by 40 percent and cost at least 150,000 jobs. Agriculture is the largest sector of the Zimbabwean economy, providing about 500,000 jobs. According to critics of the plan, most of the agricultural land previously seized by the government had deteriorated because of mismanagement or had become the property of government officials or politically connected businesses.

In March, the government cut about 600 farms from the list and in August promised to pay for all confiscated land. However, the European Union—an organization of 15 Western European nations—gave Mugabe a cool response to his plea for aid to pay for the plan. In October, the farmworkers' union reported that an estimated 12,000 workers—nearly all black—had been laid off from commercial farms. The union accused white farmers of attempting to halt land reform.   □ Simon Baynham

See also **Africa** (Facts in brief table).

Visitors at Walt Disney World's Animal Kingdom, a combination zoo and theme park that opened in Orlando, Florida in 1998, view animals and plants of the African savanna during a tour by safari vehicle.

Zoos. Oceans Pavilion, the largest aquarium in Europe, opened in May 1998 in Lisbon, Portugal, as the keynote exhibit of Expo '98, the last world fair of the 1900's. The aquarium, which contains 8,000 animals of 250 species, is based on the theme that all of Earth's oceans constitute a single ocean system. Designed by American architect Peter Chermayeff of Cambridge Seven Associates in Cambridge, Massachusetts, Oceans Pavilion cost $70 million to build.

At the center of the aquarium is a large tank, measuring 110 feet (34 meters) across by 22 feet (6.7 meters) deep, representing the open ocean. This tank, containing 1.2 million gallons (4.5 million liters) of seawater, houses more than 80 species that normally live far out at sea, including brown sharks, gray reef sharks, eagle rays, sea turtles, bluefin tuna, and large schools of mackerel and other fish. At each corner of the open ocean tank is a separate exhibit representing a coastal region in one of four different oceans—the Atlantic, Antarctic, Pacific, or Indian ocean.

Visitors enter the aquarium's upper level to find the above-water portions of the coastal habitats. The first habitat is a simulation of rocky coastal cliffs such as those along the northern Atlantic in Scotland or Newfoundland. Various seabirds, including puffins, murres, and razorbills, can be seen roosting along the cliffs and diving into the water below. At the next coastal habitat, the visitor encounters the Antarctic region, where rocky outcrops and tall grasses mimic the coasts of the Falkland Islands or southern Chile. Magellanic penguins pop in and out of the water in this habitat. Turning from this cold part of the world, the visitor reaches the temperate Pacific coastal habitat, which includes sea otters swimming in a cove pool and oyster catchers flying above them. The final corner on the aquarium's upper level displays the tropical island environment of the Indian Ocean, where numerous birds roost in palm trees and colorful fish swim among a coral reef.

The lower level of the aquarium allows visitors to see the underwater portions of the coastal habitats as well as the open ocean tank. In the underwater section of the northern Atlantic, spectators watch as puffins and other seabirds swim through the openings in the foundations of the rocky cliffs. In the temperate Pacific habitat, visitors view sea otters swimming below the water's surface and observe an underwater seaweed forest that is inhabited by such brightly colored fish as orange Garibaldis. Each of the four coastal habitats is separated from the open ocean by curved, transparent acrylic walls. As a person looks through a coastal tank and into the open ocean tank beyond, all the animals appear to be part of the same ocean environment. This illusion reinforces the aquarium's theme that all the world's oceans constitute one big ocean.

Pacific odyssey. In June, the Long Beach Aquarium of the Pacific, the fourth largest aquarium in the United States, opened on the waterfront at Long Beach, California. Its 17 major exhibit tanks and 30 smaller tanks housed more than 10,000 animals of 550 species.

Visitors enter the aquarium in the Great Hall of the Pacific, where a 143,000-gallon (541,000-liter) tank nearly three stories tall houses more than 400 predatory species common in southern California waters. Among these animals are leopard sharks, barracudas, giant sea bass, white sea bass, and giant striped sea stars.

In a gallery devoted to animal life in southern California and Mexico's Baja Peninsula, spectators view an underwater forest in which sharks and other fish weave among strands of giant seaweed called kelp. Another exhibit in this gallery simulates the shore of Santa Catalina Island. It shelters California sea lions and harbor seals that were rehabilitated after being rescued from the island in poor health. In a simulation of the Sea of Cortez, sea turtles paddle among other aquatic life of the area.

The northern Pacific gallery represents the frigid waters off Russia and northern Japan. Puffins and other diving birds rest on the rocky cliffs while northern sea otters play in the water of this exhibit. In other displays representing scenes farther from shore, visitors can see such unusual animals as the giant Pacific octopus and the Japanese spider crab, which can measure 6 feet (1.8 meter) across.

The aquarium's largest exhibit displays species found in four different coral-reef habitats in Micronesia's Palau Islands in the tropical Pacific. More than 1,000 fish, including blue-spotted stingrays, reef-tip sharks, zebra sharks, pufferfish, stinging catfish, and giant groupers, swim about in the 350,000-gallon (1.3 million-liter) tank. Scuba divers, equipped with microphones, swim among the fish and answer visitors' questions about the reef's inhabitants.

More Disney magic. Walt Disney World added more magic to its Orlando, Florida, site in April, when it opened Animal Kingdom, a combination zoo/theme park. Visitors to Animal Kingdom can go on an African safari in an open vehicle and a trip back in time to visit dinosaurs.

One-thousand animals from 200 species live on a 500-acre (202-hectare) site in Animal Kingdom. The site has been planted with numerous trees, shrubs, and grasses like those on an African savanna. The "Kilimanjaro Safari" is a 20-minute safari vehicle ride over bumpy trails that simulates an African safari on which visitors can see elephants, rhinos, hippos, lions, cheetahs, giraffes, zebras, several antelope species, and ostriches. In a "make-believe" Disney theme-park twist, the vehicle takes off in pursuit of "poachers" who have "killed" an elephant. Gorillas can be seen during a walk along a jungle trail.

The Tree of Life, a 145-foot (44-meter) tall, 170-foot (52-meter) in circumference artificial tree, stands near the entrance of Animal Kingdom. The tree, representing the diversity of animal life, is hand carved with more than 300 detailed images of animals. Animal Kingdom also includes Dinoland USA, which features life-sized robotic dinosaurs, and Camp Minnie-Mickey, where Disney's trademark cartoon characters entertain.

The north woods. In June, the Calgary Zoo in Alberta, Canada, opened the Northern Forest, the third in a series of exhibits about wildlife in Canada. Other exhibits in the series, called Canadian Wilds, are the Aspen Woodlands, which opened in 1992, and Rocky Mountains, which opened in 1995. The exhibits were designed to provide people with a better understanding of Canada's habitats and wildlife.

The new exhibit contained a 3.5-acre (1.4-hectare) forest of poplars, aspen, spruce, tamarack, and other trees. Visitors to the forest can see woodland caribou, moose, lynx, and rare whooping cranes. An interpretive center on the grounds offers visitors a look at beavers and river otters in natural-habitat displays.

□ Eugene J. Walter, Jr.

Index

How to use the index

This index covers the contents of the 1997, 1998, and 1999 editions.

Each index entry gives the edition year and the page number or numbers—for example, **Conservation, 99:** 134-135. This means that information on this topic may be found on pages 134 through 135 of the 1999 edition.

When there are many references to a topic, they are grouped alphabetically by clue words under the main topic. For example, the clue words under **Constitutions** group the references to that topic under several subtopics.

The "see" and "see also" cross-references—for example, **Coronary artery disease** and **Courts**—refer the reader to other entries in the index or to Update articles in the volumes covered by the index.

When a topic such as **Crime** appears in all capital letters, this means that there is an Update article entitled Crime in at least one of the three volumes covered by this index. References to the topic in other articles may also appear after the topic name.

When only the first letter of a topic, such as **Cyclones,** is capitalized, this means that there is no article entitled Cyclones but that information on this topic may be found in the edition and on the pages listed.

The indication (il.) means that the reference on this page is to an illustration only, as in the picture of **Bjorn Daehlie** on page 315 of the 1999 edition.

An entry followed by *WBE* refers to a new or revised *World Book Encyclopedia* article in the supplement section, as in **Dance:** *WBE* **99:** 466. This means that a *World Book Encyclopedia* article on this topic begins on page 466 of the 1999 edition.

Acknowledgments

The publishers acknowledge the following sources for illustrations. Credits read from top to bottom, left to right, on their respective pages. An asterisk (*) denotes illustrations and photographs created exclusively for this edition. All maps, charts, and diagrams were prepared by the staff unless otherwise noted.

6 Everett Collection; AP/Wide World
7 Agence France-Presse; AP/Wide World
8 Agence France-Presse; AP/Wide World
9 AP/Wide World
10 AP/Wide World; Agence France-Presse
11-13 AP/Wide World
14 Agence France-Presse
17-27 AP/Wide World
28 Agence France-Presse
31-32 AP/Wide World
35 Reuters/Archive Photos
36 Agence France-Presse
38 AP/Wide World
40 Agence France-Presse
44-47 AP/Wide World
49 © Stephanie Compoint, Sygma
51 AP/Wide World
55 © Paul Hosefros, NYT Pictures
56 © Asahi Shimbun, Sygma
60 © Kirkland Sygma
61 Archive Photos
63 © Lisa Quinones, Black Star; © Bob Riha, Liaison Agency
65 © David Heald, The Solomon R. Guggenheim Foundation
67 Reuters/Archive Photos
71 JPL/NASA
73 Agence France-Presse
75 Reuters/Archive Photos
78 Volkswagen of America, Inc.; Ford Motor Company; Rolls-Royce Motor Cars, Inc.; Ford Motor Company
81-83 AP/Wide World
85 Reuters/Archive Photos
87 AP/Wide World
90 © Antonio Dickey, Mayor's Press Office/City of Chicago
92 AP/Wide World
93 Reuters/Archive Photos
95 Reuters/Archive Photos
100 Honshu-Shikoku Bridge Authority
102 AP/Wide World
103 Agence France-Presse
104 AP/Wide World
113 © Jonathan Hayward
117 Teng and Associates, Inc.
119 Reuters/Archive Photos
124 AP/Wide World
126 Apple Computer, Inc.
127 Reuters/Archive Photos
133-137 AP/Wide World
138 © A. Lichtenstein, Sygma
147 © Rodney Freeman
149 AP/Wide World
151 Agence France-Presse
153 © Mats Bäcker, Royal Swedish Ballet
154 AP/Wide World
155 Popperfoto/Archive Photos; Archive Photos; NBC/Archive Photos
156 Reuters/Archive Photos; Archive Photos; AP/Wide World
157 AP/Wide World
158 Archive Photos; Archive Photos; AP/Wide World; Camera Press/Archive Photos
159 Archive Photos; AP/Wide World

160 Archive Photos
161 Reuters/Archive Photos
162 AP/Wide World
164 Agence France-Presse
170 AP/Wide World
173 Reuters/Archive Photos
174 © International Monetary Fund
176 AP/Wide World
177 Agence France-Presse; Reuters/Archive Photos
181-187 AP/Wide World
188-192 Reuters/Archive Photos
194 © Regis Bossu, Sygma
195-199 © European Monetary Institute
200 Steven Spicer*
203-209 AP/Wide World
211 Agence France-Presse
213 © Rusty Jarrett, Allsport
214 AP/Wide World
216 Agence France-Presse
218-219 AP/Wide World
225 Franklin D. Roosevelt Library
226 Agence France-Presse; Reuters/Archive Photos
228 Reuters/Archive Photos
231 Agence France-Presse
232-234 AP/Wide World
238-241 Agence France-Presse
242 Reuters/Archive Photos
244 © Alfred Smuskiewicz
245 © Israel Sun Ltd.; © Lemmer/Daoud from Sipa Press; © Alfred Smuskiewicz
247 © Alfred Smuskiewicz; © Lemmer/Daoud from Sipa Press; © Lemmer/Daoud from Sipa Press
249-252 Reuters/Archive Photos
254-257 AP/Wide World
259 Agence France-Presse
264 © The British Library Board
270 Granger Collection
273 AP/Wide World
276 Pfizer Inc.
278 Reuters/Archive Photos
279-281 AP/Wide World
285 Fox/Paramount from Shooting Star; AP/Wide World; AP/Wide World; AP/Wide World
288-289 AP/Wide World
291 Agence France-Presse
292 Reuters/Archive Photos
293 © Ron Cohn, The Gorilla Foundation; AP/Wide World
294 AP/Wide World
295 Agence France-Presse
296 From The New York Journal, February 1, 1898 p.1; AP/Wide World
299 The San Francisco Academy of Comic Art
300 © Corel
306-308 AP/Wide World
310 Agence France-Presse
312 Archive Photos
313 AP/Wide World
314 Reuters/Archive Photos
315 Archive Photos
316 © Shaun Botterill, Allsport
317-323 AP/Wide World
324 Reuters/Archive Photos
325 AP/Wide World

326 © Gianni Giansanti, Sygma
327-330 AP/Wide World
331 Reuters/Archive Photos
332-333 AP/Wide World
334 Reuters/Archive Photos
336 Smithsonian Institution Archives; Brian McLeod, Ph.D., Harvard - Smithsonian Center for Astrophysics
338 © Caroline Forbes, Faber and Faber Ltd.
340 AP/Wide World
342 © Frank Teti, Neal Peters Collection
344 UPI/Corbis-Bettmann
345 C.D. Collection from Shooting Star; Archive Photos
347 Everett Collection
348 AP/Wide World
350 Reuters/Archive Photos
354-355 AP/Wide World
359 Agence France-Presse
360 Archive Photos
363 © Robert Grossman, NYT Pictures
365 Reuters/Archive Photos
368 AP/Wide World
370 AP/Wide World; Agence France-Presse
371-375 AP/Wide World
379 NASA
380 Reuters/Archive Photos; AP/Wide World
382 Agence France-Presse
385-390 Reuters/Archive Photos
392 AP/Wide World
395 Agence France-Presse
398 NBC from Shooting Star
399 © 1998 Twentieth Century Fox Television. All rights reserved.
401 Agence France-Presse
402 AP/Wide World
405 © Carol Rosegg, Boneau/Bryan Brown
406 Joan Marcus © Disney Enterprises, Inc.
409 Loomis Dean, Life Magazine © Time, Inc.; Michael Cooper
410 © Frederick Charles
412 Miss Saigon ™ © Cameron Mackintosh Ltd.; Cats ™ © 1981 The Really Useful Group Ltd.; Les Miserables ™ © Cameron Mackintosh Ltd.; The Phantom of the Opera ™ 1996 The Really Useful Group Ltd.
414-415 © Joan Marcus
417 © Ragdoll Productions Ltd.; Tiger Electronics
420 Reuters/Archive Photos
421 AP/Wide World
425 © David Cairns, Sipa Press
431 Agence France-Presse
435 Reuters/Archive Photos
437 AP/Wide World
439 Reuters/Archive Photos; AP/Wide World
440 AP/Wide World; Agence France-Presse
441 Agence France-Presse; AP/Wide World; AP/Wide World
445 AP/Wide World
448 © Disney Enterprises, Inc.
465 © Corel

To help World Book owners keep their encylopedias up to date, the follwing articles are reprinted from the 1999 edition of the encyclopedia.

1998 WORLD BOOK SUPPLEMENT

© Sylvain Grandadam, Tony Stone Images

A traditional Japanese dance features colorful costumes and the expressive use of fans. Asian dance typically emphasizes gestures of the head, eyes, and especially the hands and fingers.

Dance

Dance is the movement of the human body in a rhythmic way. Dance serves many functions in human society. It is an art form, a social activity, a type of communication, and a form of recreation. People can dance by themselves, in couples, or in large groups. The dance can be spontaneous or performed in established movements. It can tell a story, explore an emotion, or serve as a form of self-expression. Many people dance as a career, but anyone can dance simply by moving in rhythm.

Dance is among the oldest human art forms. Dancing extends beyond the human species itself. For example, many animals perform complex dances during courtship.

Dance differs from other kinds of rhythmic movement, such as dribbling a basketball, because in dance the movement itself is the goal of the activity. Music usually accompanies dance, providing the rhythm, tempo, and mood for the movements.

In modern societies, many people enjoy dancing simply for entertainment. Each generation creates new dances as an expression of its own sense of life and fun. For example, rock dancing arose about 1960 with the popularity of rock music. This type of dance was created primarily by and for young people. Rock dances such as

© Joe Viesti

An American square dance is performed by groups of four couples. Many square dances originated in ancient English, Irish, and Scottish folk dances that settlers brought to America.

the *twist* did not require partners to touch each other while they danced. The dancing was free-spirited and individual, allowing each dancer to create his or her own steps spontaneously. Rock dancing stressed pure emotion underscored by the strong beat of the music.

Why people dance

Religious reasons. For thousands of years, human beings have danced for religious reasons. Many religions involve some form of dance.

William Deresiewicz, the contributor of this article, is a professional dance critic. He is also a dance teacher, administrator, and dancer.

Many religious dances are forms of prayer. Believers dance as they pray for rain, for the fertility of crops, and for success in war or in hunting. Such dances often imitate or pantomime some movement. For example, dancers may imitate the movement of the animal to be hunted, or a hunter's actions in stalking it. They may wear elaborate costumes and masks or makeup to depict deities or animals.

Religious dance also may attempt to create a state of *ecstasy* (intense joy) or trance in the worshiper. Dance may also be used as one part of a religious occasion or ritual. One example is the dancing of Jews at the festival of Simhat Torah. Another example is the dancing and whirling of members of a Muslim religious order called *dervishes*. Dancing was a formal element in Christian worship until the A.D. 1100's, when religious leaders began to prohibit it because they believed it was too worldly an activity. However, spontaneous dance has become a common element of worship among some Protestant denominations.

Social reasons. Dancing plays an important role in social functions. All societies have characteristic forms of dance. Such dancing may take place at ceremonial occasions or at informal gatherings. Like traditional foods and costumes, dance helps members of a nation or ethnic group recognize their connection to one another and to their ancestors. By dancing together, members of a group express their sense of common identity or belonging.

Dance can strengthen social connections. By dancing together, people share an intimate physical experience that is cooperative and harmonious. Social dances tend to form patterns, such as circles and chains, and to involve the mingling of couples. Examples include square dancing and line dancing. These patterns tend to reinforce a sense of unity. Because dancing involves physi-

cal contact, it also serves as a symbol of social bonds, such as when the bride and groom dance the first dance at a wedding reception.

Dance is especially important during courtship, which is one reason it is so popular among young people. Like some animals, people dance as a way of attracting a possible mate by displaying their beauty, grace, and vitality.

Recreational reasons. Many people dance for fun. Dancing allows individuals to feel their body moving freely, to release energy, and to express exuberance and joy. Dancing is also good exercise. It allows people to test the limits of what their bodies can do, as they fling their arms out, kick up their legs, and stretch and twist their bodies.

Artistic reasons. In nearly all societies, dance is an important art form. Its unique powers of self-expression and representation come from the fact that dance uses the body directly, without words, images, or sounds. Dance refines and enlarges the natural human tendency to express feelings physically. The skip of joy becomes a ballerina's leap. A stomp of rage can develop into complex patterns of stamping and clapping, as in the flamenco dance of Spain.

When a dance is performed before an audience, it can serve as a form of drama, all the more powerful because it is silent. Spoken theater can better represent complex social situations, but dance can more directly convey deep emotions and spiritual states.

Dances to take part in

Many dances are easy to learn and are designed so that almost anyone can participate in them. Social dances are common modern forms of such dances, which might be called *participatory, shared,* or *communal dances.* The most basic and widespread forms of

© Jack Vartoogian

Folk dances celebrate the history and traditions of a particular ethnic or national group. The famous Ballet Folklórico of Mexico is a highly trained company of professional dancers who perform colorful folk dances that reflect the Indian and Spanish roots of Mexican culture.

communal dances are *ritual ethnic dances* and *folk dances*. These two types often overlap, but they differ in their appearance and purpose, and in the occasions on which they are performed.

Ritual ethnic dances have traditionally been performed by peoples in such places as Africa and the Pacific Islands and by American Indians. The dances of these groups show as much variety as their languages. Dances may be performed to mark many different events, such as initiation rituals, funerals, and certain seasons, such as the harvest. But some features are commonly found in ritual ethnic dancing.

Most ritual ethnic dance is performed in groups rather than by solo dancers or by male-female couples. However, some dancers may have a special solo part or act as leader of the group. Groups of men and women usually dance separately, and different types of dances are designed for men or women. The movements of the men are often sharp and vigorous. Those of the women tend to be more subdued or subtle. A group's chiefs and priests often dance more than other members of the group. A leader may display authority by performing a certain type of dance.

Costumes or masks are often used for specific purposes and occasions in ritual ethnic dance. Dancers may also wear tall, spectacular headdresses, or leg rattles that help establish the rhythm of the dance. Ritual ethnic dances are performed in many arrangements, the most common being a circle. The use of the drum is another common feature of ritual ethnic dancing. For many peo-

ple, a drum is all they need to give a dance its rhythm. But other instruments, such as flutes, stringed instruments, and horns, are also used.

In some dances, participants may work themselves into a frenzy or trance during which they believe a god or spirit takes possession of their body. Such a dance may begin slowly and build to a hypnotic intensity, ending only when the dancers collapse in exhaustion.

The movements of ritual ethnic dances are varied. The most common movement is stamping the foot on the ground. Large groups of dancers can make the ground shake with this action. Other movements include graceful leaps, swirling motions of the pelvis, and wavelike movements or vibrations of the entire body.

Ritual ethnic dance has long served to pass along a people's culture and history to its younger generation. However, some of these dances today are performed only as entertainment and no longer have significance as rituals.

Folk dances. Folk dance is sometimes defined as a dance that developed among the common people, without the aid of choreographers or organizers. Folk dance is sometimes called *ethnic dance* when it celebrates the traditions of a specific ethnic group. Folk dance and ethnic dance are closely related. But some experts consider ethnic dance a type that is always performed in its original form, while folk dance may be changed or adapted over time.

Most folk dances are simple and easy to learn. They usually involve step patterns only, with the arms, head,

Bear Dance, Preparing for a Bear Hunt (1835-1837), an oil painting on canvas by George Catlin; National Museum of American Art, Washington, D.C. (Art Resource)

Religious dances are often forms of prayer. These Native American dancers were dancing to ask for success in bear hunting. The dancers imitated the movements of the bear as they danced. Some dancers wore bear masks to feel they were actually assuming the animal's spirit and powers.

Ballroom dancing is a form of dancing for couples. Various ballroom dances originated in Europe, the United States, and Latin America. These dances then spread throughout the rest of the world as both a popular social activity and a competitive sport.

and body held in a set position. Participants generally join hands or hold each other by the shoulders or around the waist. Most of the dances require only a modest amount of energy, with movement between a walk and a jog. Folk dancers often wear traditional clothing, such as boots; embroidered jackets and skirts; and bright hats, scarves, and leggings.

Folk dance, with its circular formations and linked lines, builds feelings of togetherness. Some folk dances are earthy and vigorous, such as the *Morris dance* from England, with its stamping and high leaps. Other forms are brisk and lively, such as the Italian *tarantella*. The *jig* and the *Highland fling* of Ireland and Scotland feature rapid footwork.

A folk dance may reflect qualities a group or nation especially admires. For example, Russian folk dances, especially those for men, seem to explode with energy. In Spain, such dances as the *flamenco, bolero*, and *fandango* express passion, pride, and sexual desire.

Some folk dances retain elements of their roots in ancient religious observances. The most familiar example

is the *Maypole dance,* traditionally celebrated on May 1. Participants in this happy rural dance welcome spring by weaving bright ribbons around a decorated pole as they dance around it. However, the dance originated as an ancient tree-worshiping ceremony practiced by the early settlers in the great forests that once covered Europe.

Many folk dances developed from peasant dances in Europe during the Middle Ages. However, like other aspects of traditional life, folk dance began to disappear in the change from rural to urban society. Starting in the early 1900's, some people attempted to preserve and revive the folk dances of their native lands. Today, most folk dances are performed at festivals and events, where people have a special interest in getting in touch with their roots.

Some types of folk dance were created in the 1900's as a way to build national identity. For example, in Israel, which was founded as a nation in 1948, the people have created new folk dances and adapted old ones, such as the Romanian *hora*. Other folk dances, such as the

Rock dancing is a popular form of social dancing created by and for young people. Rock dances are free-spirited and encourage individuals to make up their own steps. Young men and women often perform rock dances without touching any other dancers.

The waltz became the most fashionable social dance of the 1800's. It originated in Germany and Austria and soon spread to other countries. The waltz inspired some of the finest dance music of the period and also added beauty and elegance to many romantic ballets of the 1800's.

Emperor Franz Joseph at a Ball in Vienna (about 1900), a gouache painting on canvas by Wilhelm Gause; Museum der Stadt, Vienna, Austria/ET Archive, London, from Superstock

American square dance, are modern developments of older forms.

Social dances. In addition to developing into today's folk dances, the peasant dances of medieval Europe also evolved into a third type of participatory dance, called *social dance.* In social dancing, people in modern societies dance for personal pleasure. Each generation creates its own type of social dance to express its own sense of life and fun.

Social dances emerged in the late Middle Ages as the European aristocracy began to modify the dances of the common people to make the dances more suitable for the court. The traditional circle dances began to acquire more elegance and refinement. Dancers paid more attention to details of etiquette and technique, such as how to approach one's partner and how to hold one's head. Soon dancing came to be regarded as the best way to teach the graceful body movement and gracious behavior expected of the courtier.

In the late 1600's and early 1700's, King Louis XIV of France brought aristocratic life to a high state of development. Louis was especially dedicated to the art of the dance. Courtly dances of his time included the gigue, minuet, and pavane. The French court of the early 1700's also adapted English country dances into formal dances for groups of eight. These dances, called *cotillon,* soon became popular in England and other European countries. Eventually, these formal dances were carried to the United States, where their name was changed to *cotillion.* Today, a formal ball is frequently referred to as a cotillion.

Until about 1800, court dancing emphasized group participation. Then a new kind of social dance arose that put the man and woman into a dance world of their own as partners. These dances became known as *ballroom dances* because they were performed in large ballrooms. The first ballroom dance was the waltz, a light and gracious turning dance that was popularized in Vienna, Austria, and rapidly swept throughout Europe. At first the waltz caused some controversy. Never before had men and women danced so closely together.

After the waltz gained widespread acceptance, it was joined by other social dances. Many Latin American ballroom dances were introduced in the early 1900's, including the tango, rumba, and samba. Ballroom dancing has now become an international sport, with competitions held in a number of dance categories.

During the 1960's, another new type of social dance was born that gained popularity among young people. This type, based on rock music, shifted the emphasis from the couple to the individual. At concerts and parties, rock dancing meant "doing your own thing" in the individual's own style and space on the dance floor. With the strong beat of the music and the desire to be

© Jack Vartoogian

Dancers from Bali perform with their legs bent and their feet flat on the ground. They keep their torsos, elbows, and wrists flexible, creating movements that are harmonious and fluid.

Modern dance introduced a revolutionary style of dance during the 1900's. One of the central figures in modern dance was American choreographer and dancer Martha Graham. She created *Maple Leaf Rag,* her final work, *shown here,* in 1990. Although many of Graham's dances were serious or even tragic, *Maple Leaf Rag* had a lighthearted quality, with music by American ragtime composer Scott Joplin.

spontaneous and free, dance was returning to its roots in ecstasy and pure emotion.

Dances to watch

The world has two great traditions of what is usually called *theatrical dance,* the Asian tradition and the European and American tradition. Both traditions employ movements of great beauty, intricacy, and difficulty to convey emotional states and artistic ideas. Both require that the performers undergo long and rigorous training to develop the necessary control of their bodies as well as the necessary expressive qualities. For this reason, unlike participatory or communal dances, theatrical dances are usually performed by professional dancers or dedicated amateurs.

Asian theatrical dance is primarily religious in nature. In such Asian religions as Hinduism and Buddhism, dance remains a strong link between the faithful and their gods. Asian dance primarily tells stories, acts out prayers, or recounts myths of deities and heroes. It emphasizes gestures of the head, eyes, and especially the hands and fingers. Through these gestures, performers express the story's fine points and details. Asian dance also features elaborate costuming and bodily decoration, such as ankle bells, shining head pieces, and beautiful robes. Asian dancers also may wear expressive masks that represent certain types of characters.

The movements of Asian dance are generally harmonious and fluid. The dancer stands strongly on bent legs, feet flat and solid on the ground. The body is held erect, and the elbows and wrists are flexible. The changing angles of the elbows and wrists help to shape poses and gestures. The performer's face is active. The eyes dart, and the mouth grimaces or smiles. The toes usually point upward, while the heels may stamp out complex rhythms. The whole effect is one of great poise, even amidst the most vigorous action.

The Asian theatrical dance tradition originated in India. There are four major forms of Indian dance: (1) *bharata natyam,* (2) *kathakali,* (3) *kathak,* and (4) *manipuri.*

The most important form is *bharata natyam,* a solo dance traditionally performed in temples by female dancers called *devadasis.* Bharata natyam, like other

forms of Indian dance, includes a vocabulary of symbolic gestures called *mudras* or *hastas.* Each of these gestures may have a variety of meanings. Bharata natyam is danced to classical Hindu religious poetry and is accompanied by a drummer, a singer, and sometimes other musicians as well.

The *kathakali* presents stories from the *Ramayana* and the *Mahabharata,* the great epic poems of Hinduism. Themes from the *Puranas,* which are long Hindu stories told in verse, may also be used. Kathakali is physically demanding and typically requires dancers to support their weight on the outside edges of their feet.

Kathak is a form that mingles Hindu and Muslim influences. It requires great technical skill and involves speedy footwork and spectacular turns.

Manipuri is more like folk dancing. This form of dance blends solo and group dancing as it tells stories of the Hindu god Krishna.

Throughout Southeast Asia, classical Indian dance combined with local traditions to create distinctive national forms. Cambodian dancers train their fingers, elbows, and other joints to stretch well beyond the natural range. This enables them to perform odd contortions and movements that display a delicate beauty. Dance in Myanmar (formerly called Burma) relies less on symbolic gestures and uses more humor and mimicry. On the island of Java, now part of Indonesia, performances of dance-dramas called *wayang wong* exhibit the rigid, jerky quality of puppet theater, from which they developed. Traditional dances on the Indonesian island of Bali are both vigorous and elegant. Balinese dancers perform to the sounds of gongs and flutes.

The dance of China and Japan is less an independent art than part of a total theatrical form that includes singing and spoken drama. Today, the most highly developed form of Chinese dance-drama is the *Beijing opera,* also called the *Peking opera,* which is famous especially for its acrobatics. Japanese *no* theater is an old, traditional art that emphasizes exquisitely restrained and refined dance elements. *Kabuki,* another form of traditional Japanese dance-drama, is livelier and appeals to a wider audience. For more information on Chinese and Japanese dance-drama, see **Drama** (Asian drama).

European and American theatrical dance. In contrast to Asian dance, European and American theatrical dance emphasizes the lower rather than the upper body, and energetic movement rather than precise gesture. Asian dancers communicate with their hands and face, but European and American dancers emphasize their legs and feet. European and American dancers perform leaps and movements in which male dancers lift female partners into the air. In European and American dance, the body does not tell a detailed story as much as it expresses emotions through movement, whether slow and tender, sharp and angry, or large and bold.

Unlike Asian dance, European and American dance is *secular*—that is, it deals primarily with nonreligious themes. European and American dance explores the earthly rather than the divine. Its most common theme is romantic love, but it also expresses ideas about the natural world, family and community life, and social and political issues. During the 1900's, dance became a powerful artistic means for portraying the experiences of the isolated individual within modern society.

Ballet is the oldest and most highly developed form of European theatrical dance, growing out of court dances of the 1400's and 1500's. Ballet dances were later replaced by ballroom dancing as a form of social dance. In addition to performing ballets themselves, by the 1600's court aristocracy employed professional dancers to perform the ballets as staged entertainment. Academies were established to train these professional performers and encourage the development of their art.

By the late 1800's, ballet had reached a high level of refinement. Ballet companies had become expensive organizations that produced great spectacles. Ballets used elaborate scenery and costumes to help tell romantic, fairy-tale stories. For more information on the techniques and history of ballet, see the **Ballet** article.

Modern dance arose as a reaction to the ballet of the late 1800's, with its rigid organization and heavy use of scenic effects. About 1900, a young American woman named Isadora Duncan became well known for performing a kind of dance that seemed to reject everything in ballet. Duncan danced barefoot in a loosely flowing tunic. She usually danced alone, using natural movements rather than the traditional movements of ballet. Duncan began the modern dance emphasis on individuality and innovation. She called her style of movement "the dance of the future," but it became best known as *modern dance.* Duncan's supporters applauded her work as remarkably fresh and spontaneous.

Several American women continued Duncan's innovations. These dancer-teacher-choreographers included Ruth St. Denis, Doris Humphrey, and Martha Graham. Their revolutionary work was even more impressive because it came during the early 1900's, at a time when most women had little voice in society. Women artists were scarce in other art forms, and women dancers in ballet had been limited to performing rather than doing choreography.

Martha Graham became the central figure in modern dance in the mid-1900's. Through her artistry, passion, and intensity, Graham brought modern dance to the level of great art. She developed a method of movement, inspired by the act of breathing, which was based on the contraction and release of muscles. The method was designed to capture the rhythm of human emotion. Graham's method became the standard modern dance technique adopted throughout the world.

Graham created nearly 200 dances, the best revealing tremendous dramatic qualities. She was unsurpassed at translating psychological conflict and spiritual yearning into movement of startling directness and power.

Martha Graham's greatest male dancer was Merce Cunningham, who became her most important successor. Cunningham was an innovator in his dance creations. His dances were an element separate from the music that accompanied them. The dances consisted of sections that were put together in any order.

Modern dance has explored a vast array of creative themes and techniques since the 1950's due to the work of Graham, Cunningham, Doris Humphrey's follower José Limón, and such younger choreographers as Paul Taylor, Twyla Tharp, and Mark Morris. Taylor's work was noted for its inventiveness and humor. Tharp brought modern dance into contact with both social dance and ballet. Morris gained praise for his witty and passionate work distinguished for its musicality, its ele-

Shooting Star

American musical comedy has attracted some of the most creative choreographers of the 1900's. From 1955 to 1978, American director and choreographer Bob Fosse was a dominant choreographer on Broadway. He created several acclaimed dances for the 1966 musical *Sweet Charity.* In 1969, Fosse also directed the motion-picture version that starred Shirley MacLaine, *center.*

gant simplicity, and its warmly human quality.

African Americans made important contributions to modern dance. Alvin Ailey was a major figure. In creating his American Dance Theater, Ailey sought to make modern dance into a vehicle for expressing the black experience through music and movement. His company gained praise for its exuberance and energy.

Modern dance flourished not only in the United States but in European countries as well, especially Germany, Belgium, and the Netherlands. Mary Wigman led the modern dance movement in Germany during the 1920's and 1930's. The leading modern dance choreographers at the end of the 1900's included Pina Bausch of Germany and Jiří Kylián of the Czech Republic, who worked in the Netherlands.

Many younger choreographers of the late 1900's turned away from modern dance as an art that consisted purely of movement. Their work mixed and often emphasized video, spoken language, and other nondance elements.

Musical comedy is a primarily American form of theatrical entertainment that typically tells a story through songs and dialogue as well as dance. Musicals generally feature athletic, rhythmic dancing, but some also include dance pieces that resemble classical ballet. Important ballet choreographers who have created dances for musical comedies include George Balanchine, Agnes de Mille, and Jerome Robbins. Some of the greatest American musicals are known primarily for their dances, such as Robbins's *West Side Story* (1957); *A Chorus Line* (1975), with choreography by Michael Bennett; *Chicago* (1975), with choreography by Bob Fosse; *My One and Only* (1983), with choreography by Tommy Tune; and *Crazy for You* (1992), with choreography by Susan Stroman.

Other forms of theatrical dance include jazz dance and tap dancing. Both are major elements of dance in musical comedies and in motion pictures.

Jazz dance, like jazz music, relies strongly on rhythm. It is usually energetic, with dancers using different parts of the body, such as the shoulders, pelvis, and head, in isolated movement. Jazz dancing is a personal style that emphasizes individual expression and often includes humor and improvisation.

Tap dancing combines dance traditions from Britain and Africa. It resembles jazz dancing in its strong rhythms and frequent displays of improvisation. Tap dancing relies almost totally on footwork, however. The feet become musical instruments, marking out complex rhythms with the heel and toe. Tap dancing underwent a revival during the 1990's, largely due to the work of such young dancers and choreographers as Gregory Hines and Savion Glover.   William Deresiewicz

Related articles in *World Book* include:

Biographies

For biographies of ballet dancers and choreographers, see the *Related articles* in the **Ballet** article. See also:

Ailey, Alvin	Graham, Martha	Robinson, Bill
Astaire, Fred	Greco, José	Saint Denis, Ruth
Cunningham, Merce	Holm, Hanya	Shawn, Ted
	Kelly, Gene	Taylor, Paul
Duncan, Isadora	Nikolais, Alwin	Tharp, Twyla
Dunham, Katherine		

Kinds of dances

Ballet	Folk dancing	Square dancing
Ballroom dancing	Fox trot	Tango
Bolero	Minuet	Tarantella
Cotillion	Rumba	Waltz
Flamenco		

Pictures of dancers

The following articles have pictures of dancers:

Africa	Indonesia	Pygmies
Asia	Kenya	Roaring Twenties
Clothing	Latin America	Romania
Folklore	Mexico	South Dakota
France	Motion picture	Spain
Gypsies	Pacific Islands	United States
Indian, American		

Other related articles

Band (Dance bands)	Pantomime
Buffalo ceremonials	Rain dance
Castanets	Rhythm
Ghost dance	Rock music (Disco and punk)
Hawaii (Dancing and music)	Snake dance
Mask	Sun dance
Musical comedy	

Outline

I. Why people dance
  A. Religious reasons
  B. Social reasons
  C. Recreational reasons
  D. Artistic reasons
II. Dances to take part in
  A. Ritual ethnic dances
  B. Folk dances
  C. Social dances
III. Dances to watch
  A. Asian theatrical dance
  B. European and American theatrical dance

Questions

What are some features of tribal dance?
What is a *mudra?*
Who was Isadora Duncan? Martha Graham?
What are the four major forms of Indian dance?
What is the significance of a *Maypole dance?*
What are some reasons why people dance?
What are the main characteristics of jazz dance?
How do participatory or communal dances differ from theatrical dances?
What role does religion play in Asian theatrical dance?
What are some of the chief functions that dance serves in society?

Additional resources

Level I
Berger, Melvin. *The World of Dance.* Phillips, 1978.
Haskins, James. *Black Dance in America.* Crowell, 1990.
Tythacott, Louise. *Dance.* Thomson Learning, 1995.

Level II
Emery, Lynne F. *Black Dance.* 2nd ed. 1988. Reprint. Princeton Book Co., 1991.
Harris, Jane A., and others. *Dance a While: Handbook of Folk, Square, Contra, and Social Dance.* 7th ed. Macmillan, 1994.
Jonas, Gerald. *Dancing: The Pleasure, Power, and Art of Movement.* Abrams, 1992.
Quirey, Belinda, and others. *May I Have the Pleasure? The Story of Popular Dancing.* 1976. Reprint. Gordon Pr., 1986.
Sorell, Walter, ed. *The Dance Has Many Faces.* 3rd ed. A Cappella Bks., 1992.
Wright, Judy P. *Social Dance.* Human Kinetics, 1992.

Jakarta is the capital, largest city, and commercial center of Indonesia. Modern buildings surround a traffic circle in downtown Jakarta. The Welcome Monument stands in the center of the circle.

© R. Ian Lloyd

Indonesia

Indonesia is a country in Southeast Asia that consists entirely of islands, more than 13,500 of them. The islands of Indonesia stretch across more than 3,200 miles (5,150 kilometers) of tropical ocean along the equator. Indonesia has the fourth largest population in the world. Only China, India, and the United States have more people. Indonesia occupies a strategic position in Southeast Asia, and its political and economic conditions are important to the stability of the region.

Indonesia has an extremely diverse population. Its people belong to about 300 different ethnic groups and speak more than 250 languages. They had no common language until the late 1920's, when Indonesian nationalists provided one by creating a new language called Bahasa Indonesia, a modified form of the Malay language. Bahasa Indonesia, which means *language of Indonesia*, became a force for national unity. Another unifying force is Islam. Most of Indonesia's people are Muslims, and they make up the world's largest Muslim population.

Indonesia is rich in natural resources. Many of its islands were formed by volcanoes, so they are mountainous and rise steeply from the sea. Much of the soil is especially fertile because it contains volcanic ash, which is rich in nutrients. The rich soil supports bountiful fields of rice, and Indonesia ranks among the world's leading rice producers. Other major farm products include coffee, cocoa, palm oil, rubber, spices, and tea. Lush tropical rain forests cover about two-thirds of Indonesia. Teak and other valuable hardwood trees and rare plants

Dwight Y. King, the contributor of this article, is Associate Professor of Political Science at Northern Illinois University.

and animals live in the forests. Elephants, rhinoceroses, and tigers roam among the trees. Underground lie deposits of oil, natural gas, bauxite, coal, copper, gold, nickel, silver, and tin.

The Netherlands ruled Indonesia during most of the period from the 1600's to 1945. Indonesia declared its independence in 1945 and fought the Dutch until 1949, when they gave up their control.

Government

National government of Indonesia is based on a constitution written in 1945. The Constitution recognizes one God but is otherwise neutral regarding religion.

The Indonesian government is based on a set of beliefs known as Pancasila. Pancasila consists of five principles: (1) belief in one God, (2) humanitarianism, (3) the unity of Indonesia, (4) democracy based on deliberation and consensus among representatives, and (5) social justice for all people. Sukarno, Indonesia's first president, set forth the principles of Pancasila in 1945 and made it an official state doctrine. Indonesian law requires all religious, professional, and cultural organizations to adopt Pancasila. Some Islamic organizations, however, object to the government's policy of making religious traditions secondary to Pancasila.

The Constitution establishes a body called the People's Consultative Assembly as the highest government authority. The Assembly has 1,000 members. They consist of the 500 members of the House of People's Representatives, Indonesia's legislature, plus 500 representatives of regional, occupational, and other groups. The Assembly normally meets only once every five years.

The House of People's Representatives meets yearly. The 500 lawmakers in the House serve five-year terms. The voters elect 425 of the members, and the president appoints the other 75 from the nation's armed forces.

In theory, the People's Consultative Assembly establishes the general direction of government policies, and the House of People's Representatives enacts laws to carry them out. In practice, the Assembly and the House have little power. Instead, the president and and a cabinet of ministers appointed by the president make all important decisions. The president is chief of state, head of the government, and commander of the armed forces.

The People's Consultative Assembly elects the president and vice president to five-year terms. The Constitution sets no limit on the number of terms a president can serve.

Local government. Indonesia has 27 provinces. The provinces are divided into districts and municipalities. These units are further divided into subdistricts and villages. The central government appoints the officials of all local governments except the rural villages from lists of people nominated by regional legislatures. Rural villagers elect their own village officials.

Politics. Indonesia's most important political organization is Golkar. Golkar is a federation of a number of groups, including labor and the military. It is technically not a political party, but it sponsors most of the candidates in elections. Indonesia's laws ensure that Golkar candidates win a majority of seats in the legislature.

Until 1998, only two political parties were allowed to operate in Indonesia. They were the United Development Party, which represents Muslim groups, and the Indonesian Democratic Party, a coalition of nationalists and Christians. Both parties had much less influence than Golkar. In 1998, President Suharto, who had dominated the country and its politics since the 1960's, resigned. Following Suharto's resignation, a number of new political parties emerged.

Courts. Indonesia has district courts, high courts, military courts, and special religious courts that handle personal matters among Muslims, such as divorces and inheritances. The highest court is the Supreme Court. It reviews cases appealed from the high courts and settles disputes between courts in different regions or between the religious courts and other courts. The Supreme Court has no authority, however, to overturn laws it finds unconstitutional. The central government appoints judges. There are no juries.

Armed forces of Indonesia have great influence on both civilian and military affairs. The armed forces consist of the Army, Navy, Air Force, and police force. The president is the supreme commander. By law, Indonesian men may be drafted for two years. But in practice, so many people volunteer that no one is drafted.

International organizations. Indonesia belongs to many international organizations, including the United Nations and its specialized agencies. Indonesia is a founding member of the Association of Southeast Asian Nations. Indonesia is a member of the World Bank, which provides loans to poorer nations for economic development, and the International Monetary Fund, which works to improve payment arrangements and other financial dealings between countries. Indonesia also belongs to several other international finance and development agencies, including the Asian Development Bank, the Islamic Development Bank, and the International Finance Corporation.

People

Indonesia has one of the most ethnically diverse populations in the world, with people from about 300 ethnic groups. The largest ethnic group is the Javanese, who live mostly on the island of Java and make up about 45 percent of Indonesia's population. The second largest group is the Sundanese, who live in western Java and make up about 14 percent of the population. The Madurese, who live mostly on Madura, and the Malays each make up about 8 percent of Indonesia's people. The many small ethnic minorities include Arabs, Balinese, Dayaks, and Papuans. People of Chinese descent are the wealthiest ethnic group in Indonesia. Their wealth causes social tension, and they have sometimes become the targets of racial violence.

The people of Indonesia speak more than 250 different languages. Bahasa Indonesia is the official language. Indonesian nationalists created it in the late 1920's, early in the country's struggle for independence, to provide a common tongue for Indonesia's many peoples. Bahasa Indonesia was based on the Malay language spoken in eastern Sumatra, the Riau Islands, and the Malay Peninsula. It resembles Coastal Malay, which was the common language of trade in Indonesian ports. Bahasa

The Parliament Building in Jakarta is the meeting place for the People's Consultative Assembly and the House of People's Representatives.

Indonesia in brief

General information

Capital: Jakarta.
Official language: Bahasa Indonesia.
Official name: Republic of Indonesia.
National anthem: "Indonesia Raya" ("Great Indonesia").
Largest cities: (1989 official estimates)
Jakarta (6,761,886)   Bandung (1,401,108)
Surabaya (2,159,170)   Semarang (1,112,175)
Medan (1,715,670)

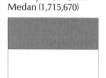

Symbols of Indonesia. Indonesia's flag was adopted on Independence Day, Aug. 17, 1945. Red stands for courage,
and white for purity. The coat of arms bears the national
motto of Indonesia, *Unity Through Diversity*. The motto
dates from the 1920's.

Land and climate

Land: Indonesia is made up of more than 13,500 islands that
lie along the equator. About two-thirds of Indonesia's land
is forested, and much of it is mountainous and volcanic.
Area: 735,358 sq. mi. (1,904,569 km²). *Greatest distances*—east-
west, about 3,200 mi. (5,120 km); north-south, about 1,200
mi. (1,930 km). *Coastline*—22,888 mi. (36,835 km).
Elevation: *Highest*—Puncak Jaya, 16,503 ft. (5,030 m) above sea
level. *Lowest*—sea level along the coasts.

Chief islands (1989 official estimates)

Island	Area In sq. mi.	In km²	Population
Greater Sunda Islands			
Borneo (Kalimantan)	208,287	539,460	8,677,500
Sulawesi (Celebes)	73,057	189,216	12,507,700
Java (including Madura)	51,037	132,186	107,513,800
Sumatra	182,812	473,481	36,882,000
Lesser Sunda Islands			
Bali	2,147	5,561	3,089,200
Flores	6,965	18,040	1,287,400
Lombok	1,706	4,419	2,448,600
Sumba	5,297	13,720	444,100
Sumbawa	6,084	15,758	959,500
Timor	11,965	30,990	1,955,600
Molucca Islands	28,767	74,505	1,814,200
Irian Jaya	162,928	421,981	1,555,700

Climate: Indonesia has a tropical climate, with hot, humid
weather and heavy rainfall most of the year. The average
temperature is 80 °F (27 °C).

Government

Form of government: The president serves as both head of
state and head of government. The president has great
power, including control of the legislative and judicial
branches. Military officers serve as key advisers to the
president and have much influence on policy.
Legislature: House of People's Representatives consisting of
500 members, 425 of whom are elected and 75 of whom
are appointed by the president.
Executive: President and Cabinet. The Cabinet is appointed
by the president.
Judiciary: Highest court is the Supreme Court.
Political subdivisions: 27 provinces.

People

Population: *1998 estimate*—206,491,000. *1990 census*—
179,378,946. *Estimated 2003 population*—220,416,000.
Population density: 281 persons per sq. mi. (108 per km²).
Distribution: 69 percent rural, 31 percent urban.
Major ethnic groups: About 45 percent Javanese, 14 percent
Sundanese, 8 percent Madurese, and 8 percent Malay.
Smaller ethnic groups include Arabs, Balinese, Chinese,
Dayaks, and Papuans.
Major religions: About 87 percent Muslim and 10 percent
Christian. The remainder are Hindu, Buddhist, or followers
of local religions.

Population trend

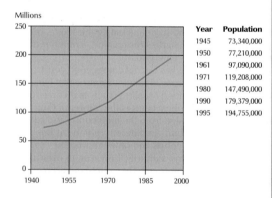

Millions

Year	Population
1945	73,340,000
1950	77,210,000
1961	97,090,000
1971	119,208,000
1980	147,490,000
1990	179,379,000
1995	194,755,000

Economy

Chief products: *Agriculture*—bananas, cassava, cocoa,
coconuts, coffee, corn, hogs, palm oil, poultry and eggs,
rice, rubber, sheep, spices, sugar cane, sweet potatoes,
tea, tobacco. *Fishing*—shrimp, tuna. *Forest industry*—
plywood, rattan, teak, timber. *Manufacturing*—cement,
chemicals, cigarettes, clothing, fertilizers, footwear,
petroleum, processed rubber products, steel products,
textiles, and wood products. *Mining*—bauxite, coal, copper, gold, natural gas, nickel, petroleum, silver, tin.
Money: *Basic unit*—rupiah. One hundred sen equal one
rupiah.
International trade: *Major exported goods*—coffee, liquefied natural gas, palm oil, rubber, tea, textiles and clothing,
tobacco, wood and wood products. *Major imported
goods*—chemicals, machinery, mineral products, transportation and electrical equipment. *Main trading
partners*—Japan is Indonesia's most important trading partner by far. Other major partners of Indonesia include Australia, Germany, Singapore, Taiwan, and the United States.

Indonesia became the language used in schools and universities. Children learn the language of their ethnic group at home and learn Bahasa Indonesia in school.

Some Indonesians, especially the Javanese, have only one name. They include the country's first two presidents, Sukarno and Suharto.

Way of life

Rural life. About two-thirds of the people of Indonesia are farmers or agricultural workers who live in small, rural villages. Life in most of these villages, called *desas,* is controlled by village headmen, religious teachers, and other traditional leaders. The village leaders govern by a traditional system that stresses cooperation. The villagers often settle disputes and solve problems by holding open discussions, called *musyawarah,* that continue until everyone reaches an agreement, known as *mufakat.*

Life in small farm villages increasingly combines modern practices with older ways of life. For example, most villagers listen to the radio, shop in nearby towns, and send their children to public school. At the same time, they follow many ancient customs. For example, some villagers still build a traditional type of Indonesian house that stands on stilts about 6 feet (1.8 meters) high. Families use the space underneath for cattle stalls or chicken coops, or to store tools and firewood. The floors and walls are made of timber or flattened bamboo. The roofs are covered with clay tiles, palm thatch, or iron.

Some ethnic groups build large communal houses in which as many as several hundred people may live. These groups include the Dayaks on Borneo, the Toraja on Sulawesi, the Batak on Sumatra, and some Papuan groups on Irian Jaya.

City life. City people live in American- and European-style houses and apartment buildings. Most of the

© Jean-Leo Dugast, Panos Pictures

Traditional Indonesian houses, such as this one in a village on Sulawesi, stand on stilts. Families typically use the space underneath for storage or as shelter for farm animals.

largest cities of Indonesia are on Java. They include Jakarta, Indonesia's largest city by far. Jakarta, Surabaya, and Medan have modern business districts with busy streets, elegant stores, and towering office buildings.

Clothing. The traditional clothing of Indonesian men and women is a colorful skirt called a *sarong* or a *kain.* A sarong is a long strip of cloth wrapped around the body. A kain is similar, but with the ends sewn together. Men wear a shirt with trousers, or a sarong. Women usually wear a long-sleeved blouse and a sarong or kain.

The men often wear a special hat or cap, and women may wear a shawl over their shoulders or on their head.

Population density

About 60 percent of all the Indonesian people live on the island of Java, though Java accounts for only about 7 percent of the country's total area. Most of Indonesia's largest cities are also on Java. The most thinly populated region is Irian Jaya.

WORLD BOOK map

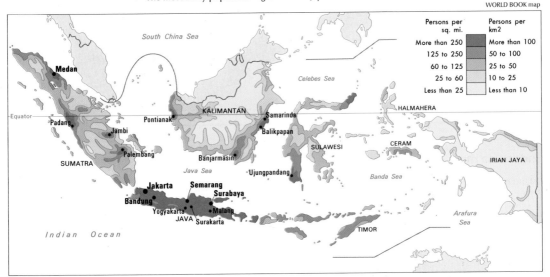

Persons per sq. mi.	Persons per km2
More than 250	More than 100
125 to 250	50 to 100
60 to 125	25 to 50
25 to 60	10 to 25
Less than 25	Less than 10

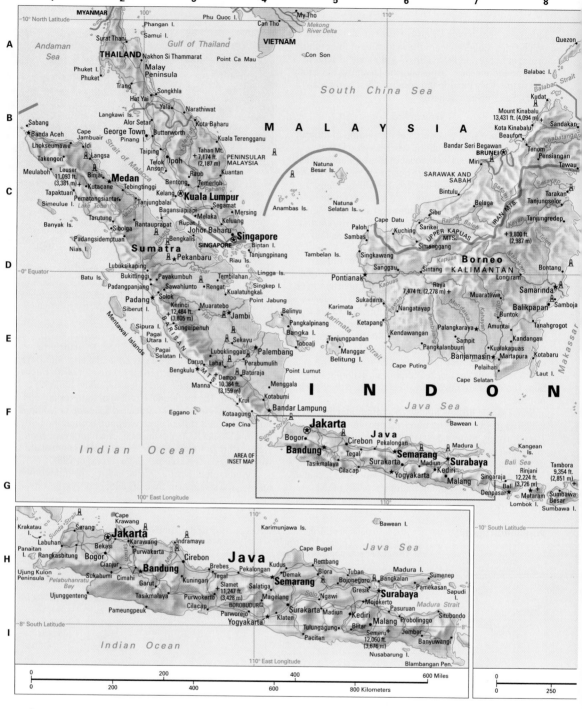

Indonesia map index

Island groups

Borneo
(Indonesian)
(Kalimantan)
.........8,677,459 ..D 7
Irian Jaya .....1,555,682 ..E 15
Java (Djawa)
(including
Madura)
.......107,513,797 ..G 6
Lesser Sunda
Islands
(Nusateng-
gara) .....10,185,381 ..G 9

Molucca
Islands
(Maluku)
...........1,814,150 ..D 12
Sulawesi
(Celebes)
...........12,507,650 ..E 9
Sumatra
(Sumatera)
...........36,881,990 ..D 3

Cities and towns

Balik-
papan ......368,724 ..E 8

Banda
Aceh ....166,323 ..B 1
Bandung ....1,401,108 ..G 5
Banjar-
masin ....436,212 ..E 7
Bengkulu ....126,099 ..E 3
Binjai ....158,357 ..C 2
Blitar ....113,937 ..I 5
Bogor ....240,036 ..H 2
Bukittinggi ...76,220 ..D 2
Cirebon .....215,041 ..H 3
Gorontalo ...110,478 ..D 10
Jakarta ....6,761,886 ..F 5
Jambi ....287,294 ..E 4
Kediri ....233,834 ..I 5

Madiun ....181,367 ..I 5
Magelang ....117,481 ..I 4
Malang ......548,193 ..I 6
Manado .....229,781 ..D 11
Medan .....1,715,670 ..C 2
Mojokerto ....94,587 ..I 6
Padang .....568,889 ..D 2
Palang-
karaya ....94,412 ..E 7
Palem-
bang ......880,732 ..E 4
Pangkalpi-
nang ....109,761 ..E 5
Parepare ....91,746 ..F 9
Pasuruan ...138,492 ..I 6

Payakum-
buh ....86,094 ..D 3
Pekanbaru ...212,704 ..D 3
Pekalon-
gan ....137,910 ..H 4
Pematang-
siantar .....198,000 ..C 2
Pontianak ....344,185 ..D 5
Probo-
linggo ......157,159 ..I 6
Salatiga ......85,524 ..H 4
Samarinda ...343,198 ..D 8
Semarang ...1,112,175 ..G 6
Sukabumi ...110,344 ..H 2
Surabaya ...2,159,170 ..G 7

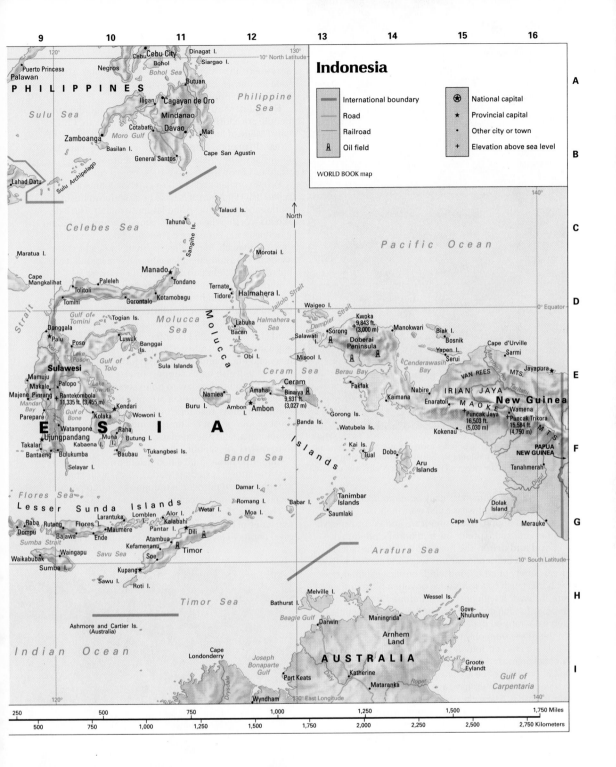

Indonesia

Legend:
- International boundary
- Road
- Railroad
- Oil field
- ⊛ National capital
- ★ Provincial capital
- • Other city or town
- + Elevation above sea level

WORLD BOOK map

Source: 1989 official estimates.

© Chuck O'Rear, Westlight

Television viewing is a popular form of entertainment throughout Indonesia. This photograph shows children watching television in a home in the village of Pabelan, near Mabelang, on Java.

Unlike Muslim women in many other countries, those in Indonesia do not wear a veil over their face. In the cities, most people wear American- and European-style clothes, but some prefer the traditional clothing.

Food and drink. The main food of Indonesians is rice, boiled or fried in various ways and served with a great variety of other foods. Indonesians eat their rice with meat, fish or a fish sauce, or vegetables; or they simply flavor it with hot spices. Indonesian cooks often simmer food in coconut milk and oil, and sometimes serve it wrapped in banana or coconut leaves.

The most commonly eaten meats are water buffalo, beef, and chicken. Indonesians eat little pork because most of them are Muslims, and their religion forbids eating it. Tea and coffee are favorite beverages.

People in the cities have a more varied diet than those in rural areas. Many city people eat Chinese, American, and European dishes as well as Indonesian foods.

Recreation. Cockfighting, though outlawed, is a popular recreation in Indonesia, especially on Bali and in the Indonesian part of Borneo, called Kalimantan. On Madura, the people hold bull races and bullfights. A martial art called *pencak silat* is popular throughout Indonesia. Practitioners fight not only with their hands and feet but also with sticks and knives.

Many Indonesians enjoy European and American sports, especially badminton and soccer. Indonesians also like to bicycle, swim, and play tennis and volleyball.

Many people spend their evenings watching television or going to motion-picture theaters. Many movies are American or European films with subtitles in Bahasa Indonesia, but action pictures from Asian countries are also popular.

Religion. More than 85 percent of the Indonesian people are Muslims, and about 10 percent are Christians. Many of Indonesia's Muslims follow Islam less strictly than other Muslims do. For example, many Indonesians combine ancestor and nature worship with Islam or Christianity.

People on Bali and western Lombok follow a religion called Bali-Hinduism. It is based on Hinduism but includes ancient Balinese and Javanese beliefs. The Bali-Hindus worship the spirits of natural features, including mountains and large trees. They also honor the spirits of ancestors which, they believe, visit them. Bali has thousands of Bali-Hindu temples where the religion's many holidays are celebrated with colorful festivals.

Buddhism and Hinduism were important religions on the islands hundreds of years ago. But Indonesia now has relatively few Buddhists or Hindus.

Education. Most of Indonesia's adult population can read and write. For the country's literacy rate, see **Literacy** (table: Literacy rates). The government provides primary and intermediate schooling for a small fee. The government also helps support private schools. Children are required by law to go to school for nine years, beginning by age 7. Some parts of Indonesia lack enough schools, teachers, or textbooks. But overall, almost all Indonesian children attend primary school, about half attend intermediate school, and nearly one-third go to high school.

Indonesia has about 50 public and private universities. The largest is Gadjah Mada University in Yogyakarta. Only about 4 percent of Indonesia's young people receive a college education.

The arts. The most famous arts of Indonesia include two types of traditional dancing: the dances of the old royal courts of Java and the dramatic folk dances of Bali.

© Photobank

A group of Muslim women gather for outdoor prayers on Java. Indonesia has no official religion, but more than 85 percent of the country's people are Muslims.

© R. Ian Lloyd

Traditional Javanese dancers wear elaborate costumes and make slow, stylized gestures rich with meaning. These dancers are performing a dance drama called the *Ramayana Ballet.*

Both types of dancers wear elaborate costumes and heavy makeup or masks. Javanese dances consist of slow, elaborate motions in which even finger gestures have a meaning. The dances may represent scenes of adventure, battle, or love. Balinese dances have quicker rhythms and more forceful movements. Many Balinese dances have a religious meaning and are based on ancient Hindu stories.

Wayang (shadow) puppet dramas are a major part of Javanese and Balinese culture. The most popular puppets are flat and made of leather, but wooden puppets are also used. The puppeteer sits behind a screen with a palm-oil lamp that throws shadows of the puppets onto the screen. Most *wayang* performances last from late night until early morning.

On Java and Bali, a traditional Indonesian orchestra called a *gamelan* accompanies dances and puppet plays. A gamelan consists chiefly of metal percussion instruments, including gongs, xylophones, and double-ended drums. The orchestra also includes flutes and *rebabs* (two-stringed instruments that resemble lutes).

Beautiful stone sculptures decorate Indonesia's many ancient Buddhist and Hindu temples. Famous temples include the Buddhist complex at Borobudur and the Hindu temples of Prambanan, both in central Java.

Early Indonesian literature consisted largely of local folk tales and traditional Hindu and Islamic stories. Literature became highly developed in many regional languages, especially Javanese. Modern literature written in Bahasa Indonesia began in the late 1920's. Much of

modern Indonesian literature is concerned with conflicts between Indonesian and European values and the relationship of traditional Indonesian values to the modern world. Pramoedya Ananta Toer, often considered the greatest Indonesian author, explored these and other themes in his series of four novels about Indonesia's struggle against colonialism. The novels, all published during the 1980's, are *This Earth of Mankind, Child of All Nations, Steps Forward,* and *House of Glass.*

Famous Indonesian crafts include *batik,* a method of waxing and dyeing cloth to make beautifully colored fabrics. Craftworkers also make ceremonial daggers called *krises.* Some Indonesian peoples carve seated wooden figures to represent their ancestors. The Dayaks sculpt objects to ward off evil spirits. The Balinese carve Hindu figures and symbols for their homes and temples.

The islands

People live on more than 6,000 of the 13,500 islands of Indonesia. The rest of the islands are uninhabited. Many geographers divide the islands into three groups: (1) the Greater Sunda Islands, (2) the Lesser Sunda Islands, and (3) the Molucca Islands. Indonesia also includes Irian Jaya, which is part of the island of New Guinea. A table in the section *Indonesia in brief* lists the areas and populations of the chief islands.

The Greater Sunda Islands include Borneo, Sulawesi (formerly called Celebes), Java (also spelled Jawa), and Sumatra (also spelled Sumatera). Most of the Indonesian people live on the Greater Sundas, and most of the nation's economic activity is centered there.

Borneo is the third largest island in the world, after Greenland and New Guinea. The southern three-fourths of Borneo is part of Indonesia. The other fourth consists of the independent nation of Brunei and two Malaysian states, Sarawak and Sabah. The Indonesian part of Borneo is called Kalimantan and is about the same size as France. Tree plantations, natural tropical rain forests, and mountains cover most of Kalimantan. The Kapuas River, the longest river in Indonesia, flows about 700 miles (1,100 kilometers) from the mountains to the sea. The low coastal plains are largely swampy. Kalimantan is thinly populated, and most of the people live along the coast. Banjarmasin is the largest city.

Sulawesi is an island with four long peninsulas. It is the most mountainous island of Indonesia. Mountains in the central region average about 10,000 feet (3,000 meters) above sea level. Many volcanoes, some of them active, rise on the northern peninsula. Forests cover most of the mountain slopes. Some inland valleys and plateaus have fertile farmlands and rich grazing lands. Many of the coastal peoples fish for a living. Ujung Pandang is the largest city of Sulawesi and a major seaport.

Java is Indonesia's most densely populated and most industrialized island. It has about 7 percent of Indonesia's total area and about 60 percent of the people. An east-west chain of mountains, including many old volcanoes, extends across the island. Wide, fertile plains lie north of the mountains, with limestone ridges to the south. A large highland plateau covers western Java.

Java's rich volcanic soil supports intensive agriculture. Thousands of small farm villages dot the island. Most of Indonesia's large cities are also on Java, includ-

Rain forests are abundant throughout Indonesia. The forests are rich in fine woods and other commercially valuable products and in wildlife. Some forests are protected nature preserves.

© Chris Stowers, Panos Pictures

ing Jakarta, the capital and largest city. Because Java is so densely populated, the government began a resettlement program in the 1960's to encourage Java residents to move to less crowded islands. Nevertheless, Java's population continues to grow, but more slowly.

Java has 112 volcanoes, some of which are active. The remnants of the island of Krakatau lie off the coast of Java, in the Sunda Strait. In 1883, Krakatau erupted. Much of the island disappeared, and huge, destructive waves called *tsunamis* washed over Java and nearby islands, killing about 36,000 people.

Sumatra is the sixth largest island in the world. The Barisan Mountains, a range of volcanic peaks along the southwestern coast, rise about 12,000 feet (3,660 meters). The mountains slope eastward to a broad plain covered mostly by tree plantations, tropical rain forests, and some farms. Much of the eastern coast of the island is swampy. To the west, the mountains drop sharply to the sea. Sumatra has rich deposits of oil and natural gas. Medan is Sumatra's largest city.

The Lesser Sunda Islands, which Indonesians call Nusa Tenggara, consist of two strings of islands extending between Bali on the west and Timor on the east. Bali has the most people and the largest city, Denpasar. Most other towns in the Lesser Sundas are small, coastal trading centers. The islands have many mountains, and many short rivers flow from the mountains to the sea.

Timor and other islands in the east have fewer tropical rain forests and more dry grasslands than the islands in the west. Corn is the main crop in the eastern islands, but rice is the principal crop in the western islands.

The Molucca Islands, which Indonesians call the Maluku Islands, lie in the northeastern section of Indonesia. Halmahera, the largest island of this group, covers 6,870 square miles (17,790 square kilometers). Halmahera, Ceram, and Buru are mountainous and

thickly forested. The Aru and Tanimbar islands are flat and swampy. The Moluccas also include hundreds of ring-shaped coral reefs called *atolls* and other small coral islands that are uninhabited.

Most of the Moluccan people live in coastal trading settlements. Ambon, an important port on an island of the same name, is the largest city in the Moluccas.

The Moluccas were formerly called the Spice Islands, and they have long been famous for growing cloves, nutmeg, and mace. Through the centuries, the spice trade attracted people from many lands. These traders, including Arabs, Dutch, and Malays, intermarried with the Moluccans and greatly influenced their way of life. On some isolated islands, however, the people have kept many old customs. On the Tanimbar Islands, for example, people still make offerings to their ancestors.

Irian Jaya covers the western half of the island of New Guinea and some small islands to the north and west. It was called Irian Barat (West Irian) until 1972, when its name was changed to Irian Jaya (Victorious Irian). The eastern half of New Guinea is part of Papua New Guinea, an independent nation.

Irian Jaya is the least developed and most thinly populated region of Indonesia. Most of the population consists of Pacific Islanders called Papuans. The Papuans belong to a number of ethnic groups, several of whom live in isolated areas and follow traditional ways of life. The Asmat people, for example, are hunter-gatherers who live by hunting wild pigs and crocodiles and gathering the pulp of the sago palm.

To ease crowding on other islands, the Indonesian government sponsors a voluntary resettlement program that helps families move to Irian Jaya and other islands. Since the late 1960's, more than 1½ million people have moved from Java and Bali to Irian Jaya and other islands under this program.

Tropical rain forests cover about 85 percent of Irian Jaya. Towering mountains extend from east to west through most of the region. These mountains include 16,503-foot (5,030-meter) Puncak Jaya, the highest mountain in Indonesia. Rich deposits of copper and gold lie deep in the mountains. Most of the coastal areas are low and swampy, and some hold pockets of oil. Jayapura, Irian Jaya's largest city, and other towns sit along the coasts. Most of the farmland also lies along the coasts.

Climate

Indonesia has a hot, humid climate. The average temperature is about 80 °F (27 °C), but temperatures are lower in the highlands. Temperatures vary little throughout the year. As a result, the seasons in Indonesia are based on differences in rainfall, not on changes in temperature. Only Java and the Lesser Sunda Islands have a distinct dry season in which less rain falls. Rainfall is fairly evenly distributed throughout the year in other parts of the country, with heavier downpours in the wet season.

The wet and dry seasons are caused largely by two winds called *monsoons.* From December to March, the winter monsoon blows from the Asian mainland. This monsoon crosses the South China Sea, where it picks up moisture, and brings heavy rains to Indonesia. From mid-June to October, the summer monsoon brings dry air from Australia. Timor, the Indonesian island most affected by this wind, has the longest dry season—five months. Borneo and Sumatra, which lie farthest from Australia, have heavy rainfall the year around.

The driest regions of Indonesia are in the Lesser Sundas, which receive from 35 to 40 inches (89 to 102 centimeters) of rain per year. The wettest islands, Borneo and Sumatra, get 120 to 145 inches (305 to 368 centimeters) per year. Some mountainous areas on Irian Jaya receive about 250 inches (635 centimeters) annually.

Economy

Indonesia's economy is a mixed one, with both privately owned firms and state-owned enterprises. The private sector accounts for about 80 percent of total national output. About half of Indonesians work in agriculture and fishing, but diversified manufacturing has become a mainstay of the economy.

Service industries, which produce services rather than goods, have become increasingly valuable to Indonesia's economy. Indonesia's main service industries include banking, government, trade, and transportation. Tourism is also an important source of income to Indonesia. Visitors flock to the island of Java to see its beautiful scenery and famous temples, and to Bali, which is renowned for its dancing and colorful festivals.

Manufacturing. Manufactured products account for more than half of Indonesia's export earnings. The major industries include the manufacture of chemicals, garments and footwear, plywood and other wood products, steel products, and textiles. Other important Indonesian manufactured goods include cement, cigarettes, electronic equipment, fertilizers, pharmaceuticals, processed rubber products, and pulp and paper. Some plants assemble automobiles, motorcycles, and light airplanes using a combination of imported and Indonesian-made parts and machinery.

Most manufacturing plants are on Java. Jakarta and Surabaya are the leading industrial centers.

Agriculture continues to be a major economic activity that employs about half of Indonesia's people. Indonesian farmers grow a large variety of crops, helped by fertile volcanic soil, a tropical climate, and plentiful rainfall. Many Indonesian farms are large plantations where workers raise crops for export, such as cocoa, palm oil, rubber, spices, sugar cane, tea, and tobacco.

Rice, the chief food crop, is grown mostly on small farms. Indonesia's government was an early supporter of the Green Revolution, an effort to boost grain production that began in the 1960's. As a result, Indonesian farmers have long planted high-yielding varieties of rice. The farmers on Java grow most of Indonesia's rice. They irrigate their fields with water from mountain streams and produce at least two rice crops a year.

Besides rice, small farms produce bananas, cassava, cloves, coconuts, coffee, corn, fruit, peanuts, soybeans, spices, and sweet potatoes. Farmers generally grow crops for sale as well as for their own use. Their major cash crop is rubber. Many farmers also raise cattle, goats, hogs, poultry, sheep, and water buffalo.

© R. Ian Lloyd

Rice is Indonesia's chief food crop. Much of it is grown in terraced fields, such as these. Indonesian farmers have boosted rice production by planting high-yielding varieties of the crop.

Indonesia's gross domestic product

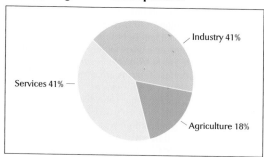

Industry 41%

Services 41%

Agriculture 18%

Indonesia's gross domestic product (GDP) was about $140,000,000,000 in 1993. The GDP is the total value of goods and services produced within a country in a year. *Services* include community, government, and personal services; finance, insurance, real estate, and business services; trade, restaurants, and hotels; transportation and communication; and utilities. *Industry* includes construction, manufacturing, and mining. *Agriculture* includes agriculture, forestry, and fishing.

Production and workers by economic activities

Economic activities	Percent of GDP produced	Employed workers Number of persons	Percent of total
Manufacturing	21	8,582,000	11
Agriculture, forestry, & fishing	18	41,969,000	52
Trade, restaurants, & hotels	17	12,451,000	15
Mining	14	619,000	1
Community, government, & personal services	10	10,378,000	13
Finance, insurance, real estate, & business services	7	620,000	1
Transportation & communication	6	2,967,000	4
Construction	6	2,564,000	3
Utilities	1	174,000	*
Total	100	80,324,000	100

*Less than one-half of 1 per cent.
Figures are for 1993.
Source: Bureau of Statistical Information Systems, Jakarta.

On several Indonesian islands, farmers practice *slash-and-burn agriculture*, also called *shifting cultivation*. They cut down forest trees and burn them, then plant crops in the clearing. The ashes from the burned trees enrich the soil. The farmers raise crops on the same land for only a few years. When the soil begins to wear out, they move.

Mining. Indonesia is one of the world's largest producers of oil and natural gas and the world's largest exporter of liquefied natural gas. Most of the country's petroleum comes from East Kalimantan and Sumatra. Pertamina, a state-owned company, is responsible for the production of petroleum and natural gas. Indonesia is also a leading copper- and tin-mining country. Irian Jaya is believed to hold the world's richest copper ore deposits. The islands of Bangka and Belitung have many tin mines. Indonesia's other mineral products include bauxite, coal, gold, nickel, silver, and tin.

Fishing industry. Fishing is a growing industry in In-

donesia, and many kinds of fish are caught in Indonesian waters. Fishing crews take anchovies, mackerel, sardines, tuna, a fish related to pompano called scad, and other fish from the sea. People raise milkfish and prawns in coastal ponds, and a variety of freshwater fish in inland ponds. Fish provide a major part of coastal people's diet. Shrimp and tuna are Indonesia's most important seafood exports.

Forestry. Indonesia has abundant forests that are rich both in commercially valuable products and in wildlife. Forests cover about two-thirds of the country. More than two-thirds of the forested area is used for commercial purposes. About 10 percent consists of nature preserves or protected areas of tropical rain forest. Indonesia's chief forest products include teak, timber, and plywood. Other products from Indonesia's forests include bamboo; mangrove bark, which is used to make dyes; and cinchona bark, which is used to make the malaria drug quinine. Most of the quinine used today comes from Indonesia.

Most of Indonesia's wood products come from Kalimantan and Sumatra. Poor inland transportation has hampered the development of lumbering in other areas.

Energy sources. Petroleum and natural gas provide about 85 percent of Indonesia's energy needs. Coal supplies about 10 percent, hydroelectric power about 3 percent, and geothermal power about 1 percent. Power plants in Indonesia are government-owned.

International trade. Indonesia is the world's largest exporter of liquefied natural gas. Oil and gas account for about 25 percent of Indonesia's total export earnings, down from more than 80 percent in the early 1980's.

Wood products, especially timber, are Indonesia's most important export after petroleum and natural gas. Indonesia once exported many valuable hardwoods, including ebony and teak logs. By the 1980's, such trees were becoming depleted. As a result, Indonesia shifted from exporting logs to exporting processed wood products, including plywood, sawn timber, rattan, and wooden furniture. Rubber ranks as Indonesia's chief agricultural export. Other major exports include coffee, palm oil, tea, textiles, and tobacco. Major imports include chemicals, machinery, mineral products, and transportation and electrical equipment.

Japan is Indonesia's most important trading partner by far. Other major partners include Australia, Germany, Singapore, Taiwan, and the United States. Indonesia belongs to the World Trade Organization, an international organization that promotes trade between nations.

Transportation and communication are difficult in much of Indonesia because of the thick forests and rugged mountains, and the wide stretches of sea that separate the islands. Less than 1 percent of all Indonesians own an automobile. Buses and six- to eight-seat vehicles called *bemos* pick up and let off passengers along most roads. There are good networks of roads on Java, Sumatra, and Bali. On most of the other islands, however, traffic must travel along jungle tracks or by riverboat. Railroads, which are owned by the government, operate on Java, Madura, and Sumatra.

A shipping company owned by the government handles most transportation among the islands. Local vessels carry passengers and freight along the coasts and

© R. Ian Lloyd

Borobudur, a magnificent Buddhist monument near Yogyakarta, is a popular tourist attraction. It was probably built in the 700's and 800's by the Buddhist rulers of the Saliendra kingdom.

between islands. Tanjung Priok, near Jakarta, is Indonesia's leading port.

A government-owned airline called Garuda Indonesia provides international and domestic air service. Another government-owned airline and several private airlines also fly within Indonesia. The main airport is Sukarno-Hatta International Airport at Cengkareng, near Jakarta.

The government operates Indonesia's postal, telegraph, and telephone systems. The government also runs the major radio and television stations. Several privately owned radio and TV stations also broadcast programs. A satellite communications system enables radio and TV programs to reach all of Indonesia's provinces. Many families have a radio or a television set.

Indonesia has approximately 60 daily newspapers and 90 weeklies. The most important daily papers include *Pos Kota* and *Kompas,* both published in Jakarta.

History

Ancient times. Scientists have found fossilized bones on Java of one of the earliest species of prehistoric human beings. This species, called *Homo erectus,* may have lived there as long as 1½ million years ago. See **Java fossils.**

As early as 2,500 B.C., the ancient Indonesians made tools and ornaments of bronze or iron, wove cloth, and sailed the sea. They traded wherever they went, and established trade routes among the islands and with the Asian mainland. Gradually, the islands became a crossroads for commerce between Arabia and China. Merchants of many lands—Arabs, Chinese, Indians, and Persians—came to Indonesia for its spices and other riches.

Hindu and Buddhist kingdoms were rivals for power in Indonesia for hundreds of years. The first strong kingdom was a Hindu state called Mataram, established in central Java in the A.D. 700's. It soon fell to a Buddhist kingdom led by a line of rulers called the Sailendras. The Sailendras lost control of Java in the 800's. Through marriage, they reappeared as rulers of a powerful Buddhist kingdom called Srivijaya, which had developed in Sumatra during the 600's. Srivijaya became the region's leading sea power. A new Hindu kingdom, also called Mataram, replaced the Sailendras in Java. Mataram and Srivijaya became bitter rivals.

In 1293, Prince Widjaya founded a kingdom called Madjapahit. Madjapahit became the first Indonesian kingdom to base its power on both agriculture and commerce. It conquered many other Indonesian lands and ended Srivijaya's power. In the 1300's, Madjapahit claimed most of the islands.

The spread of Islam. Muslim traders from Arabia and India were among the first people to bring Islam to Indonesia. But the religion's main influence came later from Melaka (also spelled Malacca), a port kingdom on the southwestern coast of the Malay Peninsula.

During the early 1400's, Melaka gained control of the important trading route through the Strait of Malacca, between Malaya and Sumatra. Melaka became a great warehouse center. Its ruler converted to Islam, and the religion spread to various parts of Indonesia.

The Madjapahit kingdom fell in the early 1500's. A new Muslim kingdom—the third kingdom in Indonesia to be called Mataram—arose on its ruins. Mataram reestablished a united kingdom in central and eastern Java.

The coming of the Europeans. In 1497 and 1498, the Portuguese explorer Vasco da Gama sailed around Africa and discovered a sea route from Europe to India. Other Portuguese explorers soon followed. The Portuguese captured Melaka in 1511, built a fort there, and tried to take over the profitable Indonesian trade.

By the end of the 1500's, the English and Dutch began to challenge the Portuguese for control of Indonesia's riches. England and the Netherlands each formed an East India Company to trade in the region, the English in 1600 and the Dutch in 1602. In 1641, the Dutch captured Melaka from the Portuguese.

Dutch rule. In 1677, the ruler of Mataram on Java asked the Dutch to help him fight a rebel uprising. The Dutch did so, and he gave them important trading rights and Javanese territories. In similar ways, or by force, the trade on other Indonesian islands passed into Dutch hands. By the late 1700's, the Dutch East India Company controlled commerce on most of the islands. The region became known as the Dutch East Indies or the Netherlands Indies.

The Dutch East India Company forced the Indonesians to produce certain crops and deliver them at prices set by the company. The company made enormous profits at first. But its costs grew rapidly during the late 1700's, and it went bankrupt. Legislation by the Dutch government in 1798 caused the company to dis-

Important dates in Indonesia

A.D. 600's-1200's The Buddhist kingdom of Srivijaya expanded from Sumatra and became a great sea power.

1300's The Hindu kingdom of Madjapahit controlled much of Indonesia.

1400's Islam spread throughout the islands.

1602 The Dutch East India Company was formed.

1620's The Dutch began to control trade in areas of Indonesia.

1799 The Dutch government took over the lands controlled by the Dutch East India Company.

1908 Indonesians began to form nationalist groups.

1942-1945 Japanese forces occupied Indonesia during World War II.

1945 Indonesia declared its independence, and Sukarno became president.

1949 The Dutch recognized Indonesia's independence.

1963 West New Guinea (now Irian Jaya) came under Indonesian control.

1966 Suharto took over much of Sukarno's power and began to reorganize the government.

1968 Suharto was named president.

1976 Indonesia annexed the Portuguese colony of East Timor.

1997-1998 Indonesia suffered one of the worst financial crises in its history.

1998 Following protests in Jakarta and other cities, Suharto resigned as president.

band the next year. The government took over the company's land.

At first, the Dutch government established effective political control mainly on Java. Beginning in 1830, the Dutch government forced peasants throughout Java and in parts of Sumatra and Sulawesi to grow such export crops as indigo and coffee on much of their land. The Dutch government collected these crops and made large profits from their sale. In 1870, it permitted Dutch investors to lease farmland in the region. In the next 30 years, many privately owned Dutch plantations went into operation, most of them on Sumatra. The Dutch government gradually extended its control throughout the East Indies, partly by conquest and partly through agreements with local rulers. By about 1910, the final extent of the Netherlands Indies had been established.

The rise of nationalism. Indonesians in several areas had long resisted Dutch rule. In 1825, a major revolt began on Java under Diponegoro, a Javanese prince. Fighting continued until the Dutch crushed the revolt in 1830.

Budi Utomo, the first nationalist organization, was founded in 1908 and won support among well-educated Javanese. It was a cultural association rather than a political party. In 1912, the Islamic Association, originally a Javanese trading society, became political and developed into a serious challenge to the Dutch. To quiet nationalist demands, the Dutch set up a People's Council with some Indonesian representatives on it. But the council had little power beyond that of debate. The Indonesian Communist Party, formed in 1920, led a series of minor revolts in 1926 and 1927. Many other anti-Dutch parties also developed, including the Indonesian National Party, founded in 1927 by Sukarno.

Independence. On Jan. 11, 1942, during World War II, Japanese forces landed in the Netherlands Indies. On February 27, the Japanese defeated an Allied fleet in the Battle of the Java Sea. In the world war, Japan fought on the side of Germany, Italy, and the other Axis nations, and the Netherlands sided with Britain, the United States, and the other Allies. The Japanese occupied the Netherlands Indies on March 7, and the Allies surrendered the next day. Many Indonesian nationalists cooperated with the Japanese but continued to work for independence. On Aug. 17, 1945, after Japan had agreed to surrender to the Allies, Sukarno and other nationalists declared Indonesia's independence. Sukarno became the nation's first president.

The Dutch tried to regain control of Indonesia. From 1945 to 1949, there were periods of fighting and a series of truces. The Dutch recaptured much territory but could not defeat the Indonesians. For the many peoples of Indonesia, the revolution strengthened their belief in nationalism and their sense of Indonesian identity. Under pressure from the United States and the United Nations (UN), the Dutch finally agreed to grant independence to all the Netherlands Indies except West New Guinea (now Irian Jaya). That territory's future was to be decided at later conferences. The Netherlands formally recognized Indonesia's independence on Dec. 27, 1949.

Indonesia under Sukarno faced serious problems. Only the natural resources needed by the Dutch had been developed. Transportation systems were inadequate. About 90 percent of the population could not read or write, and few people were qualified for high positions in government or business. Regional and ethnic differences threatened to divide the country. There was little agreement on how to solve Indonesia's serious economic and social problems. Parliamentary elections, held in 1955, continued the political confusion by failing to produce a majority party. Revolts broke out on Sumatra and Sulawesi in 1958, but Indonesian Army units from Java defeated all the rebels by 1961.

In 1960, Sukarno dissolved the elected parliament and appointed a new one. He called his system of government "guided democracy." In 1963, the People's Consultative Assembly declared him president for life.

Sukarno had repeatedly demanded that the Netherlands turn over Irian Jaya to Indonesia and threatened to seize it by force. In 1962, the Netherlands gave temporary control of Irian Jaya to the UN, which gave Indonesia responsibility for administering the area. In 1969, the West Irians voted to remain part of Indonesia, and the UN recognized Indonesia's control of Irian Jaya.

In 1963, the country of Malaysia was established over Indonesia's opposition by combining the British colonies of North Borneo (Sabah) and Sarawak with Malaya and Singapore. Indonesia claimed that the United Kingdom had granted Malaysia a false independence and kept the real power. Indonesia also declared that the British had forced North Borneo and Sarawak to join the new nation. Sukarno threatened to crush Malaysia. In 1964, he sent Indonesian forces into the new nation. They were unsuccessful, chiefly because of British military support for Malaysia. In 1965, Sukarno withdrew Indonesia from the UN to protest Malaysia's election to the UN Security Council.

The fall of Sukarno. Sukarno succeeded in giving his people a sense of national identity and pride. But the Sukarno government mismanaged Indonesia's economy, and the country almost went bankrupt. Beginning in 1957, Indonesia seized many foreign-owned plantations and industries, but it did not have enough trained peo-

Student protesters scale the Parliament Building in Jakarta in May 1998 during widespread demonstrations against President Suharto. Suharto resigned shortly after this picture was taken.

© Paula Bronstein, Gamma/Liaison

ple to run them. Most of the plantations and industrial plants came under the control of Army administrators. Sukarno spent huge sums on such projects as monuments and sports stadiums, but he neglected the development of natural resources. The country's exports fell, and its debts rose. Inflation drove prices up sharply.

During the 1960's, the Indonesian Communist Party gained strength. Communists controlled labor unions and other key organizations, but they held few government posts. In 1965, military officers associated with the Communist Party tried to overthrow the government. They killed six generals and some other officers. The Army, led by Lieutenant General Suharto, quickly defeated the rebels. Over the next several months, civilian mobs retaliated against the Communists, killing more than 200,000 people.

Indonesia under Suharto. In 1966, pressure from the Army and student groups forced Sukarno to transfer much of his power to Suharto. Suharto outlawed the Communist Party, dismissed many government officials, and appointed new ones. He ended Indonesia's opposition to Malaysia and brought Indonesia back into the UN. By 1967, Sukarno had lost his remaining power, and Suharto became acting president. The next year, the People's Consultative Assembly elected Suharto president. The Assembly reelected Suharto as president every five years from 1973 to 1998.

When Suharto became president, Indonesia's economy was weak. The country could not grow enough rice to feed its people, foreign banks would not lend money to the Indonesian government, and the inflation rate was about 1,000 percent a year. Suharto's government, backed by a strong military, created economic and political stability. The government received large amounts of foreign loans and investment. It funded projects to increase rice production, and yields rose sharply. The government also improved health conditions in Indonesia and helped raise living standards in other ways.

Indonesia invaded East Timor, a Portuguese colony, in 1975 and annexed it the following year. Many of the people of East Timor, who were mostly Roman Catholic, objected to rule by Indonesians, who were mostly Muslim. Since the annexation, opponents of Indonesian rule have battled Indonesian government troops. The UN refuses to recognize the annexation of Timor, and the United States and other countries have accused Indonesia's government of human rights violations there. In 1996, two Timorese dissidents won the Nobel Peace Prize for their attempts to end the conflict.

During the late 1960's and throughout the 1970's, several uprisings broke out in Irian Jaya. The rebels, who called themselves the Free Papua Movement, sought unification with Papua New Guinea. Indonesian government troops quickly put down the uprisings, but conflicts along the border with Papua New Guinea continued throughout the 1980's and 1990's.

World prices for petroleum products had soared in the 1970's, greatly aiding Indonesia's economy. Oil prices fell in the mid-1980's, however, slowing economic growth. As a result, Indonesia worked to diversify its economy and become less dependent on oil and gas. Exports of wood products, coffee, rubber, shrimp, and manufactured goods increased. Diversified manufacturing and strong industrial growth, particularly on Java, brought prosperity in the late 1980's and early 1990's.

The fall of Suharto. Opposition to Suharto gained strength in the mid-1990's. Many people criticized the Suharto family's immense wealth and its control of key government agencies and economic enterprises. Corruption in government also drew criticism. Megawati Sukarnoputri—a daughter of Indonesia's first president, Sukarno—and Muslim leader Amien Rais emerged as rivals to Suharto. From 1993 to 1996, Megawati had headed the opposition Indonesian Democratic Party.

In 1997 and 1998, Indonesia suffered one of the worst financial slumps in its history. The value of its currency fell, and its stock market plunged. Banks and other businesses failed, and millions of people lost their jobs.

Meanwhile, the price of food and other necessities soared. The economic downturn led to renewed calls for Suharto to step down. Violent protests broke out in Jakarta and some other major cities. In May 1998, Suharto resigned. Vice President Bacharuddin Jusuf Habibie succeeded him. Shortly after taking office, Habibie promised to pursue a program of economic, political, and social reforms.   Dwight Y. King

Outline

I. **Government**
   A. National government
   B. Local government
   C. Politics
   D. Courts
   E. Armed forces
   F. International organizations
II. **People**
III. **Way of life**
   A. Rural life
   B. City life
   C. Clothing
   D. Food and drink
   E. Recreation
   F. Religion
   G. Education
   H. The arts
IV. **The islands**
   A. The Greater Sunda Islands
   B. The Lesser Sunda Islands
   C. The Molucca Islands
   D. Irian Jaya
V. **Climate**
VI. **Economy**
   A. Service industries
   B. Manufacturing
   C. Agriculture
   D. Mining
   E. Fishing industry
   F. Forestry
   G. Energy sources
   H. International trade
   I. Transportation and communication
VII. **History**

Related articles in *World Book* include:

History

Physical features

Other related articles

Questions

How do monsoons affect the climate of Indonesia?
What are some of Indonesia's major mining products?
How did Islam spread to Indonesia during the 1400's?
On which island do about 60 percent of the Indonesians live?
What is the main food of Indonesians?
Why is much of Indonesia's soil especially fertile?
When did Indonesian nationalism begin to develop?
How many islands make up Indonesia?
What is a *gamelan? Batik?*
Why is transportation difficult in Indonesia?

Additional resources

Cribb, Robert. *Historical Dictionary of Indonesia.* Scarecrow, 1992.
Frederick, William H., and Worden, R. L., eds. *Indonesia: A Country Study.* 5th ed. U. S. Government Printing Office, 1993.
Schwarz, Adam. *A Nation in Waiting: Indonesia in the 1990s.* Westview, 1994.

Internet is a vast network of computers that connects many of the world's businesses, institutions, and individuals. The Internet, which means *interconnected network of networks,* links tens of thousands of smaller computer networks. It enables computer users throughout the world to send and receive messages, share information in a variety of forms, and even play computer games with people thousands of miles away. Computers linked to the Internet range from simple and inexpensive personal computers, often called *PC's,* to huge *mainframe* computers used by government institutions, educational institutions, and businesses.

Computers require special hardware and software to connect to the Internet. Necessary hardware includes a *modem,* a device that translates a computer's digital information into signals that can be transmitted over telephone lines (see **Modem**). Required software includes a communications program that allows the transmission and receipt of messages.

The Internet, often called simply the Net, began as a collection of text-based information. But the development and rapid growth of a part of the Internet called the World Wide Web (also known as WWW or the Web), transformed the presentation of information on the Net. In addition to text, the Web allows the use of photographs, moving pictures, and sound to create presentations approaching the visual quality of television and the audio quality of recorded music.

Uses of the Internet

The major uses of the Internet include communication, research, publishing, and sales.

Communication. Probably the most popular use of the Internet and the Web is *electronic mail,* also called *e-mail.* Virtually every Internet user is assigned an electronic address from which e-mail messages are sent and at which they are received. The Internet carries hundreds of millions of e-mail messages each day.

An *Internet service provider* (ISP) offers local telephone numbers through which an individual, using a computer and modem, can connect to the Internet. An ISP maintains its customers' e-mail addresses, routes e-mail and requests for Internet-based information to and from its users, and manages high-speed communications lines that speed up Internet sessions. An *on-line service* provides a wide range of exclusive content in addition to Internet access.

Research. The Internet is like a vast library, containing as much knowledge on every subject as might be held in millions of books. Information is available in many forms, from files consisting only of text to multimedia files that combine text, photos, animation or video, software programs, and sound. Internet resources grow larger every day.

Because of the ease with which information is stored on computers, and the speed with which it can be accessed, the Internet is a popular first stop for many people performing research. A businessperson might search Internet resources for help in developing sales or product information. Students can access databases to find material related to homework assignments or courses of study. Physicians use the Net to compare medical treatments and to review advances in medical science. Scientists share research data on the Internet.

Publishing. Publishers are increasingly using the Internet as a medium for presenting newspapers, magazines, and books. Because information on the Net is electronic, the publisher is freed from the costs of paper, printing, and distribution. More importantly, the publisher can update information instantly, making it possible to distribute far more current news than could be provided on paper.

Sales. Many businesses use the Internet to carry on commerce. Retail establishments sell nearly every type of product over the Internet. Software publishers view the Net as a convenient and inexpensive way to distribute products. Over the Internet, users can buy new programs, sample programs before purchasing them, or receive upgrades to programs they already own. Users generally make Internet purchases with credit cards.

Because tens of millions of people use the Internet every day, advertisers are eager to place messages in frequently visited spots. Those ads can be electronically linked to an advertiser's own information, which often takes the form of elaborate multimedia files. In effect, advertisers can invite Internet users to view commercials on their computer. Additionally, a user can supply the advertiser with his or her e-mail address to get further information or incentives, such as discount coupons.

The Internet also has important uses within the financial community. Many banks and stockbrokers offer their customers software to make and track investments from their computer.

Other uses. A popular feature of the Net is *chat.* Using special software, users can gather in electronic "chat rooms" and send typed messages back and forth, discussing topics of common interest. The Internet also features many Web-based games with animation, sound effects, and music. Game players can challenge players in distant countries to tournaments.

How the Internet works

Computer networks enable computers to communicate and share information and resources. The simplest networks consist of a user's computer, known as the *client,* and a resource computer, called the *host* or *server.* The client makes requests of the host, which, in turn, provides the requested resources, such as information or software.

The Internet works in much the same way, on a far vaster scale. To connect to the Net, a user *logs on* by instructing his or her computer's communication software to call the Internet service provider. To protect the user's security, this process usually requires a secret password.

Once connected to the ISP, the user has several options. For some functions, such as e-mail or text-only resources known as *newsgroups,* the user's communications software alone may provide access. Most such software includes simple word processors in which messages can be composed or read.

For more sophisticated resources, such as the World Wide Web, an additional piece of software known as a *browser* is used. With a browser running, a computer user may access millions of sites around the world. Each site has a separate electronic address, known as a *uniform resource locator* (URL). Directories of these addresses are maintained and constantly updated throughout the Internet. The addresses themselves are organized into various *domains* (categories), such as educational, commercial, or organizations. In a URL, the domain type takes the form of

a three-letter extension, such as *.edu* for *education* and *.com* for *commercial.*

By typing an address, or by clicking the computer mouse's cursor on a picture or word linked electronically to the address, the user transmits a request through the ISP and onto the larger Internet. When the request arrives at the desired destination, the server computer responds by sending the user its information. This information often takes the form of a starting page called a *home page,* which is similar to the table of contents of a book or magazine. From a home page, the user can search for further information by using links to other pages within the same Web site or to other Web sites.

Because there are tens of millions of sites, most browsers include systems for *bookmarking* (recording) the addresses of favorite or frequently visited sites. Once a site has been bookmarked, the user need simply click on the appropriate bookmark to visit the site again.

A user need not know in advance the address of the desired information. Among the most popular features of the Internet and World Wide Web are *search engines.* These programs offer users the opportunity to type in key words or phrases related to the information they seek. The search engine then reviews indexes of information and sites on the Internet and the Web, providing the user with the addresses of sites that most closely match the request. Because search engine sites are used frequently by millions of people, they are popular spots for advertisements.

The Internet and society

The Internet has made huge amounts of information accessible to more people than ever before. The development of the Web in the early 1990's made the Internet relatively easy and fun to use by adding graphics, motion, and sound and by using pictures to represent computer commands. This accessibility has raised some serious questions.

Among these questions are doubts about the appropriateness of information. Not all of the information on the Internet and the Web is accurate, and some is deliberately misleading. Many schools teach students how to evaluate information derived from the Internet.

Many parents worry about violent or pornographic material available on the Net. Criminals may lurk in chat rooms, seeking to arrange face-to-face meetings with unsuspecting victims. Special programs known as *parental control software* can help parents restrict access to sites that may be unsuitable for children.

The Internet also poses security concerns. Mischievous programmers known as *hackers* often try to break into large computer systems. Some hackers damage databases stored in these systems or attempt to steal information or electronic funds. Others may seek access to credit card numbers and other individual financial information. Many people are concerned about the security and confidentiality of credit card numbers used to make purchases over the Internet.

Software itself can become a danger on the Internet. Programs known as *viruses, e-mail bombs,* or *Trojan horses* have been distributed across the Internet and can cause damage to data on systems that receive them. Many companies produce software designed to protect users against unwanted and damaging viruses.

Glossary of Internet terms

Bulletin board is an electronic message center. Most bulletin boards serve specific interest groups. They allow users to read messages left by others and to leave their own as well.

Chat room is a location on the Internet where users can discuss topics of common interest by sending typed messages back and forth. The messages appear to other users as soon as they are typed.

Client is a user's computer.

Cookie is a piece of data placed on a client's hard drive by a server. It can be used for a variety of purposes. One such purpose would be to store a name and password so that a user would not have to enter this information every time he or she returned to the same Web site.

Download is to receive data or software over the Internet and store it so that it may be used later.

E-mail, or electronic mail, is a way of sending a message over the Internet to another specific user or group of users.

Firewall is a combination of hardware and software that prevents a visitor to an organization's Web site from gaining access to other information stored on the organization's computer network, such as corporate records or employee information.

Forum, or *newsgroup,* is an on-line discussion group in which participants with a common interest can exchange open messages.

Home page is the starting page of a Web site. It generally includes tools and indexes to help visitors navigate through the rest of the site. In many ways, a home page functions as an electronic table of contents.

Hyperlink is a programmed connection from one Web site to another. It usually appears on a Web site as a highlighted or underlined word or phrase. When a user clicks a mouse on the passage, the client connects to the related Web site.

Hypertext markup language, or HTML, is the programming language most commonly used by the World Wide Web.

Hypertext transfer protocol, or HTTP, is the set of rules governing the transfer of files between a server and a client. HTTP electronically oversees the connection of clients to Web sites.

Internet service provider is a business that provides a client with the means to connect to the Internet and maintains exchanges of information between clients and servers.

Modem is a device that converts a computer's digital information to signals that can be transmitted over telephone lines. It also converts signals it receives back to digital information.

Net is a common abbreviation for *Internet.*

Network is a communication system that links two or more computers.

On-line service is a business that provides Internet access plus a wide range of exclusive content and features, such as chat rooms, games, and news reports.

Search engine is a program that allows a user to locate information on the Internet by typing in key words or phrases. The search engine then returns addresses of Web sites that most closely match the request.

Server, or host, is a computer that provides requested resources, such as information or software, to a client via a modem or network connection.

Surfing is the process of visiting a number of Web sites in rapid succession.

Uniform resource locator, or URL, is an electronic address that identifies a Web site.

Web browser, or simply *browser,* is a piece of software that allows a user to access Web sites.

Web site is a collection of information at a specific address on the World Wide Web.

World Wide Web, or WWW for short, is a part of the Internet that includes text, graphics, video, animation, and sound.

Most people believe that the benefits of the Internet far outweigh its dangers. Although the Internet and the Web have grown quickly, they have revealed only a fraction of their potential as tools for education, research, communication, news, and entertainment.

History of the Internet

The Internet began to take shape in the late 1960's. The United States Department of Defense was concerned at the time about the possibility of devastating nuclear warfare. It began investigating means of linking various computer installations together so that their ability to communicate might withstand a war. Through its Advanced Research Projects Agency (ARPA), the Defense Department initiated *ARPANet,* a network of university and military computers.

The network's operating *protocols* (rules) laid the groundwork for relatively fast and error-free computer-to-computer communication. Other networks adopted these protocols, which in turn evolved as new computer and communications technologies became available.

Throughout the 1970's, the ARPANet grew at a slow but steady pace. Computers in other countries began to join the network. Other networks came into existence as well. These included Unix to Unix Copy (UUCP), which was established to serve users of the UNIX computer programming language, and the User's Network (USENET), a medium for posting text-based articles on a variety of subjects.

By 1981, just over 200 computers were connected to ARPANet. The U.S. military then divided the network into two organizations—ARPANet and a purely military net-

work. During the 1980's, ARPANet was absorbed by NSFNET, a more advanced network developed by the National Science Foundation. Soon, the collection of networks became known simply as the Internet.

One of the reasons for the slow growth of the early Internet was the difficulty of using the network. To access its information, users had to master complex series of programming commands that required either memorization or frequent reference to special manuals.

The Internet's breakthrough to mass popularity occurred in 1991 with the arrival of the World Wide Web. The Web was developed by Tim Berners-Lee, a British computer scientist at the European Center for Nuclear Research (CERN). This development opened the Internet to multimedia.

In addition, the programming language that the Web used, called HyperText Markup Language (HTML), made it far easier to link information from computers throughout the world. This development effectively created an interactive index that enabled users to jump easily from the resources of one computer to another, effortlessly following an information trail around the world.

The arrival of browsers in 1993 further simplified use of the Web and the Internet, and brought about staggering growth in the Internet. Today, there are tens of millions of computer users accessing the Net and the Web daily. As the Internet incorporates new technologies that add such features as spoken-word commands, instantaneous translation, and increased availability of historical and archival material, it will continue its rapid growth.   Keith Ferrell

See also **Computer** (Computer networks); **Electronic publishing; Medicine** (Computers and electronic communication); **On-line service; World Wide Web.**

Islam, *ihs LAHM,* is the name given to the religion preached by the Prophet Muhammad in the A.D. 600's. Islam is an Arabic word that means *surrender* or *submission.* God is called *Allah* (in Arabic, pronounced *ah LAH),* which means *The God.* A person who submits to Allah and follows the teachings of Islam is called a *Muslim.* This article discusses the beliefs and practices of Islam. For information about the history of Muslim people, including the history of their religion, see **Muslims.**

Muhammad was born about A.D. 570 in the Arabian city of Mecca. Muslims believe that in about 610, he began to receive revelations from Allah that were transmitted by the angel Gabriel. These revelations took place in the cities of Mecca and Medina over about a 22-year period. They were assembled in a book called the Quran (*ku RAHN),* sometimes spelled *Koran.* The Quran is the holy book of the Muslims, who believe it contains God's actual words. The Quran and the *sunna (SOON uh),* the example of the words and practices of Muhammad, make up the foundation of Islamic law.

Islam is the world's second largest religion behind Christianity. Today, Muslims live in every country in the world. Although Islam began in Arabia, more than half of the world's Muslims live in South and Southeast Asia. The countries with the largest Muslim populations are Indonesia, India, Bangladesh, and Pakistan. About one-fourth of all Muslims live in the Middle East. They make up the majority of the population in the European country of Albania and nearly half the population in Bosnia-Herzegovina. Muslims rank as the second largest religious group in Belgium, France, and Germany. Several million Muslims live in the United States.

Teachings and practices

The central concept of Islam is *tawhid (taw HEED),* the oneness of God. For Muslims, there is one God who is the lord of the universe. People owe worship and obedience to God before any other thing. God is one, the creator, the all-knowing. In relations with humanity, God is the lawgiver, judge, and restorer of life after death.

Prophets. According to the Quran, God has provided guidance for human beings in the teachings of prophets, who have appeared in many nations throughout history. In Islam, prophets do not foretell the future. Instead, God selects the prophets to urge people to worship God alone and to teach them to live according to God's commandments. The Quran mentions 25 prophets by name. According to tradition, God chose thousands of prophets beginning with Adam, the first prophet in Islam, and ending with Muhammad, the final prophet. The Quran teaches that the Prophet Abraham was the first *monotheist* (believer in one God).

The most important type of prophet in Islam is the *rasul (rah SOOL),* which means *messenger.* A rasul is a person to whom God has revealed a book for the guidance of humanity. The messengers of God in Islam include Abraham, Moses, David, Jesus, and Muhammad.

Muslims believe that children are born without sin and that all people can lead themselves to salvation once God has shown them the way. Believers in Islam achieve salvation by following the revealed books of God's messengers. Muslims believe in heaven and hell, where people go after death based on their actions during life.

The sunna of Muhammad. In Islam, Muhammad is the final messenger of God, sent to confirm the authentic teachings of previous prophets. God also sent him to correct the alterations that followers of previous religions had introduced into God's original teachings. For Muslims, Muhammad's mission includes all humanity and is not limited to a specific region, group, or community. Therefore, his life serves as a model for all men and women. The example of Muhammad's sayings and acts, the sunna, is presented in written collections called the *hadith (hah DEETH).*

Muslims do not consider Islam to be a new religion. They believe its teachings contain the same message given to all prophets and messengers since the creation of Adam. Because they confirm all of these teachings as a whole, they do not like to be called *Muhammadans.*

The Five Pillars of Islam. Every action performed in obedience to God is considered an act of worship in Islam. Most devout Muslims take care in their daily lives to respect their parents and elders, to be kind to animals and human beings, and to do their daily tasks to the best of their ability. The formal acts of worship called the Five Pillars of Islam provide the framework for all aspects of a Muslim's life. The pillars consist of (1) *shahada,* (2) prayer, (3) almsgiving, (4) fasting, and (5) pilgrimage.

Shahada is the first pillar and is considered the basis of all other pillars of the faith. *Shahada* (*shuh HAHD uh)* is an Arabic word that means *an act of bearing witness.* It consists of two statements: "I bear witness that there is no God but Allah," and "I bear witness that Muhammad is the Messenger of Allah." The first statement declares that there is only one God and that God alone is worthy of worship. The second statement says that Muhammad is God's messenger. For Muslims, the second statement also includes a declaration of belief in Muhammad's interpretation of Islam, as expressed in the sunna.

Prayer. Muslims are required to pray five times a day—just before dawn, at midday, in midafternoon, just after sunset, and at night. Prayer, called *salat (suh LAHT),* is the most important demonstration of a Muslim's devotion to God. Muslims believe that prayer reinforces belief in Islam because it reduces the likelihood of disobeying God by committing sins. A prayer's timing is determined by the movement of the sun. A crier called a *muezzin (moo EHZ ihn)* makes the call to prayer. If the prayer is performed in a *mosque (masjid* in Arabic, meaning *house of worship),* the muezzin traditionally calls worshipers from a tower called a *minaret.* Before making their prayers, Muslims must wash their hands, their face, parts of their arms and head, and their feet in a ritual manner.

The physical movements of the salat symbolize the believers' submission to God. When praying, Muslims stand facing the holy city of Mecca in Saudi Arabia. Raising their hands to their ears, they say in Arabic "God is greatest." They then recite the opening passage of the Quran, known as the Fatiha *(FAH tee hah),* followed by another verse from the Quran. After reciting these verses, they again say "God is greatest" and bow from the waist, praising God. After returning to an upright position, they say "God is greatest" a third time and fall to their knees, touching the floor with their foreheads. In this face-down posi-

© Mehmet Biber, Photo Researchers

Muslim pilgrims pray at the Kaaba, the holiest shrine of Islam. The Kaaba is an empty cube-shaped building that stands in the center of the Sacred Mosque in the city of Mecca, Saudi Arabia. According to Islamic law, all adult Muslims must, if possible, make at least one pilgrimage to Mecca during their lifetime.

tion, they again praise God. After sitting back on their heels and asking God for forgiveness, worshipers kneel with their faces down one more time and then stand, saying "God is greatest" before each new position.

Each cycle of the prayer is called a *raka (RAHK uh)*, which means *bowing* in Arabic. One cycle includes the first Quran recitation, the bow, kneeling face down twice, sitting, and standing up. After the final cycle, worshipers offer a peace greeting. Depending on the time of day, the salat may have two to four cycles. On Fridays, Muslims gather at midday to pray as a group. Before the prayer, a religious leader called an *imam (ih MAHM)* recites two short sermons. Typically, men pray at the front of the group and women pray in a separate section behind or beside them.

Almsgiving is required as a way of assisting the poor. The Arabic term for almsgiving is *zakat,* which means *purification.* Muslims "purify" their wealth by giving a certain percentage of it to the needy and recognizing that all things ultimately belong to God. Zakat is paid once a year, in the form of a tax. Most zakat donations go to mosques, Islamic centers, or welfare organizations. Some Muslims supplement zakat with a voluntary form of giving called *sadaqa (SAH dah kah),* which means *sincere gift* in Arabic.

Fasting. Every Muslim must fast in the month of Ramadan *(RAHM uh DAHN),* the ninth month of the Islamic calendar. The Islamic calendar is lunar, so each month follows the phases of the moon and lasts 29 or 30 days. As a result, Ramadan falls at different seasons of the year. Muslims believe that the first verses of the Quran were revealed to Muhammad during Ramadan about A.D. 610.

The Quran instructs Muslims to fast from dawn to sunset during Ramadan. While fasting, Muslims do not eat any food, drink any beverages, smoke, or engage in sexual relations during daylight hours. At night, they may eat, drink, and resume other normal activities. Muslims fast to practice spiritual reflection, self-restraint, concern for others, and obedience to God. Alms are normally given to the poor at the end of the fast. Because fasting can be physically demanding, some people are excused. Those excused include the sick, injured, elderly, and pregnant or nursing women. They are supposed to provide food for the poor, or if able, fast at a later time instead.

Pilgrimage. The Quran commands Muslims to make a *hajj* (pilgrimage) to Mecca at least once in their lifetime if they are physically and financially able to make the journey. The hajj takes place over the first several days of the 12th month of the Islamic calendar.

The rites of the hajj commemorate the trials and sacrifices of the Prophet Abraham, his wife Hagar, and their son the Prophet Ishmael. Muslims believe that Abraham and Ishmael built the Kaaba *(KAH bah)* as the first house of worship to God. The Kaaba is an empty cube-shaped building in the center of the Great Mosque in Mecca.

The first requirement of the hajj is that men wear two

pieces of unsewn white cloth, called the *ihram*, which means *garment of consecration*. Women must wear a long white gown and headscarf. While wearing these garments, a pilgrim may not kill any animal or insect, remove any hair from his or her body, or engage in any sexual act. The second requirement is that pilgrims walk around the Kaaba seven times in a counterclockwise direction.

Most pilgrims perform three additional rites, though they are not official parts of the hajj. While walking, many pilgrims attempt to kiss or touch the Black Stone, which Abraham and Ishmael placed in one corner of the Kaaba. Pilgrims may also run seven times along a corridor of the Great Mosque to commemorate Hagar's search for water for her infant son, Ishmael. Finally, pilgrims may take water from a well called Zamzam on the grounds of the Great Mosque.

The third part of the hajj involves standing at Arafat, a plain outside Mecca, on the ninth day of the pilgrimage month. During the afternoon prayer, pilgrims listen to an imam deliver a sermon from the heights of Mount Arafat at the edge of the plain. This act commemorates the final pilgrimage of Muhammad, who delivered his farewell sermon from this site.

To finish the pilgrimage, Muslims next spend the night at Muzdalifah, an encampment near a place called Mina, on the way back to Mecca. The next day, they throw stones at the three pillars where, according to tradition, Ishmael drove away Satan's temptations. Many pilgrims also sacrifice an animal, usually a sheep or goat, at Mina. This action commemorates Abraham's vow to sacrifice his son. The hajj pilgrimage is completed after each pilgrim returns to Mecca and walks around the Kaaba seven more times.

Holidays and celebrations. All Muslims celebrate two major holidays, the Feast of Fast-Breaking and the Feast of Sacrifice. The first is held on the day following Ramadan and marks the end of the monthlong fast. The feast is a joyous occasion in which families gather for a rich meal and children receive sweets. The Feast of Sacrifice is held on the 10th day of Dhul-Hijja, the month of the hajj. On this day, many Muslims sacrifice an animal, such as a goat or sheep. A small portion of the meat is prepared for family and friends, and the rest is given to the poor.

In some countries, Muslims celebrate the birthday of Muhammad on the 12th day of the third Islamic month. Muslims spend the day praying, reading the Quran, and reciting poems and stories written in honor of the Prophet.

Muslims celebrate their New Year at the beginning of the first month of the Islamic calendar. On the 10th day of the month, members of the Shiite division hold a celebration called Ashura that marks the massacre in 680 of Husayn, a grandson of Muhammad. Muslims from Iran, Afghanistan, and central Asian countries follow an ancient solar calendar along with the Islamic lunar calendar. They often celebrate another New Year called Nawruz *(naw ROOZ)* on the first day of spring.

Islam's social structure

The sharia. Islam has two sources of authority. The first is the word of God given in the Quran. The second is the sunna, the body of traditions that preserves the words and conduct of Muhammad. Muslim scholars use these sources to understand the principles of the *sharia (shah REE ah)*, an Arabic word that means *the way that leads to God*. It refers to the divinely revealed and inspired Islamic law that plays a central role in the lives of Muslims throughout the world. Scholars recognize four main sources for interpreting the sharia and applying it to daily life. They are (1) the Quran, (2) the sunna, (3) extending the reasoning of previous laws to new situations, and (4) the views of Muslim scholars and jurists.

In theory, all Islamic law is divine in origin. In practice, however, most sources of Muslim law are found in the sunna rather than the Quran, particularly in the

© J. Polleross, The Stock Market

Muslims pray in a house of worship called a *mosque*. The worshipers face a decorative niche called a *mihrab* that points toward the holy city of Mecca, the direction Muslims must face while praying. Next to the mihrab is a pulpit called a *mimbar*.

The symbol of Islam is a crescent and star. The symbol appears on the flags of several nations whose population has a Muslim majority, including Pakistan and Turkey.

part of the hadith that reflects Muhammad's interpretation of the Quran's rulings. The practice of deriving present-day laws from the sources of the sharia is called *fiqh* (pronounced *fihk).* There are several schools of fiqh, each named after the founder of a method of interpretation. Although most Muslims agree about the major points of Islam, differences do exist, based on the opinions of the different schools of fiqh.

Ethics and morals. Actions in Islamic law are judged on five values: (1) *obligatory* (required), (2) recommended, (3) neutral, (4) disapproved, and (5) forbidden. Most religious duties, such as the Five Pillars, are obligatory. Anyone who fails to perform them may be punished by God or the Islamic state. For example, in many Muslim countries, refusal to fast during Ramadan may result in fines or imprisonment. In some Muslim countries, special organizations ensure that people make their five daily prayers at the proper time and follow accepted standards of dress and behavior.

Most actions in Islamic law are not obligatory. People who fail to perform acts that are recommended or neutral are seldom punished. Most acts that are clearly forbidden are mentioned in the Quran. They include adultery, gambling, cheating, consuming pork or alcoholic beverages, and lending money at interest. The Quran details severe punishments for such crimes as murder, theft, and adultery. Crimes are punished harshly because they violate not only the rights of the victim, but also the commands of God. The Quran seeks to lessen the severity of these punishments, however, by urging Muslims to practice mercy and not yield to revenge.

Islamic virtues. Islam teaches respect for parents, protection for orphans and widows, and charity to the poor. It also teaches the virtues of faith in God, kindness, honesty, hard work, honor, courage, cleanliness, and generosity. Heads of families must treat household members kindly and fairly. A wife has rights against her husband and may sue for divorce in cases of physical abuse, lack of financial support, or the inability to produce a child. Islam also teaches that a person must not refuse requests for help, even if they seem unnecessary.

Divisions of Islam. There are three historic divisions in Islam. The great majority of Muslims belong to the Sunni *(SOON ee)* division. Sunni Muslims call themselves by this name because they claim to follow the sunna of Muhammad. They follow a traditional and widely held interpretation of Islam.

Most of the conservative Muslims that Westerners call *fundamentalists* are Sunnis. Like fundamentalists of other religions, these Muslims follow a strict approach to religion. They reject modern and popular interpretations of Islamic law, which they view as too permissive. They insist instead on precise adherence to the Quran and hadith, as they interpret those writings. Many Muslims dislike the name *fundamentalists,* however.

The next largest division is the Shiah *(SHEE ah),* whose members are called Shiites. Shiite Muslims honor Ali, the cousin and son-in-law of Muhammad, and Ali's descendants, whom they believe should be the leaders of the Muslim community. Shiah comes from the Arabic phrase *shiat Ali,* meaning *supporters of Ali.*

The largest group of Shiites are the Imami *(ee MAHM ee)* Shiah. They are also known as the *Ithna Ashari,* or *Twelvers.* They see authority as residing in 12 imams, starting with Ali, who was born in about 600, and ending with Muhammad al-Mahdi, who was born in about 868. They believe this last imam is still alive, in a miraculous state of concealment from human view. He will return at the end of time to restore justice on earth. A small group of Shiites, known as the Ismaili *(ihs may EE lee)* Shiah, broke away from the Imamis in the 700's. One group of Ismailis, known as the Nizaris, still follow an imam called Aga Khan IV, who lives in France.

Today, the Kharijites make up the smallest division of Islam. Their name is based on an Arabic word that means *secessionists.* They received this name because they were former followers of Ali who broke away in 657. Kharijites are strict Muslims whose beliefs are based on precise adherence to the teachings of the Quran and sunna as their community interprets them. They are most noteworthy for their belief in equality under God. In the first centuries of their existence, they elected their leaders and proclaimed that the best Muslim should lead his fellow believers, even if he was a slave. In some Kharijite communities in Algeria, female scholars and religious leaders serve the needs of women while male scholars and religious leaders serve the needs of men.　Vincent J. Cornell

Related articles in *World Book.* See the articles on **Muhammad** and **Muslims.** Other related articles include:

Allah	Feasts and festivals	Quran
Arabic literature	(In Islam)	Ramadan
Arabs	Hajj	Shiites
Crescent	Harem	Sunnites
Dervish	Islamic art	World, History of
Devil	Kaaba	the (The Islamic
Fakir	Mecca	world; The Is-
	Medina	lamic empire)

Additional resources

Braswell, George W., Jr. *Islam: Its Prophet, Peoples, Politics, and Power.* Broadman, 1996.
Esposito, John L. *Islam: The Straight Path.* 3rd ed. Oxford, 1998.
Esposito, John L., ed. *The Oxford Encyclopedia of the Modern Islamic World.* 4 vols. Oxford, 1995.
Nasr, Seyyed H. *Ideals and Realities of Islam.* Rev. ed. Kazi Pubns., 1994.
Netton, Ian R. *A Popular Dictionary of Islam.* Humanities Pr., 1992.
Renard, John. *In the Footsteps of Muhammad: Understanding the Islamic Experience.* Paulist, 1992.
Schimmel, Annemarie. *Islam: An Introduction.* State Univ. of N.Y. Pr., 1992.
Williams, John A., ed. *The Word of Islam.* Univ. of Tex. Pr., 1994. An anthology of Islamic writings.

Malaysia

Malaysia, *muh LAY zhuh* or *may LAY zhuh,* is a country in Southeast Asia that is divided into two parts. One part, known as Peninsular Malaysia, consists of the territory of Kuala Lumpur and 11 states on the Malay Peninsula. The other part consists of two states called Sarawak and Sabah along the northern and northwestern coasts of the island of Borneo and the small island territory of Labuan off the coast of Sabah. The two parts of Malaysia lie about 400 miles (640 kilometers) apart, linked by the South China Sea.

Malaysia lies close to the equator and has a tropical climate that is hot and humid. Thick rain forests cover parts of both Peninsular Malaysia and Borneo.

Malaysia is rich in natural resources. It has long ranked as a leading producer of rubber and tin, as well as timber, a vegetable oil called palm oil, natural gas, and petroleum. In the late 1900's, Malaysia also became a major manufacturing nation and a successful exporter of electronic products.

Malays, Chinese, and Indians form the largest ethnic groups in Malaysia. More than 80 percent of the people live in Peninsular Malaysia. Most of the nation's urban areas are also there, including Kuala Lumpur *(KWAH luh loom POOR),* the capital and largest city.

Europeans arrived in what is now Malaysia during the 1500's. In 1511, the Portuguese seized the commercial kingdom of Melaka from the Malays but were unsuccessful in conquering other areas on the Malay Peninsula. The Dutch defeated the Portuguese in 1641 and took over Melaka. In the late 1700's, the British arrived. They signed a treaty with the Dutch in 1824 that gave them control over the Malay Peninsula. Nevertheless, total British control was not established until the early 1900's. Peninsular Malaysia became an independent nation called Malaya in 1957. Malaya, Sarawak, Sabah, and the island of Singapore united to form the Federation of Malaysia in 1963, but Singapore withdrew two years later and became independent.

Government

Malaysia is a constitutional monarchy and a parliamentary democracy. The country is divided into 13 states and 2 federal territories. The two territories are the area surrounding Kuala Lumpur, the national capital, and the island of Labuan. Hereditary rulers, most of whom are called sultans, rule 9 of Malaysia's 13 states. From among themselves, the nine rulers choose a king called the *yang di-pertuan agong,* which means *paramount ruler.* The king is the head of state. He serves a five-year term, performing mainly ceremonial duties, before the kingship rotates to another of the nine hereditary rulers.

National government. A prime minister and a parliament run the federal government. Parliament has two houses, a house of representatives called the Dewan Rakyat and a senate called the Dewan Negara. The Dewan Rakyat has 192 members, consisting of 144 from

Leonard Y. Andaya, the contributor of this article, is Professor of History at the University of Hawaii at Manoa and coauthor of A History of Malaysia.

The Petronas Towers, the world's tallest skyscrapers, loom over Kuala Lumpur, Malaysia's capital and largest city. The towers, completed in 1996, are 1,483 feet (452 meters) high.

Facts in brief

Capital: Kuala Lumpur.
Official language: Bahasa Malaysia.
Elevation: *Highest*—Mount Kinabalu, 13,431 ft. (4,094 m) above sea level. *Lowest*—sea level along the coast.
Population: *Estimated 1998 population*—21,398,000; density, 168 persons per sq. mi. (65 per km²); distribution, 51 percent urban, 49 percent rural. *1991 census*—18,379,655. *Estimated 2003 population*—23,407,000.
Chief products: *Agriculture*—cacao, coconuts, palm oil, pepper, pineapple and other fruit, rice, rubber, timber. *Manufacturing*—air conditioners and other appliances, cement, electronic and electrical products, processed foods, rubber goods, semiconductors, textiles. *Mining*—bauxite, copper, gold, ilemite, iron ore, natural gas, petroleum, tin.
National anthem: "Negara Ku" ("My Country").
Money: *Basic unit*—ringgit (sometimes called Malaysian dollar). One hundred sen equal one ringgit.

WORLD BOOK map

Malaysia lies in Southeast Asia. One part of the country lies on the Malay Peninsula. The other part is on the island of Borneo.

Symbols of Malaysia. Malaysia's flag dates from 1963. Its 14 red-and-white stripes and 14-point gold star symbolize Malaysia's original 14 states. The crescent represents Islam. The national crest shows the symbols and colors of the states.

Malaysia map index

States

Cities and towns

Physical features

Source: 1991 census for states; 1980 census for cities and towns.

Peninsular Malaysia, 27 from Sarawak, 20 from Sabah, and 1 from Labuan. The people elect these representatives for five-year terms, unless an election is called earlier. Normally, the leader of the political party with the most seats becomes prime minister. The prime minister then chooses a cabinet. The Dewan Negara has 69 members, all of whom serve three-year terms. The 13 state legislatures elect two members apiece. The king appoints the other 43 members with the advice of the prime minister. Two of the appointed members represent Kuala Lumpur, 1 represents Labuan, and the other 40 are appointed on the basis of distinguished public service or to represent ethnic minorities.

Local government. Nine of Malaysia's 13 states were formerly kingdoms and continue to be governed by their traditional rulers. The other four states have governors appointed by the federal government. Each of the 13 states has its own constitution, legislature, and local officials.

Political parties. The most powerful political organization in Malaysia is an alliance called the National Front. The largest party in the alliance is the United Malays National Organization (UMNO). The two major opposition parties are the Democratic Action Party, the members of which are mainly Chinese, and the Islamic Party of Malaysia, which represents Muslim interests.

Courts. The Federal Court, formerly called the Supreme Court, is the highest judicial body in Malaysia. It has 10 members, who are appointed by the king on the advice of the prime minister. Below it is a Court of

Appeal, and at the next level are two high courts, one for Peninsular Malaysia, the other for Sabah and Sarawak. Lower courts include local and juvenile courts. Special religious courts issue rulings on Islamic law, called *sharia.* Jury trials were abolished in 1995.

Armed forces of Malaysia has three branches: the Malaysian Army, the Royal Malaysian Navy, and the Royal Malaysian Air Force. Malaysia's armed forces have about 111,500 active members. All service is voluntary.

People

Malaysia's population is racially and ethnically diverse. Three groups of people have lived on the Malay Peninsula since prehistoric times: (1) a forest-dwelling people called the Orang Asli, who were mainly hunters and gatherers; (2) a coastal people called the Orang Laut, who earned a living by fishing and seafaring; and (3) the Malays, who primarily farmed and fished. Today, the Malays make up more than half the country's population.

Two other large ethnic groups came to what is now Malaysia during colonial times, in the 1800's and early 1900's. These two groups were the Chinese, who came to work in tin mining or retail trade, and Indians, who came to work on rubber plantations. When Sabah and Sarawak became part of Malaysia in 1963, the peoples of Borneo added still other ethnic groups to this multiracial land. Sabah's largest ethnic group is the Kadazans. In Sarawak, the largest group is the Ibans,

also called the Sea Dayaks. Still another wave of immigration began in the 1970's because of an economic boom. Hundreds of thousands of migrant workers, mainly from Indonesia, poured into Malaysia to fill manufacturing jobs.

The Malays dominate Malaysia's government and armed forces, but the Chinese control much of the economy. Many Chinese Malaysians resent the political power of the Malays. The Malays, in turn, resent the other group's wealth. The tensions between the Chinese and the Malays have erupted in violence from time to time.

Malaysians use several different languages. The Malay language is called Bahasa Malaysia, which means *language of Malaysia.* It is the country's official language. Many Malaysians also speak English. Many Malaysians of Chinese descent speak southern Chinese dialects, though a large number also know some Mandarin Chinese. Many Indian Malaysians use a southern Indian language called Tamil. Many smaller ethnic groups, such as the Kadazans, speak their own language but can also communicate in Bahasa Malaysia.

Way of life

Rural life. Most people in the rural areas of Peninsular Malaysia are Malays who farm or fish. Rural Malays live in villages called *kampongs,* also spelled *kampungs.* Their houses are built on stilts with wooden or bamboo walls and floors, and thatched palm roofs. Such raised construction prevents flooding in the rainy

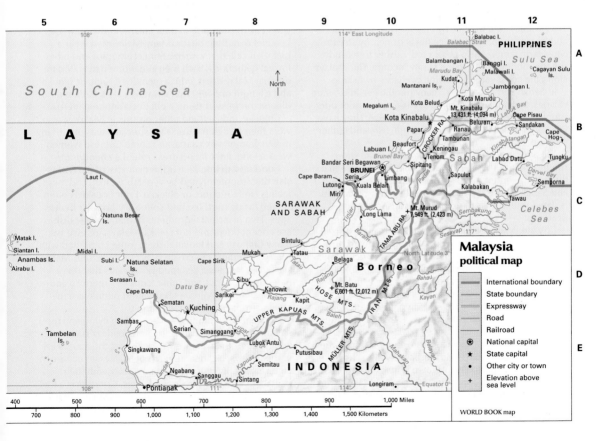

© Jonathan Kirn, Gamma/Liaison

People of various ethnic groups live in Peninsular Malaysia. Malays make up the largest group, followed by Chinese and Indians. Most of the people shown in this scene at a bus stop in Kuala Lumpur are Malays.

© R. Ian Lloyd

Sepak takraw is a traditional Malay game. Players use mainly their feet to hit a ball over a net. They cannot use their hands.

season and allows air to circulate more freely to cool the interior. Well-to-do families may have tin or tile roofs.

Most rural families grow rice as their staple food. They supplement the rice by raising fresh vegetables and by fishing in flooded rice fields or nearby streams. Most farm families also raise a few rubber trees and sell the rubber to add to the family income. The Malays along the coast earn their living primarily by fishing.

In Sabah and in Sarawak, many people live in isolated villages. Several families often live together under one roof in a large dwelling called a *long house*. They have vegetable gardens, and they also hunt, fish, and gather edible plants in the nearby jungles.

Most rural villages have one or more small shops run by Chinese merchants, who sell many articles that the people cannot make for themselves. In Sarawak and Sabah, Chinese peddlers travel upriver by boat to isolated settlements to exchange goods for forest products.

City life. Malaysia is rapidly becoming an urbanized society. More than half the population lives in urban areas. A lack of jobs in the countryside and an economic boom in the cities have contributed to urban growth.

Kuala Lumpur is a bustling, modern city with lofty skyscrapers, including the world's tallest building, Petronas Towers. This office building, the headquarters of the national oil company, stands 1,483 feet (452 meters) high.

Wealthy Malaysians live in large, comfortable homes with yards and servants. Most urban dwellers, however, live in modest apartments or town houses like those in American and European cities. Many rural Malays who have recently moved to the city live in shacks and other makeshift shelters in temporary squatter settlements.

Clothing. In everyday life, most Malaysians wear clothing similar to that worn in North America and Europe. Nearly all Malays are Muslims, and many of them choose modest styles favored by Islam. For example, many Malay women wear a loose, long-sleeved blouse, a long skirt extending to their ankles, and a shawl or kerchief over their heads. Many Malay men wear a black hat called a *songkok*. For ceremonies and other formal gatherings, both men and women may don traditional Malay dress, which includes a tunic or blouse and a length of *batik* cloth worn as a skirt. Batik is a traditional process of dying cloth in elaborate patterns.

Chinese, Indians, and other groups in Malaysia also wear their traditional dress for special occasions. Many Indian women wear saris, and some Chinese women wear a long, tight-fitting dress called a *cheongsam*.

Food and drink. Rice is the mainstay of the Malaysian diet, supplemented by vegetables, fish, and meat, mainly lamb, mutton, or chicken. Fruit or cake is often served for dessert. Tea and coffee are popular beverages. Two principal ingredients in many Malay dishes are coconut milk and hot chilies. Malaysians also eat many Chinese and Indian dishes, some combined with Malay ingredients to create tasty combinations. Malaysian cities also have fast-food restaurants that serve hamburgers, pizza, and other kinds of American and European foods. Middle-class young people are the chief patrons of such restaurants.

Recreation. Among the Malays, kite flying and top spinning are traditional sports practiced by skilled adults rather than children. *Pencak silat*, the martial art of the Malays, has become part of Malaysian national culture. Silat practitioners fight not only with their hands but also with sticks and knives. *Congkak* is a traditional Malay game of skill using a board with holes and pebbles or marbles. *Sepak takraw* is a popular game like volleyball using a rattan or plastic ball. Unlike volleyball players, however, sepak takraw players use mainly their feet. They cannot touch the ball with their hands.

The most popular Western sports in Malaysia are soccer and badminton. Malaysian teams have won several international badminton championships.

Religion. Malaysia has considerable religious diversity and widespread religious toleration. Muslim mosques, Christian churches, and Hindu and Buddhist temples stand side by side in urban areas. Islam is the religion of almost all Malays, as well as some Malaysian Indians, and is also the official religion of the state. People are allowed to follow other religions but may not try to convert Muslims to their faith. Many Chinese Malaysians are Buddhist, and others are Christian or Taoist. The Kadazans of Sabah and many Ibans of Sarawak are Christian. Most Malaysian Indians practice Hinduism. Many Malaysians make it a custom to participate in the religious holidays of other faiths.

Beginning in the 1970's, an Islamic revival called the *dakwah* movement rapidly gained strength. Most followers of the movement were young, educated urban Muslims. They sought to return to the fundamental beliefs of Islam. They were inspired by Islamic movements in other parts of the world, including the 1979 revolution that established an Islamic government in Iran. The dakwah movement contributed to a growing Islamization of Malaysian life. For example, many Malaysians adopted stricter Islamic standards of dress and behavior.

Education. Primary and secondary education are free. Children start school at 6 years old. They remain in primary school for six years and then go to secondary school. Bahasa Malaysia is the language of instruction in most schools, though some schools, especially at the primary level, also teach in Mandarin Chinese or Tamil. In all schools, English and Bahasa Malaysia are compulsory subjects. Malaysia has many universities, technical institutes, and teacher training colleges. The largest university is the University of Malaya at Kuala Lumpur.

The arts. Malaysia has attempted to preserve its traditional art forms despite the immense popularity of American and European rock music, television, and motion pictures. A traditional form of Malay drama is *mak yong* (also spelled *mak yung* or *ma'yong*), in which the performers sing, dance, and act out heroic tales about sultans and princesses. An orchestra called a *gamelan* accompanies most performances. A gamelan consists chiefly of metal percussion instruments, including gongs, xylophones, and drums.

Malaysia has had an active motion-picture industry since the founding of Malay Film Productions in the 1940's. Among its most famous stars was an actor, director, producer, singer, and composer named P. Ramlee. Ramlee appeared in films during the 1950's and 1960's.

Land and climate

Malaysia has a total area of 127,320 square miles (329,758 square kilometers). Peninsular Malaysia comprises the Federal Territory of Kuala Lumpur and 11 small states, with a total area of 50,810 square miles (131,598 square kilometers). Two much larger states—Sarawak and Sabah—lie on the island of Borneo. Sarawak covers 48,050 square miles (124,449 square kilometers). Sabah—including the Federal Territory of Labuan, a small island off the coast of Borneo—covers 28,460 square miles (73,711 square kilometers). Both the Malay Peninsula and Borneo are heavily forested and mountainous. Mount Kinabalu in Sabah is the highest peak, rising to about 13,431 feet (4,094 meters).

Malaysia has a tropical climate with hot, humid weather that varies little throughout the year. Coastal temperatures range from 70 to 90 °F (21 to 32 °C), while

© Jean-Claude Lejeune, Black Star

Tropical rain forests cover most mountain areas in Malaysia. This village is in the state of Sabah on Borneo. Mount Kinabalu, the country's highest peak, rises in the background.

© Cameramann International, Ltd. from Marilyn Gartman

Farmers grow rice, Malaysia's chief food crop, on small farms like this one near Kuala Lumpur. Malaysian farms also produce cacao, coconuts, pepper, and pineapples and other fruit.

Petroleum production is a major economic activity in Malaysia, and petroleum is the country's chief export. This refinery is in Kerteh, in eastern Peninsular Malaysia. A pipeline links the refinery to offshore wells in the South China Sea.

© Corel

mountain temperatures are usually 55 to 80 °F (13 to 27 °C). Rainfall varies slightly, with heavier downpours from October to April and less rain from May to September. Peninsular Malaysia gets an average of 100 inches (250 centimeters) of rain annually, while Sarawak and Sabah both receive about 150 inches (380 centimeters).

Many animals flourish in Malaysia. They include tigers, wild oxen, water buffaloes, tapirs, orangutans, many varieties of monkeys, cobras, crocodiles, lizards, over 500 kinds of birds, and a vast number of butterflies. Malaysia's plants are equally varied, with many types of wild orchids, tropical fruits, and exotic hardwood trees.

Economy

From the mid-1970's to the mid-1990's, Malaysia had one of the world's fastest growing economies. From 1970 to the mid-1990's, Malaysia's *gross domestic product,* the total value of all goods and services produced within the country, grew at an average annual rate of more than 7 percent. After more than two decades of robust growth, however, the Malaysian economy slowed somewhat in the late 1990's.

Malaysia's impressive economic performance has been based on rich natural resources and a diversified economy. In the 1970's, Malaysia was primarily an exporter of raw commodities, such as timber, rubber, tin, and palm oil. It still produces those basic goods, but they play a much smaller economic role. The country now derives much of its wealth from manufacturing.

Manufacturing employs about one-fourth of Malaysia's labor force and produces about one-third of the gross domestic product. Nearly all manufacturing takes place in the western half of Peninsular Malaysia, chiefly in the Kelang Valley and on the island of Penang.

The Malaysian electronics industry has been a major success. Malaysia is a leading producer of integrated circuits and other semiconductor devices.

Malaysia has also established its own automobile industry. With Japanese help, Malaysian automakers began in 1985 to produce a car called the Proton, the first Malaysian-built automobile.

Agriculture. Malaysia is the world's leading producer of palm oil, a vegetable oil made from palm tree nuts. Palm oil is used for cooking and in the production of margarine and soap. Malaysia is also the third-largest producer of natural rubber, exceeded only by Thailand and Indonesia. Nearly all of the country's palm oil and rubber are raised on large plantations for export.

Farmers grow rice, Malaysia's chief food crop, on small farms throughout the country. Malaysian farmers also grow many varieties of tropical fruit, including pineapples, mangoes, and bananas. Two local favorites are the spiky, strong-smelling durian and the juicy, reddish-purple mangosteen. Small farms also produce coconuts, vegetables, and *cacao* (seeds used in making chocolate). Some farmers raise cattle or hogs. Sarawak is one of the world's largest producers of black pepper.

Forestry. Malaysia's tropical rain forests yield many valuable products, including aromatic woods, such as camphor and sandalwood, and beautiful hardwoods, such as ebony, mahogany, and teak.

Mining. Malaysia is rich in mineral resources. The Malay Peninsula has the world's largest reserves of *alluvial tin,* easily mined tin deposits left by flowing water. The country's other minerals include *bauxite* (aluminum ore), copper, gold, and iron ore.

Fishing industry. Malaysian fishing crews take shrimp and such fishes as anchovies and mackerel from Malaysia's coastal waters. Shrimp is the country's most important seafood export.

Service industries, which produce services rather than goods, have become increasingly important to Malaysia's economy. They now employ about half the labor force. The country's main service industries include government, transportation, and retail sales. Most retail stores in Malaysia are small general stores run by

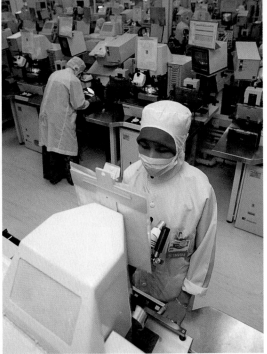

© R. Ian Lloyd

Malaysia's electronics industry produces integrated circuits and other semiconductor devices. This picture shows workers at an integrated circuit factory in Kuala Lumpur.

Chinese or Indian Malaysians. Larger retail outlets, including supermarkets and department stores, operate chiefly in urban centers. Urban areas also have the bulk of the country's other service industries, such as finance and real estate. Malaysia has a rapidly growing tourist industry that draws millions of visitors a year.

Energy sources. Malaysia is well supplied with energy. Large amounts of oil and natural gas come from offshore wells near the coasts of Terengganu and Sarawak. The heavy rainfall and rugged terrain of Peninsular Malaysia and the Borneo states furnish ample amounts of the falling water needed for hydroelectric power. Plants that burn oil, gas, or coal supply about four-fifths of Malaysia's electric power, and hydroelectric plants generate about one-fifth.

International trade. Malaysia's exports have changed greatly since the 1970's, when rubber and tin dominated. By the 1990's, manufactured goods accounted for more than half of the country's export earnings. Electrical and electronic products, particularly integrated circuits, make up the largest category of manufactured exports. Other major exports include palm oil; petroleum; rubber and rubber products, such as gloves; textiles; and wood products. Malaysia's main imports include chemicals, food, machinery, and transportation equipment. The country's major trading partners are Japan, the United States, and Singapore.

Transportation. Malaysia has a good transportation network, but rapid economic growth has stretched it to the limit. Historically, waterways were Malaysia's primary means of transportation. Even today, water travel remains important because the country's mountainous terrain and thick forests hinder movement by land. Rivers form the main thoroughfare into the interior. The Strait of Malacca, on the western side of the Malay Peninsula, serves as a major shipping lane between Eu-

rope and Asia. The South China Sea links the two parts of Malaysia and is the principal thoroughfare between East Asia and Southeast Asia. Malaysia's major seaports include George Town, Port Kelang, and Johor Baharu.

Long-distance travel in Malaysia depends heavily on aviation. Kuala Lumpur International Airport at Sepang is about 30 miles (50 kilometers) south of Kuala Lumpur. This airport opened in 1998 and helped relieve congestion at the older Subang airport. A government-owned airline called Malaysia Airlines is the major Malaysian air carrier. In 1994, a second national airline called Air Asia began operations.

Since Malaysia's economic boom began in the 1970's, the country's roads have become severely congested. More Malaysians have bought motorcycles and automobiles, adding to traffic congestion. Most middle-class families own cars, especially Malaysian-built Protons. Lower-income groups tend to ride motorcycles or use public transportation. Malaysia has an estimated 58,500 miles (94,000 kilometers) of roads, three-fourths of which are paved.

Buses provide most of Malaysia's public transportation. Railroads, which are owned by the government, operate in Peninsular Malaysia and in Sabah.

Communications. A government-run corporation called Radio Television Malaysia operates radio and television stations. Malaysia also has commercial and cable television stations. Under the Broadcasting Act of 1987, the federal minister of information has the power to monitor all radio and television programming.

Most Malaysian families have a radio or a television set, and most also have a telephone. Cellular telephones are popular among business people and the middle class, and the use of such phones has become a status symbol in modern Malaysia.

Malaysia has about 40 daily newspapers. The most important papers include *Berita Harian* and *Utusan Malaysia* in Bahasa Malaysia and the *New Straits Times* and *The Star* in English.

History

Early days. Scientists have found archaeological evidence of human inhabitants in the Niah Caves in Sarawak from about 40,000 years ago. The earliest evidence of inhabitants on the Malay Peninsula that has been found is from about 10,000 years ago. Most scholars believe the earliest settlers on the Malay Peninsula came overland from southern China in small groups over a period of thousands of years. These early inhabitants became the ancestors of the Orang Asli.

During the 1000's B.C., new groups of migrants who spoke a language related to Malay came to Malaysia. The ancestors of these people had traveled by sea from south China to Taiwan, and later from Taiwan to Borneo and the Philippines. These people became the ancestors of the Malays and the Orang Laut. The newcomers settled mainly in the coastal areas of the peninsula.

About A.D. 1400, a group of Malay-speaking migrants came to the Malay Peninsula from Srivijaya, a trading kingdom on the island of Sumatra (now part of Indonesia). Led by a Sumatran prince called Paramesvara, these newly arrived immigrants established a commercial kingdom called Melaka.

Melaka, also spelled Malacca, became an international center for the spice trade. During the middle and late 1400's, Melaka gained control over much of the Malay Peninsula, Sumatra, and the key shipping route through the Strait of Malacca. It attracted traders from throughout the world.

In the mid-1400's, Melaka became a Muslim kingdom. Islam spread throughout the Malay Peninsula and to other parts of Southeast Asia. Melaka's prosperity drew the attention of the Europeans, who wished to gain control of the valuable spice trade.

Coming of the Europeans. In 1511, the Portuguese seized Melaka from the Malays. The Malays soon moved their center to Johor at the southern end of the Malay Peninsula. Descendants of the ruling family of Melaka also founded other kingdoms on the peninsula.

The Dutch seized Melaka from the Portuguese in 1641 and ruled there for the next 150 years. By the 1700's, the Dutch controlled trade in most of the region.

In 1786, the British acquired Penang Island and established a settlement called George Town there. Gradually, Britain acquired control over more of the area to protect its shipping lanes between China and India. In 1824, the Dutch surrendered to the British their possessions on the Malay Peninsula. In 1826, the British formed a colony called the Straits Settlements that included Melaka and the islands of Penang and Singapore. In 1840, James Brooke, a wealthy English adventurer, helped the sultan of Brunei quiet a local rebellion. In return, the sultan ceded the southern part of his territory, present-day Sarawak, to Brooke in 1841 and bestowed on Brooke the title *rajah.* Brooke and his descendants, called "white rajahs," ruled Sarawak as a self-governing state until the 1940's. In 1881, North Borneo (as Sabah was then called) came under the control of a private trading company called the British North Borneo Company. The British declared North Borneo and Sarawak to be British protectorates in 1888. By 1914, Britain had either direct or

Dinamika/Information Dept.

Malaya became independent in August 1957. Tunku Abdul Rahman made the declaration and became the country's first prime minister. The country has been called Malaysia since 1963.

indirect colonial control over all the lands that now make up Malaysia, which it called British Malaya.

British rule took several forms. For example, Britain had direct colonial rule in the Straits Settlements, family control by the Brookes in Sarawak, and corporate control in North Borneo. In the kingdoms on the Malay Peninsula, the British governed indirectly, through local rulers. Britain placed a representative called a *resident* in each kingdom. The local sultan agreed to accept the resident's advice on political and economic matters.

To increase its revenues from British Malaya, the British expanded tin mining in the late 1800's. They also introduced rubber trees from Brazil and established rubber plantations in the late 1800's and early 1900's. To provide labor for these enterprises, the British imported Chinese workers for the tin mines and Indian laborers for the rubber plantations. To help feed the rapidly expanding work force, the British encouraged the Malays to farm for a living.

The British also encouraged ethnic divisions. For example, the British administered the two main ethnic communities in Kuala Lumpur separately through their Malay and Chinese leaders. By hardening the lines that divided the Malays, Chinese, and Indians, these policies helped keep the groups from uniting against the British.

Independence. World War II and its aftermath brought the end of British rule. In that war, Japan, Germany, and the other Axis nations fought against Britain, the United States, and the other Allies. Japan invaded British Malaya in 1941 and occupied it until losing the war in 1945.

Britain dissolved the Straits Settlements in 1946. In 1948, the kingdoms on the Malay Peninsula, plus Melaka and the island of Penang, united to form the Federation of Malaya, a partially independent territory under British protection. Singapore, North Borneo, and Sarawak became separate crown colonies. In 1948, the Malayan Communist Party began a guerrilla uprising against the British that became known as the Emergency. With Malay help, the British finally subdued the Emergency in 1960, three years after independence.

Important dates in Malaysia

c. 40,000 B.C. Earliest known inhabitants of what is now Malaysia lived in the Niah Caves in Sarawak.

A.D. 1400's A powerful Muslim trading kingdom called Melaka developed on the Malay Peninsula.

1511 The Portuguese took control of Melaka.

1641 The Dutch seized Melaka from the Portuguese.

1786 The British acquired Penang Island.

1824 The Dutch surrendered their possessions on the Malay Peninsula to the British.

1826 The British formed a colony called the Straits Settlements, which included Melaka and the islands of Penang and Singapore.

1846 The sultan of Brunei gave the English adventurer James Brooke the right to rule Sarawak and the title rajah.

1881-1941 The British North Borneo Company controlled Sabah.

1888 North Borneo and Sarawak became British protectorates.

1948 The Malayan Communist Party began a guerrilla uprising called the Emergency that did not end until 1960.

1957 The Federation of Malaya became an independent nation.

1963 Singapore, Sabah, and Sarawak joined Malaya to form the Federation of Malaysia, but Singapore withdrew in 1965.

1996 Petronas Towers, the world's tallest building, was erected in Kuala Lumpur, Malaysia.

1998 Kuala Lumpur International Airport opened in Sepang, Malaysia.

The Federation of Malaya had gained complete independence from Britain in 1957. Singapore, which had a mostly Chinese population, remained outside the federation as a British crown colony.

Building national unity. The first prime minister of the new nation was Tunku Abdul Rahman. Earlier in the 1950's, he and other leaders had formed a political alliance of the three main ethnic parties: the United Malays National Organization, the Malayan Chinese Association, and the Malayan Indian Congress. This three-party partnership, known as the Alliance, was the forerunner of the National Front that is Malaysia's most powerful political organization today.

In 1963, Singapore, Sabah, and Sarawak joined Malaya to form the Federation of Malaysia. The Malay majority hoped that including Sabah and Sarawak, which had ethnically diverse populations, would balance the large numbers of Chinese from Singapore. Economic and political disputes soon developed between the mostly Chinese state leaders of Singapore and the mostly Malay federal government of Malaysia. In 1965, Singapore withdrew from the federation and became independent.

In Malaysia, as in the former British Malaya, the ethnic groups followed different traditional occupations. The Malays controlled government and agriculture, while the Chinese dominated commerce and industry. The Chinese resented the political power of the Malays, and the Malays envied the economic success of the Chinese. The tensions eventually triggered racial violence. In 1969, bloody riots broke out after an election on Peninsular Malaysia. The government declared a state of emergency, suspending the Constitution and Parliament until 1971.

After the riots, Malaysia's political leaders tried to build national unity. They amended the Constitution to forbid discussion, even in Parliament, of certain "sensitive issues," including the special position of the Malays and of Borneo's ethnic groups, and the powers of the Malay sultans. The amendment also required all government bodies to use Bahasa Malaysia as their principal official language. Many non-Malays, however, resented the government's attempts to build national unity through increased emphasis on Malay culture.

Also after the riots, Malaysia's leaders determined to improve the economic conditions of the Malays. In 1971, they launched a 20-year plan called the New Economic Policy to achieve a better balance of wealth among racial groups. To minimize racial politics, the government created in 1974 a multiparty alliance called the National Front, uniting Malay, Chinese, and Islamic groups.

Recent developments. By the end of the 1990's, the New Economic Policy and its successor, the New Development Policy begun in 1991, had done much to eliminate racial tensions. Malaysia's economy had grown at a robust rate for two decades, and rapid economic growth had brought prosperity to all racial groups in the country. Government leaders announced a new goal called "Vision 2020," which aimed to make Malaysia a fully developed nation with a high standard of living by 2020. The goal suffered a setback, however, when an economic crisis spread throughout Southeast Asia. By 1998, the growth of Malaysia's economy had slowed somewhat, but Malaysia hoped to put its economic programs back on track.　　Leonard Y. Andaya

Related articles in *World Book* include:

Outline

Questions

What was the goal of the New Economic Policy that Malaysia began in 1971?

How is Malaysia's king chosen?

What is *sepak takraw? Pencak silat?*

Who were the "white rajahs" of Sarawak?

Which religion do most Malays follow?

Where in Malaysia is the world's tallest building?

What are Malaysia's three largest ethnic groups?

Why are water and air transportation so important in Malaysia?

What are some of Malaysia's major agricultural exports?

What country ruled Malaysia from the 1800's to the mid-1900's?

Additional resources

Andaya, Barbara Watson and Leonard Y. *A History of Malaysia.* St. Martin's, 1982.
Crouch, Harold. *Government and Society in Malaysia.* Cornell Univ. Pr., 1996.
Insight Guide: Malaysia. 16th ed. Houghton, 1996.
Kaur, Amarjit. *Historical Dictionary of Malaysia.* Scarecrow, 1993.
Malaysia in Pictures. Rev. ed. Lerner, 1997. Younger readers.

Muslims, *MUHZ luhmz,* sometimes spelled *Moslems,* are people who practice the religion of Islam. The Prophet Muhammad first preached the religion in the A.D. 600's. Islam originated with the Arabs in the Middle East. By the mid-700's, Muslims had built an empire that stretched from the Atlantic Ocean to the borders of China.

This article traces the history of the Muslim people throughout the world. For additional information about the religion of the Muslims, see **Islam.**

Before Muhammad

Abraham and Ishmael. According to Muslim tradition, the history of the Muslims begins with the story of Abraham and Ishmael. Both Jews and Arabs regard Abraham, who may have lived between about 1800 and 1500 B.C., as the father of their people. Abraham's wife Sarah was past childbearing age, so she gave her handmaiden Hagar to her husband as a second wife. Hagar bore a son, the prophet Ishmael. Later, Sarah and Abraham also had a son, the prophet Isaac. After Isaac's birth, Sarah pressured Abraham into expelling Hagar and Ishmael from his house.

Muslim tradition teaches that Hagar and Ishmael traveled to a valley in western Arabia called Bakka, which is now the city of Mecca. There they found a sacred well, called Zamzam, that sustained Hagar and Ishmael with its water. When Ishmael reached adulthood, Abraham visited him. Near the well of Zamzam, the two prophets built the Kaaba as a temple to God (Allah). In the eastern corner of the Kaaba, they placed the Black Stone, which Muslims believe was brought to them by an angel. The Kaaba became the holiest shrine of Islam. Muslims who perform the pilgrimage to Mecca walk around the Kaaba seven times. Many of them will try to kiss or touch the Black Stone.

The Arabs before Islam included nomads, traders, farmers, and town-dwellers. They belonged to many tribes and had many religions. Most Arabs worshiped multiple gods. Arab deities included the goddesses al-Lat, al-Uzza, and Manat, who were important in the Mecca region. The supreme deity of the Arabs was a remote heavenly god, whom they called Allah, which means "the god." The Arabs believed he was the creator of the universe, the bringer of life and rain. He was the god on whom people called in times of great danger or distress.

Muhammad

The Prophet Muhammad was born in Mecca in about A.D. 570. At that time, Mecca was a major commercial center controlled by an Arab tribe called the Quraysh (pronounced *koo RAYSH),* who had abandoned the traditional Arab nomadic way of life and become merchants. The Quraysh were divided into clans, including the Banu Umayya *(BA noo oo MAY ah)* and the Banu Hashim *(BA noo HA shihm).* The Banu Umayya were the wealthiest and most powerful clan in Mecca. The Banu Hashim, into which Muhammad

was born, were responsible for supplying food and drink for pilgrims who came to Mecca to visit the Kaaba.

In about A.D. 610, Muhammad began to receive revelations from Allah. For Muslims, the greatest miracle of Muhammad's prophethood was the Quran *(ku RAHN),* sometimes spelled Koran, the holy book of Allah's revelations. The revelation of the Quran to Muhammad took place over a period of about 22 years. Muhammad dictated the verses to his followers, who wrote them down. Several of these "Scribes of Revelation," such as Ali, Uthman *(ooth MAN),* and Muawiya *(moo AH wih yah),* became important Muslim leaders.

Several years after Muhammad's death, when Uthman was *caliph* (leader) of the Muslims, he formed a committee to collect these revelations into a single volume. Their work produced a master copy of the Quran that became the model for the book used by Muslims today.

The people of Mecca persecuted the early Muslims because Muhammad had rejected their gods and because he condemned wealthy Meccans for not helping those in need, such as widows, orphans, and the poor. Eventually, Muhammad and his followers were forced to abandon Mecca. In 622, a delegation from Medina, a town then called Yathrib which lies north of Mecca, invited him to come to that city and act as *arbitrator* (judge) between its feuding tribes. Muhammad's journey from Mecca to Medina is called the *Hijra,* also spelled *Hegira.* Muslims consider it so important that the Islamic calendar begins with the year of the Hijra. In Medina, Muhammad and his companions laid the foundations of Islamic society, which was based on the *sunna* and the *sharia.* The sunna was the example of the Prophet's sayings and behavior. The sharia was the code of Islamic law.

To defend Islam from its enemies, Muhammad launched several military campaigns against Mecca and other parts of the Arabian Peninsula. Mecca surrendered to him in 630. In 631, delegations from many tribes and clans in Arabia swore to give up the worship of multiple gods and submit to Muhammad's authority. In 632, Muhammad died in Medina.

The early caliphs

After the Prophet died, a dispute arose over his successor. On one side were members of the tribes of Medina, who wanted one of their own leaders to rule the town again. Another side included Muhammad's friend Abu Bakr, along with Umar, one of the most powerful of the early Muslims. After the death of his first wife, Muhammad had married both Abu Bakr's daughter Aisha *(ah YEE shah)* and Umar's daughter Hafsa. They were the most influential of the Prophet's wives. In addition, some Muslims thought Muhammad's cousin and son-in-law, Ali, who had adopted Islam as a child and was like a son to the Prophet, should succeed him as leader. On the day of Muhammad's death, Umar acknowledged Abu Bakr as *caliph* (successor) to the Prophet, and soon others followed his example. Umar said he took the action to prevent divisions in the Muslim community.

Abu Bakr ruled as caliph in Medina for two years.

Vincent J. Cornell is Associate Professor of Religion at Duke University.

He took political charge of the Muslim community and led prayers in the Prophet's place, but he refused to assume Muhammad's role as the interpreter of Islamic doctrine. He left interpretation to the collective judgment of the Prophet's companions. Abu Bakr's example in referring religious decisions to community leaders eventually formed the basis of the Sunni (SOON ee) division in Islam. The followers of Sunni Islam are called Sunnites.

Abu Bakr faced revolts by Arabian tribes against the authority of the Islamic state. Some tribes even put forth their own prophets. Within about a year, however, Abu Bakr put down these revolts and the tribes accepted Islam.

Umar. In 634, Abu Bakr died, naming Umar to succeed him as caliph. Umar's 10-year rule became a great period of Islamic expansion. First, he sent Quran reciters to the tribes of Arabia to teach them Islam. Next, he embarked on the full-scale conquest of the Middle East. During this period, Islam was largely a religion of the Arabs, and Umar concentrated on spreading Islam among the tribes of Syria and Iraq. Most Arabs converted to Islam at this time.

By the end of Umar's caliphate in 644, the Muslims had conquered Syria, Palestine, Egypt, and most of Iraq. Because of the great increase in the number of people under their rule, the Muslims set up an administration to govern the new territories. They sent Muslim soldiers and their families to settle in strategically located towns, which rapidly grew into major cities. Each town centered on a main *mosque* (Muslim place of worship) and was ruled by the provincial governor. Soldiers and other Muslims each received a payment from a share of the booty taken during conquests and taxes from conquered lands. The payments varied depending on how long each person had been a Muslim. Thus, the earliest converts had great political power and often made fortunes.

Uthman. Just before Umar died, he appointed a committee to choose his successor. When the committee asked Ali to become caliph and follow the rulings of his predecessors, he refused. He claimed that he knew more than the previous caliphs about Muhammad's original views and intentions. Uthman, another son-in-law of the Prophet, agreed to the request and became caliph.

Under Uthman, the Muslims completed the conquest of Iran and began to spread across North Africa from Egypt. But political conflicts broke out and marked the end of Muslim political and religious unity. Despite Uthman's piety, his enemies accused him of favoritism and a love of wealth and luxury. Political

© Superstock

The Dome of the Rock in Jerusalem is one of the holiest places in Islam. The dome encloses a rock, shown in the foreground, from which the Prophet Muhammad is believed to have ascended to heaven. The dome was built between 688 and 691, during the rule of the Umayyad caliph Abd al-Malik.

corruption and stricter economic policies in the provinces caused the Muslims of Egypt to revolt against their governor, Uthman's foster brother. Uthman's half-brother, who was the governor of Kufa in southern Iraq, disgraced himself by appearing drunk in public.

In 656, delegations from Egypt and Iraq arrived in Medina to protest Uthman's policies. Many of Medina's citizens also opposed Uthman, including Muhammad's widow Aisha and his son-in-law Ali. But Ali had no desire to start a rebellion. When Uthman appealed to him to help settle the dispute, he did so, but he asked the caliph to change his policies. Ali's attempt at a settlement failed, and protesters killed Uthman. Immediately afterward, a delegation went to Ali and proclaimed him caliph. At first, he refused because Uthman had been murdered. But he consented after other delegations from Medina and the provinces urged him to accept.

Ali. The caliphate of Ali marks the beginning of the Shiite division of Islam. As the closest living relative of Muhammad, Ali claimed a unique understanding of the Prophet's teachings. Ali's followers, the Shiah *(SHEE ah)*, considered him the only true *Imam* (Muslim

British Library, London/Art Resource

The Prophet Muhammad, according to Islam, ascended to heaven on the back of a creature called Buraq. Muhammad's face is blank because Islam forbids portraying images of living things.

leader). After Ali's death, his sons and descendants led the Shiah as Imams. Although the Shiites agreed with most Muslims on matters of doctrine, they felt their Imams should have priority in the interpretation of Islamic doctrine.

When Ali accepted the caliphate, several Muslim leaders opposed him, including Muhammad's widow Aisha and Muawiya, the governor of Syria and Uthman's cousin. From this point, Medina no longer served as the capital of the Islamic state. Ali moved to Kufa (now Al Kufah, Iraq), where most of his supporters lived. Aisha and her allies moved to Basra (now Al Basrah, Iraq). In 656, Ali and Aisha fought the Battle of the Camel, the first conflict of Muslim against Muslim. Ali won the battle, named for the camel that carried Aisha.

Ali next turned against Muawiya, who demanded that Ali produce Uthman's assassins or be considered an accomplice in the murder. In 657, the armies of Ali and Muawiya fought at Siffin, on the Euphrates River in northern Syria. During the battle, soldiers in Muawiya's army raised pages of the Quran on their spears and called for arbitrators to settle the conflict peacefully. Ali agreed, so the battle ended indecisively. Many of Ali's followers, however, opposed arbitration and turned against him. These followers, called Kharijites, which means *secessionists*, make up the third major division in Islam, along with the Sunnites and the Shiites.

The Kharijites rejected both Muawiya and Ali. They felt the best Muslim should be caliph, even if that person were a slave. In 658, Ali fought the Kharijites at Nahrawan in central Iraq. He won the battle, but many faithful Muslims were killed in the fighting, causing even more people to turn against him. In 660, Muawiya was proclaimed caliph in Jerusalem. In 661, Ali, who refused to step down as caliph, was murdered by a Kharijite assassin seeking revenge for Nahrawan.

The Muslim empire

The Umayyads. After the death of Ali, Muawiya founded the Umayyad *(oo MY ad)* caliphate and made Damascus his capital in 661. Under the Umayyads, the Islamic state became an imperial power, much like its rival, the Byzantine Empire. When choosing ruling officials, the Umayyads preferred Arabs over their non-Arab subjects. Under the Umayyads, the Muslims extended their conquests into Afghanistan and central Asia in the east and across North Africa and into Spain in the west. Their main source of power was an Arab army based in Syria. This army swore personal loyalty to the caliph and acted as his bodyguard. Administratively, the Umayyads adopted many of the customs and institutions of the Byzantine Empire and of the Sassanian Empire, which had ruled Persia until the Muslim conquest.

In 680, Muawiya died and was succeeded by his son Yazid, who became notorious for corruption and misrule. The inhabitants of Medina refused to recognize Yazid. Ali's son Husayn also rose against him. Husayn set off toward Kufa to gather support, but the Kufans refused to help him. The Umayyads massacred Husayn and his small band of followers at Karbala in southern Iraq. This violence against the Prophet's family shocked the Muslim world.

In 684, Yazid's cousin Marwan, a former aide of Uthman, succeeded to power in Syria. Abd al-Malik, Marwan's son, was proclaimed caliph in 685, and began the second phase of Umayyad rule. The later Umayyads faced a long series of revolts. Kharijites, Shiites, and other rebels agitated against them in the name of Islam, advocating a return to the religion as it was practiced by Muhammad and his companions.

The Abbasids. By the mid-700's, important changes had occurred in Muslim society. An increasing rate of conversion to Islam, combined with intermarriage between Arabs and non-Arabs, had transformed the makeup of the Muslim population. For the first time, non-Arab Muslims outnumbered Arab Muslims in many regions. Many of the Kharijite and Shiite rebels against the Umayyads came from non-Arab converts. In North Africa, the Kharijites were mainly Berbers. In eastern Iran, many Kharijites and Shiites were Persian. Such new Muslims demanded equality with Arabs. The new Muslims called for a society in which each Muslim would have the same privileges and be subject to the same taxes, regardless of ethnic background. Religious scholars, who sought a return to a higher standard of piety, supported them.

The Abbasids *(uh BAS ihdz)* took up the cause of the new Muslims. The Abbasids descended from Muhammad's uncle Abbas. At first they joined forces with the Shiites, claiming that the most qualified member of the Prophet's family should be caliph. The Abbasids eventually dominated the anti-Umayyad movement. The Abbasids called for revenge against the Umayyads for their treatment of Muhammad's family. They conquered the Umayyads in 750, after a struggle lasting only three years. When some descendants of Ali claimed that one of them should hold the office of caliph, the Abbasids suppressed them and their supporters.

From 750 to the mid-800's, the Abbasids transformed the Islamic state into an empire that blended many cultures and was ruled by an absolute monarch. The caliph continued to uphold the sunna of the Prophet and the Islamic sharia. The Abbasid caliph was a magnificent ruler, living in splendid isolation and surrounded by thousands of officials and slaves. Only the most privileged were allowed to speak with him.

The capital of the Abbasids was Baghdad in central Iraq, established in 762 by the caliph Abu Jafar al-Mansur. At the heart of Baghdad was a huge administrative complex called the City of Peace. Beyond its walls stretched Baghdad and its suburbs, with more than a million inhabitants.

The Abbasid Empire was a highly centralized monarchy, the greatest since the Roman Empire. It drew support from one of the largest and most integrated economic systems known until modern times. Through the Persian Gulf flowed the products of east Africa, Arabia, India, southeast Asia, and China. Across the desert from Syria and down the Euphrates River came goods from North Africa, Egypt, and the Mediterranean. To Muslim scholars and historians of

this period, Baghdad was the center of the world.

During the Abbasid period, the Islamic arts and sciences flourished. Several schools of Islamic law formed during this period. Study of the Quran and of Arabic grammar developed. In about 830, the caliph al-Mamun created a research library called the House of Wisdom. A staff translated the works of Plato, Aristotle, and other Greek philosophers into Arabic. These translations stimulated the development of an Islamic philosophical tradition that played a major role in reintroducing many important works and ideas from Greek philosophy into western Europe.

The Abbasid period also witnessed the emergence of Sufism, which is Islamic mysticism. The Sufis do not make up a separate division, like the Shiites and Kharijites. Most Sufis are Sunni Muslims and see Sufism as a school of thought within mainstream Islam. Most Sufis follow the sharia closely and differ from other Muslims only in their desire to create a closer personal relationship with Allah.

The fall of the Abbasids. As a highly centralized monarchy, the Abbasid Empire lasted little more than 100 years. Its authority never became fully established

Gouache manuscript painting (1588); Giraudon/Art Resource

The Ottoman Empire under Sultan Suleiman I dominated much of Europe and North Africa. Suleiman led Muslim armies as far west as the walls of Vienna, *shown here,* in 1529.

in the Islamic west. In 756, Abd al-Rahman, an Umayyad prince who had escaped to Spain, founded a second Umayyad line of rulers that lasted until 1031. In the 780's, Idris ibn Abdallah, a descendant of Ali's son Hasan, fled from Abbasid persecution and created an independent kingdom in Morocco. In the 800's, the Abbasid governors of Tunisia and Egypt broke away from Baghdad and formed their own states.

From 929 to 1031, there were three competing caliphates at one time—the Abbasids in Iraq, an Umayyad caliphate in Spain, and the Fatimids in North Africa and, from 969, in Egypt. By this time, the Abbasids ruled over the Muslim world in name only. From the mid-900's until the Mongols captured Baghdad in 1258, most of the caliphs were puppet rulers, serving at the whim of military dictators. The blending of many cultures within Islam had led to the development of multiple centers of power and culture in the Muslim world. The diversity of the Muslim world continues to this day.

The spread of Islam

The Mongols killed the last Abbasid caliph in 1258 and captured Baghdad, but the vitality of the Muslims did not diminish. Socially and culturally, the Muslim

Gouache and gold painting on paper
(1590); Victoria & Albert Museum, London/Art Resource

Babur founded the Mughal Empire in India in 1526. Babur was a cultured ruler who encouraged religious tolerance. This painting shows him supervising the laying out of a garden in Afghanistan.

world became more diverse than ever. In west Africa and what are now Malaysia and Indonesia, Muslim merchants and scholars introduced Islam and converted kings, who made Islam the state religion. In China, the Muslim population also grew from communities of merchants. In Africa south of the Sahara, large-scale conversions began in the 1400's. Most of these conversions resulted from trade and personal contact rather than conquest.

Muslim power reached a new height in the 1500's. By that century, the Muslims had established three powerful empires: (1) the Ottoman Empire, which began in what is now Turkey; (2) the Safavid dynasty in Iran; and (3) the Mughal Empire in India.

The Ottoman Empire lasted from about 1300 to 1922. The Ottomans were named after Osman I, a Turkish chieftain who founded a state in Anatolia, now Turkey, in the late 1200's. The Ottomans claimed to be the champions of Sunni Islam. In 1453, Sultan Muhammad II conquered Constantinople, the capital of the Byzantine Empire. The city, now called Istanbul, became the capital of the Ottoman Empire.

By 1600, the Ottoman Empire formed a crescent around the Mediterranean extending from Hungary in eastern Europe through Palestine and Egypt to Algeria in North Africa. Under the reign of Sultan Suleiman I in the 1500's, the Muslim world achieved its greatest level of unity since the time of the Abbasids. Under the Ottomans, many cultures maintained their identities within Muslim society. The Ottoman sultans were Turkish, but the generals, admirals, and administrators of the Ottoman Empire came from throughout the Mediterranean world. Many Ottoman aristocrats were skilled in the arts, languages, and literature, and they set the standard for culture in the Muslim world.

Many Ottoman officials came from Christian families. Each year, recruiting teams collected boys from eastern Europe. The youths were taken to Istanbul, converted to Islam, and educated. Legally, they became slaves of the sultan and were supposed to be loyal only to him. The most physically active boys became "Men of the Sword" and served in the Janissary Corps, a special division of infantry that formed the core of the Ottoman army. The more scholarly students became "Men of the Pen" and served in administrative posts, from which they could rise to the rank of grand vizier, the highest Ottoman official after the sultan.

The Safavid dynasty. The main rivals of the Ottomans were the Safavids in Iran. The Safavids, originally Sufis from northwestern Iran, rose to power as the leaders of Shiite Turks. Under Shah Ismail I in the early 1500's, Iran, formerly a Sunni country, converted to Shiism. Through the middle of the 1600's, the Ottomans and Safavids fought each other in a series of devastating wars. The wars ended in a costly stalemate that drained the resources of both empires. Safavid kings ruled Iran until 1722.

The Mughal Empire of India was founded by Babur, a central Asian prince, in 1526. Using firearms, Babur's small invasion force easily defeated much larger Indian armies. The Mughal Empire reached its peak under Akbar, who reigned from 1556 to 1605.

A religious procession in Karachi, Pakistan, honors the birthday of the Prophet Muhammad. Pakistan is one of the largest Muslim nations in the world. Although Islam originated in the Middle East, the majority of Muslims today live in other parts of the world, especially south Asia.

© Anis Hamdani, Gamma/Liaison

His empire covered two-thirds of South Asia, including most of present-day Afghanistan, Pakistan, north and central India, and Bangladesh. Mughal society under Akbar tolerated many different religious beliefs. Akbar's son Jahangir was a Muslim, but he had a Hindu mother. The empire officially was Sunni, but many Shiites held high offices. The empire grew less tolerant and declined in the 1700's. It ended in 1858.

Colonialism

Domination by the West. In 1798, the French general Napoleon invaded and conquered Egypt. The conquest shocked the Muslim world. Since the time of the Abbasids, Muslims had viewed Europe as a barbaric land, where culture and morality remained at a low level. With Egypt's defeat, Muslims faced a Europe that had superior military strength and openly challenged their social values. Muslims were impressed by Western military technology and influenced by their contacts with European scientists and historians. Muslim delegations began to travel to Europe to study the latest trends in science and philosophy.

Although the French left Egypt in 1801, they returned to the Muslim world, invading Algeria in 1830. During the last half of the 1800's and the early 1900's, Europe either directly or indirectly controlled every Muslim country except Arabia, Turkey, and Iran. Most states of north and west Africa became French colonies. British political influence and territorial control in India grew in the 1700's and 1800's. Egypt was under British control from 1882. Indonesia began to

fall under the rule of the Netherlands as early as the 1600's.

Colonialism caused drastic changes within all Muslim societies. Colonial governments brought administrative changes and built roads, railroads, and bridges. But colonial authorities also deprived Islam of its former role in the organization of social and economic life. They reorganized the Islamic sharia and supplemented it with a European system of laws. To the present day, most Muslim countries have a dual legal system. Laws governing marriage, family, inheritance, and other personal matters are usually based on the sharia, while most criminal and commercial laws are based on European models.

Reform and renewal. The most influential Muslim movement of the colonial period was the Salafiyyah (Way of the Ancestors). It was founded by Jamal al-Din al-Afghani, an Iranian politician and philosopher, and Muhammad Abduh, an Egyptian theologian and expert on Islamic law. The Salafiyyah attempted to reform Islam using modern Western concepts of reason and science. Afghani also helped found Pan-Islamism, a movement that called for the unity of all Muslims. He feared that nationalism would divide the Muslim world and believed that Muslim unity was more important than ethnic identity. Muhammad Abduh's main concerns were the reform of Islamic law and theology. He rejected the blind acceptance of the past.

The most important successors of the Salafiyyah movement were the Muslim Brotherhood, the Jamaat-i-Islami, and the Muhammadiyah. Hasan al-Banna, an

Egyptian teacher, founded the Muslim Brotherhood in 1928. The organization inspired Islamic reform movements in other Arab countries, including Jordan, Sudan, and Syria. The Muslim Brotherhood started as a religious and philanthropic society that promoted morality and good works. It eventually moved into politics and supported the replacement of nonreligious governments with governments based on Islamic principles. Today, the Muslim Brotherhood is one of the most influential movements in the Muslim world. It is affiliated with Islamic reform movements in non-Arab countries, such as Pakistan, Bangladesh, and Malaysia. It also influences Islamic centers in the United States.

The Jamaat-i-Islami was founded in 1941 in what is now Pakistan by Abu al-Ala Maududi, who was dedicated to reviving Islam in India. After British rule ended in India in 1947, he supported the creation of an Islamic republic in Pakistan. Throughout its history, the Jamaat-i-Islami has supported conservative Muslim politics. The leaders have called for curtailing the influence of minority Islamic sects in Pakistan and have stirred up opposition to nonreligious governments. Although its political influence declined after the death of its founder, the Jamaat-i-Islami continues to attract a following among university students and the lower middle class. It also has considerable influence among Pakistani immigrants in Europe and the United States.

The Muhammadiyah is the largest Muslim reform organization in Southeast Asia. It was founded on the Indonesian island of Java in 1912 and was heavily influenced by the views of Muhammad Abduh. The Muhammadiyah supports a form of Islam based on reason. It has called for the social liberation of Muslim women. Aishiya, the Muhammadiyah's women's organization, was named after the Prophet's wife. It ranks as one of the most dynamic women's organizations in the Muslim world.

The Muslim world today

A goal held by many Muslims is the formation of a unified community of believers. But the great diversity of the modern Muslim world acts against this goal. Although most Muslims believe that "Islam is one," there remain important differences of doctrine and practice within the Muslim world. The practice of Islam in Morocco, for example, differs in many ways from the practice of Islam in Iran or Oman. Only about 15 percent of Muslims are Arabs. The largest group of Muslims live in South Asia in Bangladesh, India, and Pakistan and speak languages, such as Bengali and Urdu, which are much different from Arabic. The single nation with the largest Muslim population is Indonesia in Southeast Asia. And as Islam becomes more prominent in Europe and North America, new cultural forms will add to this diversity.

Cultural differences lie behind many social controversies in Islam, especially regarding the role of women. The treatment of women varies widely throughout the Muslim world. Women in such countries as Afghanistan and Saudi Arabia live largely in seclusion and have little social or economic independence. In other countries, however, including

Bangladesh, Malaysia, Pakistan, Turkey, and Tunisia, women are elected to parliament, serve as government officials, and may even become prime minister.

Vincent J. Cornell

See the articles on countries where Muslims live, such as **Egypt** and **India**. See also:

Outline

Questions

What are the three major divisions in Islam?
Who built the Kaaba?
Where was the Mughal Empire founded?
What was the *Hijra?*
Who founded the Umayyad caliphate?
What is the goal of the Muslim Brotherhood?
What was the Salafiyyah movement?
Who was the first caliph?
What is *Sufism?*
Who were the Safavids?

Additional resources

Child, John. *The Rise of Islam.* Bedrick, 1995.
Esposito, John L., ed. *The Oxford Encyclopedia of the Modern Islamic World.* 4 vols. Oxford, 1995.
Lapidus, Ira M. *A History of Islamic Societies.* Cambridge, 1988.

© Jim Schafer

Downtown Pittsburgh lies in a triangle-shaped area bordered by two rivers, the Allegheny, spanned by the bridge at the left; and the Monongahela, at the right. Its skyscrapers house most of the city's major corporations. The area at the tip of the triangle is Point State Park.

Pittsburgh is the second largest city in Pennsylvania. Only Philadelphia has more people. Pittsburgh lies in the rolling hills of southwestern Pennsylvania, where the Allegheny and Monongahela rivers meet and form the Ohio River.

During the late 1800's, Pittsburgh became the world's leading producer of steel. Massive mills turned out steel for automobiles, ships, trains, and numerous other products. Pittsburgh earned the nickname the *Steel City.*

Steel production gave Pittsburgh a booming economy. It also caused severe pollution, however. Sometimes, the air became so polluted that during the 1940's, downtown streetlights had to be turned on during daytime. Some people mocked Pittsburgh as the "Smoky City." In the early 1950's, Pittsburgh began a major urban renewal program. The program included strict controls on industry and coal-burning furnaces. These steps greatly reduced pollution in the city.

Most of Pittsburgh's big steel mills are gone. The city is still an important steel producer, but it has a much more varied economy than it had in the past. Service industries, especially health and medical, now contribute greatly to the economy.

Settlers first came to the area that is now Pittsburgh in the 1750's. The British and the French both claimed the area. The area was a scene of fighting between the British and French during the 1750's. The British military built a fort there in 1758. They named it Fort Pitt in honor of William Pitt, who later became Britain's prime minister. British settlers established a community around the fort and named it Pittsburgh.

The city

Layout of Pittsburgh. Pittsburgh covers 56 square miles (145 square kilometers) in the center of Allegheny County. Much of downtown Pittsburgh lies in a wedge-shaped area between the fork of the Allegheny and Monongahela rivers. This area, called the Golden Triangle, features skyscrapers that house offices and shops. Most of Pittsburgh's major corporations have their headquarters in or near there. They include the Aluminum Company of America (Alcoa), Mellon Bank, PPG Industries, and USX Corporation. The 64-story USX Tower ranks as one of the tallest buildings in Pennsylvania.

The western tip of the Golden Triangle—where the Ohio River begins—is called the Point. Old factories and warehouses formerly crowded the Point. But those buildings were torn down at the start of Pittsburgh's urban renewal program in the 1950's. In their place, developers established scenic Point State Park and a new office complex called Gateway Center. Large numbers of workers commute to and from downtown Pittsburgh, mostly by automobile. Bridges over the rivers serve the cars. Pittsburgh has more than 450 bridges, more than any other United States city.

A hill called Mount Washington overlooks downtown Pittsburgh. It rises 450 feet (137 meters) and stretches for several miles along the Monongahela River. It features observation decks and restaurants that offer spectacular views of Pittsburgh and its three famous rivers. Two small cable car lines, called "inclines" by Pittsburghers, carry visitors up and down Mount Washington.

The Civic Arena stands just east of Pittsburgh's business area. Its domed roof can be opened so that musical and stage events can be held in the open air when weather permits. Three Rivers Stadium, a large outdoor sports facility, dominates the area called the North Side, just across the Allegheny River from downtown.

Residential areas spread out beyond downtown. Industrial activity is scattered throughout the region.

The metropolitan area. Pittsburgh's metropolitan area covers all of Allegheny County and parts of Beaver, Butler, Westmoreland, and Washington counties. It includes about 200 communities. Penn Hills is Pittsburgh's largest suburb. Other big suburbs include Bethel Park, McCandless, Monroeville, and Mount Lebanon.

The Pittsburgh metropolitan area includes a number of communities which, like Pittsburgh itself, formerly depended on steel production. These communities include Duquesne, Homestead, and McKeesport. When their mills closed, the towns suffered economically. Like Pittsburgh, they are working to build a varied economy.

People

Ethnic groups. Early in its history, Pittsburgh attracted people from many parts of Europe. The first settlers came from England. Large numbers of German, Irish, Italian, and Polish people settled in the city during the 1800's. Pittsburgh still has an old neighborhood called Polish Hill, where Polish is spoken as often as English. Many Croats, Hungarians, and Serbs came to work in the steel mills and settled in Pittsburgh about 1900.

African Americans account for about a fourth of Pittsburgh's population. Large numbers of African Americans began moving there in the early 1900's. From the 1930's through the 1950's, Pittsburgh's Hill District was one of the most prosperous African American communities in the United States. Today, many African Americans live near the center of the city. Some blacks live in the suburbs, including Penn Hills and Wilkinsburg.

Housing. Pittsburgh's East End includes well-kept neighborhoods with housing ranging from relatively inexpensive duplexes to lavish mansions. The part of the North Side near Three Rivers Stadium includes houses that are more than 100 years old. They have been restored to reflect their original condition and beauty. Crawford Square is a development of single-family homes, town houses, and apartments near the Civic Arena, close to downtown. The city government and private developers worked together to build it. Some of the older homes near downtown stand on the steep hillsides. The hills are so steep that many buildings are two stories high in front and four or more stories in back.

Education. The public schools of Pittsburgh serve about 40,000 students. Pittsburgh's Roman Catholic diocese, which covers six counties, has about 35,000 students in its elementary and high schools. The Pittsburgh area is also a center of higher education. It includes about 30 colleges and universities. The University of Pittsburgh ranks as the area's largest school of higher education. Other area schools include Carnegie Mellon University; Duquesne University; Pittsburgh Theological Seminary; and Carlow,

---

Facts in brief

Population: *City*—369,879. *Metropolitan area*—2,394,811.
Area: *City*—56 sq. mi. (145 km²). *Metropolitan area*—4,624 sq. mi. (11,976 km²).
Climate: *Average temperature*—January, 29 °F (−2 °C); July, 72 °F (22 °C). *Average annual precipitation* (rainfall, melted snow, and other forms of moisture)—40 in. (100 cm). For the monthly weather in Pittsburgh, see **Pennsylvania** (Climate).
Government: Mayor-council. *Terms*—4 years for the mayor and 9 council members.
Founded: 1758. Incorporated as a city in 1816.

Largest communities in the Pittsburgh area

Name	Population	Name	Population
Pittsburgh	369,879	McKeesport	26,016
Penn Hills	51,430	West Mifflin	23,644
Bethel Park	33,823	Baldwin	21,923
Mount Lebanon	33,362	Wilkinsburg	21,080
Monroeville	29,169	Scott	17,118

Symbols of Pittsburgh. The city flag and coat of arms of Pittsburgh include the crest of the Chatham family, of which William Pitt was the first earl. The castle above the crest represents Pittsburgh as a chartered municipality.

Chatham, La Roche, Point Park, and Robert Morris colleges.

Social problems. Pittsburgh, like other large urban areas, has a number of social problems. They include street crime and illegal drug sales and use. Pittsburgh formerly experienced severe air and water pollution. But controls and cooperation have led to a major reduction of the pollution problem.

Cultural life

The arts. The Pittsburgh Symphony Orchestra presents concerts downtown at Heinz Hall for the Performing Arts. The Benedum Center for the Performing Arts is the home of several groups. They are the Pittsburgh Ballet Theatre, Pittsburgh Opera, Pittsburgh Dance Council, and Civic Light Opera. The Pittsburgh Public Theater offers professional regional theater. The annual Three Rivers Arts Festival, held each June in Point State Park and the Golden Triangle, features works by painters, sculptors, and musicians. The Star Lake Amphitheatre in Washington County presents outdoor concerts.

Museums and libraries. Pittsburgh's Carnegie Institute includes the Museum of Natural History and the Museum of Art. The natural history museum features a collection of dinosaur fossils. The art museum

Pittsburgh

Pittsburgh lies in southwestern Pennsylvania. The Allegheny and Monongahela rivers join within the city to form the Ohio River. The map below shows the city and some of its landmarks. The map on the right shows Allegheny County and parts of the other counties in the Pittsburgh metropolitan area.

PENNSYLVANIA
• Pittsburgh

▦▦▦▦ City boundary	▬▬▬▬ Expressway
- - - - County boundary	▬▬▬ Other road
▨ Park or cemetery	▬▬▬ Railroad
	■ Point of interest

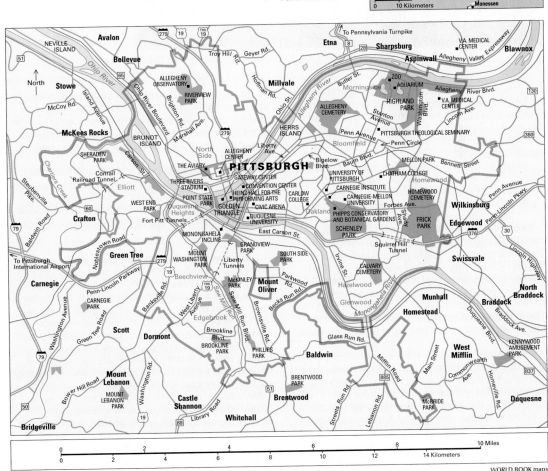

WORLD BOOK maps

Heinz Hall for the Performing Arts, in the downtown area, is the home of the world-famous Pittsburgh Symphony Orchestra.

includes the Heinz Architectural Center and Hall of Architecture. The Carnegie Science Center presents science shows and other programs. The Andy Warhol Museum houses many of the most famous works by Warhol, a major Pop artist who was born in Pittsburgh.

Carnegie Library of Pittsburgh is the city's public library. It is named for Andrew Carnegie, a Pittsburgh steel manufacturer, who founded it in 1895. The Carnegie Library of Pittsburgh system includes a main library at the Carnegie Institute and several branches.

Recreation. The Pittsburgh area has more than 150 parks, fields, playgrounds, and playlots. Schenley Park is one of Pittsburgh's largest parks. It includes the Phipps Conservatory and Botanical Gardens, which houses a rich collection of plants and flowers in one of the few remaining Victorian greenhouses in the United States. Highland Park is home of the Pittsburgh Zoo and the Aquarium. The National Aviary in Pittsburgh houses about 200 species of birds in a natural setting with plants, pools, and waterfalls. Exhibits at the Pittsburgh Children's Museum encourage personal participation. Suburban areas include several large county parks that offer biking, hiking, horse riding, swimming, and ice skating. Suburban Raccoon Creek State Park, in Hookstown, includes a large lake and a wildflower reserve. Kennywood Amusement Park, in West Mifflin, is famous for its fast roller coasters.

Each August, the Three Rivers Regatta brings spectators downtown to see speedboat races and fireworks. The riverboats of the Gateway Clipper Fleet of-fer dining, dancing, and sightseeing tours of downtown the year around. Fort Necessity National Battlefield, in Farmington south of Pittsburgh, marks the site of the Battle of Fort Necessity of 1754. The battle was one of the first of the French and Indian War, which began that year.

The Pittsburgh Steelers of the National Football League and the Pittsburgh Pirates baseball team of the National League play in Three Rivers Stadium. The Civic Arena is the home of the Pittsburgh Penguins of the National Hockey League.

Economy

The economy of the Pittsburgh area went through a major change in the 1980's. It had been dependent on heavy industry—notably steel production—but it began to develop more variety and balance. Unemployment rose as heavy industry declined, but the development of other economic activities helped improve economic conditions. Today, service industries contribute heavily to the Pittsburgh area's economy, employing about 370,000 people. Health care and retail trade are the largest service industries. Manufacturing employs more than 130,000 people.

Manufacturing. Pittsburgh's steel mills formerly produced all kinds of steel. Today's remaining mills chiefly turn out specialty steel, which is used to make tools and automobiles. This type of steel is of higher quality and more profitable than types made in earlier years. Pittsburgh factories also produce glass products, fabricated metals, chemicals, and machinery.

Pittsburgh's largest private employers include Alcoa, the world's biggest aluminum producer; USX Corporation, a leading steelmaker; and PPG Industries, a glass, paint, and chemical manufacturer. The H. J. Heinz Company makes ketchup, pickles, and other food products.

Service industries. The Pittsburgh area ranks as a major center of health care. About 90 hospitals serve the area. The University of Pittsburgh runs a medical center specializing in liver, kidney, heart, and lung transplants.

Research and development is also a major service industry. More than 170 academic, industrial, and governmental research laboratories operate in the Pittsburgh area. Their engineers, scientists, and technicians work in such fields as medical technology, computer software programming, and industrial automation.

Transportation and communication. Pittsburgh International Airport is in southwestern Allegheny County. Two major railroads and four interstate highways serve the city. A trolley-subway connects downtown with southern suburbs. Pittsburgh's rivers are used to ship raw materials to, and finished products from, the city.

Pittsburgh has one daily newspaper, the morning *Pittsburgh Post-Gazette*. The *Tribune-Review* in nearby Greensburg also publishes a Pittsburgh edition. Several smaller daily newspapers published in towns surrounding Pittsburgh serve the area's suburban population. KDKA became one of the first commercial radio stations in the United States when it began broadcasting in 1920. For more details, see **Radio** (The start of broadcasting).

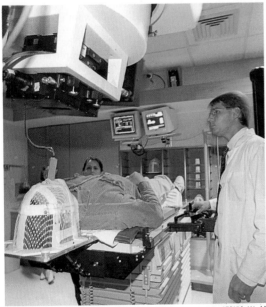

AP/Wide World

Health care is important to Pittsburgh's economy. The area has many general and specialized hospitals and other medical facilities. Medical workers provide radiation treatment in this picture.

Government

The city of Pittsburgh has a mayor-council form of government. Voters elect the mayor and the nine council members to four-year terms. Most of the city's revenues come from a wage tax and property taxes. In the 1990's, to reduce its spending, the city turned over three city institutions to private groups to own and manage. The three were the Pittsburgh Zoo, the Phipps Conserv-atory and Botanical Gardens, and the National Aviary in Pittsburgh. Pittsburgh is the seat of Allegheny County.

In addition to the city government, the Pittsburgh area has dozens of other government bodies. They include suburban municipal governments, local boards of education, and county government.

History

Early days. In the 1740's, French soldiers claimed the area that is now Pittsburgh for the king of France. Many Indians traded goods with French and Canadian traders. The Iroquois of western New York had chased the original tribes out of the area in the 1600's.

Both Britain and France sought to gain control of the region, and this competition led to the French and Indian War (1754-1763). In 1754, French troops built Fort Duquesne at the fork of the Allegheny and Monongahela rivers. George Washington built Fort Necessity south of Fort Duquesne. Washington, who later became the first president of the United States, was then a 22-year-old lieutenant colonel in Britain's Virginia militia. The French defeated Washington's troops in the Battle of Fort Necessity and forced Washington to surrender the fort. The battle marked one of the first military actions of the French and Indian War.

In spite of their early defeat, the British won control of the Pittsburgh area in 1758. They built Fort Pitt near the fork of the Allegheny and Monongahela rivers. A settlement grew up around the fort and became Pittsburgh. The American colonists won independence from Britain in the Revolutionary War (1775-1883). After the war, Pittsburgh became a starting point for pioneers traveling west. Pittsburgh became the Allegheny County seat in 1788 and was incorporated as a borough in 1794.

Industrial development. Demands from Western settlements for manufactured goods caused industry to grow rapidly in Pittsburgh. The city was incorporated in 1816. It then had a population of about 5,000. Nearby deposits of coal and oil helped make Pittsburgh an ironmaking and glassmaking center by the mid-1800's.

Transportation developments also helped industry grow in Pittsburgh. In 1811, the first steamboat to travel on the Ohio and Mississippi rivers was launched from Pittsburgh. The Pennsylvania Canal System, which connected Pittsburgh and Philadelphia, opened its main line in 1834. A railroad entered Pittsburgh in 1851. By then, more than 46,000 people lived in the city.

The American Civil War (1861-1865) created a great demand for arms and ammunition. Pittsburgh became a chief supplier for the Union Army. During the late 1800's, steel manufacturers Andrew Carnegie and

Smoke from Pittsburgh's steel mills darkened the skies in this picture from the 1940's, before industry controls reduced air pollution. But steel production also benefited Pittsburgh's economy.

Archive Photos

Henry Clay Frick built industrial empires in the city. Pittsburgh steel mills played an important role in America's growth. They supplied great amounts of steel to build bridges, factories, and railroads. Steady industrial growth attracted thousands of workers to Pittsburgh during the late 1800's. Many came from southern and central Europe. From 1870 to 1900, the city's population more than tripled, jumping from 86,076 to 321,616. By 1900, half of the world's glass and iron came from Pittsburgh's factories. The city's steel mills made two-thirds of the steel produced in the United States by 1900.

The early 1900's. The arrival of more immigrants from Europe and of many blacks from the southern United States helped boost the population of Pittsburgh to 669,817 by 1930. In 1936, the Allegheny and Monongahela rivers flooded the Golden Triangle, causing 74 deaths and damaging thousands of homes.

World War II. In December 1941, the United States joined the side of the Allies in their World War II fight against the Axis nations. From then until the Allied victory in September 1945, the Pittsburgh area's mills and factories operated at full capacity to provide steel, glass, and other products for the war effort. During the war, mills of the Pittsburgh area turned out more steel than did the Axis countries of Germany and Japan combined.

Also during World War II, Pittsburgh became one of the first cities in the United States to construct large amounts of public housing. Thousands of people moved to the city to take jobs in its booming war-related industries. The inflow of people caused a housing shortage and led the city and federal governments to construct low-rent public housing for workers.

Urban renewal. In 1946, Mayor David L. Lawrence, financier Richard K. Mellon, and many other civic and corporate leaders began an urban renewal program in Pittsburgh that would become the first such pro-

gram in the United States. The city started strict smoke-control and water pollution-control programs to clean up Pittsburgh's polluted air and water. By the 1960's, most of the clean-up efforts had been completed. Pittsburgh's population reached its highest point of 676,806 in 1950. In the 1950's and 1960's, many white residents moved out of the city to surrounding suburbs.

The first stage of urban renewal, known as Pittsburgh's Renaissance I, ended in the early 1970's. The factories and warehouses in the Golden Triangle had been torn down and replaced with Point State Park and Gateway Center in the 1950's. The Civic Arena and the USX Tower had been completed in the 1960's. Three Rivers Stadium was built during the 1970's. A second project, Renaissance II, began during the 1980's. It produced a convention center, a trolley-subway system, and several new skyscrapers, including PPG Place.

Recent developments. Between 1980 and 1990, the population of Pittsburgh dropped from 423,959 to 369,879, largely because of economic problems. Many young people in the area moved to other cities to find work. At the same time, the metropolitan area population increased from 2,218,870 to 2,394,811. During the 1990's, unemployment declined in the Pittsburgh area, as new jobs in health care and other occupations became available. Pittsburgh International Airport opened in 1992, adding to the area's role as a transportation center. Bill Steigerwald

Related articles in *World Book* include:
Allegheny River
Carnegie, Andrew
Fort Duquesne
Fort Necessity
Mellon, Andrew W.
Monongahela River
Pittsburgh, University of

Planet is a large, round heavenly body that orbits a star and shines with light reflected from the star. We know of nine planets that orbit the sun in our solar system. In the 1990's, astronomers also discovered many planets orbiting distant stars.

All but two of the planets in our solar system have smaller objects revolving around them called *satellites* or *moons.* Our solar system also contains thousands of smaller bodies known as *asteroids.* The asteroids are often called minor planets, and the term *major planet* is used to distinguish the nine planets from the asteroids. The remainder of this article uses *planet* to mean *major planet.*

The usual order of the planets in our solar system, outward from the sun, is Mercury, Venus, Earth, Mars, Jupiter, Saturn, Uranus, Neptune, and Pluto. To help remember the order, some people use the phrase *My Very Educated Mother Just Sent Us Nine Pizzas* as a memory aid. The initial letters of the words in that phrase match the initial letters of the planet names.

Pluto is not always the farthest planet from the sun, however. Its orbit is such a long oval that Pluto moves inside the path of Neptune for about 20 years every 248 years. One such 20-year period lasted from Jan. 23, 1979, to Feb. 11, 1999. After February 11, however, Pluto will again be the most distant planet for hundreds of years.

The planets of our solar system can be divided into two groups. The innermost four planets—Mercury, Venus, Earth, and Mars—are small, rocky worlds. They are called the *terrestrial* (earthlike) planets, from the Latin word for Earth, *terra.* Earth is the largest terrestrial planet. The other earthlike planets have from 38 percent to 95 percent of Earth's diameter and from 5.6 percent to 81 percent of Earth's *mass* (total quantity of matter).

The next four planets—Jupiter, Saturn, Uranus, and Neptune—are called *gas giants* or *Jovian* (Jupiterlike) *planets.* They have gaseous atmospheres and no solid surfaces. All four Jovian planets consist mainly of hydrogen and helium. Smaller amounts of other materials also occur, including traces of ammonia and methane in their atmospheres. They range from 3.9 times to 11.2 times Earth's diameter and from 15 times to 318 times Earth's mass. Jupiter, Saturn, and Neptune give off more energy than they receive from the sun. Most of this extra energy takes the form of *infrared* radiation, which is felt as heat, instead of visible light. Scientists think the source of some of the energy is probably the slow compression of the planets by their own gravity.

The ninth planet, Pluto, is only 18 percent the diameter of Earth and $\frac{1}{500}$ of its mass. As a small, rocky planet with a larger orbit than the gas giants, it does not fit in either group. Some astronomers think that Pluto may not be a major planet at all.

Observing the planets

People have known the inner six planets of our solar system for thousands of years because they are visible from Earth without a telescope. The outermost three planets—Uranus, Neptune, and Pluto—were discovered

by astronomers, beginning in the 1780's. All three can be seen from Earth with a telescope.

To the unaided eye, the planets look much like the background stars in the night sky. However, the planets move slightly from night to night in relation to the stars. The name *planet* comes from a Greek word meaning *to wander.* The planets and the moon almost always follow the same apparent path through the sky. This path, known as the *zodiac,* is about 16° wide. At its center is the *ecliptic,* the apparent path of the sun. If you see a bright object near the ecliptic at night or near sunrise or sunset, it is most likely a planet. You can even see the brightest planets in the daytime, if you know where to look.

Planets and stars also differ in the steadiness of their light when viewed from Earth's surface. Planets shine with a steady light, but stars seem to twinkle.

The twinkling is due to the moving layers of air that surround Earth. Stars are so far away that they are mere points of light in the sky, even when viewed through a telescope. The atmosphere bends the starlight passing through it. As small regions of the atmosphere move about, the points of light seem to dance and change in brightness.

Planets, which are much closer, look like tiny disks through a telescope. The atmosphere scatters light from different points on a planet's disk. However, enough light always arrives from a sufficient number of points to provide a steady appearance.

How planets move

Planets move in two main ways. They travel around their parent star in paths called *orbits.* As each planet orbits its star, it also rotates on its *axis,* an imaginary line through its center.

Orbits. Viewed from Earth's surface, the planets of the solar system and the stars appear to move around Earth. They rise in the east and set in the west each night. Most of the time, the planets move westward across the sky slightly more slowly than the stars do. As a result, the planets seem to drift eastward relative to the background stars. This motion is called *prograde.* For a while each year, however, the planets seem to reverse their direction. This backward motion is called *retrograde.*

In ancient times, most scientists thought that the moon, sun, planets, and stars actually moved around Earth. One puzzle that ancient scientists struggled to explain was the annual retrograde motion of the planets. In about A.D. 150, the Greek astronomer Ptolemy developed a theory that the planets orbited in small circles, which in turn orbited Earth in larger circles. Ptolemy thought that retrograde motion was caused by a planet moving on its small circle in an opposite direction from the motion of the small circle around the big circle.

In 1543, the Polish astronomer Nicolaus Copernicus showed that the sun is the center of the orbits of the planets. Our term *solar system* is based on Copernicus's discovery. Copernicus realized that retrograde motion occurs because Earth moves faster in its orbit than the planets that are farther from the sun. The planets that are closer to the sun move faster in their orbits than Earth travels in its orbit. Retrograde motion occurs whenever Earth passes an outer planet traveling around

Jay M. Pasachoff, the contributor of this article, is Field Memorial Professor of Astronomy and Director of the Hopkins Observatory at Williams College.

the sun or an inner planet passes Earth.

In the 1600's, the German astronomer Johannes Kepler used observations of Mars by the Danish astronomer Tycho Brahe to figure out three laws of planetary motion. Although Kepler developed his laws for the planets of our solar system, astronomers have since realized that Kepler's laws are valid for all heavenly bodies that orbit other bodies.

Kepler's first law says that planets move in *elliptical* (oval-shaped) orbits around their parent star—in our solar system, the sun. An *ellipse* is a closed curve formed around two fixed points called *foci.* The ellipse is formed by the path of a point moving so that the sum of its distances from the two foci remains the same. The orbital paths of the planets form such curves, with the parent star at one focus of the ellipse. Before Kepler, scientists had assumed that the planets moved in circular orbits.

Kepler's second law says that an imaginary line joining the parent star to its planet sweeps across equal areas of space in equal amounts of time. When a planet is close to its star, it moves relatively rapidly in its orbit. The line therefore sweeps out a short, fat, trianglelike figure. When the planet is farther from its star, it moves relatively slowly. In this case, the line sweeps out a long, thin figure that resembles a triangle. But the two figures have equal areas.

Kepler's third law says that a planet's *period* (the time it takes to complete an orbit around its star) depends on its average distance from the star. The law says that the square of the planet's period—that is, the period multiplied by itself—is proportional to the cube of the planet's average distance from its star—the distance multiplied by itself twice—for all planets in a solar system.

In 1687, the English scientist, astronomer, and mathematician Isaac Newton completed his theory of gravity and explained why Kepler's laws work. Newton showed how his expanded version of Kepler's third law could be used to find the mass of the sun or of any other object around which things orbit. Using Newton's explanation, astronomers can determine the mass of a planet by studying the period of its moon or moons and their distance from the planet.

Rotation. Planets rotate at different rates. One day is defined as how long it takes Earth to rotate once. Jupiter

Inner planets

Mercury
Venus
Earth
Mars

Outer planets

Jupiter
Saturn
Uranus
Neptune
Pluto

The orbits of the planets around the sun are shown here. Two diagrams are needed because the orbits of the outer planets would extend off the page if they were drawn to the same scale as those of the inner planets.

and Saturn spin much faster, in only about 10 hours. Venus rotates much slower, in about 243 earth-days.

Most planets rotate in the same direction in which they revolve around the sun, with their axis of rotation standing upright from their orbital path. A law of physics holds that such rotation does not change by itself. So astronomers think that the solar system formed out of a

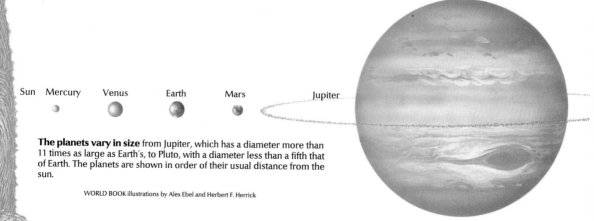

Sun   Mercury   Venus   Earth   Mars   Jupiter

The planets vary in size from Jupiter, which has a diameter more than 11 times as large as Earth's, to Pluto, with a diameter less than a fifth that of Earth. The planets are shown in order of their usual distance from the sun.

WORLD BOOK illustrations by Alex Ebel and Herbert F. Herrick

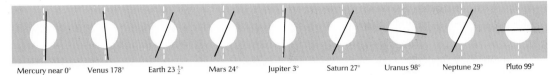

Mercury near 0° Venus 178° Earth 23 ½° Mars 24° Jupiter 3° Saturn 27° Uranus 98° Neptune 29° Pluto 99°

The axes of the planets, represented by the solid lines, are imaginary lines around which the planets rotate. A planet's axis is not perpendicular to the path of the planet's orbit around the sun. It tilts at an angle from the perpendicular position indicated by the broken line.

cloud of gas and dust that was already spinning.

Uranus and Pluto are tipped on their sides, however, so that their axes lie nearly level with their paths around the sun. Venus is tipped all the way over. Its axis is almost completely upright, but the planet rotates in the direction opposite from the direction of its revolution around the sun. Most astronomers think that some other objects in the solar system must have collided with Uranus, Pluto, and Venus and tipped them.

The planets of our solar system

Astronomers measure distances within the solar system in *astronomical units* (AU). One astronomical unit is the average distance between Earth and the sun, which is about 93 million miles (150 million kilometers). The inner planets have orbits whose diameters are 0.4, 0.7, 1.0, and 1.5 AU, respectively. The orbits of the gas giants are much larger: 5, 10, 20, and 30 AU, respectively. Because of their different distances from the sun, the temperature, surface features, and other conditions on the planets vary widely.

Mercury, the innermost planet, has no moon and almost no atmosphere. It orbits so close to the sun that temperatures on its surface can climb as high as 800 °F (430 °C). But some regions near the planet's poles may be always in shadow, and astronomers speculate that water or ice may remain there. No spacecraft has visited Mercury since the 1970's, when Mariner 10 photographed about half the planet's surface at close range.

Venus is known as Earth's twin because it resembles Earth in size and mass, though it has no moon. Venus has a dense atmosphere that consists primarily of carbon dioxide. The pressure of the atmosphere on Venus's surface is 90 times that of Earth's atmosphere. Venus's

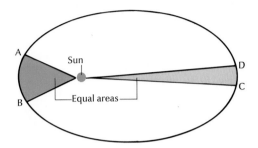

Kepler's second law shows how a planet covers equal areas of its orbit in equal lengths of time. The planet travels at a higher speed near the sun, from *A* to *B*, than far from the sun, *C* to *D*.

thick atmosphere traps energy from the sun, raising the surface temperature on Venus to about 860 °F (460 °C), hot enough to melt lead. This trapping of heat is known as the *greenhouse effect.* Scientists have warned that a similar process on Earth is causing permanent global warming. Several spacecraft have orbited or landed on Venus. In the 1990's, the Magellan spacecraft used radar—radio waves bounced off the planet—to map Venus in detail.

Earth, our home planet, has an atmosphere that is mostly nitrogen with some oxygen. Earth has oceans of liquid water and continents that rise above sea level. Many measuring devices on the surface and in space monitor conditions on our planet. In 1998, the National Aeronautics and Space Administration (NASA) launched the first of a series of satellites called the Earth Observing System (EOS). The EOS satellites will carry remote-sensing instruments to measure climate changes and other conditions on Earth's surface.

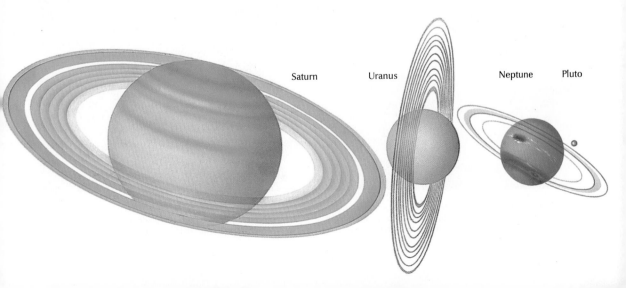

Saturn   Uranus   Neptune   Pluto

NASA/JPL/MSSS

A canyon on Mars is Earthlike in appearance. However, numerous craters produced by the impact of meteorites give the surface near the edge of the canyon a pitted, unearthly look.

NASA/JPL

The Great Red Spot of Jupiter is one of the most spectacular features in the solar system. This swirling mass of gas, which resembles a hurricane, is about three times as wide as Earth.

Mars is known as the red planet because of its reddish-brown appearance, caused by rusty dust on the Martian surface. Mars is a cold, dry world with a thin atmosphere. The *atmospheric pressure* (pressure exerted by the weight of the gases in the atmosphere) on the Martian surface is less than 1 percent the atmospheric pressure on Earth. This low surface pressure has enabled most of the water that Mars may once have had to escape into space.

The surface of Mars has giant volcanoes, a huge system of canyons, and stream beds that look as if water flowed through them in the past. Mars has two tiny moons, Phobos and Deimos. Many spacecraft have landed on or orbited Mars.

Jupiter, the largest planet in our solar system, has more mass than the other planets combined. Like the other Jovian planets, it has gaseous outer layers and may have a rocky core. A huge storm system called the Great Red Spot in Jupiter's atmosphere is larger than Earth and has raged for hundreds of years.

Jupiter's four largest moons—Io, Europa, Ganymede, and Callisto—are larger than Pluto, and Ganymede is also bigger than Mercury. Circling Jupiter's equator are three thin rings, consisting mostly of dust particles. A pair of Voyager spacecraft flew by Jupiter in 1979 and sent back close-up pictures. In 1995, the Galileo spacecraft dropped a probe into Jupiter's atmosphere and went into orbit around the planet and its moons.

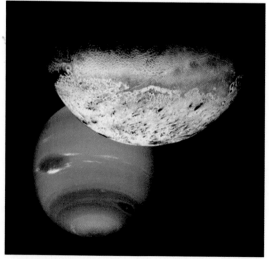

NASA/JPL

The blue clouds of Neptune are mostly frozen methane, the main chemical in natural gas—a fuel used for heating and cooking on Earth. The other object shown is Neptune's moon Triton.

NASA/JPL

A river of lava on Venus split in two as it flowed from left to right, producing a delta like those made by rivers of water on Earth. Venus's surface has many long channels of hardened lava.

Saturn, another giant planet, has a magnificent set of gleaming rings. Its gaseous atmosphere is not as colorful as Jupiter's, however. One reason Saturn is relatively drab is that its hazy upper atmosphere makes the cloud patterns below difficult to see. Another reason is that Saturn is farther than Jupiter from the sun. Because of the difference in distance, Saturn is colder than Jupiter. Due to the temperature difference, the kinds of chemical reactions that color Jupiter's atmosphere occur too slowly to do the same on Saturn.

Saturn's moon Titan is larger than Pluto and Mercury. Titan has a thick atmosphere of nitrogen and methane. In 1980 and 1981, the Voyager 2 spacecraft sent back close-up views of Saturn and its rings and moons.

The Cassini spacecraft will orbit Saturn in 2004. It will also drop a small probe into Titan's atmosphere.

Uranus was the first planet discovered with a telescope. German-born English astronomer William Herschel found it in 1781. He at first thought he had discovered a comet. Almost 200 years later, scientists detected 10 narrow rings around Uranus when the planet moved in front of a star and the rings became visible. Voyager 2 studied Uranus and its rings and moons close-up in 1986.

Neptune was first observed in 1846 by German astronomer Johann G. Galle after other astronomers predicted its position by studying how it affected Uranus's orbit. In 1989, Voyager 2 found that Neptune had a storm system called the Great Dark Spot, similar to Jupiter's Great Red Spot. But five years later, in 1994, the Hubble Space Telescope found that the Great Dark Spot had vanished. Neptune has four narrow rings, one of which has clumps of matter. Neptune's moon Triton is one of the largest in the solar system and has volcanoes that emit plumes of frozen nitrogen.

Pluto. Tiny, distant Pluto has been difficult to study because it is so far from Earth. The American astronomer Clyde W. Tombaugh discovered Pluto in 1930. Only in 1978, when astronomers discovered a moon orbiting Pluto, could they determine the planet's mass. They found that Pluto was much less massive than expected. The Hubble Space Telescope found a dozen areas of contrasting light and dark on Pluto. NASA plans to launch a mission called the Pluto-Kuiper Express in the early 2000's. The mission will send a probe to explore Pluto and the *Kuiper* (pronounced *KY pur) belt,* a band of small rocky objects orbiting beyond Neptune. Astronomers hope the probe reaches Pluto before the planet has traveled so far from the sun that its thin atmosphere freezes and snows.

Planets in other solar systems

How planets are detected. Even with the most advanced telescopes, astronomers cannot see planets orbiting other stars directly. The planets shine only by reflected light and are hidden by the brilliance of their parent stars. The planets and their stars are also much farther away than our sun. The nearest star is 4.2 light-years away, compared to 8 light-minutes for the sun. One *light-year* is the distance that light travels in one year—about 5.88 trillion miles (9.46 trillion kilometers). Thus, it takes light 4.2 years to reach Earth from the nearest star beyond the sun and only 8 minutes to reach Earth from the sun.

NASA/JPL

The rings of Saturn consist of billions of pieces of ice, ranging in size from particles the size of dust grains to chunks over 10 feet (3 meters) wide. The rings are shown here in false color.

Although astronomers cannot see planets around distant stars, they can detect the planets from tiny changes in the stars' movement. These changes are caused by the slight pull of the planet's gravity on its parent star. To find new planets, astronomers use a technique called *spectroscopy,* which breaks down the light from stars into its component rainbow of colors. The scientists look for places in the rainbow where colors are missing. At these places, dark lines known as *spectral lines* cross the rainbow. The spectral lines change their location in the rainbow slightly as a star is pulled by the gravity of an orbiting planet toward and away from Earth. These apparent changes in a star's light as the star moves are due to a phenomenon known as the *Doppler effect.* The changes not only show that a planet is present but also indicate how much mass it has.

The first discoveries. Astronomers announced the discovery of the first planets around a star other than our sun in 1992. The star is a pulsar named PSR B1257+12 in the constellation Virgo. *Pulsars* are dead stars that have collapsed until they are only about 12 miles (20 kilometers) across. They spin rapidly on their axes, sending out radio waves that arrive on Earth as pulses of radio energy. Some pulsars spin hundreds of times each second. If a pulsar has a planet, the planet pulls the star to and fro slightly as it orbits. These pulls cause slight variations in the radio pulses. From measurements of these variations, the Polish-born American astronomer Alexander Wolszczan and American Dale A. Frail discovered three planets in orbit around PSR B1257+12. The star emits such strong X rays, however, that no life could survive on its planets.

Astronomers soon began to find planets around stars more like the sun. In 1995, Swiss astronomers Michel Mayor and Didier Queloz found the first planet orbiting a sunlike star, 51 Pegasi, in the constellation Pegasus. American astronomers Geoffrey W. Marcy and R. Paul Butler confirmed the discovery and found planets of their own around other stars. By the late 1990's, the stars known to have planets included 70 Virginis in the constellation Virgo, 47 Ursae Majoris in the Big Dipper (Ursa Major), and Rho[1] Cancri in the constellation Cancer.

Some stars have planets orbiting them at a distance that could support life. Most scientists consider liquid water essential for life. For a planet to support living things, it must orbit its star at the right distance so that it is neither too hot nor too cold to have liquid water. Astronomers call this region the *habitable zone*. The planets around 70 Virginis and 47 Ursae Majoris have orbits in the habitable zone. However, all the planets found so far are probably gaseous with no solid surface.

Astronomers were surprised to find that other solar systems have huge, gaseous planets in close orbits. In our own solar system, the inner planets are rocky and small, and only the outer planets, except for Pluto, are huge and gassy. But several newly discovered planets have at least as much mass as Jupiter, the largest planet in our solar system. Unlike Jupiter, however, these massive planets race around their stars in only a few weeks. Kepler's third law says that for a planet to complete its orbit so quickly, it must be close to its parent star. Several of these giant planets, therefore, must travel around their stars even closer than our innermost planet, Mercury, orbits our sun. Such close orbits would make their surfaces too hot to support life as we know it.

Some newly discovered planets follow unusual orbits. Most planets travel around their stars on nearly circular paths, like those of the planets in our solar system. But a planet around the star 16 Cygni B follows an extremely elliptical orbit. It travels farther from its star than the planet Mars does from our sun, and then draws closer to the star than Venus does to our sun. If a planet in our solar system traveled in such an extreme oval, its gravity would disrupt the orbits of the other planets and toss them out of their paths.

How the planets formed

Astronomers have developed a theory about how our solar system formed that explains why it has small, rocky planets close to the sun and big, gaseous ones farther away. Astronomers believe our solar system formed about 4.6 billion years ago from a giant, rotating cloud of gas and dust called the *solar nebula*. Gravity pulled together a portion of gas and dust at the center of the nebula that was denser than the rest. The material accumulated into a dense, spinning clump that formed our sun.

The remaining gas and dust flattened into a disk called a *protoplanetary disk* swirling around the sun. Protoplanetary disks around distant stars were first observed through telescopes in 1983. Rocky particles within the disk collided and stuck together, forming bodies called *planetesimals*. Planetesimals later combined to form the planets. At the distances of the outer planets, gases froze into ice, creating huge balls of frozen gas that formed the Jovian planets.

Hot gases and electrically charged particles flow from our sun constantly, forming a stream called the *solar wind*. The solar wind was stronger at first than it is today. The early solar wind drove the light elements—hydrogen and helium—away from the inner planets like Earth. But the stronger gravity of the giant outer planets held on to more of the planets' hydrogen and helium, and the solar wind was weaker there. So these outer planets kept most of their light elements and wound up with much more mass than Earth.

Astronomers developed these theories when they thought that rocky planets always orbited close to the

The planets at a glance[*]

	Mercury ☿	Venus ♀	Earth ⊕	Mars ♂
Average distance from the sun	35,980,000 mi. (57,900,000 km)	67,230,000 mi. (108,200,000 km)	92,960,000 mi. (149,600,000 km)	141,000,000 mi. (227,900,000 km)
Closest approach to Earth	57,000,000 mi. (91,700,000 km)	25,700,000 mi. (41,400,000 km)	————————	34,600,000 mi. (55,700,000 km)
Length of year (earthdays) Average orbital speed	87.97 29.76 mi. per sec. (47.89 km per sec.)	224.7 21.77 mi. per sec. (35.03 km per sec.)	365.26 18.51 mi. per sec. (29.79 km per sec.)	686.98 14.99 mi. per sec. (24.13 km per sec.)
Diameter at equator	3,031 mi. (4,878 km)	7,521 mi. (12,104 km)	7,926 mi. (12,756 km)	4,223 mi. (6,796 km)
Rotation period Tilt of axis (degrees)	59 earthdays about 0	243 earthdays 178	23 hrs. 56 min. 23.44	24 hrs. 37 min. 23.98
Temperature	−280 to +800 °F (−170 to +430 °C)	+860 °F (+460 °C)	−130 to +140 °F (−90 to +60 °C)	−220 to +60 °F (−140 to +20 °C)
Mass (Earth = 1) Density (g/cm³) Gravity (Earth = 1)	0.056 5.42 0.386	0.815 5.25 0.879	1 5.52 1	0.107 3.94 0.38
Number of known satellites	0	0	1	2

[*]Many of these figures are approximations or obtained by scientific calculations.

parent star and giant planets farther out. But the "rule" was based only on our own solar system. Now that astronomers have learned something about other solar systems, they have devised new theories. Some scientists have suggested that the giant planets in other solar systems may have formed far from their parent stars and later moved in closer.   Jay M. Pasachoff

Related articles in *World Book* include:

Planets

Earth
Jupiter
Mars
Mercury
Neptune
Pluto
Saturn
Uranus
Venus

Biographies

Brahe, Tycho   Lowell, Percival
Copernicus, Nicolaus   Newton,
Galileo   Sir Isaac
Herschel, Sir William   Ptolemy
Kepler, Johannes

Other related articles

Asteroid   Moon
Astrology   Observatory
Astronomy   Orbit
Bode's law   Satellite
Day   Solar system
Doppler effect   Space exploration
Evening star   Sun
Gravitation   Telescope
Life (The search for life on oth-   Year
    er planets)   Zodiac
Meteor

Outline

I. **Observing the planets**
II. **How planets move**
   A. Orbits   B. Rotation
III. **The planets of our solar system**
   A. Mercury   B. Venus
   C. Earth   D. Mars
   E. Jupiter   F. Saturn
   G. Uranus   H. Neptune
   I. Pluto
IV. **Planets in other solar systems**
   A. How planets are detected
   B. The first discoveries
V. **How the planets formed**

Questions

Why is Venus called Earth's twin?
Which is the largest planet in our solar system? The smallest?
Why are planets in other solar systems difficult to see?
Who discovered the three laws of planetary motion?
What is an astronomical unit?
How do the four planets nearest the sun differ from the next four planets?
Why is Pluto not always the farthest planet from the sun?
What is the Kuiper belt?
How can you tell planets and stars apart in the night sky?
Which three planets have rings?

Additional resources

Level I
Dickinson, Terence. *Other Worlds: A Beginner's Guide to Planets and Moons.* Firefly Bks., 1995.
Fradin, Dennis B. *The Planet Hunters.* Margaret K. McElderry Bks., 1997.

Level II
Cattermole, Peter. *Earth and Other Planets.* Oxford, 1995.
Croswell, Ken. *Planet Quest: The Epic Discovery of Alien Solar Systems.* Free Pr., 1997.
Schaaf, Fred. *Planetology: Comparing Other Worlds to Our Own.* Watts, 1996.
Watters, Thomas R. *Planets: A Smithsonian Guide.* Macmillan, 1995.

Jupiter ♃	Saturn ♄	Uranus ♅	Neptune ♆	Pluto ♇
483,600,000 mi. (778,300,000 km)	888,200,000 mi. (1,429,400,000 km)	1,786,400,000 mi. (2,875,000,000 km)	2,798,800,000 mi. (4,504,300,000 km)	3,666,200,000 mi. (5,900,100,000 km)
390,700,000 mi. (628,760,000 km)	762,700,000 mi. (1,277,400,000 km)	1,607,000,000 mi. (2,587,000,000 km)	2,680,000,000 mi. (4,310,000,000 km)	2,670,000,000 mi. (4,290,000,000 km)
4,332.7 8.12 mi. per sec. (13.06 km per sec.)	10,759 5.99 mi. per sec. (9.64 km per sec.)	30,685 4.23 mi. per sec. (6.81 km per sec.)	60,190 3.37 mi. per sec. (5.43 km per sec.)	90,800 2.95 mi. per sec. (4.74 km per sec.)
88,846 mi. (142,984 km)	74,898 mi. (120,536 km)	31,763 mi. (51,118 km)	30,800 mi. (49,500 km)	1,430 mi. (2,300 km)
9 hrs. 55 min. 3.08	10 hrs. 39 min. 26.73	17 hrs. 14 min. 97.92	16 hrs. 7 min. 28.80	6 earthdays 98.8
−220 °F (−140 °C)	−290 °F (−180 °C)	−360 °F (−220 °C)	−350 °F (−210 °C)	−390 to −370 °F (−230 to −220 °C)
317.892 1.33 2.53	95.184 0.69 1.07	14.54 1.27 0.91	17.15 1.64 1.14	0.0022 2.0 0.07
16	18	17	8	1

Rain forest

Rain forest is a woodland of tall trees growing in a region of year-round warmth and abundant rainfall. Almost all rain forests lie at or near the equator. They form an evergreen belt of lush vegetation that encircles the planet. German botanist Andreas F. W. Schimper first coined the term *rain forest*—in German, *Regenwald*—in 1898.

Tropical rain forests occupy only 6 to 7 percent of the earth's surface. However, they support more than half of the world's plant and animal *species* (kinds). More kinds of frogs and other amphibians, birds, insects, mammals, and reptiles live in rain forests than in any other area. Scientists believe millions more rain forest species remain undiscovered.

The rain forest provides people with many benefits. Its plants produce timber, foods, medicines, and such industrial products as dyes, fibers, gums, oils, and resins. Rain forests help regulate the earth's climate and maintain clean air. The forests' lush, green beauty and rich wildlife offer a special source of enjoyment.

In addition, rain forests provide homes to millions of people. Such groups as the Yanomami of South America, the Dayaks of Southeast Asia, and the Pygmies of central Africa have lived in rain forests for centuries. They make their living by hunting, fishing, collecting forest products, and farming. Traditional forest peoples have acquired much knowledge about the rain forest's plants and animals.

In spite of these benefits, people cut down thousands of square miles or square kilometers of rain forest each year. This destruction eliminates thousands of species of animals. A number of governments and conservation organizations are working to preserve the rain forests.

Characteristics of rain forests

Climate and soil. The temperature in a tropical rain forest varies little. It rarely rises above 95 °F (35 °C) or drops below 64 °F (18 °C). In many regions, the average temperature in the hottest month is only 2 to 5 °F (1 to 3 °C) higher than the average temperature in the coldest month. Most rain forests receive more than 80 inches (203 centimeters) of rain annually. Some areas may receive more than 250 inches (635 centimeters) of rain each year. Thundershowers can occur more than 200 days a year.

Rain forest soils vary greatly from place to place. In many areas, the soil is acidic and infertile because years of heavy rains have washed out most of the *nutrients* (nourishing substances). Most rain forest nutrients are part of living plants. Small amounts of nutrients occur in a thin layer of topsoil that contains decaying vegetation.

Rain forest trees have developed several ways of capturing nutrients. For example, they obtain nourishment from rainwater that collects in their leaves or along their trunks and branches. They also withdraw nutrients from their old leaves before they shed them. The roots of most rain forest trees grow close to the surface and quickly absorb soil nutrients before they wash away. Special fungi called *mycorrhizae* grow in or on many of the roots and help them absorb minerals from the soil.

The lush rain forest houses a wide variety of plant life. Beautiful ferns grow near the bases of tall trees in the Asian rain forest pictured here. This forest lies on the island of Bali in Indonesia.

Structure and growth. Rain forests grow in four major layers: (1) the *canopy*, or top layer; (2) the *sub-canopy*, a layer of trees just below the canopy; (3) the *understory*, a shady lower area; and (4) the *floor*. The tallest trees, known as *emergents*, grow more than 165 feet (50 meters) tall. The *crowns* (tops) of these trees dominate the canopy. Emergents receive the greatest amount of sunlight, but they must endure high temperatures and strong winds. The crowns of other trees in the canopy usually form a nearly continuous covering of leaves 65 to 165 feet (20 to 50 meters) above the ground. Some tall trees have large growths called *buttresses* that extend from the base of the trunk and help support the tree.

More than 70 percent of rain forest animal and plant species reside in the canopy and sub-canopy. Many tree branches have a dense covering of *epiphytes*, plants that grow on other plants and obtain nourishment from the air and rain. Vines called *lianas* often climb on or around the trunks and branches of trees.

The shady understory shelters small palms, young trees, and *herbaceous* (nonwoody) plants that can grow in dim light. Many popular house plants, such as philodendrons, dieffenbachia, and ferns, are developed from species that live in this area. Some scientists believe only 1 percent of the sunlight available to emergent trees reaches the understory.

A thin layer of fallen leaves, seeds, fruits, and branches covers the forest floor. This layer quickly decomposes and is constantly replaced.

The layers of a rain forest continually change. Large old trees die and fall to the ground, leaving a gap in the canopy. Direct sunlight penetrates through to the understory and stimulates the growth of seedlings, saplings, and small trees below. The small trees slowly stretch upward into the canopy. As they branch and expand their crowns, they fill the gaps in the canopy. A mature rain forest consists of a mixture of closed canopies, gaps, and patches of growing trees where the canopy is being rebuilt. The regeneration of many rain forest trees depends on gaps developing regularly in the canopy.

Plants and animals. About 45 percent of the world's plant species occur in tropical rain forests. Scientists have counted over 250 species of trees in small areas of Asian and South American rain forests. A similar plot of land in a northern temperate forest would have only about 10 to 15 tree species. In addition to trees, rain forests support a great variety of bamboos, herbs, and shrubs. Climbing vines, ferns, mosses, and orchids grow directly on the trunks and branches of large trees.

Because of continual moisture and warmth, tropical rain forests stay green all year. Most rain forest trees continually lose old leaves and grow new ones. Only a few species lose all of their leaves for a brief period.

Fish, amphibians, reptiles, birds, and mammals abound in the rain forest and its rivers. However, insects rank as the most plentiful rain forest animals. An individual tree in a South American rain forest may support more than 40 species of ants. Scientists have counted about 1,200 species of beetles living in only 19 tree crowns from Panama.

Plants and animals in the rain forest depend on one another for survival. Many animal groups, especially insects and birds, pollinate the flowers of rain forest trees. Such animals receive food from the flowers' nectar. In return, they pollinate the next flowers they visit. Some trees rely on only one species of insect for pollination. Many rain forest trees also depend on animals to disperse their seeds. In the Amazon rain forest, fish disperse the seeds of some trees.

The Sepik River winds through dense rain forest on the island of New Guinea in Papua New Guinea. Many rain forest peoples and animals live along rivers.

© Jean-Paul Ferrero, Explorer

Rain forests of the world

The largest rain forests occur in tropical parts of the Americas, Asia, and Africa. Smaller areas of rain forest exist on many Pacific Islands and in parts of Australia's northeastern coast. These forests lie chiefly near the equator, in regions that receive some of the world's heaviest rainfall.

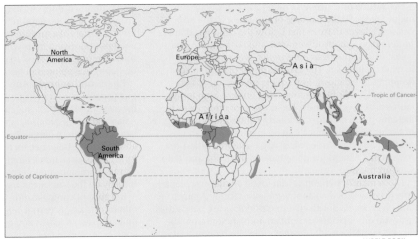

WORLD BOOK map

Rain forests around the world

The world's largest rain forests occur in tropical regions of the Americas, Asia, and Africa. Smaller areas of rain forest exist on many Pacific Islands and in parts of Australia's northeastern coast. People have also applied the term *rain forest* to such woodlands as those in North America's Pacific Northwest. However, the plant life in these forests is much less diverse than that found in tropical rain forests. For example, only a few species of large *conifers* (cone-bearing trees) dominate Pacific Northwest forests.

The Americas. About half of the world's rain forests grow in the American tropics. The largest expanse of forest—about 2 million square miles (5.2 million square kilometers)—lies in the Amazon River basin. Rain forests also occur in coastal areas from Ecuador and Brazil to southern Mexico, and in patches on many of the Caribbean islands.

American tropical rain forests support a rich assortment of plant species. More than 500 kinds of large plants may inhabit only 5 acres (2 hectares) of forest. Valuable hardwood trees include mahogany and rosewood. Over 150 species of trees produce edible fruits. Avocados, cocoa, rubber, and vanilla also grow there.

The rain forests of tropical America support more than 1,500 species of birds, 500 species of mammals, and 2,000 species of butterflies. More bats live there than live anywhere else. Monkeys, sloths, and toucans feed in the forest canopy and sub-canopy. Capybaras, the world's largest rodents, as well as ocelots and tapirs, forage along the forest floor. Emerald tree boas and arrow-poison frogs hide among foliage in the understory. The Amazon River contains more than 2,000 species of freshwater fish, including the dangerous piranha.

American rain forests provide homes to a variety of peoples. They include the Kuna of Panama, the Maya of Mexico and Central America, the Shipibo of Peru, and the Yanomami of Brazil and Venezuela. Such forest groups survive primarily by farming, but they also hunt animals and gather edible wild plants from the forest.

Asia. Rain forests cover about 1 million square miles (3 million square kilometers) of the Asian tropics. The forests grow in western and southern India and extend eastward through Vietnam. Large blocks of forest also occur in Indonesia, Malaysia, and the Philippines.

A single family of trees, the *dipterocarps,* forms a dominant part of the Asian rain forest canopy. About 380 species of dipterocarps grow in these forests. Dipterocarp trees produce valuable wood and *resins.* Resins are sticky substances that people use for varnishing and *caulking* (making objects watertight). Other important plants include the *pitcher plants,* which feed on animal life, and the *rafflesia,* the world's largest flower. A single rafflesia may grow more than 3 feet (90 centimeters) wide. Such fruits as bananas, durians, litchis, and mangoes also flourish in Asian rain forests.

Some of the best-known rain forest mammals in Asia include elephants, gibbons, orangutans, and tigers. The forests also support hundreds of reptile and amphibian species and thousands of bird and beetle species.

Rain forest peoples of Asia include the Penan of Borneo. They rely on rain forest plants and animals for subsistence and rarely farm the land. Another Bornean group, the Lun Dayeh, clear small areas of forest to make rice farms. The T'in people of Thailand and Laos harvest hundreds of wild plant species from the rain forest for food and other purposes.

Africa. Africa's tropics have about 810,000 square miles (2.1 million square kilometers) of rain forest. The forested area extends from Congo (Kinshasa) westward to the Atlantic Ocean. Patches of rain forest also occur on the east coast of Madagascar.

African rain forests do not house as many plant species as do the forests of South America or Asia. Small areas of African rain forest support from 50 to 100 species of trees. Many of these trees have their fruits dispersed by elephants. A number of valuable woods, including ebony, mahogany, and sipo, flourish in the African tropics. Other well-known plants from the region include oil palms and coffee plants.

Diverse animal life characterizes Africa's tropical rain forests. Squirrels and monkeys share the canopy and sub-canopy with other small mammals, including galagos and golden pottos, as well as hundreds of species of birds. The mandrill, a brightly colored relative of the baboon, and the okapi, a horselike relative of the giraffe, roam the forest floor. Congo peacocks and wild hogs called bush pigs also dwell on the ground. Gorillas and chimpanzees live on the ground and in trees. The forests of Madagascar support animals found almost nowhere else, including long-tailed, monkeylike lemurs.

Forest-dwelling people in the African tropics are collectively known as Pygmies. Traditionally, they have survived by hunting and gathering wild animals and plants. Pygmies live in such countries as Burundi, Cameroon, Congo (Brazzaville), Congo (Kinshasa), Gabon, and Rwanda.

Australia and the Pacific Islands. Tropical rain forests cover about 145,600 square miles (377,000 square kilometers) in northeast Australia and on many Pacific Islands. Rain forest trees of these regions include several kinds of figs, as well as the smaller lilly-pilly and brush cherry. The lacewood and Queensland maple trees produce valuable hardwoods. Coachwood and Moreton Bay chestnut trees develop brilliantly colored flowers.

Rain forests of Australia and New Guinea house unique wildlife. Such marsupials as cuscuses, sugar gliders, and tree kangaroos make their homes in the trees. Several kinds of parrots and numerous species of snakes also reside in the forests.

Rain forest peoples of this area include Australian Aborigines and Melanesian peoples from such islands as New Guinea, the Solomon Islands, and Vanuatu. Many of these cultures hunt and gather food from the rain forest. They also raise crops.

The value of rain forests

Rain forests benefit people in four major ways. They provide (1) economic, (2) scientific, (3) environmental, and (4) recreational value.

Economic value. Wood ranks as the most important rain forest product. Foresters harvest millions of trees from rain forests each year. People use about 80 percent of rain forest wood for fuel and about 20 percent for timber. International trade in tropical hardwoods averages billions of dollars a year.

Other valuable rain forest resources include fibers, fruits, nuts, oils, and resins. Indonesia and the Philippines export millions of dollars in furniture and other products made from *rattan,* a kind of palm. Amazon rain forests provide thousands of tons of Brazil nuts and rubber. Mexican and Central American forests yield various types of *chicle,* an ingredient used in chewing gum.

Scientific value. Tropical rain forests have much to teach people. Many scientists study the rain forest as an *ecosystem*—that is, they investigate the relationships among all its living things and the environment that supports them. Because of its great diversity of life, the rain forest ranks as the most complex ecosystem on land. Biologists have discovered and classified only a small percentage of the organisms believed to live there. As scientists learn more about rain forests, they can better understand how to conserve these and other ecosystems.

Rain forests provide a wealth of foods and medicines. The forest peoples of Borneo use hundreds of different plant species for food. Most of these plants have not been grown outside Borneo. About 85 wild relatives of the common avocado exist in forests of Central America. Commercial avocado growers are working with scientists to develop ways of using these species to breed avocados that are more resistant to disease.

Several important medicines come from rain forest plants. These include *quinine,* used to treat malaria; *tubocurarine,* a muscle relaxant sometimes used in heart surgery; and *pilocarpine,* used to treat the eye disease glaucoma. The rosy periwinkle plant from Madagascar yields important anticancer drugs. Scientists believe many more potential medicines may exist in rain forests.

Environmental value. Tropical rain forests help regulate the earth's environment in several ways. For example, tropical trees help control the amount of rain water that reaches the ground. These trees absorb an enormous quantity of rain. In a process called *transpiration,* much of this water evaporates from the trees' leaf pores and reenters the atmosphere as vapor. Eventually, the vapor condenses into water and falls to the earth again as rain. Transpiration may account for as much as half of the rainfall in some rain forests. By regulating rainfall, rain forest trees keep floods and droughts from becoming too severe. The dense rain forest vegetation also reduces soil erosion.

Jaguar
© Luiz Claudio Marigo, Bruce Coleman Ltd.

Tussock moth
© George D. Dodge, Bruce Coleman Inc.

Keel-billed toucan
© MPL Fogden, Bruce Coleman Ltd.

Wild orchid
© Corel

Rain forest life includes an astonishing variety of colorful animals and plants. More kinds of birds, flowers, insects, mammals, and reptiles live in the rain forests than in any other region. Biologists believe millions more rain forest species remain undiscovered. Because people are clearing the world's rain forests so quickly, many forest species may become extinct before scientists can discover them.

Carpet chameleon
© Gail Shumway, FPG

Rafflesia
© Alain Compost, Bruce Coleman Ltd.

Rain forests help control temperatures in their own regions and in other parts of the world. Rain forest trees absorb light and heat. This absorption keeps tropical climates from becoming too hot or too cold. The forests also take in and store massive amounts of carbon dioxide, preventing the build-up of this gas in the atmosphere. Scientists believe the accumulation of carbon dioxide and other gases in the atmosphere increases temperatures around the world. By absorbing carbon dioxide, tropical rain forests may help keep worldwide temperatures from becoming too warm.

Recreational value. Rain forests offer great beauty, lush vegetation, and unique wildlife for tourists. A growing number of people travel to rain forests each year. Tourism has helped increase awareness of the need to preserve these environments.

The future of rain forests

People are rapidly destroying the world's rain forests. In 1950, rain forests covered about 8,700,000 square miles (22,533,000 square kilometers) of the earth. This area would cover about three-fourths of Africa. Today, less than half the original extent of the earth's rain forest remains. In such regions as Madagascar, Sumatra, and the Atlantic coast of Brazil, only small patches still stand.

Few rain forest species can adjust to severe disturbance of their habitat. Most perish when people clear large areas of forest. Scientists estimate that tropical *deforestation* (clearing of trees) wipes out about 7,500 species per year.

Causes of deforestation. Commercial logging and the expansion of agriculture have damaged or wiped out extensive areas of rain forest. Huge mining projects, the construction of hydroelectric dams, and government resettlement programs have also taken their toll.

A complex mix of social, political, and economic factors has triggered these destructive activities. Rapid population growth and poverty often intensify the pressure to clear rain forest for short-term economic benefits. Brazil, Indonesia, and other nations have cut down huge expanses of rain forest to create new settlements that allow people to move out of overcrowded cities. Moreover, the governments of many tropical countries are deeply in debt. This debt provides a strong motivation to gather as much as possible from the rain forest as quickly as possible. After clearing the forest to harvest wood and other products, people then commonly use the land to grow crops.

Deforestation usually displaces forest peoples. When denied access to the forest, these peoples often lose important knowledge about rain forest species and their uses. Loss of such knowledge further threatens the survival of the forests.

© Philippe Guignard

Deforestation wipes out large areas of rain forests each year, threatening the wildlife in those regions. This picture shows a partially deforested area of Gabon, a country in western Africa.

Saving rain forests. Many conservation organizations, including the World Wildlife Fund, Conservation International, and the Nature Conservancy, are working with governments to conserve rain forests. Such efforts include (1) establishing protected areas, (2) promoting intelligent management of rain forests, and (3) increasing public awareness about the importance of the forests.

In the 1980's and 1990's, hundreds of protected areas were established in tropical forests. These areas included nature reserves, wildlife sanctuaries, and national parks. However, such efforts affected only a small percentage of the total area of rain forest. Moreover, many conservation areas remain only "paper parks," with little protection or enforcement on the ground.

Governments and conservation organizations also promote sound management of tropical forests by the people who use them. For example, certain organizations certify timber from loggers that harvest rain forest wood in a sustainable fashion. Certified timbers may bring a higher price on the international market. Areas of some rain forests have been set aside as *extractive reserves*. Local populations manage these reserves and practice sustainable harvesting of many forest products.

Increasing public awareness about the plight of rain forests may also aid the struggle to conserve them. Awareness has grown due to greater exposure of rain forest issues in the media, and to an increasing number of tourists who travel to rain forests.   Charles M. Peters

The index to the 1999 *World Book Year Book* begins on page 449.